2

WORLD MILITARY

TRANSPORT FLEETS 2002

An AIR-BRITAIN Publication

WORLD MILITARY TRANSPORT FLEETS 2002

Compiled and edited by
Peter Smithson and Philip Hancock

Published by: Air-Britain (Historians) Ltd

Sales Department: 41, Penhurst Road, Leigh, Tonbridge, Kent, TN11 8HL

Membership Enquiries: 1, Rose Cottages, 179 Penn Road, Hazlemere,
                         Buckinghamshire, HP15 7NE

ISBN: 0 85130 315 3

PHOTO CAPTIONS:

Front Cover:

McDonnell Douglas C-17A Globemaster III, 92-3294 of the United States Air Force at Farnborough, September 1994. (Philip Hancock)

Rear Cover:

Top: Lockheed VC-130H Hercules, 112 of the Royal Saudi Air Force at London Heathrow, August 2001.
Centre: CASA 212A Aviocar srs 100, 16503 and four others of the Portuguese Air Force at Sintra, May 2000. (Chris Chatfield)
Bottom: PADC-built Britten-Norman BN-2A-21 Islander, PCG-251 of the Philippine Coast Guard at Clark Air Base, February 2001. (Peter J Bish)

Printed by: Cromwell Press Ltd, Trowbridge, Wiltshire BA14 0XB

WORLD MILITARY TRANSPORT FLEETS 2002

CONTENTS

vi

INTRODUCTION

The aim of this book is to provide an accurate summary of the world's fixed wing military and government operated transport aircraft, and it is intended to fill a gap in the current range of Air-Britain publications. Each country is listed alphabetically with a brief introduction including a serial system summary, a listing of bases with (where available) unit details and current acquisition plans followed by as complete a listing as possible of the relevant equipment currently operated. For countries where no types within this book's scope are current, such as war-torn Sierra Leone or Somalia, an entry relating the current situation has been inserted. Some of the smaller island groups have been omitted where no military air arm or Government aircraft exist.

When deciding which types to include over and above the obvious standard transports (Hercules, Ilyushins and Antonovs etc) we elected to include patrol and SAR equipment as in many cases dual uses already apply in service. All transport types down to a Maximum Take Off Weight (MTOW) of 1600kg are included.

Only current airworthy equipment or airframes in storage (with a good chance of flying again) are listed. Aircraft in use as ground instructional airframes, dumped, broken up, written off, preserved (including historic flights) or sold are omitted from this pilot edition. Aircraft stored at the AMARC facility in the USA are included, as many will one day fly again although not maybe with US forces, details such as the park code are included.

The listing order within a country is generally in serial number order as this makes for a tidy and logical presentation for most operators. However where an air arm has no self regulated serial allocation system and relies on a previous owner's serial or construction number (c/n) as an aircraft identity (such as France and Greece) we have resorted to listing by type and then serial to make locating an individual entry easier. The CIS countries that use predominantly 'civil' style identities are listed in the order of the last five digits where two or more prefix styles may still apply across all their airframes.

The line by line layout follows the following format:

A9-662	Lockheed P-3W (L-285D) Orion	5789	N64996	11 Sqn	Cvtd P-3C-II.5
Col. 1	Col. 2	Col. 3	Col. 4	Col. 5	Col. 6

Column One - shows the aircraft serial along with the last reported code or civil registration after an oblique if applicable, the presentation is generally as worn on the aircraft.
Column Two - shows the full aircraft type reflecting the actual manufacturer where it can be determined and any local name or designation allocated by the operator in question. Where a type has been built on a primarily civil production line the equivalent civil designation is also given in brackets.
Column Three - shows the individual c/n (or manufacturers serial number-msn) where known with an applicable line number after an oblique.
Column Four - shows any the last recorded previous identity with an indication of who the last owner was if not immediately apparent.
Column Five - gives the last reported unit/operator details where known.
Column Six - is a notes field giving additional details such as role if different from that normally associated with the type, colour scheme variation, current status (i.e. stored) or an individual aircraft name where known.

This publication is intended to complement current Air-Britain titles and we have tried not to duplicate listings. We have however included many quasi-military operators and government agencies such as VIP operations, police forces, the Securité Civile in France and the Canadian provincial government operators of fire fighting tanker aircraft. This equipment was felt to warrant inclusion for completeness, as they are definitely not airline operations. The military-run airlines of South America and China are also listed, if they are formally part of the country's armed forces.

While every effort has been made to ensure complete accuracy, the sheer volume of data in this initial publication means that mistakes will get through. That being said, nothing has been assumed, where a c/n has been omitted it is because it has not been confirmed even if those around it make it appear to fit a sequence. Notes have been applied where necessary.

The majority of the text was completed before the shocking news of 11th September 2001 and the effect of any re-organizations and deployments resulting from this event have not been taken into account.

If we received an updated or even expanded volume is promised, for this your reporting and constructive comments are necessary and welcomed. Please let us know what you think and what you want.

Our thanks need to be expressed to Terry Smith, Pete Webber, Michael Austen, Dave Partington and Chris Chatfield for their constructive comments regarding what we envisaged and what was actually possible. Also thanks of course to our respective families for their patience and occasional encouragement to get on with it. Data has been gathered from numerous published sources and cross checked to ensure accuracy where possible, those most useful include Air-Britain themselves (Air-Britain News and monographs), Scramble, The Aviation Hobby Shop, Aerospace Publishing, eMail group reports (civil-spotters@yahoogroups.com and mil-spotters@yahoogroups.com) and Key Publishing (Air Forces Monthly). Checking from official sources such as www sites has been the determining factor where inconsistencies or doubts were noted.

Peter Smithson, 21 Laurel Close, Colnbrook, Berkshire, SL3 0QB, coronado@compuserve.com

Philip Hancock, 6 Weybarton, Byfleet, Surrey, KT14 7EF, hancock@tesco.net.

December 2001

IMPORTANT NOTE:

Readers are advised that access to, and in some cases even observation of, military aircraft and facilities is forbidden. Due care should be exercised at all times that appropriate official permissions have been sought and are known at local level before making notes. taking photographs or approaching military installations and aircraft, whether active, stored or derelict. Air-Britain will accept no responsibility for any transgressions of local laws by members and non-members alike.

AFGHANISTAN
Di Afganistan Islami Dawlat / Islamic State of Afghanistan   C Asia

The Soviet invasion in 1979 and their withdrawal with their own internal problems ten years later left Russian equipment in the country for the Mujahideen to inherit when the civil war 'ceased' in 1992. Subsequent conflict erupted between this new government and what became the Taliban regime, resulting in the destruction of what was left. The Taliban forces controlled the majority of the country, until November 2001, with Iranian and Pakistani support. Prior to the tragic events in the USA on September 11th 2001 it was thought that less than six An-26/32s remained although Iran may have donated a number of captured Iraqi aircraft to the Northern Alliance Forces to add to their single An-12 and small number of An-24s. Changes are clearly expected in 2002.

SERIAL SYSTEM Three digit serials are allocated in batches depending on type.

Afghan Hanai Qurah
Afghan Air Force

237	Antonov An-26	Std
247	Antonov An-26	Operational
264	Antonov An-26	Operational
284	Antonov An-26	Operational
297	Antonov An-32	Std Kabul-Bagram
389	Antonov An-12BP	Std

Northern Alliance Forces

390	Antonov An-12	Operational

ALBANIA
Republica e Shqipërisë / Republic of Albania   SE Europe

A founder member of the Warsaw Pact, but subsequent alienation from both the Soviet Union and China has left Albania in a very backward state as a country. Work began to change this in the late 1990s but this caused its own internal problems worsened by the then situation in the Balkans. The majority of the equipment is of Chinese origin and is not believed fully serviceable.

SERIAL SYSTEM Two systems are noted, one a sequential two digit batched by type (Y-5) and the other a four digit based on the last four numbers of the msn."

Aviacioni Ushtarake Shqipëtare
Albanian People's Army Air Force

UNITS/BASES	4050 Aviation Regiment, Tirana-Vlora		Y-5 (An-2)	

12	Yunshuji/Nanchang Y-5	1332015		Std Tirana
14	Yunshuji/Nanchang Y-5		4050 AvRmt	
15	Yunshuji/Nanchang Y-5	1332016		Std Tirana
20	Yunshuji/Nanchang Y-5			Std Tirana
21	Yunshuji/Nanchang Y-5	1332022		Std Tirana
22	Yunshuji/Nanchang Y-5			Std Tirana
23	Yunshuji/Nanchang Y-5	1332012		Std Tirana
30	Yunshuji/Nanchang Y-5	1332023		Std Tirana
31	Yunshuji/Nanchang Y-5	1332025		Std Tirana
32	Yunshuji/Nanchang Y-5			Std Tirana
34	Yunshuji/Nanchang Y-5	13332018		Std Tirana
12-25	Ilyushin Il-14	147001225		Std Tirana

ALGERIA
al-Jumhouriya al-Jaza'iriya dimuqratiya ash-sha'abiya   N Africa

Independent from France since 1962, the Air Force was originally also given the title Armée de l'Air Algérienne (AAA). An Arab state supported by the Soviet Union until the latter's collapse, Algeria flies an extensive transport fleet but has suffered recently from civil unrest.

SERIAL SYSTEM Civil-style registrations are used with unique AF (7T-W**) and Government (7T-VP*/VR*) blocks.

al Quwwat al Jawwija Aljaza'Eriiya
Algerian Air Force

UNITS/BASES	31 Sqn, Boufarik	C-130, L-100
	35 Sqn, Boufarik	Il-76
	68 Sqn, Oran-Tafaroui Lartige	King Air, Super King Air
	580 Sqn, Boufarik	Falcon 900, F.27, G-IV

PLANS   Il-78 tankers were noted for the first time in 2000 (presumably surplus from the CIS) and a maritime patrol type is also required (up to 12 aircraft). The Government have traded in the two Falcon 900s against a Gulfstream V and two Gulfstream IVs

Reg	Type			Sqn	Role
7T-WAM	Fokker F.27 Troopship 400M	10529	PH-FRK		Survey
7T-WCF	Beech King Air C90B	LJ-1359	N8280K	68 Sqn	
7T-WCG	Beech King Air C90B	LJ-1379	N3112K	68 Sqn	
7T-WCH	Beech King Air C90B	LJ-1380	N3128K	68 Sqn	
7T-WHA	Lockheed C-130H-30 (L-382T-56E) Hercules	4997	7T-VHA	31 Sqn	
7T-WHB	Lockheed C-130H-30 (L-382T-13F) Hercules	5224	7T-VHB	31 Sqn	
7T-WHD	Lockheed C-130H-30 (L-382T-45E) Hercules	4987		31 Sqn	
7T-WHE	Lockheed C-130H (L-382C-25E) Hercules	4935		31 Sqn	
7T-WHF	Lockheed C-130H (L-382C-25E) Hercules	4934		31 Sqn	
7T-WHI	Lockheed C-130H (L-382C-25E) Hercules	4930		31 Sqn	
7T-WHJ	Lockheed C-130H (L-382C-25E) Hercules	4928		31 Sqn	
7T-WHL	Lockheed C-130H-30 (L-382T-45E) Hercules	4989		31 Sqn	
7T-WHM	Lockheed C-130H-30 (L-382T-30E) Hercules	4919	7T-VHM	31 Sqn	
7T-WHN	Lockheed C-130H-30 (L-382T-16E) Hercules	4894	7T-VHN	31 Sqn	
7T-WHO	Lockheed C-130H-30 (L-382T-16E) Hercules	4897	7T-VHO	31 Sqn	
7T-WHP	Lockheed C-130H-30 (L-382T-30E) Hercules	4921	7T-VHP	31 Sqn	
7T-WHQ	Lockheed C-130H (L-382C-25E) Hercules	4926		31 Sqn	
7T-WHR	Lockheed C-130H (L-382C-25E) Hercules	4924		31 Sqn	
7T-WHS	Lockheed C-130H (L-382C-25E) Hercules	4912		31 Sqn	
7T-WHT	Lockheed C-130H (L-382C-25E) Hercules	4911		31 Sqn	
7T-WHY	Lockheed C-130H (L-382C-25E) Hercules	4913		31 Sqn	
7T-WHZ	Lockheed C-130H (L-382C-25D) Hercules	4914		31 Sqn	
7T-WIA	Ilyushin Il-76MD	0083489674		35 Sqn	
7T-WIB	Ilyushin Il-76MD	0093493803		35 Sqn	
7T-WIC	Ilyushin Il-76MD	1003405154		35 Sqn	
7T-WID	Ilyushin Il-76TD	1023414470	RA-76419	35 Sqn	
7T-WIE	Ilyushin Il-76TD	1023414463	RA-76406	35 Sqn	
7T-WIG	Ilyushin Il-76TD	1023413435	RA-76407	35 Sqn	
7T-WIP	Ilyushin Il-76TD	1043419636		35 Sqn	
7T-WIJ	Ilyushin Il-76TD	1023413423	RA-76440	35 Sqn	
7T-WIV	Ilyushin Il-76TD	1043419649		35 Sqn	
	Ilyushin Il-78				AAR
	Ilyushin Il-78				AAR
	Ilyushin Il-78				AAR
	Ilyushin Il-78				AAR
	Ilyushin Il-78				AAR
	Ilyushin Il-78				AAR
7T-WLA	Pilatus PC-6/B2-H4 Turbo Porter	919	HB-FLM		
7T-WLE	Pilatus PC-6/B2-H4 Turbo Porter	920	HB-FLN		
7T-WRF	Beech King Air A100	B-147	7T-VRF	68 Sqn	Calibration
7T-WRG	Beech Super King Air 200	BB-184	7T-VRG	68 Sqn	Trainer
7T-WRH	Beech Super King Air 200	BB-175	7T-VRH	68 Sqn	Trainer
7T-WRY	Beech Super King Air 200T	BT-20	7T-VRY	68 Sqn	MP
7T-WRZ	Beech Super King Air 200T	BT-21	7T-VRZ	68 Sqn	MP
	Raytheon Beech 1900D	UE-384	N32345		SIGINT
	Raytheon Beech 1900D	UE-404	N44663		
	Raytheon Beech 1900D	UE-411	N44824		
	Raytheon Beech 1900D	UE-413	N44849		
	Raytheon Beech 1900D	UE-414	N44808		
	Raytheon Beech 1900D	UE-417	N50317		Transport
	Raytheon Beech 1900D	UE-419	N50919		
	Raytheon Beech 1900D	UE-420	N50220		
	Raytheon Beech 1900D				
	Raytheon Beech 1900D				
	Raytheon Beech 1900D				
	Raytheon Beech 1900D				

Government of the Democratic & Popular Republic of Algeria

Reg	Type			Role
7T-VPC	GAC Gulfstream IVSP	1418	N418GA	VIP
7T-VPG	GAC Gulfstream V	617	N575GA	VIP
7T-VPM	GAC Gulfstream IVSP	1421	N324GA	VIP
7T-VPR	GAC Gulfstream IVSP	1288	N403GA	VIP
7T-VPS	GAC Gulfstream IVSP	1291	N412GA	VIP
7T-VRI	Beech Super King Air 200	BB-171	7T-WRI	VIP
7T-VRN	Fokker F.27 Friendship 600	10527	7T-WAN	VIP
7T-VRO	Beech Super King Air 200	BB-807	7T-WRO	VIP
7T-VRS	Beech Super King Air 200	BB-759	7T-WRS	VIP
7T-VRT	Beech Super King Air 200	BB-775	7T-WRT	VIP
7T-VRW	Fokker F.27 Troopship 400M	10556	7T-WAV	VIP

ANGOLA
República de Angola   S Africa

Called Portuguese West Africa until independence in 1975 and affected by a prolonged civil war between the South African backed guerrilla group UNITA and the Government, peace was established in the early 1990s, but broke down in 1998 with UNITA basing combat aircraft at Luca. Much of the support received by the government forces came from the Soviet Union with Cuban assistance in particular. The advisors are long gone but the available equipment is nearly all of Russian origin.

SERIAL SYSTEM   Three digit serials batched by type are prefixed with a role letter (ie T, Transporte), civil D2- markings are also dual allocated in some cases. Civil registration blocks also identify the operator (ie D2-F** and M** are Air Force, D2-E** for the Government).

Fôrça Aérea Populaire de Angola/Difesa Anti-Aviones
Angolan Air and Anti Aircraft Defence Force

UNITS/BASES   Transport bases include Kuito amd Luena

PLANS   Lockheed Martin has an MoU to supply eight ex RAF C-130Ks

R 104	Antonov An-2			
R 203	Britten-Norman BN-2A-21 Islander	543	2453	
R 206	Britten-Norman BN-2A-21 Islander	798	2456	
R 207	Britten-Norman BN-2A-21 Islander	802	2457	
R 208	Britten-Norman BN-2A-21 Islander	803	2458	
T 40	Fairchild Hiller FH-227B	563	ZS-JOZ	Std
T 200	Antonov An-26			
T 201	Antonov An-26			
T 203	Antonov An-26			
T 204	Antonov An-26			
T 205	Antonov An-26			
T 206	Antonov An-26			
T 207	Antonov An-26			
T 208	Antonov An-26			
T 209	Antonov An-26			
T 210	Antonov An-26			
T 211	Antonov An-26			
T 212	Antonov An-26			
T 213	Antonov An-26			
T 214 / D2-MHI	Antonov An-26			
T 215	Antonov An-26			
T 216	Antonov An-26			
T 217	Antonov An-26			
T 218	Antonov An-26			
T 219	Antonov An-26			
T 220	Antonov An-26			
T 221	Antonov An-26			
T 222	Antonov An-26			
T 223	Antonov An-26			
T 224	Antonov An-26			
T 226	Antonov An-26			
T 228	Antonov An-26			
T 229	Antonov An-26			
T 230	Antonov An-26			
T 231	Antonov An-26			
T 232	Antonov An-26			
T 233	Antonov An-26			
T 234	Antonov An-26			
T 235	Antonov An-26			
T 236	Antonov An-26			
T 237	Antonov An-26			
T 239	Antonov An-26			
T 240	Antonov An-26			
T 241	Antonov An-26			
T 242	Antonov An-26			
T 243	Antonov An-26			
T 244	Antonov An-26			
T 250	Antonov An-32			
T 252	Antonov An-32			
T 300	Antonov An-12			
T 301	Antonov An-12BP			
T 302	Antonov An-12			
T 303	Antonov An-12			
T 402	CASA 212 Aviocar srs 200	A53-3-330		

T 403	CASA 212 Aviocar srs 200	A53-4-331		
T 407 / D2-MAE	CASA 212 Aviocar srs 200	A53-8-340		
T 408 / D2-MKL	CASA 212 Aviocar srs 300M	380		MP
T 409 / D2-MLN	CASA 212 Aviocar srs 300M	381		MP
T 410 / D2-MNM	CASA 212 Aviocar srs 300M	384		MP
T 411 / D2-MMO	CASA 212 Aviocar srs 300M	385		MP
T 412	CASA 212 Aviocar srs 200			MP
T 450	Yakovlev Yak-40			
T 700	Antonov An-74			
T 701	Antonov An-26			
T 702	Antonov An-26			
T 704	Antonov An-26			
T 705	Antonov An-26			
T 750	Antonov An-72			
D2-FAB	Antonov An-32			
D2-FAC	Antonov An-32			
D2-FAD	Antonov An-32			
D2-FAE	Antonov An-32			
D2-MAD	Antonov An-26			
D2-MAB	Antonov An-26B	11403		
D2-MCD	Antonov An-26			
D2-MDE	Antonov An-26			
D2-MOP	Antonov An-26B	13607		
D2-MFQ	Antonov An-26B	13704		
D2-TAD	Antonov An-26	4609		

Government of the Republic of Angola

D2-EAG	Yakovlev Yak-40	9230122	I-JAKO	VIP
D2-ECB	GAC G-1159A Gulfstream III	474	N311GA	VIP
D2-ECC	Tupolev Tu-134A	349830		VIP
D2-EEO	Britten-Norman BN-2A-21 Islander	825	YR-BPI	
D2-EEP	Britten-Norman BN-2A-21 Islander	579	YR-BPG	
D2-EEQ	Britten-Norman BN-2A-21 Islander	580	YR-BPH	
D2-END	Antonov An-26			
D2-ENI	Antonov An-26			
D2-EPN	Antonov An-26	7804		
D2-EPO	Antonov An-26			
D2-EPP	Antonov An-26			
D2-EPQ	Antonov An-26	10808		
D2-EPR	Antonov An-26			
D2-ESE	Britten-Norman BN-2A-21 Islander	826	YR-BPJ	
D2-ESI	Britten-Norman BN-2A-21 Islander	827	YR-BPK	
D2-EUN	Embraer EMB-110P1A Bandeirante	110467	PT-SHV	MR
D2-EUT	Embraer EMB-110P1A Bandeirante	110465	PT-SHT	MR
D2-EZG	Antonov An-26			
D2-EZH	Antonov An-26			
D2-EZI	Antonov An-26			
D2-TPR	Boeing 707-3J6B	20715 / 870	B-2404	VIP

ARGENTINA
República Argentina   S America

Britain partly relaxed the arms embargo imposed since the 1982 Falklands war in 1998, but relations between the two countries have still not thawed completely as Argentine territorial claims on the Falkland Islands (Malvinas) remain. Increased defence spending and a re-alignment with the USA is resulting in the acquisition of better equipment.

SERIAL SYSTEM   Air Force serials consist of a one or two letter code denoting role followed by a sequential number, the Navy use a sequential four digit serial and a larger presentation code describing the role and unit. The Coast Guard, Army and National Guard have unique serial prefixes followed by a two or three digit identity, Government aircraft are civil registered sometimes in the LQ- series.

Fuerza Aérea Argentina - FAA
Argentine Air Force

ICAO code FAG, callsign Fuair

UNITS/BASES   I Brigada Aérea, BAM El Palomar-Buenos Aires
Grupo Aérea 1 de Transporte
    Escuadrón 1   C-130B/H, KC-130H, L-100-30
    Escuadrón II   F.28-1000
    Escuadrón IV   F.27-400M/600

Escuadrón V	707
II Brigada Aérea, BAM General Urquiza-Parana	
Grupo Aéreo 2 de Bombardeo	
Escuadrón II	Learjet 35A, Guarani II
III Brigada Aérea, BAM Reconquista-Santa Fe	
Escuadrilla Servicios	AC500U (support for Pucara unit)
IV Brigada Aérea, BAM El Plumerillo-Mendoza	
Grupo Aérea 4 de Caza	
Escuadrón II	Paris
Escuadrilla Servicios	AC500
V Brigada Aérea, BAM Coronel Pringles-Villa Reynolds	
Escuadrilla Servicios	AC500U (support for A-4AR units)
VI Brigada Aérea, BAM Tandil	
Escuadrilla Servicios	AC500U (support for Mirage/Dagger units)
VII Brigada Aérea, BAM Mariano Moreno	
Grupo Aéreo 7 de Helicopteros	AC500
IX Brigada Aérea, BAM Comodoro Rivadavia	
Grupo Aérea 9 de Transporte	
Escuadrón VI	F.27-400M/600
Escuadrón VII	Twin Otter
(aircraft detached to BAM Marambio in Antarctica)	
Lineas Aéreas del Estado (LADE), BAM El Palomar-Buenos Aires & BAM Comodoro Rivadavia	
(aircraft taken from 1 BA and IX BA as required)	Twin Otter, F-27-600, F.28, L-100, 707
Comando de Regiónes Aéreas	
Instituto Nacional de Aviación Civil (INAC), Moron Airport-Buenos Aires	
	PA-34, C182
Escuadrón de Aviones Presidenciales, Aeroparque Jorge Newbery	
	757, F.28, Learjet 60, Sabreliner

PLANS	Bombardier CL-415 (up to 4) being considered.				
E-202	Morane-Saulnier MS.760A Paris 1R	4	A-02	IV BA, Gr4	
E-203	Morane-Saulnier MS.760A Paris 1R	7	A-03		Std
E-204	Morane-Saulnier MS.760A Paris 1R	10	A-04		Std
E-205	Morane-Saulnier MS.760A Paris 1R	11	A-05	IV BA, Gr4	
E-206	Morane-Saulnier MS.760A Paris 1R	13	A-06		Std
E-207	Morane-Saulnier MS.760A Paris 1R	15	A-07	IV BA, Gr4	
E-208	Morane-Saulnier MS.760A Paris 1R	16	A-08	IV BA, Gr4	
E-209	Morane-Saulnier MS.760A Paris 1R	17	A-09		Std
E-210	Morane-Saulnier MS.760A Paris 1R	18	A-10		Std
E-211	Morane-Saulnier MS.760A Paris 1R	21	A-11		Std
E-212	Morane-Saulnier MS.760A Paris 1R	22	A-12	IV BA, Gr4	
E-214	Morane-Saulnier/DINFIA MS.760A Paris	A-2			Std
E-215	Morane-Saulnier/DINFIA MS.760A Paris	A-3			Std
E-216	Morane-Saulnier/DINFIA MS.760A Paris	A-4			Std
E-219	Morane-Saulnier/DINFIA MS.760A Paris	A-7			Std
E-220	Morane-Saulnier/DINFIA MS.760A Paris	A-8		IV BA, Gr4	
E-221	Morane-Saulnier/DINFIA MS.760A Paris	A-9			Std
E-222	Morane-Saulnier/DINFIA MS.760A Paris	A-10			Std
E-223	Morane-Saulnier/DINFIA MS.760A Paris	A-11			Std
E-224	Morane-Saulnier/DINFIA MS.760A Paris	A-12			Std
E-225	Morane-Saulnier/DINFIA MS.760A Paris	A-13			Std
E-226	Morane-Saulnier/DINFIA MS.760A Paris	A-14			Std
E-227	Morane-Saulnier/DINFIA MS.760A Paris	A-15		IV BA, Gr4	
E-228	Morane-Saulnier/DINFIA MS.760A Paris	A-16			Std
E-229	Morane-Saulnier/DINFIA MS.760A Paris	A-17			Std
E-230	Morane-Saulnier/DINFIA MS.760A Paris	A-18			Std
E-231	Morane-Saulnier/DINFIA MS.760A Paris	A-19			Std
E-232	Morane-Saulnier/DINFIA MS.760A Paris	A-20		IV BA, Gr4	
E-233	Morane-Saulnier/DINFIA MS.760A Paris	A-21			Std
E-234	Morane-Saulnier/DINFIA MS.760A Paris	A-22			Std
E-235	Morane-Saulnier/DINFIA MS.760A Paris	A-23			Std
E-236	Morane-Saulnier/DINFIA MS.760A Paris	A-24			Std
E-241	Morane-Saulnier/DINFIA MS.760A Paris	A-29		IV BA, Gr4	
E-242	Morane-Saulnier/DINFIA MS.760A Paris	A-30		IV BA, Gr4	
E-243	Morane-Saulnier/DINFIA MS.760A Paris	A-31			Std
E-244	Morane-Saulnier/DINFIA MS.760A Paris	A-32			Std
F-33	DINFIA IA.50B Guarani II			II BA	
PG-321	Piper/Chincul PA-34-220T Seneca III	AR34-8133039		INAC	
PG-332	Piper/Chincul PA-34-220T Seneca III	AR34-8133033		INAC	
PG-333	Piper/Chincul PA-34-220T Seneca III	AR34-8133129		INAC	
T-01	Boeing 757-23A	25487 / 470		Esc AP	*'Virgen de Lujan'*
T-02	Fokker F.28 Fellowship 1000	11048	LV-LZN	Esc AP	
T-03	Fokker F.28 Fellowship 4000	11203	PH-RRC	Esc AP	leased

T-10	Learjet 60	60-140	N140LJ	Esc AP	
T-11	Rockwell Sabreliner 75A	380-3	T-10 (FAA)	Esc AP	
T-21	Learjet 35A	35A-115		II BA, Gr2	
T-22	Learjet 35A	35A-136		II BA, Gr2	
T-23	Learjet 35A	35A-319		II BA, Gr2	
T-24	Learjet 35A	35A-369	VR-17 (FAA)	II BA, Gr2	
T-25	Learjet 35A	35A-484	VR-18 (FAA)	II BA, Gr2	
T-41	Fokker F.27 Friendship 600	10345	T-80 (FAA)	Gr 1/Gr 9 / LADE	
T-42	Fokker F.27 Friendship 600	10346	T-79 (FAA)	Gr 1/Gr 9 / LADE	
T-43	Fokker F.27 Friendship 600	10451	PH-EXA	Gr 1/Gr 9 / LADE	
T-44	Fokker F.27 Friendship 600	10454	PH-EXB	Gr9 / LADE	
T-45	Fokker F.27 Friendship 600	10368	TC-79 (FAA)	Gr9 / LADE	
T-82	DeHavilland Canada DHC-6 Twin Otter 200	167		Gr9 / LADE	Ski equipped
T-83	DeHavilland Canada DHC-6 Twin Otter 200	170		Gr9 / LADE	
T-84	DeHavilland Canada DHC-6 Twin Otter 200	214	LV-JMN	Gr9 / LADE	
T-85	DeHavilland Canada DHC-6 Twin Otter 200	173		Gr9 / LADE	
T-86	DeHavilland Canada DHC-6 Twin Otter 200	225		Gr9 / LADE	Ski equipped
T-87	DeHavilland Canada DHC-6 Twin Otter 200	185?	LV-JPX	Gr9 / LADE	Ski equipped
T-88	DeHavilland Canada DHC-6 Twin Otter 200	158	LV-JMP	Gr9 / LADE	
T-89	DeHavilland Canada DHC-6 Twin Otter 200	179	LV-JMS	Gr9 / LADE	
T-90	DeHavilland Canada DHC-6 Twin Otter 200	178	LV-JMR	Gr9 / LADE	Ski equipped
T-131	Aero Commander 500U Shrike	1742-38		V BA, Esc Ser	
T-132	Aero Commander 500U Shrike	1743-39		RANE Base Flight	
T-133	Aero Commander 500U Shrike	1744-40			Std
T-134	Aero Commander 500U Shrike	1745-41		VI BA, Gr6	
T-135	Aero Commander 500U Shrike	1746-42		RANO Base Flight	
T-136	Aero Commander 500U Shrike	1748-43			Std Quilmes
T-137	Aero Commander 500U Shrike	1749-44			Std
T-139	Aero Commander 500U Shrike	1758-47		VII BA, Gr7	
T-142	Aero Commander 500U Shrike	1769-52			Std Quilmes
T-152	Aero Commander 500B	1131-74	LV-PSS	VII BA, Gr7	
TC-52	Fokker F.28 Fellowship 1000C	11074	LV-RCS	Gr 1 / LADE	
TC-53	Fokker F.28 Fellowship 1000C	11020	PH-EXX	Gr 1 / LADE	
TC-54	Fokker F.28 Fellowship 1000C	11018	LV-VCS	Gr 1 / LADE	
TC-55	Fokker F.28 Fellowship 1000C	11024	PH-EXZ	Gr 1 / LADE	
TC-56	Lockheed C-130B (L-282-1B) Hercules	3515	58-0720 (USAF)	Gr 1/ Esc 1	
TC-57	Lockheed C-130B (L-282-1B) Hercules	3563	59-1526 (USAF)	Gr 1/ Esc 1	
TC-58	Lockheed C-130B (L-282-1B) Hercules	3538	58-0741 (USAF)	Gr 1/ Esc 1	
TC-59	Lockheed C-130B (L-282-1B) Hercules	3649	61-0964 (USAF)	Gr 1/ Esc 1	
TC-60	Lockheed C-130B (L-282-1B) Hercules	3656	61-0969 (USAF)	Gr 1/ Esc 1	
TC-61	Lockheed C-130H (L-382C-12D) Hercules	4308		Gr 1/ Esc 1	Cvtd C-130E
TC-64	Lockheed C-130H (L-382C-23D) Hercules	4436		Gr 1/ Esc 1	
TC-65	Lockheed C-130H (L-382C-23D) Hercules	4437		Gr 1/ Esc 1	
TC-66	Lockheed C-130H (L-382C-23D) Hercules	4464		Gr 1/ Esc 1	
TC-67	Lockheed C-130H (L-382C-48D) Hercules	4576		Gr 1/ Esc 1	
TC-68	Lockheed C-130H (L-382C-48D) Hercules	4578		Gr 1/ Esc 1	
TC-69	Lockheed KC-130H (L-382C-82D) Hercules	4814		Gr 1/ Esc 1	
TC-70	Lockheed KC-130H (L-382C-82D) Hercules	4816		Gr 1/ Esc 1	
TC-71	Fokker F.27 Troopship 400M	10403	PH-FOB	Gr 1/Gr 9 / LADE	
TC-73	Fokker F.27 Troopship 400M	10407	PH-FOF	Gr 1/Gr 9 / LADE	
TC-74	Fokker F.27 Troopship 400M	10408	PH-FOG	Gr 1/Gr 9 / LADE	
TC-75	Fokker F.27 Friendship 500	10621	PH-EXM	Gr9 / LADE	
TC-78	Fokker F.27 Troopship 400M	10418	PH-FOS	Gr 1/Gr 9 / LADE	
TC-79	Fokker F.27 Troopship 400M	10575	PH-EXG	Gr9 / LADE	
TC-91	Boeing 707-387B	21070 / 897	T-01	Gr1, Esc V	
TC-93	Boeing 707-387C	19962 / 755	VR-21 (FAA)	Gr1, Esc V	
TC-100	Lockheed L-100-30 (L-382G-53C) Hercules	4891	LV-APW	Gr1, Esc 1 / LADE	
VR-22	Piper PA-31P Navajo	31P-52	PG-397 (FAA)	INAC, Esc I	
LV-ISD	Boeing 707-387B	19241 / 555	TC-95 (FAA)	Gr1, Esc V	AAR
LV-LGC	Boeing 707-372C	20076 / 721	TC-93 (FAA)	Gr1, Esc V	
LV-WXL	Boeing 707-365C	19590 / 654	JY-AJM	Gr1, Esc V	AAR

Comando de Aviación Naval Argentina - COAN
Argentine Naval Aviation Command

UNITS/BASES	Fuerza Aeronavale 1, BA Punta Indio-Veronica	
	Escuadra Aeronaval 1, Escuela de Aviación Navale	Turbo Porter
	Fuerza Aeronavale 2, BA Comandante Espora-Bahia Blanca	
	Escuadra Aeronaval 2, Escuadrilla Aeronaval Antisubmarina	S-2T
	Fuerza Aeronavale 3, BA ViceAlmirante Zar-Trelew	
	Escuadra Aeronaval 6, Escuadrilla Aeronaval de Exploracion	L-188, P-3B
	Escuadra Aeronaval 6, Escuadrilla Aeronaval de Vigilancia Maritima	B200 Comoran/Petrel
	Escuadra Aeronaval 6, Escuadrilla Aeronaval de Sosten Logistico Movil	F.28-3000

0686 / 4-G-2	Pilatus/Fairchild PC-6/B1A-H2 Turbo Porter	2047		EA4, EAR	
0688 / 4-G-82	Beech Queen Air B80	LD-450			Std
0689 / 4-G-83	Beech Queen Air B80	LD-452			Std
0697 / 4-P-41	Beech Super King Air 200M Cormoran	BB-54		EAVM	
0698 / 4-G-42	Beech Super King Air 200 Petrel	BB-71		EAVM	Survey
0700 / 2-AS-21	Grumman S-2T Turbo Tracker	234C	Bu152346 (USN)	EA2, 1 esc	Cvtd S-2E
0701 / 2-AS-22	Grumman S-2T Turbo Tracker	298C	Bu152829 (USN)	EA2, 1 esc	Cvtd S-2E
0702 / 2-AS-23	Grumman S-2T Turbo Tracker	321C	4X-JYN	EA2, 1 esc	Cvtd S-2E
0704 / 2-AS-25	Grumman S-2T Turbo Tracker	333C	Bu153577 (USN)	EA2, 1 esc	Cvtd S-2E
0740 / 5-T-10	Fokker F.28 Fellowship 3000C	11147	PH-EXW	EA5, 1esc	'Stella Naris'
0741 / 5-T-20	Fokker F.28 Fellowship 3000C	11145	LV-RTC		Std Buenoa Aires/Ezeiza
0742 / 5-T-21	Fokker F.28 Fellowship 3000C	11150	PH-EXX	EA5, 2esc	'Islas Malvinas'
0743 / 4-G-43	Beech Super King Air 200 Petrel	BB-460		EAVM	
0745 / 4-G-45	Beech Super King Air 200 Petrel	BB-488		EAVM	
0747 / 6-P-47	Beech Super King Air 200M Cormoran	BB-546		EAVM	
0748 / 6-P-48	Beech Super King Air 200M Cormoran	BB-549		EAVM	
0790 / 6-P-103	Lockheed L-188W Electra Wave	1070	N5536	EA6, 1esc	
0791 / 6-P-102	Lockheed L-188W Electra Wave	1067	HR-TNN	EA6, 1esc	
0793 / 6-P-104	Lockheed L-188W Electra Wave	1072	N5534	EA6, 1esc	
0867 / 6-P-51	Lockheed P-3B (L-185) Orion	5158	Bu152718 (USN)	EA6, 1esc	
0868 / 6-P-52	Lockheed P-3B (L-185) Orion	5172	Bu152732 (USN)	EA6, 1esc	
0869 / 6-P-53	Lockheed P-3B (L-185) Orion	5186	Bu152746 (USN)	EA6, 1esc	
0870 / 6-P-54	Lockheed P-3B (L-185) Orion	5205	Bu152761 (USN)	EA6, 1esc	
0871 / 6-P-55	Lockheed P-3B (L-185) Orion	5207	Bu152763 (USN)	EA6, 1esc	
0872 / 6-P-56	Lockheed P-3B (L-185) Orion	5216	Bu153419 (USN)	EA6, 1esc	
LV-RTC	Beech Super King Air 200 Petrel	BB-471	0744 (COAN)	EA4, EAR	Survey

Servicio de Aviación de Prefectura Naval Argentina
Argentinian Coast Guard Aviation Service

UNITS/BASES	Estación Aérea Comodoro Rivadavia
PLANS	Looking at acquiring three Airtech CN235MPAs

PA-61	CASA 212 Aviocar srs 300	382	
PA-62	CASA 212 Aviocar srs 300	383	
PA-71	CASA 212 Aviocar srs 300 Patrullero	399	'Isla Soledad'
PA-72	CASA 212 Aviocar srs 300 Patrullero	400	'Isla Gran Malvina'
PA-73	CASA 212 Aviocar srs 300 Patrullero	401	'Golfo San Jorge'
PA-101	Piper PA-23-250 Aztec		

Comando de Aviación del Ejército - CAE
Army Aviation

UNITS/BASES	Escuadrón de Aviación de Apoyo de Inteligencia 601, Campo de Mayo-Buenos Aires	
		OV-1D
	Escuadrón de Aviación de Apoyo 603, Campo de Mayo-Buenos Aires	Various
	Instituto Geografico Militar, Campo de Mayo-Buenos Aires	Queen Air, Citation
	Sección Aviación de Ejército 2, Rosario-Santa Fe	Merlin IIIA
	Sección Aviación de Ejército 4, Cordoba	Merlin IIIA, C207
	Sección Aviación de Ejército 5, Bahia Blanca	Merlin IIIA, C207
PLANS	Ex-US Army C-12s have been requested for some time	

AE-020	Grumman OV-1D Mohawk	69-17008	EAAI601	
AE-021	Grumman OV-1D Mohawk	68-15932		Std
AE-024	Grumman OV-1D Mohawk	68-15941	EAAI601	
AE-025	Grumman OV-1D Mohawk	68-15951	EAAI601	
AE-026	Grumman OV-1D Mohawk	68-16991	EAAI601	
AE-027	Grumman OV-1D Mohawk	62-5865	EAAI601	SLAR
AE-028	Grumman OV-1D Mohawk	67-18921	EAAI601	
AE-029	Grumman OV-1D Mohawk	68-17009		Std
AE-030	Grumman OV-1D Mohawk	62-5887		Std
AE-031	Grumman OV-1D Mohawk	68-15963		Std
AE-032	Grumman OV-1D Mohawk	67-18918		Std
AE-033	Grumman OV-1D Mohawk	69-17012	EAAI601	
AE-034	Grumman OV-1D Mohawk	68-15933	EAAI601	
AE-035	Grumman OV-1D Mohawk	67-18895		Std
AE-036	Grumman OV-1D Mohawk	69-17026		Std
AE-037	Grumman OV-1D Mohawk	68-15954		Std
AE-038	Grumman OV-1D Mohawk	69-17002	Esc d Av	Training
AE-039	Grumman OV-1D Mohawk	69-16997	Esc d Av	Training

AE-040	Grumman OV-1D Mohawk		69-17006		Std
AE-042	Grumman OV-1D Mohawk		69-17016		Std
AE-106	DeHavilland Canada DHC-6 Twin Otter 200	136	AE-257 (CAE)	EAA603	
AE-175	Rockwell Sabreliner 75A	380-13	N65761	EAA603	
AE-176	Swearingen SA226T Merlin IIIA	T-275	N5393M		
AE-178	Swearingen SA226T Merlin IIIA	T-280	N5397M		
AE-179	Swearingen SA226T Merlin IIIA	T-281	N5399M		
AE-180	Swearingen SA226AT Merlin IVA	AT-071E	N5656M	EAA603	
AE-181	Swearingen SA226AT Merlin IVA	AT-063	TS-01 (FAA)	EAA603	
AE-182	Swearingen SA226AT Merlin IVA	AT-064	TS-02 (FAA)	EAA603	
AE-185	Cessna 500 Citation 1	500-0356/366	N36848	IGM	
AE-216	Cessna T207			EAA603	
AE-217	Cessna T207			EAA603	
AE-218	Cessna T207				
AE-219	Cessna T207				
AE-220	Cessna T207				
AE-221	Cessna T207				
AE-222	Cessna T207				
AE-223	Cessna T207A Turbo Stationair 7 II	20700481			
AE-224	Cessna T207A Turbo Stationair 7 II				
AE-261	Aeritalia G222	4011		EAA603	
AE-262	Aeritalia G222	4021		EAA603	
AE-263	DeHavilland Canada DHC-6 Twin Otter 300	594		EAA603	
AE-264	CASA 212 Aviocar srs 200	CC60-3-324	LV-RBB	EAA603	

Gendarmeria Nacional

UNITS/BASES Fixed wing aircraft are based at Campo de Mayo-Buenos Aires with the Aviación de Gendarmeria Argentina.

GN-706	Piper PA-31P Navajo		
GN-802	Cessna 206 Super Skywagon	206-0269	
GN-803	Cessna 206 Super Skywagon	206-0270	
GN-804	Pilatus PC-6/B2-H2 Turbo Porter	786	
GN-805	Pilatus PC-6/B2-H2 Turbo Porter	787	
GN-807	Pilatus PC-6/B2-H2 Turbo Porter	805	
GN-808	Pilatus PC-6/B2-H2 Turbo Porter	806	
GN-809	Pilatus PC-6/B2-H2 Turbo Porter	807	
GN-810	Pilatus PC XII	294	HB-FQI
GN-	Fairchild Metro IV		

Policia Federal
Federal Police

LQ-MRM	Cessna 500 Citation 1	500-0386/470	LV-PAX

Government of the Republic of Argentina

LQ-ZRB	Raytheon Beech King Air C90B	LJ-1552	N3132D	Santiago del Estero State Govt
LQ-ZRG	Raytheon Beech Super King Air B200	BB-1652	LV-PIF	Chaco State Govt
LV-MCW	Pilatus PC-6/B2-H2 Turbo Porter	790		Formosa State Govt
LV-MCX	Pilatus PC-6/B2-H2 Turbo Porter	791		Chaco State Govt
LV-MIS	Pilatus PC-6/B2-H2 Turbo Porter	793		Santiago del Estero State Govt
LV-MYZ	Pilatus PC-6/B2-H2 Turbo Porter	804		Formosa State Govt

---

ARMENIA
Hayastani Hanrapetutyun / Republic of Armenia   SW Asia

Not possessing an Air Force as such Armenia has a defence pact with Russia and air assets come under Army control. VIP transport is carried out with the aid of Armenian Airlines.

SERIAL SYSTEM None noted other than the use of civilian identities and presumably Soviet style two digit tactical codes.

Armenian Army Air Arm

UNITS/BASES	Yerevan-Erebuni, 15 SAP	An-24, An-32B	
	Areni, 60 UAE	An-2	
EK-48026	Antonov An-32B		Armenian AL cs
	Antonov An-2		
	Antonov An-2		
	Antonov An-2		
	Antonov An-2		

Antonov An-2
Antonov An-2
Antonov An-24

Government of the Republic of Armenia

| EK-65072 | Tupolev Tu-134A-3 | 49972 | CCCP-65072 |
| EK-65975 | Tupolev Tu-134A-3 | 3352006 | CCCP-65975 |

AUSTRALIA
| Commonwealth of Australia | Australasia |

Independent within the British Commonwealth and confirming its desire to stay that way rather than become a republic in 1999, Australia is the strongest and most stable of the Pacific Rim countries. Australia has pioneered the modern day trend for leasing rather than buying military aircraft with the Air Force Falcon 900s and then the Army Nomad replacements noted below.

SERIAL SYSTEM All RAAF serials commence with the letter 'A' followed by a one or two digit type identifier, then a dash followed by the individual identity which is either sequential or based on a previous serial or c/n. The Navy use a similar system prefixed with the letter 'N'. As all their aircraft are leased from commercial sources the Army aircraft all bear civil identities, as do leased aircraft of the RAN and RAAF.

Royal Australian Air Force

ICAO code ASY, call signs Windsor (domestic) and Aussie (international), Tanker aircraft callsign Dragon

UNITS/BASES	Air Lift Group		
	84 Wing:		
	32 Sqn, East Sale, VIC	HS.748, B200	Training
	33 Sqn, Richmond, NSW	707	VIP & AAR
	34 Sqn, Fairbairn, NSW	Falcon 900	VIP
	86 Wing:		
	35 Sqn, Townsville, QLD (Det. at Darwin, NT)	Caribou	
	36 Sqn, Richmond, NSW	C-130H	
	37 Sqn, Richmond, NSW	C-130E, (replacing with C-130J	
	38 Sqn, Amberley, QLD (Det. At Pearce, WA)	Caribou	Training
	Surveillance and Control Group		
	42 Wing:		
	2 Sqn, RAAF Williamtown, NSW	Wedgetail	(del. from 2004/5)	AEW
	(Det. of 2 aircraft at RAAF Tindall, NT)		
	Maritime Patrol Group		
	92 Wing:		
	10 Sqn, Edinburgh, SA	Orion	
	11 Sqn, Edinburgh, SA	Orion	
	Training Command		
	School of Air Navigation (SAN), East Sale, VIC	HS748, Super King Air	Nav. training
	Civilian Contractors: Pearl Aviation (ARDU support)	Super King Air	

PLANS Four BBJs on firm order for the AEW&C role as the Wedgetail, serial prefix A30, two more on option.
19 P-3C are to be modified to AP-3C standard by Raytheon in Australia, re-delivery to the RAAF of the initial air craft is still pending.
Replacement of the leased Falcon 900s and VIP 707 with Challenger and BBJ.
Replacement of the remaining HS748s with Super King Airs.
New AAR type by 2004/6 replacing the 707s
Replacement of the Caribou with the C-27J, CN235M-300 and C295M shortlisted, but no changes until 2010.
The C-130Hs and Orions will be refurbished or replaced from 2007 (A400M or C-17 buy a possibility).

A4-140	DeHavilland Canada DHC-4A Caribou	140		38 Sqn	
A4-152	DeHavilland Canada DHC-4A Caribou	152		35 Sqn	
A4-195	DeHavilland Canada DHC-4A Caribou	195		38 Sqn	
A4-199	DeHavilland Canada DHC-4A Caribou	199		38 Sqn	
A4-204	DeHavilland Canada DHC-4A Caribou	204		38 Sqn	
A4-210	DeHavilland Canada DHC-4A Caribou	210			
A4-225	DeHavilland Canada DHC-4A Caribou	225		38 Sqn	
A4-228	DeHavilland Canada DHC-4A Caribou	228		38 Sqn	
A4-231	DeHavilland Canada DHC-4A Caribou	231		38 Sqn	
A4-234	DeHavilland Canada DHC-4A Caribou	234		38 Sqn	
A4-236	DeHavilland Canada DHC-4A Caribou	236		38 Sqn	special c/s
A4-275	DeHavilland Canada DHC-4A Caribou	275		35 Sqn	
A4-285	DeHavilland Canada DHC-4A Caribou	285		35 Sqn	
A4-299	DeHavilland Canada DHC-4A Caribou	299		35 Sqn	
A9-434	Lockheed TAP-3B (L-185) Orion	5231	Bu153434 (USN)	10/11 Sqn	Trainer

A9-438	Lockheed TAP-3B (L-185) Orion	5235	Bu153438 (USN)	10/11 Sqn	Trainer
A9-439	Lockheed TAP-3B (L-185) Orion	5236	Bu153439 (USN)	10/11 Sqn	Trainer
A9-656	Lockheed P-3W (L-285D) Orion	5778	N64854	10 Sqn	Cvtd P-3C-II.5
A9-657	Lockheed AP-3C (L-285D) Sea Sentinel Orion	5780	N64911	Raytheon, Avalon	ESM Testbed
A9-658	Lockheed P-3W (L-285D) Orion	5782	N4009K	10 Sqn	Cvtd P-3C-II.5
A9-659	Lockheed P-3W (L-285D) Orion	5784	N64996	11 Sqn	Cvtd P-3C-II.5
A9-660	Lockheed P-3W (L-285D) Orion	5785	N64854	11 Sqn	Cvtd P-3C-II.5
A9-661	Lockheed P-3W (L-285D) Orion	5787	N64911	10 Sqn	Cvtd P-3C-II.5
A9-662	Lockheed P-3W (L-285D) Orion	5789	N64996	11 Sqn	Cvtd P-3C-II.5
A9-663	Lockheed P-3W (L-285D) Orion	5791	N4009K	11 Sqn	Cvtd P-3C-II.5
A9-664	Lockheed P-3W (L-285D) Orion	5793	N64854	11 Sqn	Cvtd P-3C-II.5
A9-665	Lockheed P-3W (L-285D) Orion	5795	N4009H	10 Sqn	Cvtd P-3C-II.5
A9-751	Lockheed P-3C-II (L-285D) Orion	5657	Bu160751 (FMS)	11 Sqn	
A9-752	Lockheed P-3C-II (L-285D) Orion	5658	Bu160752 (FMS)	10 Sqn	
A9-753	Lockheed P-3C-II (L-285D) Orion	5660	Bu160753 (FMS)	10 Sqn	
A9-755	Lockheed P-3C-II (L-285D) Orion	5664	Bu160755 (FMS)	11 Sqn	
A9-756	Lockheed P-3C-II (L-285D) Orion	5666	Bu160756 (FMS)	11 Sqn	
A9-757	Lockheed P-3C-II (L-285D) Orion	5668	Bu160757 (FMS)	10 Sqn	
A9-758	Lockheed P-3C-II (L-285D) Orion	5672	Bu160758 (FMS)	10 Sqn	
A9-759	Lockheed AP-3C (L-285D) Sea Sentinel Orion	5674	Bu160759 (FMS)	Raytheon, Avalon	Cvtd P-3C-II
A9-760	Lockheed AP-3C (L-285D) Sea Sentinel Orion	5676	Bu160760 (FMS)	Raytheon, Avalon	Cvtd P-3C-II
A10-601	Hawker Siddeley HS.748-228 srs 2	1601/set108	G-AVZD	32 Sqn	
A10-602	Hawker Siddeley HS.748-228 srs 2	1602/set121		32 Sqn	
A10-603	Hawker Siddeley HS.748-228 srs 2	1603/set124		32 Sqn	
A10-605	Hawker Siddeley HS.748-228 srs 2	1605/set130		32 Sqn	
A10-606	Hawker Siddeley HS.748-228 srs 2	1606/set133		32 Sqn	
A10-608	Hawker Siddeley HS.748-228 srs 2	1608/set137		32 Sqn	
A20-261	Boeing 707-368C	21261 / 919	N7486B	33 Sqn	VIP
A20-623	Boeing 707-338C	19623 / 671	C-GRYN	33 Sqn	AAR
A20-624	Boeing 707-338C	19624 / 689	VH-EAD	33 Sqn	AAR
A20-627	Boeing 707-338C	19627 / 707	VH-EAG	33 Sqn	AAR
A20-629	Boeing 707-338C	19629 / 737	C-GGAB	33 Sqn	AAR
A26-C70	Dassault Falcon 900	70	N450FJ	34 Sqn	
A26-C73	Dassault Falcon 900	73	N452FJ	34 Sqn	
A26-C74	Dassault Falcon 900	74	N453FJ	34 Sqn	
A26-C76	Dassault Falcon 900	76	N454FJ	34 Sqn	
A26-C77	Dassault Falcon 900	77	N455FJ	34 Sqn	
A32-C01	Beech Super King Air B200	BB-1125	VH-KBH	SAN	
A32-C02	Beech Super King Air B200	BB-1189	VH-KCH	SAN	
A32-C03	Beech Super King Air B200	BB-1401	VH-YDH	SAN	
A32-C04	Beech Super King Air B200	BB-1463	VH-YEH	SAN	
A97-C01	Lockheed C-130H (L-382C-71D) Hercules	4780		36 Sqn	
A97-C02	Lockheed C-130H (L-382C-71D) Hercules	4782		36 Sqn	
A97-C03	Lockheed C-130H (L-382C-71D) Hercules	4783		36 Sqn	
A97-C04	Lockheed C-130H (L-382C-71D) Hercules	4784		36 Sqn	
A97-C05	Lockheed C-130H (L-382C-71D) Hercules	4785		36 Sqn	
A97-C06	Lockheed C-130H (L-382C-71D) Hercules	4786		36 Sqn	
A97-C07	Lockheed C-130H (L-382C-71D) Hercules	4787		36 Sqn	
A97-C08	Lockheed C-130H (L-382C-71D) Hercules	4788		36 Sqn	
A97-C09	Lockheed C-130H (L-382C-71D) Hercules	4789		36 Sqn	
A97-C10	Lockheed C-130H (L-382C-71D) Hercules	4790		36 Sqn	
A97-C11	Lockheed C-130H (L-382C-71D) Hercules	4791		36 Sqn	
A97-C12	Lockheed C-130H (L-382C-71D) Hercules	4793		36 Sqn	
A97-440	Lockheed Martin C-130J-30 (L-382V-03J) Hercules II	5440	N4080M	37 Sqn	
A97-441	Lockheed Martin C-130J-30 (L-382V-03J) Hercules II	5441	N130JV	37 Sqn	
A97-442	Lockheed Martin C-130J-30 (L-382V-03J) Hercules II	5442	N130JR	37 Sqn	
A97-447	Lockheed Martin C-130J-30 (L-382V-03J) Hercules II	5447	N73232	37 Sqn	
A97-448	Lockheed Martin C-130J-30 (L-382V-03J) Hercules II	5448	N73230	37 Sqn	
A97-449	Lockheed Martin C-130J-30 (L-382V-03J) Hercules II	5449	N73233	37 Sqn	
A97-450	Lockheed Martin C-130J-30 (L-382V-03J) Hercules II	5450	N4187W	37 Sqn	
A97-464	Lockheed Martin C-130J-30 (L-382V-03J) Hercules II	5464		37 Sqn	
A97-465	Lockheed Martin C-130J-30 (L-382V-03J) Hercules II	5465		37 Sqn	
A97-466	Lockheed Martin C-130J-30 (L-382V-03J) Hercules II	5466	N4107F	37 Sqn	

A97-467	Lockheed Martin C-130J-30 (L-382V-03J) Hercules II				
		5467	N73235	37 Sqn	
A97-468	Lockheed Martin C-130J-30 (L-382V-03J) Hercules II				
		5468		37 Sqn	
VH-OYA	Beech Super King Air 200	BB-365	P2-SML	ARDU	Lsf Pearl Avn

Royal Australian Navy - RAN

UNITS/BASES	Civilian Contractors - Pel Air			Learjet (Target Support)	
PLANS	Replacement of the HS748s with a civilian contractors operation				
N15-710 / 801	Hawker Siddeley HS.748-228 srs 2	1710/set202			Std East Sale
VH-SLD	Learjet 35A	35A-145	N145GJ	Pel Air	
VH-SLE	Learjet 35A	35A-428	N17LH	Pel Air	
VH-SLF	Learjet 36A	36A-049	N136ST	Pel Air	
VH-SLJ	Learjet 36	36-014	N200Y	Pel Air	

Australian Army Aviation Corps - AAAC

UNITS/BASES	1 Aviation Regiment				
	173 Sqn, Oakey, QLD (det. At Darwin, NT)			Super King Air, Twin Otter (Surveillance)	
VH-FNT	DeHavilland Canada DHC-6 Twin Otter 300	280	P2-GVI	173 Sqn	Lsd
VH-FNY	DeHavilland Canada DHC-6 Twin Otter 300	527	VH-OHP	173 Sqn	Lsd
VH-HPJ	Beech Super King Air 350 (B300)	FL-166	N6786S	173 Sqn	RADAR testbed
VH-HPP	Beech Super King Air B200C	BL-137	ZS-NSD	173 Sqn	Lsd
VH-HPT	DeHavilland Canada DHC-6 Twin Otter 300	707	VH-USW	173 Sqn	Lsd
VH-HPX	Beech Super King Air B200	BB-1505	N3197L	173 Sqn	Lsd
VH-HPZ	Beech Super King Air B200C	BL-138	VH-AJM	173 Sqn	Lsd

Australian Customs Service / Surveillance Australia

UNITS/BASES	All aircraft are operated by the National Jet Systems subsidiary Surveillance Australia from bases at Broome, Darwin (NT), Cairns (QLD) and Horn Island			
VH-LCL	DeHavilland Canada DHC-8-202 Dash 8	492	C-GEOA	Survey
VH-ZZA	DeHavilland Canada DHC-8-202 Dash 8 MPA	419	C-FWWU	MR
VH-ZZB	DeHavilland Canada DHC-8-202 Dash 8 MPA	424	C-FXBC	MR
VH-ZZC	DeHavilland Canada DHC-8-202 Dash 8 MPA	433	C-FXFK	MR
VH-ZZE	Reims/Cessna F406 Vigilant	F406-0076	F-WZDX	MR
VH-ZZF	Reims/Cessna F406 Vigilant	F406-0078	F-WZDY	MR
VH-ZZG	Reims/Cessna F406 Vigilant	F406-0079	F-WZDZ	MR
VH-ZZI	Bombardier DeHavilland DHC-8-202 Dash 8 MPA 550		C-GDLD	MR
VH-ZZJ	Bombardier DeHavilland DHC-8-202 Dash 8 MPA 551		C-FDHI	MR
VH-ZZS	Aero Commander 500S Shrike	3071	N45WS	MR
VH-ZZT	Pilatus Britten-Norman BN-2B-20 Islander	2279	G-BVNC	MR
VH-ZZU	Pilatus Britten-Norman BN-2B-20 Islander	2280	G-BVND	MR
VH-ZZV	Pilatus Britten-Norman BN-2B-20 Islander	2281	G-BVNE	MR
VH-ZZW	Pilatus Britten-Norman BN-2B-20 Islander	2282	G-BVNF	MR
VH-ZZX	Pilatus Britten-Norman BN-2B-20 Islander	2283	G-BVSG	MR
VH-ZZY	Pilatus Britten-Norman BN-2B-20 Islander	2284	G-BVSH	MR

AUSTRIA
Republik Österreich   C Europe

Becoming independent again in 1955 after Allied occupation following World War II, Austria's defence spending is the lowest in Europe despite the country's wealth and Austria remains non-aligned and neutral. Larger transports are leased as required.

SERIAL SYSTEM   Each type is given a two character alphanumeric code which is followed by a two letter identifier, sequential by type commencing *A.

Österreichische Luftstreitkrafte - OLK
Austrian Air Defence Forces

UNITS/BASES	Fliegerregiment 1, Tulln-Langenlebarn	
	4 Flachenstaffel	Skyvan, PC-6, CN.235
	detachment at Wiener-Neustadt	

PLANS	2/4 new transports are required, a CN235 is leased for evaluation, but the final choice may be C-130s.			
3G-EA	Pilatus PC-6B2/H2 Turbo Porter	752		4 FlaSta
3G-EB	Pilatus PC-6B2/H2 Turbo Porter	758		4 FlaSta
3G-EC	Pilatus PC-6B2/H2 Turbo Porter	764		4 FlaSta
3G-ED	Pilatus PC-6B2/H2 Turbo Porter	765		4 FlaSta
3G-EE	Pilatus PC-6B2/H2 Turbo Porter	766		4 FlaSta
3G-EF	Pilatus PC-6B2/H2 Turbo Porter	769		4 FlaSta
3G-EG	Pilatus PC-6B2/H2 Turbo Porter	770		4 FlaSta
3G-EH	Pilatus PC-6B2/H2 Turbo Porter	771		4 FlaSta
3G-EJ	Pilatus PC-6B2/H2 Turbo Porter	775		4 FlaSta
3G-EK	Pilatus PC-6B2/H2 Turbo Porter	776		4 FlaSta
3G-EL	Pilatus PC-6B2/H2 Turbo Porter	777		4 FlaSta
3G-EM	Pilatus PC-6B2/H2 Turbo Porter	856		4 FlaSta
5S-TA	Shorts SC.7 Skyvan srs 3M	SH.1855	G-14-27	4 FlaSta
5S-TB	Shorts SC.7 Skyvan srs 3M	SH.1860	G-14-32	4 FlaSta
6T-AA	Airtech/CASA CN235-300	C130	EC-101	4 FlaSta	Leased from CASA

Bundesministerium Für Inneres - Flugpolizei
Federal Ministry of the Interior (Air Police)

UNITS/BASES	Aircraft are based at Vienna-Meidling		
OE-BIA	Pilatus PC-6B2-H2 Turbo Porter	664	OE-BBL
OE-BIB	Cessna 207 Skywagon	20700165	OE-DEX

AZERBAIJAN
Azarbaycan Respublikasy   SW Asia

This CIS member bordering Iran experienced an oil boom in the 1990s and fought their other neighbour, Armenia, over the Nagorno-Karabakh territory. Russia brokered a ceasefire in 1994 and little new equipment has been acquired since.

SERIAL SYSTEM Serials are based on the former Soviet identities with new civil prefixes.

Azeri Air Forces and Air Defence Forces

UNITS/BASES	Gyandzha, OO-VTA		An-12, An-24, IL-76, Tu-134	
4K-12425	Antonov An-12BP	2401103	CCCP-12425	
	Antonov An-24			
4K-65496	Tupolev Tu-135 (Tu-134A-3)	63468	4K-65985	
4K-86810	Ilyushin Il-76M	053404094	RA-86810	Aeroflot cs

Government of the Republic of Azerbaijan

4K-AZ10	Tupolev Tu-154M	98A-1013		Azerbaijan AL cs
4K-85729	Tupolev Tu-154M	92A-911	CCCP-85729	Azerbaijan AL cs
4K-65711	Tupolev Tu-134B-3	63498	AL-65711	

BAHAMAS
Commonwealth of the Bahamas   W Indies

Independent within the Commonwealth since 1973 but still nominally reliant on the UK for defence. The Defence Force is primarily a Coastguard air support operation, given that the state consists of several hundred small islands.

SERIAL SYSTEM Defence Force aircraft are prefixed DF followed by a four digit serial, the Police aircraft carry the RBPF prefix.

Royal Bahamas Defence Force - Air Wing

UNITS/EASES	Aircraft based at Nassau-Windsor Field, New Providence Island.		
DF-1001	Cessna 421C Golden Eagle III	421C-1206	HK-2997

Royal Bahamas Police Force

UNITS/EASES	The Air Element operates from Nassau-Windsor Field, New Providence Island.			
RBPF-1	Colemill Panther Navajo	31-8212034	HK-2939	cvtd PA-31-325
RBPF-2	Colemill Panther Navajo	(no c/n plate)		cvtd PA-31-325

BAHRAIN

Dawlat al Bahrain

SW Asia

Independent from the United Kingdom in 1971 and now a close US ally frequently hosting US military deployments. Equipment is almost exclusively of US origin. The combat air arm the Bahrain Amiri Air Force do not currently operate transports although C-130s are earmarked for acquisition. The civil registered VIP fleet is operated by the Amiri Flight.

SERIAL SYSTEM Civilian registrations are allocated for the Amiri Flight

Bahrain Amiri Flight

ICAO code BAH, Callsign Bahrain One

UNITS/BASES All aircraft are based at Sintrah-Shaikh Isa AB

A9C-BA	Boeing 727-2M7 Advanced (Super 27)	21824 / 1595	N740RW	'Al Bahrain'
A9C-BAH	GAC Gulfstream IV-SP	1353	N353GA	
A9C-BDF1	Avro RJ85	E2390	G-6-390	
A9C-BG	Grumman G-1159 Gulfstream IITT	202	N17586	
A9C-HHH	Boeing 747SP-21	21649 / 373	V8-AC1	

BANGLADESH

Gana Prajatantri Bangladesh / People's Republic of Bangladesh

S Asia

Originally became independent from India in 1972 as East Pakistan and considered politically stable since 1991. The Soviet and Chinese equipment operated since the Air Force was established in 1973 now look ready for replacement by Western types subject to finance being made available.

SERIAL SYSTEM A civilian style registration is allocated but the aircraft also display the c/n or previous identity as a military serial.

Bangladesh Biman Bahini
Bangladesh Defence Force Air Wing

UNITS/BASES 3 (Unicorn) Sqn, Jessore/Matiur Rahman AB   An-32

1701 / S3-ACA	Antonov An-32	1701		3 Sqn
1702 / S3-ACB	Antonov An-32	1702		Std Tejgoan
3505 / S3-ACD	Antonov An-32	3505		3 Sqn
10962	Lockheed C-130B (L-282-1B) Hercules	3647	61-0962 (USAF)	On order
12640 / S3-AGD	Lockheed C-130B (L-282-1B) Hercules	3676	61-2640 (USAF)	On order
80754	Lockheed C-130B (L-282-1B) Hercules	3553	58-0754 (USAF)	On order
91537	Lockheed C-130B (L-282-1B) Hercules	3589	59-1537 (USAF)	On order

Government of the People's Republic of Bangladesh

S3-BHN	Piper PA-31T Cheyenne 1A	31T-1104007	N2436W

BARBADOS

W Indies

Despite making moves to become a Republic the Barbados Islands remain independent within the British Commonwealth. The new Regional Security Systems organisation appears to have been established with US assistance as a counter-drug operation.

SERIAL SYSTEM The DF aircraft remain civil registered while the new Regional Security Systems aircraft are prefixed RSS.

Barbados Defence Force

UNITS/BASES The Defence Wing is based at Bridgetown-Grantly Adams International.

8P-DFA	Cessna 402C	402C-0427	N6788P

Regional Security Systems

UNITS/BASES Operate from Bridgetown-Grantly Adams International.

RSS-A1	Fairchild C-26A Metro (SA.227AC)	(USAF)
RSS-A2	Fairchild C-26A Metro (SA.227AC)	(USAF)

BELARUS
Respublika Belarus   E Europe

Belarus (or Byelorussia-White Russia) retains close ties with Russia through a defence pact and many of its military aircraft retain the Soviet red star marking. Russian forces still operate from Belarus sites. The Il-76 transports operated by the commercial carrier Belavia are also reported as being Air Force owned, all being former Soviet military equipment.

SERIAL SYSTEM Aircraft either bear the former Soviet civil registration, usually with the 'EW-' Belarus prefix, or the old Soviet style two digit tactical code.

Voyenno-Vozdushnyve Sily
Military Air Forces

UNITS/BASES	Minsk-Machulishchi, 50 TAB		An-26, An-24, An-12, Il-76, Tu-134	
EW-63955	Tupolev Tu-135 (Tu-134A)	63955	CCCP-63955	Command Post
CCCP-76709	Ilyushin Il-76MD	0063473173		Aeroflot cs
CCCP-78761	Ilyushin Il-76MD	0083486570		
EW-78763	Ilyushin Il-76MD	0083486582	CCCP-78763	Aeroflot cs
EW-78793	Ilyushin Il-76MD	0093490721	CCCP-78793	Aeroflot cs
EW-78302	Ilyushin Il-76MD	0093492771	CCCP-78802	Aeroflot cs
CCCP-86646	Ilyushin Il-76	043402053		
01 yellow	Antonov An-24B	09902203		
02 yellow	Antonov An-26	5501		
03 yellow	Antonov An-26	3501		
03 yellow	Antonov An-2	116047308		
04 yellow	Antonov/PZL-Mielec An-2T	1G160-54		
08 yellow	Antonov An-12BP	4342108		
10 yellow	Antonov An-12BP	7345210		
11 yellow	Antonov An-12BP	8345410		
12 yellow	Antonov An-12BP	00347407		
14 yellow	Antonov/PZL-Mielec An-2T	1G108-03		
21 yellow	Antonov An-26	4708		
23 yellow	Antonov An-26	1503		
24 yellow	Antonov An-26RTR	1504		
25 yellow	Antonov An-26	6604		
26 yellow	Antonov An-26	6006		
61 yellow	Antonov/PZL-Mielec An-2T	1G195-59		
86 black	Antonov/PZL-Mielec An-2T	1G237-01		

Government of the Republic of Belarus

EW-85315	Tupolev Tu-154M	95A-1010		VIP
EW-88202	Yakovlev Yak-40	9630449	CCCP-88202	Belavia cs

BELGIUM
Koninkrijk België/Royaume de Belgique   W Europe

A founder member of NATO and location of its headquarters, Belgium is a dual-language kingdom. Its former African colonies (the Congo (DR), Rwanda and Burundi) have all been given independence but still receive support in times of crisis. Until October 2000 the Gendarmarie operated a Turbine Islander, but this was damaged beyond repair in a ground accident and replacement has not yet been confirmed.

SERIAL SYSTEM Each AF aircraft type is allocated a two letter designation the first letter of which determines the role (ie C for cargo/transport), individual aircraft are then identified with a sequential number. The Army uses a similar system but with a single letter prefix.

Force Aérienne Belge / Belgische Luchtmacht
Belgian Air Force

ICAO code AFB, callsign Belgian Air Force

UNITS/BASES	15 Wing, 20 Smaldeel, Brussels-Melsbroek	C-130H
	15 Wing, 21 Smaldeel, Brussels-Melsbroek	A310, Falcon 20/900, Merlin, HS748, ERJ-135

PLANS	Seven A400M are to be budgeted for (reduced from 12).
	The four ERJs will replace the Merlins and HS748s.
	Two more ERJs (this time VIP Legacy models) are required to replace the three Falcons of 21sm.

CA-01	Airbus Industrie A310-222	372	9V-STN	15w/21sm	
CA-02	Airbus Industrie A310-222	367	9V-STM	15w/21sm	
CD-01	Dassault Falcon 900B	109	G-BTIB	15w/21sm	
CE-01	Embraer ERJ-135LR	145449	PT-SUU	15w/21sm	
CE-02	Embraer ERJ-135LR	145486		15w/21sm	
CE-03	Embraer ERJ-145			15w/21sm	on order 2002
CE-04	Embraer ERJ-145			15w/21sm	on order 2002
CF-01	Swearingen SA226T Merlin IIIA	T-259	N5374M		Std Weelde
CF-02	Swearingen SA226T Merlin IIIA	T-260	N5373M		Std Melsbroek
CF-04	Swearingen SA226T Merlin IIIA	T-264	N5378M	15w/21sm	
CF-05	Swearingen SA226T Merlin IIIA	T-265	N5381M	15w/21sm	
CF-06	Swearingen SA226T Merlin IIIA	T-267	N5382M		Std Melsbroek
CH-01	Lockheed C-130H (L-382C-25D) Hercules	4455	71-1797 (FMS)	15w/20sm	
CH-02	Lockheed C-130H (L-382C-25D) Hercules	4460	71-1798 (FMS)	15w/20sm	
CH-03	Lockheed C-130H (L-382C-25D) Hercules	4461	71-1799 (FMS)	15w/20sm	
CH-04	Lockheed C-130H (L-382C-25D) Hercules	4467	71-1800 (FMS)	15w/20sm	
CH-05	Lockheed C-130H (L-382C-25D) Hercules	4470	71-1801 (FMS)	15w/20sm	
CH-07	Lockheed C-130H (L-382C-25D) Hercules	4476	71-1803 (FMS)	15w/20sm	
CH-08	Lockheed C-130H (L-382C-25D) Hercules	4478	71-1804 (FMS)	15w/20sm	
CH-09	Lockheed C-130H (L-382C-25D) Hercules	4479	71-1805 (FMS)	15w/20sm	
CH-10	Lockheed C-130H (L-382C-25D) Hercules	4481	71-1806 (FMS)	15w/20sm	Open skies aircraft
CH-11	Lockheed C-130H (L-382C-25D) Hercules	4482	71-1807 (FMS)	15w/20sm	
CH-12	Lockheed C-130H (L-382C-25D) Hercules	4483	71-1808 (FMS)	15w/20sm	
CM-01	Dassault Falcon 20E	276	F-WNGL	15w/21sm	c/s BAF31
CM-02	Dassault Falcon 20E	278	F-WNGM	15w/21sm	c/s BAF32
CS-01	Hawker Siddeley HS.748-288 srs 2A (LFD)	1741/set222		15w/21sm	
CS-02	Hawker Siddeley HS.748-288 srs 2A (LFD)	1742/set223		15w/21sm	
CS-03	Hawker Siddeley HS.748-288 srs 2A (LFD)	1743/set224	G-BEEM		Std Weelde

Aviation Légère de la Force Terrestre / Licht Vliegwezen van de Landmacht
Belgian Army - Light Aviation Group

UNITS/BASES	16 Regiment, Liége-Bierset AB			Islander	
	École d'Aviation Légère/School Licht Vliegwezen, Brasschaat AAF			Islander	
B-01 / LA	Britten-Norman BN-2A-21 Islander	466	G-BDJA		c/s 'OT-ALA'
B-02 / LB	Britten-Norman BN-2B-21 Islander	468	G-BDHG	Min of Enviroment	c/s 'OT-ALB'
B-03 / LC	Britten-Norman BN-2B-21 Islander	476	G-BDJV		c/s 'OT-ALC'
B-04 / LD	Britten-Norman BN-2B-21 Islander	498	G-BDPN		c/s 'OT-ALD'
B-07 / LG	Britten-Norman BN-2B-21 Islander	523	G-BDVX	16 Reg	c/s 'OT-ALG'
B-08 / LH	Britten-Norman BN-2B-21 Islander	531	G-BDZI		c/s 'OT-ALH'
B-09 / LI	Britten-Norman BN-2B-21 Islander	533	G-BDZK		c/s 'OT-ALI'
B-10 / LJ	Britten-Norman BN-2B-21 Islander	541	G-BEDW		c/s 'OT-ALJ'
B-11 / LK	Britten-Norman BN-2B-21 Islander	549	G-BEED		c/s 'OT-ALK'
B-12 / LL	Britten-Norman BN-2B-21 Islander	553	G-BEFI	Nat Geografic Inst.	c/s 'OT-ALL'

BELIZE

C America

Formerly known as British Honduras, all UK forces but for a small British Army training unit have now been withdrawn although a lot of UK interests remain. The Air Wing was formed in 1983. US DEA aircraft operate within the country to enforce anti drug policing.

SERIAL SYSTEM The Defence Force aircraft are prefixed BDF followed by a two digit serial.

Belize Defence Force Air Wing

UNITS/BASES	All aircraft are based at Belize City		
BDF-01	Pilatus Britten-Norman BN-2B-21 Defender	2137	G-BJYR
BDF-02	Pilatus Britten-Norman BN-2B-21 Defender	2136	G-BJYP

BENIN
République du Benin   W Africa

Formerly the French colony of Dahomey, Benin was granted independence in 1960, Benin has a dependence on Nigeria for industrial products and the two countries are regarded as close. Antonov An-26s have also been reported as being operated in conjunction with a national airline.

SERIAL SYSTEM Civil registrations are allocated in a unique TY-A** block, the Twin Otter technically being owned by the Government is in a separate sequence.

Force Aérienne du Benin
Benin Air Force

UNITS/BASES   The Twin Otter operates from Cotonou with the Department Vols Commerciaux

TY-AAA	Aero Commander 500B	1110-65	N6241X	
TY-AAK	Dornier 28D-2 Skyservant	4348	D-IAVH	Std Cotonou
TY-AAL	Dornier 28D-2 Skyservant	4349	D-IAVI	Std Cotonou
TY-BBS	DeHavilland Canada DHC-6 Twin Otter 300	807	C-GESR	

BHUTAN
Druk Gyal Khab   SE Asia

Independent Eastern Himalayan Kingdom strongly influenced by India in external affairs. The Army operated Dornier is often quoted as being in service but has never been reported, it is assumed to be an Indian HAL-built aircraft.

SERIAL SYSTEM No details are known, the country's civil prefix is A5-.

Royal Bhutan Army

UNITS/BASES   Based at Thimpu Airport

-               Dornier 228

BOLIVIA
República de Bolivia   S America

Despite support from the USA to assist with the anti drug operations the FAB still gets by with limited funding. Flying the military air-line (TAM) to parts of the country that would not support a commercial operation, the FAB also have TAB leasing DC-8s when required from the USA. Being landlocked it is odd that Bolivia has a Navy but it does and it too has a patrol aircraft to monitor rivers and lakes. It is believed that the Bolivian Army (Ejercito) currently has no applicable fixed wing aircraft in service.

SERIAL SYSTEM Air Force serials are allocated by type in blocks and are prefixed on the aircraft 'FAB' unless operated by TAM in which case that prefix is substituted. These can change as equipment is exchanged. The Navy and Police use prefixes AB and CB respectively.

Fuerza Aérea Bolivana
Bolivian Air Force

UNITS/BASES   I Brigada Aéreo, BA General Walter Arze, El Alto-La Paz

Grupo Aéreo de Caza 31, Escuadrón 311	Various (supporting AT-33)
Grupo Aéreo 71, Escuadrón 711	C-130A/H
Grupo Aéreo 71, Escuadrón 712	F-27, CV580, Arava, Electra
- aircraft operate for Transporte Aéreo Militair (TAM)	
Grupo Aéreo 91, Escuadrón 911	Learjet, Super King Air
Servicio Nacional de Aerofotogrametrica	Learjet, C402, Aztec
Escuadrilla Ejecutiva	Various VIP transports
II Brigada Aéreo	
Grupo Aéreo Mixto, BA de Colcapiru-Cochabamba	Turbo Porter
Grupo Aéreo 61, Escuadrón 611, BA Jorge Wilsterman,Rebore	Turbo Porter
Grupo Aéreo 62, Escuadrón 621, Riberalta	Various
Grupo Aéreo 72, Escuadrón 721, BA Jorge Wilsterman, Rebore	BT-67
III Brigada Aéreo, BA El Trompillo, Santa Cruz de la Sierra	
Grupo Aéreo de Caza 32, Escuadrón 321	Baron (supporting AT-33)

001	Rockwell Sabreliner 60	306-115	N2118J	Esc Ejec	
003	Cessna 402B	402B-0108	N7858Q		
005	Cessna 421B Golden Eagle				
008	Learjet 25B	25B-192		SNA	Survey
010	Learjet 25D	25D-211	N3514F		
018	Beech Super King Air 200C	BL-28			
021	Cessna 402C	402C-0614	N68790	SNA	
026	Beech King Air			Gr 31	
029	Beech Baron 58	TH-1260	N1804Z	Gr 32	
031	Beech Baron 58			Gr 31	
041	Beech Baron 55			Gr 31	
66	Lockheed C-130B (L-282-1B) Hercules	3560	59-1524 (USAF)	Gr 71	
71	Convair 580 (cvtd CV440-47)	370	TAM71 (FABo)		Std la Paz
72	Convair 580 (cvtd CV340-31)	132	TAM72 (FABo)	Gr 71	
73	Convair 580 (cvtd CV340-60)	170	TAM73 (FABo)	Gr 71	
76	IAI Arava srs 201	0024	TAM76 (FABo)	Gr 71	
90	Fokker F.27 Troopship 400M	10578	TAM90 (FABo)	Gr 71	
91	Fokker F.27 Troopship 400M	10580	TAM91 (FABo)	Gr 71	
92	Fokker F.27 Troopship 400M	10584	TAM92 (FABo)	Gr 71	
94	Fokker F.27 Troopship 400M	10600	CP-2282	Gr 71	
207	Cessna U206				
211	Cessna U206				
222	Cessna U206C Super Skywagon	U206-0980			
227	Cessna 210				
229	Cessna U206F Stationair	U20601735			
237	Cessna U206G Stationair 6 II	U20605929			
238	Cessna U206G Stationair 6 II	U20605996			
239	Cessna U206G Stationair 6 II	U20606046			
240	Cessna U206G Stationair 6 II	U20606075			
241	Cessna U206G Stationair 6 II	U20606089			
242	Cessna U206G Stationair 6 II	U20606098			
243	Cessna U206G Stationair 6 II	U20606121			
251	Cessna U206				
261	Cessna T210L Turbo Centurion II	21059975	FAB238		
271	Cessna U206				
273	Cessna U206				
280	Cessna U206				
290	Cessna U206G Stationair 6 II				
293	Cessna U206G Stationair 6 II				
294	Cessna U206				
306	Cessna U206				
320	Cessna U206				
324	Cessna U206				
325	Cessna U206				
326	Cessna U206				
331	Cessna U206G Stationair 6 II				
338	Cessna U206				
339	Cessna 210				
346	Cessna 210L Centurion II	21061251			
TAM01	Lockheed L-188A Electra	1125	TAM69 (FABo)		Std La Paz
TAM25	Basler BT-67 Turbo Dakota	32626	44-76294	Gr 72	Cvtd C-47
TAM38	Basler BT-67 Turbo Dakota	20507	FAB1038 (FABo)	Gr 72	Cvtd C-47A
TAM61	Lockheed C-130A (L-182-1A) Hercules	3181	57-0474 (USAF)		Std La Paz
TAM68	Lockheed C-130B (L-282-1B) Hercules	3655	61-0968 (USAF)		Std La Paz
TAM69	Lockheed C-130H (L-382C-72D) Hercules	4759	TAM91 (FABo)	TAM/Gr 71	
TAM70	Convair 580 (cvtd CV340-31)	94	N73140		Std La Paz
TAM74	Convair 580 (cvtd CV440-12)	367	N73164		Std La Paz
TAM75	IAI Arava srs 201	0021	4X-IAT	TAM/Gr 71	
TAM78	IAI Arava srs 201	0030	4X-IBC	TAM/Gr 71	
TAM79	IAI Arava srs 201	0032	4X-IBE	TAM/Gr 71	
TAM80	IAI Arava srs 201	0042	4X-IBO	TAM/Gr 71	
TAM85	CASA 212 Aviocar srs 100	90	221 (FAS)		Std La Paz
TAM93	Fokker F.27 Troopship 400M	10599	PH-EXC		Std La Paz
TAM95	Fokker F.27 Troopship 400M	10601	PH-FTW		Std La Paz

Armada Boliviano
Bolivian Navy

UNITS/BASES The single aircraft is based at La Paz-El Alto

AB-102	Cessna 402C	402C0605	C-GNJM

Carabinero Boliviano
Bolivian Police

CB-001   Cessna 421B Golden Eagle

BOSNIA-HERZEGOVINA
Republika Bosnia i Hercegovina   SE Europe

Initial independence from Yugoslavia in 1991 had to be supported by United Nations peacekeepers (UNPROFOR) following prolonged and brutal fighting. Peace was finally achieved in 1995 following NATO airstrikes and a subsequent occupation by NATO forces as IFOR and later SFOR. Two armed forces exist within the country, the Vojska Federacije of the Bosniac and Croat Federation and the Serbian Republika Srpska, however neither operate transport aircraft.

Government of the Srpska Republic

T9-SEA   Cessna 550 Citation II

BOTSWANA
Republic of Botswana   S Africa

Independent within the British Commonwealth since 1966, the Defence Force was established in 1977 to support Police operations. A true combat capability was obtained in 1997 with ex Canadian CF-5s, until then only transport and light strike duties were performed.

SERIAL SYSTEM   All serials commence with the letter 'O' the second letter is unique to type, individual aircraft being identified with a sequential number.

Botswana Defence Force Air Arm

UNITS/BASES   All aircraft are now reported as being based at the new base at Molepolole

Z1 Sqn	CN235, Defender
Z2 Sqn	Defender
Z3 Sqn	Defender
Z10 Sqn	Aviocar
Z12 Sqn	G-IV, Defender

PLANS   The C-130Bs are being internally upgraded in the USA

OA1	Britten-Norman BN-2A-21 Defender	791	G-BDTC	Z1 Sqn	
OA2	Britten-Norman BN-2A-21 Defender	783	G-BDRP	Z1 Sqn	
OA3	Britten-Norman BN-2A-21 Defender	799	G-BDTK	Z3 Sqn	
OA4	Britten-Norman BN-2A-21 Defender	772	G-BDMT	Z2 Sqn	
OA5	Britten-Norman BN-2A-21 Defender	836	G-BEMN	Z3 Sqn	
OA6	Britten-Norman BN-2A-21 Defender	918	G-BIUC	Z3 Sqn	
OA7	Pilatus Britten-Norman BN-2B-20 Defender	2226	G-BRSS	Z12 Sqn	
OA8	Pilatus Britten-Norman BN-2B-20 Defender	2227	G-BRST	Z12 Sqn	
OA9	Pilatus Britten-Norman BN-2B-20 Defender	2257	G-BTVK	Z12 Sqn	
OA10	Pilatus Britten-Norman BN-2B-20 Defender	2258	G-BTVL	Z12 Sqn	
OA11	Pilatus Britten-Norman BN-2B-20 Defender	2265	G-BUBH	Z12 Sqn	
OA12	Pilatus Britten-Norman BN-2B-20 Defender	2295	G-BWNE	Z12 Sqn	
OB1	Beech Super King Air B200	BB-1352	N5568V		
OC1	CASA 212 Aviocar srs 300	392	EC-006	Z12 Sqn	
OC2	CASA 212 Aviocar srs 300	394		Z12 Sqn	
OG1	Airtech/CASA CN235M-100	C008		Z12 Sqn	
OG2	Airtech/CASA CN235M-100	C009		Z12 Sqn	
OK1	GAC Gulfstream IV	1173	N17587	Z12 Sqn	Government
OM1	Lockheed C-130B (L-282-1B) Hercules	3506	58-0711 (USAF)		
OM2	Lockheed C-130B (L-282-1B) Hercules	3544	58-0746 (USAF)		
OM3	Lockheed C-130B (L-282-1B) Hercules	3539	58-0742 (USAF)		
	Cessna O-2A Super Skymaster	M337-0205	68-10840 (USAF)		
	Cessna O-2A Super Skymaster	M337-0322	68-11046 (USAF)		
	Cessna O-2A Super Skymaster	M337-0326	68-11050 (USAF)		
	Cessna O-2A Super Skymaster	M337-0394	68-11169 (USAF)		
	Cessna O-2A Super Skymaster	M337-0397	68-11172 (USAF)		
	Cessna O-2A Super Skymaster	M337-0413	69-7615 (USAF)		
	Cessna O-2A Super Skymaster	M337-0448	69-7650 (USAF)		
	Cessna O-2A Super Skymaster	M337-0460	69-7662 (USAF)		
	Cessna O-2A Super Skymaster	M337-0464	69-7666 (USAF)		

BRAZIL

República Federativa do Brasil	S America

Brazil has the largest land mass in South America and its military forces are correspondingly large. These are backed up by the most successful aircraft manufacturing company on the continent, Embraer. Financial difficulties through the 1980s have now been rectified and a major acquisition programme is being established.

SERIAL SYSTEM Four digit serials are allocated in blocks unique to a type, the first digit denoting the primary role (ie 2***, transport). When presented on the aircraft the serial is prefixed with the local designation, usually derived from the standard US system, these are shown below in brackets after the aircraft type.

Fôrça Aérea Brasileira
Brazilian Air Force

UNITS/BASES	Grupo de Transport Especial (GTE), Brasilia	VU-9, C-35A, VU-93, VC-96
	Comando Geral do Ar	
	COMAR 1, 1 ETA, Belem	C-95B, C-98
	COMAR 2, 2 ETA, Recife	C-95
	COMAR 3, 3 ETA, Galeao	C-95. C-95B
	COMAR 4, 4 ETA, Sao Paulo	C-95, C-95A
	COMAR 5, 5 ETA, Porte Alegre	C-95A
	COMAR 6, 6 ETA, Anapolis	C-95C, VC-97, VU-9
	COMAR 7, 7 ETA, Manaus	C-95C, VC-97, VU-9
	II Forca Aérea	
	1 GAE ' Cardeal', Santa Cruz	P-95B
	7 GAv, 2 Esq 'Phoenix', Florianapolis	P-95B
	7 GAv, 3 Esq 'Netuno', Belem	P-95A
	8 GAv, 4 Esq, Santa Cruz	P-3 from 2002)
	8 GAv, 5 Esq 'Pantera', Santa Maria	U-7
	8 GAv, 7 Esq 'Falcao', Manaus	U-7
	10 GAv, 2 Esq 'Pelicano', Campo Grande	SC-95B
	2 Esq de Ligacao & Observacao (2ELO), Sao Pedro de Aldeia	U-7 (support to AT-27)
	III Forca Aérea	
	6 GAv, 1 Esq 'Carcara', Recife	R-35A, R-95
	6 GAv, 2 Esq, Recife	R-99A/B
	V Forca Aérea	
	1 GTT, 1 Esq 'Gordo', Afonsos	C-130E
	1 GTT, 2 Esq 'Cascavel', Afonsos	C-115
	1 GT, 1 Esq 'Coral', Galeao	SC-130E, C-130H, KC-130H
	2 GT, 1 Esq 'Condor', Galeao	C-91
	2 GT, 2 Esq 'Corsario', Galeao	KC-137
	9 GAv, 1 Esq 'Arara', Manaus	C-115
	15 GAv, 1 Esq 'Onca', Campo Grande	C-95B
	Comando Geral de Apoio (COMGAP)	
	Grupo de Eletronica E Prot. Ao Voo (GEIV), Santos Dumont	EC-95, EU-93
	Departamento de Pesquisas e Desenvolvimento (DEPED)	
	Centro Tecnico Aeroespacial (CTA), Sao Jose dos Campos	XC-95, XC-97, XU-93
	Departamento de Ensino (DEPENS)	
	Academia de Fôrça Aérea (AFA), Pirassununga	C-95A, U-7 (support to Air Force Academy)
	Escola do Especialistas de Aeronautica (EEAR), Guaratingueta	C-95

PLANS Eight ex USN P-3A/Bs are being reworked in Brazil with Lockheed Martin assistance to replace P-95As and S-2s from 2002, twelve aircraft were taken from the AMARC store to select from, the other 4 airframes will be use for training and spares.
The CLX programme is being formulated to replace the Buffalos, with the CASA C295 being considered.
Ten ex Italian AF C-130Hs have been acquired through Lockheed Martin.

2000	Embraer EMB-120 Brasilia (YC-97)	120003	PT-ZBB		
2002	Embraer EMB-120 Brasilia (VC-97)	120040	PT-SJO	6ETA	
2003	Embraer EMB-120 Brasilia (VC-97)	120055	PT-SJY	6ETA	
2004	Embraer EMB-120 Brasilia (VC-97)	120066	PT-SKJ	6ETA	
2005	Embraer EMB-120ER Brasilia (C-97)	120337	PT-SZA		
2006	Embraer EMB-120 Brasilia (C-97)	120107	N31711		
2007	Embraer EMB-120 Brasilia (C-97)	120138	N16719		
2008	Embraer EMB-120 Brasilia (C-97)	120101	N12709		
2009	Embraer EMB-120 Brasilia (C-97)	120106	N16710		
	Embraer EMB-120 Brasilia (C-97)	120166	N47722		
2113	Hawker Siddeley 125-3A-RA (VC-93)	25136/NA701	N125HS	GTE	
2114	Hawker Siddeley 125-400A (VU-93)	25212/NA740	N702P	GTE	
2115	Boeing 737-2N3 Advanced (VC-96)	21165 / 441		GTE	
2116	Boeing 737-2N3 Advanced (VC-96)	21166 / 445		GTE	
2117	Hawker Siddeley 125-400A (XU-93)	25210/NA738	N702D	CTA	

2118	Hawker Siddeley 125-400A (VU-93)	25200/NA729	N702SS	GTE	
2119	Hawker Siddeley 125-403B (EU-93)	25274	G-5-20	GEIV	
2120	Hawker Siddeley 125-3B-RC (VC-93)	25162		GTE	
2121	Hawker Siddeley 125-3B-RC (EU-93)	25165		GEIV	
2123	Hawker Siddeley 125-3B-RC (VU-93)	25167		GTE	
2124	Hawker Siddeley 125-3B-RC (VC-93)	25168		GTE	
2125	Hawker Siddeley 125-3B-RC (EU-93)	25164		GEIV	
2126	Hawker Siddeley 125-403B (VU-93)	25277	G-5-11	GTE	
2127	Hawker Siddeley 125-403B (VU-93)	25288		GTE	
2128	Hawker Siddeley 125-403B (VU-93)	25289	G-5-16	GTE	
2134	Embraer EMB-110C Bandeirante (C-95)	110003			
2135	Embraer EMB-110C Bandeirante (C-95)	110007			
2136	Embraer EMB-110C Bandeirante (C-95)	110008			
2137	Embraer EMB-110C Bandeirante (C-95)	110014			
2138	Embraer EMB-110C Bandeirante (C-95)	110015			
2140	Embraer EMB-110C Bandeirante (C-95)	110020			
2141	Embraer EMB-110C Bandeirante (C-95)	110027			
2142	Embraer EMB-110C Bandeirante (C-95)	110028			
2146	Embraer EMB-110C Bandeirante (C-95)	110036		CTA	
2150	Embraer EMB-110C Bandeirante (C-95)	110042		3ETA	
2151	Embraer EMB-110C Bandeirante (C-95)	110043		2ETA	
2155	Embraer EMB-110C Bandeirante (C-95)	110052		3ETA	
2156	Embraer EMB-110C Bandeirante (C-95)	110053			
2161	Embraer EMB-110C Bandeirante (C-95)	110060			
2162	Embraer EMB-110C Bandeirante (C-95)	110061			
2164	Embraer EMB-110C Bandeirante (C-95)	110064			
2165	Embraer EMB-110C Bandeirante (C-95)	110067		3ETA	
2166	Embraer EMB-110C Bandeirante (C-95)	110068			
2168	Embraer EMB-110C Bandeirante (C-95)	110073			
2170	Embraer EMB-110C Bandeirante (C-95)	110077			
2171	Embraer EMB-110C Bandeirante (C-95)	110078		3ETA	
2172	Embraer EMB-110C Bandeirante (C-95)	110080		AFA	
2175	Embraer EMB-110A Bandeirante (EC-95)	110095			
2176	Embraer EMB-110A Bandeirante (EC-95)	110097		GEIV	
2177	Embraer EMB-110A Bandeirante (EC-95)	110099		GEIV	
2178	Embraer EMB-110A Bandeirante (EC-95)	110100		GEIV	
2183	Embraer EMB-110C Bandeirante (C-95)	110110			
2187	Embraer EMB-110C Bandeirante (C-95)	110118			
2190	Embraer EMB-110A Bandeirante (EC-95)	110123		GEIV	
2191	Embraer EMB-110A Bandeirante (EC-95)	110124		GEIV	
2240	Embraer EMB-110B Bandeirante (R-95)	110133		1/6GAv	
2241	Embraer EMB-110B Bandeirante (R-95)	110134		1/6GAv	
2242	Embraer EMB-110B Bandeirante (R-95)	110135		1/6GAv	
2244	Embraer EMB-110B Bandeirante (R-95)	110140		1/6GAv	
2245	Embraer EMB-110B Bandeirante (R-95)	110141		1/6GAv	
2280	Embraer EMB-110K1 Bandeirante (C-95A)	110139			
2281	Embraer EMB-110K1 Bandeirante (C-95A)	110148		PMARF	
2282	Embraer EMB-110K1 Bandeirante (C-95A)	110149			
2283	Embraer EMB-110K1 Bandeirante (C-95A)	110143	PT-GLA		
2284	Embraer EMB-110K1 Bandeirante (C-95A)	110152			
2285	Embraer EMB-110K1 Bandeirante (C-95A)	110160			
2286	Embraer EMB-110K1 Bandeirante (EC-95A)	110164		GEIV	Cvtd C-95A
2287	Embraer EMB-110K1 Bandeirante (C-95A)	110168		EEAR	
2288	Embraer EMB-110K1 Bandeirante (C-95A)	110169	PT-GLE	PAMRF	
2289	Embraer EMB-110K1 Bandeirante (C-95A)	110170			
2290	Embraer EMB-110K1 Bandeirante (C-95A)	110172			
2291	Embraer EMB-110K1 Bandeirante (C-95A)	110173			
2292	Embraer EMB-110K1 Bandeirante (C-95A)	110174			
2293	Embraer EMB-110K1 Bandeirante (C-95A)	110175			
2294	Embraer EMB-110K1 Bandeirante (C-95A)	110176			
2295	Embraer EMB-110K1 Bandeirante (C-95A)	110177		2ETA	
2296	Embraer EMB-110K1 Bandeirante (C-95A)	110178			
2297	Embraer EMB-110K1 Bandeirante (C-95A)	110180			
2298	Embraer EMB-110K1 Bandeirante (C-95A)	110181		2ETA	
2299	Embraer EMB-110K1 Bandeirante (C-95A)	110183		Base Flt	Pirassununga
2300	Embraer EMB-110P1 Bandeirante (C-95B)	110246	(PT-SAM)	1ETA	
2301	Embraer EMB-110P1 Bandeirante (C-95B)	110247	(PT-SAN)	1ETA	
2303	Embraer EMB-110P1 Bandeirante (C-95B)	110264		2/2GT	
2304	Embraer EMB-110P1 Bandeirante (C-95B)	110269			
2305	Embraer EMB-110P1 Bandeirante (C-95B)	110276	PP-ZKK		
2306	Embraer EMB-110P1 Bandeirante (C-95B)	110282		CATRE	
2307	Embraer EMB-110P1 Bandeirante (EC-95B)	110291			Cvtd C-95B
2308	Embraer EMB-110P1 Bandeirante (C-95B)	110299			
2309	Embraer EMB-110P1 Bandeirante (C-95B)	110306		CATRE	

2311	Embraer EMB-110P1 Bandeirante (C-95B)	110320		1/15GAv	
2312	Embraer EMB-110P1 Bandeirante (C-95B)	110326		3ETA	
2313	Embraer EMB-110P1 Bandeirante (C-95B)	110332		3ETA	
2314	Embraer EMB-110P1 Bandeirante (C-95B)	110337			
2316	Embraer EMB-110P1 Bandeirante (C-95B)	110390	PT-SFH		
2317	Embraer EMB-110P1 Bandeirante (C-95B)	110429	PT-SGV		
2318	Embraer EMB-110P1 Bandeirante (C-95B)	110430			
2319	Embraer EMB-110P1 Bandeirante (C-95B)	110431			
2320	Embraer EMB-110P1 Bandeirante (C-95B)	110432			
2321	Embraer EMB-110P1 Bandeirante (C-95B)	110433		1/15GAv	
2323	Embraer EMB-110P1 Bandeirante (C-95B)	110435			
2325	Embraer EMB-110P1 Bandeirante (C-95B)	110440			
2326	Embraer EMB-110P1 Bandeirante (C-95B)	110443		3ETA	
2327	Embraer EMB-110P1 Bandeirante (EC-95B)	110450		GEIV	Cv'd C-95B
2328	Embraer EMB-110P1 Bandeirante (EC-95B)	110452			Cv'd C-95B
2329	Embraer EMB-110P1 Bandeirante (C-95B)	110454			
2330	Embraer EMB-110P1 Bandeirante (C-95B)	110457			
2331	Embraer EMB-110P1K Bandeirante (C-95C)	110471		6ETA	
2332	Embraer EMB-110P1K Bandeirante (C-95C)	110472		6ETA	
2334	Embraer EMB-110P1K Bandeirante (C-95C)	110476		6ETA	
2335	Embraer EMB-110P1K Bandeirante (C-95C)	110477		6ETA	
2336	Embraer EMB-110P1K Bandeirante (C-95C)	110478		6ETA	
2337	Embraer EMB-110P1K Bandeirante (C-95C)	110479	PT-SHZ	6ETA	
2338	Embraer EMB-110P1K Bandeirante (C-95C)	110480	PT-SOA	6ETA	
2339	Embraer EMB-110P1K Bandeirante (C-95C)	110481	PT-SOB	6ETA	
2340	Embraer EMB-110P1K Bandeirante (C-95C)	110482	PT-SOD	6ETA	
2341	Embraer EMB-110P1K Bandeirante (C-95C)	110484	PT-SOE	6ETA	
2342	Embraer EMB-110P1K Bandeirante (C-95C)	110491		6ETA	
2343	Embraer EMB-110P1K Bandeirante (C-95C)	110492			
2344	Embraer EMB-110P1K Bandeirante (C-95C)	110493			
2345	Embraer EMB-110P1K Bandeirante (C-95C)	110495			
2346	Embraer EMB-110P1K Bandeirante (C-95C)	110497			
2347	Embraer EMB-110P1K Bandeirante (C-95C)	110499			
2348	Embraer EMB-110P1K Bandeirante (C-95C)	110500			
2351	DeHavilland Canada DHC-5D Buffalo (C-115)	17	CF-DJU		
2352	DeHavilland Canada DHC-5D Buffalo (C-115)	18			
2353	DeHavilland Canada DHC-5D Buffalo (C-115)	20			
2354	DeHavilland Canada DHC-5D Buffalo (C-115)	22			
2355	DeHavilland Canada DHC-5D Buffalo (C-115)	24			
2357	DeHavilland Canada DHC-5D Buffalo (C-115)	27			
2358	DeHavilland Canada DHC-5D Buffalo (C-115)	28			
2360	DeHavilland Canada DHC-5D Buffalo (C-115)	30			
2361	DeHavilland Canada DHC-5D Buffalo (C-115)	31			
2362	DeHavilland Canada DHC-5D Buffalo (C-115)	32			
2363	DeHavilland Canada DHC-5D Buffalo (C-115)	33			
2364	DeHavilland Canada DHC-5D Buffalo (C-115)	34			
2365	DeHavilland Canada DHC-5D Buffalo (C-115)	35		2/1GTT	
2367	DeHavilland Canada DHC-5D Buffalo (C-115)	37			
2368	DeHavilland Canada DHC-5D Buffalo (C-115)	38		2/1GTT	
2369	DeHavilland Canada DHC-5D Buffalo (C-115)	39			
2370	DeHavilland Canada DHC-5D Buffalo (C-115)	40		2/1GTT	
2371	DeHavilland Canada DHC-5D Buffalo (C-115)	41		2/1GTT	
2373	DeHavilland Canada DHC-5D Buffalo (C-115)	43			
2401	Boeing 707-345C (C-137)	19840 / 679	PP-VJY	2/2GT	Std Galeao
2402	Boeing 707-345C (KC-137)	19842 / 712	PP-VJX	2/2GT	AAR
2403	Boeing 707-320C (KC-137)	20008 / 739	PP-VJH	2/2GT	AAR
2404	Boeing 707-324C (KC-137)	19870 / 702	PP-VLK	2/2GT	AAR
2451	Lockheed C-130E (L-382-16B) Hercules	4092		2/1GT	
2453	Lockheed C-130E (L-382-16B) Hercules	4113		2/1GT	
2454	Lockheed C-130E (L-382-16B) Hercules	4114		2/1GT	
2455	Lockheed C-130E (L-382C-5D) Hercules	4202			WO
2456	Lockheed C-130E (L-382C-8D) Hercules	4287		1/1GT	
2458	Lockheed SC-130E (L-382C-8D) Hercules	4291	N7983R	1/1GT	SAR
2459	Lockheed SC-130E (L-382C-8D) Hercules	4292		1/1GT	SAR
2461	Lockheed KC-130H (L-382C-47D) Hercules	4625		1/1GT	AAR
2462	Lockheed KC-130H (L-382C-47D) Hercules	4636		1/1GT	AAR
2463	Lockheed C-130H (L-382C-45D) Hercules	4570		1/1GT	
2464	Lockheed C-130H (L-382C-45D) Hercules	4602		1/1GT	
2465	Lockheed C-130H (L-382C-45D) Hercules	4630		1/1GT	
2466	Lockheed C-130H (L-382C-80E) Hercules	4990	N4187W	1/1GT	
2467	Lockheed C-130H (L-382C-80E) Hercules	4991	N4187W	1/1GT	
2500	Hawker Siddeley HS.748-204 srs 2 (C-91)	1550/set19	(VR-AAU)	1/2GT	
2501	Hawker Siddeley HS.748-205 srs 2 (C-91)	1551/set22	(VR-AAV)	1/2GT	
2502	Hawker Siddeley HS.748-205 srs 2 (C-91)	1552/set21	(VR-AAW)	1/2GT	

2503	Hawker Siddeley HS.748-205 srs 2 (C-91)	1553/set23		1/2GT	
2504	Hawker Siddeley HS.748-205 srs 2 (C-91)	1554/set24		1/2GT	
2505	Hawker Siddeley HS.748-205 srs 2 (C-91)	1555/set25		1/2GT	
2506	Hawker Siddeley HS.748-281 srs 2A LFD (C-91)	1729/set205		1/2GT	
2507	Hawker Siddeley HS.748-281 srs 2A LFD (C-91)	1730/set206		1/2GT	
2508	Hawker Siddeley HS.748-281 srs 2A LFD (C-91)	1731/set207		1/2GT	
2510	Hawker Siddeley HS.748-281 srs 2A LFD (C-91)	1733/set211		1/2GT	
2511	Hawker Siddeley HS.748-281 srs 2A LFD (C-91)	1734/set212		1/2GT	
2600	Embraer EMB-810C (PA-34-220T Seneca III) (U-7)	810130	PT-ENU		
2603	Embraer EMB-810C (PA-34-220T Seneca III) (U-7)	810139	PT-EOD		
2607	Embraer EMB-810C (PA-34-220T Seneca III) (U-7)	810149	PT-EPQ		
2608	Embraer EMB-810C (PA-34-220T Seneca III) (U-7)	810151	PT-EQP		
2613	Embraer EMB-810D (PA-34-220T Seneca III) (U-7A)	810360			
2615	Embraer EMB-810D (PA-34-220T Seneca III) (U-7A)	810370			
2616	Embraer EMB-810D (PA-34-220T Seneca III) (U-7A)	810371		Base Flt	Pirassununga
2617	Embraer EMB-810D (PA-34-220T Seneca III) (U-7A)	810380			
2621	Embraer EMB-810D (PA-34-220T Seneca III) (U-7A)	810396			
2623	Embraer EMB-810D (PA-34-220T Seneca III) (U-7A)	810403			
2625	Embraer EMB-810D (PA-34-220T Seneca III) (U-7A)	810413			
2626	Embraer EMB-810D (PA-34-220T Seneca III) (U-7A)	810416			
2628	Embraer EMB-810D (PA-34-220T Seneca III) (U-7A)	810428			
2630	Embraer EMB-810D (PA-34-220T Seneca III) (U-7A)	810526			
2631	Embraer EMB-810D (PA-34-220T Seneca III) (U-7A)	810527			
2632	Embraer EMB-810D (PA-34-220T Seneca III) (U-7A)				
2633	Embraer EMB-810D (PA-34-220T Seneca III) (U-7A)				
2634	Embraer EMB-810D (PA-34-220T Seneca III) (U-7B)			PAMA-SP	Campo de Marte
2650	Embraer EMB-121E Xingu (VU-9)	121002	PP-ZXI		
2651	Embraer EMB-121E Xingu (VU-9)	121003			
2652	Embraer EMB-121E Xingu (VU-9)	121004			
2653	Embraer EMB-121E Xingu (VU-9)	121005		6ETA	
2654	Embraer EMB-121E Xingu (VU-9)	121006		6ETA	
2656	Embraer EMB-121E Xingu (VU-9)	121060			
2657	Embraer EMB-121A Xingu (VU-9)	121037	PT-MBE		
2701	Cessna 208 Caravan 1 (C-98)	20800052	N9429F	7ETA	
2702	Cessna 208 Caravan 1 (C-98)	20800132	N9702F	7ETA	
2703	Cessna 208 Caravan 1 (C-98)	20800133	N9704F	7ETA	
2704	Cessna 208 Caravan 1 (C-98)	20800167	N9744F	7ETA	
2705	Cessna 208 Caravan 1 (C-98)	20800168	N9745F	7ETA	
2706	Cessna 208 Caravan 1 (C-98)	20800169	N9746F	7ETA	
2707	Cessna 208 Caravan 1 (C-98)	20800170	N9748F	7ETA	
2708	Cessna 208 Caravan 1 (C-98)	20800176	N9756F	7ETA	
2710	Learjet 35A (VU-35A)	35A-631	N3818G	GTE	
2711	Learjet 35A (VU-35A)	35A-632	N1461B	GTE	
2712	Learjet 35A (VU-35A)	35A-633	N39416	GTE	
2713	Learjet 35A (VU-35A)	35A-636	N1476B	GTE	
2714	Learjet 35A (VU-35A)	35A-638	N39412	GTE	
2715	Learjet 35A (VU-35A)	35A-639	N6317V	GTE	
2716	Learjet 35A (VU-35A)	35A-640	N8568Y	GTE	
2717	Learjet 35A (VU-35A)	35A-641	N7261H	GTE	
2718	Learjet 35A (VU-35A)	35A-642	N7262X	GTE	
	Cessna 208B Caravan 1 (C-98)	208B0678	N5263U		
2720	Cessna 208B Caravan 1 (C-98)	208B0821	N52626		
6000	Learjet 35A (R-35A)	35A-613	N4289X	1/6GAv	
6001	Learjet 35A (R-35A)	35A-615	N7260E	1/6GAv	

6002	Learjet 35A (R-35A)	35A-617	N4289Z	1/6GAv	
6050	Raytheon Hawker 800XP (EU-93A)	258401	N23592	GEIV	
6051	Raytheon Hawker 800XP (EU-93A)	258421	N31820	GEIV	
6052	Raytheon Hawker 800XP (EU-93A)	258434	N40027	GEIV	
6053	Raytheon Hawker 800XP (EU-93A)	258447	N40310	GEIV	
6100	Learjet 55C	55C-140	PT-OCA		
6542	Embraer EMB-110P1K Bandeirante (SC-95B)	110349	2315 (FABr)	2/10GAv	SAR
6543	Embraer EMB-110P1K Bandeirante (SC-95B)	110356?		2/10GAv	SAR
6544	Embraer EMB-110P1K Bandeirante (SC-95B)	110361		2/10GAv	SAR
6545	Embraer EMB-110P1K Bandeirante (SC-95B)	110367		2/10GAv	SAR
6546	Embraer EMB-110P1K Bandeirante (SC-95B)	110374	PP-ZAD	2/10GAv	SAR
6701	Embraer EMB-145SA (R-99A)	145104	PP-XSA		
6702	Embraer EMB-145SA (R-99A)	145122	PP-XSB		
6703	Embraer EMB-145SA (R-99A)	145263	PP-XSC		
	Embraer EMB-145SA (R-99A)	145365			
	Embraer EMB-145SA (R-99A)				
6750	Embraer EMB-145RS (R-99B)	145140	PP-XRS	2/6GAv	
6751	Embraer EMB-145RS (R-99B)	145154	PP-XRT	2/6GAv	
	Embraer EMB-145RS (R-99B)	145257			
7051	Embraer EMB-111A(A) Bandeirulha (P-95)	110151	2261 (FABr)	3/7GAv	'Pelicano'
7052	Embraer EMB-111A(A) Bandeirulha (P-95)	110155	2262 (FABr)	3/7GAv	'Taiacu'
7054	Embraer EMB-111A(A) Bandeirulha (P-95)	110163	2264 (FABr)	3/7GAv	'Martin Pescador'
7055	Embraer EMB-111A(A) Bandeirulha (P-95)	110167	2265 (FABr)	3/7GAv	'Talhar Mar'
7056	Embraer EMB-111A(A) Bandeirulha (P-95)	110171	2266 (FABr)	3/7GAv	'Albatroz'
7057	Embraer EMB-111A(A) Bandeirulha (P-95)	110179	2267 (FABr)	3/7GAv	'Bigua'
7058	Embraer EMB-111A(A) Bandeirulha (P-95)	110182	6-P-201 (COAN)	3/7GAv	'Alca'
7059	Embraer EMB-111A(A) Bandeirulha (P-95)	110185	2269 (FABr)	3/7GAv	'Picargo'
7060	Embraer EMB-111A(A) Bandeirulha (P-95)	110188	6-P-202 (COAN)	3/7GAv	'Gaivota'
7061	Embraer EMB-111A(A) Bandeirulha (P-95)	110191	2271 (FABr)	3/7GAv	'Alcatraz'
7101	Embraer EMB-111A Bandeirulha (P-95B)	110483		1/7GAv	
7103	Embraer EMB-111A Bandeirulha (P-95B)	110488			
7104	Embraer EMB-111A Bandeirulha (P-95B)	110489		1/7GAv	
7105	Embraer EMB-111A Bandeirulha (P-95B)	110491			
7106	Embraer EMB-111A Bandeirulha (P-95B)	110493			
7107	Embraer EMB-111A Bandeirulha (P-95B)	110495			
	Lockheed P-3C II Orion		Bu	on order, Cvtd USN P-3A/B	
	Lockheed P-3C II Orion		Bu	on order, Cvtd USN P-3A/B	
	Lockheed P-3C II Orion		Bu	on order, Cvtd USN P-3A/B	
	Lockheed P-3C II Orion		Bu	on order, Cvtd USN P-3A/B	
	Lockheed P-3C II Orion		Bu	on order, Cvtd USN P-3A/B	
	Lockheed P-3C II Orion		Bu	on order, Cvtd USN P-3A/B	
	Lockheed P-3C II Orion		Bu	on order, Cvtd USN P-3A/B	
	Lockheed P-3C II Orion		Bu	on order, Cvtd USN P-3A/B	
	Reims/Cessna F406 Caravan II				on order
	Reims/Cessna F406 Caravan II				on order
	Reims/Cessna F406 Caravan II				on order
	Reims/Cessna F406 Caravan II				on order
	Reims/Cessna F406 Caravan II Vigilant Frontier				on order

Fôrça Aéronaval da Marinha do Brasil - FAMB
Brazilian Naval Aviation

PLANS   To complete the fixed wing complement on the aircraft carrier "Sao Paulo" the acquisition of S-2F3T Trackers, modified by Embraer and Marsh Aviation is likely.

BRUNEI
Negara Brunei Darussalam / Islamic Sultanate of Brunei   SE Asia

Oil rich and ASEAN member Brunei has been responsible for its own defence since 1984 but still only possesses a helicopter based armed capability. Construction of a new military airfield to handle the proposed BAe Hawk purchase should move the air arm to a different level. The once huge VIP flight has been rationalised following an investigation by the Sultan into its operation. The British Army maintain a helicopter detachment at Seria supporting a Gurkha Battalion and training facilities.

SERIAL SYSTEM Three digit serials are allocated in batches by type prefixed with the Armed Forces initials.

Angkatan Tentara Udara Diraja Brunei
Royal Brunei Armed Forces

UNITS/BASES   The transport aircraft is currently based at Brunei IAP with 4 Sqn.

PLANS	Three IPTN-built CN235MPAs were on order, but are reported as being on hold due to a budget restriction, an additional CN235M may be acquired instead.			
ATU-DB-501	Airtech/IPTN CN235M-100	N033		4 Sqn

Sultan's Flight

P4-ABJ	Airbus Industrie A310-304	431	P4-DPD	Operated by Praeda AVV
V8-001	GAC Gulfstream V	515	V8-007	
V8-AC3	Airbus Industrie A340-213X	204	F-WWJB	Std Berlin
V8-AL⁻	Boeing 747-430	26426 / 910	D-ABVM	
V8-EKH	Airbus Industrie A340-212	046	V8-PJB	Royal Brunei AL cs
V8-MHB	Boeing 767-27GER	25537 / 517	V8-MJB	Royal Brunei AL cs

BULGARIA
Narodna Republika Bulgaria   SE Europe

Struggling to support its Soviet-supplied fleet by the late 1990s, Bulgaria has declared its desire to join NATO. This will eventually lead to US and European equipment replacing what was until 1989 a force as well trained and equipped as any the Warsaw Pact countries. Current budgetary restrictions will not allow this until 2010 however.

SERIAL SYSTEM An almost sequential serial allocation system is in use with the transport aircraft in the three digit batch commencing '0'. VIP aircraft bear identities with the country's civil prefix LZ, some in the block used by the former national airline.

Bulgarski Voenno Vozdushni Sili - BVVS
Bulgarian Air Defence Force Military Aviation

UNITS/BASES	16th Transportna Aviobasa, 1/16 Eskadrila, Sofia-Vrazhdebna			An-24, An-26, An-30, L-410
	Corpus Takticheska Aviatzia HQ, Plovdiv			An-2
	Corpus Protivovazdushna Otbarana HQ, Sofia-Dobroslavtzy			An-2
026	Antonov/PZL-Mielec An-2T	1G157-01		CTA HQ
027	Antonov/PZL-Mielec An-2T	1G157-02		CPO HQ
034	Antonov An-24			16 TrAB
055	Antonov An-30	0802		16 TrAB	Open Skies survey
062	Let 410UVP	841225	CCCP-67460	16 TrAB
063	Let 410UVP	841226	CCCP-67461	16 TrAB
064	Let 410UVP	902524	LZ-RME	16 TrAB
065	Let 410UVP	841333		16 TrAB
066	Let 410UVP-E	892337		16 TrAB
067	Let 410UVP-E	892338		16 TrAB
068	Let 410UVP-E3	902522		16 TrAB
069	Let 410UVP	902523	LZ-LSC	16 TrAB
070	Antonov An-26	13708		16 TrAB
075	Antonov An-26	13709		16 TrAB
080	Antonov An-26	13710		16 TrAB
087	Antonov An-26	14209		16 TrAB
090	Antonov An-26	14303		16 TrAB

Upravlenie za Predkasarmena Podgotovka na Mladezhta - UPPM
Directorate of Youth Training

UNITS/BASES	The An-2s are based with the following Aeroclubs:
	HQ Sofia (Bozhuriste), Krumovo, Montana, Shoumen, Sliven, Bourgas, Varna and Targovishte.

LZ-906	Antonov An-2	115747308
LZ-907	Antonov An-2	117047305
LZ-909	Antonov/PZL-Mielec An-2R	1G56-44
LZ-911	Antonov/PZL-Mielec An-2T	1G181-60
LZ-912	Antonov/PZL-Mielec An-2R	1G33-13
LZ-913	Antonov/PZL-Mielec An-2R	1G55-06
LZ-914	Antonov/PZL-Mielec An-2R	1G55-26
LZ-915	Antonov/PZL-Mielec An-2R	1G55-29
LZ-916	Antonov/PZL-Mielec An-2R	1G55-22
LZ-917	Antonov/PZL-Mielec An-2R	1G86-08
LZ-920	Antonov/PZL-Mielec An-2R	1G92-04
LZ-921	Antonov/PZL-Mielec An-2R	1G79-27
LZ-923	Antonov/PZL-Mielec An-2R	1G55-09

Pratvitelstven Aviootryad 28
Government Air Transport Group 28

UNITS/BASES   All aircraft are based at Sofia International Airport.

LZ-BTZ	Tupolev Tu-154M	88A-781		Leased to Balkan Bulgarian
LZ-OOI	Dassault Falcon 2000	123		
LZ-TUG	Tupolev Tu-134A-3	49858	OK-BYT	

BURKINA FASO
République Démocratique et Populaire de Burkino Faso   W Africa

Independent from France since 1960 and known as Upper Volta until 1984, Burkina Faso is regarded as the poorest country in Africa. The Air Force created with French assistance in 1964 received Soviet aid in the 1980's and is still a primarily transport orientated organisation.

SERIAL SYSTEM   Civil registrations are allocated in a unique AF sequence, XT-M**.

Force Aérienne de Burkina Faso
Air Force of Burkina Faso

UNITS/BASES   Aircraft are based at the country's main airport, Ouagadougou.

XT-MAD	Aero Commander 500B	1109-64	XT-AAA
XT-MAG	Reims F337E Super Skymaster	F3370006/ 01220	
XT-MAJ	Nord 262C Frégate	36	F-BPXA
XT-MAK	Nord 262C Frégate	98	
XT-MAL	Hawker Siddeley HS.748-320 srs 2A LFD 1754/set229		
XT-MAN	Hawker Siddeley HS.748-369 srs 2A LFD 1775/set255		G-11-13
XT-MAX	Beech Super King Air 200	BB-742	G-BPWJ

Government of the People's Democratic Republic of Burkina Faso

XT-BBE	Boeing 727-14	18990 / 238	N21UC

BURUNDI
République du Burundi   C Africa

Part of the Belgian colony of Ruanda-Urundi until independence in 1962 and separation in 1966 (the other half becoming Rwanda). Tribal fighting has resulted in civil war here and in Rwanda since 1993. The Armée Nationale du Burundi operate what remains of the country's military aircraft, but only the Government are reported to have the equipment that qualifies for inclusion in this publication.

Government of the Republic of Burundi

UNITS/BASES   Based at Bujumbura International

9U-BTB	Dassault Falcon 50	66	N4413N

CAMBODIA
Preah Reacheanachakr Kampuchea / Kingdom of Cambodia   SE Asia

Becoming independent from France in 1953 initial assistance for the Royal Khmer Aviation came from France and the USA. Subsequently support came from the USSR too as both super powers tried to maintain control of this Vietnamese neighbour state during the 1960s and early 1970s. Renamed the Khmer Republic in 1970 and Kampuchea in 1975, the name Cambodia being restored in 1989 when the Vietnamese withdrew. After years of civil war a UN ceasefire was agreed in 1991; the monarchy was reinstated in 1993 and the current Air Force title was then adopted.

SERIAL SYSTEM   All serials bear the civil prefix of XU, followed usually by three digits, but sometimes a full civil style identity.

Royal Cambodian Air Force

UNITS/BASES   All transports are based at Phnom Penh-Pochentong Airport.

XU-016	Yunshuji/Harbin Y-12 II	0083	XU-701
XU-017	Yunshuji/Harbin Y-12 II	0084	XU-702
XU-MLA	Britten-Norman BN-2A-21 Defender	401	XU-MTA

| XU-MLB | Britten-Norman BN-2A-21 Defender | 414 | XU-MTB | |
| XU-MLC | Britten-Norman BN-2A-21 Defender | 400 | N7071C | |

Council of Ministry

UNITS/BASES Aircraft bear Air Force titles but are government operated from Phnom Penh-Pochentong Airport.

XU-008	Dassault Falcon 20E	323	OE-GLF	
XU-012	Cessna 421C Golden Eagle III	421C0325	VH-CMR	tie up unconfirmed
XU-311	Antonov An-24RV	27307803	CCCP-47261	
XU-312	Antonov An-24RV	37308904	CCCP-46638	

CAMEROON
République de Cameroun   W Africa

Still French-speaking following independence in 1960 and more advanced industrially than most of it neighbours thanks to petroleum production since the late 1970s, the Cameroon Air Force and Government operate a predominantly transport orientated inventory.

SERIAL SYSTEM Civil registrations are allocated in a unique block, TJ-X**, the presentation often appearing at TJX-**.

l'Armée de l'Air du Cameroun
Cameroon Air Force

UNITS/BASES Transports are presumed based at Yaounde-Nsimalen.

TJ-XAD	Lockheed C-130H (L-382C-69D) Hercules	4752	TJX-AD	
TJ-XAM	Dornier 28A-1 Skyservant	3085	TJ-XAH	
TJX-AR	Piper PA-23-250 Aztec	27-4473	N13830	
TJX-AU	Piper PA-23-250 Aztec			
TJ-XBM	DeHavilland Canada DHC-5D Buffalo	105	C-GDAF	
TJ-XBN	DeHavilland Canada DHC-5D Buffalo	106	C-GDAI	Std Douala
TJ-XBP	Dornier 128-6MPA Turbo Skyservant	6003	D-IDDA	
TJ-XBQ	Dornier 128-6MPA Turbo Skyservant	6004	D-IDIL	
TJ-XBR	DeHavilland Canada DHC-5D Buffalo	120	C-GEAY	
TJ-XBS	DeHavilland Canada DHC-5D Buffalo	121	C-GDWT	Std Douala
TJ-XBT	DeHavilland Canada DHC-5D Buffalo	122	C-GHSV	Std Douala
TJ-XCA	IAI Arava 102	105		
TJ-XCE	Lockheed C-130H-30 (L-382T-20E) Hercules	4933	TJX-CE	

Government of the Republic of Cameroon

TJ-AAJ	Dornier 28B Skyservant	3054	TJX-AG	
TJ-AAM	Boeing 727-2R1 Advanced	21636 / 1414		Section Liasion Air
TJ-AAS	IAI Arava 101B	81	4X-CUP	
TJ-AAT	Cessna U206G Stationair 6 II	U20606915	(N9643R)	
TJ-AAW	GAC G-1159A Gulfstream III	486	N316GA	Section Liasion Air

CANADA
N America

Canada has been a member of NATO since its creation in 1948. The Royal Canadian Air Force was merged with the Army and Royal Canadian Navy in 1968 to form the current single military body and now operates as the Air Command within the Camadian Forces, Maritime Command being the Navy and Mobile Command the Army.

SERIAL SYSTEM Each type is allocated a two letter and three digit code (ie CC-130, Canadian Transport 130). The serial is five/six digit number the first three numbers of which are this code followed by a two or three digit sequential number.

Canadian Forces

ICAO code CFC, callsign Canforce

UNITS/BASES	7 Wing, CFB Ottawa, Ontario	
	412 Transport & Rescue Sqn	CC-144
	8 Wing, CFB Trenton, Ontario	
	424 'Tiger' Transport & Rescue Sqn	CC-130E/H (pooled aircraft)
	426 Transport Training Sqn	CC-130E/H (pooled aircraft)
	429 Transport Sqn	CC-130E/H (pooled aircraft)
	436 Transport Sqn	CC-130E/H (pooled aircraft)
	437 'Husky' Transport & Tanker Sqn	CC-150

14 Wing, CFB Greenwood, Nova Scotia
  404 'Buffalos' MP and Training Sqn   CP-140/A (pooled aircraft)
  405 'Pathfinders' MP Sqn   CP-140/A (pooled aircraft)
  413 'Tusker' Transport & Rescue Sqn   CC-130E
  415 'Swordfishes' MP Sqn   CP-140/A (pooled aircraft)
17 Wing, CFB Winnipeg, Manitoba
  Central Flying School   CT-145
  402 Squadron (Air Reserve)   CT-142, CC-142
18 Wing, CFB Edmonton, Alberta
  435 Transport Sqn   CC-130E/H/T
  440 'Bat' Transport & Rescue Sqn   CC-138   (det. at Yellowknife, NWT)
19 Wing, CFB Comox, British Columbia
  407 'Demons' MP Sqn   CP-140
  442 Transport & Rescue Sqn   CC-115

Civilian Contractors: Bombardier
Canadian Aviation Training Centre, 3 CFFTS, Portage la Prairie, Manitoba   King Air

PLANS   Four options are being reviewed as the Future Strategic Airlift Project (FSAP), 13 westernised An-70s, 13 Airbus A400Ms, 6 Boeing C-17s or a commercial leasing arrangement with aircraft in CF colours.
Related to FSAP is the C-130E replacement tactical transport purchase which, although separate, will depend on the choice of larger aircraft but will probably consist of 12 C-130J-30s.

15001	Airbus Industrie CC-150 Polaris (A-310-304)	446	F-WQCQ	437 Sqn
15002	Airbus Industrie CC-150 Polaris (A-310-304(F))	482	C-GLWD	437 Sqn
15003	Airbus Industrie CC-150 Polaris (A-310-304(F))	425	C-FWDX	437 Sqn
15004	Airbus Industrie CC-150 Polaris (A-310-304(F))	444	C-FNWD	437 Sqn
15005	Airbus Industrie CC-150 Polaris (A-310-304(F))	441	F-ZJEP	437 Sqn
144601	Canadair CC-144 Challenger (CL-600S)	1040	C-GLYM	412 Sqn
144614	Canadair CC-144 Challenger (CL-601)	3036	C-GCUP	412 Sqn
144615	Canadair CC-144 Challenger (CL-601)	3037	C-GCUR	412 Sqn
144616	Canadair CC-144 Challenger (CL-601)	3038	C-GCUT	412 Sqn
115451	DeHavilland Canada CC-115 Buffalo (DHC-5)	5	CAF 9451	442 Sqn
115452	DeHavilland Canada CC-115 Buffalo (DHC-5)	6	CAF 9452	442 Sqn
115456	DeHavilland Canada CC-115 Buffalo (DHC-5)	10	CAF 9456	442 Sqn
115457	DeHavilland Canada CC-115 Buffalo (DHC-5)	11	CAF 9457	442 Sqn
115462	DeHavilland Canada CC-115 Buffalo (DHC-5)	19	C-GNUZ	442 Sqn
115465	DeHavilland Canada CC-115 Buffalo (DHC-5)	25	CAF 9465	442 Sqn
130305	Lockheed CC-130E (L-382-15B) Hercules	4020	CAF 10305	8 Wg
130306	Lockheed CC-130E (L-382-15B) Hercules	4026	CAF 10306	413 Sqn
130307	Lockheed CC-130E (L-382-15B) Hercules	4041	CAF 10307	8 Wg
130308	Lockheed CC-130E (L-382-15B) Hercules	4042	CAF 10308	8 Wg
130310	Lockheed CC-130E (L-382-15B) Hercules	4051	CAF 10310	413 Sqn
130311	Lockheed CC-130E (L-382-15B) Hercules	4060	CAF 10311	8 Wg
130313	Lockheed CC-130E (L-382-15B) Hercules	4066	CAF 10313	8 Wg
130314	Lockheed CC-130E (L-382-15B) Hercules	4067	CAF 10314	413 Sqn
130315	Lockheed CC-130E (L-382-15B) Hercules	4070	CAF 10315	8 Wg
130316	Lockheed CC-130E (L-382-15B) Hercules	4075	CAF 10316	8 Wg
130317	Lockheed CC-130E (L-382-15B) Hercules	4122	CAF 10317	8 Wg
130319	Lockheed CC-130E (L-382-15B) Hercules	4095	CAF 10319	8 Wg
130320	Lockheed CC-130E (L-382-15B) Hercules	4096	CAF 10320	8 Wg
130323	Lockheed CC-130E (L-382-15B) Hercules	4193	CAF 10323	8 Wg
130324	Lockheed CC-130E (L-382-15B) Hercules	4194	CAF 10324	8 Wg
130325	Lockheed CC-130E (L-382C-7D) Hercules	4285	CAF 10325	8 Wg
130326	Lockheed CC-130E (L-382C-7D) Hercules	4286	CAF 10326	8 Wg
130327	Lockheed CC-130E (L-382C-7D) Hercules	4288	CAF 10327	8 Wg
130328	Lockheed CC-130E (L-382C-7D) Hercules	4289	CAF 10328	8 Wg
130332	Lockheed CC-130H (L-382C-51D) Hercules	4568	73-1596 (FMS)	CAE Avtn
130333	Lockheed CC-130H (L-382C-51D) Hercules	4574	73-1599 (FMS)	8 Wg
130334	Lockheed CC-130H (L-382C-63E) Hercules	4994		8 Wg
130335	Lockheed CC-130H (L-382C-63E) Hercules	4995		8 Wg
130336	Lockheed CC-130H (L-382C-40D) Hercules	4580	N4246M	8 Wg
130337	Lockheed CC-130H (L-382C-40D) Hercules	4584	N4247M	8 Wg
130338	Lockheed CC-130H (L-382C-26F) Hercules	5175		435 Sqn
130339	Lockheed CC-130H (L-382C-26F) Hercules	5177		AETE
130340	Lockheed CC-130H (L-382C-26F) Hercules	5189		435 Sqn
130341	Lockheed CC-130H (L-382C-26F) Hercules	5200		435 Sqn
130342	Lockheed CC-130H (L-382C-26F) Hercules	5207		435 Sqn
130343	Lockheed CC-130H-30 (L-382G-71C) Hercules	5307	N41030	8 Wg
130344	Lockheed CC-130H-30 (L-382G-71C) Hercules	5320	N4080M	8 Wg
13802	DeHavilland Canada CC-138 (DHC-6)	304		440 Sqn
13803	DeHavilland Canada CC-138 (DHC-6)	305		440 Sqn
13804	DeHavilland Canada CC-138 (DHC-6)	306		440 Sqn
13805	DeHavilland Canada CC-138 (DHC-6)	307		440 Sqn

140101	Lockheed CP-140 (L-285B) Aurora	5682	N64996	14 Wg
140102	Lockheed CP-140 (L-285B) Aurora	5689	N64959	14 Wg
140103	Lockheed CP-140 (L-285B) Aurora	5693	N64854	407 Sqn
140104	Lockheed CP-140 (L-285B) Aurora	5697	N48354	14 Wg
140105	Lockheed CP-140 (L-285B) Aurora	5704	N4007A	14 Wg
140106	Lockheed CP-140 (L-285B) Aurora	5706	N40035	407 Sqn
140107	Lockheed CP-140 (L-285B) Aurora	5708	N40065	407 Sqn
140108	Lockheed CP-140 (L-285B) Aurora	5709	N4008R	14 Wg
140109	Lockheed CP-140 (L-285B) Aurora	5711	N4009K	14 Wg
140110	Lockheed CP-140 (L-285B) Aurora	5712	N48354	14 Wg
140111	Lockheed CP-140 (L-285B) Aurora	5714	N64996	14 Wg
140112	Lockheed CP-140 (L-285B) Aurora	5715	N64854	407 Sqn
140113	Lockheed CP-140 (L-285B) Aurora	5717	N4007A	14 Wg
140114	Lockheed CP-140 (L-285B) Aurora	5719	N40035	14 Wg
140115	Lockheed CP-140 (L-285B) Aurora	5720	N64959	407 Sqn
140116	Lockheed CP-140 (L-285B) Aurora	5722	N40065	407 Sqn
140117	Lockheed CP-140 (L-285B) Aurora	5723	N4008R	14 Wg
140118	Lockheed CP-140 (L-285B) Aurora	5725	N4009K	407 Sqn
140119	Lockheed CP-140A (L-285B) Arcturus	5828	N6563L	14 Wg
140120	Lockheed CP-140A (L-285B) Arcturus	5829	N6564K	14 Wg
140121	Lockheed CP-140A (L-285B) Arcturus	5830	N65672	14 Wg
142801	DeHavilland Canada CC-142 (DHC-8)	38	C-GJBT	402 Sqn
142802	DeHavilland Canada CC-142 (DHC-8)	46	C-GIQG	402 Sqn
142803	DeHavilland Canada CT-142 (DHC-8)	71	C-GESR	402 Sqn
142804	DeHavilland Canada CT-142 (DHC-8)	80	C-GFRP	402 Sqn
142805	DeHavilland Canada CT-142 (DHC-8)	103	C-GDNG	402 Sqn
142806	DeHavilland Canada CT-142 (DHC-8)	107	C-GFQL	402 Sqn
C-GMBC / 901	Beech King Air C90B	LJ-1300		CATC
C-GMBD / 902	Beech King Air C90B	LJ-1301		CATC
C-GMBG / 903	Beech King Air C90B	LJ-1304		CATC
C-GMBH / 904	Beech King Air C90B	LJ-1309		CATC
C-GMBW / 905	Beech King Air C90B	LJ-1310		CATC
C-GMBX / 906	Beech King Air C90B	LJ-1313		CATC
C-GMBY / 907	Beech King Air C90B	LJ-1317		CATC
C-GMBZ / 908	Beech King Air C90B	LJ-1319		CATC

Province of Alberta

ICAO code GOA, callsign Alberta.
Based at Edmonton, operates as Air Transportation Services, part of the Department of Public Works Supply and Services.

C-FTUU / 205	Canadair CL-215	1011	CF-TUU	Tanker
C-FTUW / 206	Canadair CL-215	1030	CF-TUW	Tanker
C-GFSA	Beech Super King Air 350	FL-174		
C-GFSG	Beech Super King Air 200	BB-671		
C-GFSH	Beech Super King Air 200	BB-912		
C-GFSJ	DeHavilland Canada DHC-8-103 Dash 8	017		
C-GFSK / 201	Canadair CL-215	1085	C-GKDN	Tanker
C-GFSL / 202	Canadair CL-215	1086	C-GKDP	Tanker
C-GFSM / 203	Canadair CL-215	1098	C-GKDP	Tanker
C-GFSN / 204	Canadair CL-215	1099	C-GKDY	Tanker

Province of Manitoba - Air Services

Based at Winnipeg International and Thompson, Manitoba. Operates as Air Services, a division of the Dept. of Government Services.

C-FEMA	Cessna S550 Citation S/II	S550-0040	(N1269D)	
C-FMAU	DeHavilland Canada DHC-3 Otter	74	CF-MAU	
C-FMAX	DeHavilland Canada DHC-3 Otter	267	CF-MAX	
C-FODY	DeHavilland Canada DHC-3 Otter	429	CF-ODY	
C-FTUV / 256	Canadair CL-215	1020	CF-TUV	Tanker
C-FTXI / 255	Canadair CL-215	1016	CF-TXI	Tanker
C-GBNE	Cessna 500 Citation 1	500-0378/461	N3156M	
C-GBOW / 253	Canadair CL-215	1087	C-GKDY	Tanker
C-GDAT	Cessna 310R II	310R1883	N315U	
C-GKCE	Cessna 310R II	310R0649	N98920	
C-GMAF / 250	Canadair CL-215	1044	C-GUMW	Tanker
C-GMAK / 254	Canadair CL-215	1107	C-GKEA	Tanker
C-GMLN	Cessna 310R II	310R1884	N316U	
C-GRNE	Piper PA-31-350 Navajo	31-7952224	N91834	
C-GUMW / 251	Canadair CL-215	1065		Tanker
C-GYJB / 252	Canadair CL-215	1068		Tanker
C-GYNE	Cessna 310R II	310R1367	N4086C	

Province of Newfoundland

Based at St.Johns, operates as the Air Services Division.

C-FAYN / 282	Canadair CL-215	1105	C-GKET		Tanker
C-FAYU / 283	Canadair CL-215	1106			Tanker
C-FGNL	Beech King Air A100	B-184	CF-GNL		EMS
C-FIZU	Consolidated PBY-5A Catalina	46655	N10015		Tanker
C-FNJC	Consolidated PBY-5A Canso	CV-430	44-33929		Tanker
C-FTXA / 284	Canadair CL-215	1006	CF-TXA		Tanker
C-FYWP / 285	Canadair CL-215	1002	CF-YWP		Tanker
C-GDKW / 280	Canadair CL-215	1095			Tanker
C-GDKY / 281	Canadair CL-215	1096			Tanker
C-GLFY	Cessna 337G Super Skymaster	33701700	(N53557)		Surveyer

NWT Government

Based at Hay River Airport, North West Territories and operated by Buffalo Airways (ICAO code BFL, callsign Buffalo).

C-GBPD / 291	Canadair CL-215	1084		Tanker
C-GBYU / 290	Canadair CL-215	1083	C-GKEA	Tanker
C-GCSX / 295	Canadair CL-215	1088	C-GKEA	Tanker
C-GDHN / 296	Canadair CL-215	1089	C-GKEE	Tanker

Province of Ontario

ICAO code TRI, callsign Trillium.
Based at Sault St.Marie, Ontario, operates as MNR Aviation Services, a division of the Ministry of Natural Resources.

CF-OBS	DeHavilland Canada DHC-2 Beaver I	2		
C-FODU	DeHavilland Canada DHC-3 Otter	369	CF-ODU	
C-FOEH	DeHavilland Canada DHC-2 Turbo Beaver III	1644TB24	CF-OEH	
C-FOEK	DeHavilland Canada DHC-2 Turbo Beaver III	1650TB28	CF-OEK	
C-FOER	DeHavilland Canada DHC-2 Turbo Beaver III	1671TB41	CF-OER	
C-FOEU	DeHavilland Canada DHC-2 Turbo Beaver III	1678TB46	CF-OEU	
C-FOEW	DeHavilland Canada DHC-2 Turbo Beaver III	1682TB50	CF-OEW	
C-FOPA	DeHavilland Canada DHC-2 Turbo Beaver III	1688TB56	CF-OPA	
C-FOPG	DeHavilland Canada DHC-6 Twin Otter 300	232	CF-OPG	
C-FOPI	DeHavilland Canada DHC-6 Twin Otter 300	243	CF-OPI	
C-FOPJ	DeHavilland Canada DHC-6 Twin Otter 300	344	CF-OPJ	
C-GCJX	Piper PA-31-350 Navajo Chieftain	31-7552064	N4WE	Survey
C-GOGA	DeHavilland Canada DHC-6 Twin Otter 300	739		
C-GOGB	DeHavilland Canada DHC-6 Twin Otter 300	761		
C-GOGC	DeHavilland Canada DHC-6 Twin Otter 300	750		
C-GOGD / 270	Bombardier Canadair CL-415	2028	C-GAOI	Tanker
C-GOGE / 271	Bombardier Canadair CL-415	2031	C-GAUR	Tanker
C-GOGF / 272	Bombardier Canadair CL-415	2032	C-GBGE	Tanker
C-GOGG / 273	Bombardier Canadair CL-415	2033	C-GBFY	Tanker
C-GOGH / 274	Bombardier Canadair CL-415	2034	C-GCNO	Tanker
C-GOGT	Beech Super King Air 200	BB-535		Executive
C-GOGW / 275	Bombardier Canadair CL-415	2037	C-GBPM	Tanker
C-GOGX / 276	Bombardier Canadair CL-415	2038	C-GBPU	Tanker
C-GOGY / 277	Bombardier Canadair CL-415	2040		Tanker
C-GOGZ / 278	Bombardier Canadair CL-415	2043		Tanker
C-GQNJ	Beech Super King Air 200	BB-275		Executive

Gouvernement du Québec

ICAO code QUE, callsign Québec.
Based at Québec, operated by the Service Aérien Gouvernemental a Division of the Ministère du Conseil du Trésor.

C-FASE / 238	Canadair CL-215T	1114	1114 (Greek AF)	Tanker
C-FAWQ / 239	Canadair CL-215T	1115	1115 (Greek AF)	Tanker
C-FPQH	Fairchild F-27F Friendship	84	N1410	
C-FPQI	Fairchild F-27F Friendship	66	N42Q	
C-FTXG / 228	Canadair CL-215	1014	CF-TXG	Tanker
C-FTXJ / 230	Canadair CL-215	1017	CF-TXJ	Tanker
C-FTXK / 231	Canadair CL-215	1018	CF-TXK	Tanker

C-FURG	Canadair CL-601-1A Challenger	3063	C-GLYH	Ambulance
C-GFQB / 237	Canadair CL-215	1092	C-GKDP	Tanker
C-GCBA / 240	Bombardier Canadair CL-415	2005	C-GKDN	Tanker
C-GCBC / 241	Bombardier Canadair CL-415	2012	C-GKET	Tanker
C-GCBD / 242	Bombardier Canadair CL-415	2016	C-GBPU	Tanker
C-GCBE / 243	Bombardier Canadair CL-415	2017	C-GKEA	Tanker
C-GCBF / 244	Bombardier Canadair CL-415	2019	C-FVKV	Tanker
C-GCBG / 245	Bombardier Canadair CL-415	2022	C-FVLW	Tanker
C-GCBI / 246	Bombardier Canadair CL-415	2023	C-FVLI	Tanker
C-GCBK / 247	Bombardier Canadair CL-415	2026	C-FVLY	Tanker
C-GCBQ	Canadair CL-601-3A Challenger	5051	N300KC	
C-GCBT	DeHavilland Canada DHC-8-202 Dash 8Q	470	P2-ANL	

Province of Saskatchewan

ICAO code SGS, callsign Saskatchewan (also uses SLG and Lifeguard for EMS flights).
Based at Regina, Saskatoon and La Ronge, operates as Air Transportation Services.

C-FAFN / 216	Canadair CL-215	1093	C-GKDY	Tanker
C-FAFO / 217	Canadair CL-215	1094	C-GKEO	Tanker
C-FAFP / 218	Canadair CL-215	1100	C-GKEA	Tanker
C-FAFQ / 219	Canadair CL-215	1101	C-GKEE	Tanker
C-FHAO	Piper Aerostar 600A	60-0737-8061227	N6079U	
C-FVWO / 214	Canadair CL-215	1003	CF-YWO	Tanker
C-FVXG / 215	Canadair CL-215	1009	CF-YXG	Tanker
C-GEAS	Raytheon Beech King Air 350	FL-17	N56872	
C-GEHP / 1	Grumman CS2F-2 Tracker	DHC-97	12198 (CAF)	Tanker
C-GEHR / 3	Grumman CS2F-2 Tracker	DHC-51	12185 (CAF)	Tanker
C-GEQC / 4	Grumman CS2F-2 Tracker	DHC-53	12187 (CAF)	Tanker
C-GEQD / 5	Grumman CS2F-2 Tracker	DHC-98	12199 (CAF)	Tanker
C-GEQE / 6	Grumman CS2F-2 Tracker	DHC-92	12193 (CAF)	Tanker
C-GGPS	Piper PA-31T Cheyenne II	31T-7820023	N9662N	
C-GJPT	Piper PA-31T Cheyenne II	31T-7520039	N531PT	
C-GNKP	Piper PA-31T Cheyenne II	31T-7520008	N1017T	
C-GEAA	Piper PA-42-720 Cheyenne IIIA	42-5501057	OE-FAA	
C-GEAE	Raytheon Beech Super King Air B200	BB-1748	N50848	
C-GWDQ	Piper PA-31-350 Navajo Chieftain	31-8152119	N40869	
C-GWHK / 2	Grumman CS2F-1 Firecat	DHC-37	1538 (RCN)	Tanker
C-GZJR	Piper Aerostar 600A	60-0764-8061231	N6082Y	

Province of New Brunswick

Based at Frederiction and operated by Executive Flight Service.

| C-GXBF | Piper PA-31T Cheyenne II | 31T-7620010 | N9748N | |

Royal Canadian Mounted Police - RCMP

Based at Ottawa, Ontario, the aircraft are operated by GRC Air Services (GRC standing for Gendarmerie Royale du Canada).

C-FVPA	Pilatus PC-XII/45	164	(N164PB)	
C-FVPB	Pilatus PC-XII/45	283	N283PC	
C-FVPC	DeHavilland Canada DHC-6 Twin Otter 300	311	CF-MPC	
C-FVPL	DeHavilland Canada DHC-6 Twin Otter 300	320	CF-MPL	
C-FVPN	Pilatus PC-XII/45	296	HB-FQK	
C-FVPO	Pilatus PC-XII/45	229	HB-FRA	
C-FVPW	Pilatus PC-XII/45	315	HB-FRA	
C-FRPH	Cessna 208B Grand Caravan	208B0377	N1118B	
C-FSUJ	Cessna 208B Grand Caravan	208B0373	N973CC	
C-GFLA	Pilatus PC-XII/45	293	N293PC	
C-GHQG	Beech Super King Air 300	FA-39	N339WD	
C-GMPE	Pilatus PC-XII/45	184	HB-FSS	
C-GMPI	Pilatus PC-XII/45	239	HB-FRJ	
C-GMPJ	DeHavilland Canada DHC-6 Twin Otter 300	534		
C-GMPW	Pilatus PC-XII/45	274	N274PC	
C-GMPX	DeHavilland Canada DHC-6 Twin Otter 300	588		
C-GMPY	Pilatus PC-XII/45	311	N311PB	
C-GMPZ	Pilatus PC-XII/45	272	N272PC	

CAPE VERDE ISLANDS
República de Cabo Verde   W African coast

Cabo Verde consists of an archipelago 650 km off the coast of Senegal. Independent from Portugal since 1975, favour was found with the Soviet Union until the latter's collapse. The Coast Guard Dornier operates commercial flights when required but along with the Bandeirante is tasked primarily with MR/SAR duties.

SERIAL SYSTEM   A sequential number is issued with an 'FAC' prefix. As the Dornier also operates commercially a civil registration is allocated.

Fôrça Aérea Caboverdaine
Cabo Verde Air Force

UNITS/BASES   Aircraft based at Amilcar Cabral International on Sal Island.

FAC-01	Antonov An-26	
FAC-02	Antonov An-26	
	Antonov An-26	

Guarda Costeira de Cabo Verde
Cape Verde Coast Guard - Air Wing

UNITS/BASES   Aircraft based at Amilcar Cabral International on Sal Island.

FAC-03	Embraer EMB110P1 Bandeirante	110474	
D4-CBK	Dornier 228-212	8222	7Q-YKS

CENTRAL AFRICAN REPUBLIC
République Centrafricaine   C Africa

It is reported that through lack of funds only two aircraft currently fly for the national air arm, although the former French colony of Ubangi-Shari may hold other aircraft in storage. As a former colony a detachment of French Air Force aircraft is usually present how-ever, including Mirage F1s and Transalls.

SERIAL SYSTEM   Civil style registrations are issued in a unique sequence, 'TL-K**'.

Escadrille Centrafricaine
Central African Flight

UNITS/BASES   Based at Bangui-M'Poko International Airport

TL-KAA	Britten Norman BN-2 Islander	Std Bangui
TL-KAC	Britten Norman BN-2 Islander	Ministry of Water and Forest

CHAD
République du Tchad   C Africa

Despite independence from France in 1960, a large French military presence is retained in the country with regular deployments of Mirages and Jaguars to bolster the based ALAT forces due to continued border disputes with Libya and a history of guerilla conflict and civil war.

SERIAL SYSTEM   Civil style registrations are allocated in a sequence with each type commencing TT-*AA. Government aircraft markings are issued sequentially in the TT-AA* block.

Forces Aériennes Tchadiennes
Chad Air Force

UNITS/BASES   Transports are based at N'djamena Airport

TT-KAA	Pilatus PC-6B2/H2 Turbo Porter	762	HB-FGM
TT-LAA	Fokker F.27 Friendship 600	10648	5A-DLS
TT-LAM	Antonov An-26		
TT-LAN	Antonov An-26	14308	RA-26234
TT-MAA	Reims F337E Super Skymaster	F33700017/ 01285	TT-MAE
TT-MAB	Reims F337E Super Skymaster	F33700014/ 01273	
TT-MAD	Reims F337F Super Skymaster	F33700028/ 01345	
TT-MAI	Reims F337F Super Skymaster	F33700038/ 01371	

TT-PAA	Lockheed C-130A (L-182-1A) Hercules	3208	N4445V
TT-PAF	Lockheed C-130H (L-382C-04F) Hercules	5141	N73238
	Antonov An-72		UK-

Government of the Republic of Chad

| TT-AAH | Lockheed C-130H-30 (L-382T-09F) Hercules | 5184 | |
| TT-AAI | Grumman G-1159 Gulfstream II | 240 | 5A-DDR |

CHILE
República de Chile   S America

Despite its relatively small size Chile has a modern air arm, with a number of upgraded types in service, although the recent economic situation has slowed new acquisitions.

SERIAL SYSTEM   Three digit serials are allocated in batches by type for the AF, Army and Navy, Army aircraft usually being prefixed with an E and Navy sometimes with the initials ARC. Police two digit sequential serials are prefixed C.

Fuerza Aérea de Chile - FAC
Chilean Air Force

UNITS/BASES   I Brigada Aérea
   Ala 4, Grupo 1, Escuadrón de Enlace, BA Los Condores-Iquique
   Aviocar, Twin Otter (supporting A-36)

   II Brigada Aérea
   Ala 2, Grupo 2, BA Los Condores-Iquique   Beech 99
   Ala 2, Grupo 10, Benitez IAP-Santiago   C-130B/H, Boeing 707, Beech 99,
      Super King Air, Twin Otter
   Servicio Aerofotogrametrico   Learjet
   III Brigada Aérea
   Ala 5, Grupo 5, BA El Tepual-Puerto Montt   Twin Otter, Aviocar, CitationJet
   IV Brigada Aérea
   Ala 3, Grupo 6, BA Carlos Ibanez-Punta Arenas   Twin Otter
   Grupo 19, BA Teniente Marsh, Antarctica   Twin Otter

PLANS   VIP 707 replacement with CFM powered 737 or similar reported.
   The USA has offered KC-135s to supplement/replace the converted 707s as part of an F-16 package.
   Two Xian Y-7H were reported as delivered but have never been reported as seen.

261	Cessna O-2A Super Skymaster	M337-0441	69-7643 (USAF)		SAR
	Cessna O-2A Super Skymaster				
	Cessna O-2A Super Skymaster				
	Cessna O-2A Super Skymaster				
	Cessna O-2A Super Skymaster				
	Cessna O-2A Super Skymaster				
	Cessna O-2A Super Skymaster				
	Cessna O-2A Super Skymaster				
	Cessna O-2A Super Skymaster				
	Cessna O-2A Super Skymaster				
	Cessna O-2A Super Skymaster				
	Cessna O-2A Super Skymaster				
301	Beech 99A	U-138	CC-EFP	II BA	
302	Beech 99A	U-139	CC-EFQ	II BA	
303	Beech 99A Petrel	U-140	CC-EFR	II BA, Gr 2	
304	Beech 99A	U-141	CC-EFS	II BA	
307	Beech 99A	U-144	CC-EFV	II BA	
331	Beech King Air A100	B-219	CC-ESA	II BA, Gr 10	
336	Beech Super King Air B200	BB-1530		II BA, Gr 10	
351	Learjet 35	35-050	CC-ECO	II BA, SA	
352	Learjet 35	35-066	CC-ECP	II BA, SA	
361	Cessna 525 CitationJet 1	525-0463	N1284D	III BA, Gr 5	
362	Cessna 525 CitationJet 1	525-0464	N1284P	III BA, Gr 5	
363	Cessna 525 CitationJet 1	525-0465	N1285P	III BA, Gr 5	
902	Boeing 707-351C	19443 / 611	CC-CCK	II BA, Gr 10	
903	Boeing 707-330B	18926 / 446	CC-CEA	II BA, Gr 10	AAR, *'Aguila'*
904	Boeing 707-385C	19000 / 447	905 (FACh)	II BA, Gr 10	AEW, *'Condor'*
911	GAC Gulfstream IV	1089	N53MU	II BA, Gr 10	
921	Boeing 737-58N	28866 / 2929	N1786B	II BA, Gr 10	
922	Boeing 737-330(F)	23524 / 1272	D-ABXC	II BA, Gr 10	
932	DeHavilland Canada DHC-6 Twin Otter 300	583		IV BA, Gr 6	Ski equipped
933	DeHavilland Canada DHC-6 Twin Otter 300	584			

936	DeHavilland Canada DHC-6 Twin Otter 100	10			
937	DeHavilland Canada DHC-6 Twin Otter 100	11		II BA, Gr 10	
938	DeHavilland Canada DHC-6 Twin Otter 300	586		IV BA, Gr 6	Ski equipped
939	DeHavilland Canada DHC-6 Twin Otter 100	20			
940	DeHavilland Canada DHC-6 Twin Otter 100	24		II BA, Gr 10	
941	DeHavilland Canada DHC-6 Twin Otter 300	589			
942	DeHavilland Canada DHC-6 Twin Otter 300	590		IV BA, Gr 6	Ski equipped
943	DeHavilland Canada DHC-6 Twin Otter 300	396	CC-CAE		
944	DeHavilland Canada DHC-6 Twin Otter 300	397	CC-CBB	III BA, Gr 5	
945	DeHavilland Canada DHC-6 Twin Otter 300	398	CC-CBF	III BA, Gr 5	
946	DeHavilland Canada DHC-6 Twin Otter 300	399	CC-CBH	III BA, Gr 5	
947	DeHavilland Canada DHC-6 Twin Otter 300	404	CC-CBM	III BA, Gr 5	
960	CASA 212 Aviocar srs 200	350	EC-006	I BA, Gr 1	
961	CASA 212 Aviocar srs 200	355		I BA, Gr 1	
965	CASA 212 Aviocar srs 300DF	442		III BA, Gr 5	
966	CASA 212 Aviocar srs 300DF	443		III BA, Gr 5	
994	Lockheed C-130B (L-282-1B) Hercules	3622	60-0310 (USAF)	II BA, Gr 10	
995	Lockheed C-130H (L-382C-28D) Hercules	4453		II BA, Gr 10	
996	Lockheed C-130H (L-382C-28D) Hercules	4496		II BA, Gr 10	
997	Lockheed C-130B (L-282-1B) Hercules	3551	58-0752 (USAF)	II BA, Gr 10	
998	Lockheed C-130B (L-282-1B) Hercules	3690	61-2647 (USAF)	II BA, Gr 10	

Servicio de Aviación de la Armada de Chile
Chilean Naval Aviation Service

UNITS/BASES	Squadron VC-1, Vina del Mar-Torquemada AB	Aviocar, Bandeirante, P-3ACH
	One Aviocar detached to Punta Arenas	
	Squadron VP-1, Vina del Mar-Torquemada AB	P-3ACH, Bandeirante
	EMB-111AN detached to Iquique Puerto Montt and Talcahuano	
	Squadron VT-1, Vina del Mar-Torquemada AB	O-2

PLANS	The two stored Orions will be modified and updated for MR service when funds allow.

107	Embraer EMB-110CN Bandeirante	110101	PT-GKF	VC-1	
108	Embraer EMB-110CN Bandeirante	110102	PT-GKG	VC-1	
109	Embraer EMB-110CN Bandeirante	110108	PT-GKH	VC-1	
145	CASA 212 Aviocar srs 100	A11-1-134		VC-1	
146	CASA 212 Aviocar srs 100	A11-2-135		VC-1	
147	CASA 212 Aviocar srs 100	A11-3-137		VC-1	
261	Embraer EMB-111AN Bandeirante	110147		VP-1	
262	Embraer EMB-111AN Bandeirante	110150		VP-1	
263	Embraer EMB-111AN Bandeirante	110154		VC-1	
264	Embraer EMB-111AN Bandeirante	110158		VP-1	
265	Embraer EMB-111AN Bandeirante	110162		VP-1	
266	Embraer EMB-111AN Bandeirante	110166		VP-1	
330	Cessna O-2A Super Skymaster	M337-0350	68-11125 (USAF)	VT-1	
331	Cessna O-2A Super Skymaster	M337-0234	68-10869 (USAF)	VT-1	
332	Cessna O-2A Super Skymaster	M337-0439	69-7641 (USAF)	VT-1	
333	Cessna O-2A Super Skymaster	M337-0351	68-11126 (USAF)	VT-1	
334	Cessna O-2A Super Skymaster	M337-0407	69-7609 (USAF)	VT-1	Dam 21Jan01
335	Cessna O-2A Super Skymaster	M337-0402	69-7604 (USAF)	VT-1	
CC-LHB	Cessna O-2A Super Skymaster	M337-0425	69-7627 (USAF)	Navy Aero Club	
337	Cessna O-2A Super Skymaster	M337-0348	CC-LHI	VT-1	originally 68-11123
401	Lockheed UP-3A (L-185) Orion	5044	Bu150518 (USN)		Std Vina del Mar
402	Lockheed P-3ACH (L-185) Orion	5033	Bu150507 (USN)	VP-1	Cvtd UP-3A
404	Lockheed P-3ACH (L-185) Orion	5135	Bu152165 (USN)	VP-1	Cvtd UP-3A
406	Lockheed UP-3A (L-185) Orion	5059	Bu150607 (USN)		Std Vina del Mar
407	Lockheed P-3ACH (L-185) Orion	5097	Bu151384 (USN)	VP-1	Cvtd UP-3A
408	Lockheed P-3ACH (L-185) Orion	5111	Bu152141 (USN)	VC-1	VIP, Cvtd UP-3A

Comando de Aviación del Ejército de Chile
Chilean Army Aviation Command

UNITS/BASES	Regimento de Aviación 1, Rancagua, deployed countrywide as required.

PLANS	Five futher Cessna 208B's were reported as on order but no sightings have been reported.

E-131	Cessna 208B Grand Caravan	208B0651	N5262Z	Reg Av 1
E-132	Cessna 208B Grand Caravan	208B0652	N52623	Reg Av 1
E-133	Cessna 208B Grand Caravan	208B0653	N5264M	Reg Av 1
204	Piper PA-31 Navajo			Reg Av 1
208	Beech Baron 58			Reg Av 1
209	Beech King Air 90			Reg Av 1

E-21●	CASA 212 Aviocar srs 100	A10-1-103		Reg Av 1	
E-21⁻	CASA 212 Aviocar srs 100	A10-2-106		Reg Av 1	
E-21**3**	CASA 212 Aviocar srs 100	A10-4-117		Reg Av 1	
E-21⌐	CASA 212 Aviocar srs 100	A10-5-118		Reg Av 1	
E-21**5**	CASA 212 Aviocar srs 100	A10-6-126		Reg Av 1	
E-21**6**	Airtech/CASA CN235M-100	C020		Reg Av 1	
E-21**8**	Airtech/CASA CN235M-100	C022		Reg Av 1	
E-21**9**	Airtech/CASA CN235M-100	C019	250 (IAC)	Reg Av 1	
	Airtech/CASA CN235M-100				on order
	Airtech/CASA CN235M-100				on order
231	CASA 212 Aviocar srs 300	AB10-2-455		Reg Av 1	
232	CASA 212 Aviocar srs 300	AB10-3-456		Reg Av 1	
E-30⁻	Cessna 550 Citation II	550-0104/146	CC-ECN	Reg Av 1	
E-30**3**	Cessna 650 Citation III	650-0131	CC-ECL	Reg Av 1	

Prefectura Aérea de los Carabineros de Chile
Chilean Air Police

C-05	Cessna U206G Stationair		
C-51	Piper PA-31T-620 Cheyenne II	31T-8020090	CC-CMZ
	Cessna 208B Grand Caravan	208B0657	N1241X

CHINA
Zhonghua Renmin Gongheguo / People's Republic of China — E Asia

The post W.W.II communist revolution and subsequent rift with the Soviet Union has hindered what is viewed by most observers as the single biggest threat to world stability. Despite having the world's largest population China's military forces, while large, have a disappointing capability. Air transport has been particularly ignored with major reliance placed on railways to move equipment, leaving an almost non-existent strategic capability given the size of force to mobilize. The Air Force established a commercial arm in 1985 as China United Airlines to operate scheduled services to the more remote parts of the country and VIP flights on demand. The Antonov An-2, or at least its Chinese counterpart the Y-5, is reported to be the most numerous type on strength but serial details are limited for the 300 plus aircraft reported in service.
Also see the separate entry for the semi-autonomous territory of Hong Kong.

SERIAL SYSTEM   No clear system of military serial allocation has been noted, although aircraft in the civil sequence B-4*** all appear to have a Government affiliation.

Zhongkuo Shenmin Taifang Tsunputai
People's Liberation Army Air Force (PLAAF)

UNITS/BASES   Reported transport bases include:
Beijing-Nan Yuan — Tu-154, Il-76, Y-7 (China United Airlines - CUA)
Chengdu, Sichuan Province — Il-76
Wuhan, Hubei Province — An-26
Xian-Yanliang, Shaanxi Province — Citation, Y-12, Y-5 (Zhongfei AL, Divn of Flight Test Establishment)

Airborne Troop units are based at::
Kaifeng, Henan Province, 43rd Brigade
Yingshan, Hubei Province, 44th Brigade
Huangpi, Hubei Province, 45th Brigade

PLANS   The acquisition of state of the art AEW capabilty was thwarted in 2000 when US pressure stopped Israeli work on the modified Beriev Ilyushin AI-50 (Il-76, RA-74780), China intends to lease up to two A-50s from Russia while the A-50E is developed and will acquire four of the latter version. The purchase of up to 38 new build Il-76s is being negotiated with Uzbekistan.

741	Antonov An-26	2306
742	Antonov An-26	2308
743	Antonov An-26	2309
744	Antonov An-26	2310
745	Antonov An-26	2401
746	Antonov An-26	2402
747	Antonov An-26	2403
748	Antonov An-26	2404
749	Antonov An-26	2405
750	Antonov An-26	2502
751	Antonov An-26	2503
752	Antonov An-26	2507
753	Antonov An-26	2509
754	Antonov An-26	2510
755	Antonov An-26	2601

756	Antonov An-26	2902		
757	Antonov An-26	2903		
759	Antonov An-26	2905		
760	Antonov An-26	3105		
761	Antonov An-26	3003		
762	Antonov An-26	3004		
763	Antonov An-26	3005		
764	Antonov An-26	3110		
765	Antonov An-26	3106		
766	Antonov An-26	3108		
767	Antonov An-26	3109		
768	Antonov An-26	3302		
769	Antonov An-26	3408		
770	Antonov An-26	3409		
771	Antonov An-26	3903		
772	Antonov An-26	3905		
773	Antonov An-26	3906		
774	Antonov An-26	3908		
775	Antonov An-26	4003		
776	Antonov An-26	4004		
778	Antonov An-26	4107		
779	Antonov An-26	4108		CUA
780	Antonov An-26	4201		
781	Antonov An-26	4202		
782	Antonov An-26	4203		
783	Antonov An-26	4207		
784	Antonov An-26	4301		CUA
785	Antonov An-26	4302		
786	Antonov An-26	4303		
787	Antonov An-26	4306		
788	Antonov An-26	4307		
789	Antonov An-26	4310		CUA
790	Antonov An-26	4401		
791	Antonov An-26	7304		
792	Antonov An-26	7305		
793	Antonov An-26	7307		
794	Antonov An-26	7308		
795	Antonov An-26	7310		
796	Antonov An-26	8903		
797	Antonov An-26	8908		
798	Antonov An-26	8909		
799	Antonov An-26	9007		
800	Antonov An-26	9008		
801	Antonov An-26	9010		
802	Antonov An-26	9103		
803	Antonov An-26	10204		
804	Antonov An-26	10206		
805	Antonov An-26	10207		
806	Antonov An-26	10303		
807	Antonov An-26	10307		
808	Antonov An-26	10309		
809	Antonov An-26	10402		
33041	Antonov An-26			
33042	Antonov An-26			
33043	Antonov An-26			
33044	Antonov An-26			
33045	Antonov An-26			
33046	Antonov An-26			
33047	Antonov An-26			
33048	Antonov An-26			
33049	Antonov An-26			
33141	Antonov An-26			
33142	Antonov An-26			
51054	Antonov An-26	2904	759 (PLAAF)	
51057	Antonov An-26			CUA
51058	Antonov An-26			CUA
71290	Antonov An-26			
871	Antonov An-30	0902		
872	Antonov An-30	0903		CUA
873	Antonov An-30	1001		
874	Antonov An-30	1002		
875	Antonov An-30	1003		
879	Antonov An-30	1507		
880	Antonov An-30	1508		

881	Antonov An-30	1509			
882	Antonov An-30	1510			
883	Antonov An-30	1601			
B-4103 / 091	Cessna 550 Citation II	550-0301/357	N6799T	Zhongfei AL	Survey
B-4104 / 092	Cessna 550 Citation II	550-0297/362	N68003	Zhongfei AL	Survey
B-4105 / 090	Cessna 550 Citation II	550-0305/359	N67999	Zhongfei AL	Survey
B-4030	Ilyushin Il-76MD	1013407233		CUA	
B-4031	Ilyushin Il-76MD	1013408254		CUA	
B-4032	Ilyushin Il-76MD	1013409289		CUA	
B-4033	Ilyushin Il-76MD	1033416512		CUA	
B-4034	Ilyushin Il-76MD	1033416524		CUA	
B-4035	Ilyushin Il-76MD	1033416529		CUA	
B-4036	Ilyushin Il-76MD	1033417550		CUA	
B-4037	Ilyushin Il-76MD	1033417557		CUA	
B-4038	Ilyushin Il-76MD	1033417567		CUA	
B-4039	Ilyushin Il-76MD	1043418576		CUA	
B-4040	Ilyushin Il-76MD	1053419656		CUA	
B-4041	Ilyushin Il-76MD	1053420663		CUA	
B-4042	Ilyushin Il-76MD	1063418587		CUA	
B-4043	Ilyushin Il-76MD	1063420671		CUA	
B-4044	Ilyushin Il-76MD			CUA	
B-4045	Ilyushin Il-76MD			CUA	
B-4046	Ilyushin Il-76MD			CUA	
B-4047	Ilyushin Il-76MD			CUA	
B-4048	Ilyushin Il-76MD			CUA	
B-4049	Ilyushin Il-76MD			CUA	
181	Yunshuji/Shaanxi Y-8				
982	Yunshuji/Shaanxi Y-8				
987	Yunshuji/Shaanxi Y-8				
989	Yunshuji/Shaanxi Y-8				
31044	Yunshuji/Shaanxi Y-8	020803			
31140	Yunshuji/Shaanxi Y-8	030805			
94004 / LH	Yunshuji/Shaanxi Y-8				
B-4001	Tupolev Tu-154M	85A-711		CUA	
B-4003	Tupolev Tu-154M	85A-713		CUA	
B-4004	Tupolev Tu-154M	85A-714		CUA	
B-40 4	Tupolev Tu-154M	90A-847		CUA	
B-40 5	Tupolev Tu-154M	90A-856		CUA	
B-40 6	Tupolev Tu-154M	91A-872		CUA	
B-40 7	Tupolev Tu-154M	91A-873		CUA	
B-4022	Tupolev Tu-154M	87A-765	OK-SCA	CUA	
B-4023	Tupolev Tu-154M	88A-770	OK-TCB	CUA	
B-4024	Tupolev Tu-154M	88A-789	OK-TCC	CUA	
B-4027	Tupolev Tu-154M	92A-943		CUA	VIP
B-4028	Tupolev Tu-154M	93A-967	RA-85783	CUA	VIP
B-4029	Tupolev Tu-154M	93A-950		CUA	VIP
B-4050	Tupolev Tu-154M	86A-730	B-2612	CUA	
B-4051	Tupolev Tu-154M	86A-741	B-2614	CUA	
B-4138	Tupolev Tu-154M	85A-712	B-4002	CUA	VIP/ELINT
3158	Yunshuji Y-5				
5261	Yunshuji Y-5				
5301	Yunshuji Y-5				
11978	Yunshuji Y-5				
21597	Yunshuji Y-5				
30913	Yunshuji Y-5				
B-8482	Yunshuji/Shijiazhuang Y-5	0608		Zhongfei AL	Survey
3179	Yunshuji/Xian Y-7	01703	B-3433		
3418	Yunshuji/Xian Y-7-100	10709			
4510	Yunshuji/Xian Y-7-100	10710			
4520	Yunshuji/Xian Y-7H	027H02			Cloud seeder
5010	Yunshuji/Xian Y-7-100	10708			
5011	Yunshuji/Xian Y-7-100	11701			
5066	Yunshuji/Xian Y-7-100	10705			
5813	Yunshuji/Xian Y-7-100	10706			
5853	Yunshuji/Xian Y-7				
5863	Yunshuji/Xian Y-7				
8192	Yunshuji/Xian Y-7	01704	B-3434		
9032	Yunshuji/Xian Y-7-100	10703			
9042	Yunshuji/Xian Y-7-100	10704			
12603	Yunshuji/Xian Y-7	01702			
33140	Yunshuji/Xian Y-7-200	057H03			
33141	Yunshuji/Xian Y-7				
51053	Yunshuji/Xian Y-7-100				
B-3820	Yunshuji/Harbin Y-12 II	0031		Zhongfei AL	Survey

People's Republic of China Naval Aviation

UNITS/BASES	Beijing-Nan Yuan	Yak-42D	

PLANS Development of an AEW version of the Y-8 is underway using the RACAL Skymaster radar system.

B-4012	Yakovlev Yak-42D	4520424914375	VIP
B-4013	Yakovlev Yak-42D		VIP

Government of the People's Republic of China

UNITS/BASES	Xijiao, CAAC Military Division			

B-4005	Bombardier CRJ 200ER	7138	C-FZAT	VIP
B-4006	Bombardier CRJ 200ER	7149	C-FZIS	VIP
B-4007	Bombardier CRJ 200ER	7180	C-GATM	VIP
B-4008	Boeing 737-3T0	23839 / 1507	N19357	VIP
B-4009	Boeing 737-3T0	23840 / 1516	N27358	VIP
B-4010	Bombardier CRJ 200ER	7189	C-GATY	VIP
B-4011	Bombardier CRJ 200ER	7193	C-GBFR	VIP
B-4018	Boeing 737-33A	25502 / 2310		
B-4019	Boeing 737-33A	25503 / 2313		
B-4020	Boeing 737-34N	28081 / 2746		VIP
B-4021	Boeing 737-34N	28082 / 2747		VIP
B-4025	Boeing 767-332ER	30597 / 797	N179DZ	
B-4052	Boeing 737-3Q8	24701 / 1957	PK-GWI	
B-4053	Boeing 737-3Q8	24702 / 1994	PK-GWJ	
B-4106	Cessna 650 Citation VI	650-0220	N6830T	Calibrator
B-4107	Cessna 650 Citation VI	650-0221	N1301A	Calibrator

Airborne Remote Sensing Services - Poly Technologies

UNITS/BASES	Beijing-Nan Yuan			

B-4101	Cessna S550 Citation S/II	S550-0049	N1270K	Survey
B-4102	Cessna S550 Citation S/II	S550-0050	N1270S	Survey
HY-984	Learjet 36A	36A-053	N39418	Survey
HY-985	Learjet 36A	36A-034	N763R	Survey
HY-986	Learjet 35A	35A-601	N3818G	Survey
HY-987	Learjet 35A	35A-602	N10873	Survey
HY-988	Learjet 35A	35A-603	N1471B	Survey

COLOMBIA
República de Colombia   S America

Columbia's reputation as the world centre for drug production is being fought against with increasing US assistance, other problems include active guerrilla units for which an extensive COIN capability is maintained. The Air Force also operates an airline (SATENA) connecting Bogota to areas that are not commercially viable. Many light transports have been acquired by all the air arms when intercepting drug runners, most if airworthy are used for a while and then dumped as there is steady source of new additions.

SERIAL SYSTEM All AF aircraft are prefixed FAC, The Army, Navy and Police have different prefixes based on their initials.

Fuerza Aérea Colombiana - FAC
Colombian Air Force

UNITS/BASES	Comando Aéreo de Combat - CACOM 1	
	Grupo 21, Escuadrón Aerotactico 214, BA German Olano-Palanquero	AC-47, PA-31T
	Comando Aéreo de Combat - CACOM 2	
	Grupo 31, Escuadrón Aerotactico 313, BA Luis F Gomez Nino-Apiay	AC-47, C402C
	Comando Aéreo de Combat - CACOM 3	
	Grupo 41, Escuadrón Aerotactico 412, BA del Atlantico-Barranquilla	AC-47, QueenAir, Baron
	Comando Aereo de Apoyo Tactico - CAATA 1	
	Grupo 51, Escuadrón Artillados 515, BA Luis F Pinto-Melgar	C210
	Comando Aéreo de Transporte Militar - CATAM	
	Escuadrón 711, BA Camilo Daza, El Dorado-Bogota	C-130B/H
	Escuadrón 712, BA Camilo Daza, El Dorado-Bogota	Various
	Escuadrón Aerofotografico, BA Camilo Daza, El Dorado-Bogota	RC695A
	Escuadrón Presidencial, BA Camilo Daza, El Dorado-Bogota	707, F.28
	Servicio de Aeronavegacion a Territorios Nacionales - SATENA, El Dorado-Bogota	
		F.28, 727, Do328, Aviocar

Escuela Militar de Aviación
   Escuadrón de Transporte 613, BA Marco Fidel Suarez- Cali   C310
Grupo Aéreo del Sur - GASUR
   Escaudrón de Enlace, BA Ernesto Esguerra-Tres Esquinas   C-47, Beaver, PA-23

PLANS   Further C-130Bs (or even C-130Es) are being requested from the USA.

Serial	Type	c/n	Reg	Operator	Notes
0001	Fokker F.28 Fellowship 1000	11992	001 (FACo)	Esc Pres.	
123	Piper PA-44-180 Seminole				
169	Cessna 401				
509	Piper PA-31 Navajo				
512	Piper PA-23-250D Aztec				
516	Cessna 340				
517	Cessna 404 Titan				
520	Piper PA-31 Navajo				
522	Piper PA-31 Navajo				
527	Cessna 310				
529	Cessna 310				
535	Cessna 404 Titan				
538	GAC Commander 695 (Jetprop 980)				
542	Aero Commander 680V	1563-19	HK-2539G		
558	Beech Queen Air 65	LC-223	N4BL		
560	Beech Queen Air 65	LC-221	N9536Q		
561	Beech Queen Air 65	LC-	N6811C		
571	Beech Baron D55	TE-380	N2765T		
581	Beech Queen Air				
1001	Lockheed C-130B (L-282-1B) Hercules	3575	N4653	Esc 711	
1004	Lockheed C-130H (L-382C-42E) Hercules	4964	N4080M	Esc 711	
1005	Lockheed C-130H (L-382C-42E) Hercules	4965	N41030	Esc 711	
1006	Lockheed C-130B (L-282-1B) Hercules	3512	58-0717 (USAF)		Std El Dorado
1009	Lockheed C-130B (L-282-1B) Hercules	3697	62-3487 (USAF)		
1010	Lockheed C-130B (L-282-1B) Hercules	3521	58-0726 (USAF)		
1012	Lockheed C-130B (L-282-1B) Hercules	3635	61-0956 (USAF)		
	Lockheed C-130B (L-282-1B) Hercules	3675	61-2639 (USAF)		
1120	Cessna 208 Caravan 1			SATENA	
1121	Cessna 208 Caravan 1			SATENA	
1141	Fokker F.28 Fellowship 3000C	11162	PH-EZL	SATENA	'El Llanero'
1146	Boeing 727-95(F)	19595 / 467	HK-3771X	SATENA	
1147	Boeing 727-2B7	20303 / 793	HK-3872X	SATENA	
1154	CASA 212 Aviocar srs 200	CD51-05-317			Dam, WFU?
1156	CASA 212 Aviocar srs 300	A51-01-370		SATENA	'Vaupes'
1157	CASA 212 Aviocar srs 300	A51-02-372		SATENA	'Amazonas'
1158	CASA 212 Aviocar srs 300	A51-03-391			'Uraba'
1160	Dornier 328-120	3079	D-CDXB	SATENA	'Maipures'
1161	Dornier 328-120	3080	D-CDXH	SATENA	'La Macarena'
1162	Dornier 328-120	3082	D-CDXP	SATENA	'Bahia Solano'
1163	Dornier 328-120	3081	D-CDXM	SATENA	'El Antioqueno'
1164	Dornier 328-120	3092	D-CDXO	SATENA	
1165	Dornier 328-120	3103	D-CDXW	SATENA	'El Guambiano'
1201	Boeing 707-373C	19716 / 644	HL7425	Esc Pres.	
1211	Cessna 550 Citation II	550-0582/582	(N1301A)	Esc 712	
1250	CASA 212A Aviocar srs 300	A74-1-449	1701 (FACo)	Esc 712	Dam Oct97, on rebuild
1260	Airtech/CASA CN235-100	C109?			
1261	Airtech/CASA CN235-100	C118			
1262	Airtech/CASA CN235-100	C121			
1270	Embraer EMB-110P1K Bandeirante	110494	PT-SOH	Esc 712	
1271	Embraer EMB-110P1K Bandeirante	110496	PT-SOI	Esc 712	
1654	Basler BT-67 Turbo Dakota	26292		Basler, Oshkosh	on order, cvtd C-47
1658	Basler BT-67 Turbo Dakota	32541/conv37	N91BF	Basler, Oshkosh	on order, cvtd C-47
1667	Basler BT-67 Turbo Dakota	19052		Basler, Oshkosh	on order, cvtd C-47
1670	Basler BT-67 Turbo Dakota	19125/conv36	N40359	GASUR	Cvtd C-47
1681	Basler BT-67 Turbo Dakota	16500/33248			Cvtd C-47
1686	Basler BT-67 Turbo Dakota				Cvtd C-47
1952	IAI Arava srs 201	0066	952 (FACo)	Esc 712	
2144	Piper PA-34-200T Seneca II	34-7870368	HK-2144		
3111	Swearingen Merlin				
3180	Cessna 402				
5050	Cessna 208 Caravan 1				Std Caracas, Venezuela
5054	Cessna 208 Caravan 1	20800285	N5264A		
5055	Cessna 208 Caravan 1	20800286	N5263D		
5056	Cessna 208 Caravan 1	20800287	N5265N		

5059	Cessna 208 Caravan 1				
5060	El Gavilan Gavilan 358				
	El Gavilan Gavilan 358		HK-4148Z		
	El Gavilan Gavilan 358		HK-4165Z		
	El Gavilan Gavilan 358				
	El Gavilan Gavilan 358				
	El Gavilan Gavilan 358				
	El Gavilan Gavilan 358				
	El Gavilan Gavilan 358				
	El Gavilan Gavilan 358				
	El Gavilan Gavilan 358				
	El Gavilan Gavilan 358				
	El Gavilan Gavilan 358				
5122	Cessna 210N Centurion	21063061			
5153	Piper PA-23 Aztec				
5183	Beech Baron 55				
5190	Piper PA-31 Navajo				
5194	Piper PA-31T Cheyenne II				
5198	GAC Commander 695A (Jetprop 1000)	96030	N73H	Esc Afg	
5200	Piper PA-34 Seneca				
5507	Cessna 404 Titan				
5513	Piper PA-34-220T Seneca III	34-7770158			
5527	Cessna 310R			Esc 613	
5533	Cessna 310				
5535	Cessna 402				
5553	GAC Commander 695 (Jetprop 980)	95055	N29SA		
5557	Beech Queen Air				
5570	Beech King Air C90	LJ-752	570 (FACo)	Esc 711	
5591	GAC Commander 695 (Jetprop 980)				
5601	Rockwell Commander 690				
5603	Beech Queen Air				
5606	Piper PA-34 Seneca				
5620	Beech Queen Air				
5625	Beech Super King Air 200				
5741	Piper PA-31T Cheyenne II				
5750	Beech Super King Air 300				
6111	Beech Super King Air 200				

Armada República de Colombia
Colombian Navy

UNITS/BASES   The Grupo Aeronaval del Atlantico is based at Rafael Nunoz Intl Airport at Cartagena-Bolivar.

ARC-101	Beech Super King Air 350			GAA	
ARC-301	Piper PA-31T-620 Cheyenne	31T-7520014	5739 (FACo)	GAA	
ARC-408	Cessna 206			GAA	
ARC-504	Aero Commander 680			GAA	
ARC-506	Piper PA-31 Navajo			GAA	
ARC-507	Colemill Panther Navajo				Std Cartagena
ARC-508	Piper PA-31 Navajo			GAA	
ARC-509	Colemill Panther Navajo				Std Cartagena
ARC-510	Piper PA-31 Navajo			GAA	
ARC-601	Rockwell Commander 690C			GAA	
ARC-603	Rockwell Commander 690			GAA	
ARC-605	Rockwell Commander 690			GAA	
ARC-606	Rockwell Commander 690C				Std Cartagena

Ejército de Colombia
Colombian Army

UNITS/BASES   Most aircraft are based at El Dorado-Bogota, with detachments where required.

EJC-017	Cessna 404 Titan				
EJC-103	GAC Commander 695A (Jetprop 1000)				
EJC-105	Piper PA-34 Seneca				c/n plate removed
EJC-108	Beech Super King Air 200				
EJC-109	Piper PA-34 Seneca				
EJC-111	Piper PA-31 Navajo				
EJC-115	GAC Commander 695 (Jetprop 980)	95066	XB-ORA		
EJC-116	Beech King Air 90				
EJC-117	Beech Super King Air 200				
EJC-119	Cessna 206				
EJC-120	Cessna U206G Stationair				
EJC-121	Convair 580	62 / 88	HK-3559		

Policia Nacionales de Colombia - PNC
Colombian Police

UNITS/BASES   Based at Bogota with detachments at Guaymaral and Cartagena.

PNC-201	DeHavilland Canada DHC-6 Twin Otter 300	727	HK-2777G	
PNC-202	DeHavilland Canada DHC-6 Twin Otter 300	829	C-GDIU	
PNC-203	Beech Super King Air 200			
PNC-204	Cessna 441 Conquest II	441-0031		
PNC-205	GAC Commander 695A (Jetprop 1000)			
PNC-208	Beech Super King Air 300			
PNC-209	Beech Super King Air 200	BB-212	N910P	
PNC-2˙0	Beech Super King Air 200			
PNC-2˙1	Basler BT-67 Turbo Dakota	14222/25667	N95BF	Cvtd C-47
PNC-2˙2	Basler BT-67 Turbo Dakota	13110	N145ZA	Cvtd C-47
PNC-2˙3	Basler BT-67 Turbo Dakota			Cvtd C-47
PNC-2˙8	Cessna 208 Caravan 1			
PNC-2˙9	Cessna 208 Caravan 1			
PNC-221	Beech Super King Air 200	BB-833	XA-RZH	
PNC-222	Fairchild C-26A Metro (SA.227AC)		ex USAF	
PNC-223	Fairchild C-26A Metro (SA.227AC)		ex USAF	
	Fairchild C-26A Metro (SA.227AC)		ex USAF	
	Fairchild C-26A Metro (SA.227AC)		ex USAF	
	Fairchild C-26A Metro (SA.227AC)		ex USAF	
PNC-238	CASA 212 Aviocar			
PNC-240	CASA 212 Aviocar			
PNC-287	Cessna 206 Super Skywagon			

COMOROS
Jumhuriya al-Qumur al-Itthadiya al-Islamiya / Federal & Islamic Republic of the Comoros
SE African coast

A former French Overseas Territory until independence in 1975, the Comores Islands sit in the Mozambique Channel halfway between Mozambique and Madagascar. The last fixed wing aircraft based at Moroni-Hahaia International Airport was reported sold in 1998 leaving only a helicopter in operation.

SERIAL SYSTEM   Aircraft carry a civilian registration prefixed D6-EC*, 'EC' denoting Etat Comorien.

CONGO
République Démocratique du Congo
C Africa

Following independence from Belgium in July 1960 the Congo was split when the rich Katanga province attempted to break away, precipitating a civil war which continued with varying intensity until 1997. Known as the Republic of Zaire from 1971 until 1997, though it is not thought that much of the former Force Aérienne Zairoise equipment is operational at present. The details below reflect the situation prior to the 1997 changes as no accurate reports have been received since.

SERIAL SYSTEM   Both military serials (alphanumeric) and civil markings are in use, the civil-style prefix '9T-' usually being used as call-signs, particularly for the transports. Government aircraft use the civil '9Q-' prefix.

Air Force of the Democratic Republic of Congo

UNITS/BASES				
	12 Wing, Kinshasa		C.310	Training, communications
	19 Wing, 191 Escadrille, Kinshasa		C-130, C-47, Islander	
	21 Wing, Kamina		C.337	COIN
	22 Wing, 221 Escadrille, Kamina		DHC-5	

9T-CBA	DeHavilland Canada DHC-5D Buffalo	72		221 Ecs	
9T-CBC	DeHavilland Canada DHC-5D Buffalo	74		221 Ecs	
9T-CBD	CASA 212 Aviocar srs 200	CC34-2-235	9Q-CZC		Std Kinshasa
9T-TCA	Lockheed C-130H (L-382C-21D) Hercules	4411		191 Esc	Std Bordeaux
9T-TCE	Lockheed C-130H (L-382C-21D) Hercules	4416		191 Esc	Std Milan
AT-2008	Cessna 310R			12 Wg	
AT-2009	Cessna 310R			12 Wg	
AT-2010	Cessna 310R			12 Wg	
AT-2011	Cessna 310R			12 Wg	
AT-2012	Cessna 310R			12 Wg	
AT-2013	Cessna 310R			12 Wg	
AT-2014	Cessna 310R			12 Wg	
AT-2015	Cessna 310R			12 Wg	

AT-2016	Cessna 310R				12 Wg
AT-2017	Cessna 310R	310R0178	N5058J		12 Wg
AT-2018	Cessna 310R	310R0183	N5063J		12 Wg
AT-2019	Cessna 310R				12 Wg
AT-2020	Cessna 310R				12 Wg
AT-2021	Cessna 310R	310R0213	N5093J		12 Wg
AT-2022	Cessna 310R				12 Wg

Known Cessna 310R c/ns supplied include 310R0076, 0080, 0218, 0226 and 0236, serial tie-ups not known.

Government of the Democratic Republic of Congo

9Q-CDC	Boeing 727-30	18934 / 222	9Q-RDZ	*'Hewa Bora'*
9T-MSS	Boeing 707-382B	19969 / 751	9Q-MNS	Std Lisbon

CONGO
République Populaire du Congo   C Africa

A former French colony independent since 1960 and supported by various communist regimes until the early 1990s. The majority of the Air Force equipment is withdrawn from service with no spares support, being mostly of Soviet origin.

SERIAL SYSTEM Three digit individual numbers are prefixed with the civil 'TN-' prefix.

Force Aerienne Congolaise
Congo Air Force

UNITS/BASES Aircraft are based at Brazzaville-Maya Maya Airport with the Escadrille de Transporte.

TN 222	Antonov An-24V	17306606	TN-111 (FACon)	Std
TN 223	Antonov An-24V	1021804	TN-103 (FACon)	Std Maya Maya
TN 224	Antonov An-24RV	17306607	TN-ABY	Std Maya Maya
TN 401	Cessna 310			Std Maya Maya

Government of the People's Republic of Congo

TN-ADI	Aerospatiale SN601 Corvette	9	F-OCRN

COSTA RICA
República de Costa Rica   C America

Despite the precarious history of its bordering countries Costa Rica is now the most stable and developed of the smaller Central American countries. Following a civil war in 1948 the armed forces were abolished and a Civil Guard established. The air arm is actually part of the Polica de Fronteras, its aircraft carrying the title Fuerza Publica.

SERIAL SYSTEM A sequential system is used for all types prefixed with the initials MSP.

Servicio Vigilancia Ministerio Seguridad - Vigilancia Aérea
Ministry of Security, Aerial Surveillance Service

ICAO code MSP, callsign Seguridad.

UNITS/BASES	Escuadrilla de Communicaciones, BA 1 San Jose, BA 2 Liberia-Guanacaste	Various
	Escuadrilla de Apoya a La Guardia Costera	
	(Coast Guard Support Squadron), Base Aeronaval Golfito	O-2

MSP001	Colemill Panther Navajo	31-8012033	N35527	EC	Cvtd PA-31-310
MSP002	DeHavilland Canada DHC-4A (C-7A) Caribou	149	63-9718 (US Army)	EC	
MSP003	Colemill Panther Navajo	31-8352002	HK-3026P	EC	Cvtd PA-31-350
MSP004	Cessna U206G Turbo Stationair 6 II	U20606879		EC	Soloy conversion
MSP005	Cessna U206G Turbo Stationair 6 II	U20606880	TI-SPB	EC	Soloy conversion
MSP006	Cessna U206G Turbo Stationair 6 II	U20606895	TI-SPC	EC	Soloy conversion
MSP007	Cessna U206G Turbo Stationair 6 II	U20606972		EC	Soloy conversion
MSP010	Cessna O-2A Super Skymaster	M337-0446	TI-SPE	EAGC	Std ?
	Cessna O-2A Super Skymaster		TI-SPF	EAGC	
	Cessna O-2A Super Skymaster	M337-0412	TI-SPG	EAGC	
MSP017	Piper PA-34-220T Seneca III	3433028		EC	

CROATIA
Republika Hrvatska   SE Europe

Croatia declared independence from Yugoslavia in June 1991 but within months was subjected to attacks from the Serbian led government forces. Although a ceasefire was agreed in early 1992 sporadic fighting continued until a final peace was achieved in 1995 by which time Croatia had reclaimed the last of its territory. The arms embargo was lifted and a steady re-equipment with former CIS types continues, NATO membership is sought but is unlikely at present given recent history.

SERIAL SYSTEM No clear system has been defined with both three digit and civil prefixed registrations being reported.

Hrvatsko Zracne Snage - HZS
Croatian Air Force

UNITS/BASES	91 Zrakoplovna Baza Pleso,				
	27 Eskadrila Transportinih Zrakoplova, Zagreb-Pleso			An-32B, An-2	
PLANS	Reported as negotiating with TAI in Turkey for CN235Ms, but funding is a problem.				
	Only two An-32s are believed in service but at least three serials were reported in early 2001 !				

013	Antonov An-2	19347313	OK-MYB		Std Velika Gorica
014	Antonov An-2			27 Esk	
016	Antonov An-2			27 Esk	
707	Antonov An-32B		RA-48005	27 Esk	white cs
710	Antonov An-32			27 Esk	
727	Antonov An-32B	2810	021 (HZS)	27 Esk	
9A-BAB	Antonov An-32B	3310		27 Esk	reserialed?
9A-BFT	Antonov/PZL-Mielec An-2R	1G99-16	YU-BFT	27 Esk	
9A-BHT	Antonov/PZL-Mielec An-2R	1G135-43	YU-BHT	27 Esk	
9A-BHJ	Antonov/PZL-Mielec An-2R	1G135-45	YU-BHV	27 Esk	
9A-BKA	Antonov/PZL-Mielec An-2	1G167-05	YU-BKA	27 Esk	yellow cs
9A-BKC	Antonov/PZL-Mielec An-2R	1G167-07	YU-BKC	27 Esk	
9A-BMA	Antonov/PZL-Mielec An-2R	1G181-46	RC-BMA	27 Esk	
9A-BOF	Antonov/PZL-Mielec An-2R	1G223-56	RC-BOF	27 Esk	white cs
9A-BOG	Antonov/PZL-Mielec An-2TP	1G214-08	YU-BOG	27 Esk	white cs
9A-BZB	Antonov/PZL-Mielec An-2R	1G225-4	CCCP-33321	27 Esk	
9A-ISC	Dornier 28D2 Skyservant	4171	58+96 (WGAF)		Std Velika Gorica

Croatian Ministry of the Interior

UNITS/BASES	Based at Split, now thought transferred to the HZS.			

9A-CAB / 22	Canadair CL-215	1004	C-FYWQ	Fire bomber
9A-CAC / 33	Canadair CL-215	1012	C-FTZE	Fire bomber
9A-CAG / 44	Bombardier Canadair CL-415	2027	C-FZQZ	Fire bomber
855	Bombardier Canadair CL-415	2041	9A-CAH	Fire bomber
C-FTXB / 225	Canadair CL-215	1007	CF-TXB	Fire bomber, Lsf Bombardier
C-GFNF / 27	Canadair CL-215	1027	F-ZBBI	Fire bomber, Lsf Bombardier

Government Flight Service of the Republic of Croatia - GFS

UNITS/BASES	Based at Zagreb-Pleso.			

9A-CRO	Bombardier Canadair CL-604 Challenger	5322	N604CL	
9A-CRT	Canadair CL-601-3A Challenger	5067	9A-CRO	

CUBA
República de Cuba   W Indies

Until 1959 a US satellite state, but following the overthrow of the Batista dictatorship by Fidel Castro much support was received from Soviet Union nearly taking the world to nuclear war in 1962. The Air Force, despite having received much material, is now operationally a shadow of its former self. Commercial charter and freight work is carried out by the Air Force operated airline, Aerogaviota.

SERIAL SYSTEM While operating with Aerogaviota the civil marks are used but these aircraft are believed to revert to military identities with the deletion of the CU-T prefix (eg. CU-T1401 would become 14-01).

Defense Anti-Aérea y Fuerza Aérea Revolucionaria - DAAFAR
Anti-Aircraft Defence and Revolutionary Air Force

UNITS/BASES	151 Escuadrón de Transporte, Cienfuegos		An-26, An-2

	251 Escuadrón de Transporte, Havana-Jose Marti International Airport			Il-76, Yak-40, An-32, An-24, An-2
	252 Escuadrón de Transporte, San Antonio de los Banos			An-26, An-2
	351 Escuadrón de Transporte, Santiago de Cuba			An-26, An-2

PLANS   Antonov An-32s have been advised as delivered but with no sightings.

CU-T1232	Yakovlev Yak-40	9011060		Aerogaviota	
CU-T1238	Antonov An-26	7803	CCCP-47324	Aerogaviota	
CU-T1239	Antonov An-26	7907	CCCP-47325	Aerogaviota	
CU-C1258	Ilyushin Il-76MD	0043454615		Cubana	Cubana cs
CU-C1271	Ilyushin Il-76MD	0053459767		Std Havana, Cubana cs	
12-46	Antonov An-24B				
CU-T1448	Yakovlev Yak-40	9011160		Aerogaviota	
CU-T1449	Yakovlev Yak-40	9021260	12-49 (DAFAAR)	Aerogaviota	
CU-T1450	Yakovlev Yak-40	9021360	12-50 (DAAFAR)	Aerogaviota	
CU-T1401	Antonov An-26B	12604		Aerogaviota	
CU-T1402	Antonov An-26B	12605		Aerogaviota	
CU-T1403	Antonov An-26B	12905		Aerogaviota	
CU-T1404	Antonov An-26B	12906		Aerogaviota	
CU-T1405	Antonov An-26B	13501		Aerogaviota	
CU-T1406	Antonov An-26B	13502		Aerogaviota	
CU-T1407	Antonov An-26	14306			
CU-T1408	Antonov An-26	6903	CCCP-47328	Aerogaviota	
CU-T1420	Antonov An-26	6607	CCCP-47324	Aerogaviota	
CU-T1421	Antonov An-26	6610	CCCP-47325	Aerogaviota	
CU-T1422	Antonov An-26	3805			Std?
CU-T1423	Antonov An-26	3806	D2-MIR	Aerogaviota	Std?
CU-T1425	Antonov An-26	6904	CCCP-47329	Aerogaviota	
CU-T1426	Antonov An-26	5603	CCCP-47323	Aerogaviota	
CU-T1428	Antonov An-26	11303		Aerogaviota	
CU-T1429	Antonov An-26	7006	CCCP-47331	Aerogaviota	
CU-T1432	Antonov An-26	7306	CCCP-47335	Aerogaviota	
CU-T1433	Antonov An-26	7309	CCCP-47336	Aerogaviota	
CU-T1434	Antonov An-26	7701	CCCP-47338	Aerogaviota	
CU-T1435	Antonov An-26	7702	CCCP-47339	Aerogaviota	
CU-T1440	Yakovlev Yak-40	9631249		Cubana cs	
CU-T1443	Yakovlev Yak-40	9710752		Cubana cs	
CU-F1444	Antonov An-30			Aerogaviota	
CU-T1445	Antonov An-30			Aerogaviota	

953	Antonov An-2

About 20 An-2 remain in service, no further serial details are known at this time.

CYPRUS
Kypriaki Dimokratia   SE Europe

Since 1974 Cyprus has been divided into two following Turkish occupation of the Northern part of the island. Only Turkey recognises and supports the Republic of Northern Cyprus declared in 1983, while the Greek Cypriot area operates a common defence policy with Greece. Although currently peaceful and discussing resolution of the dispute prior to EU entry in 2004, the two halves have experienced tension, most recently in 1996 when the Greek Cypriots were threatened with air strikes for deploying surface-to-air missiles. What is now the Air Force was known as the National Guard Air Arm until 1996.

SERIAL SYSTEM Both civil and military markings are employed. Civil registrations are prefixed '5B-' and military serials use the c/n in modified form.

Cyprus Air Force

UNITS/BASES   Aircraft are based at Lakatamia and Paphos.

12106	Pilatus Britten-Norman BN-2B-21 Maritime Defender			
		2106	5B-ICV	1000th BN-2

Cyprus Police Air Wing

5B-CPA	Pilatus Britten-Norman BN-2T Turbine Islander	2207	G-CYPP

52

CZECH REPUBLIC

Ceska Republika   C Europe

Part of Czechoslovakia until January 1993 when the country was divided by mutual consent, the other half becoming Slovakia. The former (Ceskoslovenske Letectvo) Czechoslovakian Air Force inventory was divided with a 66/33 split in favour of the Czech Republic. A member of NATO since 1999.

SERIAL SYSTEM The serials reflect the last four digits of the c/n.

Ceske Letectvo a Protivzdusna Obrana
Czech Air Force and Air Defence

ICAO code CEF, call sign Czech Air Force.

UNITS/BASES   6 Zakladna Dopravniho Letectva, 61 Dopravni Letka (61dlt), Prague-Kbely   Tu-154, An-24, An-26,
L-41T/UVP, Challenger, Yak-40

34 Zakladna Skolniho Letectva, 344 Pruzkumna Dopravni Letka (344 pzdlt), Pardubice
An-30FG, L-410M/FG, An-26Z-1

PLANS   FMS funding requested for four ex USAF C-130B Hercules, but also considering C-27 and CN235.

0005	Let L-610	910005	OK-134	61 dlt	
0260	Yakovlev Yak-40K	9940260	OK-BYK	61 dlt	VIP
0402	Let L-410M	750402		344 pzdlt	
0403	Let L-410M	750403		344 pzdlt	
0501	Let L-410M	750501	OK-160	344 pzdlt	
0503	Let L-410M	760503		344 pzdlt	
0601	Tupolev Tu-154B2	84A-601	OK-BYD	61 dlt	VIP
0712	Let L-410UVP	810712		61 dlt	
0926	Let L-410T	820926		61 dlt	
0928	Let L-410T	820928		61 dlt	
0929	Let L-410T	820929		61 dlt	
1003	Tupolev Tu-154M	9?A-1003		61 dlt	
1016	Tupolev Tu-154M	96A-1016	OK-BYZ	61 dlt	VIP
1107	Antonov An-30	1107	LZ-AEG	344 pzdlt	Open Skies Survey
1132	Let L-410T	831132		61 dlt	
1134	Let L-410T	831134		61 dlt	
1257	Yakovlev Yak-40K	9821257	OK-BYJ	61 dlt	VIP
1504	Let L-410UVP	851504	(CCCP-67537)	61 dlt	
1525	Let L-410FG	851525		344 pzdlt	
1526	Let L-410FG	851526		344 pzdlt	
2312	Let L-410UVP-E14	892312		61 dlt	
2408	Antonov An-26	12408		61 dlt	
2409	Antonov An-26	12409		61 dlt	
2507	Antonov An-26	12507		61 dlt	
2601	Let L-410UVP-E	912601	(CCCP-67671)	61 dlt	
2602	Let L-410UVP-E	912602	(CCCP-67672)	61 dlt	
2710	Let L-410UVP-E20C	922710	OK-BYF	61 dlt	VIP
3209	Antonov An-26Z-1	13209		344 pzdlt	EW
4201	Antonov An-26	14201	UN-26206	61 dlt	
5105	Canadair CL601-3A Challenger	5105	OK-BYA	61 dlt	VIP
7109	Antonov An-24V	17307109		61 dlt	
7110	Antonov An-24V	17307110		61 dlt	

DENMARK

Kongeriget Danmark   N Europe

As a NATO member since 1949 Denmark's main role was to defend the Kattegat which Soviet ships would have to pass through coming into or out of the Baltic Sea. Even though this requirement is now less important both Greenland and the Faeroe Island are part of the Danish Kingdom and are therefore supported by the RDAF for SAR and maritime reconnaissance.

SERIAL SYSTEM Each type is identified with a letter prefix followed by a three digit number, usually derived from the previous operator's serial or the c/n (eg. B-680 ex FMS 73-1680).

Kongelige Danske Flyvevben - KDF
Royal Danish Air Force - RDAF

ICAO code DAE, callsign Danish Airforce.

UNITS/BASES   Eskadrille 721, Vaerlose   Challenger, Gulfstream III, C-130H

PLANS	A fourth C-130J is on option.				
B-678	Lockheed C-130H (L-382C-38D) Hercules	4572	73-1678 (FMS)	Esk 721	
B-679	Lockheed C-130H (L-382C-38D) Hercules	4587	73-1679 (FMS)	Esk 721	
B-680	Lockheed C-130H (L-382C-38D) Hercules	4599	73-1680 (FMS)	Esk 721	
C-080	Bombardier Canadair CL-604 Challenger	5380	C-GEGM	Esk 721	
C-168	Bombardier Canadair CL-604 Challenger	5468	C-GHRJ	Esk 721	
C-172	Bombardier Canadair CL-604 Challenger	5472	C-GHRZ	Esk 721	
F-249	GAC G-1159A Gulfstream III	249	N901GA	Esk 721	
F-313	GAC G-1159A Gulfstream III	313		Esk 721	
	Lockheed Martin C-130J (L-382V-36J) Hercules II				
		5536			On Order 2003
	Lockheed Martin C-130J (L-382V-36J) Hercules II				
		5537			On Order 2003
	Lockheed Martin C-130J (L-382V-36J) Hercules II				
		5538			On Order 2003

DJIBOUTI
al-Jumhouriya al-Djibouti / Republic of Djibouti   NE Africa

Originally French Somaliland, but renamed the French Territory of Afars and Issas in 1967 before finally being granted independence and adopting its current name in 1977. The French armed forces are still present in the country to act as a deterrent given the unstable nature of its neighbours.

SERIAL SYSTEM Civil registrations are allocated in the J2-M** batch. The usual presentation shows only the last two digits like a code.

Force Aérienne Djiboutienne
Djibouti Air Force

UNITS/BASES   Aircraft are based at Djibouti-Ambouli Airport.

J2-MAE	Cessna U206G Stationair 6 II	U20605433	N6334U	Reims-assembly no.0019
J2-MAH	Cessna 402C	402C1010		Std Ambouli
J2-MAI	Cessna 208 Caravan 1	20800185	N9766F	
J2-MAT	Antonov An-28			

Government of the Republic of Djibouti

J2-KBA	Boeing 727-191	19394 / 418	N727X

DOMINICAN REPUBLIC
República Dominicana   W Indies

Sharing the island of Hispaniola with Haiti, Dominica has been stable since a 1965 civil war and is relatively prosperous compared to its neighbour thanks mainly to tourism. The Air Force was depleted in 1998 during Hurricane George, when two hangars and their contents were damaged or destroyed.

SERIAL SYSTEM Four digit serials are allocated in batches depending on the role.

Fuerza Aérea Dominicana - FAD

UNITS/BASES   Escuadron de Transporte Aereo, San Isidro   Aviocar, Duke, Super King Air, C206

1535	Colemill Panther Navajo	31-283	HK-1589P	Esc Trans	Cvtd PA-31
1537	Cessna 207			Esc Trans	
1538	Beech Duke 60	P-476	HI-322	Esc Trans	
3500	CASA 212 Aviocar srs 400	468		Esc Trans	
3501	CASA 212 Aviocar srs 400	469		Esc Trans	
3502	CASA 212 Aviocar srs 400			Esc Trans	

ECUADOR
República de Ecuador   S America

As a recipient of US aid since 1948 Ecuador has one of the better-equipped South American air forces, although recent border disputes and conflicts have meant closer scrutiny of acquisitions. The Air Force operates an airline on a commercial basis (it was re-titled from Transportes Aereos Militares Ecuatorianos in 1990) and the aircraft remain at Air Force disposal despite mainly civilian management.

SERIAL SYSTEM   The Air Force allocates three digit serials based on the c/n for the majority of the transports and these are also sometimes prefixed FAE. Civil identities are also issued, particularly for service with TAME. The Navy and Army also allocate three digit serials and prefix them with the operators initials.

Fuerza Aérea Ecuatoriana - FAE
Ecuadorean Air Force

UNITS/BASES			
I Zona Aerea, BA Mariscal Sucre-Quito			
Ala de Transporte 11			
Escuadron de Transporte 1111	C-130, Twin Otter		
Escuadron Presidencial	HS748, Sabreliner		
Transportes Aereos Mercantiles Ecuatorianos (TAME)		Boeing 727, F.28, HS748	
II Zona Aerea, BA Simon Bolivar- Guayaquil			
Ala de Combate 22			
Escuadron de Rescate 2212	Twin Otter		

PLANS   A replacement for the recently retired Presidential HS.748 is being sought, a 50 seat twin jet being specified.

001 / HC-AUK	Hawker Siddeley HS.748-267 srs 2A	1684/set155	684 (FAE)		Damaged and std
001A	Rockwell Sabreliner 60	306-117	N22MY	Esc Pres	
043	North American Sabreliner 40R	282-43	N4469F	Esc Pres	
047	Rockwell Sabreliner 40A	282-109	N77AT	Esc Pres	
049	Rockwell Sabreliner 60	306-68	N265DP	Esc Pres	
078 / HC-BHM	Boeing 727-2T3 Advanced	22078 / 1644	N1293E	TAME	'Cotopaxi'
112 / HC-BZU	Fokker F.28 Fellowship 4000	11112	SE-DGE	TAME	
220 / HC-BMD	Fokker F.28 Fellowship 4000	11220	PH-ZCH	TAME	Dam 17Jul2001
328 / HC-BLV	Boeing 727-17	20328 / 806	G-BKCG	TAME	
447	DeHavilland Canada DHC-6 Twin Otter 300	832		Esc 1111	
448	DeHavilland Canada DHC-6 Twin Otter 300	833		Esc 1111	
449	DeHavilland Canada DHC-6 Twin Otter 300	834		Esc 1111	
451	DeHavilland Canada DHC-6 Twin Otter 300			Esc 1111	
524	Piper PA-34-220T Seneca III	34-8533020	HC-BOC	Ala 22	
525	Cessna U206G Stationair 6 II	U20606683			
618 / HC-BZR	Boeing 727-230 Advanced	21618 / 1404	TC-AFT	TAME	
620 / HC-BZS	Boeing 727-230 Advanced	21620 / 1419	TC-AFO	TAME	
682 / HC-AUD	Hawker Siddeley HS.748-246 srs 2A	1682/set168		TAME	
691 / HC-BLE	Boeing 727-134	19691 / 487	RP-C1240	TAME	
692 / HC-BLF	Boeing 727-134	19692 / 498	RP-C1241	TAME	
739 / HC-BEY	Hawker Siddeley HS.748-285 srs 2A (LFD)1739/set220			TAME	
788 / HC-BSC	Boeing 727-230 Advanced	20788 / 1011	D-ABRI	TAME	
892	Lockheed C-130H (L-382C-87D) Hercules	4812	812 (FAE)	Esc 1111	
893	Lockheed L-100-30 (L-382G-54C) Hercules	4893	N4175M	Esc 1111	
894	Lockheed C-130B (L-282-1B) Hercules	3501	57-0525 (USAF)	Esc 1111	
895	Lockheed C-130B (L-282-1B) Hercules	3505	57-0529 (USAF)	Esc 1111	
896	Lockheed C-130B (L-282-1B) Hercules	3528	58-0733 (USAF)		Std Quito
897	Lockheed C-130B (L-282-1B) Hercules	3683	61-2645 (USAF)		Std Quito

Aviación Naval Ecuatoriana - ANE
Ecuadorian Naval Aviation

UNITS/BASES			
1 Escuadrilla de Enlace, BA Simon Bolivar-Guayaquil		C.320, Super King Air	
2 Escuadrilla de Transportes, BA Simon Bolivar-Guayaquil		CN235M, Super King Air	

AN-202	Airtech/CASA CN235M-100	C016		2 Esc
AN-204	Airtech/CASA CN235M-100	C017		2 Esc
	Cessna 320E Skyknight			1 Esc
AN-231	Beech Super King Air 200	BB-771	N3831Q	
AN-232	Beech Super King Air 300	FA-75	N7247A	
AN-233	Beech Super King Air 200	BB-580	N67PC	
AN-234	Beech Super King Air 200	BB-458	N169DB	

Servicio Aéreo del Ejército Ecuatoriana - AEE
Ecuadorian Army Aviation Service

UNITS/BASES	19 Brigada Aerea del Ejercito				
	Grupo Aereo 43, BA Simon Bolivar-Guayaquil		CN235M, Arava, Turbo Porter		
	Grupo Aereo 45, BA Mariscal Sucre-Quito		DHC-5, Arava, Super King Air		
	Instituto Geografico Militar, BA Mariscal Sucre-Quito		Citation, King Air, Turbo Porter		

AEE-101	Beech Super King Air 200	BB-811	AEE-001 (AEE)	Gr 45	
AEE-202	IAI Arava srs 201	0012	T-202 (AEE)		
AEE-203	IAI Arava srs 201	0015	T-203 (AEE)		
AEE-204	IAI Arava srs 201	0019	T-204 (AEE)		
AEE-206	IAI Arava srs 201	0086	T-206 (AEE)		
AEE-207	IAI Arava srs 201	0091	T-207 (AEE)		
AEE-501	DeHavilland Canada DHC-5D Buffalo	104		Gr 45	
AEE-502	Airtech/CASA CN235M-100	C015		Gr 43	
E-190	Pilatus PC-6/B2-H2 Turbo Porter	754			
E-195	Pilatus PC-6/B2-H4 Turbo Porter	879			
IGM-240	Beech King Air A100	B-242		IGM	Survey
IGM-628	Cessna 550 Citation II	550-0628/628	N183AB	IGM	Survey

EGYPT
Jumhouriya Misr al-Arabiya / Arab Republic of Egypt   NE Africa

The reward for Egyptian support of the ongoing Middle East peace process has been much US assistance. The formerly British and Soviet equipped air force now has aircraft of American origin and regularly hosts exercises with the US military.

SERIAL SYSTEM   Three/four digit serials are displayed usually in Arabic numerals, fortunately most transport types are also allocated a civil (SU-) registration.

al Quwwat al Jawwiya il Misriya
Egyptian Air Force

UNITS/BASES	2 Sqn, Cairo East-Almaza		Buffalo	
	4 Sqn, Cairo East-Almaza		C-130H	
	16 Sqn, Cairo East-Almaza		VC-130H, EC-130H	VIP, ELINT
	87 Sqn, Cairo-West		E-2C	AEW
	Bilbeis, Air Navigation School		Buffalo	Training
	Cairo East-Almaza		King Air, Beech 1900	Survey, ECM

PLANS	The Hawkeyes are to be upgraded by Northrop Grumman in Egypt from 2003.	

850 / SU-BAX	Beech Super King Air 200	BB-353	SU-AYD		Survey
1161 / SU-BFA	DeHavilland Canada DHC-5D Buffalo	110	1210 (EAF)		
1162 / SU-BFB	DeHavilland Canada DHC-5D Buffalo	111	1211 (EAF)		
1163 / SU-BFC	DeHavilland Canada DHC-5D Buffalo	112	1212 (EAF)		
1164 / SU-BFD	DeHavilland Canada DHC-5D Buffalo	113	1213 (EAF)		
1165 / SU-BFE	DeHavilland Canada DHC-5D Buffalo	114	1214 (EAF)		
1166 / SU-BFF	DeHavilland Canada DHC-5D Buffalo	115	1215 (EAF)		
1167 / SU-BFG	DeHavilland Canada DHC-5D Buffalo	116	1216 (EAF)		
1168 / SU-BFH	DeHavilland Canada DHC-5D Buffalo	117	1217 (EAF)		
1170 / SU-BFJ	DeHavilland Canada DHC-5D Buffalo	119	1219 (EAF)		
1271 / SU-BAB	Lockheed C-130H (L-382C-64D) Hercules	4709	76-1599 (FMS)	4 Sqn	
1272 / SU-BAC	Lockheed C-130H (L-382C-64D) Hercules	4714	76-1600 (FMS)	4 Sqn	
1273 / SU-BAD	Lockheed C-130H (L-382C-64D) Hercules	4719	76-1601 (FMS)	4 Sqn	
1274 / SU-BAE	Lockheed C-130H (L-382C-64D) Hercules	4721	76-1602 (FMS)	4 Sqn	
1275 / SU-BAF	Lockheed C-130H (L-382C-64D) Hercules	4728	76-1603 (FMS)	4 Sqn	
1277 / SU-BAI	Lockheed C-130H (L-382C-81D) Hercules	4794	78-756 (FMS)	4 Sqn	
1278 / SU-BAJ	Lockheed C-130H (L-382C-81D) Hercules	4795	78-757 (FMS)	4 Sqn	
1279 / SU-BAK	Lockheed C-130H (L-382C-81D) Hercules	4797	78-758 (FMS)	4 Sqn	
1280 / SU-BAL	Lockheed C-130H (L-382C-81D) Hercules	4802	78-759 (FMS)	4 Sqn	
1281 / SU-BAM	Lockheed VC-130H (L-382C-81D) Hercules	4803	78-760 (FMS)	16 Sqn	
1282 / SU-BAN	Lockheed C-130H (L-382C-81D) Hercules	4804	78-761 (FMS)	4 Sqn	
1283 / SU-BAP	Lockheed C-130H (L-382C-81D) Hercules	4805	78-762 (FMS)	4 Sqn	
1284 / SU-BAQ	Lockheed C-130H (L-382C-81D) Hercules	4806	78-763 (FMS)	4 Sqn	
1285 / SU-BAR	Lockheed C-130H (L-382C-81D) Hercules	4807	78-764 (FMS)	4 Sqn	
1286 / SU-BAS	Lockheed C-130H (L-382C-81D) Hercules	4808	78-765 (FMS)	4 Sqn	
1287 / SU-BAT	Lockheed C-130H (L-382C-81D) Hercules	4809	78-766 (FMS)	4 Sqn	
1288 / SU-BAU	Lockheed C-130H (L-382C-81D) Hercules	4810	78-767 (FMS)	4 Sqn	
1289 / SU-BAV	Lockheed VC-130H (L-382C-81D) Hercules	4811	78-768 (FMS)	16 Sqn	
1290 / SU-BEW	Lockheed C-130H (L-382C-24E) Hercules	4936	82-0080 (FMS)	4 Sqn	

1291 / SU-BEX	Lockheed C-130H (L-382C-24E) Hercules	4937	82-0081 (FMS)	4 Sqn	
1292 / SU-BEY	Lockheed C-130H (L-382C-24E) Hercules	4938	82-0082 (FMS)	4 Sqn	
1293 / SU-BKS	Lockheed C-130H-30 (L-382T-10F) Hercules	5187		4 Sqn	
1294 / SU-BKT	Lockheed C-130H-30 (L-382T-10F) Hercules	5191		4 Sqn	
1295 / SU-BKU	Lockheed C-130H-30 (L-382T-10F) Hercules	5206		4 Sqn	
4801 / SU-BKV	Beech 1900C-1 Airliner	UC-10	N7242C		
4802 / SU-BLA	Beech 1900C-1 Airliner	UC-33	N7242U		
4803 / SU-BKW	Beech 1900C-1 Airliner	UC-15	N7242D		
4804 / SU-BKX	Beech 1900C-1 Airliner	UC-16	N7242L		
4805 / SU-BKY	Beech 1900C-1 Airliner	UC-18	N7242M		
4806 / SU-BKZ	Beech 1900C-1 Airliner	UC-21	N7242Q		
	Beech 1900C-1 Airliner	UC-51	N31527		Elint
	Beech 1900C-1 Airliner	UC-52	N31544		Elint
	Grumman E-2C Hawkeye		Bu162791 (FMS)	87 Sqn	
	Grumman E-2C Hawkeye		Bu162792 (FMS)	87 Sqn	
	Grumman E-2C Hawkeye		Bu162823 (FMS)	87 Sqn	
	Grumman E-2C Hawkeye		Bu162824 (FMS)	87 Sqn	
	Grumman E-2C Hawkeye		Bu162825 (FMS)	87 Sqn	
	Grumman E-2C Hawkeye		Bu163565 (FMS)	87 Sqn	
	Grumman E-2C Hawkeye		Bu164626 (FMS)	87 Sqn	

Government of the Arab Republic of Egypt

UNITS/BASES   All aircraft based at Cairo East-Almaza.

SU-AXJ	Boeing 707-366C	20919 / 888		c/s Egyptian 01
SU-AXN	Dassault Falcon 20E-5	294	F-BVPM	
SU-AYD	Dassault Falcon 20F-5	361	F-WMKF	
SU-AZJ	Dassault Falcon 20F-5	358	F-WRQY	
SU-BGM	GAC Gulfstream IV	1048	N448GA	
SU-BGU	GAC G-1159A Gulfstream III	439	N17586	
SU-BGV	GAC G-1159A Gulfstream III	442	N17587	
SU-BNC	GAC Gulfstream IV	1329	N329GA	
SU-BND	GAC Gulfstream IV	1332	N332GA	
SU-BNO	GAC Gulfstream IV-SP	1424	N328GA	
SU-BNF	GAC Gulfstream IV-SP	1427	N427GA	
SU-GGG	Airbus Industrie A340-212	061	F-WWJI	

EL SALVADOR
República de El Salvador   C America

Renamed from the Fuerza Aérea Salvadorena following the end of the civil war against the Marxist FMLN guerrillas in 1992 which the El Salvador Government fought with US backing.

SERIAL SYSTEM   Three digit serials are are allocated in blocks by aircraft type.

Fuerza Aérea El Salvador - FAES
Salvadorean Air Force

UNITS/BASES	Grupo de Transporte, Ilopango	BT-67, C-47, C337, Merlin	
	Grupo de Caza y Bombardeo, San Salvador-Comalapa Int'l Airport	O-2	FAC
PLANS	The FAES was requesting three surplus USAF C-27A's.		

99	Swearingen SA.226T Merlin IIIB	T-372	N1010V		VIP
106	Douglas C-47			GdT	
116	Basler BT-67 Turbo Dakota	33282/16534	F-OGDZ	GdT	Cvtd C-47
117	Basler BT-67 Turbo Dakota	24509		GdT	Cvtd C-47
118	Basler BT-67 Turbo Dakota	33238/16490	N10801	GdT	Cvtd C-47
119	Basler BT-67 Turbo Dakota	6204	N721A	GdT	Cvtd C-47
123	Douglas AC-47			GdT	Cvtd C-47
608	Cessna 337G Super Skymaster			GdT	
610	Cessna O-2B Super Skymaster			GdC-B	
613	Cessna O-2A Super Skymaster			GdC-B	
614	Cessna O-2A Super Skymaster			GdC-B	
615	Cessna O-2A Super Skymaster			GdC-B	
616	Cessna O-2A Super Skymaster			GdC-B	
617	Cessna O-2A Super Skymaster			GdC-B	
619	Cessna O-2B Super Skymaster			GdC-B	
620	Cessna O-2A Super Skymaster			GdC-B	
621	Cessna O-2A Super Skymaster			GdC-B	

624	Cessna O-2A Super Skymaster			GdC-B
625	Cessna O-2A Super Skymaster			GdC-B
626	Cessna O-2A Super Skymaster			GdC-B
629	Cessna O-2A Super Skymaster			GdC-B
	Cessna O-2A Super Skymaster			GdC-B
	Cessna O-2A Super Skymaster			GdC-B

EQUATORIAL GUINEA
República de Guinea Ecuatorial   W Africa

Becoming independent from Spain in 1968 the country is situated on mainland Africa and the Island of Bioko (Fernando Poo). Support was forthcoming from the Soviet Union which no doubt viewed it as a future naval base, but little of the material supplied is thought to be currently airworthy. It is believed that the aircraft are flown by the Government rather that the National Guard.

SERIAL SYSTEM   Serials are allocated using the civil prefix 3C- in the sequence 3C-*GE (for Guinea Ecuatorial), numbers are used rather than letters to complete the identity, the first Yak-40 with the 'C' marking signifying 'Council'. The leased Falcon's French markings are self explanatory.

Government of the Republic of Equatorial Guinea

UNITS/BASES   Based at Malabo on the Island of Bioko.

3C-1GE	Antonov An-24	1970		
3C-4GE	Yakovlev Yak-40	9940660		Std
3C-5GE	Antonov An-32	1609		'Enrique Nvo Okene'
3C-CGE	Yakovlev Yak-40	9821557	3C-MNB	
F-GUEQ	Dassault Falcon 900B	167	F-WWFO	Lsf Dassault Falcon Service

ERITREA
Dawlat al Eritrea / State of Eritrea   NE Africa

Having fought a long civil war Eritrea declared itself independent from Ethiopia in 1993 but was left a country with major problems. Holding the Red Sea ports that were once part of Ethiopia means that tensions still exist which bubble over in border conflict, despite both countries' financial and famine difficulties.

SERIAL SYSTEM   Three digit numbers are prefixed with the ERAF air arm identifier.

Eritrean Air Force

UNITS/BASES   All aircraft appear to based at Asmara, no unit details are known.

ERAF 800	Yunshuji/Harbin Y-12 II
ERAF 801	Yunshuji/Harbin Y-12 II
ERAF 802	Yunshuji/Harbin Y-12 II
ERAF 803	Yunshuji/Harbin Y-12 II
	Dornier 228

ESTONIA
Eesti Vabariik / Republic of Estonia   NE Europe

Estonia declared independence from the USSR in 1991 but had little equipment left behind when the Soviet military pulled out. The Let 410s were donated by the German Government but further equipment offers have been declined because of the lack of support to keep them in service.

SERIAL SYSTEM   Serials for the Army Aviation element appear sequential by type, the Border Guard aircraft being civil registered.

Eesti Ohu Vagi
Estonian Army Aviation

UNITS/BASES   Pievalve Lennu Eskadril, Amari-Lennubas.

40	Antonov/PZL-Mielec An-2T	1G43-25		
41	Antonov An-2	111747320	ES-BAD	
	Antonov/PZL-Mielec An-2T	1G160-28	ES-BAG	on overhaul

Eesti Piirivalve Lennusalk
Estonian Border Guard Aviation Group

UNITS/BASES   Aircraft based at Dmari-Tallinn.

ES-PLW	Let 410UVP	810726	ES-EPA
ES-PLY	Let 410UVP	810727	ES-EPI

ETHIOPIA
Federal Democratic Republic of Ethiopia   NE Africa

Formerly the Italian controlled Abyssinia, Ethiopia has fought drought, famine and civil war since the 1970s when the monarchy was abolished. The independence of the former province of Eritrea is the latest catalyst for instability combined with renewed drought in 2000. Serviceability of the mainly Soviet-supplied equipment is poor as the communist backed regime was overthrown at the same time as the Soviet Union collapsed.

SERIAL SYSTEM   Three and four digit serials are issued in blocks by type.

Ye Ityopya ayer Hayl
Ethiopian Air Force

UNITS/BASES   Bishoftu & Addis Ababa-Bole   An-12, An-32, C-130B

1502	Antonov An-12BP	401802	
1503	Antonov An-12BP	402009	Soviet AF
1505	Antonov An-12BP	5342907	Soviet AF
1511	Antonov An-12		
1513	Antonov An-12		
1551	Antonov An-32		
1561	Lockheed C-130B (L-282-1B) Hercules	3633	61-0954 (USAF)
1562	Lockheed C-130B (L-282-1B) Hercules	3671	61-2635 (USAF)
1563	Lockheed C-130B (L-282-1B) Hercules	3672	61-2636 (USAF)
1564	Lockheed C-130B (L-282-1B) Hercules	3674	61-2638 (USAF)
1601	Yakovlev Yak-40		

Ethiopian Army Aviation

EA 62	DeHavilland Canada DHC-6 Twin Otter 300	506	C-GQFF
EA 63	DeHavilland Canada DHC-6 Twin Otter 300	508	C-GQFG
	Cessna 401		

Ethiopian Police Force

EP 104	Reims F337E Super Skymaster	F33700002/ 01197	D-GCAB
EP 201	Dornier 28D-1 Skyservant	4054	D-IDCB
EP 202	Dornier 28D-1 Skyservant	4059	D-IDCG

Government of the Federal Democratic Republic of Ethiopia

ET-AID	DeHavilland Canada DHC-6 Twin Otter 300	504	EA 61 (Eth AA)

FALKLAND ISLANDS
British Crown Colony of the Falkland Islands & Dependencies   S Atlantic

Scene of the first of the modern 'televised' conflicts when an Argentinian occupation was repulsed by a British expeditionary force in 1982. Still with a based UK military deterent force at RAF Mount Pleasant and regular support flights from the UK.

SERIAL SYSTEM   All aircraft are civil registered using the Falkland Island prefix.

Falklands Islands Government Air Service - FIGAS

UNITS/BASES   Aircraft are based at Port Stanley.

VP-FBD	Pilatus Britten-Norman BN-2B-26 Islander	2160	G-BKJK
VP-FBI	Pilatus Britten-Norman BN-2B-26 Islander	2188	G-BLNI
VP-FBM	Pilatus Britten-Norman BN-2B-26 Islander	2200	G-BLNZ
VP-FBN	Pilatus Britten-Norman BN-2B-26 Islander	2216	G-BRFY
VP-FBO	Pilatus Britten-Norman BN-2B-26 Islander	2218	G-BRGA
VP-FBR	Pilatus Britten-Norman BN-2B-26 Islander	2252	G-BTLX

FINLAND
Suomen Tasavalta / Republic of Finland   N Europe

While remaining non-aligned, Finland's chief defence worry has always been from over the border in the East, though the breakup of the Soviet Union has eased some of these concerns. Most recent acquisitions have been of Western origin whereas the older equipment was bought with neutrality in mind.

SERIAL SYSTEM Each type is allocated a two digit code (based on its name), this is followed by a sequential number.

Suomen Ilmavoimat
Finnish Air Force

ICAO code FNF, callsign Finnforce.

UNITS/BASES		
Havittajalentolaivue 11, 4th Flight, Rovaniemi	PA-31 (supporting Draken and Hawk units)	
Havittajalentolaivue 21, 4th Flight, Tampere-Pirkkala	PA-31 (supporting F-18 and Hawk units)	
Havittajalentolaivue 31, 4th Flight, Kuopio-Rissala	PA-31 (supporting F-18 and Hawk units)	
Koulutuslentolaivue, Kauhava	PA-31	Training
Tukilentolaivue, 1st Flight, Kuopio-Rissala	F.27, Learjet	Special Mission
Tukilentolaivue, 3rd Flight, Kuopio-Rissala	F.27	
Tukilentolaivue, 4th Flight, Kuopio-Rissala	PA-31	

PLANS   The F.27s are reaching the replacement stage, the ELINT aircraft being looked at first with a Gulfstream based system having been reviewed.

FF-1	Fokker F.27 Friendship 100	10274	OH-KFA	TukiLLv	ELINT
FF-2	Fokker F.27 Friendship 100	10300	OH-LKC	TukiLLv	
FF-3	Fokker F.27 Troopship 400M	10662	PH-EXL	TukiLLv	
LJ-1	Learjet 35A	35A-430	N10870	TukiLLv	
LJ-2	Learjet 35A	35A-451	N1462B	TukiLLv	
LJ-3	Learjet 35A	35A-470	N3810G	TukiLLv	
PC-1	Piper PA-31-350 Navajo Chieftain	31-8252076	OH-PAJ		
PC-2	Piper PA-31-350 Navajo Chieftain	31-8252077	OH-PAL		
PC-3	Piper PA-31-350 Navajo Chieftain	31-8252081	OH-PAO		
PC-4	Piper PA-31-350 Navajo Chieftain	31-8252083	OH-PAP		
PC-5	Piper PA-31-350 Navajo Chieftain	31-8252041	OH-PAU		
PC-6	Piper PA-31-350 Navajo Chieftain	31-8252042	OH-PAV		

Rajavartiolaitos
Frontier Guard - Air Patrol Squadron

UNITS/BASES   Based at Helsinki, aircraft are detached to Turku and Rovaniemi, callsign Finnguard.

OH-MVN	Dornier 228-212	8233	D-CATE	MR
OH-MVO	Dornier 228-212	8232	D-CATD	MR

FRANCE
République Française   W Europe

France has relinquished control of the majority of its overseas colonies but those that remain still have Air Force units based. Having been a NATO founder member France left in 1965 and has pursued an independent line since, including maintaining its own nuclear deterrent. This looks set to change as it becomes a cornerstone of the new EU military force while again co-operating in NATO operations as it did recently in the Balkans.

SERIAL SYSTEM   Serials are usually derived from the c/n or previous identity, they are usually shortened. F-**** callsigns are also allocated, sometimes being partially visible externally as part of a code (if displayed), the numeric part of the code showing the unit. The callsign changes when the aircraft moves units. The Army use three letter codes and the Navy has no code system. The Customs and Securité Civile use civil style registrations in the F-Z*** sequence, the fire fighting aircraft also carrying large two digit codes to aid recognition at a distance.

L'Armée de l'Air

ICAO codes FAF (callsign French Air Force), CTM (callsign COTAM)

UNITS/BASES		
Commandement de Forces Aériennes Stratégiques - CFAS		
ERV00.093 'Bretagne', BA125 Istres	Stratotanker	AAR
CITac00.339, BA116 Luxeuil-St Sauveur	Falcon 20	RADAR Training
Commandement de la Force Aérienne de Combat - CFAC		
EE00.54 'Dunkerque'	C.160G	ELINT/COMINT

Commandement de la Force Aérienne de Projection - CFAP

Unit	Aircraft	
CIET00.340, BA101 Toulouse-Francazal	C.160R, N262	
EC00.70 'Chateaudun', BA279 Chateaudun	TBM700, Twin Otter	
EE00.51 'Aubrac', BA105 Evreux-Fauville	DC-8	ELINT/COMINT
ET03.060 'Esterel', BA110 Creil	A310, DC-8	
ET01.061 'Touraine', BA123 Orléans-Bricy	C.160R	
ET02.061 'Franche-Comte', BA123 Orleans-Bricy	C-130H/H-30	
ET03.061 'Poitou', BA123 Orleans-Bricy	C.160R	
ET01.062 'Vercours', BA110 Creil	CN235	
ET01.064 'Bearn', BA105 Evreux-Fauville	C.160R	
ET02.064 'Anjou', BA105 Evreux-Fauville	C.160R	
ETE00.041 'Verdun', BA128 Metz-Frescaty	TBM700, N262	
ETE00.042 'Ventoux', BA118 Mont-de-Marsan	N262, Twin Otter	
ETE00.043 'Medoc', BA106 Bordeaux-Merignac	TBM700	
ETE00.044 'Mistral', BA114 Salon-de-Provence	TBM700, N262	
ETEC00.065, BA107 Villacoublay-Vélizy	Falcon 20/50/900, TBM700, N262	VIP
ETOM00.050 'Reunion', BA181 St Denis, La Réunion	C.160R	
ETOM00.052 'La Tontouta', DA376 Numea, New Caledonia	CN235	
ETOM00.055 'Ouessant', DA160 Dakar-Ouakam, Senegal	C.160R	
ETOM00.058 'Antilles', DA365 Fort-de-France, Martinique	C.160R	
ETOM00.082 'Maine', BA190 Tahiti-Faaa	CN235	
ETOM00.088 ' Larzac', DA188 Djibouti	C.160R	
GAM00.056 'Vaucluse', BA105 Evreux-Fauville	C.160R, Twin Otter	

Commandement Air des Systèmes de Surveillance, d'Information et de Communication - CASSIC

Unit	Aircraft	
EDCA00.036, BA 702 Avord	E-3F	AEW

Commandement de Ecoles de l'Armée de l'Air - CEAA

Unit	Aircraft
EAT00.319, BA 702 Avord	Xingu
ENOSA00.316, BA101 Toulouse-Francazal	Paris, N262
ETO00.8, 1D/120 'Eracles', BA120 Cazaux	Falcon 20

Centre d'Expériences Aériennes Militaires - CEAM

Unit	Aircraft
EET06.0330 'Albret', BA118 Mont-de-Marsan	CN235M, Twin Otter, C-160, TBM-700

PLANS

The two A319s will replace 2 VIP Falcon 20 and 3 Nord 262s.
A total of 50 Airbus A400Ms are required, with deliveries from 2008.

418 / F-FADC	Airbus Industrie A310-304	418	F-WQIC	ET03.060	
421 / F-FADA	Airbus Industrie A310-304	421	F-ODVD	ET03.060	
422 / F-FADB	Airbus Industrie A310-304	422	F-ODVE	ET03.060	
1485 / F-RBFA	Airbus Industrie A319-115X(CJ)	1485	F-GXFA	ETEC00.065	
1556 / F-RBFB	Airbus Industrie A319-115X(CJ)	1556	F-GXFB		on order
470 / 93-CA	Boeing C-135FR Stratotanker	18679 / C2001	63-8470 (FMS)	ERV00.093	F-UKCA
471 / 93-CB	Boeing C-135FR Stratotanker	18680 / C2002	63-8471 (FMS)	ERV00.093	F-UKCB
472 / 93-CC	Boeing C-135FR Stratotanker	18681 / C2003	63-8472 (FMS)	ERV00.093	F-UKCC
38474 / 93-CE	Boeing C-135FR Stratotanker	18683 / C2005	63-8474 (FMS)	ERV00.093	F-UKCE
475 / 93-CF	Boeing C-135FR Stratotanker	18684 / C2006	63-8475 (FMS)	ERV00.093	F-UKCF
735 / 93-CG	Boeing C-135FR Stratotanker	18695 / C2007	63-12735 (FMS)	ERV00.093	F-UKCG
312736 / 93-CH	Boeing C-135FR Stratotanker	18696 / C2008	63-12736 (FMS)	ERV00.093	F-UKCH
312737 / 93-CI	Boeing C-135FR Stratotanker	18697 / C2009	63-12737 (FMS)	ERV00.093	F-UKCI
738 / 93-CJ	Boeing C-135FR Stratotanker	18698 / C2010	63-12738 (FMS)	ERV00.093	F-UKCJ
739 / 93-CK	Boeing C-135FR Stratotanker	18699 / C2011	63-12739 (FMS)	ERV00.093	F-UKCK
740 / 93-CL	Boeing C-135FR Stratotanker	18700 / C2012	63-12740 (FMS)	ERV00.093	F-UKCL
23497 / 93-CM	Boeing C-135FR Stratotanker Cvtd KC-135R	18480 / T0548	62-3497 (USAF)	ERV00.093	F-UKCM
23516 / 93-CO	Boeing C-135FR Stratotanker Cvtd KC-135R	18499 / T0567	62-3516 (USAF)	ERV00.093	F-UKCO
23525 / 93-CN	Boeing C-135FR Stratotanker Cvtd KC-135R	18508 / T0576	62-3525 (USAF)	ERV00.093	F-UKCN
23574 / 93-CP	Boeing C-135FR Stratotanker Cvtd KC-135R	18557 / T0625	62-3574 (USAF)	ERV00.093	F-UKCP
201 / 36-CA	Boeing E-3F Sentry (707)	24115 / 1000		EDCA00.036	F-ZBCA
202 / 36-CB	Boeing E-3F Sentry (707)	24116 / 1003		EDCA00.036	F-ZBCB
203 / 36-CC	Boeing E-3F Sentry (707)	24117 / 1006		EDCA00.036	F-ZBCC
204 / 36-CD	Boeing E-3F Sentry (707)	24510 / 1009		EDCA00.036	F-ZBCD
043 / 62-IA	Airtech/CASA CN235M-200	C043		ET01.062	
045 / 62-IB	Airtech/CASA CN235M-200	C045		ET01.062	
065 / 82-IC	Airtech/CASA CN235M-200	C065		ETOM00.082	
066 / 62-ID	Airtech/CASA CN235M-200	C066		ET01.062	
071 / 62-IE	Airtech/CASA CN235M-200	C071		ET01.062	
072 / 82-IF	Airtech/CASA CN235M-200	C072		ETOM00.082	
105 / 62-IG	Airtech/CASA CN235M-200	C105		ET01.062	
107 / 52-IH	Airtech/CASA CN235M-200	C107		ETOM00.052	

111 / 62-II	Airtech/CASA CN235M-200	C111		ET01.062	
114 / 62-IJ	Airtech/CASA CN235M-200	C114		ET01.062	
123 / 62-IM	Airtech/CASA CN235M-200	C123		ET01.062	
128 / 62-IK	Airtech/CASA CN235M-200	C128		ET01.062	
129 / 62-IL	Airtech/CASA CN235M-200	C129		ET01.062	F-ZVLY
137 / 62-IN	Airtech/CASA CN235M-200	C137		ET01.062	
141 / 62-IO	Airtech/CASA CN235M-200	C141		ET01.062	
49 / 120-FA	Dassault Falcon 20C	49/408	F-TEOA	ETO00.8	F-RHFA
93 / ED	Dassault Falcon 20C	93		ETEC00.065	F-RAED
167 / EB	Dassault Falcon 20C	167		ETEC00.065	F-RAEB
238 / EE	Dassault Falcon 20C	238		ETEC00.065	F-RAEE
268 / EF	Dassault Falcon 20C	268		ETEC00.065	F-RAEF
291 / 65-EG	Dassault Falcon 20E	291		ETEC00.065	F-RAEG
115 / 339-JG	Dassault Falcon 20	115/432	F-WJML	CITac00.339	F-UKJG
					Std Chateaudun
182 / 339-JA	Dassault Falcon 20C	182/461	F-ZJTA	CITac00.339	F-UKJA
260 / A	Dassault Falcon 20E	260/488	F-WMKJ	ETEC00.065	F-RAEA
342 / C	Dassault Falcon 20F	342/532	F-RAEG	ETEC00.065	F-RAEC
422 / 65-EH	Dassault Falcon 20F	422	F-RCAL	ETEC00.065	F-RAEH
451 / 339-JC	Dassault Falcon 20F	451	F-ZJTS	CITac00.339	F-UKJC
483 / 339-JI	Dassault Falcon 20F	483	F-WRQQ	CITac00.339	F-UKJI
5	Dassault Falcon 50	5		ETEC00.065	F-RAFI
27	Dassault Falcon 50	27	F-WGTG	ETEC00.065	F-RAFK
34	Dassault Falcon 50	34	F-WEFS	ETEC00.065	F-RAFL
78	Dassault Falcon 50	78	F-GEOY	ETEC00.065	F-RAFJ
2	Dassault Falcon 900	2	F-GFJC	ETEC00.065	F-RAFP
4	Dassault Falcon 900	4	F-WWFA	ETEC00.065	F-RAFQ
292 / CC	DeHavilland Canada DHC-6 Twin Otter 200	292	F-BTOQ	GAM00.056	
298 / CD	DeHavilland Canada DHC-6 Twin Otter 200	298	F-BTOR	GAM00.056	
300 / CE	DeHavilland Canada DHC-6 Twin Otter 200	300	F-BTOT	GAM00.056	
730 / CA	DeHavilland Canada DHC-6 Twin Otter 300	730		ETE00.042	
742 / CB	DeHavilland Canada DHC-6 Twin Otter 300	742		ETE00.042	
745 / CV	DeHavilland Canada DHC-6 Twin Otter 300	745		ETE00.042	
786 / CT	DeHavilland Canada DHC-6 Twin Otter 300	786		ETE00.042	
790 / CW	DeHavilland Canada DHC-6 Twin Otter 300	790		ETE00.042	
45819	Douglas DC-8-55F	45819 / 238	F-BNLD		Std Le Bourget
46013	Douglas DC-8-72F	46013 / 427	OH-LFT	ET03.060	F-RAFG
46130	Douglas DC-8-72F	46130 / 542	OH-LFY	ET03.060	F-RAFF
054 / 319-YX	Embraer EMB-121AA Xingu	121054	PT-MBW	EAT00.319	F-TEYX
055 / 319-YZ	Embraer EMB-121AN Xingu	121055	55 (Fr Navy)	EAT00.319	F-TEYZ
064 / 319-YY	Embraer EMB-121AN Xingu	121064		EAT00.319	F-TEYY
066	Embraer EMB-121AN Xingu	121066	66 (Fr Navy)	EAT00.319	
069	Embraer EMB-121AN Xingu	121069	69 (Fr Navy)	EAT00.319	
070 / 319-	Embraer EMB-121AN Xingu	121070	70 (Fr Navy)	EAT00.319	
072 / 319-YA	Embraer EMB-121AA Xingu	121072	PP-ZXJ	EAT00.319	F-TEYA
073 / 319-YB	Embraer EMB-121AA Xingu	121073	PP-ZXL	EAT00.319	F-TEYB
075 / 319-YC	Embraer EMB-121AA Xingu	121075	PP-ZXN	EAT00.319	F-TEYC
076 / 319-YD	Embraer EMB-121AA Xingu	121076	PP-ZXO	EAT00.319	F-TEYD
077	Embraer EMB-121AN Xingu	121077	77 (Fr Navy)	EAT00.319	
078 / 319-YE	Embraer EMB-121AA Xingu	121078	PP-ZXQ	EAT00.319	F-TEYE
080 / 319-YF	Embraer EMB-121AA Xingu	121080	PP-ZXS	EAT00.319	F-TEYF
082 / 319-YG	Embraer EMB-121AA Xingu	121082	PP-ZXX	EAT00.319	F-TEYG
083 / 319-ZE	Embraer EMB-121AN Xingu	121083	83 (Fr Navy)	EAT00.319	
084 / 319-YH	Embraer EMB-121AA Xingu	121084	PP-ZXW	EAT00.319	F-TEYH
086 / 319-YI	Embraer EMB-121AA Xingu	121086	PP-ZYA	EAT00.319	F-TEYI
089 / 319-YJ	Embraer EMB-121AA Xingu	121089	PP-ZYC	EAT00.319	F-TEYJ
090 / 319-ZF	Embraer EMB-121AN Xingu	121090	90 (Fr Navy)	EAT00.319	
091 / 319-YK	Embraer EMB-121AA Xingu	121091	PP-ZYE	EAT00.319	F-TEYK
092 / 319-YL	Embraer EMB-121AA Xingu	121092	PP-ZYF	EAT00.319	F-TEYL
095 / 319-YM	Embraer EMB-121AA Xingu	121095	PP-ZYG	EAT00.319	F-TEYM
096 / 319-YN	Embraer EMB-121AA Xingu	121096	PP-ZYH	EAT00.319	F-TEYN
098 / 319-YO	Embraer EMB-121AA Xingu	121098	PP-ZYI	EAT00.319	F-TEYO
099 / 319-YP	Embraer EMB-121AA Xingu	121099	PP-ZYJ	EAT00.319	F-TEYP
101 / 319-YR	Embraer EMB-121AA Xingu	121101		EAT00.319	F-TEYR
102 / 319-YS	Embraer EMB-121AA Xingu	121102		EAT00.319	F-TEYS
103 / 319-YT	Embraer EMB-121AA Xingu	121103		EAT00.319	F-TEYT
105 / 319-YU	Embraer EMB-121AA Xingu	121105		EAT00.319	F-TEYU
107 / 319-YV	Embraer EMB-121AA Xingu	121107		EAT00.319	F-TEYV
108 / 319-YW	Embraer EMB-121AA Xingu	121108		EAT00.319	F-TEYW
111 / 319-YQ	Embraer EMB-121AA Xingu	121111		EAT00.319	F-TEYQ
4588 / 61-PM	Lockheed C-130H (L-382C-36D) Hercules	4588	F-ZJEP	ET02.061	F-RAPM
4589 / 61-PN	Lockheed C-130H (L-382C-36D) Hercules	4589	9T-TCC	ET02.061	F-RAPN
5114 / 61-PA	Lockheed C-130H (L-382C-92E) Hercules	5114		ET02.061	F-RAPA
5116 / 61-PB	Lockheed C-130H (L-382C-92E) Hercules	5116		ET02.061	F-RAPB

5119 / 61-PC	Lockheed C-130H (L-382C-92E) Hercules	5119		ET02.061	F-RAPC
5140 / 61-PD	Lockheed C-130H-30 (L-382T-91E) Hercules	5140		ET02.061	F-RAPD
5142 / 61-PE	Lockheed C-130H-30 (L-382T-91E) Hercules	5142		ET02.061	F-RAPE
5144 / 61-PF	Lockheed C-130H-30 (L-382T-91E) Hercules	5144		ET02.061	F-RAPF
5150 / 61-PG	Lockheed C-130H-30 (L-382T-94E) Hercules	5150	N4242N	ET02.061	F-RAPG
5151 / 61-PH	Lockheed C-130H-30 (L-382T-94E) Hercules	5151		ET02.061	F-RAPH
5152 / 61-PI	Lockheed C-130H-30 (L-382T-94E) Hercules	5152		ET02.061	F-RAPI
5153 / 61-PJ	Lockheed C-130H-30 (L-382T-94E) Hercules	5153	N73235	ET02.061	F-RAPJ
5226 / 61-PK	Lockheed C-130H-30 (L-382T-20F) Hercules	5226		ET02.061	F-RAPK
5227 / 61-PL	Lockheed C-130H-30 (L-382T-20F) Hercules	5227		ET02.061	F-RAPL
1 / 330-DB	Morane Saulnier 760 Paris IIR	001			Std Chateaudun
27 / 316-DQ	Morane Saulnier 760 Paris 1R	027			
30 / 65-LI	Morane Saulnier 760 Paris	030			
34 / 115-MH	Morane Saulnier 760 Paris 1R	034		EAM 09.115	F-SCBB
38 / 132-CN	Morane Saulnier 760 Paris	038		EAM 09.132	
44 / 115-CB	Morane Saulnier 760 Paris 1R	044			F-RBLD
					Std Chateaudun
45 / 115-MJ	Morane Saulnier 760 Paris 1R	045		EAM.09-115	
54 / 115-MG	Morane Saulnier 760 Paris 1R	054	C41-2913 (FAB)	EAM 09.115	
57 / 316-DJ	Morane Saulnier 760 Paris 1R	057	C41-2918 (FAB)		
58 / 126-HH	Morane Saulnier 760 Paris	058	C41-2920 (FAB)	SAL 09.126	
61 / 316-DI	Morane Saulnier 760 Paris 1R	061	C41-2919 (FAB)		
65 / 314-DD	Morane Saulnier 760 Paris	065	C41-2924 (FAB)	EAC 00.314	
71 / 316-DO	Morane Saulnier 760 Paris	071	C41-2929 (FAB)		
92	Morane Saulnier 760 Paris	092			
93 / 316-DS	Morane Saulnier 760 Paris 1R	093			
94 / 116-CC	Morane Saulnier 760 Paris 1R	094		EAM 09.116	
64 / AA	Nord 262D-51 Frégate	64		ETEC00.065	F-RBAA
66 / AB	Nord 262D-51 Frégate	66		ETEC00.065	F-RBAB
68 / AC	Nord 262D-51 Frégate	68		ETEC00.065	
77 / AK	Nord 262D-51 Frégate	77		ETE00.044	
80 / AW	Nord 262D-51 Frégate	80		ETEC00.065	
81 / AH	Nord 262D-51 Frégate	81		ETE00.041	F-RBAH
83 / DB	Nord 262D-51 Frégate	83			Std Chateaudun
87 / DC	Nord 262D-51 Frégate	87			Std Chateaudun
88 / AL	Nord 262D-51 Frégate	88		ETE00.042	
89 / AZ	Nord 262D-51 Frégate	89		ETE00.041	
91 / AT	Nord 262D-51 Frégate	91		ETE00.042	F-RBAT
92 / DE	Nord 262D-51 Frégate	92			Std Chateaudun
93 / AP	Nord 262D-51 Frégate	93		ETEC00.065	
94 / AU	Nord 262D-51 Frégate	94		ETEC00.065	
95 / AR	Nord 262D-51 Frégate	95		ETEC00.065	
105 / AE	Nord 262D-51 Frégate	105		ETEC00.065	
106 / AY	Nord 262D-51 Frégate	106		ETE00.041	
107 / AX	Nord 262D-51 Frégate	107		ETEC00.065	
108 / AG	Nord 262D-51 Frégate	108		ETE00.041	
109 / AM	Nord 262D-51 Frégate	109		ETE00.043	
110 / AS	Nord 262D-51 Frégate	110		ETEC00.065	
33 / XA	SOCATA TBM-700	33		ETE00.043	F-RAXA
35 / XB	SOCATA TBM-700	35		ETE00.043	F-RAXB
70 / 43-XC	SOCATA TBM-700	70		ETE00.043	F-RAXC
77 / 65-XD	SOCATA TBM-700	77		ETEC00.065	F-RAXD
78 / 65-XE	SOCATA TBM-700	78		ETEC00.065	F-RAXE
80 / 41-XF	SOCATA TBM-700	80		ETE00.041	F-RAXF
93 / XL	SOCATA TBM-700	93		ETE00.043	F-RAXL
94 / 65-XG	SOCATA TBM-700	94		ETEC00.065	F-RAXG
95 / 65-XH	SOCATA TBM-700	95		ETEC00.065	F-RAXH
103 / 41-XI	SOCATA TBM-700	103		ETE00.041	F-RAXI
104 / XJ	SOCATA TBM-700	104		EC00.070	F-RAXJ
105 / 65-XK	SOCATA TBM-700	105		ETEC00.065	F-RAXK
110 / 41-XP	SOCATA TBM-700	110		ETE00.041	F-RAXP
111 / 65-XM	SOCATA TBM-700	111		ETEC00.065	F-RAXM
117 / 44-XN	SOCATA TBM-700	117		ETE00.044	F-RAXN
125 / 65-XO	SOCATA TBM-700	125		ETEC00.065	F-RAXO
131 / 65-XQ	SOCATA TBM-700	131		ETEC00.065	F-RAXQ
146 / 65-XR	SOCATA TBM-700	146		ETEC00.065	F-RAXR
147 / 65-XS	SOCATA TBM-700	147		ETEC00.065	F-RAXS
RA02 / 61-MI	Transall/VFW C-160R	A02	F-SDBS	ET00.061	F-RAMI
RA04 / 61-MS	Transall/Nord C-160R	A04	F-SDBT	ET01.061	F-RAZA
RA06 / 61-ZB	Transall/MBB C-160R	A06	F-SDBU	ET03.061	F-RAZB
R1 / 61-MA	Transall/VFW C-160R	F1	KM+101 (WGAF)	ET01.061	F-RAMA
R2 / 61-MB	Transall/MBB C-160R	F2	KA+201 (WGAF)	ET01.061	F-RAMB
R3 / 61-MC	Transall/Nord C-160R	F3	F-ZJYF	ET01.061	F-RAMC
R4 / 61-MD	Transall/VFW C-160R	F4	KM+104 (WGAF)	ET01.061	F-RAMD

R5 / 61-ME	Transall/MBB C-160R	F5	KA+202 (WGAF)	ET01.061	F-RAME
R11 / 61-MF	Transall/MBB C-160R	F11	KA+203 (WGAF)	ET01.061	F-RAMF
R12 / 61-MG	Transall/Nord C-160R	F12		ET01.061	F-RAMG
R13 / 61-MH	Transall/VFW C-160R	F13	KM+105 (WGAF)	ETOM00.050	F-RAMH
R15 / 61-MJ	Transall/Nord C-160R	F15		ET01.061	F-RAMJ
R17 / 61-ML	Transall/MBB C-160R	F17	KA+205 (WGAF)	ET01.061	F-RAML
R18 / 61-MM	Transall/Nord C-160R	F18		ET01.061	F-RAMM
R42 / 61-MN	Transall/MBB C-160R	F42	KA+206 (WGAF)	ET01.061	White cs, F-RAMN
R43 / 61-MO	Transall/VFW C-160R	F43	KM+108 (WGAF)	ET01.061	F-RAMO
R44 / 61-MP	Transall/MBB C-160R	F44	KA+207 (WGAF)	ET01.061	F-RAMP
R45 / 61-MQ	Transall/Nord C-160R	F45		ET01.061	F-RAMQ
R46 / 61-MR	Transall/VFW C-160R	F46	KM+109 (WGAF)	ET01.061	F-RAMR
R48 / 61-MT	Transall/Nord C-160R	F48		ET01.061	F-RAMT
R50 / 61-MV	Transall/VFW C-160R	F50	F-BUFS	ET01.061	F-RAMV
R51 / 61-MW	Transall/Nord C-160R	F51		ET01.061	F-RAMW
R52 / 61-MX	Transall/VFW C-160R	F52	KM+111 (WGAF)	ET01.061	F-RAMX
R53 / 61-MY	Transall/MBB C-160R	F53	KA+209 (WGAF)	ET01.061	F-RAMY
R54 / 61-MZ	Transall/Nord C-160R	F54		ET01.061	F-RAMZ
R55 / 61-ZC	Transall/Nord C-160R	F55		ET01.061	F-RAZC
R86 / 61-ZD	Transall/MBB C-160R	F86	KA+210 (WGAF)	ET01.061	F-RAZD
R87 / 61-ZE	Transall/Nord C-160R	F87		ETOM00.050	F-RAZE
R88 / 61-ZF	Transall/MBB C-160R	F88	KA+211 (WGAF)	ET03.061	F-RAZF
R89 / 61-ZG	Transall/Nord C-160R	F89		ET03.061	F-RAZG
R90 / 61-ZH	Transall/MBB C-160R	F90	KA+212 (WGAF)	ET03.061	F-RAZH
R91 / 61-ZI	Transall/VFW C-160R	F91	KM+112 (WGAF)	ET03.061	F-RAZI
R92 / 61-ZJ	Transall/MBB C-160R	F92	KA+213 (WGAF)	ET03.061	F-RAZJ
R93 / 61-ZK	Transall/Nord C-160R	F93		ET03.061	F-RAZK
R94 / 61-ZL	Transall/VFW C-160R	F94	KM+113 (WGAF)	ET03.061	F-RAZL
R95 / 61-ZM	Transall/MBB C-160R	F95	KA+214 (WGAF)	ET03.061	F-RAZM
R96 / 61-ZN	Transall/Nord C-160R	F96		ET03.061	F-RAZN
R97 / 61-ZO	Transall/VFW C-160R	F97	KM+114 (WGAF)	ET03.061	F-RAZO
R98 / 61-ZP	Transall/MBB C-160R	F98	KA+215 (WGAF)	ET01.061	F-RAZP
R99 / 61-ZQ	Transall/Nord C-160R	F99		ET03.061	F-RAZQ
R100 / 61-ZR	Transall/VFW C-160R	F100	KM+115 (WGAF)	ET03.061	F-RAZR
R153 / 61-ZS	Transall/Nord C-160R	F153		ET03.061	F-RAZS
R154 / 61-ZT	Transall/Nord C-160R	F154		ET03.061	F-RAZT
R157 / 61-ZW	Transall/Nord C-160R	F157		ET03.061	F-RAZW
R158 / 61-ZX	Transall/Nord C-160R	F158		ET03.061	F-RAZX
R159 / 61-ZY	Transall/Nord C-160R	F159		ET03.061	F-RAZY
R160 / 61-ZZ	Transall/Nord C-160R	F160		ET03.061	F-RAZZ
R201 / 64-GA	Aérospatiale C-160R Transall	201	F-ZJUA	ET01.064	Cvtd C-160NG
R202 / 64-GB	Aérospatiale C-160R Transall	202	F-ZJUB	ET02.064	Cvtd C-160NG
R203 / 64-GC	Aérospatiale C-160R Transall	203	F-ZJUC	ET02.064	Cvtd C-160NG
R204 / 64-GD	Aérospatiale C-160R Transall	204	F-ZJUD	ET02.064	Cvtd C-160NG
R205 / 64-GE	Aérospatiale C-160R Transall	206	F-ZJUE	ET01.064	Cvtd C-160NG
R206 / 64-GF	Aérospatiale C-160R Transall	209	F-ZJUF	ET02.064	Cvtd C-160NG
R207 / 64-GG	Aérospatiale C-160R Transall	210	F-ZJUG	ET01.064	Cvtd C-160NG
R208 / 64-GH	Aérospatiale C-160R Transall	211	F-ZJUH	ET02.064	Cvtd C-160NG
R210 / 64-GJ	Aérospatiale C-160R Transall	213	F-ZJUJ	ET02.064	Cvtd C-160NG
R211 / 64-GK	Aérospatiale C-160R Transall	214	F-ZJUK	ET01.064	Cvtd C-160NG
R212 / 64-GL	Aérospatiale C-160R Transall	215	F-ZJUL	ET02.064	Cvtd C-160NG
R213 / 64-GM	Aérospatiale C-160R Transall	216	F-ZJUM	ET01.064	Cvtd C-160NG
R214 / 64-GN	Aérospatiale C-160R Transall	217	F-ZJUN	ET02.064	Cvtd C-160NG
R215 / 64-GO	Aérospatiale C-160R Transall	218	F-ZJUO	ET01.064	Cvtd C-160NG
F216 / GT	Aérospatiale C-160NG Transall 'Gabriel'	219	F-ZJUP	ET01.061	
R217 / 64-GQ	Aérospatiale C-160R Transall	220	F-ZJUQ	ET01.064	Cvtd C-160NG
R218 / 64-GR	Aérospatiale C-160R Transall	221	F-ZJUR	ET02.064	Cvtd C-160NG
F221 / GS	Aérospatiale C-160NG Transall 'Gabriel'	224	F-ZJUU	ET01.061	
F223 / 64-GW	Aérospatiale C-160NG Transall	226	F-ZJUW	ET01.064	
R224 / 64-GX	Aérospatiale C-160R Transall	227	F-ZJUX	ET02.064	Cvtd C-160NG
R225 / 64-GY	Aérospatiale C-160R Transall	228	F-ZJUY	ET01.064	Cvtd C-160NG
R226 / 64-GZ	Aérospatiale C-160R Transall	229	F-ZJUZ	ET02.064	Cvtd C-160NG
F227 / 64-GP	Aérospatiale C-160NG Transall	230	F-ZJUA		
H01 / 59-BA	Aérospatiale C-160H Transall	222	F-ZJUS		Std Chateaudun
H02 / 59-BB	Aérospatiale C-160H Transall	223	F-ZJUT		Std Chateaudun
H03 / 59-BC	Aérospatiale C-160H Transall	231	F-ZJUB		Std Chateaudun
H04 / 59-BD	Aérospatiale C-160H Transall	232	F-ZJUC		Std Chateaudun

Marine National, Aéronavale
Naval Aviation

ICAO code FNY.

UNITS/BASES		
Flotille 4 (4F), Lann-Bihoue*	Hawkeye	(*deployed on aircraft carrier 'Charles de Gaulle')
Flotille 21 (21F), Nimes-Garons	Atlantique 2	
Flotille 23 (23F), Lann-Bihoue	Atlantique 2	
Flotille 24 (24F), Lann-Bihoue	Falcon 50, Xingu, Nord 262	
Flotille 25 (25F), Noumea-La Tontouta/Tahiti-Faaa	Guardian	
Flotille 28 (28F), Hyeres	Xingu, Nord 262	
Escadrille 56 (56S), Nimes-Garons	Nord 262	
Escadrille 57 (57S), Landivisau	Falcon 10MER	

PLANS — Two more new E-2Cs to be acquired.

Code	Type	c/n	Reg	Unit	Reg2
01	AMD-BA Atlantique 2	01	42 (Fr Navy)		Cvtd Br1150
04	AMD-BA Atlantique 2	04		21F	
1	AMD-BA Atlantique 2	1		21F	
2	AMD-BA Atlantique 2	2		21F	
3	AMD-BA Atlantique 2	3		23F	
5	AMD-BA Atlantique 2	5		23F	
6	AMD-BA Atlantique 2	6		21F	
7	AMD-BA Atlantique 2	7		21F	
8	AMD-BA Atlantique 2	8		21F	
9	AMD-BA Atlantique 2	9		21F	
10	AMD-BA Atlantique 2	10		23F	
11	AMD-BA Atlantique 2	11		23F	
12	AMD-BA Atlantique 2	12		23F	
13	AMD-BA Atlantique 2	13		21F	
14	AMD-BA Atlantique 2	14		21F	
15	AMD-BA Atlantique 2	15		21F	
16	AMD-BA Atlantique 2	16		21F	
17	AMD-BA Atlantique 2	17		23F	
18	AMD-BA Atlantique 2	18		21F	
19	AMD-BA Atlantique 2	19		23F	
20	AMD-BA Atlantique 2	20		23F	
21	AMD-BA Atlantique 2	21		21F	
22	AMD-BA Atlantique 2	22		21F	
23	AMD-BA Atlantique 2	23		21F	
24	AMD-BA Atlantique 2	24		21F	
25	AMD-BA Atlantique 2	25		21F	
26	AMD-BA Atlantique 2	26		23F	
27	AMD-BA Atlantique 2	27		23F	
28	AMD-BA Atlantique 2	28		21F	
29	AMD-BA Atlantique 2	29			
30	AMD-BA Atlantique 2	30			
32	Dassault Falcon 10MER	32		57S	
101	Dassault Falcon 10MER	101		57S	
129	Dassault Falcon 10MER	129		57S	
133	Dassault Falcon 10MER	133		57S	
143	Dassault Falcon 10MER	143		57S	
185	Dassault Falcon 10MER	185		57S	
7	Dassault Falcon 50M	7	F-WQBN	25F	
30	Dassault Falcon 50M	30	F-WQFZ	24F	F-ZVMB
36	Dassault Falcon 50M	36	F-ZWTA	24F	F-ZJTL
	Dassault Falcon 50M			24F	
	Dassault Falcon 50M			24F	
48	Dassault Falcon 20G Gardian	448	F-WJMK	25F	F-ZWVF
65	Dassault Falcon 20G Gardian	465		25F	F-ZJTS
72	Dassault Falcon 20G Gardian	472		25F	
77	Dassault Falcon 20G Gardian	477		25F	
80	Dassault Falcon 20G Gardian	480		25F	F-ZJSA
27	Embraer EMB-121AN Xingu	121027	PT-MAT		
30	Embraer EMB-121AN Xingu	121030	G-XTWO	24F	
47	Embraer EMB-121AN Xingu	121047	PT-MBP	2S	
56	Embraer EMB-121AN Xingu	121056	PT-MBY		
61	Embraer EMB-121AN Xingu	121061	PT-MCC		
65	Embraer EMB-121AN Xingu	121065		2S	
67	Embraer EMB-121AN Xingu	121067		2S	F-YDNC
68	Embraer EMB-121AN Xingu	121068		2S	
71	Embraer EMB-121AN Xingu	121071	PP-ZXH	28F	
74	Embraer EMB-121AN Xingu	121074	PP-ZXM	24F	

79	Embraer EMB-121AN Xingu	121079	PP-ZXR	2S	
81	Embraer EMB-121AN Xingu	121081	PP-ZXT	2S	
85	Embraer EMB-121AN Xingu	121085	PP-ZXZ	28F	
87	Embraer EMB-121AN Xingu	121087	PP-ZYB	2S	
100	Embraer EMB-121AN Xingu	121100			
1	Grumman E-2C Hawkeye		Bu165455 (FMS)	4F	
2	Grumman E-2C Hawkeye		Bu165456 (FMS)	4F	
3	Grumman E-2C Hawkeye			4F	On order
32	Morane Saulnier 760 Paris	32		57S	
33	Morane Saulnier 760 Paris	33		57S	
40	Morane Saulnier 760 Paris	40		57S	
42	Morane Saulnier 760 Paris	42		57S	
46	Morane Saulnier 760 Paris	46		57S	
85	Morane Saulnier 760 Paris	85		57S	
45	Nord 262A-34 Frégate	45		56S	F-RBOC
46	Nord 262A-34 Frégate	46		56S	F-RBOD
51	Nord 262A-34 Frégate	51		2S	F-RBOE
52	Nord 262A-34 Frégate	52		56S	F-RBOF
53	Nord 262A-34 Frégate	53		2S	
63	Nord 262A-29 Frégate	63		28F	
69	Nord 262A-26 Frégate	69	F-WJAK	56S	
70	Nord 262A-29 Frégate	70		56S	
71	Nord 262A-29 Frégate	71		56S	
72	Nord 262A-29 Frégate	72		56S	
73	Nord 262A-29 Frégate	73		56S	
75	Nord 262A-29 Frégate	75		56S	
79	Nord 262A-29 Frégate	79		28F	
100	Nord 262A-45 Frégate	100	F-GBEH	2S	F-YDCY
227	Piper PA-31-350 Navajo	31-7401227	F-ETBB	3S	
925	Piper PA-31-350 Navajo	31-7300925	F-BTMR	3S	

Aviation Légère de l'Armée de Terre - ALAT
Army Aviation

UNITS/BASES	Escadrille Avions de l'Armée de Terre (EAAT), Rennes-St Jacques		Caravan II, TBM700	
	Etablissement de Réserve Générale du Materiel (ERGM), Montauban		Turbo Porter	

0008 / ABM	Reims/Cessna F406 Caravan II	F406-0008		EAAT	F-MAGM
0010 / ABN	Reims/Cessna F406 Caravan II	F406-0010		EAAT	F-MAGN
887 / MCA	Pilatus PC-6B2/H4 Turbo Porter	887	HB-FKU	ERGM	F-MMCA
888 / MCB	Pilatus PC-6B2/H4 Turbo Porter	888	HB-FKV	ERGM	F-MMCB
889 / MCC	Pilatus PC-6B2/H4 Turbo Porter	889	HB-FKW	ERGM	F-MMCC
890 / MCD	Pilatus PC-6B2/H4 Turbo Porter	890	HB-FKX	ERGM	F-MMCD
891 / MCE	Pilatus PC-6B2/H4 Turbo Porter	891	HB-FKY	ERGM	F-MMCE
99 / ABO	SOCATA TBM-700	99		EAAT	F-MABO
100 / ABP	SOCATA TBM-700	100		EAAT	F-MABP
115 / ABQ	SOCATA TBM-700	115		EAAT	F-MABQ
136 / ABR	SOCATA TBM-700	136		EAAT	F-MABR
139 / ABS	SOCATA TBM-700	139		EAAT	F-MABS
156 / ABT	SOCATA TBM-700	156		EAAT	F-MABT
159 / ABU	SOCATA TBM-700	159		EAAT	F-MABU
160 / ABV	SOCATA TBM-700	160		EAAT	F-MABV

Délégation Générale pour l'Armament - DGA

UNITS/BASES	Centre d'Essais en Vol (CEV), Istres		Falcon 20, Transall, Nord 262	
	Centre d'Essais en Vol (CEV), Cazaux		Falcon 20, Aviocar	
	École du Personnel Navigants d'Essais et de Réception (EPNER), Istres		Nord 262, Falcon 20	

1 / MV	Aérospatiale SN601 Corvette	1	F-BUAS	CEV	F-ZVMV
2 / MW	Aérospatiale SN601 Corvette	2	F-BRNZ	CEV	F-ZVMW
10 / MX	Aérospatiale SN601 Corvette	10	F-GFEJ	CEV	F-ZVMX
03	Airbus Industrie A300B2-103	03	F-BUAD	CEV	NOVESPACE
03	AMD-BA Atlantique 2	03		CEV	
377 / MO	CASA 212 Aviocar srs 300	A12-01-377		CEV	F-ZVMO
378 / MP	CASA 212 Aviocar srs 300	A12-02-378		CEV	F-ZVMP
386 / MQ	CASA 212 Aviocar srs 300	A12-03-386		CEV	F-ZVMQ
387 / MR	CASA 212 Aviocar srs 300	A12-04-387		CEV	F-ZVMR
388 / MS	CASA 212 Aviocar srs 300	A12-05-388		CEV	F-ZVMS
0242 / AB	Cessna 310K	310K0242	F-BOEJ	CEV	
0244 / AX	Cessna 310K	310K0244	F-BOEX	CEV	
045 / AU	Cessna 310L	310L0045	F-BOJR	CEV	
046 / AV	Cessna 310L	310L0046	F-BOJS	CEV	

0185 / AC	Cessna 310N	310N0185	F-BPUM	CEV	
0187 / BJ	Cessna 310N	310N0187	F-BPUQ	CEV	
0188 / BK	Cessna 310N	310N0188	F-BPUR	CEV	
0190 / BL	Cessna 310N	310N0190	F-BPUS	CEV	
0192 / BM	Cessna 310N	310N0192	F-BPUT	CEV	
0193 / BG	Cessna 310N	310N0193	F-BPUN	CEV	
0194 / BH	Cessna 310N	310N0194	F-BPUO	CEV	
0513 / BE	Cessna 310Q	310Q0513		CEV	
0693 / BI	Cessna 310Q	310Q0693		CEV	
0820 / CL	Cessna 310Q	310Q0820		CEV	
0981 / BF	Cessna 310R	310R0981		CEV	
185 / AC	Cessna 411	411-0185/F001	F-RAFY	CEV	
248 / AB	Cessna 411	411-0248/F002		CEV	
250 / AD	Cessna 411	411-0250/F006		CEV	
F008 / AE	Cessna 411	F008	F-ZARC	CEV	
22 / CS	Dassault Falcon 20C	22/404	F-BMKK	CEV	F-ZACS
79 / CT	Dassault Falcon 20C	79/415		CEV	F-ZACT
86 / CG	Dassault Falcon 20C	86		CEV	F-ZACG
96 / CB	Dassault Falcon 20C	96		CEV	F-ZACB
104 / CW	Dassault Falcon 20C	104	F-BOXV	CEV	F-ZACW
124 / CC	Dassault Falcon 20C	124/433	F-WJMJ	CEV	F-ZACC
131 / CD	Dassault Falcon 20C	131/437	F-WJMD	CEV	F-ZACD
138 / CR	Dassault Falcon 20C	138/440	F-BUIC	CEV	F-ZACR
145 / CU	Dassault Falcon 20C	145/443	F-GCGY	CEV	F-ZACU
188 / CX	Dassault Falcon 20C	188/464	F-BRPK	CEV	F-ZACX
252 / CA	Dassault Falcon 20E	252/485	I-GIAZ	CEV	F-ZACA
263 / CY	Dassault Falcon 20E	263/489	F-BSBU	CEV	F-ZACY
288 / CV	Dassault Falcon 20E	288/499	F-BUYE	CEV	F-ZACV
375 / CZ	Dassault Falcon 20F	375/547	F-GBMD	CEV	F-ZACZ
46043	Douglas DC-8-72F	46043 / 443	OH-LFV	CEV	F-ZWMT
68 / NB	Morane Saulnier 760 Paris 2R	068	C41-2927 (FAB)	CEV	F-ZJNB
113 / NI	Morane Saulnier 760 Paris	113		CEV	F-ZJNI
114 / NJ	Morane Saulnier 760 Paris	114		CEV	F-ZJNJ
115 / OV	Morane Saulnier 760 Paris	115		CEV	F-ZJOV
116 / ON	Morane Saulnier 760 Paris	116		CEV	F-ZJON
117 / AZ	Morane Saulnier 760 Paris	117		CEV	F-ZJAZ
118 / NQ	Morane Saulnier 760 Paris	118		CEV	F-ZJNQ
119 / NL	Morane Saulnier 760 Paris	119		CEV	F-ZLNL
55 / MH	Nord 262A-40 Frégate	55		CEV	F-ZVMH
58 / MJ	Nord 262A-41 Frégate	58		EPNER	F-ZVMJ
67 / MI	Nord 262A-41 Frégate	67		CEV	F-ZVMI
62 / GU	Reims/Cessna FTB337G Turbo Skymaster	FTB33700062		CEV	
106 / MN	SOCATA TBM-700	106		CEV	F-ZVMN
R49 / 59-MU	Transall/MBB C-160R	F49	F-BUFR	CEV	F-RAMU

Douanes Françaises
French Customs Service

ICAO code FDO, callsign French Custom

UNITS/BASES	Brigade de Surveillance Aéroterrestre		C210, Titan, C310R
	Brigade de Surveillance Aéromaritime		Caravan II, Titan
	Hyères-Le Palyvestre		

F-ZBAB	Reims/Cessna F406 Caravan II Vigilant	F406-0025	F-GEUL
F-ZBEB	Reims/Cessna F406 Caravan II Vigilant	F406-0039	F-WZDS
F-ZBEZ	Cessna 404 Titan	404-0054	F-GAJX
F-ZBCE	Reims/Cessna F406 Caravan II Vigilant	F406-0042	F-GKRA
F-ZBCF	Reims/Cessna F406 Caravan II SurMar	F406-0077	F-WZDZ
F-ZBCG	Reims/Cessna F406 Caravan II PolMar II	F406-0066	F-WZDT
F-ZBCH	Reims/Cessna F406 Caravan II SurMar	F406-0075	
F-ZBCI	Reims/Cessna F406 Caravan II Vigilant	F406-0070	
F-ZBCJ	Reims/Cessna F406 Caravan II SurMar	F406-0074	F-WZDJ
F-ZBDW	Cessna 404 Titan	404-0640	F-BIPJ
F-ZBDX	Cessna 404 Titan	404-0692	F-GCQM
F-ZBDZ	Cessna 310R-II	310R0569	F-GAJI
F-ZBEP	Reims/Cessna F406 Caravan II Vigilant	F406-0006	
F-ZBER	Cessna 404 Titan	404-0608	F-GAMZ
F-ZBES	Reims/Cessna F406 Caravan II Vigilant	F406-0017	
F-ZBFA	Reims/Cessna F406 Caravan II PolMar I	F406-0001	F-GGRA
F-ZBGA	Reims/Cessna F406 Caravan II SurMar	F406-0086	F-WWSR

Securité Civile

UNITS/BASES   All fixed wing aircraft are based at Marseille-Marignane with the Groupement Moyens Aériens.

PLANS   All CL-215s are stored pending disposal.

F-ZBAA / 22	Conair Turbo-Firecat	456/027	F-WEOL	Tanker	cvtd US-2B Tracker
F-ZBAP / 12	Conair Turbo-Firecat	567/026	F-ZBDA	Tanker	cvtd US-2B Tracker
F-ZBAR / 21	Canadair CL-215 1A-10	1021		Tanker	Std Marseille-Marignane
F-ZBAU / 02	Conair Turbo-Firecat	09/DHC-32	F-WZLQ	Tanker	
F-ZBAY / 23	Canadair CL-215 1A-10	1023		Tanker	Std Marseille-Marignane
F-ZBAZ / 01	Conair Turbo-Firecat	08/DHC-57	F-WEOL	Tanker	
F-ZBBD / 29	Canadair CL-215 1A-10	1029		Tanker	
F-ZBBE / 5	Canadair CL-215 1A-10	1005	CF-YWN	Tanker	Std Marseille-Marignane
F-ZBBH / 26	Canadair CL-215 1A-10	1026		Tanker	Std Marseille-Marignane
F-ZBBJ / 28	Canadair CL-215 1A-10	1028		Tanker	Std Marseille-Marignane
F-ZBBL / 19	Conair Turbo-Firecat	626/024	F-WEOK	Tanker	cvtd US-2B Tracker
F-ZBBV / 46	Canadair CL-215	1046	C-GAOS	Tanker	Std Marseille-Marignane
F-ZBBW / 47	Canadair CL-215	1047		Tanker	Std Marseille-Marignane
F-ZBCZ / 23	Conair Turbo-Firecat	036/DHC-94	F-ZBCA	Tanker	
F-ZBDD / 24	Canadair CL-215 1A-10	1024		Tanker	Std Marseille-Marignane
F-ZBEG / 39	Bombardier Canadair CL-415	2015	C-FXBH	Tanker	
F-ZBEH / 20	Conair Turbo-Firecat	410/035	F-WEOJ	Tanker	
F-ZBEO / 36	Bombardier Canadair CL-415	2011	C-FWPD	Tanker	
F-ZBET / 15	Conair Turbo-Firecat	710/028	F-WEOJ	Tanker	
F-ZBEU / 42	Bombardier Canadair CL-415	2024	C-FZDE	Tanker	
F-ZBEW / 11	Conair Turbo-Firecat	621/025	F-WEOL	Tanker	
F-ZBEY / 07	Conair Turbo-Firecat	400/017	F-WEOK	Tanker	
F-ZBEZ / 41	Bombardier Canadair CL-415	2018	C-FXBX	Tanker	
F-ZBFE / 17	Conair Turbo-Firecat	656/032	F-WEOK	Tanker	
F-ZBFF / 71	Conair Firefighter (F-27-600)	10432/003	C-FGDS	Tanker	
F-ZBFG / 72	Conair Firefighter (F-27-600)	10440/002	C-FBDY	Tanker	
F-ZBFJ / 98	Beech Super King Air B200	BB-1102	D-IWAN	Logistic	
F-ZBFK / 97	Beech Super King Air B200	BB-876	F-GHSC	Logistic	
F-ZBFN / 33	Bombardier Canadair CL-415	2006	C-FVUK	Tanker	
F-ZBFP / 31	Bombardier Canadair CL-415	2002	C-FBET	Tanker	
F-ZBFS / 32	Bombardier Canadair CL-415	2001	C-GSCT	Tanker	
F-ZBFV / 37	Bombardier Canadair CL-415	2013	C-FWPE	Tanker	
F-ZBFW / 38	Bombardier Canadair CL-415	2014	C-FWZH	Tanker	
F-ZBFX / 34	Bombardier Canadair CL-415	2007	C-FVUJ	Tanker	
F-ZBFY / 35	Bombardier Canadair CL-415	2010	C-FVDY	Tanker	
F-ZBMA / 24	Conair Turbo-Firecat	461/021	C-GFZG	Tanker	
F-ZBMB / 97	Beech Super King Air B200	BB-1379	F-GJFD	Logistic	
	Conair Turbo-Firecat	DHC-58	C-FLRA	Tanker	on order

GABON
République Gabonaise   W Africa

Originally part of French Equatorial Africa until independence in 1960, Gabon has developed better than most of its neighbours in terms of manufacturing and infrastructure. Dependent on France for defence support through an agreement, the armed forces are primarily transport and patrol orientated.

SERIAL SYSTEM   Civil style registrations are allocated, AF aircraft receiving marks in the TR-K** batch.

Force Aérienne Gabonaise
Gabonese Air Force

UNITS/BASES   All transports are based at Libreville-Leon M'Ba Airport.

TR-KDA	Cessna 337D Super Skymaster	33701132	N86260	
TR-KJC	Nord 262C-62 Frégate	97		
TR-KJE	Airtech/CASA CN235-100	C044		
TR-KKC	Lockheed C-130H (L-382C-79D) Hercules	4765		
TR-KKD	Lockheed C-130H-30 (L-382G-56C) Hercules	4895		
TR-KNA	Embraer EMB-110P1K Bandeirante	110268	TR-KMA	
TR-KNB	Embraer EMB-110P1K Bandeirante	110297	TR-KMB	
TR-KNC	Embraer EMB-111A Bandeirante	110360		MR

La Garde Présidentielle
Presidential Guard

TR-KJD	ATR-42F-300	131	F-WWEB

Government of the Republic of Gabon

TR-KSP	GAC Gulfstream IV-SP	1327	(TR-KHD)	
TR-LEX	Dassault Falcon 900EX	24	F-WWFU	
TR-LSB	Piper PA-31-350 Navajo Chieftain	31-7405141	N74993	
TR-LTZ	Douglas DC-8-73F (CF)	46053 / 446	N8638	Cvtd 63F, 'Franceville'

GEORGIA
Sakartvelos Respublikis   SW Asia

What equipment this CIS Republic has is what was left by the Soviets when they departed in 1991. Internal ethnic divisions arose during the mid 1990s and although no recent fighting has taken place the territories of Adjaria and Abkhazia are still seeking independence. US aid, initially in the form of UH-1 helicopters, was promised in 1999. No fixed wing transports are flown by the Air Force, although civil aircraft are drawn on when required.

SERIAL SYSTEM Government aircraft bear the civil registration prefix.

Government of the Republic of Georgia

4L-65993	Tupolev Tu-134A	63860	RA-65993	VIP

GERMANY
Bundesrepublik Deutschland   C Europe

Reunification in 1990 of the two German states partitioned in 1945 was greeted enthusiastically by the population but resulted in economic problems for the country. The East German equipment was absorbed and for the most part discarded by the Air Force with only the M G-29s now remaining. Participation in the proposed European military force is guaranteed in addition to the support of existing NATO commitments.

SERIAL SYSTEM Each type is allocated a block, the first two digits being common for the series and remaining numbers being sequential. Presentation is as two numbers either side of the national insignia, this is reflected in the listing below for clarity although the cross is not actually part of the serial.

Luftwaffe
Air Force

ICAO code GAF, callsign German Air Force.

UNITS/BASES	Lufttransportgeschwader 61 (LTG 61), 611 & 612 Staffeln, Landsberg AB	Transall	
	Lufttransportgeschwader 62 (LTG 62), 621 & 622 Staffeln, Wunsdorf AB	Transall	
	Lufttransportgeschwader 63 (LTG 63), 631 & 632 Staffeln, Hohn AB	Transall	
	Flugbereitschaftstaffel (FBS), 1 Staffel, Köln-Bonn Airport	A310, Challenger	VIP

PLANS Purchase of 75 Airbus Industrie A400M to re-equip LTG61 and LTG63, although this may be reduced to just 40. Four of the A310s are to be converted to MRTT standard for AAR operation. Privatisation of the FBS Challenger operation is being reviewed.

10+21	Airbus Industrie A310-304ET	498	D-AOAA	FBS/1st	
10+22	Airbus Industrie A310-304ET	499	D-AOAB	FBS/1st	
10+23	Airbus Industrie A310-304ET	503	D-AOAC	FBS/1st	
10+24	Airbus Industrie A310-304(F)	434	D-AIDA	FBS/1st	AAR
10+25	Airbus Industrie A310-304(F)	484	D-AIDB	FBS/1st	AAR
10+26	Airbus Industrie A310-304(F)	522	D-AIDE	FBS/1st	AAR
10+27	Airbus Industrie A310-304(F)	523	D-AIDI	FBS/1st	AAR
12+02	Canadair CL-601-1A Challenger	3040	N608CL	FBS/1st	
12+03	Canadair CL-601-1A Challenger	3043	N609CL	FBS/1st	
12+04	Canadair CL-601-1A Challenger	3049	N610CL	FBS/1st	
12+05	Canadair CL-601-1A Challenger	3053	N604CL	FBS/1st	
12+06	Canadair CL-601-1A Challenger	3056	N612CL	FBS/1st	
12+07	Canadair CL-601-1A Challenger	3059	N614CL	FBS/1st	
50+06	Transall/Nord C-160D	D6		LTG 61	
50+07	Transall/VFW C-160D	D7	KM+102	LTG 61	
50+08	Transall/Nord C-160D	D8		LTG 63	

50+09	Transall/Nord C-160D	D9		LTG 62
50+10	Transall/VFW C-160D	D10	KM+103	LTG 62
50+33	Transall/VFW C-160D	D41		LTG 62
50+34	Transall/MBB C-160D	D56		LTG 63
50+35	Transall/VFW C-160D	D57		LTG 62
50+36	Transall/MBB C-160D	D58		LTG 62
50+37	Transall/VFW C-160D	D59		LTG 62
50+38	Transall/MBB C-160D	D60	PK-PTA	LTG 62
50+40	Transall/VFW C-160D	D62		LTG 61
50+41	Transall/VFW C-160D	D63		LTG 62
50+42	Transall/VFW C-160D	D64		LTG 63
50+43	Transall/MBB C-160D	D65		LTG 61
50+44	Transall/MBB C-160D	D66		LTG 62
50+45	Transall/MBB C-160D	D67		LTG 63
50+46	Transall/VFW C-160D	D68		LTG 62
50+47	Transall/MBB C-160D	D69		LTG 61
50+48	Transall/VFW C-160D	D70		LTG 61
50+49	Transall/VFW C-160D	D71		LTG 63
50+50	Transall/MBB C-160D	D72		LTG 62
50+51	Transall/VFW C-160D	D73		LTG 61
50+52	Transall/MBB C-160D	D74		LTG 62
50+53	Transall/VFW C-160D	D75		LTG 61
50+54	Transall/MBB C-160D	D76		LTG 63
50+55	Transall/VFW C-160D	D77		LTG 62
50+56	Transall/MBB C-160D	D78		LTG 63
50+58	Transall/MBB C-160D	D80		LTG 62
50+59	Transall/VFW C-160D	D81		LTG 63
50+60	Transall/MBB C-160D	D82		LTG 62
50+61	Transall/Nord C-160D	D83		LTG 63
50+62	Transall/Nord C-160D	D84		LTG 62
50+64	Transall/MBB C-160D	D101		LTG 61
50+65	Transall/Nord C-160D	D102		LTG 62
50+66	Transall/VFW C-160D	D103		LTG 61
50+67	Transall/MBB C-160D	D104	PK-PTC	LTG 63
50+68	Transall/Nord C-160D	D105		LTG 61
50+69	Transall/VFW C-160D	D106		LTG 63
50+70	Transall/MBB C-160D	D107		LTG 63
50+71	Transall/Nord C-160D	D108		LTG 63
50+72	Transall/VFW C-160D	D109		LTG 63
50+73	Transall/MBB C-160D	D110		LTG 63
50+74	Transall/Nord C-160D	D111		LTG 61
50+75	Transall/VFW C-160D	D112		LTG 63
50+76	Transall/MBB C-160D	D113		LTG 63
50+77	Transall/Nord C-160D	D114		LTG 63
50+78	Transall/VFW C-160D	D115		LTG 62
50+79	Transall/MBB C-160D	D116		LTG 63
50+81	Transall/VFW C-160D	D118		LTG 62
50+82	Transall/MBB C-160D	D119		LTG 63
50+83	Transall/Nord C-160D	D120		LTG 62
50+84	Transall/VFW C-160D	D121		LTG 61
50+85	Transall/MBB C-160D	D122		LTG 63
50+86	Transall/Nord C-160D	D123		LTG 61
50+87	Transall/VFW C-160D	D124		LTG 63
50+88	Transall/MBB C-160D	D125		LTG 61
50+89	Transall/Nord C-160D	D126		LTG 62
50+90	Transall/VFW C-160D	D127		LTG 62
50+91	Transall/MBB C-160D	D128		LTG 62
50+92	Transall/Nord C-160D	D129	D-ACTR	LTG 61
50+93	Transall/VFW C-160D	D130		LTG 61
50+94	Transall/MBB C-160D	D131		LTG 63
50+95	Transall/Nord C-160D	D132		LTG 63
50+96	Transall/VFW C-160D	D133		LTG 61
50+97	Transall/MBB C-160D	D134		LTG 62
50+98	Transall/Nord C-160D	D135		LTG 61
50+99	Transall/VFW C-160D	D136		LTG 61
51+00	Transall/MBB C-160D	D137		LTG 62
51+01	Transall/Nord C-160D	D138		LTG 62
51+02	Transall/VFW C-160D	D139		LTG 63
51+03	Transall/MBB C-160D	D140		LTG 62
51+04	Transall/Nord C-160D	D141		LTG 61
51+05	Transall/VFW C-160D	D142		LTG 62
51+06	Transall/MBB C-160D	D143		LTG 63
51+07	Transall/Nord C-160D	D144		LTG 62
51+09	Transall/MBB C-160D	D146		LTG 63

51– 0	Transall/Nord C-160D	D147		LTG 61
51– 1	Transall/VFW C-160D	D148		LTG 62
51– 2	Transall/MBB C-160D	D149	D-AMBV	LTG 63
51– 3	Transall/Nord C-160D	D150		LTG 61
51– 4	Transall/VFW C-160D	D151		LTG 63
51– 5	Transall/MBB C-160D	D152		LTG 61

Bundesmarine - Marineflieger
Federal Navy - Naval Aviation

ICAO code GNY, callsign German Navy

UNITS/BASES   Marinefliegergeschwader 3, 1 & 2 Staffel, Nordholz   Atlantic, Do228

PLANS   The Atlantics are being upgraded to keep them in service until at least 2010.

61+01	Breguet 1151 Atlantic	2			GIA Manching
61+02	Breguet 1151 Atlantic	4		MFG-3	ELINT
61+03	Breguet 1151 Atlantic	6		MFG-3	ELINT
61+04	Breguet 1151 Atlantic	8		MFG-3	
61+05	Breguet 1151 Atlantic	10		MFG-3	
61+06	Breguet 1151 Atlantic	12		MFG-3	ELINT
61+08	Breguet 1151 Atlantic	14		MFG-3	
61+09	Breguet 1151 Atlantic	16		MFG-3	
61+10	Breguet 1151 Atlantic	18		MFG-3	
61+11	Breguet 1151 Atlantic	20		MFG-3	
61+12	Breguet 1151 Atlantic	22		MFG-3	
61+13	Breguet 1151 Atlantic	24		MFG-3	
61+14	Breguet 1151 Atlantic	26		MFG-3	
61+15	Breguet 1151 Atlantic	28		MFG-3	
61+16	Breguet 1151 Atlantic	30		MFG-3	
61+17	Breguet 1151 Atlantic	32		MFG-3	
61+19	Breguet 1151 Atlantic	59		MFG-3	ELINT
61+20	Breguet 1151 Atlantic	60		MFG-3	ELINT
57+01	Dornier 228-212LM	8185	98+77	MFG-3	
57+02	Dornier 228-212LM	8211	D-CBDX	MFG-3	
57+03	Dornier 228-212	8212		MFG-3	
57+04	Dornier 228-212LM	8214		MFG-3	

Ministry of Defence

UNITS/BASES	Wehrtechnische Dienstelle für Luftfahrzeuge 61 (WTD61), Manching			Transall	Support for test ops
	Civilian Contractors: Gesellschaft für Flugzieldarsellung GmbH, Hohn			Learjet	Target Duties
	Civilian Contractors: Holstenair, Lübeck-Blankensee			Westwind	Target Duties

50+57	Transall/VFW C-160D	D79		WTD 61	
51+08	Transall/VFW C-160D	D145		WTD 61	
98+78	Dornier 228-200	8068	D-CENT	WTD 61	
D-CGFA	Learjet 35A	35A-179	N801PF	GFD	TT
D-CGFB	Learjet 35A	35A-268	N2U	GFD	TT
D-CGFC	Learjet 35A	35A-331	N435JW	GFD	TT
D-CGFD	Learjet 35A	35A-139	N15SC	GFD	TT
D-CGFE	Learjet 36A	36A-062	N4291N	GFD	TT
D-CGFF	Learjet 36A	36A-063	N1048X	GFD	TT
D-CHAL	IAI 1124 Westwind	207	N666K	Holstenair	TT
D-CHBL	IAI 1124 Westwind	226	N120S	Holstenair	TT
D-CHCL	IAI 1124 Westwind I	277	N504JC	Holstenair	TT
D-CHDL	IAI 1124 Westwind	199	N999MS	Holstenair	TT

GHANA
Republic of Ghana   W Africa

The Air Force was established quickly after independence from Britain in 1957, the country formerly being known as the Gold Coast. Initial equipment and support came from India, Israel and the UK. The mainly transport orientated air arm has operated in support of the UN and Organisation for African Unity.

SERIAL SYSTEM Each type is allocated a three digit batch, this is prefixed with the letter G (no dash) and displayed usually with a single letter code.

Ghana Air Force

UNITS/BASES 1 Sqn, Takoradi, det. at Accra with Defenders   Skyvan, Defender
               2 Sqn, Accra   F.27, F.28
               Transport Sqn, Accra   Gulfstream

G360	Pilatus Britten-Norman BN-2T Defender	2225	G-BRSR	1 Sqn	Camo cs
G361	Pilatus Britten-Norman BN-2T Defender	2222	G-BRPB	1 Sqn	
G362	Pilatus Britten-Norman BN-2T Defender	2223	G-BRPC	1 Sqn	
G363	Pilatus Britten-Norman BN-2T Defender	2229	G-BRSV	1 Sqn	
G450	Shorts SC.7 Skyvan srs 3M-400	SH.1930	G-BCFI	1 Sqn	
G451	Shorts SC.7 Skyvan srs 3M-400	SH.1928	G-BCFG	1 Sqn	
G452	Shorts SC.7 Skyvan srs 3M-400	SH.1929	G-BCFH	1 Sqn	
G453	Shorts SC.7 Skyvan srs 3M-400	SH.1931	G-BCFJ	1 Sqn	
G454 / E	Shorts SC.7 Skyvan srs 3M-400	SH.1932	G-BCFK	1 Sqn	White cs '9G-VRB'
G455 / F	Shorts SC.7 Skyvan srs 3M-400	SH.1933	G-BCFL	1 Sqn	Camo cs
G520 / A	Fokker F.27 Friendship 600	10505	PH-FRF	2 Sqn	White cs
G521 / B	Fokker F.27 Troopship 400M	10507	PH-FRE	2 Sqn	Camo cs
G522 / C	Fokker F.27 Troopship 400M	10518	PH-FRH	2 Sqn	Camo cs, Std
G525 / F	Fokker F.27 Troopship 400M	10520	G-523/D	2 Sqn	White cs
G530	Fokker F.28 Fellowship 3000	11125	PH-EXP	2 Sqn	Gvmt use
G540	GAC G-1159A Gulfstream III	493	N40QJ		VIP

GREECE
Elleniki Dimokratia / Hellenic Republic   SE Europe

Having joined NATO at the same time as their traditional enemy Turkey in 1952, Greece also joined the EU in 1981. Much US assistance has been received to reward Greek support for NATO's southern flank (along with Turkey). A common defence policy was agreed with (southern) Cyprus in 1993. Political tension with Turkey over the Aegean Islands and Cyprus still simmers despite joint exercise participation.

SERIAL SYSTEM No universal system is in use, only the Air Force C-130s appearing in a unique batch. Usually the serial is derived from the c/n or previous identity.

Elliniki Polemiki Aeroporia
Hellenic Air Force - HAF

ICAO code HAF, callsign Hellenic Air Force.

UNITS/BASES Diikissi Aeroporikis Ipostirixis
               112 Pteriga Mahis, Elefsis
                  353 Mira Naftikis Aeroporikis Sinergasias 'Triaina (Albatross)'   P-3B
                  355 Mira Taktikon Metaforon 'Ifaistos (Vulcan)'   CL-215, CL-415, Do28D
                  356 Mira Taktikon Metaforon 'Ilraklios (Hercules)'   C-130B/H, ERJ-145, YS-11
                  380 Mira Aeroporiko Systima Enaeriou & Epitirsis   Saab 340AEW

               Taktiki Aeroporikis Dynamis
               113 Pteriga Machis, Thessaloniki-Mikra
                  356 Mira Taktikon Metaforon, Det 1, Sedes   Skyservant
                  Det TACHQ, Larissa   Skyservant

PLANS Five Bombardier CL-415GR held on option. Reported as interested in a Boeing C-17 purchase.
         Four Embraer ERJ-145 AEW airframes with Ericsson Erieye radar are on order, 2 RSwAF Saab 340 are being leased pending delivery.
         Being offered six C-27Js as a YS-11 replacement, with lease of ex AMI C-130/G222s to cover before delivery.
         Two ex AMI C-130Hs are reported to have been acquired through Lockheed Martin, although one was though DBR in AMI service.

2039	Bombardier Canadair CL-415GR	2039	C-GELJ	355 Mira	
2041	Bombardier Canadair CL-415GR	2041			on order

2042	Bombardier Canadair CL-415GR	2042	C-GFBX	355 Mira	
2044	Bombardier Canadair CL-415GR	2044	C-GFOJ	355 Mira	
2049	Bombardier Canadair CL-415GR	2049	C-GGIF	355 Mira	
2050	Bombardier Canadair CL-415GR	2050		355 Mira	
2052	Bombardier Canadair CL-415GR	2052	C-GHMP	355 Mira	
2053	Bombardier Canadair CL-415GR	2053		355 Mira	
2054	Bombardier Canadair CL-415GR	2054		355 Mira	
	Bombardier Canadair CL-415GR				on order
1039	Canadair CL-215	1039		355 Mira	
1041	Canadair CL-215	1041	C-GAJN	355 Mira	
1045	Canadair CL-215	1045	C-GUMW	355 Mira	
1055	Canadair CL-215	1055		355 Mira	
1060	Canadair CL-215	1060	C-GUMW	355 Mira	
1064	Canadair CL-215	1064		355 Mira	
1067	Canadair CL-215	1067	YU-BRE	355 Mira	
1069	Canadair CL-215	1069	YU-BRF	355 Mira	
1070	Canadair CL-215	1070	YU-BRG	355 Mira	
1073	Canadair CL-215	1073	C-GKDT	355 Mira	
1075	Canadair CL-215	1075	C-GKDT	355 Mira	
1110	Canadair CL-215	1110	YU-BRH	355 Mira	
1111	Canadair CL-215	1111	C-GKEA	355 Mira	
1112	Canadair CL-215	1112	C-GKON	355 Mira	
1123	Canadair CL-215	1123	C-GKEV	355 Mira	
4082	Dornier 28D-2 Skyservant	4082	58+07 (WGAF)	355 Mira	Std Elefsis
4086	Dornier 28D-2 Skyservant	4086	58+11 (WGAF)	355 Mira	
4087	Dornier 28D-2 Skyservant	4087	58+12 (WGAF)	355 Mira	
4094	Dornier 28D-2 Skyservant	4094	58+19 (WGAF)	355 Mira	Std Elefsis
4097	Dornier 28D-2 Skyservant	4097	58+22 (WGAF)	355 Mira	Std Elefsis
4100	Dornier 28D-2 Skyservant	4100	58+25 (WGAF)	355 Mira	Std Elefsis
4102	Dornier 28D-2 Skyservant	4102	58+27 (WGAF)	355 Mira	Std Elefsis
4108	Dornier 28D-2 Skyservant	4108	58+33 (WGAF)	355 Mira	Std Elefsis
4110	Dornier 28D-2 Skyservant	4110	58+35 (WGAF)	355 Mira	Std Elefsis
4117	Dornier 28D-2 Skyservant	4117	58+42 (WGAF)	355 Mira	
4120	Dornier 28D-2 Skyservant	4120	58+45 (WGAF)	355 Mira	Std Elefsis
4123	Dornier 28D-2 Skyservant	4123	58+48 (WGAF)	355 Mira	
4131	Dornier 28D-2 Skyservant	4131	58+56 (WGAF)	355 Mira	Std Elefsis
4138	Dornier 28D-2 Skyservant	4138	58+63 (WGAF)	355 Mira	Std Elefsis
4166	Dornier 28D-2 Skyservant	4166	58+91 (WGAF)	355 Mira	Std Elefsis
209	Embraer EMB-135LR	145209	PT-SFX	VIP Flt	
374	Embraer EMB-135LR	145374			
0296	Lockheed C-130B (L-282-1B) Hercules	3597	60-0296 (USAF)	356 Mira	Std Elefsis
0300	Lockheed C-130B (L-282-1B) Hercules	3604	60-0300 (USAF)	356 Mira	Std
303	Lockheed C-130B (L-282-1B) Hercules	3613	60-0303 (USAF)	356 Mira	
948	Lockheed C-130B (L-282-1B) Hercules	3624	61-0948 (USAF)	356 Mira	Std Elefsis
723	Lockheed C-130B (L-282-1B) Hercules	3518	58-0723 (USAF)	356 Mira	Std Elefsis
741	Lockheed C-130H (L-382C-54D) Hercules	4622		356 Mira	ECM
742	Lockheed C-130H (L-382C-54D) Hercules	4632		356 Mira	
743	Lockheed C-130H (L-382C-54D) Hercules	4665		356 Mira	
744	Lockheed C-130H (L-382C-54D) Hercules	4672		356 Mira	
745	Lockheed C-130H (L-382C-59D) Hercules	4716	75-0542 (FMS)	356 Mira	
746	Lockheed C-130H (L-382C-59D) Hercules	4720	75-0543 (FMS)	356 Mira	
747	Lockheed C-130H (L-382C-59D) Hercules	4723	75-0544 (FMS)	356 Mira	
749	Lockheed C-130H (L-382C-59D) Hercules	4727	75-0546 (FMS)	356 Mira	
751	Lockheed C-130H (L-382C-59D) Hercules	4732	75-0548 (FMS)	356 Mira	
752	Lockheed C-130H (L-382C-59D) Hercules	4734	75-0549 (FMS)	356 Mira	
	Lockheed C-130H (L-382C-22D) Hercules	4495	MM61999 (AMI)	356 Mira	
	Lockheed C-130H (L-382C-22D) Hercules	4498	MM62001 (AMI)	356 Mira	
152181	Lockheed P-3A (L-185) Orion	5151	Bu152181 (USN)		Std Tanagra (Spares use)
152183	Lockheed P-3A (L-185) Orion	5153	Bu152183 (USN)		Std Elefsis (Spares use)
744	Lockheed P-3B LW (L-185) Orion	5184	Bu152744 (USN)	353 Mira	
747	Lockheed P-3B LW (L-185) Orion	5187	Bu152747 (USN)	353 Mira	
415	Lockheed P-3B LW (L-185) Orion	5212	Bu153415 (USN)	353 Mira	
424	Lockheed P-3B LW (L-185) Orion	5221	Bu153424 (USN)	353 Mira	
427	Lockheed P-3B LW (L-185) Orion	5224	Bu153427 (USN)	353 Mira	
441	Lockheed P-3B LW (L-185) Orion	5238	Bu153441 (USN)	353 Mira	
151366	Lockheed UP-3A (L-185) Orion	5079	Bu151366 (USN)		Std Tanagra (Spares use)
151389	Lockheed UP-3A (L-185) Orion	5102	Bu151389 (USN)		Std Tanagra (Spares use)
2136	NAMC YS-11A-520	2136	SX-BBG	355 Mira	Std Elefsis
2137	NAMC YS-11A-520	2137	SX-BBH	355 Mira	Std Elefsis
2143	NAMC YS-11A-520	2143	SX-BBI	355 Mira	Std Elefsis
2145	NAMC YS-11A-520	2145	SX-BBL	355 Mira	Std Elefsis
2153	NAMC YS-11A-520	2153	SX-BBP	355 Mira	Std Elefsis
100004 / 004	Saab 340B Argus (S100B)	340B-395	100004 (RSwAF)	380 Mira	AEW&C
	Saab 340B Argus (S100B)		(RSwAF)	380 Mira	on order, AEW&C

Elliniki Aeroporia Stratou
Hellenic Army Aviation - HAA

UNITS/BASES	4 TEAS, Pahi AB, Megara, Attiki		C-12C	
PLANS	Two Raytheon C-12R/AP survey aircraft due for delivery from 2001.			
401	Beech C-12C (Super King Air 200)	BC-34	4 TEAS	
	Raytheon Beech C-12R/AP (Super King Air 200)			Survey, for del 2001
	Raytheon Beech C-12R/AP (Super King Air 200)			Survey, for del 2002

Liminiki Astonomia
Hellenic Coast Guard

UNITS/BASES	All aircraft are based at Dekelia.				
AC-21	Reims/Cessna F406 Caravan II SurPolMar	F406-0087	F-GJJK		
AC-22	Reims/Cessna F406 Caravan II SurPolMar	F406-0088	F-GJJN		On order
AC-23	Reims/Cessna F406 Caravan II SurPolMar	F406-0089	F-GJJO		On order

Government of the Hellenic Republic

UNITS/BASES	Based at Athens-Spata Airport with Olympic Airways.				
SX-ECH	Dassault Falcon 900	26	HB-IAC		'King Minos'
					Std/Dam Geneva

GUATEMALA
República de Guatemala   C America

A US arms embargo was lifted in 1983 which meant that some rebuilding of the guerrilla war strained Air Force was possible, most notably with the Turbo Dakotas. Full support remains hard to fund however and re-equipment in the immediate future seems unlikely.

SERIAL SYSTEM The first digit of the three digit serial denotes the type, the remaining numbers being sequenced through the batch. Some aircraft including the Presidential transports remain civil registered.

Fuerza Aérea Guatemalteca
Guatemalan Air Force

UNITS/BASES	5 Escuadron de Transporte, BA La Aurora-Guatemala City			BT-67	
	8 Escuadron de Transporte, BA La Aurora-Guatemala City			Arava	
	Escuadron de Enlace, BA La Aurora-Guatemala City			C206, C210, PA-31	
	Grupo Presidencial, BA La Aurora-Guatemala City			Super King Air	
018	Piper PA-31 Navajo			EdE	confiscated drug runner
30	Cessna 206		HK-	EdE	confiscated drug runner
31	Cessna 206		HK-	EdE	confiscated drug runner
050	Cessna T210 Turbo Centurion			EdE	confiscated drug runner
060	Cessna T210 Turbo Centurion			EdE	confiscated drug runner
065	Cessna T210 Turbo Centurion			EdE	confiscated drug runner
080	Colemill Panther Navajo			EdE	Cvtd PA-31
530	Basler BT-67 Turbo Dakota	20031	43-15565	5 Esc	Cvtd C-47A
555	Basler BT-67 Turbo Dakota	16751/33499	44-77167	5 Esc	Cvtd C-47
560	Basler BT-67 Turbo Dakota	17131/34398	45-1128	5 Esc	Cvtd C-47
575	Basler BT-67 Turbo Dakota	19674	N62102	5 Esc	Cvtd C-47
580	Basler BT-67 Turbo Dakota	9100	N510NR		Std La Aurora
590	Basler BT-67 Turbo Dakota	16794/33542	N29R	5 Esc	Cvtd C-47
848	IAI Arava srs 201	0033	4X-IBF	8 Esc	
864	IAI Arava srs 201	0045	4X-IBR	8 Esc	
880	IAI Arava srs 201	0048	4X-IBU	8 Esc	
897	IAI Arava srs 101A	0004	4X-IAB		Std La Aurora
1467	Fokker F.27 Troopship 400M	10270	TG-ACA		
1770	Fokker F.27 Troopship 400M	10493	1470 (FAG)		Std La Aurora
TG-CFA	Beech King Air F90	LA-181	HK-2888	Gr. Presidencial	
					confiscated drug runner
TG-FAC	Cessna U206G Stationair 6	U20606522	N9484Z	EdE	
TG-FAD	Cessna U206G Stationair 6	U20606732	(N9896Z)		Std La Aurora
TG-MAR	Cessna T210M Turbo Centurion	21061609	N732LZ		Std La Aurora
TG-MDN	Beech Super King Air 300	FA-105	HK-3628	Gr. Presidencial	
TG-PES	Cessna T210N Turbo Centurion	21063717	N5211C		

GUINEA
République de Guinée   W Africa

Shortly after independence from France in 1958, support was accepted from the Soviet Union in return for provision of a staging post for their MR and transport aircraft. Despite recent helicopter acquisitions from France the serviceability of the transport and combat elements of the air arm must by now be stretched.

Force Aérienne de Guinée
Guinea Air Force

UNITS/BASES   The transport squadron operates from Conakry-Gbessia Airport.

3X-GEA	Antonov An-12B	02348008	Opb Air Guinée
3X-GEB	Antonov An-12B	02348009	Opb Air Guinée
3X-GEC	Antonov An-12BP	7345001	Opb Air Guinée
3X-GED	Antonov An-12BP	7345002	Opb Air Guinée

GUINEA-BISSAU
República da Guiné-Bissau   W Africa

Known as Portuguese Guinea until independence in 1974 after a prolonged civil war ended as a result of a change of power in Portugal. The Force Aerienne de Guinea-Bissau was primarily set up with Soviet help in 1978 although some French equipment is now also operated. Transports were shared with the National Airline Air Bissau (formerly TAGB), but it is not currently trading.

SERIAL SYSTEM Civil registrations are issued using the standard 'J5-' prefix.

Guinea Bissau Coast Guard

J5-GAE	Reims Cessna FTB337G Milirole	FTB33700060	04-AV-P

GUYANA
Co-operative Republic of Guyana   S America

As the former colony of British Guiana until 1966, all the fixed wing aircraft now flown are of UK origin but are only transports with no combat capabilty. Serviceability is a problem due to spares shortage.

SERIAL SYSTEM Aircraft bear civil registrations.

Guyana Defense Force - G.D.F.

UNITS/BASES   The Air Corps operate from Timehri Airport-Georgetown.

8R-GFN	Britten-Norman BN-2A-2 Islander	289	N4249Y	WO 8Jan01?
8R-GGK	Shorts SC.7 Skyvan srs 3-100	SH.1980	8P-ASG	
8R-GRR	Shorts SC.7 Skyvan srs 3M-100	SH.1976	G-BJDA	

Government of the Co-operative Republic of Guyana

8R-GEG	Cessna U206F Stationair	U20602113	N70989	Min of Communications

HAITI
République d'Haiti   W Indies

French-speaking and occupying one third of the island of Hispaniola. After a 1994 US led invasion to restore the deposed President the armed forces were disbanded. The current status is not known and the last known equipment is detailed below.

SERIAL SYSTEM Aircraft bear a sequential four digit serial, the last allocations being in the 12** range.

Corps Aérien d'Haiti

UNITS/BASES   All aircraft were based at Bowen Field, Port-au-Prince and are presumed stored.

1251	Beech Baron B55	TH-531		
1252	Summit Sentry O2-337	33701624	N53440	Cvtd Cessna 337G
1253	Summit Sentry O2-337	33701625	N53441	Cvtd Cessna 337G

1254	Summit Sentry O2-337	33701626	N53442		Cvtd Cessna 337G
1255	Summit Sentry O2-337	33701627	N53443		Cvtd Cessna 337G
1256	Summit Sentry O2-337	33701628	N53444		Cvtd Cessna 337G
1257	Summit Sentry O2-337	33701629	N53445		Cvtd Cessna 337G
1259	Cessna 402B	402B0901	N5214J		Cvtd Cessna 337G
1275	Douglas C-47				
1278	Douglas C-47				
1283	IAI Arava 201	085	4X-CUT		
1288	Piper PA-34 Seneca				
1292	Beech King Air 90				

HONDURAS
República de Honduras — C America

Border tensions have eased recently but have led to conflicts in the past (including the 'Football War' with El Salvador). The Honduran Air Force is one of the better equipped in the region but is, like most neighbouring air forces, under-funded.

SERIAL SYSTEM Three digit serials are are allocated in blocks by aircraft role.The VIP aircraft bear civil identities.

Fuerza Aerea Hondurena - FAH
Honduran Air Force

UNITS/BASES	Base Aerea Teniente-Coronel Hernan Acosta Meija (HAM), Tegucigalpa-Toncontin				
				Various transports	
	Base Aerea Coronel Armando Escalon Espinal (AEE), San Pedro Sula-La Mesa			C401B (supporting A-37 unit)	
PLANS	Conversion of C-47 by Basler to BT-67 standard.				

006	Gulfstream 695A Jetprop 1000	96060	HK-3194X	HAM	
007	Cessna 401B			AEE	
009	Cessna 310R			HAM	
010	Piper PA-31T Cheyenne		001 (FAH)	HAM	
011	Piper PA-31-350 Navajo Chieftain			HAM	
303	Douglas C-47B	14301/25746	43-48485	HAM	
304	Douglas C-47A	12962	42-93089	HAM	
305	Douglas C-47A	19426	42-100963	HAM	VIP
306	Douglas C-47A	13642	42-93701	HAM	
308	Douglas C-47			HAM	
309	Douglas C-47			HAM	
311	Douglas C-47			HAM	
314	Douglas C-47			HAM	
319	Douglas C-47			HAM	
557	Lockheed C-130A (L-182-1A) Hercules	3030	55-0003 (USAF)		Std Toncontin
558	Lockheed C-130A (L-182-1A) Hercules	3042	55-0015 (USAF)	HAM	
560	Lockheed C-130A (L-182-1A) Hercules	3022	54-1635 (USAF)		Std Toncontin
HR-CEF	IAI 1124A Westwind II	333	HR-002		
HR-EMA	Lockheed L-188A Electra	1028	555 (FAH)		VIP
HR-JFA	Piper PA-42 Cheyenne III	42-8001056			

HONG KONG
Special Administrative Region of China — SE Asia

British colonial rule ended in July 1997 when control reverted to China. Despite fears that the change would radically alter the way that business was allowed to be conducted from this important regional hub seem to have been largely unfounded. The contract for the supply of the two uniquely configured Jetstreams was one of the last items agreed by the outgoing British administration.

Government Flying Service - GFS

| *UNITS/BASES* | Hong Kong International Airport - Chep Lap Kok. | | | | |

| B-HRS | British Aerospace 4124 Jetstream 41MPA | 41102 | G-BXWM | | MR |
| B-HRT | British Aerospace 4124 Jetstream 41MPA | 41104 | G-BXWN | | MR |

HUNGARY
Magyar Népköztársasg   C Europe

A member of NATO since 1999, Hungary has gone through major force cuts to achieve this status. An application for EU membership has also been made.

SERIAL SYSTEM The three digit serials are taken from the last three numbers of the aircraft c/n.

Magyar Honvédség Repülö Csapatai
Hungarian Air Defence Group

UNITS/BASES   89 Vegyes Szallito Repulo Dandar, 1 Szallito Repulo Szazad, Szolnok   An-26

PLANS   Looking at acquiring up to 6 ex RAF C-130K Hercules through Lockheed Martin.

203	Antonov An-26	2203		Std Szolnok
204	Antonov An-26	2204		Std Szolnok
208	Antonov An-26	2208		Std Szolnok
209	Antonov An-26	2209		Std Szolnok
403	Antonov An-26	3403	89 VSRD	
405	Antonov An-26	3405	89 VSRD	
406	Antonov An-26	3406	89 VSRD	
407	Antonov An-26	3407	89 VSRD	
603	Antonov An-26	3603	89 VSRD	

ICELAND
Lýdhveldidh Ísland   N Atlantic

In a strategically very important position and a member of NATO, Iceland has only a Coast Guard operation to enforce its fishery protection laws. Sustaining a combat force and the need for a transport element is not considered viable with a population of around 300,000. However as a NATO member its defence is assured and US military aircraft are both based and frequent visitors.

SERIAL SYSTEM Aircraft wear standard Icelandic civil registrations.

Landhelgisgaeslan
Icelandic Coast Guard

ICAO code ICG, callsign Iceland Coast

UNITS/BASES   Flight Department aircraft are based at Reykjavík Airport.

TF-SYN	Fokker F.27 Friendship 200	10545	PH-EXC	Flight Dept	SAR/VIP

INDIA
Bharatka Ganatantra   S Asia

After achieving independence from Britain in 1947 the Indian armed forces have grown into one the largest among the world's non-aligned nations. Equipment is primarily of Soviet origin or indigenous assembly as the Hindustan Aeronautics company has developed extensive capabilities. The continuing tension with Pakistan and nuclear testing may hold up future acquisitions due to embargoes, with restrictions currently in place in the UK and the USA.

SERIAL SYSTEM Air Force serial numbers are allocated sequentially and are prefixed with a one or two letter code denoting the role. The Navy and Coast Guard allocate three digit serials in blocks by type and prefix them with the air arms respective initials.

Bharatiya Vayu Sena - BVS
Indian Air Force - IAF

ICAO code IFC, callsign Indian Airforce.

UNITS/BASES   11 'Rhinos' Sqn, Gwalior   HAL-748
                  12 'Bisons' Sqn, Agra   An-32
                  25 'Himalayan Eagles' Sqn, Chandigarh   Il-76, An-32
                  41 'Otters' Sqn, Palam   Do228, HAL-748
                  43 'Ibexes' Sqn, Jorhat   An-32
                  44 'Mountain Geese' Sqn, Agra   Il-76
                  48 'Camels' Sqn, Chandigarh   An-32

49 'Para Spears' Sqn, Jorhat			An-32		
59 'Hornbills' Sqn, Gauhati			Do228		
106 'Lynxes' Sqn, Agra			HAL-748		
Air HQ Communications 'Pegasus' Sqn, New Delhi-Palam			737, HAL-748, Do228, An-32		
Aircraft and Systems Testing Establishment (ASTE), Bangalore-Yelahanka			HAL-748		
Aviation Research Centre, Research and Analysis Wing, New Delhi-Palam			An-32, 707, G-1159A		
Centre for Airborne Systems (CABS)			HAL-748		
Navigation and Signals School, Begumpet			HAL-748		
Paratroop Training School, Agra			An-32		
Transport Training Wing, Bangalore-Yelahanka			An-32, HAL-748, Do228		

PLANS   The purchase of three new Il-76TD airframes to be converted to A-50Ehl status by IAI and Beriev was reported in June 2001, delivery from 2005.
Up to six IAI Astras are reported to have been acquired for use as ELINT platforms.
Six Il-78 AAR versions are being bought from Kazakhstan.
HAL and Ilyushin are co-operating in the design of the twin jet Il-214 as a replacement for the An-32.

BH-572	Hawker Siddeley/HAL 748-103 srs 1	HAL/K/500 / 2	VT-DRF	HAL	
BH-573	Hawker Siddeley/HAL 748-104 srs 1	HAL/K/501 / 8			*'Jumbo'*
BH-574	Hawker Siddeley/HAL 748-104 srs 1	HAL/K/502 / 9			
HM-667 / K	Dornier/HAL 228-201	8081/HAL2008			
HM-668	Dornier/HAL 228-201	8082/HAL2009			
HM-669 / M	Dornier/HAL 228-201	8089/HAL2010			
HM-670	Dornier/HAL 228-201	8098/HAL2011			
HM-671 / J	Dornier/HAL 228-201	8055/HAL1007			
HM-672	Dornier/HAL 228-101	8I-3023			
HM-673 / Q	Dornier/HAL 228-101	8I-3024		TTW	
HM-674	Dornier/HAL 228-101	8I-3025			
HM-675	Dornier/HAL 228-101	8I-3026			
HM-676 / S	Dornier/HAL 228-101	8I-3027		TTW	
HM-677	Dornier/HAL 228-201	8I-4030			
HM-678	Dornier/HAL 228-201	8I-4031			
HM-679	Dornier/HAL 228-201	8I-4032			
HM-680	Dornier/HAL 228-201	8I-4033			
HM-681	Dornier/HAL 228-201	8I-4034			
HM-682	Dornier/HAL 228-201	8I-4028	VT-EQV		
HM-683	Dornier/HAL 228-201	8I-4029	VT-EQW		
HM-684	Dornier/HAL 228-201	8I-4040			
HM-685	Dornier/HAL 228-201			TTW	
HM-689 / G	Dornier/HAL 228-201				
HM-690	Dornier/HAL 228-201	81-4047			
HM-691 / H	Dornier/HAL 228-201				
H-913 / A	Hawker Siddeley/HAL 748-203 srs 2	HAL/K/510 / 51			
H-914	Hawker Siddeley/HAL 748-218 srs 2	HAL/K/516 / 78			
H-915	Hawker Siddeley/HAL 748-218 srs 2	HAL/K/517 / 79			
BH-1010	Hawker Siddeley/HAL 748-203 srs 2	HAL/K/505 / 32	VT-DTR		
BH-1011	Hawker Siddeley/HAL 748-203 srs 2	HAL/K/507 / 41			
BH-1012	Hawker Siddeley/HAL 748-203 srs 2	HAL/K/508 / 42			
BH-1013	Hawker Siddeley/HAL 748-203 srs 2	HAL/K/509 / 43			
H-1030 / A	Hawker Siddeley/HAL 748-219 srs 2	HAL/K/526 / 98			
H-1031	Hawker Siddeley/HAL 748-219 srs 2	HAL/K/527 / 99			
H-1033 / D	Hawker Siddeley/HAL 748-219 srs 2	HAL/K/529			
H-1034	Hawker Siddeley/HAL 748-219 srs 2	HAL/K/530			
BH-1047	Hawker Siddeley/HAL 748-104 srs 1	HAL/K/503 / 11			
BH-1048	Hawker Siddeley/HAL 748-203 srs 2	HAL/K/504 / 31			
H-1175	Hawker Siddeley/HAL 748-219 srs 2	HAL/K/531			
H-1176	Hawker Siddeley/HAL 748-218 srs 2	HAL/K/532			
H-1177 / E	Hawker Siddeley/HAL 748-218 srs 2	HAL/K/533			
H-1178 / F	Hawker Siddeley/HAL 748-218 srs 2	HAL/K/534			
H-1179 / I	Hawker Siddeley/HAL 748-218 srs 2	HAL/K/535			
H-1180	Hawker Siddeley/HAL 748-218 srs 2	HAL/K/536			
H-1181	Hawker Siddeley/HAL 748-218 srs 2	HAL/K/537			
H-1182	Hawker Siddeley/HAL 748-220 srs 2	HAL/K/538			
H-1386	Hawker Siddeley/HAL 748-220 srs 2	HAL/K/539			
H-1512 / J	Hawker Siddeley/HAL 748-218 srs 2	HAL/K/550			
H-1513	Hawker Siddeley/HAL 748-247 srs 2	HAL/K/551			
H-1514 / B	Hawker Siddeley/HAL 748-247 srs 2	HAL/K/552			
H-1515	Hawker Siddeley/HAL 748-247 srs 2	HAL/K/553			
H-1516 / C	Hawker Siddeley/HAL 748-247 srs 2	HAL/K/554			
H-1517	Hawker Siddeley/HAL 748-247 srs 2	HAL/K/555			
H-1518	Hawker Siddeley/HAL 748-247 srs 2	HAL/K/556			
H-1519	Hawker Siddeley/HAL 748-247 srs 2	HAL/K/557		HQ TCF	
H-1521	Hawker Siddeley/HAL 748-247 srs 2	HAL/K/559			
H-1522	Hawker Siddeley/HAL 748-247 srs 2	HAL/K/560			

H-1523	Hawker Siddeley/HAL 748-247 srs 2	HAL/K/561		
H-1524	Hawker Siddeley/HAL 748-247 srs 2	HAL/K/562		
H-1525	Hawker Siddeley/HAL 748-247 srs 2	HAL/K/563		
H-1526	Hawker Siddeley/HAL 748-247 srs 2	HAL/K/564		
H-1527	Hawker Siddeley/HAL 748-247 srs 2	HAL/K/565		
H-1528	Hawker Siddeley/HAL 748-247 srs 2	HAL/K/566		
H-1529 ' A	Hawker Siddeley/HAL 748-247 srs 2	HAL/K/567		
H-1530	Hawker Siddeley/HAL 748-247 srs 2	HAL/K/568		
H-2064	Hawker Siddeley/HAL 748-224 srs 2	HAL/K/543	(VT-EAW)	
H-2065	Hawker Siddeley/HAL 748-224 srs 2	HAL/K/544	(VT-EAX)	
H-2066 ' P	Hawker Siddeley/HAL 748-224 srs 2	HAL/K/545	(VT-EAY)	
H-2176	Hawker Siddeley/HAL 748 srs 2M (LFD)	HAL/K/570		CABS	Avionics testbed
H-2177	Hawker Siddeley/HAL 748 srs 2M (LFD)	HAL/K/571		
H-2179	Hawker Siddeley/HAL 748 srs 2M (LFD)	HAL/K/573		
H-2180	Hawker Siddeley/HAL 748 srs 2M (LFD)	HAL/K/574		
H-2181	Hawker Siddeley/HAL 748 srs 2M (LFD)	HAL/K/575		
H-2182	Hawker Siddeley/HAL 748 srs 2M (LFD)	HAL/K/576		
H-2183	Hawker Siddeley/HAL 748 srs 2M (LFD)	HAL/K/577		
H-2184	Hawker Siddeley/HAL 748 srs 2M (LFD)	HAL/K/578		
H-2372	Hawker Siddeley/HAL 748 srs 2M (LFD)	HAL/K/579		
H-2373	Hawker Siddeley/HAL 748 srs 2M (LFD)	HAL/K/580		
H-2374	Hawker Siddeley/HAL 748 srs 2M (LFD)	HAL/K/581		
H-2375 ' C	Hawker Siddeley/HAL 748 srs 2M (LFD)	HAL/K/582		
H-2376	Hawker Siddeley/HAL 748 srs 2M (LFD)	HAL/K/583		
H-2377	Hawker Siddeley/HAL 748 srs 2M (LFD)	HAL/K/584		
H-2378 ' Q	Hawker Siddeley/HAL 748 srs 2M (LFD)	HAL/K/585		
H-2379	Hawker Siddeley/HAL 748 srs 2M (LFD)	HAL/K/586		
H-2381	Hawker Siddeley/HAL 748 srs 2M (LFD)	HAL/K/588		
K-2412	Boeing 737-2A8 Advanced	23036 / 977	VT-EHW	AFHQ Comms Flt
K-2413	Boeing 737-2A8 Advanced	23037 / 982	VT-EHX	
K-2661 ' Y	Ilyushin Il-76MD Gajraj	0053458722		
K-2662 ' B	Ilyushin Il-76MD Gajraj	0053458725		44 Sqn
K-2663 ' C	Ilyushin Il-76MD Gajraj	0053458731		44 Sqn
K-2664 ' D	Ilyushin Il-76MD Gajraj	0053461849		44 Sqn	grey cs
K-2665 ' E	Ilyushin Il-76MD Gajraj	0053462856		44 Sqn
K-2666 ' F	Ilyushin Il-76MD Gajraj	0053462857		44 Sqn
K-2667	Antonov An-32 Sutlej			
K-2668 ' N	Antonov An-32 Sutlej			
K-2669 ' A	Antonov An-32 Sutlej			
K-2670 ' B	Antonov An-32 Sutlej			
K-2671 ' F	Antonov An-32 Sutlej			
K-2672 ' B-A	Antonov An-32 Sutlej	0107		
K-2674 ' M	Antonov An-32 Sutlej	0109		
K-2675 ' C	Antonov An-32 Sutlej			
K-2676	Antonov An-32 Sutlej			
K-2677 ' E	Antonov An-32 Sutlej	0202		
K-2678 ' F	Antonov An-32 Sutlej	0203		PTS
K-2679 ' K	Antonov An-32 Sutlej			
K-2680	Antonov An-32 Sutlej	0205		
K-2681	Antonov An-32 Sutlej	0206		
K-2682 ' K	Antonov An-32 Sutlej			
K-2683	Antonov An-32 Sutlej			
K-2684	Antonov An-32 Sutlej	0209		
K-2685	Antonov An-32 Sutlej			
K-2686	Antonov An-32 Sutlej			
K-2687 ' M	Antonov An-32 Sutlej	0302		
K-2688 ' H	Antonov An-32 Sutlej			
K-2690	Antonov An-32 Sutlej			
K-2691	Antonov An-32 Sutlej			
K-2692	Antonov An-32 Sutlej			
K-2693 ' F	Antonov An-32 Sutlej	0308		
K-2694 ' W	Antonov An-32 Sutlej	0309		TTW
K-2695 ' X	Antonov An-32 Sutlej			
K-2696 ' C	Antonov An-32 Sutlej			
K-2697	Antonov An-32 Sutlej	0402		
K-2698	Antonov An-32 Sutlej	0403		
K-2699	Antonov An-32 Sutlej			
K-2700	Antonov An-32 Sutlej			
K-2701	Antonov An-32 Sutlej			
K-2702	Antonov An-32 Sutlej			
K-2703	Antonov An-32 Sutlej	0408		
K-2704 ' E	Antonov An-32 Sutlej	0409		
K-2705	Antonov An-32 Sutlej	0410		
K-2706 ' J	Antonov An-32 Sutlej			

K-2707	Antonov An-32 Sutlej	0502			
K-2708	Antonov An-32 Sutlej				
K-2709	Antonov An-32 Sutlej	0504			
K-2710	Antonov An-32 Sutlej				
K-2711 / K	Antonov An-32 Sutlej				
K-2712	Antonov An-32 Sutlej	0507			
K-2713	Antonov An-32 Sutlej				
K-2714 / F	Antonov An-32 Sutlej	0509			'Agatti'
K-2715 / N	Antonov An-32 Sutlej				
K-2716	Antonov An-32 Sutlej	0601			
K-2717	Antonov An-32 Sutlej				
K-2718	Antonov An-32 Sutlej				
K-2719	Antonov An-32 Sutlej				
K-2720	Antonov An-32 Sutlej				
K-2721 / O	Antonov An-32 Sutlej				
K-2722	Antonov An-32 Sutlej				
K-2723	Antonov An-32 Sutlej				
K-2724	Antonov An-32 Sutlej				
K-2725	Antonov An-32 Sutlej				
K-2726	Antonov An-32 Sutlej				
K-2727	Antonov An-32 Sutlej				
K-2728 / T	Antonov An-32 Sutlej	0704		48 Sqn	
K-2730 / K	Antonov An-32 Sutlej	0706		TTW	
K-2731	Antonov An-32 Sutlej				
K-2732 / N	Antonov An-32 Sutlej				
K-2733 / D	Antonov An-32 Sutlej				
K-2734	Antonov An-32 Sutlej				
K-2735 / F	Antonov An-32 Sutlej				
K-2736 / D	Antonov An-32 Sutlej				
K-2737 / B	Antonov An-32 Sutlej				
K-2738	Antonov An-32 Sutlej				
K-2739	Antonov An-32 Sutlej				
K-2740 / Q	Antonov An-32 Sutlej				
K-2741	Antonov An-32 Sutlej	0807			
K-2742 / U	Antonov An-32 Sutlej				
K-2743	Antonov An-32 Sutlej				
K-2744	Antonov An-32 Sutlej	0810			
K-2745 / E	Antonov An-32 Sutlej	0901			
K-2746	Antonov An-32 Sutlej				
K-2747 / P	Antonov An-32 Sutlej				
K-2748	Antonov An-32 Sutlej				
K-2749	Antonov An-32 Sutlej				grey cs
K-2750 / H	Antonov An-32 Sutlej				
K-2751 / D	Antonov An-32 Sutlej				
K-2752	Antonov An-32 Sutlej	1009			
K-2753	Antonov An-32 Sutlej				
K-2754 / N	Antonov An-32 Sutlej				
K-2755	Antonov An-32 Sutlej			48 Sqn	
K-2756 / B	Antonov An-32 Sutlej	1201			'Brahmaputra'
K-2757	Antonov An-32 Sutlej	1202			
K-2758 / Z	Antonov An-32 Sutlej				
K-2759 / B	Antonov An-32 Sutlej	1205			
K-2760	Antonov An-32 Sutlej				
K-2761	Antonov An-32 Sutlej				
K-2762 / P	Antonov An-32 Sutlej	1208			
K-2862 / G	Antonov An-32 Sutlej				
K-2863	Antonov An-32 Sutlej				
K-2864 / W	Antonov An-32 Sutlej				
K-2878 / G	Ilyushin Il-76MD Gajraj	0063465970		25 Sqn	
K-2879 / H	Ilyushin Il-76MD Gajraj	0063465973		44 Sqn	
K-2885	Antonov An-32 Sutlej				
K-2893 / K	Antonov An-32 Sutlej				
K-2899	Boeing 707-337C	19988 / 736	VT-DXT	ARC	
K-2900	Boeing 707-337B	19248 / 549	VT-DVB	ARC	
K-2901	Ilyushin Il-76MD Gajraj	0073478343			
K-2902 / M	Ilyushin Il-76MD Gajraj	0073478353			
K-2961	GAC G-1159A Gulfstream III	494	N370GA	ARC	
K-2962	GAC G-1159A Gulfstream III	495	N371GA	ARC	
K-2999 / U	Ilyushin Il-76MD Gajraj	0073480410		44 Sqn	
K-3000	Ilyushin Il-76MD Gajraj	0073480419		25 Sqn	
K-3012	Ilyushin Il-76MD Gajraj	0083487614			
K-3013	Ilyushin Il-76MD Gajraj	0083488629			
K-3014	Ilyushin Il-76MD Gajraj	0093491750			
K-3055	Antonov An-32 Sutlej				

Serial	Type	MSN	Regn	Unit	Notes
K-3056	Antonov An-32 Sutlej				
K-3057 / Q	Antonov An-32 Sutlej	1803		TTW	
K-3058	Antonov An-32 Sutlej				
K-3059	Antonov An-32 Sutlej				
K-3060 / G	Antonov An-32 Sutlej				
K-3061	Antonov An-32 Sutlej				
K-3062 / N	Antonov An-32 Sutlej				'Narmanda'
K-3063 / B	Antonov An-32 Sutlej			12 Sqn	
K-3064 / S	Antonov An-32 Sutlej				'Saraswati'
K-3065	Antonov An-32 Sutlej				
K-3066	Antonov An-32 Sutlej				
K-3067 / E-T	Antonov An-32 Sutlej				
K-3068 / G	Antonov An-32 Sutlej	2308			'Godavari'
K-3069 / B	Antonov An-32 Sutlej				
K-3070	Antonov An-32 Sutlej				
K-3073 / Q	Antonov An-32 Sutlej				
K-3074 / G	Antonov An-32 Sutlej	2507			
K-3077 / V	Ilyushin Il-76MD Gajraj	0093496892		44 Sqn	
K-3078 / W	Ilyushin Il-76MD Gajraj	0093496912		25 Sqn	
K-3082	Antonov An-32 Sutlej				
K-3186	Boeing 737-2A8	20484 / 275	VT-EAK		
K-3187	Boeing 737-2A8	20483 / 273	VT-EAJ		
VT-ENR	GAC G-1159A Gulfstream III	420			Serial K-2980 reported

Indian Navy

UNITS/BASES					
	INAS 310 'Cobras', INS Hansa, Goa-Dabolim			Do228	code DAB
	INAS 312 'Albatross', INS Hansa, Goa-Dabolim			Tu-142M	code ARK
	INAS 315 'Winged Stallions', INS Hansa, Goa-Dabolim			Il-38	code DAB
	INAS 318, INS Utkrosh, Port Blair			Defender	
	INAS 550 'Fish', INS Garuda, Cochin			Defender	code COC
	INAS ???, INS Garuda, Cochin			Do228	code COC

PLANS	The Il-38s and Tu-142s are being upgraded in Russia.				
IN126	Britten-Norman BN-2T Turbine Defender	477	G-BDJW	INAS 318	Cvtd BN-2A-21
IN127	Britten-Norman BN-2A-21 Defender	480	G-BDJZ	INAS 318	
IN128	Britten-Norman BN-2T Turbine Defender	481	G-BDKX	INAS 318	Cvtd BN-2A-21
IN129	Britten-Norman BN-2T Turbine Defender	506	G-BDPS	INAS 318	Cvtd BN-2A-21
IN130	Britten-Norman BN-2A-21 Defender	507	G-BDPT	INAS 318	
IN132	Pilatus Britten-Norman BN-2A-21 Maritime Defender	875	G-BFNS	INAS 318	
IN133	Pilatus Britten-Norman BN-2A-21 Maritime Defender	886	G-BFTI	INAS 318	
IN134	Pilatus Britten-Norman BN-2A-21 Maritime Defender	887	G-BFTJ	INAS 318	
IN135	Pilatus Britten-Norman BN-2T Turbine Defender	888	G-BFTK	INAS 318	Cvtd BN-2A-21
IN136	Pilatus Britten-Norman BN-2A-21 Maritime Defender	889	G-BFTL	INAS 318	
IN137	Pilatus Britten-Norman BN-2B-21 Islander	2123	G-BJEH	INAS 550	
IN138	Pilatus Britten-Norman BN-2B-21 Islander	2134	G-BJOS	INAS 550	
IN139	Pilatus Britten-Norman BN-2B-21 Islander	2135	G-BJOU	INAS 550	
IN140	Pilatus Britten-Norman BN-2B-21 Islander	2148	G-BKEC	INAS 550	
IN141	Pilatus Britten-Norman BN-2B-21 Islander	2149	G-BKED	INAS 550	
IN142	Pilatus Britten-Norman BN-2B-21 Islander	2150	G-BKEE	INAS 550	
IN-221	Dornier/HAL 228-201	8I-4035		INAS 310	grey cs
IN-222	Dornier/HAL 228-201	8I-4036		INAS 310	grey cs
IN-223	Dornier/HAL 228-201	8I-4037		INAS 310	dark grey cs
IN-224	Dornier/HAL 228-201	8I-4038		INAS 310	
IN-225	Dornier 228-201	8164	D-CAFE	INAS 310	grey cs
IN-228	Dornier/HAL 228-201			COC	
IN-229	Dornier/HAL 228-201			COC	
IN-231	Dornier/HAL 228-201	8I-4059		HAL	Surveillance testbed
IN301	Ilyushin Il-38			INAS 315	
IN302	Ilyushin Il-38			INAS 315	
IN303	Ilyushin Il-38			INAS 315	
IN304	Ilyushin Il-38			INAS 315	
IN305	Ilyushin Il-38			INAS 315	
IN311	Tupolev Tu-142M			INAS 312	
IN312	Tupolev Tu-142M	7609686		INAS 312	
IN313	Tupolev Tu-142M			INAS 312	
IN314	Tupolev Tu-142M			INAS 312	

IN315	Tupolev Tu-142M			INAS 312
IN316	Tupolev Tu-142M			INAS 312
IN317	Tupolev Tu-142M			INAS 312
IN318	Tupolev Tu-142M			INAS 312

Coast Guard Air Wing

| *UNITS/BASES* | CGAS 744, Meenambakam | | | Do228 |
| | CGAS 750, Daman | | | Do228 |

| *PLANS* | Seven additional Do228s order from HAL for delivery between 2001/03. |

CG-751	Dornier 228-101	7053	D-CILA	
CG-752	Dornier 228-101	7059	D-CAOT	
CG-753	Dornier 228-101	7062	D-CAOR	
CG-754	Dornier/HAL 228-101	7113/HAL2012		
CG-755	Dornier/HAL 228-101	7105/HAL1014		
CG-756	Dornier/HAL 228-101	7106/HAL1015		
CG-757	Dornier/HAL 228-101	7114/HAL2015		Std
CG-758	Dornier/HAL 228-101	8I-3018		
CG-759	Dornier/HAL 228-101	8I-3019		
CG-760	Dornier/HAL 228-101	8I-3039		
CG-761	Dornier/HAL 228-101	8I-3021		
CG-762	Dornier/HAL 228-101	8I-3022		
CG-763	Dornier/HAL 228-101	8I-3044		
	Dornier/HAL 228-101			
	Dornier/HAL 228-101			
CG-766	Dornier/HAL 228-101			
	Dornier/HAL 228-101			
	Dornier/HAL 228-101			
	Dornier/HAL 228-101			
	Dornier/HAL 228-101			
	Dornier/HAL 228-101			
	Dornier/HAL 228-101			
	Dornier/HAL 228-101			
	Dornier/HAL 228-101			
	Dornier/HAL 228-101			
	Dornier/HAL 228-101			
	Dornier/HAL 228-101			
	Dornier/HAL 228-101			
	Dornier/HAL 228-101			
	Dornier/HAL 228-101			
	Dornier/HAL 228-101			
	Dornier/HAL 228-101			
	Dornier/HAL 228-101			
	Dornier/HAL 228-101			

Border Security Force

| *UNITS/BASES* | Flying Unit, based at Indira Ghandi IAP, Delhi |

| *PLANS* | Two An-32s were intended to replace two retired C-47s |

VT-BSA	Beech Super King Air B200	BB-1485	N1509X	
VT-DXH	Hawker Siddeley/HAL HS748-224 srs 2	HAL/K/513		Std Delhi
VT-EAT	Hawker Siddeley/HAL HS748-224 srs 2	HAL/K/540		
VT-EAV	Hawker Siddeley/HAL HS748-224 srs 2	HAL/K/542		
VT-EHK	Beech Super King Air B200	BB-985	N1841Z	
VT-EHL	Hawker Siddeley/HAL HS748-224 srs 2	HAL/K/549	VT-EBC	
VT-EIR	Hawker Siddeley/HAL HS748-224 srs 2	HAL/K/587	H2380 (BVS)	Std Delhi

Government of the Republic of India

VT-EFG	Beech King Air C90	LJ-719	N23917	Govt of Bihar,Patna
VT-EFP	Beech King Air C90	LJ-720	N23929	Govt of Madhya Pradesh,Bhopal
VT-EGR	Beech King Air C90	LJ-967	N3832X	Govt of Maharashtra, Bombay
VT-EHB	Beech Super King Air 200	BB-972	N18409	Govt of Orissa, Cuttack
VT-EHS	Learjet 29	29-003	N289CA	Aviation Research Centre, Delhi
VT-EHY	Beech King Air C90	LJ-1008	N1842A	Govt of Punjab, Chandigarh
VT-EID	Beech Super King Air 200C	BL-56	N1844C	Govt of Madhya Pradesh,Bhopal
VT-EIE	Beech Super King Air 200C	BL-63	N6921D	Govt of Uttar Pradesh, Lucknow

VT-EIH	Learjet 29	29-004	N294CA		Aviation Research Centre, Delhi
VT-EJZ	Beech King Air C90A	LJ-1100	N7219K		Govt of Haryana, Ambala
VT-ENL	Beech Super King Air B200	BB-1248	N7256G		Aviation Research Centre, Cuttack
VT-ENM	Beech Super King Air B200	BB-1236	N72473		Aviation Research Centre, Cuttack
VT-EPA	Beech Super King Air B200	BB-1254	N2646K		Aviation Research Centre, Cuttack
VT-EPY	Beech Super King Air B200	BB-1277	N7241L		Govt of Maharashtra, Bombay
VT-EQN	Beech King Air C90A	LJ-1167	N31174		Govt of Rajasthan, Jaipur
VT-EQO	Beech King Air C90A	LJ-1153	N70491		Govt of Uttar Pradesh, Lucknow
VT-GUJ	Raytheon Beech Super King Air B200	BB-1687	N3117V		Govt of Gujarat, Ahmedabad
VT-MPG	Raytheon Beech Super King Air B200	BB-1445	N8121M		Govt of Chattigarh, Raipur
VT-UFA	Beech Super King Air 300	FA-230	N80679		Govt of Uttar Pradesh, Lucknow
VT-UFZ	Raytheon Beech King Air C90B	LJ-1400	N3239K		Govt of Uttar Pradesh, Lucknow

INDONESIA
Republik Indonesia   SE Asia

A former Dutch colony independent since 1945 and occupying a string of islands over 4800km in length, Indonesia was perhaps worst hit by the 1997 Pacific Rim economic crash. Civil unrest has been caused by decentralisation of the population to outlying islands which itself is creating ethnic tensions. This has resulted in limited trade sanctions at a time of poor prosperity. A capable manufacturing industry, Dirgantara Indonesia (formerly IPTN and Nurtanio), has built a number of European types under licence and now also some of their own design. A member of the ASEAN.

SERIAL SYSTEM In the case of the Air Force a letter denoting the role is followed by a sequential four digit number beginning with two digits referring to the type. With the other air arms the letter denotes the air arm or unit and the three or four digit number is part of a batch for a type.

Tentara Nasional Indonesia - Angkatan Udara   -   TNI-AU
Indonesian National Armed Forces - Air Force

UNITS/BASES	Markas Komando Operasi (KOOPSAU) 1	
	Skuadron Udara 2, Halim-Perdanakusuma AB, Java	F.27, CN235
	Skuadron Udara 17, Halim-Perdanakusuma AB, Java	707, F.27, C-130H-30, L-100-30
	Skuadron Udara 31, Halim-Perdanakusuma AB, Java	C-130H/H-30
	Markas Komando Operasi (KOOPSAU) 2	
	Skuadron Udara 4, Malang-Abdulrachman Saleh AB, Java	Aviocar
	Skuadron Udara 5, Hasanuddin-Ujing Pandang AB, Sulawesi	737MP
	Skuadron Udara 32, Malang-Abdulrachman Saleh AB, Java	C-130B/KC-130B

A-1301	Lockheed C-130B (L-282-7B) Hercules	3546	PK-VHD	SkU 32	Std Bandung
A-1302	Lockheed C-130B (L-282-7B) Hercules	3578	T-1302	SkU 32	
A-1303	Lockheed C-130B (L-282-7B) Hercules	3580	N9298R	SkU 32	
A-1304	Lockheed C-130B (L-282-7B) Hercules	3582	N9297R	SkU 32	
A-1305	Lockheed C-130B (L-282-7B) Hercules	3583	T-1305	SkU 32	
A-1308	Lockheed C-130B (L-282-7B) Hercules	3601	PK-VHA	SkU 32	
A-1309	Lockheed KC-130B (L-282-7B) Hercules	3615	T-1309	SkU 32	AAR, cvtd C-130B
A-1310	Lockheed KC-130B (L-282-7B) Hercules	3616	T-1310	SkU 32	AAR, cvtd C-130B
A-1311	Lockheed C-130B (L-282-1B) Hercules	3614	T-1311	SkU 32	
A-1312	Lockheed C-130B (L-282-1B) Hercules	3617	T-1312	SkU 32	
A-1313	Lockheed C-130B (L-282-1B) Hercules	3621	T-1313	SkU 32	
A-1314	Lockheed L-100-30 (L-382G-41C) Hercules	4800	N4304M	SkU 17	VIP
A-1315	Lockheed C-130H (L-382C-94D) Hercules	4838		SkU 31	
A-1316	Lockheed C-130H (L-382C-94D) Hercules	4840		SkU 31	
A-1317	Lockheed C-130H-30 (L-382T-3E) Hercules	4864		SkU 31	
A-1318	Lockheed C-130H-30 (L-382T-3E) Hercules	4865		SkU 31	
A-1319	Lockheed C-130H-30 (L-382T-3E) Hercules	4868		SkU 31	
A-1320	Lockheed C-130H-30 (L-382T-3E) Hercules	4869		SkU 31	
A-1321	Lockheed C-130H-30 (L-382T-21E) Hercules	4925		SkU 31	
A-1323	Lockheed C-130H (L-382C-15E) Hercules	4899		SkU 31	
A-	Lockheed L-100-30 (L-382G-57C) Hercules	4917	PK-MLS	SkU 31	
A-	Lockheed L-100-30 (L-382G-57C) Hercules	4923	PK-MLT	SkU 31	
A-	Lockheed L-100-30 (L-382G-43C) Hercules	4824	PK-PLU	SkU 31	
A-	Lockheed L-100-30 (L-382G-43C) Hercules	4828	PK-PLW	SkU 31	
A-	Lockheed L-100-30 (L-382G-52C) Hercules	4889	PK-PLR	SkU 31	
A-1341	Lockheed C-130H-30 (L-382T-3E) Hercules	4870	A-1321	SkU 17	VIP
A-2103	CASA/IPTN NC212M Aviocar srs 200	225/N65	PK-XDN	SkU 4	
A-2104	CASA/IPTN NC212M Aviocar srs 200	226/N66	PK-NZK	SkU 4	
A-2105	CASA/IPTN NC212M Aviocar srs 200	227/N67	PK-XDP	SkU 4	
A-2106	CASA/IPTN NC212M Aviocar srs 200	228/N68	PK-XDQ	SkU 4	

A-2107	CASA/IPTN NC212M Aviocar srs 200	249/N69	PK-XDR	SkU 4	
A-2108	CASA/IPTN NC212M Aviocar srs 200	250/N70	PK-XDS	SkU 4	
A-2109	CASA/IPTN NC212M Aviocar srs 200	251/N71	PK-XDT	SkU 4	
A-2110	CASA/IPTN NC212M Aviocar srs 200	252/N72	PK-XDU	SkU 4	
A-2111	CASA/IPTN NC212M Aviocar srs 200			SkU 4	
A-2112	CASA/IPTN NC212M Aviocar srs 200			SkU 4	
A-2301	Airtech/IPTN CN235M-10 Tetuko	N016	AX-2301	SkU 2	
A-2302	Airtech/IPTN CN235M-10 Tetuko	N017	AX-2302	SkU 2	
A-2303	Airtech/IPTN CN235M-10 Tetuko	N022	AX-2303	SkU 2	
A-2304	Airtech/IPTN CN235M-10 Tetuko	N023	AX-2304	SkU 2	
A-2305	Airtech/IPTN CN235M-10 Tetuko	N024	AX-2305	SkU 2	
A-2306	Airtech/IPTN CN235M-10 Tetuko	N025	AX-2306	SkU 2	
	Airtech/IPTN CN235MPA	N021	AX-2314		on order
	Airtech/IPTN CN235MPA	N040			on order
	Airtech/IPTN CN235MPA				on order
A-2701	Fokker F.27 Troopship 400M	10536	T-2701	SkU 2	
A-2703	Fokker F.27 Troopship 400M	10538	PK-VFE	SkU 2	
A-2704	Fokker F.27 Troopship 400M	10540	T-2704		Std
A-2705	Fokker F.27 Troopship 400M	10541	T-2705		Std
A-2706	Fokker F.27 Troopship 400M	10542	T-2706	SkU 2	
A-2707	Fokker F.27 Troopship 400M	10544	T-2707	SkU 2	
A-2708	Fokker F.27 Troopship 400M	10546	T-2708	SkU 2	
A-2801	Fokker F.28 Fellowship 1000	11042	PK-PJT	SkU 17	
A-2802	Fokker F.28 Fellowship 3000	11113	PK-GFR	SkU 17	
A-2803	Fokker F.28 Fellowship 3000	11117	PK-GFQ	SkU 17	
A-7002	Boeing 707-3M1C	21092 / 899	PK-GAU	SkU 17	
AI-7301	Boeing 737-2X9 Advanced Surveiller	22777 / 868	N1779B	SkU 5	MR
AI-7302	Boeing 737-2X9 Advanced Surveiller	22778 / 947	N8288V	SkU 5	MR
AI-7303	Boeing 737-2X9 Advanced Surveiller	22779 / 985	N1786B	SkU 5	MR
L 4011	Cessna 401A	401A0067	N6267Q	SkU 4	
L 4012	Cessna 401A	401A0068	N6268Q	SkU 4	
L 4013	Cessna 401A	401A0069	N6269Q		
L 4014	Cessna 401A	401A0070	N6270Q		

The L-100s are serialled between A-1325 and A-1332 but the tie up is unknown

Tentara Nasional Indonesia - Angkatan Laut (TNI-AL)
Indonesian National Armed Forces - Naval Aviation

UNITS/BASES	Skuadron Udara 200, Juanda, Surabaya		RC695A
	Skuadron Udara 600, Juanda, Surabaya		Aviocar, Buffalo
	- detached to Tanjung Pinang and Manado		
	Skuadron Udara 800, Juanda, Surabaya		Nomad

PLANS   Seven CN235MPAs are planned for delivery from 2003 and four NC212 for ELINT work are also expec:ed.

AL-5001	DeHavilland Canada DHC-5D Buffalo	79	AX-5001	SkU 600	Re-serialled U-630?
AL-5002	DeHavilland Canada DHC-5D Buffalo	80	AX-5002	SkU 600	Re-serialled U-631?
U 610	CASA/IPTN NC212M Aviocar srs 200	220/N60	PK-XDI	SkU 600	
U 611	CASA/IPTN NC212MP Aviocar srs 200	221/N61	PK-XDJ	SkU 600	
U 612	CASA/IPTN NC212M Aviocar srs 200	222/N62	PK-XDK	SkU 600	
U 615	CASA/IPTN NC212MP Aviocar srs 200	278/N83	PK-XEG	SkU 600	
U 616	CASA/IPTN NC212MP Aviocar srs 200	279/N84	PK-XEH	SkU 600	
U 617	CASA/IPTN NC212MP Aviocar srs 200	280/N85	PK-XEI	SkU 600	
U 618	CASA/IPTN NC212M Aviocar srs 200	281/N86	PK-XEJ	SkU 600	
U 619	CASA/IPTN NC212M Aviocar srs 200		AX-2103	SkU 600	
U 620	CASA/IPTN NC212M Aviocar srs 200		AX-2106	SkU 600	
U 621	CASA/IPTN NC212M Aviocar srs 200			SkU 600	
P 801	GAF N22B Nomad	8		SkU 800	
P 802	GAF N22B Nomad	9		SkU 800	
P 803	GAF N22B Nomad	16		SkU 800	
P 804	GAF N22B Nomad	17		SkU 800	
P 805	GAF N22B Nomad	24		SkU 800	
P 806	GAF N22B Nomad	31		SkU 800	
P 807	GAF N22B Nomad	85		SkU 800	
P 808	GAF N22B Nomad	88		SkU 800	
P 809	GAF N22B Nomad	91		SkU 800	
P 811	GAF N22B Nomad	97		SkU 800	
P 812	GAF N22B Nomad	100		SkU 800	
P 813	GAF N22SL Nomad Searchmaster	110		SkU 800	
P 815	GAF N22SL Nomad Searchmaster	116		SkU 800	
P 816	GAF N22SL Nomad Searchmaster	118		SkU 800	
P 817	GAF N22SL Nomad Searchmaster	125		SkU 800	
P 818	GAF N22SL Nomad Searchmaster	126		SkU 800	

P 822	GAF N22 Nomad	40	A18-304 (RAA)	SkU 800	
P 823	GAF N22 Nomad	47	A18-308 (RAA)	SkU 800	
P 824	GAF N22 Nomad	48	A18-309 (RAA)	SkU 800	
P 825	GAF N22 Nomad	49	A18-310 (RAA)	SkU 800	
P 826	GAF N22 Nomad	51	A18-311 (RAA)		
P 827	GAF N22B Nomad	63	A18-312 (RAA)		
P 828	GAF N22B Nomad	65	A18-313 (RAA)		
P 829	GAF N22B Nomad	131	A18-314 (RAA)		
P 830	GAF N22B Nomad	132	A18-315 (RAA)		
P 831	GAF N24A Nomad	166	A18-317 (RAA)	SkU 800	
P 832	GAF N24A Nomad	167	A18-317 (RAA)		
P 833	GAF N24A Nomad	168	A18-319 (RAA)		
P 834	GAF N24A Nomad	169	A18-320 (RAA)		
P 835	GAF N24A Nomad	170	A18-321 (RAA)		
P 836	GAF N24A Nomad	130	A18-402 (RAA)		
P 837	GAF N24A Nomad	135	A18-403 (RAA)	SkU 800	
P 838	GAF N24A Nomad	136	A18-404 (RAA)	SkU 800	
P 839	GAF N24A Nomad	139	A18-405 (RAA)	SkU 800	
P 840	GAF N24A Nomad	140	A18-406 (RAA)		
P 841	GAF N24A Nomad	142	A18-407 (RAA)		

Tentara Nasional Indonesia - Angkatan Darat - TNI-AD
Indonesian National Armed Forces - Army Air Arm

UNITS/BASES Skuadron Udara Angkatan Darat 2, Pondok Cabe-Jakarta (Pelita) Airport.

PLANS Six additional Aviocars were planned but the order status requires confirmation.

A-2003	Aero Commander 680FL	1511-95	N6393U	SkU AD 2	
A-2004	Aero Commander 680FL	1517-98	N6378U	SkU AD 2	
AD-5003	DeHavilland Canada DHC-5D Buffalo	81	AX-5003	SkU AD 2	Re-serialled A-9121?
AD-5004	DeHavilland Canada DHC-5D Buffalo	82	AX-5004	SkU AD 2	Re-serialled A-9122?
AD-5005	DeHavilland Canada DHC-5D Buffalo	109	AX-5005	SkU AD 2	VIP
A-9031	CASA/IPTN NC212M Aviocar srs 200	212/N52	PK-TRG	SkU AD 2	
A-9032	CASA/IPTN NC212M Aviocar srs 200	213/N53	PK-XDA	SkU AD 2	
A-9034	CASA/IPTN NC212M Aviocar srs 200	219/N59	PK-XDC	SkU AD 2	
A-9035	CASA/IPTN NC212M Aviocar srs 200	214/N54	PK-XDH	SkU AD 2	
A-9113	CASA/IPTN NC212M Aviocar srs 200			SkU AD 2	
A-9152	CASA/IPTN NC212M Aviocar srs 300	427/N107		SkU AD 2	
A-12201	Britten-Norman BN-2A-27R Islander	713	G-BBZW	SkU AD 2	

Polisi
Police Air Wing

PLANS Four additional Aviocars were planned but the order status requires confirmation.

P-1006	Cessna 206
P-2022	Beech H18
P-2023	Beech H18
P-2031	CASA/IPTN NC212M Aviocar srs 100
P-2032	CASA/IPTN NC212M Aviocar srs 100

Satuan Udara Pertonian

UNITS/BASES The Air Force Agricultural Unit is based at Kalijati.

ST-0601	Pilatus PC-6/B2-H2 Turbo Porter	785	AG-601		Crop sprayer
ST-0602	Pilatus PC-6/B2-H2 Turbo Porter	792	AG-602		Crop sprayer
ST-0603	Pilatus PC-6/B2-H2 Turbo Porter	796	AG-603		Crop sprayer
ST-0604	Pilatus PC-6/B2-H2 Turbo Porter	799	AG-604		Crop sprayer
ST-0605	Pilatus PC-6/B2-H2 Turbo Porter	801	AG-605		Crop sprayer

Satuan Udara Federasi Aerosport Indonesia - FASI

UNITS/BASES Aerosport Federation aircraft are based at Halim-Perdanakusuma, Kalijati, Yogyakartz, Surabaya and Malang.

AF-702	Shorts SC.7-3M Skyvan srs 400	SH.1881	T-702 (TNI-AU)		
L-1821	Antonov An-2		(TNI-AU)		Para dropping
AF-4015	Cessna 401A	401A0071	L-4015 (TNI-AU)		
AF-4775	Douglas C-47A				'Seulawah'
AF-4776	Douglas C-47A	13334	PK-VTO		
AF-4777	Douglas C-47B	34228	PK-VTM		'Djakarta'
AF-4790	Douglas C-47A				

IRAN

Joumhouri-e-Islami-e-Iran / Islamic Republic of Iran   SW Asia

The Islamic revolution in 1979 put an end to many years of US support that began after World War II, the Imperial Iranian Air Force (IIAF) originally being organised along the same lines as the USAF. Serviceability problems due to embargo and the 1980s war with Iraq meant that in order to survive and grow the country has developed an indigenous manufacturing capability.

SERIAL SYSTEM Blocks are allocated for each type and commence with a one or two digit prefix followed usually by four numbers.

Islamic Republic of Iran Air Force - IRIAF

UNITS/BASES			
Shiraz, TAB 7	F.27, C-130H, Il-76, Falcon 20, AC681, P-3F
Tehran-Doshan Tappeh, TAB 12	PC-6B, VIP aircraft
Tehran-Ghale Morghi, TAB 11	Falcon 50, AC681
Tehran-Mehrabad, TAB 1	C-130H, B707, B747

PLANS   Il-76s were acquired from Iraq (11) and Russia (4). Chinese Y-7s (14) and Y-12s (10) are believed to be on order. Plans exist to build the Antonov An-140 under licence (as the Iran-140) for transport, MR, AEW and EW missions.

1001	Boeing 707-386C	21396 / 928	EP-NHY	
1002	Boeing 707-370C	20890 / 891	YI-AGF	
1003	Lockheed L-1329 JetStar II	5203	EP-VLP	WO?
1004	Lockheed L-1329-8 JetStar	5137	EP-VRP	
4-9801	Pilatus PC-6/B2-H2 Turbo Porter	825	HB-FHV	
4-9802	Pilatus PC-6/B2-H2 Turbo Porter	826	HB-FHW	
4-9803	Pilatus PC-6/B2-H2 Turbo Porter	827	HB-FHX	
4-9804	Pilatus PC-6/B2-H2 Turbo Porter	828	HB-FHY	
4-9805	Pilatus PC-6/B2-H2 Turbo Porter	829	HB-FIA	
4-9806	Pilatus PC-6/B2-H2 Turbo Porter	830	HB-FIB	
4-9807	Pilatus PC-6/B2-H2 Turbo Porter	831	HB-FIC	
4-9808	Pilatus PC-6/B2-H2 Turbo Porter	832	HB-FID	
4-9809	Pilatus PC-6/B2-H2 Turbo Porter	833	HB-FIF	
4-9810	Pilatus PC-6/B2-H2 Turbo Porter	834	HB-FIG	
4-9811	Pilatus PC-6/B2-H2 Turbo Porter	835	HB-FIH	
4-9812	Pilatus PC-6/B2-H2 Turbo Porter	836	HB-FII	
4-9813	Pilatus PC-6/B2-H2 Turbo Porter	837	HB-FIK	
4-9814	Pilatus PC-6/B2-H2 Turbo Porter	838	HB-FIL	
4-9815	Pilatus PC-6/B2-H2 Turbo Porter	839	HB-FIN	
5-2250	Antonov An-74T200			
5-2254	Antonov An-74T200			
5-2255	Antonov An-74T200			
5-280	Rockwell 681B Turbo Commander	6062		
5-281	Rockwell 681B Turbo Commander	6068		
5-59	Rockwell 681 Hawk Commander	6009	N9059N	
5-8101	Boeing 747-131(F)	19667 / 5	EP-NHV	
5-8102	Boeing 747-131(F)	19678 / 78	EP-NHT	
5-8106	Boeing 747-131(F)	19668 / 8	EP-NHK	
5-8108	Boeing 747-131(F)	19669 / 9	EP-NHD	
5-8203	Ilyushin Il-76		Iraqi AF?	
5-8205	Ilyushin Il-76		Iraqi AF?	
5-8206	Ilyushin Il-76		Iraqi AF?	
5-8207	Ilyushin Il-76		Iraqi AF?	
5-8210	Ilyushin Il-76		Iraqi AF?	
5-8302	Boeing 707-3J9C	20831 / 881	5-242 (IIAF)	
5-8303	Boeing 707-3J9C	20832 / 886	5-243 (IIAF)	
5-8305	Boeing 707-3J9C	20834 / 894	EP-NHW	
5-8306	Boeing 707-3J9C	20835 / 895	5-246 (IIAF)	
5-8308	Boeing 707-3J9C	21124 / 910		
5-8309	Boeing 707-3J9C	21125 / 912		
5-8310	Boeing 707-3J9C	21126 / 914		
5-8313	Boeing 707-3J9C	21129 / 918		
5-8314	Boeing 707-3J9C	21475 / 936		
5-8501	Lockheed C-130E (L-382C-1D) Hercules	4115	5-101 (IIAF)	
5-8502	Lockheed C-130E (L-382C-1D) Hercules	4149	5-105 (IIAF)	
5-8503	Lockheed C-130E (L-382C-6D) Hercules	4276	5-107 (IIAF)	
5-8504	Lockheed C-130E (L-382C-6D) Hercules	4283	5-109 (IIAF)	
5-8505	Lockheed C-130E (L-382C-6D) Hercules	4284	5-110 (IIAF)	
5-8507	Lockheed C-130E (L-382C-10D) Hercules	4295	5-112 (IIAF)	
5-8508	Lockheed C-130E (L-382C-10D) Hercules	4296	5-113 (IIAF)	
5-8509	Lockheed C-130E (L-382C-10D) Hercules	4297	5-114 (IIAF)	
5-8510	Lockheed C-130E (L-382C-10D) Hercules	4298	5-115 (IIAF)	
5-8511	Lockheed C-130E (L-382C-17D) Hercules	4365	5-116 (IIAF)	

5-8512	Lockheed C-130E (L-382C-17D) Hercules	4386	5-117 (IIAF)	
5-8513	Lockheed C-130E (L-382C-17D) Hercules	4387	5-118 (IIAF)	
5-8514	Lockheed C-130E (L-382C-17D) Hercules	4389	5-119 (IIAF)	
5-8515	Lockheed C-130E (L-382C-17D) Hercules	4390	5-120 (IIAF)	
5-8516	Lockheed C-130E (L-382C-17D) Hercules	4392	5-121 (IIAF)	
5-8517	Lockheed C-130E (L-382C-17D) Hercules	4394	5-123 (IIAF)	
5-8518	Lockheed C-130E (L-382C-17D) Hercules	4398	5-124 (IIAF)	
5-8519	Lockheed C-130E (L-382C-17D) Hercules	4399	5-125 (IIAF)	
5-8522	Lockheed C-130H (L-382C-17D) Hercules	4433	5-128 (IIAF)	
5-8523	Lockheed C-130H (L-382C-17D) Hercules	4438	5-129 (IIAF)	
5-8524	Lockheed C-130H (L-382C-17D) Hercules	4439	5-130 (IIAF)	
5-8525	Lockheed C-130H (L-382C-17D) Hercules	4440	5-131 (IIAF)	
5-8526	Lockheed C-130H (L-382C-17D) Hercules	4442	5-132 (IIAF)	
5-8527	Lockheed C-130H (L-382C-17D) Hercules	4444	5-133 (IIAF)	
5-8528	Lockheed C-130H (L-382C-17D) Hercules	4445	5-134 (IIAF)	
5-8529	Lockheed C-130H (L-382C-17D) Hercules	4448	5-135 (IIAF)	
5-8530	Lockheed C-130H (L-382C-17D) Hercules	4454	5-136 (IIAF)	
5-8531	Lockheed C-130H (L-382C-17D) Hercules	4456	5-137 (IIAF)	
5-8533	Lockheed C-130H (L-382C-17D) Hercules	4458	5-139 (IIAF)	
5-8534	Lockheed C-130H (L-382C-17D) Hercules	4459	5-140 (IIAF)	
5-8535	Lockheed C-130H (L-382C-17D) Hercules	4462	5-141 (IIAF)	
5-8537	Lockheed C-130H (L-382C-17D) Hercules	4465	5-143 (IIAF)	
5-8538	Lockheed C-130H (L-382C-17D) Hercules	4466	5-144 (IIAF)	
5-8539	Lockheed C-130H (L-382C-17D) Hercules	4468	5-145 (IIAF)	
5-8540	Lockheed C-130H (L-382C-17D) Hercules	4469	5-146 (IIAF)	
5-8541	Lockheed C-130H (L-382C-17D) Hercules	4471	5-147 (IIAF)	
5-8542	Lockheed C-130H (L-382C-17D) Hercules	4474	5-148 (IIAF)	
5-8543	Lockheed C-130H (L-382C-17D) Hercules	4480	5-149 (IIAF)	
5-8544	Lockheed C-130H (L-382C-17D) Hercules	4484	5-150 (IIAF)	
5-8545	Lockheed C-130H (L-382C-17D) Hercules	4485	5-151 (IIAF)	
5-8546	Lockheed C-130H (L-382C-17D) Hercules	4486	5-152 (IIAF)	
5-8547	Lockheed C-130H (L-382C-17D) Hercules	4487	5-153 (IIAF)	
5-8548	Lockheed C-130H (L-382C-17D) Hercules	4488	5-154 (IIAF)	
5-8549	Lockheed C-130H (L-382C-17D) Hercules	4489	5-155 (IIAF)	
5-8550	Lockheed C-130H (L-382C-17D) Hercules	4490	5-156 (IIAF)	
5-8551	Lockheed C-130H (L-382C-37D) Hercules	4591	5-157 (IIAF)	
5-8701	Lockheed P-3F (L-685A) Orion	6001	5-251 (IIAF)	
5-8703	Lockheed P-3F (L-685A) Orion	6003	5-253 (IIAF)	
5-8704	Lockheed P-3F (L-685A) Orion	6004	5-254 (IIAF)	
5-8705	Lockheed P-3F (L-685A) Orion	6005	5-255 (IIAF)	
5-8706	Lockheed P-3F (L-685A) Orion	6006	5-256 (IIAF)	
5-8803	Fokker F.27 Troopship 400M	10478	5-203 (IIAF)	
5-8804	Fokker F.27 Troopship 400M	10479	5-204 (IIAF)	
5-8805	Fokker F.27 Troopship 400M	10480	5-205 (IIAF)	
5-8807	Fokker F.27 Troopship 400M	10482	5-207 (IIAF)	
5-8808	Fokker F.27 Troopship 400M	10483	5-208 (IIAF)	
5-8809	Fokker F.27 Troopship 400M	10485	5-210 (IIAF)	
5-8810	Fokker F.27 Troopship 400M	10486	5-210 (IIAF)	
5-8811	Fokker F.27 Troopship 400M	10491	5-212 (IIAF)	
5-8812	Fokker F.27 Troopship 400M	10492	5-213 (IIAF)	
5-8813	Fokker F.27 Troopship 400M	10497	5-214 (IIAF)	
5-8814	Fokker F.27 Troopship 400M	10498	5-215 (IIAF)	
5-8816	Fokker F.27 Troopship 400M	10500	5-217 (IIAF)	
5-8817	Fokker F.27 Troopship 400M	10502	5-218 (IIAF)	
5-8818	Fokker F.27 Friendship 600	10504	5-219 (IIAF)	
5-9001	Dassault Falcon 20F	351	F-WMKJ	
5-9002	Dassault Falcon 20F	353	F-WRQP	
5-9003	Dassault Falcon 20F	354	F-WRQR	
5-9011	Dassault Falcon 50		YI-	"c/n 101,120 or 122"
5-9012	Dassault Falcon 50		YI-	"c/n 101,120 or 122"
5-9013	Dassault Falcon 50		YI-	"c/n 101,120 or 122"

Islamic Republic of Iran Navy Aviation - IRINA

UNITS/BASES	Transport Squadron, TAB 7 Shiraz		F.27	
501	Rockwell 690 Commander	11076		
5-2505	Rockwell 690A Commander	11183		
5-2601	Fokker F.27 Troopship 400M	10512	PH-FRG	
5-2602	Fokker F.27 Troopship 400M	10510	PH-EXC	
5-2603	Fokker F.27 Troopship 400M	10511	PH-EXD	
5-2604	Fokker F.27 Troopship 400M	10509	PH-EXB	reserialled 6-9704?
5-2802	Dassault Falcon 20E	336	F-WRQP	
5-2803	Dassault Falcon 20E	340	F-WRQX	

5-2804	Dassault Falcon 20E	346	F-WRQP
5-4035	Rockwell 690A Commander	11294	N9187N
5-4036	Rockwell 690A Commander	11295	N81427
5-4037	Rockwell 690A Commander	11333	N57196
5-4038	Rockwell 690A Commander	11334	N81467

Islamic Republic of Iran Army Aviation- IRIAA

4-901	Rockwell 690 Commander	11077	
4-902	Rockwell 690 Commander	11078	
4-903	Rockwell 690 Commander	11079	
5-3021	Dassault Falcon 20E	350	5-4040 (IIA)
5-3031	Fokker F.27 Friendship 600	10567	5-4041 (IIA)
5-3032	Fokker F.27 Troopship 400M	10568	5-4042 (IIA)

Islamic Revolutionary Guard Air Arm

15-2250	Antonov An-74TK200		
15-2258	Antonov An-74TK200		
15-2259	Antonov An-74TK200		
	Antonov An-74TK200		
	Antonov An-74TK200		
	Antonov An-74TK200		
15-2237	Yunshuji/Harbin Y-12 II		
15-2238	Yunshuji/Harbin Y-12 II		
15-2241	Yunshuji/Harbin Y-12 II		
15-2243	Yunshuji/Harbin Y-12 II		
15-2245	Yunshuji/Harbin Y-12 II		
15-2248	Yunshuji/Harbin Y-12 II		
15-2254	Yunshuji/Harbin Y-12 II		
5-2255	Ilyushin Il-76		Iraqi AF?
5-2283	Ilyushin Il-76		Iraqi AF?
5-2291	Ilyushin Il-76		Iraqi AF?

Iranian Gendarmerie
Police Wing

| 6-3201 | Rockwell 690A Commander | 11181 | N57196 |
| 6-3202 | Rockwell 690A Commander | 11293 | N81467 |

National Cartographic Center

UNITS/BASES	Flight Dept, Tehran			
EP-TAA	Dornier 228-212	8210	D-CRAM	Survey
EP-TCC	Dornier 228-212	8195	D-CNCC	Survey
EP-THA	Dornier 228-212	8207	D-CIME	Survey
EP-TKH	Dornier 228-212	8204	D-CIMO	Survey
EP-TZA	Dornier 228-212	8208	D-CIMU	Survey

Government of the Islamic Republic of Iran

EP-AGA	Boeing 737-286 Advanced	21317 / 483		VIP
EP-AGV	Rockwell 690 Commander	11045		Prime Minister's Office
EP-AGW	Rockwell 690 Commander	11047		Prime Minister's Office
EP-GDS	Boeing 727-81	19557 / 405	1002 (IIAF)	S:d Tehran
EP-PAZ	Fokker F.28 Fellowship 1000	11104	F-GIAK	VIP, operated by Iran Asseman
EP-PLN	Boeing 727-30	18363 / 35	EP-SHP	S:d Tehran

IRAQ
al-Jumhouriya al-Iraqiya   SW Asia

The exact state of the Iraqi Air Force has never fully been determined since the end of the 1991 Gulf war. It is undoubtedly an operational shadow of its former self and while Saddam Hussein remains in control of the country it is likely to stay depleted.

SERIAL SYSTEM Current aircraft all bear civil registrations, in the past these usually shadowed a four digit serial.

al Quwwat al Jawwiya al Iraqiya
Iraqi Air Force

UNITS/BASES	Baghdad-Muthenna, Habbaniyah and Qayyarah are thought to have been restored to use.			
YI-ALA	Antonov An-26	3810		Iraqi AW titles
YI-ALV	Ilyushin Il-76MD	0033448409		Iraqi AW cs

Government of the Republic of Iraq

All assumed stored unless destroyed earlier.

YI-AHH	Dassault Falcon 20F	337	F-WRQR	Survey
YI-AHJ	Dassault Falcon 20F	343	F-WRQR	Survey
YI-AKB	Lockheed L-1329 JetStar II	5235	N4055M	Std Nouakchott?
YI-AKC	Lockheed L-1329 JetStar II	5237	N4058M	Std Nouakchott?
YI-AKD	Lockheed L-1329 JetStar II	5238	N4062M	Std Nouakchott?
YI-AKE	Lockheed L-1329 JetStar II	5239	N4063M	Std Nouakchott?
YI-AKF	Lockheed L-1329 JetStar II	5240	N4065M	Std Nouakchott?

IRELAND
Republic of Ireland / Eire   W Europe

The Irish Air Corps operates in policing and surveillance roles supporting the Army and Navy. A 1998 review made several recommendations that have yet to be actioned despite the current prosperity of the country courtesy of its EU membership. So far the only commitment to new equipment has been the allocation of funds to buy a new VIP aircraft.

SERIAL SYSTEM Serial allocation is sequential with the series currently in the mid 250's.

Aer Chor nah-Eireann
Irish Air Corps

ICAO code IRL, callsign Irish.

UNITS/BASES	No 1 Support Wing, Maritime Sqn, Baldonnel-Casement			CN235
	No 1 Support Wing, Ministerial Air Transport Sqn, Baldonnel-Casement			Super King Air, G-IV

PLANS   Funds allocated to replace the G-IV (G-V, A319CJ or BBJ).
More CN235s recommended to replace the Super King Air and improve MR.
One C-130J is also required to support UN peacekeeping commitments.
Four Cessna Caravans are required to replace the Cessna 172 for utility work.

240	Beech Super King Air 200	BB-672		1 SW
251	GAC Gulfstream IV	1160	N17584	1 SW
252	Airtech/CASA CN235M-100MP	C085		1 SW
253	Airtech/CASA CN235M-100MP	C094		1 SW

Garda
Police

UNITS/BASES	Garda Air Support Unit, Baldonnel-Casement			Defender

254	Pilatus Britten-Norman BN-2T-4S Turbine Defender 4000			
		4008	G-BWPN	Garda Air Support Unit

ISRAEL
Medinat Yisrael   SW Asia

The creation of Israel as the Jewish state immediately after the Second World War has been the source of a large proportion of the world's conflicts ever since. Despite US brokered negotiation involving Arab countries and most recently the creation of the Arab Palestinian Authority within its borders, violence continues. The Israeli armed forces remain among the best equipped and trained in the modern world, as they need to be given their location. The Air Force allocates each type a Hebrew name, indicated below in brackets and italics.

SERIAL SYSTEM The serials appear random although types do tend to be concentrated in blocks, civil style '4X-' registrations are also allocated, usually when operating outside the country.

Tsvah Haganah le Israel - Heyl Ha'Avir
Israeli Defence Force - Air Force   - IDF/AF

ICAO code IAF

UNITS/BASES			
	100 'Flying Camel' Sqn, Sde Dov, Tel Aviv-Dov Hoz AP		Super King Air, Do28
	103 'Flying Elephant' Sqn, Lod, Tel Aviv-Ben Gurion IAP		C-130E/H, KC-130E
	120 'International' Sqn, Lod, Tel Aviv-Ben Gurion IAP		707
	122 'Dakota' Sqn, Lod, Tel Aviv-Ben Gurion IAP		C-47, Arava	EW
	131 'Hercules/Yellowbird' Sqn, Lod, Tel Aviv-Ben Gurion IAP		C-130E/H, KC-130E
	135 'Light Transportation' Sqn, Sde Dov, Tel Aviv-Dov Hoz AP		Super King Air, Queen Air
	191 Sqn, Sde Dov, Tel Aviv-Dov Hoz AP		RC-12D/K
	192 'Hawkeyes' Sqn, Hatzerim AB		E-2C (non-operational)
	195 Sqn, Lod, Tel Aviv-Ben Gurion IAP		Westwind

PLANS — Reported as negotiating with TAI in Turkey for CN235Ms.
14 Super King Airs are to be supplied through the US DoD to replace the remaining Do28s, Queen Airs and C-47s.
On the required list as reward for peace 'concessions' are J-STARS and AWACS capability, C-130Js and AAR airframes.
A mix of C-130Js and C-27Js is also being considered.
Two EW airframes are required from 2005 to replace the tasked 707s, the choice is between the G V and 737.

Serial	Type	c/n	Prev id	Unit	Role
002	Dornier 28B Skyservant (Agur)	3102			Std
006	Dornier 28B Skyservant (Agur)	3117			Std
007 / 4X-FNA	Douglas C-47A (Peres)	26792/15347	43-49531		Std
011	Dornier 28B Skyservant (Agur)	3118			Std
020	Dornier 28B Skyservant (Agur)	3109			Std
022	Dornier 28B Skyservant (Agur)	3097			Std
022 / 4X-FNQ	Douglas C-47A (Peres)				Std
024	Dornier 28B Skyservant (Agur)	3067			Std
026	Dornier 28B Skyservant (Agur)	3088			Std
030	Dornier 28B Skyservant (Agur)	3074			Std
034	Dornier 28B Skyservant (Agur)			100 Sqn	
038	Dornier 28B Skyservant (Agur)			100 Sqn	
040 / 4X-FMF	Douglas C-47A (Peres)				Std
041	Dornier 28B Skyservant (Agur)	3112			Std
101 / 4X-JUA	IAI Arava srs 202	0003	4X-FDA	122 Sqn	
101	Beech 65 Queen Air B80 (Zamir)	LD-478		135 Sqn	
102	Beech 65 Queen Air B80 (Zamir)	LD-479			
102 / 4X-FBA	Lockheed C-130H (L-382C-24D) Hercules (Karnaf)	4430	4X-JUA	103/131 Sqn	
103	Beech 65 Queen Air B80 (Zamir)	LD-480	N7322R	135 Sqn	
104	Beech 65 Queen Air B80 (Zamir)	LD-481	N7323R	135 Sqn	
105	Beech 65 Queen Air B80 (Zamir)	LD-484	N7326R	135 Sqn	
106	Beech 65 Queen Air B80 (Zamir)	LD-485	N7327R	135 Sqn	
106 / 4X-FBB	Lockheed C-130H (L-382C-24D) Hercules (Karnaf)	4431	4X-JUB	103/131 Sqn	
107	Beech 65 Queen Air B80 (Zamir)	LD-486	N7328R	135 Sqn	
108	Beech 65 Queen Air B80 (Zamir)	LD-487	N7329R	135 Sqn	
109	Beech 65 Queen Air B80 (Zamir)	LD-489	N7331R	135 Sqn	
110	Beech 65 Queen Air B80 (Zamir)	LD-490	N7324R	135 Sqn	
111	Beech 65 Queen Air B80 (Zamir)	LD-491	N7325R	135 Sqn	
112	Beech 65 Queen Air B80 (Zamir)	LD-492	N8597R	135 Sqn	
120 / 4X-JYP	Boeing 707-328	17921 / 160	N90287	120 Sqn/IAI	SIGINT
128 / 4X-JYL	Boeing 707-329 (Re'em)	18374 / 283	4X-BYL	120 Sqn	AAR
137 / 4X-JYM	Boeing 707-329	18460 / 328	4X-BYM	120 Sqn	SIGINT
140 / 4X-JYT	Boeing 707-329 (Re'em)	17625 / 99	4X-BYT	120 Sqn	AAR
201	IAI Arava				
203 / 4X-FBO	Lockheed C-130E (L-382-8B) Hercules (Karnaf) 3993		64-0509 (USAF)		Std
203 / 4X-JUB	IAI Arava srs 202			122 Sqn	ECM
205 / 4X-FDD	IAI Arava srs 202			122 Sqn	ECM
206	IAI Arava srs 202			122 Sqn	ECM
207	IAI Arava srs 202			122 Sqn	
208 / 4X-FBP	Lockheed C-130H (L-382C-34D) Hercules (Karnaf)4533		73-1601 (FMS)	103/131 Sqn	
209 / 4X-JUE	IAI Arava srs 202			122 Sqn	ECM
211 / 4X-JUF	IAI Arava srs 202			122 Sqn	
212 / 4X-JUG	IAI Arava srs 202			122 Sqn	ECM
214	IAI Arava				
215 / 4X-JUH	IAI Arava srs 202			122 Sqn	
216	IAI Arava				
217 / 4X-JUI	IAI Arava srs 202			122 Sqn	ECM
225	IAI Arava				
242 / 4X-JYQ	Boeing 707-344C (Re'em)	20110 / 800	4X-BYQ	120 Sqn/IAI	VIP/AAR
246 / 4X-JYS	Boeing 707-344C	20230 / 819	4X-BYS	120 Sqn	AEW

248 / 4X-JYU	Boeing 707-331C *(Re'em)*	20429 / 846	N794TW	120 Sqn	AAR
250 / 4X-JYY	Boeing 707-331C *(Re'em)*	20428 / 845	4X-BYY	120 Sqn	AAR
255 / 4X-JYB	Boeing 707-3H7C	20629 / 863	4X-BYR	120 Sqn	EW
258 / 4X-JYC	Boeing 707-328B	19291 / 536	N2090B	120 Sqn	EW
260 / 4X-JYN	Boeing 707-3J6B *(Re'em)*	20716 / 880	B-2406	120 Sqn	AAR/VIP
264 / 4X-JYH	Boeing 707-3J6C *(Re'em)*	20721 / 875	B-2416	120 Sqn	VIP
272 / 4X-JYV	Boeing 707-3J6B *(Re'em)*	20715 / 870	B-2404	120 Sqn	VIP
275	Boeing 707-3L6C *(Re'em)*	21096 / 900	A6-HRM	120 Sqn	AAR
290	Boeing 707-3W6C *(Re'em)*	21956 / 941	N707JU	120 Sqn	VIP
	Boeing 707-3P1C	21334 / 923	A7-AAA		
301 / 4X-FBF	Lockheed C-130E (L-382) Hercules *(Karnaf)*			103/131 Sqn	
303	Lockheed C-130E (L-382) Hercules *(Karnaf)*			103/131 Sqn	
303 / 4X-JUC	IAI Arava srs 202				
304 / 4X-FBE	Lockheed C-130E (L-382-8B) Hercules *(Karnaf)*	4000	014 (IDF/AF)		Std Lod
305 / 4X-FBJ	Lockheed C-130E (L-382) Hercules *(Karnaf)*	3913	312/4X-FBH	103/131 Sqn	
307 / 4X-FBN	Lockheed C-130E (L-382-4B) Hercules *(Karnaf)*	3925	63-7855 (USAF)		Std Tel Aviv
309 / 4X-FBC	Lockheed C-130H (L-382C-34D) Hercules *(Karnaf)*	4530	009 (IDF/AF)	103/131 Sqn	
310 / 4X-FBG	Lockheed C-130E (L-382-8B) Hercules *(Karnaf)*	3880	63-7810 (USAF)	103/131 Sqn	
311 / 4X-FBD	Lockheed C-130E (L-382-8B) Hercules *(Karnaf)*	3940	63-7870 (USAF)		Std Lod
312 / 4X-FBH	Lockheed C-130E (L-382-4B) Hercules *(Karnaf)*	3747	62-1796 (USAF)	103/131 Sqn	
313 / 4X-FBL	Lockheed C-130E (L-382-4B) Hercules *(Karnaf)*	3932	63-7862 (USAF)	103/131 Sqn	
314 / 4X-FBI	Lockheed C-130E (L-382-8B) Hercules *(Karnaf)*	3840	63-7774 (USAF)	103/131 Sqn	
316 / 4X-FBM	Lockheed C-130E (L-382-4B) Hercules *(Karnaf)*	3943	63-7873 (USAF)	103/131 Sqn	
318 / 4X-FBK	Lockheed C-130E (L-382-8B) Hercules *(Karnaf)*	4014	64-0528 (USAF)	103/131 Sqn	
420 / 4X-FBQ	Lockheed KC-130H (L-382C-52D) Hercules *(Karnaf)*				
		4653		103/131 Sqn	Cvtd C-130H
427 / 4X-FBS	Lockheed C-130H (L-382C-52D) Hercules *(Karnaf)*				
		4662		103/131 Sqn	
428 / 4X-FBX	Lockheed C-130H (L-382C-52D) Hercules *(Karnaf)*				
		4692		103/131 Sqn	
435 / 4X-FBT	Lockheed C-130H (L-382C-52D) Hercules *(Karnaf)*				
		4668		103/131 Sqn	
436 / 4X-FBW	Lockheed C-130H (L-382C-52D) Hercules *(Karnaf)*				
		4686	116 (IDF/AF)	103/131 Sqn	
501 / 4X-FEA	Beech Super King Air B200 *(Zufit)*	BB-1385	009 (IDF/AF)	100/135 Sqn	
504 / 4X-FEB	Beech Super King Air B200 *(Zufit)*	BB-1386	008 (IDF/AF)	100/135 Sqn	
507 / 4X-FEC	Beech Super King Air B200 *(Zufit)*	BB-1387	007 (IDF/AF)	100/135 Sqn	
510 / 4X-FED	Beech Super King Air B200 *(Zufit)*	BB-1388	006 (IDF/AF)	100/135 Sqn	
522 / 4X-FBY	Lockheed KC-130H (L-382C-53D) Hercules *(Karnaf)*				
		4660	422 (IDF/AF)	103/131 Sqn	
545 / 4X-FBZ	Lockheed KC-130H (L-382C-53D) Hercules *(Karnaf)*				
		4664	445 (IDF/AF)	103/131 Sqn	
927 / 4X-JYJ	IAI 1124N Seascan *(Shahaf)*	185	027 (IDF/AF)	195 Sqn	
929 / 4X-JYR	IAI 1124N Seascan *(Shahaf)*	152	035 (IDF/AF)	195 Sqn	
931 / 4X-JYO	IAI 1124N Seascan *(Shahaf)*	186	031 (IDF/AF)	195 Sqn	
941	Grumman E-2C Hawkeye *(Daya)*	A52-41	Bu160771 (FMS)	ex 192 Sqn	Std Hatzerim
942	Grumman E-2C Hawkeye *(Daya)*	A52-42	Bu160772 (FMS)	ex 192 Sqn	Std Hatzerim
944	Grumman E-2C Hawkeye *(Daya)*	A52-44	Bu160773 (FMS)	ex 192 Sqn	Std Hatzerim
946	Grumman E-2C Hawkeye *(Daya)*	A52-46	Bu160774 (FMS)	ex 192 Sqn	Std Hatzerim
974 / 4X-FSA	Beech RC-12D (Super King Air B200, *Kokiya*)	BP-7	81-23638 (FMS)	191 Sqn	
977 / 4X-FSB	Beech RC-12D (Super King Air B200, *Kokiya*)	BP-8	81-23639 (FMS)	191 Sqn	
980 / 4X-FSC	Beech RC-12D (Super King Air B200, *Kokiya*)	BP-9	81-23640 (FMS)	191 Sqn	
982 / 4X-FSD	Beech RC-12D (Super King Air B200, *Kokiya*)	BP-10	81-23641 (FMS)	191 Sqn	
985 / 4X-FSE	Beech RC-12D (Super King Air B200, *Kokiya*)	BP-11	81-23642 (FMS)	191 Sqn	
987 / 4X-FSF	Beech RC-12D (Super King Air B200, *Kokiya*)	FG-1		191 Sqn	
990 / 4X-FSG	Beech RC-12D (Super King Air B200, *Kokiya*)	FG-2		191 Sqn	
	Raytheon Beech Super King Air B200CT/T *(Zufit)*				
		BT-39/BB-1684	N32268	100 Sqn	622 noted 2001
	Raytheon Beech Super King Air B200CT/T *(Zufit)*				
		BT-40/BB-1717	N44717	100 Sqn	625 noted 2001
	Raytheon Beech Super King Air B200CT/T *(Zufit)*				
		BT-41/BB-1721	N44721	100 Sqn	629 noted 2001
	Raytheon Beech Super King Air B200CT/T *(Zufit)*				
		BT-42/BB-1724	N44724	100 Sqn	633 noted 2001
	Raytheon Beech Super King Air B200CT/T *(Zufit)*				
		BT-43/BB-1727	N42327	100 Sqn	636 noted 2001
4X-JUD	IAI Arava				
4X-JUK	IAI Arava srs 202				

ITALY
Repubblica Italiana   S Europe

Italy has been part on NATO since 1949 and has an aircraft manufacturing industry that has strongly influenced the types operated by its numerous air arms. The Air Force adopted its current title in 1943 and operates the Atlantics on behalf of the Navy as until recently the Marina were forbidden by law from operating fixed wing aircraft.

SERIAL SYSTEM Regardless of the service operating them all aircraft are issued a serial in a batch determining role and prefixed with the initials MM for Matricula Militare (Military Number). The transport batch commenced at MM60000. All air craft wear codes denoting the operator/unit and an individual aircraft number.

Aeronautica Militare Italiana - AMI
Italian Air Force

Callsign India**** (four digits)

UNITS/BASES	Brigata Caccia Intercettori		
	36 Stormo, 636 sqn coll., Gioia del Colle	Piaggio 180	Communications
	Brigata Caccia Bombardieri Ricognitori		
	53 Stormo, 653 sqn coll., Cameri	Piaggio 180	Communications
	Brigata Aerea Supporto e SAR		
	14 Stormo, 8 Gruppo, Pratica di Mare	G222, Boeing 707	Calibration, AAR/transport
	14 Stormo, 71 Gruppo, Pratica di Mare	G222, PD808	EW
	15 Stormo, 303 Gruppo Autonomo, Guidonia	Piaggio 166	Survey
	Brigata Aerea Transporti		
	46 Brigata Aerea		
	2 Gruppo, Pisa-San Giusto	C-130J	
	98 Gruppo, Pisa-San Giusto	G222 (to take C-27J)	
	50 Gruppo, Pisa-San Giusto	C-130H (to take C-130J-30)	
	31 Stormo, 93 Gruppo, Rome-Ciampino	Falcon 50	VIP/Medevac
	31 Stormo. 306 Gruppo, Rome-Ciampino	Falcon 900 to replace G-III, A319CJ to replace DC-9	
	Ufficio Ispettore Aviazione per la Marina		
	30 Stormo, 86 Gruppo, Cagliari	Atlantic	MR
	41 Stormo, 88 Gruppo, Catania-Sigonella	Atlantic	MR
	Commando Logistico		
	Reparto Sperimentale di Volo (RSV)		
	311 Gruppo, Pratica di Mare	Various	Test

PLANS Two C-130J-30 held on option and additional P180 Avantis are to be acquired.
Five C-27Js are on order, with seven on option. The original requirement was for 18 in total.
Four 767 tanker transports were ordered from Boeing in mid 2001 with deliveries between 2004 and 2006 to replace the 707s.
A proposed A400M purchase was cancelled in late 2001.
An independent AEW capability is sought, probably to be based around 3 or 4 C-130s.

MM578/ RS-5	Piaggio PD-808TA	502	14 Stormo
MM25153/ 303-20	Piaggio P-166DL-3/APH	472/121	
MM25154/ 303-21	Piaggio P-166DL-3/APH	473/122	
MM25155/ 303-22	Piaggio P-166DL-3/APH	474/123	
MM25156/ 303-23	Piaggio P-166DL-3/APH	475/124	
MM25157/ 303-24	Piaggio P-166DL-3/APH	476/125	
MM25158/ 303-25	Piaggio P-166DL-3/APH	477/126	
MM40108/ 41-70	Breguet 1151 Atlantic	70	41 Stormo
MM40109/ 30-71	Breguet 1151 Atlantic	71	30 Stormo
MM40110/ 41-72	Breguet 1151 Atlantic	72	41 Stormo
MM40111/ 41-73	Breguet 1151 Atlantic	73	41 Stormo
MM40112/ 30-74	Breguet 1151 Atlantic	74	30 Stormo
MM40113/ 30-75	Breguet 1151 Atlantic	75	30 Stormo
MM40114/ 41-76	Breguet 1151 Atlantic	76	41 Stormo
MM40115/ 41-77	Breguet 1151 Atlantic	77	41 Stormo
MM40116/ 30-01	Breguet 1151 Atlantic	78	30 Stormo
MM40117/ 41-02	Breguet 1151 Atlantic	79	41 Stormo
MM40118/ 30-03	Breguet 1151 Atlantic	80	30 Stormo
MM40119/ 30-04	Breguet 1151 Atlantic	81	30 Stormo
MM40120/ 41-05	Breguet 1151 Atlantic	82	41 Stormo
MM40121/ 41-06	Breguet 1151 Atlantic	83	41 Stormo
MM40122/ 30-07	Breguet 1151 Atlantic	84	30 Stormo
MM40123/ 30-10	Breguet 1151 Atlantic	85	30 Stormo
MM40124/ 41-11	Breguet 1151 Atlantic	86	41 Stormo
MM40125/ 30-12	Breguet 1151 Atlantic	87	41 Stormo
MM61917/ SP-37	Piaggio P-166ML1	429/78	
MM61919	Piaggio P-166ML1	431/80	

MM61950	Piaggio PD-808VIP	508		14 Stormo	
MM61952	Piaggio PD-808GE	510		14 Stormo	
MM61954	Piaggio PD-808TP	512		31 Stormo	
MM61955	Piaggio PD-808TP	513		14 Stormo	
MM61960	Piaggio PD-808GE	517		14 Stormo	
MM61961	Piaggio PD-808GE	518		14 Stormo	
MM61962	Piaggio PD-808GE	519		14 Stormo	
MM61988/ 46-02	Lockheed C-130H (L-382C-22D) Hercules	4441		46BA/50Gr	
MM61989/ 46-03	Lockheed C-130H (L-382C-22D) Hercules	4443		46BA/50Gr	
MM61990/ 46-04	Lockheed C-130H (L-382C-22D) Hercules	4446		46BA/50Gr	
MM61991/ 46-05	Lockheed C-130H (L-382C-22D) Hercules	4447		46BA/50Gr	
MM61992/ 46-06	Lockheed C-130H (L-382C-22D) Hercules	4449		46BA/50Gr	
MM61993/ 46-07	Lockheed C-130H (L-382C-22D) Hercules	4451		46BA/50Gr	
MM61994/ 46-08	Lockheed C-130H (L-382C-22D) Hercules	4452		46BA/50Gr	
MM61995/ 46-09	Lockheed C-130H (L-382C-22D) Hercules	4491		46BA/50Gr	
MM61997/ 46-11	Lockheed C-130H (L-382C-22D) Hercules	4493		46BA/50Gr	
MM61998/ 46-12	Lockheed C-130H (L-382C-22D) Hercules	4494		46BA/50Gr	
MM620 2	Douglas DC-9-32	47595 / 709		31 Stormo	
MM620 4	Piaggio PD-808RM	521		14 Stormo	
MM62020	Dassault Falcon 50	151	F-WPXD	31 Stormo	
MM62021	Dassault Falcon 50	155	F-WPXH	31 Stormo	
MM62022	GAC G-1159A Gulfstream III	451	N330GA	31 Stormo	
MM62025	GAC G-1159A Gulfstream III	479	N319GA	31 Stormo	
MM62026	Dassault Falcon 50	193	F-WWHH	31 Stormo	
MM62029	Dassault Falcon 50	211	F-WWHR	31 Stormo	
MM62101/ RS-45	Aeritalia G-222TCM	4003	I-CERK	RSV	Std Pratica Di Mare
MM62102/ 46-20	Aeritalia G-222TCM	4004			Std Pisa
MM62103/ 46-37	Aeritalia G-222TCM	4005			Std Pisa
MM62104/ 46-91	Aeritalia G-222TCM	4007		46BA/98Gr	
MM62105/ 46-82	Aeritalia G-222TCM	4008		46BA/98Gr	
MM62107	Aeritalia G-222VS	4012		14 Stormo	
MM62108/ 46-30	Aeritalia G-222TCM	4013			Std Pisa
MM62109/ 46-96	Aeritalia G-222TCM	4014		46BA/98Gr	
MM62110/ 46-81	Aeritalia G-222TCM	4015			Std Pisa
MM62111/ 46-83	Aeritalia G-222TCM	4016		46BA/98Gr	
MM62112/ 46-85	Aeritalia G-222TCM	4018			Std Pisa
MM62114/ 46-80	Aeritalia G-222TCM	4019			Std Pisa
MM62117/ 46-25	Aeritalia G-222TCM	4023	I-MAIT	46BA/98Gr	
MM62118/ 46-24	Aeritalia G-222TCM	4024			Std Pisa
MM62119/ 46-21	Aeritalia G-222TCM	4025		46BA/98Gr	
MM62120/ 46-90	Aeritalia G-222TCM	4026			Std Pisa
MM62121/ 46-86	Aeritalia G-222TCM	4027			Std Pisa
MM62122/ 46-23	Aeritalia G-222TCM	4028			Std Pisa
MM62123/ 46-28	Aeritalia G-222TCM	4029			Std Pisa
MM62124/ 46-88	Aeritalia G-222TCM	4030		46BA/98Gr	
MM62125/ 14-24	Aeritalia G-222TCM	4031		14 Stormo	
MM62126/ 46-26	Aeritalia G-222TCM	4032		46BA/98Gr	
MM62130/ 46-31	Aeritalia G-222TCM	4037			Std Pisa
MM62132/ 46-32	Aeritalia G-222TCM	4045			Std Pisa
MM62134/ 46-33	Aeritalia G-222TCM	4047			Std Pisa
MM62135/ 46-94	Aeritalia G-222TCM	4048		46BA/98Gr	
MM62136/ 46-97	Aeritalia G-222TCM	4049		46BA/98Gr	
MM62137/ 46-95	Aeritalia G-222TCM	4050		46BA/98Gr	
MM62138	Aeritalia G-222VS	4051		14 Stormo	
MM62139/ 14-20	Aeritalia G-222RM	4057		14 Stormo	
MM62140/ 14-21	Aeritalia G-222RM	4069		14 Stormo	
MM62141/ 14-22	Aeritalia G-222RM	4076		14 Stormo	
MM62142/ 14-23	Aeritalia G-222RM	4077		14 Stormo	
MM62143/ 46-36	Aeritalia G-222TCM	4085			Std Pisa
MM62144/ 46-98	Aeritalia G-222TCM	4086		46BA/98Gr	
MM62145/ 46-50	Aeritalia G-222TCM	4088		46BA/98Gr	
MM62146/ 46-51	Aeritalia G-222TCM	4089		46BA/98Gr	
MM62147/ 46-52	Aeritalia G-222TCM	4091			Std Pisa
MM62148/ 14-01	Boeing 707-382B	19740 / 676	CS-TBC	14 Stormo	
MM62149/ 14-02	Boeing 707-382B	20298 / 840	CS-TBG	14 Stormo	
MM62150/ 14-03	Boeing 707-3F5C	20514 / 857	CS-TBT	14 Stormo	
MM62151/ 14-04	Boeing 707-3F5C	20515 / 859	CS-TBU	14 Stormo	
MM62152/ RS-45	Aeritalia G-222TCM	4092		RSV	Std Lire
MM62153/ RS-46	Aeritalia G-222TCM	4095		RSV	
MM62154/ 46-54	Aeritalia G-222TCM	4087			Std Pisa
MM62155/ 46-53	Aeritalia G-222TCM	4090		46BA/98Gr	
MM62159	Piaggio P-180 Avanti	1024		RSV	
MM62160/ 54	Piaggio P-180 Avanti	1025		RSV	
MM62161	Piaggio P-180 Avanti	1023			

MM62162	Piaggio P-180 Avanti	1028			
MM62163	Piaggio P-180 Avanti	1029		RSV	
CMX62164	Piaggio P-180 Avanti	1030	MM62164	RSV	
MM62171	Dassault Falcon 900EX	45	F-WWFJ	31 Stormo	
MM62172	Dassault Falcon 900EX	52	F-WWFV	31 Stormo	
MM62173	Airbus Industrie A319-115CJ	1002	D-AJWF	31 Stormo	
MM62174	Airbus Industrie A319-115CJ	1157	D-AACI	31 Stormo	
MM62175/ 46-40	Lockheed Martin C-130J (L-382U-13J) Hercules II	5495	N4099R	46BA/2Gr	
MM62176/ 46-41	Lockheed Martin C-130J (L-382U-13J) Hercules II	5497		46BA/2Gr	
MM62177/ 46-42	Lockheed Martin C-130J (L-382U-13J) Hercules II	5498		46BA/2Gr	
MM62178/ 46-43	Lockheed Martin C-130J (L-382U-13J) Hercules II	5503		46BA/2Gr	
MM62179/ 46-44	Lockheed Martin C-130J (L-382U-13J) Hercules II	5504		46BA/2Gr	
MM62180/ 46-45	Lockheed Martin C-130J (L-382U-13J) Hercules II	5505		46BA/2Gr	
MM62181	Lockheed Martin C-130J (L-382U-31J) Hercules II	5510		46BA/2Gr	On order 2001
MM62182	Lockheed Martin C-130J (L-382U-31J) Hercules II	5511		46BA/2Gr	On order 2001
MM62183	Lockheed Martin C-130J (L-382U-31J) Hercules II	5512		46BA/2Gr	On order 2001
MM62184	Lockheed Martin C-130J (L-382U-31J) Hercules II	5513		46BA/2Gr	On order 2001
MM62185	Lockheed Martin C-130J (L-382U-31J) Hercules II	5514		46BA/2Gr	On order 2001
MM62186	Lockheed Martin C-130J (L-382U-31J) Hercules II	5520		46BA/2Gr	On order 2001
MM62187	Lockheed Martin C-130J-30 (L-382V-34J) Hercules II	5521		46BA/50Gr	On order 2001
	Lockheed Martin C-130J-30 (L-382V-34J) Hercules II	5523		46BA/50Gr	On order 2001
	Lockheed Martin C-130J-30 (L-382V-34J) Hercules II	5529		46BA/50Gr	On order 2002
	Lockheed Martin C-130J-30 (L-382V-34J) Hercules II	5530		46BA/50Gr	On order 2002
	Lockheed Martin C-130J-30 (L-382V-34J) Hercules II	5531		46BA/50Gr	On order 2002
	Lockheed Martin C-130J-30 (L-382V-34J) Hercules II	5539		46BA/50Gr	On order 2003
	Lockheed Martin C-130J-30 (L-382V-34J) Hercules II	5540		46BA/50Gr	On order 2003
	Lockheed Martin C-130J-30 (L-382V-34J) Hercules II	5550		46BA/50Gr	On order 2004
	Lockheed Martin C-130J-30 (L-382V-34J) Hercules II	5551		46BA/50Gr	On order 2004
	Lockheed Martin C-130J-30 (L-382V-34J) Hercules II	5552		46BA/50Gr	On order 2004
MM62199	Piaggio P-180AM Avanti		CSX62199		
	LMATTS/Alenia C-27J				On order
	LMATTS/Alenia C-27J				On order
	LMATTS/Alenia C-27J				On order
	LMATTS/Alenia C-27J				On order
	LMATTS/Alenia C-27J				On order

Esercito Italiano - Cavalleria dell'Aria
Italian Army

UNITS/BASES	4 Reggimento 'Altair'		
	28 Gruppo Squadroni (28 Gr.Sqd), 'Tucano'		
	Sqn ACTL, Viterbo	Do228	
	Sqd ACTR, Rome-Ciampino	Piaggio 180	VIP/Medevac
PLANS	Two additional Do228 to be funded.		

MM62156/ EI-101	Dornier 228-212 (ACTL)	8202	D-CAOT	28 Gr
MM62157/ EI-102	Dornier 228-212 (ACTL)	8203	D-CAOS	28 Gr
MM62158/ EI-103	Dornier 228-212 (ACTL)	8209	D-CLOZ	28 Gr
MM62167	Piaggio P-180 Avanti (ACTR)	1026		28 Gr
MM62168	Piaggio P-180 Avanti (ACTR)	1027	F-GMRM	28 Gr
MM62169	Piaggio P-180 Avanti (ACTR)	1031		28 Gr

Guardia di Finanza - G di F
Customs Services

UNITS/BASES	1 Gruppo Aereo Addestramento Avanzato, Pratica di Mare		P.166	
	2 Gruppo Aereo Esplorazione Aeromarittima, Pratica di Mare		ATR42	

MM25 71/ GF-01	Piaggio P-166DL-3/SEM1	465/114	MM61922	1 Gr
MM25 72/ GF-02	Piaggio P-166DL-3/SEM1	466/115	MM61923	1 Gr
MM25 73/ GF-03	Piaggio P-166DL-3/SEM2	490/141		1 Gr
MM25 74/ GF-04	Piaggio P-166DL-3/SEM2	491/142		1 Gr
MM25 75/ GF-05	Piaggio P-166DL-3/SEM2	492/143		1 Gr
MM25 76/ GF-06	Piaggio P-166DL-3/SEM2	493/144		1 Gr
MM25 77/ GF-07	Piaggio P-166DL-3/SEM2	494/145		1 Gr
MM25 78/ GF-08	Piaggio P-166DL-3/SEM2	495/146		1 Gr
MM25 79/ GF-09	Piaggio P-166DL-3/SEM2	496/147		1 Gr
MM25 80/ GF-10	Piaggio P-166DL-3/SEM2	497/148		1 Gr
MM25 81/ GF-11	Piaggio P-166DL-3/SEM2	498/149		1 Gr
MM25 82/ GF-12	Piaggio P-166DL-3/SEM2	499/150		1 Gr
MM62 65/ GF-13	ATR-42-400MP	500	F-WWEW	2 Gr
MM62 66/ GF-14	ATR-42-400MP	502	F-WWEM	2 Gr

Guardia Costiera / Capitanerie di Porto
Coast Guard

UNITS/BASES	3 Nucleo Aereo CP, Pescara		P-166, ATR-42MP
PLANS	A second ATR42MP is due for delivery in March 2003.		

MM25 159/ 8-01	Piaggio P-166DL-3/SEM1	478/127		3 NACP
MM25 160/ 8-02	Piaggio P-166DL-3/SEM1	479/128		3 NACP
MM25 161/ 8-03	Piaggio P-166DL-3/SEM1	480/129		3 NACP
MM25 162/ 8-04	Piaggio P-166DL-3/SEM1	481/130		3 NACP
MM25 163/ 8-05	Piaggio P-166DL-3/SEM1	482/131		3 NACP
MM25 164/ 8-06	Piaggio P-166DL-3/SEM1	483/132		3 NACP
MM25 165/ 8-07	Piaggio P-166DL-3/SEM1	484/133		3 NACP
MM25 166/ 8-08	Piaggio P-166DL-3/SEM1	485/134		3 NACP
MM25 167/ 8-09	Piaggio P-166DL-3/SEM1	486/135		3 NACP
MM25 168/ 8-10	Piaggio P-166DL-3/SEM1	487/136		3 NACP
MM25 169/ 8-11	Piaggio P-166DL-3/SEM1	488/137		3 NACP
MM25 60/ 8-12	Piaggio P-166DL-3/SEM1	489/138		3 NACP
MM62 70/ 10-01	ATR-42-400MP	466	CSX62170	3 NACP

Polizia di Stato
Police

PS-A95	Partenavia P-68C-OBS Observer	336-23/OBS
PS-A96	Partenavia P-68C-OBS Observer	337-24/OBS
PS-A97	Partenavia P-68TC-OBS Observer 2	338-25/OBS
PS-A98	Partenavia P-68TC-OBS Observer 2	339-26/OBS
PS-A99	Partenavia P-68TC-OBS Observer 2	378-31/OBS
PS-B01	Partenavia P-68TC-OBS Observer 2	
PS-B02	Partenavia P-68TC-OBS Observer 2	382-35/OBS
PS-B03	Partenavia P-68TC-OBS Observer 2	383-36/OBS
PS-B04	Partenavia P-68TC-OBS Observer 2	385-37/OBS
PS-B05	Partenavia P-68TC-OBS Observer 2	386-38/OBS
PS-B06	Partenavia P-68TC-OBS Observer 2	388-39/OBS
PS-B07	Vulcanair P-68TC-OBS Observer 2	401-08/OBS
PS-B08	Vulcanair P-68TC-OBS Observer 2	403-09/OBS
PS-B09	Vulcanair P-68TC-OBS Observer 2	404-10/OBS
PS-B10	Vulcanair P-68TC-OBS Observer 2	405-11/OBS
PS-B11	Vulcanair P-68TC-OBS Observer 2	406-12/OBS
PS-B12	Vulcanair P-68TC-OBS Observer 2	408-14/OBS
PS-B13	Vulcanair P-68TC-OBS Observer 2	409-15/OBS
PS-B14	Vulcanair P-68TC-OBS Observer 2	410-16/OBS

IVORY COAST
République de Côte d'Ivoire   W Africa

Granted independence by France in 1960 and the Air Force was established shortly afterwards with French help. France still stands by the Defence agreement to support the country if required.

SERIAL SYSTEM Civil style marks are issued in a unique sequence, 'TU-V**'.

Force Aérienne de Côte d'Ivoire
Ivory Coast Air Force

UNITS/BASES   Groupe Aérien Transportes & Liaison (GATL), Abidjan IAP.

TU-VAA	Fokker 100	11245	PH-CDI	GATL
TU-VAD	GAC Gulfstream IV	1019	N17584	GATL
TU-VAF	GAC G-1159A Gulfstream III	462	N303GA	GATL
TU-VBA	Cessna 421C Golden Eagle	421C0436	N4943J	GATL
	Cessna O-2A Super Skymaster	M337-0459	69-7661 (USAF)	
	Cessna O-2A Super Skymaster	M337-0416	69-7618 (USAF)	

JAMAICA
W Indies

Independent from Britain from 1962. The Air Wing's main task is police support, including anti-drug operations, coastal patrol and Medevac duties. The USCG also patrol Jamaican waters.

SERIAL SYSTEM Serials are sequential and include a code denoting the type of aircraft (ie T, Transport).

Jamaica Defence Force Air Wing

UNITS/BASES   All fixed wing aircraft are based at Kingston-Manley Int'l Airport with No.1 'Eagle' Flight.

PLANS   An MPA type is required for Coast Guard duties.

A-7	Cessna 210M Centurion	21062742	JDFA-7	1 Flt
T-2	Britten-Norman BN-2A-3 Defender	699	JDFT-2	1 Flt
T-3	Beech King Air A100	B-216	JDFT-3	1 Flt

JAPAN
Nihon Koku   E Asia

Consisting of four main Islands, Honshu, Hokkaido, Shikoku and Kyushu, Japan's armed forces were re-established and orientated towards defence (from Russia and China) with much US assistance from the 1950s. With increasing indigenous production today's forces are very capable and among the largest in the world.

SERIAL SYSTEM The JASDF serials start with a two digit number representing the year of acceptance and the type being followed by a dash then a four digit number the first digit of which denotes the role and the remainder sequential but not necessarily starting at 001. JMSDF serials are issued in four digit batches commencing with the role and batched after that by type. JGSDF markings are also allocated in batches by type, the aircraft also wear codes denoting the unit.

Nihon Koku Jieitai
Japan Air Self Defense Force - JASDF

UNITS/BASES	Koku Sotai (Air Defence Command)		
	83 Koku-gun, Nansei Sien Hiko-han, Naha AB	B65 (supporting an F-4 unit)	
	Sotai Sireibu Hiko-tai, Iruma AB	U-4	VIP, Medevac
	Densi-Sien-tai, Iruma AB	YS-11E/EA/EL, EC-1	ECM
	Keikai Koku-tai, 601 Hiko-tai, Misawa AB	E-2C, E-767	AEW
	Koko Sien Shudan (Air Support Command)		
	Koku Kyunan-dan, Kyunan Kyoiku-tai, Komaki AB	U-125A	ASR
	Koku Kyunan-dan, Kyunan-tai, Chitose AB	U-125A	ASR
	Koku Kyunan-dan, Kyunan-tai, Matsushima AB	MU-2S	ASR
	Koku Kyunan-dan, Kyunan-tai, Hyakuri AB	MU-2S	ASR
	Koku Kyunan-dan, Kyunan-tai, Hamamatsu AB	MU-2S	ASR
	Koku Kyunan-dan, Kyunan-tai, Akita Airport	MU-2S	ASR

Koku Kyunan-dan, Kyunan-tai, Komatsu AB	U-125A		ASR
Koku Kyunan-dan, Kyunan-tai, Niigata Airport	MU-2S		ASR
Koku Kyunan-dan, Kyunan-tai, Ashiya AB	MU-2S		ASR
Koku Kyunan-dan, Kyunan-tai, Naha AB	U-125A		ASR
Koku Kyunan-dan, Kyunan-tai, Nyutabaru AB	MU-2S		ASR
1 Yuso Koku-tai, 401 Hiko-tai, Komaki AB	C-130H		
2 Yuso Koku-tai, 402 Hiko-tai, Iruma AB	C-1, YS-11P/C, U-4		
3 Yuso Koku-tai, 403 Hiko-tai, Miho AB	C-1, YS-11P/PC/NT		
41 Kyoiku Hiko-tai, Miho AB	T-400		Training
Hiko Tenken-tai, Iruma AB	YS-11FC, U-125		Calibration
Tokubeto Koku Yuso-tai, 701 Hiko-tai, Chitose AB	747-400		VIP

Koku Kaihatsu Jikken Shudan (Air Development & Test Command)
Hiko Kaihatsu Jikken-dan, Gifu AB   Various

PLANS   Requires four AAR aircraft (KC-X) , favorite will be the 767-200, but also considering A310.
A further four AWACS 767s are under consideration.
Development funds awarded in 2001 to start work on a new Maritime Patrol (MP-X) and Transport (C-X)
indigenous design.
Four more G-IV (U-4) are to be funded.

41-5051	Beech 400T Beechjet (T-400)	TX-1	N82884	41 KH tai	
41-5052	Beech 400T Beechjet (T-400)	TX-2	N82885	41 KH tai	
41-5053	Beech 400T Beechjet (T-400)	TX-3	N82886	41 KH tai	
41-5054	Beech 400T Beechjet (T-400)	TX-4	N3195K	41 KH tai	
41-5055	Beech 400T Beechjet (T-400)	TX-5	N3195Q	41 KH tai	
51-5056	Beech 400T Beechjet (T-400)	TX-6	N3195X	41 KH tai	
51-5057	Beech 400T Beechjet (T-400)	TX-7	N3228M	41 KH tai	
51-5058	Beech 400T Beechjet (T-400)	TX-8	N3228V	41 KH tai	
71-5059	Beech 400T Beechjet (T-400)	TX-9	N1069L	41 KH tai	
01-5060	Beech 400T Beechjet (T-400)	TX-10	N3221Z	41 KH tai	
20-1101	Boeing 747-47C	24730 / 816	JA8091	701 H tai	
20-1102	Boeing 747-47C	24731 / 839	JA8092	701 H tai	
62-3501	Boeing 767-27C	27385 / 557	N767JA	HKJ dan	
62-3502	Boeing 767-27C	27391 / 588	N767JB	HKJ dan	
74-3503	Boeing 767-27C	28016 / 618	N767JC	601 H tai	
84-3504	Boeing 767-27C	28017 / 642	N767JD	601 H tai	
52-3001	Raytheon Hawker 800 (U-125A)	258245	G-JHSX	K tai, Komaki	
52-3002	Raytheon Hawker 800 (U-125A)	258247	G-BVRF	K tai, Komaki	
52-3003	Raytheon Hawker 800 (U-125A)	258250	G-BVRG	K tai, Nyutabaru	
62-3004	Raytheon Hawker 800 (U-125A)	258268	N809H	K tai, Chitose	
72-3005	Raytheon Hawker 800 (U-125A)	258288	N816H	K tai	
72-3006	Raytheon Hawker 800 (U-125A)	258305	N305XP	K tai, Komaki	
82-3007	Raytheon Hawker 800 (U-125A)	258306	N1103U	K tai, Chitose	
82-3008	Raytheon Hawker 800 (U-125A)	258325	N1112N	K tai, Komatsu	
82-3009	Raytheon Hawker 800 (U-125A)	258333	N3261Y	K tai, Nyutabaru	
92-3010	Raytheon Hawker 800 (U-125A)	258341	N3251M	K tai, Chitose	
92-3011	Raytheon Hawker 800 (U-125A)	258348	N2175W	K tai	
92-3012	Raytheon Hawker 800 (U-125A)	258360	N3189H	K tai, Komatsu	
92-3013	Raytheon Hawker 800 (U-125A)	258370	N23556	K tai	
02-3014	Raytheon Hawker 800 (U-125A)	258381	N23566	K tai, Chitose	
02-3015	Raytheon Hawker 800 (U-125A)	258407	N30562	K tai, Hyakuri	
02-3016	Raytheon Hawker 800 (U-125A)	258427	N31833	K tai, Hyakuri	
12-3017	Raytheon Hawker 800 (U-125A)	258445	N40708	K tai	
12-3018	Raytheon Hawker 800 (U-125A)	258469	N43079	K tai	
?2-3019	Raytheon Hawker 800 (U-125A)	258493	N40933	K tai	on order
?2-3020	Raytheon Hawker 800 (U-125A)	258513	N50513	K tai	on order
?2-3021	Raytheon Hawker 800 (U-125A)	258533	N50733	K tai	on order
29-3041	British Aerospace 125-800B (U-125)	258215	G-JFCX	HT tai	
39-3042	British Aerospace 125-800B (U-125)	258227	G-BUUW	HT tai	
49-3043	British Aerospace 125-800B (U-125)	258242	G-BVFE	HT tai	
75-3251	GAC Gulfstream IVSP (U-4A)	1270	N442GA	402 H tai	
75-3252	GAC Gulfstream IVSP (U-4A)	1271	N452GA	402 H tai	
85-3253	GAC Gulfstream IVSP (U-4A)	1303	N435GA	SSH tai	
95-3254	GAC Gulfstream IVSP (U-4A)	1326	N325GA	SSH tai	
05-3255	GAC Gulfstream IVSP (U-4A)	1359	N359GA	402 H tai	
34-3451	Grumman E-2C Hawkeye	A52-71	Bu161400 (FMS)	601 H tai	
34-3452	Grumman E-2C Hawkeye	A52-73	Bu161401 (FMS)	601 H tai	
34-3453	Grumman E-2C Hawkeye	A52-76	Bu161402 (FMS)	601 H tai	
34-3454	Grumman E-2C Hawkeye	A52-77	Bu161403 (FMS)	601 H tai	
54-3455	Grumman E-2C Hawkeye		Bu161786 (FMS)	601 H tai	
54-3456	Grumman E-2C Hawkeye		Bu161787 (FMS)	601 H tai	
54-3457	Grumman E-2C Hawkeye		Bu161788 (FMS)	601 H tai	
54-3458	Grumman E-2C Hawkeye		Bu161789 (FMS)	601 H tai	

34-3459	Grumman E-2C Hawkeye		Bu164621 (FMS)	601 H tai	
34-3460	Grumman E-2C Hawkeye		Bu164622 (FMS)	601 H tai	
34-3461	Grumman E-2C Hawkeye		Bu164623 (FMS)	601 H tai	
44-3462	Grumman E-2C Hawkeye		Bu164624 (FMS)	601 H tai	
44-3463	Grumman E-2C Hawkeye		Bu164625 (FMS)	601 H tai	
28-1001	Kawasaki C-1A	8001	18-1001 (JASDF)	HKJ dan	
28-1002	Kawasaki C-1A	8002	18-1002 (JASDF)	HKJ dan	
38-1003	Kawasaki C-1A	8003		403 H tai	
48-1004	Kawasaki C-1A	8004	38-1004 (JASDF)	402 H tai	
48-1005	Kawasaki C-1A	8005		402 H tai	
58-1006	Kawasaki C-1A	8006		403 H tai	
58-1007	Kawasaki C-1A	8007		403 H tai	
58-1008	Kawasaki C-1A	8008		402 H tai	
58-1010	Kawasaki C-1A (SKE)	8010			
58-1011	Kawasaki C-1A (SKE)	8011		402 H tai	
58-1012	Kawasaki C-1A	8012		402 H tai	
58-1013	Kawasaki C-1A	8013		403 H tai	
68-1014	Kawasaki C-1A	8014		402 H tai	
68-1016	Kawasaki C-1A	8016		403 H tai	
68-1017	Kawasaki C-1A	8017		402 H tai	
68-1018	Kawasaki C-1A	8018		403 H tai	
68-1019	Kawasaki C-1A-kai	8019		402 H tai	
68-1020	Kawasaki C-1A	8020		403 H tai	
78-1021	Kawasaki EC-1	8021		DS tai	Cvtd C-1A
78-1022	Kawasaki C-1A	8022		402 H tai	
78-1023	Kawasaki C-1A	8023		402 H tai	
78-1024	Kawasaki C-1A	8024		403 H tai	
78-1025	Kawasaki C-1A	8025		402 H tai	
78-1026	Kawasaki C-1A	8026		403 H tai	
88-1028	Kawasaki C-1A	8028		403 H tai	
98-1029	Kawasaki C-1A	8029		402 H tai	
08-1030	Kawasaki C-1A	8030		402 H tai	
18-1031	Kawasaki C-1A	8031		402 H tai	
35-1071	Lockheed C-130H (L-382C-27E) Hercules	4976	82-0051 (FMS)	401 H tai	
35-1072	Lockheed C-130H (L-382C-27E) Hercules	4980	82-0050 (FMS)	401 H tai	
45-1073	Lockheed C-130H (L-382C-44E) Hercules	5015	83-0001 (FMS)	401 H tai	
45-1074	Lockheed C-130H (L-382C-44E) Hercules	5017	83-0002 (FMS)	401 H tai	
75-1075	Lockheed C-130H (L-382C-68E) Hercules	5088	85-0025 (FMS)	401 H tai	
75-1076	Lockheed C-130H (L-382C-68E) Hercules	5090	85-0026 (FMS)	401 H tai	
75-1077	Lockheed C-130H (L-382C-75E) Hercules	5108	86-0372 (FMS)	401 H tai	
75-1078	Lockheed C-130H (L-382C-75E) Hercules	5109	86-0373 (FMS)	401 H tai	
85-1079	Lockheed C-130H (L-382C-82E) Hercules	5136	87-0137 (FMS)	401 H tai	
85-1080	Lockheed C-130H (L-382C-82E) Hercules	5138	87-0138 (FMS)	401 H tai	
95-1081	Lockheed C-130H (L-382C-90E) Hercules	5170	88-1800 (FMS)	401 H tai	
95-1082	Lockheed C-130H (L-382C-90E) Hercules	5171	88-1801 (FMS)	401 H tai	
95-1083	Lockheed C-130H (L-382C-90E) Hercules	5172	88-1802 (FMS)	401 H tai	
05-1084	Lockheed C-130H (L-382C-02F) Hercules	5213	89-0118 (FMS)	401 H tai	
05-1085	Lockheed C-130H (L-382C-02F) Hercules	5214	89-0119 (FMS)	401 H tai	
75-1086	Lockheed C-130H (L-382C-60F) Hercules	5435		401 H tai	
73-3201	Mitsubishi MU-2S	901/112		K tai, Hyakuri	
83-3204	Mitsubishi MU-2S	904/148		K tai, Matsushima	
93-3206	Mitsubishi MU-2S	906/176		K tai	
03-3208	Mitsubishi MU-2S	908/186		K tai, Matsushima	
13-3209	Mitsubishi MU-2S	909/200			WFU ?
13-3210	Mitsubishi MU-2S	910/201		K tai, Hyakuri	
13-3211	Mitsubishi MU-2S	911/202		K tai, Komaki	
13-3212	Mitsubishi MU-2S	912/203		K tai, Matsushima	
23-3213	Mitsubishi MU-2S	913/225		K tai, Komaki	
23-3214	Mitsubishi MU-2S	914/227		K tai, Komatsu	
33-3215	Mitsubishi MU-2S	915/234		K tai, Matsushima	
33-3216	Mitsubishi MU-2S	916/235		K tai, Komaki	
33-3217	Mitsubishi MU-2S	917/278		K tai, Matsushima	
43-3218	Mitsubishi MU-2S	918/279		K tai, Ashiya	
63-3220	Mitsubishi MU-2S	920/335		K tai, Ashiya	
63-3221	Mitsubishi MU-2S	921/336		K tai, Niigata	
73-3222	Mitsubishi MU-2S	922/360		K tai Hamamatsu	
83-3223	Mitsubishi MU-2S	923/377		K tai, Hyakuri	
83-3224	Mitsubishi MU-2S	924/378		K tai, Ashiya	
13-3225	Mitsubishi MU-2S	925/445		K tai Akita	
23-3226	Mitsubishi MU-2S	926/455		K tai, Hamamatsu	
33-3227	Mitsubishi MU-2S	927/464		K tai, Nyutabaru	
63-3228	Mitsubishi MU-2S	928		K tai, Matsushima	
53-3271	Mitsubishi MU-2J	951/654			WFU?
73-3272	Mitsubishi MU-2J	952/715			WFU?

83-3273	Mitsubishi MU-2J	953/716		WFU?
93-3274	Mitsubishi MU-2J	954/717		WFU?
52-115ᵀ	NAMC YS-11P-103	2008	402 H tai	
52-1152	NAMC YS-11P-103	2009	402 H tai	
62-1153	NAMC YS-11P-105	2018	402 H tai	
82-1155	NAMC YS-11FC-305	2074	DS tai	cvtd A
92-1156	NAMC YS-11NT-402	2124	403 H tai	cvtd A
92-1157	NAMC YS-11C-402	2125	403 H tai	cvtd A
02-1158	NAMC YS-11C-402	2150	403 H tai	cvtd A
02-1159	NAMC YS-11C-402	2151	403 H tai	cvtd A
12-1161	NAMC YS-11E/EL-402	2160	DS tai	cvtd A
12-1162	NAMC YS-11E-402	2161	DS tai	cvtd A
12-1163	NAMC YS-11E-402	2162	DS tai	cvtd A
12-1160	NAMC YS-11FC-218	2159	HT tai	cvtd A

Nihon Kaijyo Jieitai
Japan Maritime Self-Defense Force - JMSDF

UNITS/BASES	Koku Shudan (Fleet Air Force)	
	1 Koku-gun, 1 Koku-tai (VP-1), Kanoya AB	P-3C, LC-90
	1 Koku-gun, 7 Koku-tai (VP-7), Kanoya AB	P-3C
	2 Koku-gun, 2 Koku-tai (VP-2), Hachinohe AB	P-3C
	2 Koku-gun, 4 Koku-tai (VP-4), Hachinohe AB	P-3C
	4 Koku-gun, 3 Koku-tai (VP-3), Atsugi AB	P-3C
	4 Koku-gun, 6 Koku-tai (VP-6), Atsugi AB	P-3C
	5 Koku-gun, 5 Koku-tai (VP-5), Naha AB	P-3C
	5 Koku-gun, 9 Koku-tai (VP-9), Naha AB	P-3C
	31 Koku-gun, 8 Koku-tai (VP-8), Iwakuni AB	P-3C
	31 Koku-gun, 71 Koku-tai, Iwakuni AB	US-1A
	31 Koku-gun, 71 Koku-tai, Atusgi Haken-tai, Atsugi AB	US-1A
	31 Koku-gun, 81 Koku-tai (VQ-81), Iwakuni AB	EP-3, UP-3D, U-36, LC-90
	Chokkatsu Butai	
	51 Koku-Tai (VX-51), 511 Hiko-tai, Atsugi AB	P-3C, UP-3C, OP-3C
	61 Koku-tai (VR-61), Atsugi AB	YS-11M/M-A, LC-90
	Kyoiku Koku Shudan (Air Training Command)	
	Shimofusa Kyoiku Koku-gun	
	203 Kyoiku Koku-tai (VT-203), Shimofusa AB	P-3C
	205 Kyoiku Koku-tai (VT-205), Shimofusa AB	YS-11T-A
	Tokushima Kyoiku Koku-gun	
	202 Kyoiku Koku-tai (VT-202), Tokushima AB	TC-90, UC-90

PLANS	A study for an Orion replacement from 2010 is underway.

5001	Lockheed P-3C-II.5 (L-785A) Orion	7001	Bu161267 (FMS)	6 K tai	
5002	Lockheed P-3C-II.5 (L-785A) Orion	7002	Bu161268 (FMS)	3 K tai	
5003	Lockheed P-3C-III (L-785A) Orion	7003	Bu161269 (FMS)	3 K tai	Cvtd P-3C-II.5
5004	Lockheed/Kawasaki P-3C-III Orion	9001		3 K tai	Cvtd P-3C-II.5
5005	Lockheed/Kawasaki P-3C-II.5 Orion	9002		2 K tai	
5006	Lockheed/Kawasaki P-3C-II.5 Orion	9003		2 K tai	
5007	Lockheed/Kawasaki P-3C-III Orion	9004		2 K tai	Cvtd P-3C-II.5
5008	Lockheed/Kawasaki P-3C-II.5 Orion	9005		2 K tai	
5009	Lockheed/Kawasaki P-3C-II.5 Orion	9006		2 K tai	
5010	Lockheed/Kawasaki P-3C-II.5 Orion	9007		51 K tai	
5011	Lockheed/Kawasaki P-3C-III Orion	9008		6 K tai	Cvtd P-3C-II.5
5012	Lockheed/Kawasaki P-3C-III Orion	9009		6 K tai	Cvtd P-3C-II.5
5013	Lockheed/Kawasaki P-3C-II.5 Orion	9010		5 K tai	
5014	Lockheed/Kawasaki P-3C-II.5 Orion	9011		5 K tai	
5015	Lockheed/Kawasaki P-3C-II.5 Orion	9012		51 K tai	
5016	Lockheed/Kawasaki P-3C-II.5 Orion	9013		3 K tai	
5017	Lockheed/Kawasaki P-3C-III Orion	9014		3 K tai	Cvtd P-3C-II.5
5018	Lockheed/Kawasaki P-3C-II.5 Orion	9015		6 K tai	
5019	Lockheed/Kawasaki P-3C-II.5 Orion	9016		51 K tai	
5020	Lockheed/Kawasaki P-3C-II.5 Orion	9017		6 K tai	
5021	Lockheed/Kawasaki P-3C-II.5 Orion	9018		3 K tai	
5022	Lockheed/Kawasaki P-3C-II.5 Orion	9019		203 KK tai	
5023	Lockheed/Kawasaki P-3C-II.5 Orion	9020		9 K tai	
5024	Lockheed/Kawasaki P-3C-II.5 Orion	9021		7 K tai	
5025	Lockheed/Kawasaki P-3C-II.5 Orion	9022		8 K tai	
5026	Lockheed/Kawasaki P-3C-II.5 Orion	9023		203 KK tai	
5027	Lockheed/Kawasaki P-3C-II.5 Orion	9024		5 K tai	
5028	Lockheed/Kawasaki P-3C-II.5 Orion	9025		9 K tai	
5029	Lockheed/Kawasaki P-3C-II.5 Orion	9026		203 KK tai	

5030	Lockheed/Kawasaki P-3C-II.5 Orion	9027		203 KK tai	
5031	Lockheed/Kawasaki P-3C-II.5 Orion	9028		5 K tai	
5033	Lockheed/Kawasaki P-3C-II.5 Orion	9030		203 KK tai	
5034	Lockheed/Kawasaki P-3C-II.5 Orion	9031		8 K tai	
5035	Lockheed/Kawasaki P-3C-II.5 Orion	9032		9 K tai	
5036	Lockheed/Kawasaki P-3C-II.5 Orion	9033		203 KK tai	
5037	Lockheed/Kawasaki P-3C-II.5 Orion	9034		5 K tai	
5038	Lockheed/Kawasaki P-3C-II.5 Orion	9035		203 KK tai	
5039	Lockheed/Kawasaki P-3C-II.5 Orion	9036		5 K tai	
5040	Lockheed/Kawasaki P-3C-II.5 Orion	9037		6 K tai	
5041	Lockheed/Kawasaki P-3C-II.5 Orion	9038		3 K tai	
5042	Lockheed/Kawasaki P-3C-II.5 Orion	9039		203 KK tai	
5043	Lockheed/Kawasaki OP-3C Orion	9040		51 K tai	Cvtd P-3C-II.5
5044	Lockheed/Kawasaki P-3C-II.5 Orion	9041		6 K tai	
5045	Lockheed/Kawasaki P-3C-II.5 Orion	9042		9 K tai	
5046	Lockheed/Kawasaki P-3C-II.5 Orion	9043		8 K tai	
5047	Lockheed/Kawasaki P-3C-II.5 Orion	9044		9 K tai	
5048	Lockheed/Kawasaki P-3C-II.5 Orion	9045		7 K tai	
5049	Lockheed/Kawasaki P-3C-II.5 Orion	9046		7 K tai	
5050	Lockheed/Kawasaki P-3C-II.5 Orion	9047		7 K tai	
5051	Lockheed/Kawasaki P-3C-II.5 Orion	9048		203 KK tai	
5052	Lockheed/Kawasaki P-3C-II.5 Orion	9049		8 K tai	
5053	Lockheed/Kawasaki P-3C-II.5 Orion	9050		9 K tai	
5054	Lockheed/Kawasaki P-3C-II.5 Orion	9051		9 K tai	
5055	Lockheed/Kawasaki P-3C-II.5 Orion	9052		203 KK tai	
5056	Lockheed/Kawasaki P-3C-II.5 Orion	9053		203 KK tai	
5057	Lockheed/Kawasaki P-3C-II.5 Orion	9054		203 KK tai	
5058	Lockheed/Kawasaki P-3C-II.5 Orion	9055		9 K tai	
5059	Lockheed/Kawasaki P-3C-II.5 Orion	9056		5 K tai	
5060	Lockheed/Kawasaki P-3C-II.5 Orion	9057		203 KK tai	
5061	Lockheed/Kawasaki P-3C-II.5 Orion	9058		9 K tai	
5062	Lockheed/Kawasaki P-3C-II.5 Orion	9059		5 K tai	
5063	Lockheed/Kawasaki P-3C-II.5 Orion	9060		203 KK tai	
5064	Lockheed/Kawasaki P-3C-II.5 Orion	9061		8 K tai	
5065	Lockheed/Kawasaki P-3C-II.5 Orion	9062		203 KK tai	
5066	Lockheed/Kawasaki P-3C-II.5 Orion	9063		5 K tai	
5067	Lockheed/Kawasaki P-3C-II.5 Orion	9064		9 K tai	
5068	Lockheed/Kawasaki P-3C-II.5 Orion	9065		5 K tai	
5069	Lockheed/Kawasaki P-3C-II.5 Orion	9066		9 K tai	
5070	Lockheed/Kawasaki P-3C-III Orion	9067		7 K tai	
5071	Lockheed/Kawasaki P-3C-III Orion	9068		1 K tai	
5072	Lockheed/Kawasaki P-3C-III Orion	9069		1 K tai	
5073	Lockheed/Kawasaki P-3C-III Orion	9070		1 K tai	
5074	Lockheed/Kawasaki P-3C-III Orion	9071		1 K tai	
5075	Lockheed/Kawasaki P-3C-III Orion	9072		7 K tai	
5076	Lockheed/Kawasaki P-3C-III Orion	9073		7 K tai	
5077	Lockheed/Kawasaki P-3C-III Orion	9074		7 K tai	
5078	Lockheed/Kawasaki P-3C-III Orion	9075		1 K tai	
5079	Lockheed/Kawasaki P-3C-III Orion	9076		3 K tai	
5080	Lockheed/Kawasaki P-3C-III Orion	9077		4 K tai	
5081	Lockheed/Kawasaki P-3C-III Orion	9078		4 K tai	
5082	Lockheed/Kawasaki P-3C-III Orion	9079		6 K tai	
5083	Lockheed/Kawasaki P-3C-III Orion	9080		7 K tai	
5084	Lockheed/Kawasaki P-3C-III Orion	9081		4 K tai	
5085	Lockheed/Kawasaki P-3C-III Orion	9082		1 K tai	
5086	Lockheed/Kawasaki P-3C-III Orion	9083		7 K tai	
5087	Lockheed/Kawasaki P-3C-III Orion	9084		1 K tai	
5088	Lockheed/Kawasaki P-3C-III Orion	9085		51 K tai	
5089	Lockheed/Kawasaki P-3C-III Orion	9086		51 K tai	
5090	Lockheed/Kawasaki P-3C-III Orion	9087		3 K tai	
5091	Lockheed/Kawasaki P-3C-III Orion	9088		4 K tai	
5092	Lockheed/Kawasaki P-3C-III Orion	9089		4 K tai	
5093	Lockheed/Kawasaki P-3C-III Orion	9090		2 K tai	
5094	Lockheed/Kawasaki P-3C-III Orion	9091		4 K tai	
5095	Lockheed/Kawasaki P-3C-III Orion	9092		4 K tai	
5096	Lockheed/Kawasaki P-3C-III Orion	9093		2 K tai	
5097	Lockheed/Kawasaki P-3C-III Orion	9094		2 K tai	
5098	Lockheed/Kawasaki P-3C-III Orion	9095		6 K tai	
5099	Lockheed/Kawasaki P-3C-III Orion	9096		4 K tai	
5100	Lockheed/Kawasaki P-3C-III+ Orion	9097		51 K tai	
5101	Lockheed/Kawasaki P-3C-III+ Orion	9098		2 K tai	
6801	Beech TC-90 King Air	LJ-597	N1845W	202 KK tai	
6802	Beech TC-90 King Air	LJ-598	N1846W	202 KK tai	
6803	Beech TC-90 King Air	LJ-599	N1847W	202 KK tai	

6804	Beech TC-90 King Air	LJ-642	N7312R	202 KK tai	
6805	Beech TC-90 King Air	LJ-670	N9395	202 KK tai	
6806	Beech TC-90 King Air	LJ-778	N23780	202 KK tai	
6807	Beech TC-90 King Air	LJ-855	N6062X	202 KK tai	
6808	Beech TC-90 King Air	LJ-916	N67233	202 KK tai	
6809	Beech TC-90 King Air	LJ-917	N6724D	202 KK tai	
6810	Beech TC-90 King Air	LJ-976	N3832G	202 KK tai	
6811	Beech TC-90 King Air	LJ-980	N3832K	202 KK tai	
6812	Beech TC-90 King Air	LJ-1042	N18460	202 KK tai	
6813	Beech TC-90 King Air	LJ-1043	N1846B	202 KK tai	
6814	Beech TC-90 King Air	LJ-1044	N1846D	202 KK tai	
6815	Beech TC-90 King Air	LJ-1047	N1846F	202 KK tai	
6816	Beech TC-90 King Air	LJ-1060	N1875Z	202 KK tai	
6817	Beech TC-90 King Air	LJ-1061	N1876Z	202 KK tai	
6818	Beech TC-90 King Air	LJ-1062	N6886S	202 KK tai	
6819	Beech TC-90 King Air	LJ-1083	N6923Z	202 KK tai	
6820	Beech TC-90 King Air	LJ-1084	N69237	202 KK tai	
6821	Beech TC-90 King Air	LJ-1110	N7238J	202 KK tai	
6822	Beech TC-90 King Air	LJ-1146	N72400	202 KK tai	
6823	Beech TC-90 King Air	LJ-1335	N82323	202 KK tai	
6824	Beech TC-90 King Air	LJ-1336	N82326	202 KK tai	
6825	Beech TC-90 King Air	LJ-1337	N82349	202 KK tai	
6826	Beech TC-90 King Air	LJ-1338	N82366	202 KK tai	
6827	Beech TC-90 King Air	LJ-1339	N82376	202 KK tai	
6901	NAMC YS-11T-A-206	2100		205 KK tai	Crew Trainer
6902	NAMC YS-11T-A-206	2123		205 KK tai	Crew Trainer
6903	NAMC YS-11T-A-206	2132		205 KK tai	Crew Trainer
6904	NAMC YS-11T-A-206	2148		205 KK tai	Crew Trainer
6905	NAMC YS-11T-A-624	2180		205 KK tai	Crew Trainer
6906	NAMC YS-11T-A-624	2181		205 KK tai	Crew Trainer
9041	NAMC YS-11M-112	2033		61 K tai	Transport
9042	NAMC YS-11M-112	2058		61 K tai	Transport
9043	NAMC YS-11M-A-404	2174		61 K tai	Transport
9044	NAMC YS-11M-A-325	2182		61 K tai	Transport
9072	Shin Meiwa US-1	2002			
9073	Shin Meiwa US-1	2003			
9074	Shin Meiwa US-1	2004			
9075	Shin Meiwa US-1A	2005			Cvtd US-1
9076	Shin Meiwa US-1	2006			
9077	Shin Meiwa US-1	2007		71 K tai	
9078	Shin Meiwa US-1	2008			
9079	Shin Meiwa US-1A	2009		71 K tai	
9081	Shin Meiwa US-1A	2011		71 K tai	
9082	Shin Meiwa US-1A	2012		71 K tai	
9083	Shin Meiwa US-1A	2013		71 K tai	
9084	Shin Meiwa US-1A	2014		71 K tai	
9085	Shin Meiwa US-1A	2015		71 K tai	
9086	Shin Meiwa US-1A	2016		71 K tai	
9087	Shin Meiwa US-1A	2017		71 K tai	
9088	Shin Meiwa US-1A	2018		71 K tai	
9102	Beech UC-90 King Air	LJ-1038	N1839D	202 KK tai	
9151	Lockheed/Kawasaki UP-3C Orion			51 K tai	Test & evaluation
9161	Lockheed/Kawasaki UP-3D Orion	3001		81 K tai	EW trainer
9162	Lockheed/Kawasaki UP-3D Orion	3002		81 K tai	EW trainer
9163	Lockheed/Kawasaki UP-3D Orion	3003		81 K tai	EW trainer
9171	Lockheed/Kawasaki EP-3 Orion			81 K tai	EW
9172	Lockheed/Kawasaki EP-3 Orion			81 K tai	EW
9173	Lockheed/Kawasaki EP-3 Orion			81 K tai	EW
9174	Lockheed/Kawasaki EP-3 Orion			81 K tai	EW
9175	Lockheed/Kawasaki EP-3 Orion			81 K tai	EW
9201	Learjet U-36A	36A-054	N1087Z	81 K tai	
9202	Learjet U-36A	36A-056	N3802G	81 K tai	
9204	Learjet U-36A	36A-059	N1087Z	81 K tai	
9205	Learjet U-36A	36A-060	N1088A	81 K tai	
9206	Learjet U-36A	36A-061	N50154	81 K tai	
9301	Beech LC-90 King Air	LJ-1182	N3228V	1 K tai	
9302	Beech LC-90 King Air	LJ-1248	N56633	61 K tai	
9303	Beech LC-90 King Air	LJ-1249	N56638	81 K tai	
9304	Beech LC-90 King Air	LJ-1281	N81538	81 K tai	
9305	Beech LC-90 King Air	LJ-1282	N8154G	61 K tai	
9364	Beech LC-90 King Air	LJ-			

Nihon Rikujyo Jieitai
Japan Ground Self Defense Force - JGSDF

UNITS/BASES	1 Konsei-dan, 101 Hiko-tai, Naha AB			MU-2C/B300 (code IB)
	Chubu Homen Koku-tai Honbu Zuki-tai, Yao AAB			MU-2C (code M)
	Dan-Honbu oyobi Honbu Kanri Chu-tai, Kisarazu AAB			MU-2C/B300 (code IHB)
	Hokubu Homen Koku-tai Honbu Zuki-tai, Okadama AAB			MU-2C (code N)
	Seibu Homen Koku-tai Honbu Zuki-tai, Takayubara AAB			MU-2C (code W)
	Tobu Homen Koku-tai Honbu Zuki-tai, Tachikawa AAB			MU-2C (code E)
	Tohoku Homen Koku-tai Honbu Zuki-tai, Kasuminome AAB			MU-2C (code NE)
	Utsunomiya Bunko, Kita-Utsunomiya AAB			B300 (code SU)

PLANS   Up to 20 LR-2s (Super King Air 350s) are planned to replace the LR-1/MU-2s.

22003	Mitsubishi LR-1 (MU-2C)	803/230		IHB
22004	Mitsubishi LR-1 (MU-2C)	804/236		N
22005	Mitsubishi LR-1 (MU-2C)	805/275		IHB
22006	Mitsubishi LR-1 (MU-2C)	806/317		SU
22007	Mitsubishi LR-1 (MU-2C)	807/334		M
22008	Mitsubishi LR-1 (MU-2C)	808/359		NE
22009	Mitsubishi LR-1 (MU-2C)	809/376		W
22010	Mitsubishi LR-1 (MU-2C)	810/394		IB
22013	Mitsubishi LR-1 (MU-2C)	813/442		N
22014	Mitsubishi LR-1 (MU-2C)	814/443		W
22015	Mitsubishi LR-1 (MU-2C)	815/444		M
22016	Mitsubishi LR-1 (MU-2C)	816/456		SU
22017	Mitsubishi LR-1 (MU-2C)	817/457		E
22018	Mitsubishi LR-1 (MU-2C)	818/465		IHB
22019	Mitsubishi LR-1 (MU-2C)	819/463		IB
22020	Mitsubishi LR-1 (MU-2C)	820/466		NE
23051	Raytheon Beech LR-2 (Super King Air 350 (B300))			
		FL-176	N11309	SU
23052	Raytheon Beech LR-2 (Super King Air 350 (B300))			
		FL-186	N11310	IHB
23053	Raytheon Beech LR-2 (Super King Air 350 (B300))			
		FL-266	N31379	IB

Kaijo Hoan-cho
Maritime Safety Agency

UNITS/BASES   Aircraft are based at Tokyo-Haneda Airport and deployed to 13 other bases.

JA8570	Dassault Falcon 900	53	N438FJ	
JA8571	Dassault Falcon 900	56	N440FJ	
JA861A	Raytheon Beech Super King Air 350 (B300)	FL-180	N18237	
JA862A	Raytheon Beech Super King Air 350 (B300)	FL-188	N18297	
JA863A	Raytheon Beech Super King Air 350 (B300)	FL-191	N11191	
JA864A	Raytheon Beech Super King Air 350 (B300)	FL-193	N11250	
JA865A	Raytheon Beech Super King Air 350 (B300)	FL-195	N11278	
JA866A	Raytheon Beech Super King Air 350 (B300)	FL-218	N2352N	
JA867A	Raytheon Beech Super King Air 350 (B300)	FL-222	N23272	
JA868A	Raytheon Beech Super King Air 350 (B300)	FL-292	N3192N	On order
JA869A	Raytheon Beech Super King Air 350 (B300)	FL-295	N3195T	On order
JA870A	Raytheon Beech Super King Air 350 (B300)	FL-297	N3197N	On order
JA8701	NAMC YS-11A-207	2093		
JA8702	NAMC YS-11A-207	2175		
JA8780	NAMC YS-11A-213	2164		
JA8782	NAMC YS-11A-213	2167		
JA8791	NAMC YS-11A-213	2177		
JA8814	Beech Super King Air 200T	BT-9/BB-551	N2071Z	cv:d 200
JA8815	Beech Super King Air 200T	BT-11/BB-573	N60576	cv:d 200
JA8816	Beech Super King Air 200T	BT-12/BB-591	N60581	cv:d 200
JA8817	Beech Super King Air 200T	BT-13/BB-609	N60587	cv:d 200
JA8818	Beech Super King Air 200T	BT-14/BB-627	N6059C	cvtd 200
JA8819	Beech Super King Air 200T	BT-15/BB-647	N6059D	cvtd 200
JA8820	Beech Super King Air 200T	BT-16/BB-665	N60603	cvtd 200
JA8824	Beech Super King Air 200T	BT-17/BB-798	N3718Q	cvtd 200
JA8829	Beech Super King Air 200T	BT-22/BB-991	N1841K	cvtd 200
JA8833	Beech Super King Air 200T	BT-28/BB-1117	N1846M	cvtd 200
JA8854	Beech Super King Air B200T	BT-31/BB-1264	N72392	cvtd B200
JA8860	Beech Super King Air B200T	BT-32/BB-1289	N3184A	cvtd B200
JA8951	Saab 340B-SAR200	340B-385	SE-C85	
JA8952	Saab 340B-SAR200	340B-405	SE-B05	

JORDAN
al Mamlaka al-Urduniyah al-Hashemiyah / Hashemite Kingdom of Jordan   SW Asia

Another Arab country that has benefited from working closely with the USA in the Middle East peace negotiations, Jordan has taken a wider line than Egypt however as it relied economically upon embargoed Iraq to a greater extent. Current equipment is in need of update or renewal.

SERIAL SYSTEM The serials commence with the squadron number the aircraft is issued to and are then sequential, with different types starting further up the series. Government aircraft are civil registered.

Royal Jordanian Air Force

ICAO code RJZ, callsign Jordan Air Force

UNITS/BASES	3 Sqn, King Abdullah AB, Amman-Marka		C-130H, Aviocar, CN235M		
324	CASA 212A Aviocar srs 100	A3-2-52	124 (RJAF)	3 Sqn	
326	CASA 212A Aviocar srs 100	AV3-1-68	126 (RJAF)	3 Sqn	
330	Britten-Norman BN-2B-21 Islander	861	JY-CAA	3 Sqn	
340	Lockheed C-130B (L-282-1B) Hercules	3612	140 (RJAF)	3 Sqn	Std Amman
341	Lockheed C-130B (L-282-1B) Hercules	3610	141 (RJAF)	3 Sqn	Std Amman
344	Lockheed C-130H (L-382C-83D) Hercules	4779	744 (RJAF)	3 Sqn	
345	Lockheed C-130H (L-382C-89D) Hercules	4813		3 Sqn	
346	Lockheed C-130H (L-382C-28E) Hercules	4920		3 Sqn	
347	Lockheed C-130H (L-382C-28E) Hercules	4929	N4204M	3 Sqn	
350	Airtech/CASA/TAI CN235M-100	C115	115 (THK)	3 Sqn	Lsf THK
351	Airtech/CASA/TAI CN235M-100	C116	116 (THK)	3 Sqn	Lsf THK

Government of the Hashemite Kingdom of Jordan

UNITS/BASES	The Royal Flight is based at Amman-Marka (King Abdullah AB)			
JY-ABH	Airbus Industrie A340-211	009	V8-AM1	Royal Flight
JY-HKJ	Lockheed L-1011-293A TriStar 500	1247	N64854	Royal Flight
JY-ONE	Bombardier Canadair CL-604 Challenger	5426	N604JA	Royal Flight
JY-TWO	Bombardier Canadair CL-604 Challenger	5443	N605JA	Royal Flight

KAZAKSTAN
Qazaqstan Respublikasy   C Asia

Still dependent on Russia for its defence through membership of the Union of Sovereign Republics in addition to the CIS, Belarus and Kyrgyzstan. The transport equipment operated is all of Soviet forces origin.

SERIAL SYSTEM Aircraft are either alloted a civil registration or wear a Soviet style two digit tactical code.

Kazakstan Air Force

UNITS/BASES	Transports based at Alma-Ata Airport.			
UN-11367	Antonov An-12BP	3341201		
UN-11373	Antonov An-12BP	02348304		
CCCP-11377	Antonov An-12B			
UN-30031	Antonov An-30	0606		
UN-46459/ 03 red	Antonov An-24T	9911008	CCCP-46459	
UN-65683	Tupolev Tu-135 (Tu-134A)	62199	CCCP-65683	
UN-72904	Antonov An-72		CCCP-72904	Aeroflot cs
UN-75915	Ilyushin Il-22M-40 Bison	2964017101	CCCP-75915	
UN-85464	Tupolev Tu-154B-2	80A-464	CCCP-85464	HF antennas
UN-87816	Yakovlev Yak-40	9230724	CCCP-87816	
UN-87850	Yakovlev Yak-40	9441738	CCCP-87850	
01 red	Antonov An-24B	99902104		
01 red	Antonov An-72			
01 yellow	Antonov An-2	18047314		Aeroclub
02 red	Antonov An-76 (An-72P)			
02 red	Antonov An-26	12107		
06 red	Antonov An-26			
08 blue	Antonov An-12BP	1340209		
09 red	Antonov An-26	1408		

12 red	Antonov An-12BP	402212		
18 red	Antonov An-12BP			
19 red	Antonov An-12BP	3340905		
54 red	Antonov An-26	2109		
79 red	Antonov An-12BP	5342902		
85 red	Antonov An-26	9708		
86 red	Antonov An-26			

Government of the Republic of Kazakstan

UNITS/BASES   Based at Alma-Ata. The Boeing uses an Aruba civil registration.

P4-NSN	Boeing 757-2M6	23454 / 102	VR-CRK
UN-65799	Tupolev Tu-134B-3	63187	YL-LBN

KENYA
Jamhuri ya Kenya / Republic of Kenya   E Africa

The Air Force was established with British help in 1964 following independence the previous year. A 1982 coup attempt by Air Force personnel saw it disbanded and re-formed as the '82 Air Force' under Army control, independence was regained in 1994.

SERIAL SYSTEM   Three digit serials are allocated in batches by type and are sometimes presented with a KAF prefix.

Kenya Air Force

UNITS/BASES   The transports operate from Nairobi-Moi (formerly Eastleigh).

112	Dornier 28D-2 Skyservant	4319	D-ILFM	Std
113	Dornier 28D-2 Skyservant	4320	D-ILFM	Std
114	Dornier 28D-2 Skyservant	4326	D-IAVM	Std
115	Dornier 28D-2 Skyservant	4327	D-IAVN	Std
116	Dornier 28D-2 Skyservant	4328	D-IAVO	Std
117	Dornier 28D-2 Skyservant	4329	D-IAVP	Std
118	Dornier 28D-2 Skyservant	4344	D-IAVD	Std
119	Dornier 28D-2 Skyservant	4345	D-IAVE	Std
128	Yunshuji/Harbin Y-12 II			
129	Yunshuji/Harbin Y-12 II			
130	Yunshuji/Harbin Y-12 II			
134	Yunshuji/Harbin Y-12 II			
136	Yunshuji/Harbin Y-12 II			
138	Yunshuji/Harbin Y-12 II			
207	DeHavilland Canada DHC-5D Buffalo	75	C-GQFR	
208	DeHavilland Canada DHC-5D Buffalo	76	C-GQFS	
209	DeHavilland Canada DHC-5D Buffalo	77	C-GQFT	
210	DeHavilland Canada DHC-5D Buffalo	78	C-GCFU	
211	DeHavilland Canada DHC-5D Buffalo	89		
212	DeHavilland Canada DHC-5D Buffalo	90		
216	DeHavilland Canada DHC-5D Buffalo	124	C-GFHZ	
218	DeHavilland Canada DHC-5D Buffalo	125	C-GJFO	
220	DeHavilland Canada DHC-5D Buffalo	126	C-GJFH	
304	DeHavilland Canada DHC-8 Dash 8 srs 103	189	C-GLOT	
305	DeHavilland Canada DHC-8 Dash 8 srs 103	219	C-GFCF	
306	DeHavilland Canada DHC-8 Dash 8 srs 103	223	C-GFBW	
308	Fokker 70ER	11557	PH-MXM	VIP

Kenya Police Air Wing

UNITS/BASES   Based at Nairobi-Wilson.

5Y-KPA	Cessna 310R II	310R-2110	N6831E
5Y-PAW	Cessna 310R II	310R-0907	N3734G
5Y-PAX	Cessna 404 Titan II	404-0104	N37094

KOREA, NORTH
Chcson Minjujuui In'min Konghwaguk / Democratic People's Republic of Korea   SE Asia

Still ruled by a hard-line communist Government since its separation in 1953 from the more developed South Korea at the 38th par-
allel. Much support and equipment still comes from neighbouring China and, despite financial pressure, spending on defence continues almost undiminished. Regarded in the West always as potential flash point for war, recent attempts at conciliation between the
two Koreas are slow in having an effect. Application for ASEAN membership withdrawn in 1998.

SERIAL SYSTEM No details are known other than some aircraft wear civil registrations as they operate for the state airline Air Koryo.
The registration prefix P- is believed to be used unofficially.

Korean People's Army Air Force

The most populous type on the inventory is reported to be the Antonov An-2/Y-5 with up to 300 reported in service, known serial details
are minimal. The An-24, Tu-134B, Tu-154B and Il-18 aircraft of Air Koryo are sometimes reported as being AF operated.

UNITS/BASES   Air Koryo operate from Pyongyang-Sunan Airport, no other details are known.

P-912	Ilyushin Il-76MD	1003403104	Air Koryo cs
P-913	Ilyushin Il-76MD	1003404126	Air Koryo cs
P-914	Ilyushin Il-76MD	1003404146	Air Koryo cs
08	Yunshuji Y-5		
12	Yunshuji Y-5		
17	Yunshuji Y-5		
18	Yunshuji Y-5		
31	Yunshuji Y-5		
35	Yunshuji Y-5		
44	Yunshuji Y-5		
26095	Antonov An-12/Yunshuji/Shaanxi Y-8		

Government of the People's Republic of Korea

P-618	Ilyushin Il-62M	2546624	
P-881	Ilyushin Il-62M	3647853	Air Koryo cs
P-882	Ilyushin Il-62M	2850236	Air Koryo cs

KOREA, SOUTH
Tae Han Minguk / Republic of Korea   SE Asia

Korea has existed as two states since the conclusion of the Korean war in 1953. The Southern half of the country is heavily supported by the USA and most equipment is of US origin. More recently local production has been developed and now major components
are built and exported to the US and Europe. South Korea was badly affected by the late 1990's economic crash. A member of ASEAN.

SERIAL SYSTEM The Air Force primarily use the c/n or previous identity to serial the aircraft. The Navy six digit serials commence
with the year of purchase followed by a four digit number batched by type. The omission of the number four is for
superstitious reasons.

Republic of Korea Air Force - ROKAF

UNITS/BASES	12 TCW, 237 TCS, Kangnun	O-2A
	255 TAS, Pusan/Kim Hae	C-130H
	236 TAS, Pusan/Kim Hae	CN.235M

PLANS   Delivery of the Hawker 800s will give the ROKAF control of the SIGINT function currently undertaken by the US
Army with RC-12s.
Four AEW aircraft are required, the late 90s economic slump meant that the competition was re-opened in 2000,
current bidders offer the 737, A310, Gulfstream V or ERJ-145 as the base airframe.
Twenty C-130Js are required.

507	Aero Commander 560F	1219-48	N78365	
078	Airtech/CASA CN235M-100	C078		236 TAS
081	Airtech/CASA CN235M-100	C081		236 TAS
082	Airtech/CASA CN235M-100	C082		236 TAS
084	Airtech/CASA CN235M-100	C084		236 TAS
087	Airtech/CASA CN235M-100	C087		236 TAS
088	Airtech/CASA CN235M-100	C088		236 TAS
090	Airtech/CASA CN235M-100	C090		236 TAS
092	Airtech/CASA CN235M-100	C092		236 TAS
096	Airtech/CASA CN235M-100	C096		236 TAS
098	Airtech/CASA CN235M-100	C098		236 TAS

100	Airtech/CASA CN235M-100	C100		236 TAS	
102	Airtech/CASA CN235M-100	C102		236 TAS	
	Airtech/IPTN CN235M	N044	AX-2322		
	Airtech/IPTN CN235M	N045	AX-2323		
	Airtech/IPTN CN235M	N046	AX-2324		
	Airtech/IPTN CN235M	N047			
	Airtech/IPTN CN235M	N048			
	Airtech/IPTN CN235M	N049			
	Airtech/IPTN CN235M				on order
	Airtech/IPTN CN235M				on order
85101	Boeing 737-3Z8	23152 / 1073			VIP, Oof Govt
10834	Cessna O-2A Super Skymaster	M337-0199	68-10834 (USAF)	237 TCS	
11059	Cessna O-2A Super Skymaster	M337-0335	68-11059 (USAF)	237 TCS	
11128	Cessna O-2A Super Skymaster	M337-0353	68-11128 (USAF)	237 TCS	
11129	Cessna O-2A Super Skymaster	M337-0354	68-11129 (USAF)	237 TCS	
11131	Cessna O-2A Super Skymaster	M337-0356	68-11131 (USAF)	237 TCS	
11133	Cessna O-2A Super Skymaster	M337-0358	68-11133 (USAF)	237 TCS	
11136	Cessna O-2A Super Skymaster	M337-0361	68-11136 (USAF)	237 TCS	
11137	Cessna O-2A Super Skymaster	M337-0362	68-11137 (USAF)	237 TCS	
11138	Cessna O-2A Super Skymaster	M337-0363	68-11138 (USAF)	237 TCS	
11139	Cessna O-2A Super Skymaster	M337-0364	68-11139 (USAF)	237 TCS	
11140	Cessna O-2A Super Skymaster	M337-0365	68-11140 (USAF)	237 TCS	
11143	Cessna O-2A Super Skymaster	M337-0368	68-11143 (USAF)	237 TCS	
11147	Cessna O-2A Super Skymaster	M337-0372	68-11147 (USAF)	237 TCS	
11148	Cessna O-2A Super Skymaster	M337-0373	68-11148 (USAF)	237 TCS	
1713	Hawker Siddeley HS.748-248 srs 2A	1713/set191	G-BBGY		
1718	Hawker Siddeley HS.748-248 srs 2A	1718/set194	G-BABJ		
5006	Lockheed C-130H-30 (L-382T-51E) Hercules	5006	N4080M	255 TAS	
5019	Lockheed C-130H-30 (L-382T-51E) Hercules	5019	N73232	255 TAS	
5030	Lockheed C-130H-30 (L-382T-62E) Hercules	5030	N4249Y	255 TAS	
5036	Lockheed C-130H-30 (L-382T-62E) Hercules	5036	N4161T	255 TAS	
5178	Lockheed C-130H (L-382C-06F) Hercules	5178		255 TAS	
5179	Lockheed C-130H (L-382C-06F) Hercules	5179		255 TAS	
5180	Lockheed C-130H (L-382C-06F) Hercules	5180		255 TAS	
5181	Lockheed C-130H (L-382C-06F) Hercules	5181		255 TAS	
5182	Lockheed C-130H (L-382C-06F) Hercules	5182		255 TAS	
5183	Lockheed C-130H (L-382C-06F) Hercules	5183	N73233	255 TAS	
5185	Lockheed C-130H (L-382C-06F) Hercules	5185	N41030	255 TAS	
5186	Lockheed C-130H (L-382C-06F) Hercules	5186		255 TAS	
258-342	Raytheon Hawker 800SIG	258342	N2320J		SIGINT
258-343	Raytheon Hawker 800RA	258343	N1102U		Surveillance
258-346	Raytheon Hawker 800RA	258346	N23204		Surveillance
258-351	Raytheon Hawker 800SIG	258351	N23208		SIGINT
258-352	Raytheon Hawker 800SIG	258352	N2321S		SIGINT
258-353	Raytheon Hawker 800RA	258353	N2321V		Surveillance
258-357	Raytheon Hawker 800SIG	258357	N2321Z		SIGINT
258-360	Raytheon Hawker 800RA	258350	N23207		Surveillance

Republic of Korea Navy - ROKN

| UNITS/BASES | Air Wing 6, 613 Sqn, Pohang AB | | Orion | MR |
| | | | Caravan II | Utility, Target Towing |

PLANS — Options on 8 more Orions have been reported to be cancelled, although refurbished P-3A/Bs may be acquired instead.

981001	Reims/Cessna F406 Caravan II	F406-0081	F-WWSR	
981002	Reims/Cessna F406 Caravan II	F406-0082	F-WWSS	
981003	Reims/Cessna F406 Caravan II	F406-0083		
981005	Reims/Cessna F406 Caravan II	F406-0084		
981006	Reims/Cessna F406 Caravan II	F406-0085		
950901	Lockheed P-3C-III+ (L-285K) Orion	5831	N4080M	613 Sqn
950902	Lockheed P-3C-III+ (L-285K) Orion	5832	N4081M	613 Sqn
950903	Lockheed P-3C-III+ (L-285K) Orion	5833	N4099R	613 Sqn
950905	Lockheed P-3C-III+ (L-285K) Orion	5834	N4107F	613 Sqn
950906	Lockheed P-3C-III+ (L-285K) Orion	5835	Bu165102 (FMS)	613 Sqn
950907	Lockheed P-3C-III+ (L-285K) Orion	5836	Bu165103 (FMS)	613 Sqn
950908	Lockheed P-3C-III+ (L-285K) Orion	5837	Bu165104 (FMS)	613 Sqn
950909	Lockheed P-3C-III+ (L-285K) Orion	5838	Bu165105 (FMS)	613 Sqn

Republic of Korea National Maritime Police Agency - KNMP

| | Bombardier Canadair Challenger CL-604 | 5429 | N604KM | | on order |

KUWAIT
Dawlat al-Kuwait / State of Kuwait   SW Asia

Re-supplied since the repelled Iraqi invasion in 1990, Kuwait still relies upon outside forces to deter its neighbour's territorial claims. The transport force is still depleted compared to the pre-Gulf War force but plans have been made to bring it up to date.

SERIAL SYSTEM   Air Force transport serials are allocated sequentially from 300, Government/VIP aircraft are allocated in the Kuwait Airways civil registration blocks.

al Quwwat al Jawwiya al Kuwaitiya
Kuwait Air Force

UNITS/BASES   41 Sqn, Ali Salim Sabah AB   L-100

PLANS   Four C-130J are being budgeted for purchase to supplement the existing L-100-30s, in addition to tanker versions.

323	Lockheed L-100-30 (L-382G-59C) Hercules	4951	N4349Y	41 Sqn
324	Lockheed L-100-30 (L-382G-59C) Hercules	4953	N4242N	41 Sqn
325	Lockheed L-100-30 (L-382G-59C) Hercules	4955	N4232B	41 Sqn

Government of the State of Kuwait

3B-AGC	McDonnell Douglas MD-83	49809 / 1843	9K-AGC	
9K-ADE	Boeing 747-469 (SCD)	27338 / 1046		Kuwait AW cs
9K-AHI	Airbus Industrie A300C4-620	344	PK-MAY	Kuwait AW cs
9K-ALD	Airbus Industrie A310-308	648	F-WWCR	Kuwait AW cs
9K-AJD	GAC Gulfstream V	560	N660GA	Kuwait AW cs
9K-AJE	GAC Gulfstream V	569	N469GA	Kuwait AW cs
9K-AJF	GAC Gulfstream V	573	N573GA	Kuwait AW cs

KYRGYZSTAN
Kyrgyz Respublikasy   C Asia

Also known as Kirghizia, no transports have been reported as having been left by departing Soviet forces or having been acquired since creation within the CIS in 1991. The state airline Kyrghyzstan Airlines does not even appear to operate a dedicated VIP aircraft for the Government.

LAOS
Sathalanalat Paxathipatai Paxaxon Lao / Lao People's Democratic Republic   SE Asia

This former French colony took its current title in 1975 and until the late 1980s was occupied and controlled by a number of its neighbours. The majority of the equipment is now of Chinese origin and the Air Force is not believed to operate many of its own transports, aircraft being shared with Lao Aviation as shown below.

SERIAL SYSTEM   Because of their joint civil operation civil registrations are carried, sometimes however the aircraft have been noted with the RDPL- prefix omitted.

Lao People's Democratic Republic Air Force

UNITS/BASES   The transport aircraft are based at Vientiane-Wattay.

RDPL-34002	Yakovlev Yak-40	9840559		Lao Aviation cs
RDPL-34015	Yunshuji/Xian Y7-100C	12703	Govt	
RDPL-34016	Yunshuji/Xian Y7-100C	12704	Govt	
RDPL-34018	Antonov An-74TK-100		Govt	
RDPL-34036	Antonov An-26	5010		Lao Aviation cs
RDPL-34038	Antonov An-26	2504		Lao Aviation cs
RDPL-34039	Antonov An-26	2302		Lao Aviation cs
RDPL-34114	Antonov An-26			Lao Aviation cs
RDPL-34115	Yunshuji/Harbin Y-12 II	0033		Lao Aviation
RDPL-34116	Yunshuji/Harbin Y-12 II	0034		Lao Aviation
RDPL-34118	Yunshuji/Harbin Y-12 II	0043		Std Vientiane
RDPL-34119	Yunshuji/Xian Y7-100C	10707		Lao Aviation
RDPL-34127	Yunshuji/Xian Y7-100C	12706		Lao Aviation
RDPL-34128	Yunshuji/Xian Y7-100C	13701		Lao Aviation
RDPL-34129	Yunshuji/Harbin Y-12 II	0085		Std Vientiane
RDPL-34130	Yunshuji/Harbin Y-12 II	0086		Lao Aviation
RDPL-34131	Yunshuji/Harbin Y-12 II	0087		Lao Aviation

LATVIA
Latvijas Republika   NE Europe

Declaring independence from the Soviet Union in May 1990 and recognised as such in January 1991, Latvia like its neighbours Estonia and Lithiuania did not join the CIS when formed and are looking to join the EU. The Defence Force operates to support mainly army operations including medevac duties.

SERIAL SYSTEM Three digit serials are carried in distinct batches to differentiate the air arms.

Latvijas Republikas Gaisa Speki
Latvian Republic Defence Force

UNITS/BASES   Aircraft based at Lielvarde.

PLANS   Larger fixed wing aircraft such as the An-26 are being sought.

145	Let 410UVP	820737	45 (LRGS)	
147	Antonov/PZL-Mielec An-2R	1G172-15	CCCP-40743	
148	Antonov/PZL-Mielec An-2R	1G225-60	CCCP-33341	WFU?

Latvijas Republikas Zemessardzes
Latvian Republic National Guard

UNITS/BASES   Based at Riga-Spilve, but deployed to Daugavpils, Rezekne, Limbazi and Cesis.

247	Antonov An-2		
249	Antonov/PZL-Mielec An-2R	1G214-33	CCCP-40675
250	Antonov An-2		
251	Antonov An-2		
253	Antonov/PZL-Mielec An-2R	1G192-11	YL-LET
255	Antonov An-2		
256	Antonov An-2		
257	Antonov/PZL-Mielec An-2R	1G197-45	CCCP-31422

LEBANON
al-Jumhouriya al-Lubananiya / Republic of Lebanon   SW Asia

Having been devastated by civil war through the late 1970s and 80s the situation has now improved but the Air Force has acquired no fixed wing aircraft since the start of the conflict 25 years ago. The Air Force has no transports, VIP flying was performed by a government Falcon 20 but this is now sold.

LESOTHO
Mmuso wa Lesotho / Kingdom of Lesotho   S Africa

Totally enclosed by South Africa, Lesotho gained independence in 1966 having been known as the British Protectorate of Basutoland. The air arm was formed in 1978 as the Police Mobile Unit (PMU) and was later re-titled the Royal Lesotho Defence Force Air Wing. The Air Squadron operates to support the paramilitary Police force, rapid transport by anything but air being impractical in this mountainous location.

SERIAL SYSTEM A two digit sequential number is now prefixed with the initials L.D.F.

Lesotho Defence Force Air Squadron

UNITS/BASES   The fixed-wing aircraft are based at the Old Maseru Airport, but deploy to locations such as Quachas Nek.

| LDF-46 | CASA 212 Aviocar srs 300 | A71-3-408 | RLDF-45 |

LIBERIA
Republic of Liberia   W Africa

Liberia is unusual in Africa as it has no colonial ancestry, being founded as a homeland for former slaves and constituted in 1847. It is best known as being one of the first 'flag of convenience' countries with many ships and now aircraft carrying Liberian registry but not residing in the country. Previously dependent on US support, a presidential assassination in 1990 and the ensuing civil war left the country under West African peacekeeping control and serviceability of the Air Unit is thought low or non-existent. The ARU was originally known as the Justice Air Wing (JAW).

SERIAL SYSTEM A sequential three digit number is prefixed with the air arm initials ARU, some aircraft retain civil registrations.

Air Reconnaissance Unit   - ARU

UNITS/BASES Aircraft were based at Monrovia-Roberts IAP and Spriggs Payne.

ARU-015	Cessna 206			Std
ARU-016	Piper PA-23-250 Aztec			Std
ARU-022	Cessna 208 Caravan 1	208-0058	N9454F	Std
EL-AJG	IAI 101B Arava	077	4X-CUD	Std
EL-AJH	IAI 101B Arava	078	4X-CUJ	WO 08Oct89?
	DeHavilland Canada DHC-4 Caribou	219	N999NC	Std

LIBYA
al-Jamahiriya al-Arabiya al-Ishtirakia al-Sha'abiya al-Libya
/ Socialist People's Libyan Arab Republic   N Africa

Recent signs are that the American led embargo of Libya (formerly so close to the USA) is beginning to be relaxed. Colonel Qaddafi is one of the longest serving leaders in the region (albeit through dictatorship) despite his anti-Israeli and anti-USA policies that have meant that new equipment acquisitions have virtually stopped since the demise of the USSR.

SERIAL SYSTEM No single system exists with civil registrations, sequential blocks and c/n derived serials being worn.

al Quwwat al Jawwiya al Jamahirian al Libya
Libyan Arab Republic Air Force

UNITS/BASES Tripoli International Airport-Uqba ben Nafi   G II, Il-76*, L-100*
                        *operated by Libyan Arab Air Cargo (ICAO code LCR, callsign Libac)
                        Al Jufra-Hun   G222
                        Benina   C-130
                        Umm Aitiqah   An-26

PLANS   The acquisition of the An-124s noted below is presumably for quasi-military operation.

221	Aeritalia G-222T	4034	I-GAIT	
222	Aeritalia G-222T	4038		
223	Aeritalia G-222T	4040		VIP
224	Aeritalia G-222T	4052		
225	Aeritalia G-222T	4053		
226	Aeritalia G-222T	4054		
227	Aeritalia G-222T	4056		
228	Aeritalia G-222T	4058		
229	Aeritalia G-222T	4059		
230	Aeritalia G-222T	4060		
231	Aeritalia G-222T	4061		
232	Aeritalia G-222T	4062		
233	Aeritalia G-222T	4063		
234	Aeritalia G-222T	4064		
235	Aeritalia G-222T	4065		
236	Aeritalia G-222T	4066		
237	Aeritalia G-222T	4067		
238	Aeritalia G-222T	4068		
239	Aeritalia G-222T			
240	Aeritalia G-222T			
8202	Antonov An-26	11807	1 Sqn	
8203	Antonov An-26	11809	1 Sqn	
8204	Antonov An-26			
8205	Antonov An-26	12301		
8206	Antonov An-26	12303		
8207	Antonov An-26	12306		
8208	Antonov An-26	12307	1 Sqn	
8209	Antonov An-26	12308		
8210	Antonov An-26	12309	1 Sqn	
8211	Antonov An-26	12310		
8212	Antonov An-26	12406		
8213	Antonov An-26	12407	1 Sqn	
8305	Antonov An-26	13102	1 Sqn	
8306	Antonov An-26	13103	1 Sqn	
8307	Antonov An-26	13104	1 Sqn	
8308	Antonov An-26	13105		
8309	Antonov An-26	13106		

8310	Antonov An-26	13107		
8311	Antonov An-26	13108		
8315	Antonov An-26	13205		1 Sqn
0931	Let L-410T	820931	OK-MXH	
0932	Let L-410T	820932	OK-MXI	
0933	Let L-410T	820933	OK-MXJ	
0934	Let L-410T	820934	OK-MXK	
1126	Let L-410UVP	831126	OK-NZA	
1127	Let L-410UVP	831127	OK-NZB	
1128	Let L-410UVP	831128	OK-NZC	
1129	Let L-410UVP	831129	OK-NZD	
1130	Let L-410UVP	831130	OK-NZE	
1131	Let L-410UVP	831131	OK-NZF	
1533	Let L-410T	851533	OK-PXJ	
1534	Let L-410T	851534	OK-PXK	
1535	Let L-410T	851535	OK-PXL	
1536	Let L-410T	851536	OK-RXA	
1537	Let L-410T	851537	OK-RXB	
1538	Let L-410T	851538	OK-RXC	
LC 111	Lockheed C-130H (L-382C-18D) Hercules	4366		
LC 112	Lockheed C-130H (L-382C-18D) Hercules	4369		
LC 113	Lockheed C-130H (L-382C-18D) Hercules	4373		
LC 114	Lockheed C-130H (L-382C-18D) Hercules	4395		
LC 115	Lockheed C-130H (L-382C-18D) Hercules	4400		
LC 117	Lockheed C-130H (L-382C-18D) Hercules	4403		
LC 118	Lockheed C-130H (L-382C-18D) Hercules	4405		
LC 119	Lockheed C-130H (L-382C-30D) Hercules	4515		Std Gelac, GA
LC 120	Lockheed C-130H (L-382C-30D) Hercules	4518		Std Gelac, GA
LC 121	Lockheed C-130H (L-382C-30D) Hercules	4523		Std Gelac, GA
LC 122	Lockheed C-130H (L-382C-30D) Hercules	4525		Std Gelac, GA
LC 123	Lockheed C-130H (L-382C-30D) Hercules	4536		Std Gelac, GA
LC 124	Lockheed C-130H (L-382C-30D) Hercules	4538		Std Gelac, GA
LC 125	Lockheed C-130H (L-382C-30D) Hercules	4540		Std Gelac, GA
LC 126	Lockheed C-130H (L-382C-30D) Hercules	4541		Std Gelac, GA

Government of the Socialist People's Libyan Arab Republic

5A-DAK	Boeing 707-3L5C	21228 / 911		
5A-DCM	Dassault Falcon 50	68		
5A-DHI	Lockheed L-382E-19C (L-100-30) Hercules	4355	5A-DHO	cpb LCR
5A-DJQ	Lockheed L-382G-40C (L-100-30) Hercules	4798	N501AK	cpb LCR
5A-DJR	Lockheed L-382E-15C (L-100-20) Hercules	4302	RP-C99	cpb LCR
5A-DNA	Ilyushin Il-76TD	0023439140		Std Moscow Bykovo
5A-DNB	Ilyushin Il-76TD	0023437086		cpb LCR
5A-DNC	Ilyushin Il-76TD	0023437084		cpb LCR
5A-DND	Ilyushin Il-76TD	0033445299		cpb LCR
5A-DNE	Ilyushin Il-76T	0013432952		cpb LCR
5A-DNG	Ilyushin Il-76T	0013432961		cpb LCR
5A-DNH	Ilyushin Il-76TD	0033446356		opb LCR
5A-DNI	Ilyushin Il-76T	0013430878		opb LCR
5A-DNJ	Ilyushin Il-76T	0013430869		opb LCR
5A-DNK	Ilyushin Il-76T	0013430882		opb LCR
5A-DNO	Ilyushin Il-76TD	0043451509		opb LCR
5A-DNP	Ilyushin Il-76TD	0043451516		opb LCR
5A-DNQ	Ilyushin Il-76TD	0043454641		opb LCR
5A-DNS	Ilyushin Il-76TD	0023439145		opb LCR
5A-DNT	Ilyushin Il-76TD	0023439141		opb LCR
5A-DNU	Ilyushin Il-76TD	0043454651		opb LCR
5A-DNV	Ilyushin Il-76TD	0043454645		opb LCR
5A-DOM	Lockheed L-382G-62C (L-100-30) Hercules	4992	N4268M	opb LCR
5A-DRR	Ilyushin Il-76M	083415469		opb LCR
	Antonov An-124	19530502761	UR-82066	
	Antonov An-124	19530502792	UR-82003	

LITHUANIA
Lietuvos Respublika   NE Europe

One of the first Soviet Republics to declare independence in 1990, it was finally recognised in August 1991 despite Moscow's efforts to disuade it through military means. The last Soviet aircraft left in 1993 leaving Lithuania to acquire its own equipment from the new Europe.

SERIAL SYSTEM Sequential codes are allocated by type commencing 01, the colours indicating the unit/operator.

Lietuvos Karines Oro Pajegos - KOP
Lithuanian Military Air Forces

UNITS/BASES	I Aviacijos Baze, 12 Transporto Eskadrile, Zokniai-Siauliau			L410, An-2	codes in blue
	II Aviacijos Baze, 22 Transporto Eskadrile, Pajouste-Panevezys			An-2, An-26B	codes in yellow

01	Let 410UVP	820738	53+04 (Luftwaffe)	12 TE	
01	Antonov/PZL-Mielec An-2R *Kukuruzininkas*	1G141-38	LY-AEF	12 TE	
02	Let 410UVP	820739	53+05 (Luftwaffe)	12 TE	
02	Antonov/PZL-Mielec An-2R *Kukuruzininkas*	1G206-49	LY-AED	12 TE	
03	Antonov An-26B	11503	LY-AAL	22 TE	
04	Antonov An-26B	10101	LY-AAJ	22 TE	
05	Antonov An-26B	11203	LY-AAK	22 TE	
05	Antonov/PZL-Mielec An-2R *Kukuruzininkas*	1G226-60	LY-ADT	12 TE	
07	Antonov/PZL-Mielec An-2R *Kukuruzininkas*	1G201-07	LY-ADY	12 TE	Std Zokniai
09	Antonov/PZL-Mielec An-2R *Kukuruzininkas*	1G206-52	LY-AEA	12 TE	
10	Antonov/PZL-Mielec An-2R *Kukuruzininkas*	1G195-33	LY-ADU	12 TE	
12	Antonov/PZL-Mielec An-2R *Kukuruzininkas*	1G172-44	LY-ACP	22 TE	
14	Antonov/PZL-Mielec An-2R *Kukuruzininkas*	1G173-17	LY-ACS	22 TE	
15	Antonov/PZL-Mielec An-2R *Kukuruzininkas*	1G195-17	LY-ADB	22 TE	
16	Antonov/PZL-Mielec An-2R *Kukuruzininkas*	1G201-03	LY-ADH	22 TE	Std Pajuoste
17	Antonov/PZL-Mielec An-2R *Kukuruzininkas*	1G177-56	LY-AEE	22 TE	
18	Antonov/PZL-Mielec An-2R *Kukuruzininkas*	1G196-54	LY-ADF	22 TE	
20	Antonov/PZL-Mielec An-2R *Kukuruzininkas*	1G172-37	LY-ACO	22 TE	
21	Antonov/PZL-Mielec An-2R *Kukuruzininkas*			22 TE	
68115	Antonov/PZL-Mielec An-2R *Kukuruzininkas*	1G195-20	LY-ADC		
	Antonov/PZL-Mielec An-2R *Kukuruzininkas*	1G173-14	LY-ACR		
	Antonov/PZL-Mielec An-2R *Kukuruzininkas*	1G191-46	LY-ADA		

Savanoriskoji Krasto Apsaugos Tarnyba - SKAT
Home Guard

UNITS/BASES	Vilniaus Dariaus Ir Gereno Eskadrile, Vilnius-Kyviskis			An-2
	Silutes Aviacijos Eskadrile, Silute			An-2

22	Antonov/PZL-Mielec An-2R	1G206-53	LY-ADZ	SAE
25	Antonov An-2			
26	Antonov/PZL-Mielec An-2T	1G194-18		VDGE
30	Antonov/PZL-Mielec An-2TP	1G65-11		

LUXEMBOURG
Grand Duchy of Luxembourg   W Europe

Luxembourg does not actually have an Air Force although the NATO AEW Force of E-3 Sentries bears LX- civil prefixed serials as the country is a founder member. The acquisition of more surveillance aircraft is likely (see the NATO entry for details) and Luxembourg is to purchase one A400M to be based with the Belgian Air Force examples at Brussels.

MACEDONIA
Republika Makedonija   SE Europe

A former Yugoslav Republic obtaining a peaceful split from the parent in 1991 and expressing an interest in joining NATO. However internal fighting began between ethnic groups in early 2001. The Army (Armija Republika Macedonija) operates only light aircraft and helicopters at present.

SERIAL SYSTEM   Government transports currently operate in civil marks.

PLANS   Five CN235Ms have been selected when expansion is possible as the UN arms embargo was lifted in 1996. Recent local press reports also stated interest in up to 10 Britten-Norman Defender 4000s and a single Antonov An-70.

Government of the Republic of Macedonia

Z3-BFA	Learjet 25B	25B-205	YU-BKJ
Z3-BFB	Beech Super King Air 200	BB-652	YU-BMF

MADAGASCAR
Repoblika Demokratika n'i Madagaskar   SE Africa coast

Becoming independent from France as the Malagasy Republic in 1960, the Air Force was formed with French assistance in 1961. The military government that took power in the 1970s renamed the country and acquired Soviet equipment supported by North Korean 'advisors', although support and presumably therefore serviceability is now dwindling.

SERIAL SYSTEM Civil registrations are allocated in the normal 5R-M** block.

Armée de l'Air Malgache
Air Force

UNITS/BASES   Transports are based at Antananarivo-Ivato Airport.

5R-MMG/525	Douglas C-47A	19525	N97BF	
5R-MND	Max Holste MH-1521 Broussard	243		
5R-MQA	Reims F337E Super Skymaster	F3370015/ 01271		
5R-MQB	Reims F337F Super Skymaster	F3370035/ 01365		
5R-MQC	Reims F337E Super Skymaster	F3370012/ 01256		
5R-MRA	Piper PA-23-250 Aztec D	27-4339	5R-MCX	
5R-MTK	Cessna 310R			
5R-MUA	Yakovlev Yak-40	9840859		
5R-MUB	Yakovlev Yak-40	9940760		
5R-MUG	Antonov An-26			Std
5R-MUK	Antonov An-26			Std
5R-MUL	Antonov An-26			Std
5R-MUM	Antonov An-26			
5R-MUN	Antonov An-26			
5R-MUO	Antonov An-26			Std
5R-MUT	British Aerospace 748-261 srs 2B	1780/set362	5R-MTI	Std Rand, RSA
5R-MUP / 8305	Antonov An-26	8305		
5R-MVP	Antonov An-26	10208	RA-26021	

MALAWI
Mfuko la Malawi   C Africa

Until Independence in 1964 Malawi was known as the British Protectorate of Nyasaland and was part of the Central African Federation. The Army formed an Air Wing in 1966 to support its operations, but very little funding is available in what is a very poor country. The four Do228s have recently been sold and no replacement is thought to have been planned.

SERIAL SYSTEM A single role letter followed by a sequential number is prefixed with the air arm initials, codes are also apparent.

Malawi Army Air Wing - MAAW

UNITS/BASES   Fixed-wing transports are based at Blantyre-Chileka.

MAAW-J1	British Aerospace 125-800B	258064	G-5-514	VIP
76-20	Douglas C-47	13850	N46938	
76-21	Douglas C-47B	15560/27005	N5009	

Malawi Police Air Wing

7Q-YAU	Pilatus Britten-Norman BN-2T Defender	2151	G-BKEF	Std
7Q-YAV	Pilatus Britten-Norman BN-2T Defender	2158	G-BKJI	Std
7Q-YAW	Pilatus Britten-Norman BN-2T Defender	2141	G-BJYV	Std

MALAYSIA
Perskutan Tanah Malaysia   SE Asia

Part of the British Empire until independence in 1957. A civil war was fought against Communist-led guerillas until 1954. The Federation formed in 1963 exists in two halves, West Malaysia (Malaya) and East Malaysia (Borneo including the states of Sabah and Sarawak). The Pacific Rim economic crisis stopped a re-equipment programme that is now just being re-evaluated. A member of ASEAN.

SERIAL SYSTEM Each type is allocated a separate prefix number commencing M**, followed by individual identities commencing 01 and continuing sequentially.

Tentara Udara Diraja Malaysia - TUDM
Royal Malaysian Air Force

ICAO ccde RMF, callsign Angkasa

UNITS/BASES	Markas Besar Operasi Udara	
	16 Sku, Kuala Lumpur-Subang	Super King Air
	Markas Bantuan Udara	
	1 Sku, Kuching	Caribou, CN235MPA
	2 Sku, Kuala Lumpur-Subang	F.28, Falcon 900, Global Express
	14 Sku, Labuan	C-130
	20 Sku, Kuala Lumpur-Subang	C-130
	20 Sku, Kuala Lumpur-Sungai Besi	Cessna 402
	21 Sku, Kuala Lumpur-Subang (moving to Kuching?)	CN235

PLANS	Replacement of the Caribou subject to selection of a suitable type (not the CN235).
	Four C-130H to be upgraded (stretched) to C-130H-30 standard, and 2 more converted to C-130T (Tanker).

M21-01	DeHavilland Canada DHC-4A Caribou	245			Std Kuching
M21-02	DeHavilland Canada DHC-4A Caribou	246			
M21-03	DeHavilland Canada DHC-4A Caribou	247			Std Kuching
M21-06	DeHavilland Canada DHC-4A Caribou	273			Std Kuching
M21-07	DeHavilland Canada DHC-4A Caribou	274			Std Kuching
M21-08	DeHavilland Canada DHC-4A Caribou	276			Std Kuching
M21-11	DeHavilland Canada DHC-4A Caribou	279			Std Kuching
M21-12	DeHavilland Canada DHC-4A Caribou	280			Std Sungai Besi
M21-13	DeHavilland Canada DHC-4A Caribou	281		1 Sku	
M21-15	DeHavilland Canada DHC-4A Caribou	304			Std Kuching
M21-16	DeHavilland Canada DHC-4A Caribou	305		1 Sku	
M21-17	DeHavilland Canada DHC-4A Caribou	306		1 Sku	
M21-18	DeHavilland Canada DHC-4A Caribou	307		1 Sku	
M27-01	Cessna 402B	402B0893	FM2301 (TUDM)	20 Sku	N5206J
M27-02	Cessna 402B		FM2302 (TUDM)	20 Sku	
M27-04	Cessna 402B		FM2304 (TUDM)	20 Sku	
M27-05	Cessna 402B		FM2305 (TUDM)	20 Sku	
M27-06	Cessna 402B		FM2306 (TUDM)	20 Sku	
M27-07	Cessna 402B		FM2307 (TUDM)	20 Sku	
M27-08	Cessna 402B		FM2308 (TUDM)	20 Sku	
M27-09	Cessna 402B		FM2309 (TUDM)	20 Sku	
M27-10	Cessna 402B		FM2310 (TUDM)	20 Sku	
M27-11	Cessna 402B		FM2311 (TUDM)	20 Sku	
M27-12	Cessna 402B		FM2312 (TUDM)	20 Sku	
M28-01	Fokker F.28 Fellowship 1000	11088	FM2101 (TUDM)	2 Sku	c/s 9M-EBE
M30-01	Lockheed C-130H-MP (L-382C-57D) Hercules	4656	FM2401 (TUDM)	14 Sku	MR
M30-02	Lockheed C-130H (L-382C-57D) Hercules	4661	FM2402 (TUDM)	14 Sku	
M30-04	Lockheed C-130H (L-382C-57D) Hercules	4685	FM2404 (TUDM)	14 Sku	
M30-05	Lockheed C-130H (L-382C-57D) Hercules	4690	FM2405 (TUDM)	14 Sku	
M30-06	Lockheed C-130H (L-382C-57D) Hercules	4697	FM2406 (TUDM)	14 Sku	
M30-07	Lockheed C-130T (L-382C-97D) Hercules	4847	FM2451 (TUDM)	20 Sku	
				AAR, conv. PC-130H-MP	
M30-08	Lockheed C-130T (L-382C-97D) Hercules	4849	FM2452 (TUDM)	20 Sku	
				AAR, conv. PC-130H-MP	
M30-09	Lockheed C-130T (L-382C-97D) Hercules	4866	FM2453 (TUDM)	20 Sku	
				AAR, conv. PC-130H-MP	
M30-10	Lockheed C-130H-30 (L-382T-28F) Hercules	5268		20 Sku	
M30-11	Lockheed C-130H-30 (L-382T-44F) Hercules	5309		20 Sku	
M30-12	Lockheed C-130H-30 (L-382T-34F) Hercules	5277		20 Sku	
M30-14	Lockheed C-130H-30 (L-382T-44F) Hercules	5311		20 Sku	
M30-15	Lockheed C-130H-30 (L-382T-44F) Hercules	5316		20 Sku	
M30-16	Lockheed C-130H-30 (L-382T-44F) Hercules	5319		20 Sku	
M37-01	Dassault Falcon 900	64	N446FJ	2 Sku	
M41-01	Beech Super King Air B200TB	BT-35/BB-1448	N15509	16 Sku	
M41-02	Beech Super King Air B200TB	BT-36/BB-1451	N80024	16 Sku	
M41-03	Beech Super King Air B200TB	BT-37/BB-1454	N80027	16 Sku	
M41-04	Beech Super King Air B200TB	BT-38/BB-1457	N80048	16 Sku	
M44-01	Airtech/IPTN CN235M-200MPA	N034	AX-2315	8 Sku	
M44-02	Airtech/IPTN CN235M-200MPA	N035	AX-2316	8 Sku	
M44-03	Airtech/IPTN CN235M-200MPA	N036	AX-2317	8 Sku	
M44-04	Airtech/IPTN CN235M-220M	N037	AX-2318	21 Sku	
M44-05	Airtech/IPTN CN235M-220M	N038	AX-2319	21 Sku	
M44-06	Airtech/IPTN CN235M-220M	N039	AX-2320	21 Sku	
M48-01	Bombardier BL901 Global Express	9007	C-GCRW	2 Sku	

The Cessna 402s have c/ns 402B0869, 0871, 0873, 0882, 0889, 0891, 0899, 0906, 0916 and 0919, the tie up does not appear sequential.

Polis Diraja Malaysia - Air Wing
Royal Malaysian Police - Air Wing

UNITS/BASES   All aircraft are based at Kuala Lumpur-Sungai Besi.

9M-PMA	Cessna 208B Grand Caravan	208B0800	N2178M
9M-PMB	Cessna 208B Grand Caravan	208B0801	N2178N
9M-PSA	Cessna U206G Stationair 6 II	U20605115	
9M-PSB	Cessna U206G Stationair 6 II	U20605006	
9M-PSD	Cessna U206G Stationair 6 II	U20605262	
9M-PSE	Pilatus PC-6/B2-H4 Turbo Porter	849	HB-FIT
9M-PSF	Pilatus PC-6/B2-H4 Turbo Porter	850	HB-FIU
9M-PSG	Pilatus PC-6/B2-H4 Turbo Porter	851	HB-FIV
9M-PSH	Pilatus PC-6/B2-H4 Turbo Porter	852	HB-FIW
9M-PSI	Pilatus PC-6/B2-H4 Turbo Porter	853	HB-FIX
9M-PSK	Pilatus PC-6/B2-H4 Turbo Porter	855	HB-FIZ
9M-PSL	Cessna 208 Caravan 1	20800229	N9826F
9M-PSM	Cessna 208 Caravan 1	20800230	N9829F
9M-PSN	Cessna 208 Caravan 1	20800231	N9833F
9M-PSO	Cessna 208 Caravan 1	20800232	N9834F
9M-PSP	Cessna 208 Caravan 1	20800233	N9835F
9M-PSQ	Cessna 208 Caravan 1	20800234	N9836F

Government of the Federation of Malaysia

9M-AZZ	British Aerospace 125-800B	258219	G-5-740	Govt of Sarawak
9M-ISJ	GAC Gulfstream IV	1106	N17608	Govt of Johore

MALI
République de Mali   W Africa

Following independence from France in 1960, Mali was soon befriended by the Soviet Union. More recently purchases have been made in the USA.

SERIAL SYSTEM   Three digit numbers are preceded by the country's civil prefix, TZ-.

Force Aérienne de la République de Mali
Mali Republic Air Force

UNITS/BASES   Transports are reported based at Bamako-Senou Airport.

TZ-353	Antonov An-24			
TZ-359	Antonov An-26	5306		
TZ-390	Basler BT-67 Turbo DC-3	13383	N103BF	Cvtd C-47
	Pilatus Britten-Norman BN-2B-21 Islander	2182	TZ-APV	
	Britten-Norman BN-2A-3 Islander	330	TZ-ACF	

MALTA
Repubblika ta'Malta   SE Europe

Until independence in 1964 (although remaining part of the Commonwealth) Malta was always a major strategic military base for British Forces. Today Malta is applying for EU membership and already has strong trading ties with Italy (who base jointly-controlled SAR helicopters on the island).

SERIAL SYSTEM   In the recently changed serial allocation system, all aircraft are prefixed 'AS', followed by the year of purchase. then order of purchase. eg, AS9516 is a BN-2 purchased in 1995 and it was the 16th aircraft of this type acquired.

Armed Force of Malta Air Squadron

UNITS/BASES   2 Regiment, Flight Squadron, Luqa   Islander   Patrol

PLANS   It is reported that at least one of the Islanders is up for disposal.

AS9516	Pilatus Britten Norman BN-2B-26 Islander	2159	9H-ACU	2 Reg/FS
AS9819	Pilatus Britten Norman BN-2B-26 Islander	2156	9H-ADF	2 Reg/FS

MAURITANIA
al-Jumhouriya al-Muslimiya al-Mauritaniyah   NW Africa

A former French colony, independent since 1960, Mauritania has had to patrol and defend its borders since the rise of the Polisario guerilla activity in Western Sahara, a disputed territory which Mauritania occupied from 1976 to 1979. Military coups in 1978 and 1984 together with border disturbances with Senegal between 1989-92 contributed to slowing a re-equipment programme.

SERIAL SYSTEM   Civil registrations are allocated in the 5T-M** block.

Force Aérienne Islamique de Mauritanie
Islamic Air Force of Mauritania

UNITS/BASES   The majority of aircraft are based at Nouakchott Airport.

5T-MAB	Piper PA-31T Cheyenne II	31T-8120024	N2470X	
5T-MAC	Piper PA-31T Cheyenne II	31T-8120026	N2483X	
5T-MAD	Yunshuji/Harbin Y-12 II			
5T-MAE	Yunshuji/Harbin Y-12 II		B-530L	
5T-MAH	Basler BT-67 Turbo Dakota			Cvtd C-47
5T-MA	Reims F337F Super Skymaster	F3370038/ 01371	N1771M	
5T-MAC	Reims/Cessna F337F Skymaster	F3370054/ 01438	F-WLIN	
5T-MAP	Reims/Cessna F337F Skymaster	F3370055/ 01435		
5T-MAS	Britten Norman BN-2A-21 Defender	747	G-BCVR	
5T-MAV	Britten Norman BN-2A-21 Defender	574	G-BEIX	
5T-MAZ	Britten Norman BN-2A-21 Defender	576	G-BEJC	
5T-MBA	Britten Norman BN-2A-21 Defender	577	G-BEJF	

MAURITIUS
République d'île Maurice   Indian Ocean

Independent within the British Commonwealth since 1968and an independent republic since 1992, an aerial capability was obtained by the Coast Guard in 1992.

SERIAL SYSTEM   A sequential number is preceded by the air arm initials.

Mauritius Coast Guard

UNITS/BASES   The aircraft are based at Plaisance-Sir Seewooagur Ramgoolam International Airport.

MP-CG-01	HAL/Dornier 228-101		
MP-CG-02	Pilatus Britten-Norman BN-2T Islander	2238	G-BSPR

MEXICO
Estados Unidos Mexicanos   C America

Primarily a transport force with a COIN capability being reduced in importance, Mexico has always relied on the USA for new equipment. However, with the availability of Eastern European equipment since the early 1990s a number of examples have joined the services here.

SERIAL SYSTEM   Air Force VIP aircraft wear a 'TP-**' code and a Government sequence (XC-) civil registration. Other units wear a four digit code commencing with their Group number. Navy aircraft bear a two letter code starting with 'M' defining the role followed by a three digit serial starting with the Squadron number. Police aircraft wear Government 'XC-' registrations along with a 'PF' prefixed three digit code.

Fuerza Aerea Mexicana - FAM
Mexican Air Force

UNITS/BASES	Grupo 3 , BAM 1 Santa Lucia	
	Escuadrón 301	Arava
	Escuadrón 302	C-130, L-100, 727
	- aircraft also operate from EAM 1 Mexico City IAP	
	Escuadrón 501	AC500, RC690/695
	Escuadrón 502	Metro, PC-6B, King Air
	Ala de Reconocimientoy Transporte	An-32B
	Coordinación General de Transport	Learjet
	Presidencial Flight, EAM 1 Mexico City IAP	757, 737, G-1159A, Super King Air
	Special Operations Escuadrón, Mexico City IAP	King Air 90

PLANS Three EMB-145 (one with Ericsson Erieye AEW RADAR) are on order.

Reserialling is believed to have taken place for all the Grupo 3 transports, details not yet confirmed.

TP-01/ XC-CBD	Boeing 757-225	22690 / 151		Pres. Flt	*'Presidente Juarez'*
TP-02/ XC-UJB	Boeing 737-33A	24095 / 1737	N731XL	Pres. Flt	
TP-03/ XC-UJL	Boeing 737-112	19772 / 217	XB-IBV	Pres. Flt	*'Presidente Cardinas'*
TP-06/ XC-UJN	GAC G-1159A Gulfstream III	352	HB-ITM	Pres. Flt	
TP-07/ XC-UJO	GAC G-1159A Gulfstream III	386	N902KB	Pres. Flt	
TP-102/ XC-UJD	Rockwell Sabreliner 75A	380-68	TP-104 (FAM)		
TP-103/ XC-UJE	Rockwell Sabreliner 60	306-139	TP-105 (FAM)		
TP-104	Learjet 35	35-028	XC-IPP	CGT	
TP-105/ XC-UJR	Learjet 36A	36A-050	XC-AA24	CGT	
TP-106/ XC-UJF	Rockwell Sabreliner 60	306-144	XC-AA63		
TP-201/ XC-UTA	Lockheed L-188A (PF) Electra	1051	TP-04 (FAM)		*'Morelos'*
TP-209	Beech Super King Air 200	BB-725	XC-SLP	Pres. Flt	
TP-0216/ XC-UTI	Shorts SC.7 Skyvan srs 3-100	SH.1952	G-BELY		
TR-301	Pilatus PC-6/B2-H4 Turbo Porter	880		Gr3, Esc502	
TR-302	Pilatus PC-6/B2-H4 Turbo Porter	881		Gr3, Esc502	
TR-303	Pilatus PC-6/B2-H4 Turbo Porter	883		Gr3, Esc502	
TR-304	Pilatus PC-6/B2-H4 Turbo Porter	884		Gr3, Esc502	
ETE-1304	Beech King Air 90			Gr3, Esc502	
TEG-1317	Grumman G-159 Gulfstream 1	179	XC-AA53		
ETE-1318	GAC Commander 695A (Jetprop 1000)	96041	HK-2912	Gr3, Esc501	
ETE-1329	Cessna 500 Citation 1	500-0090/0090	XB-EFR		
ETE-1332	Rockwell Commander 690B	11494	YV-2302P	Gr3, Esc501	:o 3932?
ETE-1363	GAC Commander 695 (Jetprop 980)	95010	HK-3412	Gr3, Esc501	
2201	Beech King Air C90A	LJ-1166	N3100W	Spl Ops Esc	
2202	Beech King Air C90A	LJ-1168	N3082W	Spl Ops Esc	
2203	Beech King Air C90A	LJ-1171	N3086C	Spl Ops Esc	
2204	Beech King Air C90A	LJ-1175	N3139T	Spl Ops Esc	
2205	Beech King Air C90A	LJ-1176	N3108K	Spl Ops Esc	
3001	IAI Arava srs 201	0005	XC-GAW (FAM)	Gr3, Esc301	
3002	IAI Arava srs 201	0007	XC-GAX (FAM)	Gr3, Esc301	
3003	IAI Arava srs 201	0008	XC-GEB (FAM)	Gr3, Esc301	
3004	IAI Arava srs 201	0009	XC-GEC (FAM)	Gr3, Esc301	
3005	IAI Arava srs 201	0010	XC-GED (FAM)	Gr3, Esc301	
3006	IAI Arava srs 201	0036	XC-BIW (FAM)	Gr3, Esc301	
3007	IAI Arava srs 201	0039	XC-BIX (FAM)	Gr3, Esc301	
3008	IAI Arava srs 201	0035	XC-BIY (FAM)	Gr3, Esc301	
3009	IAI Arava srs 201	0037	XC-BIZ (FAM)	Gr3, Esc301	
3010	IAI Arava srs 201	0040	XC-BOA (FAM)	Gr3, Esc301	
3101	Antonov An-32B			Gr3	
3102	Antonov An-32B			Gr3	
	Antonov An-32B			Gr3	
	Antonov An-32B			Gr3	
	(One of the An-32Bs is c/n 2910 ex UR-48060)				
3609	Lockheed C-130A (L-182-1A) Hercules	3087	10609 (FAM)	Gr3, Esc302	
3611	Lockheed L-100-30 (L-382G-48C) Hercules	4851	10611 (FAM)	Gr3, Esc302	
3901	Fairchild C-26A Metro (SA.227AC)			Gr3, Esc502	
3902	Fairchild C-26A Metro (SA.227AC)			Gr3, Esc502	
3903	Fairchild C-26A Metro (SA.227AC)			Gr3, Esc502	
3904	Fairchild C-26A Metro (SA.227AC)			Gr3, Esc502	
JS-10201	Lockheed L-1329-8 JetStar	5144	DN-01 (FAM)	Pres. Flt	to 3908?
10501/ XC-FAD	Boeing 727-14	18912 / 169	XA-SEP	Gr3, Esc302	
10503/ XC-FAY	Boeing 727-14	18908 / 133	XA-SER		Std Benito Juares
10504/ XC-FAZ	Boeing 727-14	18909 / 150	XA-SEU	Gr3, Esc302	
10601	Lockheed C-130A (L-182-1A) Hercules	3004	53-3132 (USAF)	Gr3, Esc302	to 3601?
10602	Lockheed C-130A (L-182-1A) Hercules	3007	53-3135 (USAF)	Gr3, Esc302	to 3602?
10603	Lockheed C-130A (L-182-1A) Hercules	3025	54-1638 (USAF)	Gr3, Esc302	to 3603?
10604	Lockheed C-130A (L-182-1A) Hercules	3055	55-0028 (USAF)	Gr3, Esc302	to 3604?
10605	Lockheed C-130A (L-182-1A) Hercules	3058	55-0031 (USAF)	Gr3, Esc302	to 3605?
	Embraer EMB145SA			AEW&C, on order	
	Embraer EMB145MP			MR, on order	
	Embraer EMB145MP			MR, on order	

Aviación de la Armada de Mexico - AAM
Mexican Naval Aviation

UNITS/BASES	1 Escuadrón Aeronaval, Chetumal	Aviocar	MR
	2 Escuadrón Aeronaval, Mexico City-Benito Juarez IAP	F-27/FH-227, Aviocar, King Air	MR
	2 Escuadrón de Patrulla , La Paz Baja California Sur	An-32B	MR
	3 Escuadrón Aeronaval, Vera Cruz-Las Bajadas	Aviocar, PA-23	MR
	4 Escuadrón Aeronaval, La Paz Baja California Sur	Aviocar, PA-23	MR

5 Escuadrón Aeronaval, Campeche		Aviocar, C404, C402			MR
Escuadrón Avanzado, La Paz Baja California Sur		Baron			Training
Escuadrón Aeronaval de Transport, Mexico City-Benito Juarez IAP					
		Various			VIP

PLANS   A further Dash 8 is held on option.

Code	Type	C/n	Reg	Unit	Role
ME-051	Beech Baron B55	TC-1900		Esc Av	
ME-052	Beech Baron B55	TC-1901		Esc Av	
ME-055	Beech Baron B55			Esc Av	
ME-058	Beech Baron B55			Esc Av	
ME-060	Beech Baron B55			Esc Av	
ME-061	Beech Baron B55			Esc Av	
ME-062	Beech Baron B55			Esc Av	
MP-110	Piper PA-23 Aztec				
MP-111	CASA 212 Aviocar srs 200	S5-1-327		1 EA	
MP-112	CASA 212 Aviocar srs 200	S5-2-333		1 EA	
MP-311	CASA 212 Aviocar srs 200	S5-4-338		3 EA	
MP-312	CASA 212 Aviocar srs 200	S5-7-344		3 EA	
MP-313	CASA 212 Aviocar srs 200	S5-9-360		3 EA	
MP-316	Antonov An-32B	3306	UR-48006	2 EP	
MP-319	Antonov An-32B	3008	UR-48008	2 EP	
MP-320	Antonov An-32B			2 EP	
MP-411	CASA 212 Aviocar srs 200	S5-10-361		4 EA	
MP-412	CASA 212 Aviocar srs 200	S5-5-341	MP-312 (AAM)	4 EA	
MP-413	CASA 212 Aviocar srs 200	S5-3-335	MP-113 (AAM)	4 EA	
MP-508	Cessna 404 Titan			5 EA	
MP-510	CASA 212 Aviocar srs 200			5 EA	
MP-600	Piper PA-31 Navajo			5 EA	
MP-601	Beech Baron B55			Esc Av	
MP-602	Beech Baron B55			Esc Av	
MT-101	Piper PA-23 Aztec			4 EA	
MT-205	Fairchild F-27 Friendship	25	N4305F	2 EA	
MT-211	CASA 212-200 Aviocar	S5-6-342		2 EA	VIP
MT-213	Beech King Air A90	LJ-270	XC-UTG	2 EA	
MT-214	GAC Commander 695A (Jetprop 1000)	96040	N900JP	Esc AT	
MT-216	Fairchild-Hiller FH-227D	578	XC-DOU	2 EA	
MT-217	GAC Commander 695A (Jetprop 1000)	96026	HK-3157W	Esc AT	
MT-218	GAC Commander 695A (Jetprop 1000)	96013	XC-HHZ		Std Benito Juares
MT-219	GAC Commander 695 (Jetprop 980)	95040	XB-AOC	Esc AT	
MT-220	DeHavilland Canada DHC-5 Buffalo	100		2 EA	
MT-221	GAC Commander 695 (Jetprop 980)	95046	XB-DSA	Esc AT	
MT-222	GAC Commander 695 (Jetprop 980)	95082	HK-3453	Esc AT	
MT-223	Mitsubishi MU-2F (B-20)	122	N98MA	Esc AT	
MT-224	Cessna 441 Conquest II	441-0101	N412PW	2 EA	
MT-317	Antonov An-32B		.	2 EP	
MT-318	Antonov An-32B			2 EP	
MT-319	Antonov An-32B			2 EP	
MT-321	Piper PA-23 Aztec			3 EA	
MTX-01	Learjet 60	60-152	N50126	Esc AT	VIP
MTX-02	Learjet 31A	31A-174	N9VL	Esc AT	VIP
MTX-03	Learjet 25D	25D-339	N21HR	Esc AT	VIP
MTX-04	Rockwell Sabreliner 60	306-34	XC-DDA	Esc AT	VIP
MU-1550	Mitsubishi MU-2J (B-35)	566	N210MA	Esc AT	
	Bombardier DeHavilland DHC-8Q-200 Dash 8	558	C-GEOA		
	Bombardier DeHavilland DHC-8Q-200 Dash 8	559	C-GEOZ		

Policia Federal Preventiva de Mexico
Mexican Federal Police

XC-HIE / PF-201	Learjet 29	29-002	XC-DFS
XC-PFB	GAC Commander 695 (Jetprop 980)	95018	N123LA
XC-PFH	Airtech/CASA CN235-100QC	C041	EC-GEJ
XC-PFJ / PF-211	Dassault Falcon 20		
XC-PFP	Learjet 24D	24-260	XA-GBA
XC-PFT / PF-210	Grumman G-1159 Gulfstream IISP	175	XA-FNY
XC-PFW	Airtech/CASA CN235M-10	C011	N100FN
XC-PPF	GAC Commander 695 (Jetprop 980)	95061	XC-AA15
XC- / PF-239	Dassault Falcon 20		
	Antonov An-32		
	Antonov An-32		
	DeHavilland Canada DHC-6 Twin Otter		
	DeHavilland Canada DHC-6 Twin Otter		

MOLDOVA
Republica Moldova   E Europe

Moldova, also reported sometimes as Moldavia, is a former Soviet Republic between Ukraine and Romania. In the late 1990s the USAF bought the unit of MiG-29 fighters that was declared surplus by the Moldovan Air Force to prevent its acquisition by what were deemed to be unsuitable customers.

SERIAL SYSTEM Either the civil prefix is applied to the former Soviet registration or the Soviet tactical code system is retained.

FARM
Moldovan Air Force

UNITS/BASES   Transports are based at Kishinev.

ER-72932	Antonov An-72	36572070696	CCCP-72932
ER-72933	Antonov An-72		CCCP-72933
	Antonov An-72		
10 yellow	Antonov/PZL-Mielec An-2T	1G65-40	

Government of the Republic of Moldova

ER-65094	Tupolev Tu-134A-3	60255	CCCP-65094

MONGOLIA
Bügd Nayramdakh Mongol Ard Uls   E Asia

When the Soviet Union withdrew their substantial based forces in the early 1990s Mongolian defences virtually ceased to exist. Transport helicopters are thought to be the only surviving airworthy equipment although a number of Antonov An-2 and 24/26 types may have been passed on or are shared with the national airline MIAT. Achieved ASEAN membership in 1998.

SERIAL SYSTEM Three digit serials have been noted but the aircraft may now remain in civil markings.

Air Force of the Mongolian Peoples Army

UNITS/BASES   Bases at Ulaanbaatar, Altai, Choir, Choybalsan, Moron and Darhan.

MT-6046	Antonov An-24RV	47309810	BNMAU-9810
103	Antonov An-26		
107	Antonov An-26		
108	Antonov An-26		

Government of the State of Mongolia

JU-7050	Antonov An-24

MOROCCO
al-Mamlakah al-Maghrebiya / The Kingdom of Morocco   NW Africa

Maintaining a western-equipped air force, Morocco fought an extensive war with an Algerian-backed guerrilla group (Polisario) during the late 1970s and 1980s in the Western Sahara and despite a ceasefire being monitored by the UN in the area the issue has never been finally resolved. Until this happens new equipment is unlikely because of a lack of funding and international support.

SERIAL SYSTEM Civil style registrations are allocated in a unique block, CN-A**, the presentation often appearing as CNA-**. Government aircraft are registered in the normal civil sequence CN-T**.

Force Aérienne Royale Marocaine
Royal Moroccan Air Force

UNITS/BASES	1 Air Base, Rabat-Sale	Gulfstream, Falcon 50, Citation, Do28, Super King Air
	3 Air Base, Kenitra	C-130, 707, CN235, Falcon 20, King Air

CNA-MA	Airtech/CASA CN235M-100	AL05-1-C023
CNA-MB	Airtech/CASA CN235M-100	AL05-2-C024
CNA-MC	Airtech/CASA CN235M-100	AL05-3-C025
CNA-MD	Airtech/CASA CN235M-100	AL05-3-C026

CNA-ME	Airtech/CASA CN235M-100	AL05-4-C027		
CNA-MF	Airtech/CASA CN235M-100	AL05-6-C028		
CNA-MG	Airtech/CASA CN235M-100	AL01-10-C031		VIP
CNA-NB	Beech King Air A100	B-181		
CNA-NC	Beech King Air A100	B-182		
CNA-ND	Beech King Air A100	B-183		
CNA-NE	Beech King Air A100	B-186		
CNA-NF	Beech King Air A100	B-187		
CNA-NG	Beech Super King Air B200	BB-1072		
CNA-NH	Beech Super King Air B200	BB-1073		
CNA-NI	Beech Super King Air B200C	BL-57		
CNA-NL	Grumman G-1159TT Gulfstream II	182	N17589	VIP
CNA-NM	Dassault Falcon 20ECM	165	CN-MBH	
CNA-NN	Dassault Falcon 20ECM	152	CN-MBG	
CNA-NO	Dassault Falcon 50	12	F-WZHC	VIP
CNA-NP	Dornier 28D-2 Skyservant	4336	D-ILIE	
CNA-NQ	Dornier 28D-2 Skyservant	4340	D-IAUT	
CNA-NU	GAC G-1159A Gulfstream III	365		VIP
CNA-NV	Cessna 560 Citation V	560-0025	N12285	VIP
CNA-NW	Cessna 560 Citation V	560-0039		VIP
CNA-NX	Beech Super King Air 300	FA-207		
CNA-NY	Beech Super King Air 300	FA-208		
CNA-OA	Lockheed C-130H (L-382C-35D) Hercules	4535		
CNA-OC	Lockheed C-130H (L-382C-35D) Hercules	4551		
CNA-OD	Lockheed C-130H (L-382C-35D) Hercules	4575		MAWS Equipped
CNA-OE	Lockheed C-130H (L-382C-35D) Hercules	4581		
CNA-OF	Lockheed C-130H (L-382C-35D) Hercules	4583		MAWS Equipped
CNA-OG	Lockheed C-130H (L-382C-67D) Hercules	4713		
CNA-OI	Lockheed C-130H (L-382C-67D) Hercules	4733		
CNA-OJ	Lockheed C-130H (L-382C-67D) Hercules	4738		MAWS Equipped
CNA-OK	Lockheed C-130H (L-382C-67D) Hercules	4739		
CNA-OL	Lockheed C-130H (L-382C-67D) Hercules	4742		
CNA-OM	Lockheed C-130H (L-382C-11E) Hercules	4875	N4130M	MAFFS Equipped
CNA-ON	Lockheed C-130H (L-382C-11E) Hercules	4876	N4133M	
CNA-OO	Lockheed C-130H (L-382C-11E) Hercules	4877	N4137M	
CNA-OP	Lockheed C-130H (L-382C-11E) Hercules	4888	N4162M	SLAR Equipped
CNA-OQ	Lockheed C-130H (L-382C-11E) Hercules	4892		SLAR Equipped
CNA-OR	Lockheed KC-130H (L-382C-12E) Hercules	4907	N4216M	
CNA-OS	Lockheed KC-130H (L-382C-12E) Hercules	4909	N4221M	

Government of the Kingdom of Morocco

CN-TNC	Beech Super King Air 300	FA-107	I-ADLA

Ministère de l'Agriculture et de la Réforme Agraire
Ministry of Fisheries and Merchant Marine

UNITS/BASES   Based at Rabat-Sale Airport.

CN-TWK	Pilatus Britten-Norman BN-2T Defender	2213	G-BPXT
CN-TWL	Pilatus Britten-Norman BN-2T Defender	2214	G-BPXU
CN-TWM	Pilatus Britten-Norman BN-2T Defender	2215	G-BPXV
CN-TWN	Pilatus Britten-Norman BN-2T Defender	2228	G-BRSU
CN-TWR	Pilatus Britten-Norman BN-2T Defender	2259	G-BTVM
CN-TWS	Pilatus Britten-Norman BN-2T Defender	2261	G-BUBD
CN-TWT	Pilatus Britten-Norman BN-2T Defender	2262	G-BUBE
CN-TWU	Pilatus Britten-Norman BN-2T Defender	2266	G-BUBI
CN-TWV	Pilatus Britten-Norman BN-2T Defender	2273	G-BVFG
CN-TWW	Pilatus Britten-Norman BN-2T Defender	2274	G-BVFH
CN-TWX	Pilatus Britten-Norman BN-2T Defender	2275	G-BVFJ

MOZAMBIQUE
República de Moçambique   SE Africa

Granted independence from Portugal in 1975 and subsequently plunged into civil war between a Marxist Government and RENAMO guerillas from which Mozambique only emerged in 1992. The former Portuguese-equipped air force (Fôrça Popular Aérea) acquired Soviet equipment through the late 1970s and 1980s and took its current title after the fighting stopped. Current serviceability and the chances of re-equipment are deemed low.

SERIAL SYSTEM   Three digit serials are allocated in blocks by type.

Fôrça Aérea de Moçambique
Mozambique Air Force

UNITS/BASES   Reported military bases include Maputo, Beira, Nacala, Quelimane, Nampula and Cuamba.

022	Antonov An-26	6402
024	Antonov An-26	6405
026	Antonov An-26	
028	Antonov An-26	
030	Antonov An-26	10805
032	Antonov An-26	10806
034	Antonov An-26	
036	Antonov An-26	
038	Antonov An-26	

MYANMAR
Pyeidaungzu Myanma Naingngandaw / Union of Myanmar   SE Asia

Formerly known as Burma (until 1989) and for many years a very insular country, things have slowly changed but following a military coup in 1988 and disputed election results Myanmar has been internally economically unstable, subjected to some trade sanctions and is now close to China when it comes to acquisitions. Became an ASEAN member in 1997.

SERIAL SYSTEM   Four digit serials are used appearing to be blocked by type.

Tamdaw Lay
Armed Forces

UNITS/BASES   The transports mainly operate from Mingaladon (formerly Rangoon) Airport.

0002	Fokker F.27 Friendship 500	10617	XY-AEJ	
4400	Cessna 550 Citation II	550-0358/389	N6801Q	Survey
5001 / XY-AEB	Fokker F.27 Friendship 600	10392	OY-SRR	
5002	Fairchild-Hiller FH-227E	501	N2657	
5004	Fairchild-Hiller FH-227B (LCD)	549	N708U	
5005	Fairchild-Hiller FH-227B (LCD)	552	N709U	
5006	Fairchild-Hiller FH-227B (LCD)	554	N710U	
5815	Yunshuji/Shaanxi Y-8	080803		
5816	Yunshuji/Shaanxi Y-8			
5817	Yunshuji/Shaanxi Y-8	090801		
5818	Yunshuji/Shaanxi Y-8	090802		
6001	Pilatus PC-6/B2-H2 Turbo Porter	772	4001	
6002	Pilatus PC-6/B2-H2 Turbo Porter	773	4002	
6003	Pilatus PC-6/B2-H2 Turbo Porter	780	4003	
6004	Pilatus PC-6/B2-H2 Turbo Porter	781	4004	
6005	Pilatus PC-6/B2-H2 Turbo Porter	795	4005	
6006	Pilatus PC-6/B2-H2 Turbo Porter	796	4006	
6007	Pilatus PC-6/B2-H2 Turbo Porter	797	4007	

NAMIBIA
Republic of Namibia   SW Africa

Known as South-West Africa until independence from South African administration in 1990 the Defence Force's prime role is a policing one covering maritime patrol, anti-smuggling and anti-poaching operations.

SERIAL SYSTEM   Older aircraft use a modified form of the previous operator's serial number. Newer aircraft serials are prefixed NDF and employ a fiscal year system, eg 9-7640 Cessna O-2A is ex 69-7640 (USAF).

Namibia Defence Force

UNITS/BASES   Air Squadron, based at Windhoek-Eros Airport but deployed to other locations as required.

NDF97-639	Yunshuji/Harbin Y-12 II		
	Yunshuji/Harbin Y-12 II		
8-0872	Cessna O-2A Super Skymaster	M337-0237	68-10872 (USAF)
9-7628	Cessna O-2A Super Skymaster	M337-0426	69-7628 (USAF)
69-602	Cessna O-2A Super Skymaster	M337-0400	69-7602 (USAF)
69-605	Cessna O-2A Super Skymaster	M337-0403	69-7605 (USAF)
69-651	Cessna O-2A Super Skymaster	M337-0449	69-7651 (USAF)
9-7640	Cessna O-2A Super Skymaster	M337-0438	69-7640 (USAF)

Government of the Republic of Namibia

V5-EEZ	Reims/Cessna F406 Caravan II	F406-0004	F-WIVD
V5-LSW	Beech 58 Baron	TH-1505	ZS-LSW
V5-NAG	Learjet 31A	31A-091	N5019Y
V5-NAM	Dassault Falcon 900B	103	F-WWFJ

NATO
North Atlantic Treaty Organisation

The North Atlantic Treaty Organisation was founded in 1948 by the USA, UK, France, Canada, Belgium, the Netherlands and Luxembourg. Subsequent members comprised Denmark, Iceland, Italy, Norway and Portugal in 1949 when the formal Treaty signing was conducted in Washington, Greece and Turkey (both in 1952), West Germany (1955) and Spain (in 1982). France left in 1965 to pursue a more independent stance, but has always remained close to NATO participating in exercises and more recently in policing operations (such as those in Iraq and the Balkans). The latest members are Hungary, the Czech Republic and Poland in March 1999. The AEWF was formed to operate the AEW E-3 Sentries from Germany but with crews from twelve member countries. The Royal Air Force's E-3D Sentries are also nominally part of the force but are crewed only by British personnel.

SERIAL SYSTEM The aircraft wear Luxembourg prefixes signifying that country's participation although they have no aircraft to assign to NATO. The numbers themselves refer to either the c/n or FMS previous identity.

NATO Airborne Early Warning Force - NAEWF

UNITS/BASES	E-3A Component, 1 sqn, Geilenkirchen, Germany	E-3A (pooled aircraft)
	E-3A Component, 2 sqn, Geilenkirchen, Germany	E-3A (pooled aircraft)
	E-3A Component, 3 sqn, Geilenkirchen, Germany	E-3A (pooled aircraft)
	E-3A Component, 4 sqn, Geilenkirchen, Germany	E-3A (pooled aircraft), Boeing 707

E-3As are also deployed to Konya (Turkey), Preveza (Greece), Trapani (Italy) and Orland (Norway)

PLANS A NATO-operated air-ground surveillance force is planned with about 6 aircraft (perhaps A321), to be used operationally in the same manner as the E-3As. A programme is being reviewed ro re-engine the E-3s with CFM56 or JT8D-200 powerplants.

LX-N19996	Boeing 707-329C (TCA)	19996 / 748	OO-SJL	NAEWF	Cvtd 707-329C
LX-N19997	Boeing 707-307C	19997 / 747	10+01 (GAF)	NAEWF	
LX-N19999	Boeing 707-307C	19999 / 756	10+03 (GAF)	NAEWF	
LX-N20C00	Boeing 707-307C (TCA)	20000 / 759	10+04 (GAF)	NAEWF	Cvtd 707-307C
LX-N20199	Boeing 707-329C (TCA)	20199 / 816	OO-SJN	NAEWF	Cvtd 707-329C
LX-N90442	Boeing E-3A Sentry	22855 / 945	79-0442 (FMS)	NAEWF	
LX-N90443	Boeing E-3A Sentry	22838 / 947	79-0443 (FMS)	NAEWF	
LX-N90444	Boeing E-3A Sentry	22839 / 949	79-0444 (FMS)	NAEWF	
LX-N90445	Boeing E-3A Sentry	22840 / 953	79-0445 (FMS)	NAEWF	
LX-N90446	Boeing E-3A Sentry	22841 / 954	79-0446 (FMS)	NAEWF	
LX-N90447	Boeing E-3A Sentry	22842 / 955	79-0447 (FMS)	NAEWF	
LX-N90448	Boeing E-3A Sentry	22843 / 956	79-0448 (FMS)	NAEWF	
LX-N90449	Boeing E-3A Sentry	22844 / 957	79-0449 (FMS)	NAEWF	
LX-N90450	Boeing E-3A Sentry	22845 / 959	79-0450 (FMS)	NAEWF	
LX-N90451	Boeing E-3A Sentry	22846 / 961	79-0451 (FMS)	NAEWF	
LX-N90452	Boeing E-3A Sentry	22847 / 963	79-0452 (FMS)	NAEWF	
LX-N90453	Boeing E-3A Sentry	22848 / 964	79-0453 (FMS)	NAEWF	
LX-N90454	Boeing E-3A Sentry	22849 / 966	79-0454 (FMS)	NAEWF	
LX-N90455	Boeing E-3A Sentry	22850 / 967	79-0455 (FMS)	NAEWF	
LX-N90456	Boeing E-3A Sentry	22851 / 968	79-0456 (FMS)	NAEWF	
LX-N90458	Boeing E-3A Sentry	22853 / 970	79-0458 (FMS)	NAEWF	
LX-N90459	Boeing E-3A Sentry	22854 / 971	79-0459 (FMS)	NAEWF	

NEPAL
Nepal Adhirajya / Kingdom of Nepal   S Asia

Nepal first acquired fixed wing aircraft for the Royal Flight and Army in the early 1970s. Currently the Royal Flight only operate helicopters. The country, which contains contrasting terrain from the Himalayas, including Mt. Everest, to sub-tropical jungle, is home to many Tibetan refugees and has recently suffered internal disruption from Chinese-backed communist militia.

SERIAL SYSTEM Sequential serials are allocated for the Army Air Service prefixed with RAN.

Royal Nepalese Army Air Service

UNITS/BASES	1 Brigade (Aviation), Kathmandu-Tribuvan Airport	HS.748, Skyvan

PLANS	A BAE Systems RJ100 was reported as having been ordered late in 2000.			
RAN-14	Shorts SC.7 Skyvan srs 3M-400	SH.1894	9N-RF14 (Govt)	
RAN-20	Hawker Siddeley HS.748-271 srs 2A	1698/set190	9N-RAC	

NETHERLANDS
Koninkrijk der Nederlanden   W Europe

A founder member of NATO and recipient and operator of mainly US equipment, although locally built Fokker aircraft have served continuously since the establishment of a separate Air Force in 1953. Former colonies in SE Asia have been returned to independence but support is still given to the Netherlands Antilles in the Caribbean with MR cover provided by the Navy.

SERIAL SYSTEM The Air Force uses a two or three digit number, either sequential or derived from the c/n or line number, prefixed with a type defining letter code. The Navy allocate a three digit serial in blocks by type.

Koninklijke Luchtmacht - KLu
Royal (Netherlands) Air Force

ICAO code NAF, callsign Netherlands Air Force

UNITS/BASES	334 Sqn, Eindhoven				F50, F60, C-130H-30, KDC-10, G-IV
G-273	Lockheed C-130H-30 (L-382T-50F) Hercules	5273	N4080M	334 Sqn	'Ben Swagerman'
G-275	Lockheed C-130H-30 (L-382T-50F) Hercules	5275	N4080M	334 Sqn	'Joop Mulder'
T-235	McDonnell Douglas KDC-10-30F	46956 / 235	PH-MBP	334 Sqn	'Jar. Scheffer'
T-264	McDonnell Douglas KDC-10-30F	46985 / 264	PH-MBT	334 Sqn	'Prins Bernhard'
U-01	Fokker 60UTA-N	20321	PH-UTL	334 Sqn	'Marinus van Meel'
U-02	Fokker 60UTA-N	20324	PH-UTN	334 Sqn	'Willem Versteegh'
U-03	Fokker 60UTA-N	20327	PH-UTP	334 Sqn	'Jan Borghouts'
U-04	Fokker 60UTA-N	20329	PH-UTR	334 Sqn	'Jules Zeegers'
U-05	Fokker 50	20253	PH-KXO	334 Sqn	VIP, 'Fons Aler'
U-06	Fokker 50	20287	PH-MXI	334 Sqn	VIP, 'Robbie Wijting'
V-11	GAC Gulfstream IV	1009	VR-BOY	334 Sqn	VIP

Marine Luchtvaartdienst - MLD
Naval Air Service

ICAO code NRN, callsign Netherlands Navy

UNITS/BASES	Groep Maritieme Patrouillevliegtuigen - MARPAT			
	320 Sqn, MVK Valkenburg	P-3C	(pooled aircraft)	
	321 Sqn, MVK Valkenburg	P-3C	(pooled aircraft)	
	- Three P-3C detached to Curacao, Netherland Antilles.			
	2 MOTU, operated by NLS from Maastricht	Super King Air		

PLANS	Three P-3C to be retired in 2001, seven to be upgraded in the USA under the Capabilty Upkeep Programme.			
300	Lockheed P-3C-II.5 (L-285E) Orion	5733	Bu161368 (FMS)	320/321 Sqn
301	Lockheed P-3C-II.5 (L-285E) Orion	5737	Bu161369 (FMS)	320/321 Sqn
302	Lockheed P-3C-II.5 (L-285E) Orion	5741	Bu161370 (FMS)	320/321 Sqn
303	Lockheed P-3C-II.5 (L-285E) Orion	5745	Bu161371 (FMS)	320/321 Sqn
304	Lockheed P-3C-II.5 (L-285E) Orion	5750	Bu161372 (FMS)	320/321 Sqn
305	Lockheed P-3C-II.5 (L-285E) Orion	5754	Bu161373 (FMS)	320/321 Sqn
306	Lockheed P-3C-II.5 (L-285E) Orion	5758	Bu161374 (FMS)	320/321 Sqn
307	Lockheed P-3C-II.5 (L-285E) Orion	5762	Bu161375 (FMS)	320/321 Sqn
308	Lockheed P-3C-II.5 (L-285E) Orion	5765	Bu161376 (FMS)	320/321 Sqn
309	Lockheed P-3C-II.5 (L-285E) Orion	5769	Bu161377 (FMS)	320/321 Sqn
310	Lockheed P-3C-II.5 (L-285E) Orion	5773	Bu161378 (FMS)	Std Valkenburg
311	Lockheed P-3C-II.5 (L-285E) Orion	5774	Bu161379 (FMS)	320/321 Sqn
312	Lockheed P-3C-II.5 (L-285E) Orion	5776	Bu161380 (FMS)	320/321 Sqn
PH-SBK	Beech Super King Air 200	BB-180	G-BHVX	2 MOTU	Trainer

Dutch Royal Flight

UNITS/BASES	Operated from Amsterdam-Schiphol by Martinair Holland NV.		
PH-KBX	Fokker 70	11547	VIP

NEW ZEALAND
Dominion of New Zealand
Australasia

New Zealand has been an independent sovereign state since 1907 but still remains happily in the British Commonwealth. The native Maori name for the country is Aotearoa. The Air Force was established in 1923 as the New Zealand Permanent Air Force and the current title was adopted in 1934. The majority of the aircraft in service have been with the Air Force since the 1970s and while replacements are most definitely required funding continues to be tight, even for upgrades. Most recently announced was a decision to scrap the RNZAF combat capabilty by retiring A-4s and MB339s.

SERIAL SYSTEM Four digit serials are allocated prefixed with NZ and batched by type.

Royal New Zealand Air Force

ICAO code KIW, callsign Kiwi

UNITS/BASES		
5 Sqn, RNZAF Whenuapai-Auckland	P-3K	
40 Sqn, RNZAF Whenuapai-Auckland	C-130, 727	
42 Sqn, RNZAF Whenuapai-Auckland	Super King Air	

PLANS Six P-3Ks are also due to complete Project Kestrel by 2003 extending the airframe life for a further 20 years, this work is being done by Hawker Pacific in Australia. The aircraft may lose their ASW capabilty in the near future to save costs.
Looking at leasing C-130Js from Lockheed Martin to replace the C-130Hs.
The 727s are due for replacement in 2004.

NZ1881	Beech Super King Air B200	BB-1054	ZK-KAB	42 Sqn	
NZ1882	Beech Super King Air B200	BB-1008	ZK-KAC	42 Sqn	
NZ1883	Beech Super King Air B200	BB-1087	N65WM	42 Sqn	
NZ4201	Lockheed P-3K (L-185) Orion	5190	Bu152886 (FMS)	5 Sqn	Cvtd P-3B
NZ4202	Lockheed P-3K (L-185) Orion	5192	Bu152887 (FMS)	5 Sqn	Cvtd P-3B
NZ4203	Lockheed P-3K (L-185) Orion	5200	Bu152888 (FMS)	5 Sqn	Cvtd P-3B
NZ4204	Lockheed P-3K (L-185) Orion	5202	Bu152889 (FMS)	5 Sqn	Cvtd P-3B
NZ4205	Lockheed P-3K (L-185) Orion	5208	Bu152890 (FMS)	5 Sqn	Cvtd P-3B
NZ4206	Lockheed P-3K (L-185B) Orion	5401	A9-291 (RAAF)	5 Sqn	Cvtd P-3B
NZ7001	Lockheed C-130H (L-382C-14B) Hercules	4052	64-15094 (FMS)	40 Sqn	
NZ7002	Lockheed C-130H (L-382C-14B) Hercules	4053	64-15095 (FMS)	40 Sqn	
NZ7003	Lockheed C-130H (L-382C-14B) Hercules	4054	64-15096 (FMS)	40 Sqn	
NZ7004	Lockheed C-130H (L-382C-13D) Hercules	4312	68-8218 (FMS)	40 Sqn	
NZ7005	Lockheed C-130H (L-382C-13D) Hercules	4313	68-8219 (FMS)	40 Sqn	
NZ7271	Boeing 727-22C	19892 / 640	N7435U	40 Sqn	
NZ7272	Boeing 727-22C	19895 / 658	N7438U	40 Sqn	

NICARAGUA
República de Nicaragua
C America

Civil war since 1970 between the Soviet-backed Sandinista Government and the CONTRA rebels ended (with US help) in 1990 following elections. The Air Arm (formerly Fuerza Aerea Sandinista) was renamed in 1996 and replacement of Russian equipment is continuing slowly. Hurricane Mitch caused a temporary setback in Nov 1998.

SERIAL SYSTEM No clear system is in place with two and three digit serials and civil registrations in current use.

Fuerza Aérea Nicaraguense - FAN
Nicaraguan Air Force

UNITS/BASES	
No units details are known, but military airfields are reported at:	
Managua-Sandino, Punta Huete, Puerto Cabezas, Esteli, Bluefields, Montelimar, La Rosita,	
El Bluff and Puerto Sandino.	

FA 003	Cessna 404 Titan		VIP
78	Antonov/PZL Mielec An-2TP	1G214-05	
79	Antonov/PZL Mielec An-2T	1G214-11	
80	Antonov/PZL Mielec An-2T	1G214-12	
FA 151	Antonov An-26		Std Managua-Sandino
YN-CEE	Antonov An-26	14203	
YN-BYW	Antonov An-26	12404	Std Managua-Sandino
YN-CBG	Antonov An-26		Std Managua-Sandino

NIGER

République de Niger   W Africa

Still having strong economic ties with France despite independence in 1960 and also still with a small French military presence. The Air Squadron operates only transport aircraft (no helicopters or combat types), the Antonov An-26 being donated by Libya following the loss of the first Hercules.

SERIAL SYSTEM Civil style registrations are allocated in the batch 5U-M**.

Escadrille Nationale du Niger

UNITS/BASES Aircraft are based at Niamey Ad Airport.

5U-MAS	Cessna 337E Super Skymaster	33701173	N86401	
5U-MAT	Reims F337F Super Skymaster	F33700026/ 01335	N1735M	
5U-MBA	Dornier 28D-2 Skyservant	4332	D-ILIA	
5U-	Dornier 28D-2 Skyservant	4338	D-IAUR	
5U-MBH	Lockheed C-130H (L-382C-90D) Hercules	4831		
5U-MBI	Dornier 228-201	8074	D-CELO	Std Germany
5U-	Antonov An-26		Libyan AF	

Government of the Republic of Niger

5U-BAG	Boeing 737-2N9C Advanced	21499 / 513	*'Monts Baghezan'*

NIGERIA

Federal Republic of Nigeria   W Africa

Achieved independence from Britain (within the Commonwealth) in 1963 after existing as a Federation of 19 states since 1954. Various civil conflicts have been fought internally, the most notable of which was the attempted secession of Biafra in the late 1960s. Oil revenue should allow Nigeria to be the strongest and most stable country in the immediate region but it is dogged by scandal, although a manufacturing capability is slowly developing. Whilst being the largest Air Force in the area, now with mainly Western equipment, major investment is required to enable it to contribute to the African peace-keeping role it has been tasked to support.

SERIAL SYSTEM Three or four digit numbers are allocated in batches by type and prefixed with the air arms initials, NAF.

Federal Nigerian Air Force

UNITS/BASES The Transport Force is reported as based at Lagos-Murtala Muhammed Airport.

PLANS The USA is funding the restoration of the eight C-130s service, so that the NAF can assist in African peace-keeping duties.
Reported to be bartering crude oil with Dirgantara Indonesia for 20 CN235s.

NAF	Dornier 128-D2 Turbo Skyservant	4346	D-IAVF
NAF	Dornier 128-D2 Turbo Skyservant	4347	D-IAVG
NAF	Dornier 128-6 Turbo Skyservant	6006	D-IBLA
NAF	Dornier 128-6 Turbo Skyservant	6008	D-IDHA
NAF	Dornier 128-6 Turbo Skyservant	6009	D-IDHC
NAF	Dornier 128-6 Turbo Skyservant	6010	D-IDHB
NAF	Dornier 128-6 Turbo Skyservant	6011	D-ICLA
NAF	Dornier 128-6 Turbo Skyservant	6012	D-ICLB
NAF	Dornier 128-6 Turbo Skyservant	6013	D-ICLC
NAF	Dornier 128-6 Turbo Skyservant	6014	D-ICLD
NAF	Dornier 128-6 Turbo Skyservant	6019	D-IDLD
NAF	Dornier 128-6 Turbo Skyservant	6020	D-IDLE
NAF	Dornier 128-6 Turbo Skyservant	6021	D-IDLF
NAF	Dornier 128-6 Turbo Skyservant	6022	D-ICLG
NAF-027	Dornier 228-101	7043	D-IBLS
NAF-028	Dornier 228-201	8031	D-IDBC
NAF-030	Dornier 228-212	8219	D-CBDI
NAF-031	Dornier 228-212	8221	D-CBDJ
NAF-032	Dornier 228-212	8225	D-CBDL
NAF-033	Dornier 228-212	8229	D-CBDK
NAF-034	Dornier 228-212	8230	D-CBDA
NAF-035	Dornier 228-212	8231	D-CBDN
NAF-036	Dornier 228-212	8241	D-CBDM
NAF-180	Dornier 28D-1 Skyservant	4055	D-IDCC
NAF-181	Dornier 28D-1 Skyservant	4056	D-IDCD
NAF-182	Dornier 28D-1 Skyservant	4057	D-IDCE

NAF-183	Dornier 28D-1 Skyservant	4058	D-IDCF	
NAF-184	Dornier 28D-1 Skyservant	4303	D-IHOP	
NAF-185	Dornier 28D-1 Skyservant	4308	D-IAUD	
NAF-186	Dornier 28D-1 Skyservant	4309	D-IAUC	
NAF-187	Dornier 28D-1 Skyservant	4310	D-IAUB	
NAF-188	Dornier 28D-1 Skyservant	4311	D-IAUA	
NAF-189	Dornier 28D-1 Skyservant	4312	D-IAUE	
NAF-190	Dornier 28D-1 Skyservant	4314	D-IAUG	
NAF-191	Dornier 28D-1 Skyservant	4315	D-IAUI	
NAF-192	Dornier 28D-1 Skyservant	4316	D-IAUH	
NAF-193	Dornier 28D-1 Skyservant	4317	D-IAUK	
NAF-194	Dornier 28D-1 Skyservant	4318	D-IAUJ	
NAF-195	Dornier 28D-1 Skyservant	4321	D-ILFK	
NAF-196	Dornier 28D-1 Skyservant	4322	D-ILFJ	
NAF-197	Dornier 28D-1 Skyservant	4323	D-ILFI	
NAF-198	Dornier 28D-1 Skyservant	4324	D-ILFH	
NAF-199	Dornier 28D-1 Skyservant	4325	D-IAUL	
NAF-910	Lockheed C-130H (L-382C-49D) Hercules	4619	AT619 (NAF)	
NAF-912	Lockheed C-130H (L-382C-49D) Hercules	4638	AT638 (NAF)	
NAF-913	Lockheed C-130H (L-382C-49D) Hercules	4639	AT639 (NAF)	
NAF-914	Lockheed C-130H (L-382C-49D) Hercules	4649	AT649 (NAF)	Std
NAF-915	Lockheed C-130H (L-382C-49D) Hercules	4650	AT650 (NAF)	Std Lagos
NAF-916	Lockheed C-130H-30 (L-382T-40E) Hercules	4962	N4081M	Std Lagos
NAF-917	Lockheed C-130H-30 (L-382T-40E) Hercules	4963	N4099R	
NAF-918	Lockheed C-130H-30 (L-382T-41E) Hercules	5001		
NAF-950	Aeritalia G-222			
NAF-951	Aeritalia G-222			
NAF-952	Aeritalia G-222			
NAF-953	Aeritalia G-222			
NAF-954	Aeritalia G-222	4084		
NAF-1001	Piper PA-31 Navajo	31-7300162	5N-AVA	
NAF-1002	Piper PA-31 Navajo	31-7300163	5N-AVB	
NAF-1003	Piper PA-31-350 Navajo Chieftain	31-7305122	5N-AVC	

Nigerian Police Force

5N-APV	Cessna 500 Citation 1	500-0286/286	N286CC
5N-NPF	Cessna 550 Citation II	550-0125/138	N125RR

Air Border Patrol Unit

5N-AUV	Dornier 228-101	7011	D-ICIP
5N-AUW	Dornier 228-101	7018	D-IBLB
5N-AUX	Dornier 228-101	7095	D-CAGE
5N-AUY	Dornier 228-101	7116	D-CIMA
5N-AUZ	Dornier 228-101	7167	D-CAFA

Government of the Federal Republic of Nigeria

5N-AGV	Grumman G-1159 Gulfstream II	177	N17587
5N-AGZ	British Aerospace 125-800B	258143	5N-NPF
5N-AYA	Cessna 550 Citation II	550-0632/632	N12570
5N-FGE	Dassault Falcon 900	96	5N-OIL
5N-FGM	Boeing 727-2N6 Advanced	22825 / 1805	5N-AGY
5N-FGO	Dassault Falcon 900	52	F-WWFC
5N-FGF	GAC Gulfstream IV	1126	N426GA
5N-FGR	British Aerospace 125-1000B	259018	G-5-741
5N-FGS	GAC Gulfstream V	643	N523GA

NORWAY
Kongeriket Norge / Kingdom of Norway   N Europe

A founding member of NATO, Norway no longer has to worry about the monitoring and defence of the Norwegian Sea to the same extent since the breakup of the USSR. Future plans include involvement in the Rapid Reaction Forces being created by NATO and Europe and worldwide UN peace keeping support. The P-3Ns have no ASW capabilty and operate to support the Coastguard.

SERIAL SYSTEM Three or four digit serials are allocated, they are derived from the c/n or previous identity.

Kongelige Norske Luftforsvaret - KNL
Royal Norwegian Air Force - RNoAF

ICAO code NOW, callsign Norwegian

UNITS/BASES				
	333 Skvadron, Andøya	P-3C/N		
	335 Skvadron, Oslo-Gardermoen	C-130H	c/s Husky	
	717 Skvadron, Rygge	Falcon 20	EW , VIP, c/s Raven	
	719 Skvadron, Bodø (disbanded in January 2001)	DHC-6	Liaison	

PLANS	
	Reported as interested in a Boeing C-17 purchase.
	Six C-130J-30 required from 2007, maybe leased rather than bought.
	The four P-3Cs are undergoing a UIP to P-3C-III standard at Greenville, SC.

041	Dassault Falcon 20CECM	41	LN-FOI	335 Skv	ELINT
053	Dassault Falcon 20CECM	53	LN-FOD	335 Skv	ELINT
0125	Dassault Falcon 20C-5	125	LN-FOE	335 Skv	VIP, Cvtd 20C
057	DeHavilland Canada DHC-6 Twin Otter 100	57	67-057 (KNL)		Std
062	DeHavilland Canada DHC-6 Twin Otter 100	62	67-062 (KNL)		Std
184	DeHavilland Canada DHC-6 Twin Otter 200	184	N1455T		Std
952	Lockheed C-130H (L-382C-14D) Hercules	4334	68-10952 (FMS)	335 Skv	'Odin'
953	Lockheed C-130H (L-382C-14D) Hercules	4335	68-10953 (FMS)	335 Skv	'Tor', Std Oslo
954	Lockheed C-130H (L-382C-14D) Hercules	4336	68-10954 (FMS)	335 Skv	'Balder'
955	Lockheed C-130H (L-382C-14D) Hercules	4337	68-10955 (FMS)	335 Skv	'Froy'
956	Lockheed C-130H (L-382C-14D) Hercules	4338	68-10956 (FMS)	335 Skv	'Ty'
957	Lockheed C-130H (L-382C-14D) Hercules	4339	68-10957 (FMS)	335 Skv	'Brage'
3296	Lockheed P-3C UIP (L-285H) Orion	5817	Bu163296 (FMS)	333 Skv	Cvtd P-3C-III 'Vingtor'
3297	Lockheed P-3C UIP (L-285H) Orion	5818	Bu163297 (FMS)	333 Skv	Cvtd P-3C-III 'Jossing'
3298	Lockheed P-3C UIP (L-285H) Orion	5819	Bu163298 (FMS)	333 Skv	Cvtd P-3C-III 'Viking'
3299	Lockheed P-3C-UIP (L-285H) Orion	5820	Bu163299 (FMS)	333 Skv	Cvtd P-3C-III 'Ulabrand'
4576	Lockheed P-3N (L-185) Orion	5257	Bu154576 (USN)	333 Skv	Cvtd F-3B HW
6603	Lockheed P-3N (L-185C) Orion	5305	Bu156603 (USN)	333 Skv	Cvtd F-3B HW

OMAN
Saltanat Uman / Sultanate of Oman   SW Asia

Britain established the air arm as the Sultan of Oman Air Force in 1959 and Oman has remained a primarily UK customer since, although a lack of choice has now led to mainly US transport purchases. While some combat aircraft have been upgraded recently only the VIP part of the transport fleet has changed over the past few years.

SERIAL SYSTEM   Three digit serials are allocated and presented on the aircraft in Arabic, allocations are batched by type.

Royal Air Force of Oman - RAFO

ICAO code MJN, callsign Majan

UNITS/BASES			
	2 Sqn, Muscat-Seeb International Airport	Skyvan	
	4 Sqn, Muscat-Seeb International Airport	C-130, BAC 1-11	
	5 Sqn, Salalah	Skyvan	MPA, SAR

PLANS	
	A good prospect (subject to funding) for C-130Js, also requires an affordable AEW system (Saab 340, E-2C0 Hawkeye or EMB145?).

501	Lockheed C-130H (L-382C-13E) Hercules	4878	N4138M	4 Sqn	
502	Lockheed C-130H (L-382C-19E) Hercules	4916	82-0050 (FMS)	4 Sqn	
503	Lockheed C-130H (L-382C-33E) Hercules	4948	82-0053 (FMS)	4 Sqn	
551	BAC One-Eleven 485GD (F)	247	1001 (SOAF)	4 Sqn	
552	BAC One-Eleven 485GD (F)	249	1002 (SOAF)	4 Sqn	
553	BAC One-Eleven 485GD (F)	251	1003 (SOAF)	4 Sqn	
901	Shorts SC.7 Skyvan srs 3M-400	SH.1879	G-AYDP		Std Seeb
902	Shorts SC.7 Skyvan srs 3M-400	SH.1875	G-14-47		Std Seeb
903	Shorts SC.7 Skyvan srs 3M-400	SH.1876	G-AYCS		
904	Shorts SC.7 Skyvan srs 3M-400	SH.1877	G-14-49		Std Seeb
905	Shorts SC.7 Skyvan srs 3M-400	SH.1878	G-14-50		
907	Shorts SC.7 Skyvan srs 3M-400	SH.1895	G-14-67		
908	Shorts SC.7 Skyvan srs 3M-400	SH.1896	(G-14-68)		Std Seeb
911	Shorts SC.7 Skyvan srs 3M-400	SH.1867	G-AXPT		
912	Shorts SC.7 Skyvan srs 3M-400	SH.1866	G-AXWU		
913	Shorts SC.7 Skyvan srs 3M-400	SH.1940	G-14-108		Std Seeb
914	Shorts SC.7 Skyvan srs 3M-400	SH.1941	G-14-109		
915	Shorts SC.7 Skyvan srs 3M-400 Seavan	SH.1942	G-14-110		
916	Shorts SC.7 Skyvan srs 3M-400 Seavan	SH.1944	G-BDBT		Std Seeb

Oman Royal Flight

ICAO code ORF, callsign Oman

UNITS/BASES   Aircraft are based at Muscat-Seeb International Airport.

A4O-AB	GAC Gulfstream IV	1168	N462GA
A4O-AC	GAC Gulfstream IV	1196	N420GA
A4O-SO	Boeing 747SP-27	21785 / 405	N351AS
A4O-SP	Boeing 747SP-27	21992 / 447	N150UA

Royal Oman Police - Flight Operations

ICAO code ROP

UNITS/BASES   Aircraft are based at Muscat-Seeb International Airport.

A4O-CQ	Dornier 228-100	7028	D-IBLN
A4O-CJ	Airtech/CASA CN235M-100	C062	
A4O-CV	Airtech/CASA CN235M-100	C063	

PAKISTAN
Islami Jamhuriya-e-Pakistan / Islamic Repiblic of Pakistan   S Asia

Following its partitioning from India in 1947 relations between these two countries have never been warm particularly over the disputed Kashmir territory, while recent nuclear and missile tests have resulted in restrictions being applied to exports to them both. Pakistan's military is, while smaller than India's, still well equipped and since a 1999 coup is also in control of the country. The latest acquisitions and projects have been with China.

SERIAL SYSTEM   All air arms use either the c/n or previous operator's identity as a serial, a system of single letter codes used by the Air Force appears to have been discontinued. The Navy has allocated civil style registrations in addition to their Coastguard aircraft, two digit serials are derived from the squadron number and a further sequential digit.

Pakistan Fiza'ya
Pakistan Air Force

UNITS/BASES	Central Air Command, 38 (Multi-Role) Wing		
	24 Sqn 'Blinders', Sargodha	Falcon 20	EW
	Southern Air Command, 35 Composite		
	(Air Transport) Wing, Chaklala-Islamabad		
	6 Sqn, 'Antelopes'	C-130B/E, L-100	
	12 Sqn	707, F.27, Falcon 20	VIP
	41 Sqn	Various	Liasion

PLANS   An AEW capability is required, possibly in collaboration with China.
Negotiating for 10 Tusas built Airtech CN235Ms.
The CN235M is being evaluated to supplement the remaining C-130s.

TC-1887	Beech Baron 55	TC-1887	AP-AYL	41 Sqn	
927	Beech Super King Air 200	BB-927	N18262	41 Sqn	
68-19866	Boeing 707-340C	19866 / 738	AP-AWY	12 Sqn	
68-19635	Boeing 707-351B	19635 / 706	AP-BAA	12 Sqn	c/s Pakistan 1
J 468	Dassault Falcon 20F	468	F-WMKG	24 Sqn	'Lohdi'
J 469	Dassault Falcon 20F	469	F-WMKI	24 Sqn	'Iqbal'
J 753	Dassault Falcon 20E	277	F-WPXD		c/s AP-TVC
J 752	Fokker F.27 Friendship 200	10281	AP-ATW	12 Sqn	
54	Fokker F.27 Friendship 200	10254	AR-NYA	12 Sqn	
10689	Lockheed C-130E (L-382-1D) Hercules	4119	5-103 (IIAF)	6 Sqn	
12646	Lockheed C-130B (L-282-1B) Hercules	3689	61-2646 (USAF)	6 Sqn	
14727	Lockheed C-130E (L-382-6D) Hercules	4282	5-108 (IIAF)	6 Sqn	
23492	Lockheed C-130B (L-282-1B) Hercules	3702	62-3492 (USAF)	6 Sqn	
24140	Lockheed C-130B (L-282-1B) Hercules	3751	62-4140 (MAP)	6 Sqn	
24141	Lockheed C-130B (L-282-1B) Hercules	3766	62-4141 (MAP)	6 Sqn	
58739	Lockheed C-130B (L-282-1B) Hercules	3536	58-0739 (USAF)	6 Sqn	
64144	Lockheed L-100 (L-382B-4C) Hercules	4144	AP-AUT	6 Sqn	
64310	Lockheed C-130E (L-382-1D) Hercules	4148	5-104 (IIAF)	6 Sqn	
64312	Lockheed C-130E (L-382-1D) Hercules	4153	5-106 (IIAF)	6 Sqn	
97706	Lockheed C-130E (L-382C-10D) Hercules	4294	5-8506 (IRIAF)	6 Sqn	
70168	Piper PA-34-200T Seneca II			41 Sqn	
96-035	Yunshuji/Harbin Y-12 II			41 Sqn	

Pakistan Naval Aviation

UNITS/BASES	27 Sqn, PNS Drigh Road		F.27	MR
	29 Sqn, PNS Sharea Faisal-Karachi		P-3C, Atlantic	MR
	93 Sqn, PNS Mehran-Karachi		Islander	EEZ patrol

81	Lockheed P-3C-II.75 (L-285D) Orion	5825	25 (Pak Navy)	29 Sqn
82	Lockheed P-3C-II.75 (L-285D) Orion	5826	26 (Pak Navy)	29 Sqn
AR-NYB / 42	Pilatus Britten-Norman BN-2T Islander	2242	G-BSWN	93 Sqn
AR-NYC / 46	Pilatus Britten-Norman BN-2T Islander	2246	G-BSWS	93 Sqn
AR-NZB / 92	Breguet Br1150 Atlantic	40	40 (FN)	29 Sqn
AR-NZC / 93	Breguet Br1150 Atlantic	46	46 (FN)	29 Sqn
94	Breguet Br1150 Atlantic	63	F-YELY	29 Sqn
AR-NZE / 62	Fokker F.27 Friendship 200	10262	AR-MLF	27 Sqn
AR-NZQ / 52	Fokker F.27 Friendship 200	10252	AP-BDG	27 Sqn
AR-NZV / 45	Fokker F.27 Friendship 200	10445	ZK-DCB	27 Sqn
AR-NZW / 69	Fokker F.27 Troopship 400M	10469	VR-BLY	27 Sqn
AR-NZZ / 44	Fokker F.27 Friendship 200	10444	ZK-DCA	27 Sqn

Pakistan Army Aviation Corps

UNITS Fixed wing aircraft are based at Rawalpindi-Qasimaab with the VIP flight.

0222	Cessna 421C Golden Eagle III	421C0222	AP-AZQ
0233	Cessna 560 Citation V	560-0233	N1288A
11667	GAC Commander 690C (Jetprop 840)	11667	N5919K
11733	GAC Commander 690C (Jetprop 840)	11733	N56GA

Government of Pakistan

AP-BEK	Learjet 31A	31A-062	N25997	Govt of Balochistan
AP-BEX	Beech Beechjet 400A	RK-80	N8180Q	Govt of Punjab

PALESTINE
SW Asia

Now a semi-autonomous state within Israel, conflict continues despite US brokered peace negotiations. The government has a small helicopter fleet and a former Iraqi Government JetStar as Yassir Arafat's personal transport, although a leased Challenger has also recently been noted.

Government of Palestine

OE-IYA	Bombardier Canadair CL-604 Challenger	5435	N604PN	LF Transair, Vienna
7T-VHP	Lockheed L-1329 JetStar II	5233	YI-AKA	

PANAMA
República de Panamá — C America

Following the 1989 US invasion to oust General Noriega, the government abolished the armed forces. US forces have now withdrawn from the country created with much US help in 1903 to build the famous canal. The Air Service now remaining is effectively part of a Police force known as the Panamanian Public Forces.

SERIAL SYSTEM Three digit serials commencing at 200 and currently ascending in 5s are allocated.

Panamá Servicio Aéreo Nacional
Panama National Air Service

UNITS/BASES The Maritime Patrol and transport squadrons are based at Tocumen International Airport-Panama City.

200	Piper PA-31T Cheyenne		HP-111A	c/n 31T-7620046 reported
212	Piper PA-34 Seneca			
220	CASA 212 Aviocar srs 200	A31-2-241		
225	CASA 212 Aviocar srs 200	A31-3-243		
250	CASA 212 Aviocar srs 300	AA31-01-374		
255	CASA 212 Aviocar srs 300	AA31-02-375		
260	CASA 212 Aviocar srs 300	AA31-03-376		
265	Airtech/CASA CN235M-10	C011		

Government of the Republic of Panama

HP-1A	Grumman G-1159 Gulfstream II SP	78	N90HH

PAPUA NEW GUINEA
Independent State of Papua New Guinea   Australasia

Funding problems grounded the PNG-DF fixed wing aircraft from 1996 at a time when a civil war was being fought against Bougainville rebels. Australia has assisted in support of operations, particularly following a natural disaster in 1998. Serviceability appears now to be being restored.

SERIAL SYSTEM Three or four digit serials batched by type and preceded with the civil P2 prefix are worn.

Papua New Guinea Defence Force

UNITS/BASES   Aircraft operate from Port Moresby.

PLANS   Negotiating to acquire two more IPTN-built CN235s, and to have IPTN rework the two grounded CASA built aircraft.

P2-012	GAF N22B Nomad	54	P2-DFO	Std Jackson, PNG
P2-013	GAF N22SB Nomad Searchmaster	67	P2-DFP	Std Jackson, PNG
P2-015	GAF N22SL Nomad Searchmaster	113		Std Jackson, PNG
P2-016	GAF N22SL Nomad Searchmaster	143		Std Jackson, PNG
P2-021	IAI Arava srs 201	0082	4X-CUQ	Std
P2-022	IAI Arava srs 201	0083	4X-CUR	Std
P2-023	IAI Arava srs 201	0084	4X-CUS	Std
P2-0501	Airtech/CASA CN235M-100	C048		Std
P2-0502	Airtech/CASA CN235M-100	C049		

Government Flying Unit

UNITS/BASES   Aircraft flies from Port Moresby.

P2-PNG	Beech Super King Air 350 (B300)	FL-79	N8246Q

PARAGUAY
República de Paraguay   S America

Landlocked and with a military government, Paraguay has the typical South American air force run airline, TAM, to operate routes that could not be flown commercially. Having no coast line the Navy patrols the country's extensive river system.

SERIAL SYSTEM Four digit serials are allocated for the majority of Air Force aircraft with liaison types commencing 02** and transports 20**, the exceptions being the VIP aircraft which are always serialed FAP-01, 02 etc. The Navy use a three digit sequential number prefixed NAVAL.

Fuerza Aérea Paraguaya - FAP

UNITS/BASES   Grupo Aéreo de Transporte Especiales (GATE), Asunción IAP   Various Light Transports
                   also operates the Escuadrilla Presidencial   707, Twin Otter
                   Grupo de Transporte Aéreo (GdTA), Asunción-Silvo Pettirossi IAP
                   operates as Transporte Aéreo Militar (TAM)   Aviocar, C-47

PLANS   Looking at acquiring CASA 212-400s.

FAP-01	Boeing 707-321B	18957 / 472	ZP-CCF		Std Asuncion?
FAP-02	DeHavilland Canada DHC-6 Twin Otter 200	137	FAP-01 (FAPar)		VIP
0210	Cessna U206G Stationair 6 II	U20605365			
0212	Cessna U206G Stationair 6 II	U20605497			
0218	Cessna 210	"21069780"?			
0219	Cessna 210N Centurion II	21064346	ZP-TVB		
0220	Piper PA-23-160 Apache	23-1916	LV-GOE		
0221	Cessna 402B	402B1360			
0222	Cessna 402B	402B0052			
0223	Embraer EMB-810C (PA-34-220T Seneca III)	810095			
2010	Douglas C-47B	32620/15872	T-81 (FAPar)	TAM	
2027	CASA 212A Aviocar srs 200	A52-1-307		TAM	
2029	CASA 212A Aviocar srs 200	A52-2-310		TAM	
2030	Douglas C-47A	12557	(FACh)	TAM	
2031	CASA 212A Aviocar srs 200	A52-3-315		TAM	

2032	Douglas C-47B	27098/15653	2090 (FABr)	TAM	
2033	CASA 212A Aviocar srs 200	AC52-3-316		TAM	

Aviación de la Armada Nacional Paraguaya
Naval Aviation

UNITS/BASES   Fixed wing aircraft are based at Asunción-Silvo Pettirossi IAP.

NAVAL-134	Cessna 210N Centurion II	21063005	ZP-TOI
NAVAL-142	Cessna 310K	310K0142	ZP-TJN
NAVAL-144	Cessna 310		
NAVAL-146	Cessna 401B	401B0217	N7998Q

Arma Aérea del Ejércíto Paraguayo
Army Aviation

UNITS/BASES   Fixed wing aircraft are based at Asunción-Silvo Pettirossi IAP.

TE-02	Beech Baron 58	TH-1278	N18101
TE-03	Cessna 310R	310R1337	
TE-04	Cessna U206G Stationair 6 II		

Ministerio de Defensa Nacional

ZP-MDA	Cessna 310R	310R0275	TE-01 (Ejer.Para)
ZP-MDC	Cessna U206G Stationair 6 II	U20603981	ZP-PLN

PERU
República de Perú   S America

Peru operates equipment acquired from just about every manufacturing country in the world including, uniquely for a South American country, large numbers of Russian aircraft. The Air Force-run airline is titled TANS and features float-equipped Twin Otters, Turbo Porters and even Y-12s.

SERIAL SYSTEM   The FAP use three digit serials, most transports being in the 300 sequence and the liaison types in the 700 batch. Civil registrations are also allocated to most of the larger types. VIP aircraft have their own unique serials. The other air arms all display three digits prefixed with a two letter role code by the Navy and EP and PNP by the Army and Police respectively.

Fuerza Aérea del Perú - FAP
Peruvian Air Force

UNITS/BASES   Grupo Aéreo de Transportes 8, BA Jorge Chavez, Callao IAP-Lima
    Escuadrón de Transporte 841   C-130A/L-100, 707, F.28
    Escuadrón de Transporte 842   An-32
    Escuadrón de Transporte 843   C421, Queen Air
    Escuadrilla Presidencial   737, DC-8, F.28

Grupo Aéreo de Transporte 42, BA Coronel Francisco Secada Vignetta, Iquitos
    Transporte Aéreo Nacionales de Selva (TANS)   Y-12, Turbo Porter, DHC-6

Grupo Aéreo Entrenamiento 51, BA Las Palmas, Lima
    Escuadrón de Instruccion Primaria 511   Queen Air

Servicio Aerofotographico Nacional, BA Las Palmas, Lima
    Escuadrón de Aerofotografico 331   Learjet, Falcon 20

300 / OB-1433	Dassault Falcon 20F	434	F-WRQP	EA 331	VIP
302 / OB-1157	DeHavilland Canada DHC-6 Twin Otter 300	378		TANS	
303 / OB-1336	DeHavilland Canada DHC-6 Twin Otter 300	483		TANS	
305 / OB-1154	DeHavilland Canada DHC-6 Twin Otter 300	274	N86TC	TANS	
308 / OB-1157	DeHavilland Canada DHC-6 Twin Otter 300	266	N85TC	TANS	
311 / OB-1159	DeHavilland Canada DHC-6 Twin Otter 300	385		TANS	
312 / OB-1160	DeHavilland Canada DHC-6 Twin Otter 300	322		TANS	Floats
316 / OB-1164	Pilatus PC-6/B2-H2 Turbo Porter	760		TANS	Floats
319 / OB-1371	Boeing 707-323C	19575 / 714	HP-1028	ET 841	AAR
320 / OB-1165	Pilatus PC-6/B2-H2 Turbo Porter	720		TANS	Floats
322 / OB-1640	Antonov An-32B	3002	TS-LCA	ET 842	
323 / OB-1641	Antonov An-32B	2809	48052 (UN)	ET 842	
324 / OB-1642	Antonov An-32B	2907	RA-48129	ET 842	
326 / OB-1685	Antonov An-32B	3407		ET 842	

327 / OB-1686	Antonov An-32B	3207	RA-48063	ET 842	
331 / OB-1166	Pilatus PC-6/B2-H2 Turbo Porter	722		TANS	Floats
335 / OB-1500	Yunshuji/Harbin Y-12 II	0051		TANS	
336 / OB-1501	Yunshuji/Harbin Y-12 II	0052		TANS	
337 / OB-1502	Yunshuji/Harbin Y-12 II	0053		TANS	
338 / OB-1503	Yunshuji/Harbin Y-12 II	0054		TANS	
341	Fairchild C-26A Metro (SA.227AC)				
	Fairchild C-26A Metro (SA.227AC)				
	Fairchild C-26A Metro (SA.227AC)				
	Fairchild C-26A Metro (SA.227AC)				
OB-1621	Yunshuji/Harbin Y-12 II	0072		TANS	
OB-1622	Yunshuji/Harbin Y-12 II	0073		TANS	
OB-1623	Yunshuji/Harbin Y-12 II	0074		TANS	
350 / OB-1713	Boeing 737-244	19707 / 82	XA-SFR	TANS	
352 / OB-1724	Boeing 737-282 Advanced	23042 / 967	VT-PDC	TANS	
OB-1718	Boeing 737-248	19424 / 147	CC-CVA	TANS	
OB-1719	Boeing 737-248	20221 / 227	CC-CVB	TANS	
OB-1743	Boeing 737-2N7 Advanced	21226 / 458	N119SW	TANS	Lsd
356 / PRP-001	Boeing 737-528	27426 / 2739	(F-GJNR)	Esc Pres	
362 / CB-1379	Antonov An-32	0909		ET 842	
363 / CB-1380	Antonov An-32	0910		ET 842	
366 / CB-1381	Antonov An-32	1001		ET 842	
367 / CB-1382	Antonov An-32	1002		ET 842	
369 / CB-1486	Antonov An-72	1501			Std Lima
OB-1487	Antonov An-72				Std Lima
370 / CB-1372	Douglas DC-8-62F (CF)	46078 / 475	HB-IDK	Esc Pres	
371 / CB-1373	Douglas DC-8-62F (CF)	45984 / 370	HB-IDH		Std Lima
374 / OB-1384	Antonov An-32	1106		ET 842	
375 / OB-1389	Antonov An-32	1304		ET 842	
376 / OB-1383	Antonov An-32	1003		ET 842	
378 / OB-1385	Antonov An-32	1107		ET 842	
379 / OB-1386	Antonov An-32	1108		ET 842	
381 / OB-1394	Lockheed KC-130A (L-182-1A) Hercules	3058	55-0330 (USAF)	ET 841	
382 / OB-1377	Lockheed L-100-20 (L-382E-37C) Hercules	4706	OB-R-1183	ET 841	
384 / OB-1378	Lockheed L-100-20 (L-382E-37C) Hercules	4715		ET 841	
386 / OB-1387	Antonov An-32	1109		ET 842	
387 / OB-1393	Antonov An-32	1305		ET 842	
389 / OB-1390	Antonov An-32	1301		ET 842	
390 / OB-1396	Fokker F.28 Fellowship 1000	11100		TANS	
391 / OB-1391	Antonov An-32	1302		ET 842	
392 / OB-1392	Antonov An-32	1303		ET 842	
393	Lockheed C-130A (L-182-1A) Hercules			ET 841	
394 / OB-1374	Lockheed L-100-20 (L-382E-26C) Hercules	4358	OB-R-1188	ET 841	
396 / OB-1395	Lockheed C-130A (L-182-1A) Hercules	3177	57-0470 (USAF)		Std Lima
397 / OB-1375	Lockheed L-100-20 (L-382E-47C) Hercules	4850	N4115M	ET 841	
398 / OB-1376	Lockheed L-100-20 (L-382E-47C) Hercules	4853	N4119M	ET 841	
524 / OB-1431	Learjet 36A	36A-051	N4290J	EA 331	Survey
525 / OB-1432	Learjet 36A	36A-052	N4291K	EA 331	Survey
703	Cessna 421			ET 843	
704	Piper PA-34-200T Seneca II	34-7570186	CP-1181		
708	Rockwell Commander 690				
716	Piper PA-34-200 Seneca				
718	Cessna 210				
729	Beech 65 Queen Air A80	LD-245			
730	Beech 65 Queen Air A80	LD-251			
731	Beech 65 Queen Air A80	LD-254			
732	Beech 65 Queen Air A80	LD-247			
733	Beech 65 Queen Air A80	LD-248			
734	Beech 65 Queen Air A80	LD-252			
735	Beech 65 Queen Air A80	LD-253			
736	Beech 65 Queen Air A80	LD-258			
737	Beech 65 Queen Air A80	LD-259			
740	Beech 65 Queen Air A80	LD-262			
742	Beech 65 Queen Air A80	LD-265			
743	Beech 65 Queen Air A80	LD-266			
745	Beech 65 Queen Air A80	LD-268			
900 / OB-1565	Beech 65 Queen Air A80	LD-260	738 (FAP)		
901 / OB-1566	Beech 65 Queen Air A80	LD-264	741 (FAP)		

Servicio Aeronavale de la Marine
Navy Air Arm

UNITS/BASES	Escuadrón Aeronavale 11, Lima-Jorge Chavez IAP	F.27, Super King Air	ASW
	Escuadrón Aeronavale 32, Callao	An-32B, Super King Air	

	Escuadrón de Amazonos, Iquitos (Guardacosta titles)			Twin Otter, F.27	MR
AB-582	Fokker F.27-200 Friendship	10355	OB-1510	Guardacosta	
AB-583	DeHavilland Canada DHC-6 Twin Otter			Guardacosta	Floats
AB-584	Fokker F.27-600 Friendship	10322	C-FAFE	Guardacosta	
AE-562	Fokker F.27-500F Friendship	10524	OB-1446	EAN 11	
AE-571	Beech Super King Air 200CT	BL-58/BN-2		EAN 32	
AE-572	Beech Super King Air 200CT	BL-59/BN-3		EAN 32	
AE-573	Beech Super King Air 200CT	BL-60/BN-4		EAN 32	
AE-574	Beech Super King Air 200T	BB-1096/BT-25		EAN 11	
AE-575	Beech Super King Air 200T	BB-1098/BT-26		EAN 11	
AT 528	Cessna 206			EAN 32	
AT-530 / OB-1612	Antonov An-32B	3403		EAN 32	
AT-531 / OB-1613	Antonov An-32B	3408		EAN 32	

Aviación del Ejércíto Peruana
Peruvian Army Aviation

UNITS/BASES	Aircraft are based at Lima-Jorge Chavez IAP, and deployed when necessary.			
EP-807	Cessna U206G Stationair			
EP-808	Cessna U206G Stationair			
EP-809	Cessna U206G Stationair			
EP-810	Cessna U206G Stationair			
EP-811	Cessna U206G Stationair			
EP-819	Piper PA-34 Seneca			
EP-821	Piper PA-31 Navajo			
EP-823	Piper PA-31 Navajo			
EP-825	Beech Super King Air 350 (B300)	FL-21	N666RH	
EP-826	Antonov An-28	1AJ005-	RA-	
EP-827	Antonov An-28	1AJ005-	RA-	
EP-830	Let 410			
EP-831	Antonov An-32			
EP-833	Antonov An-32			
EP-835	Antonov An-32			
EP-837	Antonov An-32B	3506		

The two An-28 have c/n's 1AJ005-07 and 1AJ005-21.

Policia Nacional del Peru

UNITS/BASES	All fixed wing aircraft are operated by Escuadrón 500 at Lima-Jorge Chavez IAP.				
FP-18	Beech Super King Air 300	FA-41	HK-3495	Guardia Civil	
PNP-215	Pilatus Britten-Norman BN-2B-27R Islander	2176	FP-15 (Gda. Civil)	Esc 500	
PNP-216	Aero Commander 680			Esc 500	
PNP-217	Britten-Norman BN-2 Islander			Esc 500	
PNP-218	Aero Commander 680			Esc 500	
PNP-225	Yunshuji/Harbin Y-12 II			Esc 500	
PNP-226	Yunshuji/Harbin Y-12 II			Esc 500	
PNP-227 / OB-1624	Antonov An-32B	3307	YL-LDD	Esc 500	
PNP-228 / OB-1625	Antonov An-32B	3308	YL-LDE	Esc 500	
PNP-229	Colemill Panther Navajo			Esc 500	Cvtd PA-31
PNP-230	Beech King Air E90	LW-36	OB-1598	Esc 500	
PNP-231	Piper PA-34 Seneca			Esc 500	
PNP-233	Antonov An-32	2501	RA-48066	Esc 500	
PNP-234	Antonov An-32	2502	RA-48067	Esc 500	
PNP-323	Antonov An-32			Esc 500	
PNP-345	Antonov An-32			Esc 500	

PHILIPPINES
República Ng Pilipinas   SE Asia

The Philippines consist of over 7000 islands and was relatively prosperous in the early 1990s following removal of the Marcos dictatorship. The economic crash in the Pacific Rim has slowed an ambitious modernisation programme and left the armed forces operating on a reduced budget. A member of ASEAN.

Hukbong Himpapawid ng Pilipinas / Philippine Air Force

UNITS/BASES	220th Airlift Wing, 221st Airlift sqn, Villamor AB-Pasay City	F.27, F.27MPA
	220th Airlift Wing, 222nd Heavy Airlift sqn, Mactan AB, Cebu	C-130/L-100

220th Airlift Wing, 223rd Airlift sqn, Mactan AB, Cebu				Nomad	
250th Presidential Airlift Wing, 702nd sqn, Villamor AB-Pasay City				F.28, F.27	VIP

PLANS 4-6 new Maritime Patrol Aircraft are required, the ATR42MP and DHC-8 have been short listed.
Four ex RAF C-130Ks have been purchased from Lockheed Martin.

225	Cessna T210 Turbo Centurion				
59-0259	Fokker F.27 Friendship 200	10115	PH-FAM	702 Sqn	cvtd 100, Std Villamor
10246	Fokker F.27 Friendship 200	10246	PI-C507	221 Sqn	cvtd 100, Std Villamor
10267	Fokker F.27 Friendship 200	10267	PI-C516	221 Sqn	cvtd 100, Std Villamor
10296	Fokker F.27 Friendship 200	10296	PI-C528	221 Sqn	cvtd 100, Std Villamor
10310	Fokker F.27 Friendship 200	10310	PI-C531	221 Sqn	cvtd 100
10327	Fokker F.27 Friendship 200	10327	PI-C534	221 Sqn	cvtd 100
10620	Fokker F.27 Friendship 200MAR	10620	PH-EXI	221 Sqn	cvtd 100
RP-1250	Fokker F.28 Fellowship 3000	11153	RP-C1177	702 Sqn	
5	GAF N22B Nomad Missionmaster	5		223 Sqn	
6	GAF N22B Nomad Missionmaster	6			Std Mactan AB?
12	GAF N22B Nomad Missionmaster	12			Std Mactan AB?
15	GAF N22B Nomad Missionmaster	15		223 Sqn	
18	GAF N22B Nomad Missionmaster	18		223 Sqn	
19	GAF N22B Nomad Missionmaster	19		223 Sqn	
20	GAF N22B Nomad Missionmaster	20		223 Sqn	
22	GAF N22B Nomad Missionmaster	22		223 Sqn	
23	GAF N22B Nomad Missionmaster	23		223 Sqn	
53	GAF N22B Nomad Missionmaster	53	VH-CRI	223 Sqn	reported as a Searchmaster
68	GAF N22B Nomad Missionmaster	68	VH-MSE	223 Sqn	reported as a Searchmaster
86	GAF N22SL Nomad Searchmaster	86	VH-SBY	223 Sqn	
87	GAF N22SL Nomad Searchmaster	87	VH-SDZ	223 Sqn	
0294	Lockheed C-130B (L-282-1B) Hercules	3593	60-0294 (USAF)		Std?
0738	Lockheed C-130B (L-282-1B) Hercules	3535	58-0738 (USAF)	222 Sqn	
3545	Lockheed C-130B (L-282-1B) Hercules	3545	58-0747 (USAF)	222 Sqn	
3552	Lockheed C-130B (L-282-1B) Hercules	3552	58-0753 (USAF)	222 Sqn	
3946	Lockheed L-100 (L-382-17B) Hercules	3946	RP-C97	222 Sqn	
4593	Lockheed L-100-20 (L-382E-33C) Hercules	4593	RP-C101	222 Sqn	
4704	Lockheed C-130H (L-382C-63D) Hercules	4704		222 Sqn	
4726	Lockheed C-130H (L-382C-63D) Hercules	4726		222 Sqn	

Philippine Naval Aviation

UNITS/BASES All aircraft are normally based at Sangley Point AB.

301	Britten-Norman BN-2A-21 Defender	428	428 (Phil Navy)
302	Britten-Norman/PADC BN-2A-21 Defender	453	453 (Phil Navy)
303	Britten-Norman/PADC BN-2A-21 Defender	460	460 (Phil Navy)
304	Britten-Norman BN-2A-21 Defender	456	456 (Phil Navy)
310	Britten-Norman BN-2A-21 Defender	430	430 (Phil AF)
311	Britten-Norman/PADC BN-2A-21 Defender	538	538 (Phil AF)
312	Britten-Norman/PADC BN-2A-21 Defender	567	567 (Phil AF)
314	Britten-Norman/PADC BN-2A-21 Defender	568	568 (Phil AF)
320	Britten-Norman/PADC BN-2A-21 Defender	552	552 (Phil AF)

Philippine Army

UNITS/BASES Based at Ft.Magsaysay but deployed as required.

PA-701	Beech 65 Queen Air 80	LD-149	RP-C701
PA-9-1	Cessna P206A Super Skylane	P206-0260	RP-C66
PA-9-2	Cessna U206A Super Skywagon	U206-0438	RP-C756

Philippine Coast Guard Auxillary

UNITS/BASES Based at Manila Domestic Airport with 402 Sqn.

PCG-251	Britten-Norman/PADC BN-2A-21 Islander	3002	RP-C251
PCG-684	Britten-Norman BN-2A-21 Islander	723	RP-C684
RP-C1242	Cessna 421B Golden Eagle	421B0032	N500ES
RP-3101	SIAI-Marchetti SF.600A Canguro	009	
VH-PQD	Cessna P206 Super Skylane	P206-0134	(RP-C3165)

Integrated National Police Force

UNITS/BASES   Based at Manila Domestic Airport, carrying Pulisya titles.

RP-462	Britten-Norman/PADC BN-2A-21 Islander	462	RP-2164
RP-2169	Britten-Norman BN-2A-21 Islander	463	RP-463

Government of the Republic of the Philippines

11250	Rockwell Commander 690A	11250	N44WV
RP-C4007	Boeing 737-332	25996 / 2488	RP-C2000

POLAND
Rzeczpospolita Polska   E Europe

Poland became a NATO member in March 1999 having re-organised and in some cases upgraded the Soviet built equipment operated. The capable local manufacturing and maintenance capability of WSK-PZL has allowed the withdrawal from Russian influence to
be less damaging than with other ex Warsaw Pact members.

Polskie Wojska Lotnicze i Obrony Powietrznej - PWL
Polish Air Force and Air Defence

ICAO code PLF, callsign Polish Air Force

UNITS/BASES	36 Specjalny Pulk Lotnictwa Transportowego (36 SPLT), Warsaw-Okecie	Yak-40, Tu-154M	VIP
	2 Korpus Obrony Powietrznej (2 KOP), Bydgoszcz	An-2, M-28	HQ Flt
	19 Lotnicza Eskadra Holownicza (19 LEH), Slupsk	Yak-40	TT (with Iskra)
	(probably disbanded with Yak-40 going to 36 SPLT)		
	3 Korpus Obrony Powietrznej (3 KOP), Poznan-Lawica	An-2	HQ Flt
	13 Pulk Lotnictwa Transportowego (13 PLT), Krakow-Balice	An-26, An-28, An-2	
	Wyzsza Szkola Oficerska Sil Powietrznych		
	23 Lotnicza Eskadra Specjalna (23 LEz), Deblin	An-2	
		(support to MiG-21, Orlik and Iskra)	
	LGPR, "Land Rescue Unit", Bydgoszcz	M-28	

PLANS	The An-26s are being replaced from 2002/3 with the CASA C295, eight are on order and two C-130 size aircraft are also required.
	Ten M-28 Skytrucks have been ordered with deliveries to commence late in 2001.

032	Yakovlev Yak-40	9331129		36 SPLT	
034	Yakovlev Yak-40	9331229		36 SPLT	
037	Yakovlev Yak-40	9510238		36 SPLT	
038	Yakovlev Yak-40	9441237		36 SPLT	
039	Yakovlev Yak-40	9441137		36 SPLT	
040	Yakovlev Yak-40	9541643		36 SPLT	
041	Yakovlev Yak-40	9541843	SP-LEB	36 SPLT	
042	Yakovlev Yak-40	9541943	SP-LEC	36 SPLT	
043	Yakovlev Yak-40	9542043	SP-LED	36 SPLT	For sale, Okecie
044	Yakovlev Yak-40	9840659		36 SPLT	
045	Yakovlev Yak-40	9840759		36 SPLT	
047	Yakovlev Yak-40	9021560	SP-LEE	36 SPLT	
048	Yakovlev Yak-40	9021660	SP-LEA	36 SPLT	
101	Tupolev Tu-154M	90A-837	837 (PWL)	36 SPLT	
102	Tupolev Tu-154M	90A-862	862 (PWL)	36 SPLT	
0723	PZL-Mielec M-28B1	AJBP01-01	SP-PDE	LGPR	cvtd PZL An-28TD Land Rescue aircraft
0852	Antonov/PZL-Mielec An-2T	1G108-52			
0853	Antonov/PZL-Mielec An-2T	1G108-53		13 PLT	
0856	Antonov/PZL-Mielec An-2T	1G108-56			
0861	Antonov/PZL-Mielec An-2T	1G108-61		13 PLT	
1003	Antonov An-28TD	1AJB001-01		13 PLT	
1310	Antonov An-26	1310		13 PLT	
1402	Antonov An-26	1402		13 PLT	
1403	Antonov An-26	1403		13 PLT	
1406	Antonov An-26	1406		13 PLT	
1407	Antonov An-26	1407		13 PLT	
1463	Antonov/PZL-Mielec An-2P	1G114-63		23 LESz	
1464	Antonov/PZL-Mielec An-2P	1G114-64			
1508	Antonov An-26	1508		13 PLT	
1509	Antonov An-26	1509		13 PLT	
1602	Antonov An-26	1602	SP-KWC	13 PLT	

1603	Antonov An-26	1603	SP-LWB	13 PLT	
1604	Antonov An-26	1604	SP-LWA	13 PLT	
1851	Antonov/PZL-Mielec An-2T	1G118-51		2 KOP	
1852	Antonov/PZL-Mielec An-2T	1G118-52		2 KOP	
1853	Antonov/PZL-Mielec An-2T	1G118-53		2 KOP	
4719	Antonov/PZL-Mielec An-2T	1G147-19		23 LESz	
4720	Antonov/PZL-Mielec An-2T	1G147-20		23 LESz	
4722	Antonov/PZL-Mielec An-2T	1G147-22		13 PLT	
5706	Antonov/PZL-Mielec An-2T	1G157-06		13 PLT	
5707	Antonov/PZL-Mielec An-2T	1G157-07			
5708	Antonov/PZL-Mielec An-2T	1G157-08		Olesnica Ground School	Inst.
7445	Antonov/PZL-Mielec An-2T	1G74-45			
7447	Antonov/PZL-Mielec An-2T	1G74-47		13 PLT	
7809	Antonov/PZL-Mielec An-2P	1G178-09			
7810	Antonov/PZL-Mielec An-2P	1G178-10			
8552	Antonov/PZL-Mielec An-2T	1G85-52			
8554	Antonov/PZL-Mielec An-2T	1G85-54		2 KOP	or Navy?
9855	Antonov/PZL-Mielec An-2T	1G98-55		23 LESz	
9860	Antonov/PZL Mielec An-2TD	1G98-60			
9865	Antonov/PZL-Mielec An-2T	1G98-65			
9866	Antonov/PZL-Mielec An-2T	1G98-66		23 LESz	
9869	Antonov/PZL-Mielec An-2T	1G98-69		23 LESz	

Lotnictwo Marynarki Wojennej
Polish Naval Avition

UNITS/BASES	1 Dywizjon Lotnictwa MW, C Sqn, Babie Doly AB			An-28
	3 Dywizjon Lotnictwa MW, SAR Sqn, Siemirowice AB			An-28RM, An-2

0404	Antonov/PZL Mielec An-28T	1AJ004-04		1 DLMW	
0405	Antonov/PZL Mielec An-28M 2000	1AJ004-05		1 DLMW	Patrol
0810	PZL-Mielec M-28B Skytruck Bryza 1R	1AJGP1-01	SP-PDC	3 DLMW	cvtd An-28RM
1006	PZL-Mielec M-28B Skytruck Bryza 1R	AJG001-04		3 DLMW	
1007	PZL-Mielec M-28B Skytruck Bryza 1R	1AJHP1-01		1 DLMW	cvtd An-28RM
1008	PZL-Mielec M-28B Skytruck Bryza 1R	AJG001-01		3 DLMW	cvtd An-28RM
1017	PZL-Mielec M-28B Skytruck Bryza 1R	AJG001-03		3 DLMW	cvtd An-28RM
1022	PZL-Mielec M-28B Skytruck Bryza 1R	1AJG001-01		3 DLMW	cvtd An-28RM
1114	PZL-Mielec M-28B Skytruck Bryza 1R	AJG001-05		3 DLMW	
1115	PZL-Mielec M-28B Skytruck Bryza 1R	AJG001-06			
1115	PZL-Mielec M-28B Skytruck Bryza 1R	AJG001-07			
	PZL-Mielec M-28B Skytruck Bryza 1R	AJG001-08			
	PZL-Mielec M-28B Skytruck Bryza 1R				on order 2001
	PZL-Mielec M-28B Skytruck Bryza 1R				on order 2001
1316	Antonov/PZL-Mielec An-2T	1G113-16			
1320	Antonov/PZL-Mielec An-2T	1G113-20			

Lotnictwo Straz Graniczna
Polish Border Guard

PL-50YG	PZL-Mielec M-20 Mewa (PA-34 Seneca II)	1AH002-15	215 (PWL)		MR

PORTUGAL
República Portuguesa   SW Europe

Until the 1974 revolution overthrowing a dictatorship Portugal had control of a number of overseas colonies. These have now all gained independence and the need for a large transport fleet to support them has gone. Portugal has been a NATO member since its the organisation's creation and has received equipment primarily from the USA and Germany. The government-owned maintenance facility at Alverca (OGMA) is a major repair site, particularly for Lockheed products from Europe and Africa.

SERIAL SYSTEM A four digit system allocated in blocks by type was lengthend in the early 1990s when all serials were prefixed with the number 1, creating five digit identities.

Forca Aerea Portuguesa - FAP
Portuguese Air Force

ICAO code AFP, callsign Portuguese Air Force

UNITS/BASES	Esquadra 401, Base Aerea 1 Sintra	Aviocar	Survey, Fishery Patrol
	Esquadra 501, Lisbon & BA 6 Montijo	C-130H	
	Esquadra 502, Base Aerea 1 Sintra	Aviocar	Transport, ECM, Trainer
	Esquadra 504, Lisbon Airport	Falcon 20, Falcon 50	VIP, Calibration

Esquadra 505, Base Aerea 1 Sintra		Super Skymaster	Liasion
Esquadra 601 'Lobos', Base Aerea 6 Montijo		P-3P	
Esquadra 711, Base Aerea 4 Lajes-Azores		Aviocar	

PLANS   The Orions are to undergo a life extension and improvement programme between 2002 and 2008.
Two A310s to form a new Esquadra at Lisbon in 2000 with Tanker capability.
C-130Js are deemed desirable, but the Aviocars may need replacing first.
Re-joined the A400M programme in early 2001 with a requirement for 8 aircraft.

13701	Reims/Cessna FTB337G Milirole (Super Skymaster)				
	FTB3370002		CS-AAY	Esq 505	
13704	Reims/Cessna FTB337G Milirole (Super Skymaster)				
	FTB3370005		CS-AKQ	Esq 505	
13705	Reims/Cessna FTB337G Milirole (Super Skymaster)				
	FTB3370006		CS-ALL	Esq 505	
13706	Reims/Cessna FTB337G Milirole (Super Skymaster)				
	FTB3370007		CS-ANX	Esq 505	
3707	Reims/Cessna FTB337G Milirole (Super Skymaster)				
	FTB3370008				Std Ota
13709	Reims/Cessna FTB337G Milirole (Super Skymaster)				
	FTB3370010		CS-ANZ	Esq 505	
13710	Reims/Cessna FTB337G Milirole (Super Skymaster)				
	FTB3370011		CS-APK	Esq 505	
13711	Reims/Cessna FTB337G Milirole (Super Skymaster)				
	FTB3370012		CS-APL	Esq 505	
13715	Reims/Cessna FTB337G Milirole (Super Skymaster)				
	FTB3370016		CS-AAN	Esq 505	
3719	Reims/Cessna FTB337G Milirole (Super Skymaster)				
	FTB3370020				Std Ota
13729	Reims/Cessna FTB337G Milirole (Super Skymaster)				
	FTB3370030		CS-ABN	Esq 505	
13730	Reims/Cessna FTB337G Milirole (Super Skymaster)				
	FTB3370031		CS-ABP	Esq 505	
13732	Reims/Cessna FTB337G Milirole (Super Skymaster)				
	FTB3370033		CS-ABS	Esq 505	
16501	CASA EC212-A1 Galaktron srs 100	13	6501 (FAP)	Esq 502	
16502	CASA EC212-A1 Galaktron srs 100	14	6502 (FAP)	Esq 401	
16503	CASA 212-A1 Aviocar srs 100	17	6503 (FAP)	Esq 502	
16504	CASA 212-A1 Aviocar srs 100	18	6504 (FAP)	Esq 502	
16505	CASA 212-A2 Aviocar srs 100	25	6505 (FAP)	Esq 502	
16506	CASA 212-A2 Aviocar srs 100	26	6506 (FAP)	Esq 502	
16507	CASA 212-A2 Aviocar srs 100	28	6507 (FAP)	Esq 502	
16508	CASA 212-A2 Aviocar srs 100	29	6508 (FAP)	Esq 502	
16509	CASA 212-A2 Aviocar srs 100	32	6509 (FAP)	Esq 502	
16510	CASA 212-A2 Aviocar srs 100	33	6510 (FAP)	Esq 401	
16511	CASA 212-A2 Aviocar srs 100	35	6511 (FAP)	Esq 502	
16512	CASA 212-A2 Aviocar srs 100	36	6512 (FAP)	Esq 401	
16513	CASA 212-A2 Aviocar srs 100	37	6513 (FAP)	Esq 711	
16514	CASA 212-A2 Aviocar srs 100	38	6514 (FAP)	Esq 711	
16515	CASA 212-A2 Aviocar srs 100	41	6515 (FAP)	Esq 711	
16517	CASA 212-A2 Aviocar srs 100	49	6517 (FAP)	Esq 711	
16519	CASA 212-A2 Aviocar srs 100	53	6519 (FAP)	Esq 401	
16520	CASA 212-A2 Aviocar srs 100	54	6520 (FAP)	Esq 711	
16521	CASA 212-B2 Aviocar srs 100	56	6521 (FAP)	Esq 502	
16522	CASA 212-B2 Aviocar srs 100	57	6522 (FAP)	Esq 401	
16523	CASA 212-B2 Aviocar srs 100	61	6523 (FAP)	Esq 401	
16524	CASA 212-B2 Aviocar srs 100	62	6524 (FAP)	Esq 401	MAD boom
16801	Lockheed C-130H-30 (L-382C-73D) Hercules	4749	6801 (FAP)	Esq 501	Cvtd C-130H
16802	Lockheed C-130H-30 (L-382C-73D) Hercules	4753	6802 (FAP)	Esq 501	Cvtd C-130H
16803	Lockheed C-130H-30 (L-382C-78D) Hercules	4772	6803 (FAP)	Esq 501	
16804	Lockheed C-130H-30 (L-382C-77D) Hercules	4777	6804 (FAP)	Esq 501	
16805	Lockheed C-130H-30 (L-382C-78D) Hercules	4778	6805 (FAP)	Esq 501	
16806	Lockheed C-130H-30 (L-382T-25F) Hercules	5264	6806 (FAP)	Esq 501	
17103	Dassault Falcon 20D	217	8103 (FAP)	Esq 504	
17201	CASA 212 Aviocar srs 300M Patrullero	459		Esq 401	
17202	CASA 212 Aviocar srs 300M Patrullero	460		Esq 401	
17401	Dassault Falcon 50	195	7401 (FAP)	Esq 504	
17402	Dassault Falcon 50	198	7402 (FAP)	Esq 504	
17403	Dassault Falcon 50	221	7403 (FAP)	Esq 504	
14801	Lockheed P-3P (L-185B) Orion	5402	4801 (FAP)	Esc 601	Cvtd P-3B HW
14802	Lockheed P-3P (L-185B) Orion	5403	4802 (FAP)	Esc 601	Cvtd P-3B HW
14803	Lockheed P-3P (L-185B) Orion	5404	4803 (FAP)	Esc 601	Cvtd P-3B HW
14804	Lockheed P-3P (L-185B) Orion	5405	4804 (FAP)	Esc 601	Cvtd P-3B HW
14805	Lockheed P-3P (L-185B) Orion	5407	4805 (FAP)	Esc 601	Cvtd P-3B HW
14806	Lockheed P-3P (L-185B) Orion	5408	4806 (FAP)	Esc 601	Std

QATAR
Dawlat al-Qatar   SW Asia

Following independence from Britain in 1971 Qatar chose not to join the states forming the United Arab Emirates. The European-equipped air force operates no transports, all VIP flying being performed by the Amiri Flight.

Qatar Amiri Flight

ICAO code QAF, callsign Amiri

UNITS/BASES   All aircraft are based at Doha International Airport.

A7-AAG	Airbus Industrie A320-232	927	F-WWBA
A7-HHJ	Airbus Industrie A319-133X(CJ)	1335	A7-ABZ
A7-HHK	Airbus Industrie A340-211	026	F-WWJQ

Government of the State of Qatar

VP-BAT	Boeing 747SP-21	21648 / 367	VR-BAT

ROMÂNIA
Republica România   E Europe

Always a little more independent than some of its former Warsaw Pact partners, particularly on account of its local manufacturing capability that has worked with British and French companies in licence building projects and more recently with Israel on upgrades. Romania ousted the Ceauşescu dictatorship in 1989 and has been making slow progress towards joining the new Europe since. Future plans include NATO membership from 2006.

UNITS/BASES	Boboc (ex Buzau)	An-2TP	Training
	90 ATB, Bucharest-Otopeni	C-130B	
	19 Flotila Militara de Transport, Bucharest-Otopeni	An-24, An-26, An-30	

PLANS   The An-24 and An-26s are to be retired by 2003, more C-130s are required subject to funding.

28	Antonov/PZL-Mielec An-2R	1G124-28	YR-APH		
30	Antonov/PZL-Mielec An-2R	1G124-30	YR-APJ		
31	Antonov/PZL-Mielec An-2R	1G124-31	YR-APK		Std Bacau
32	Antonov/PZL-Mielec An-2R	1G124-32	YR-ANW		
34	Antonov/PZL-Mielec An-2R	1G124-34	YR-APM		Std Bacau
35	Antonov/PZL-Mielec An-2R	1G124-35	YR-APN		
37	Antonov/PZL-Mielec An-2R	1G124-42	YR-APW		Std Bacau
38	Antonov/PZL-Mielec An-2R	1G124-38	YR-APS		
47	Antonov/PZL-Mielec An-2R	1G124-47	YR-PAB		
53	Antonov/PZL-Mielec An-2T	1G194-53			
54	Antonov/PZL-Mielec An-2T	1G194-54			
55	Antonov/PZL-Mielec An-2T	1G194-55			
56	Antonov/PZL-Mielec An-2T	1G194-56			
57	Antonov/PZL-Mielec An-2T	1G194-57			
58	Antonov/PZL-Mielec An-2T	1G194-58			
59	Antonov/PZL-Mielec An-2T	1G194-59			
60	Antonov/PZL-Mielec An-2T	1G194-60			
206	Antonov An-26	2206	UR-26229		Std Otopeni
207	Antonov An-26	2207	YR-ADE	19 FMT	
307	Antonov An-26	13307	YR-ADJ		Std Otopeni
606	Antonov An-26	12606	YR-ADG	19 FMT	
706	Antonov An-26	2706	YR-ADC	19 FMT	
707	Antonov An-26	2707	YR-ADB		Std Otopeni
710	Antonov An-26	12710	YR-ADH	19 FMT	
801	Antonov An-26	2801	YR-ADA		Std Otopeni
808	Antonov An-26	13808	YR-ADL	19 FMT	
809	Antonov An-26	13809	YR-ADM	19 FMT	
810	Antonov An-26	13810	YR-ADN	19 FMT	
1103	Antonov An-30	1103	103	19 FMT	
1104	Antonov An-30	1104	104		Std Otopeni
1105	Antonov An-30	1105	105	19 FMT	
1801	Antonov An-24TV	1021801	YR-AML		Std Otopeni
1802	Antonov An-24TV	1021802	YR-AMM	19 FMT	
1911	Antonov An-24TV	1021911	YR-AMS	19 FMT	
1912	Antonov An-24TV	1021912	YR-AMU		Std Otopeni
5022	Antonov An-24RT	1025022	YR-AMO	19 FMT	

5024	Antonov An-24RT	1025024	YR-AMN	19 FMT
5927	Lockheed C-130B (L-282-1B) Hercules	3568	59-1527 (USAF)	90 ATB
5930	Lockheed C-130B (L-282-1B) Hercules	3576	59-1530 (USAF)	90 ATB
6150	Lockheed C-130B (L-282-1B) Hercules	3626	61-0950 (USAF)	90 ATB
6166	Lockheed C-130B (L-282-1B) Hercules	3653	61-0966 (USAF)	90 ATB

Government of Romania

YR-BRE	British Aerospace/RomBac One Eleven 561RC	405	Opb Romavia

---

RUSSIA
Rossiiskaya Federatsiya - Rossia   E Europe/Asia

Formerly possessing a transport aviation division larger than even that of the USAF (albeit the majority were in the Aeroflot colours), the Russian fleet has been drastically reduced since the breakup of the Soviet Union. Some aircraft have been passed on to (or just left with) the new CIS countries, many more have been abandoned for lack of resources to keep them operational. New programmes are definitely required, but funding them is next to impossible. The serial data below is as reported over the past ten years with known deletions omitted. Aircraft bearing the two digit tactical codes are only listed if a c/n was also known. The unit data is known to be incomplete but is in an understandable state of flux.

Voenno-Vozdushnive Sily - V-VS
Military Air Force

ICAO code RFF

UNITS/BASES	Chkalovskiy	8 ADON	Various

Voennaya Transportanya Aviatsiya - VTA (Military Transport Aviation)

Ivanovo-Severnyy	517 VTAP	Il-76MD
	? VTAE	An-12
Novgorod-Krechevitsy	110 VTAP	Il-76M, Il-76MD
	3 VTAD	An-12
	12 VTAD	An-12
Pskov	334 VTAP	Il-76MD
Setsja	566 VTAP	An-124
Smolensk	103 VTAP	Il-76M, Il-76MD
Tver-Michailovo	196 VTAP	Il-76MD
	8 VTAP	An-22A (retired in 2000?)

VT-A aircraft operate for the 223 Letny Otrayd (Moscow-Chkalovskaya, ICAO code CHD) and 224 Letny Otrayd (Bryansk and Tver, ICAO code TTF) on a semi-commercial basis for use by Russian companies. Aircraft so allocated are marked below.

Frontovaya Aviatsiya - FA (Frontal/Tactical Aviation)

Chita	? OSAP	An-12BP, An-26
Chrabrovo	? OSAP	An-12BP, An-24, An-26
Khabarovsk-Bolshoy	257 OSAP	An-12BP, An-26
Kubinka	226 OSAP	An-12BP, An-24, An-26, Tu-134
Levashevo	202 OSAP	An-12BP, An-26
Rostov-Na-Donu	535 OSAP	An-12BP, An-24, An-26, Tu-134

Dal'nyaya Aviatsiya - DA (Long-range Aviation)

Engels (reported as closed in July 2000)	230 APSZ	Il-78, Il-78M	aircraft to Ryazan ?
Ostafyevo	271 OSAP	An-12BP, An-24, An-26	
Tambov	652 UAVP	Tu-134UB	

Air Academies

Balashov	An-24. An-26
Petrovsk	L-410
Rtischevo	L-410

Chelyabinsk, ChVVAUSh	Tu-134

PLANS	164 Antonov An-70 to be procured from Aviakor in the Ukraine by 2018, replacing An-12s.
	120 Il-76MD were planned to be lengthened to Il-76MF standard in Tashkent. First 2 deliveries planned for 2001.
	The Ilyushin Il-112V has been selected as an An-26 replacement, quantity and timescale to be determined.

RA-08832	Antonov An-22A	053484317	CCCP-08832	Std, Aeroflot cs
'RA-09309'	Antonov An-22A	043481250	CCCP-09309	Marks not carried externally
RA-09312	Antonov An-22A	043481256	CCCP-09312	Std, Aeroflot cs
RA-09319	Antonov An-22	02340406	CCCP-09319	Aeroflot cs
RA-09337	Antonov An-22A	033480225	CCCP-09337	Std, Aeroflot cs

RA-09338	Antonov An-22A	033480228	CCCP-09338		Std, Aeroflot cs
RA-09340	Antonov An-22A	033481234	CCCP-09340		Std, Aeroflot cs
RA-09341	Antonov An-22A	043482266	CCCP-09341		Aeroflot cs
RA-09343	Antonov An-22A	043482272	CCCP-09343		Std, Aeroflot cs
RA-09344	Antonov An-22A	053482288	CCCP-09344		Aeroflot cs
RA-11037	Antonov An-12BP		CCCP-11037		Aeroflot cs
RA-11039	Antonov An-12BP	3341001			Aeroflot cs
RA-11178	Antonov An-12BP				Aeroflot cs
RA-11240	Antonov An-12BP	402706	CCCP-11240		Aeroflot cs
RA-11241	Antonov An-12BP	402103	CCCP-11241		Aeroflot cs
RA-11265	Antonov An-12BP	402107	CCCP-11265		Aeroflot cs
RA-11266	Antonov An-12BP				Aeroflot cs
RA-11275	Antonov An-12BP				Aeroflot cs
RA-11387	Antonov An-12BP	00347208			Aeroflot cs
RA-11400	Antonov An-12BP				Aeroflot cs
RA-11401	Antonov An-12BP	5343402	CCCP-11401		Aeroflot titles
RA-11406	Antonov An-12BP				Aeroflot cs
RA-11412	Antonov An-12BP				Aeroflot cs
RA-11414	Antonov An-12				Aeroflot cs
RA-11420	Antonov An-12				Aeroflot cs
RA-11426	Antonov An-12BP	4342204			
RA-11431	Antonov An-12BP	5343001	CCCP-11431		Aeroflot cs
RA-11432	Antonov An-12				Aeroflot cs
RA-11653	Antonov An-12BP				Aeroflot cs
RA-11654	Antonov An-12MGA	402708	CCCP-11654		Aeroflot cs
RA-11660	Antonov An-12BP				Aeroflot cs
RA-11680	Antonov An-12BP	9900805	CCCP-11680		Aeroflot cs
RA-11719	Antonov An-12BP		CCCP-11719		Aeroflot cs
RA-11732	Antonov An-12BP				Aeroflot cs
RA-11742	Antonov An-12BP				Aeroflot cs
RA-11786	Antonov An-12BP				Aeroflot cs
RA-11792	Antonov An-12MGA	402701			Aeroflot cs
RA-11803	Antonov An-12BP	8345806	CCCP-11803		Aeroflot cs
RA-11835	Antonov An-12BP				Aeroflot cs
RA-11844	Antonov An-12BP				
RA-11864	Antonov An-12BP	2401704	CCCP-11864		Aeroflot cs
CCCP-11871	Antonov An-12BP	1340109			Aeroflot cs
RA-11877	Antonov An-12BP				Aeroflot cs
RA-11923	Antonov An-12BP	1340101			
RA-11924	Antonov An-12BP	6344508	CCCP-11924		Aeroflot cs
RA-11931	Antonov An-12BP				
RA-11936	Antonov An-12BP	2340507			Aeroflot cs
RA-11945	Antonov An-12BP				
RA-11965	Antonov An-12BP				
RA-12101	Antonov An-12BP	402509	CCCP-12101		Aeroflot cs
RA-12103	Antonov An-12BP				WFU Ivanova
RA-12115	Antonov An-12BP				Aeroflot cs
RA-12121	Antonov An-12BP	401912	CCCP-12121		Aeroflot cs
RA-12122	Antonov An-12BP				Aeroflot cs
RA-12123	Antonov An-12BP	402004	CCCP-12123		Aeroflot cs
RA-12124	Antonov An-12BP	402505	CCCP-12124		Aeroflot cs
RA-12126	Antonov An-12BP	402507	CCCP-12126		Aeroflot cs
RA-12129	Antonov An-12	7344906	CCCP-12129		Aeroflot cs
RA-12132	Antonov An-12BP				Aeroflot cs
RA-12133	Antonov An-12BP				Aeroflot cs
RA-12137	Antonov An-12BP				Aeroflot cs
RA-12143	Antonov An-12BP				Aeroflot cs
RA-12330	Antonov An-12BP				Aeroflot cs
RA-26157	Antonov An-26	13610			Aeroflot cs
RA-26642	Antonov An-26	2101	CCCP-26642		Aeroflot cs
RA-26696	Antonov An-26				Aeroflot cs
RA-26697	Antonov An-26				Aeroflot cs
RA-26698	Antonov An-26				Aeroflot cs
RA-27205	Antonov An-30	0709	CCCP-27205		Open Skies survey
RA-30078	Antonov An-30	0507	CCCP-30078		Open Skies survey
RA-46454	Antonov An-26		CCCP-46454		ELINT, Aeroflot cs
RA-46824	Antonov An-24B		CCCP-46824	223 LO	coded 824?
RA-47403	Antonov An-26				Aeroflot cs
RA-47407	Antonov An-26				Aeroflot cs
RA-47410	Antonov An-26	6003			Aeroflot cs
RA-47411	Antonov An-26				Aeroflot cs
RA-47413	Antonov An-26				Aeroflot cs
RA-47414	Antonov An-26				Aeroflot cs
RA-47707	Antonov An-24B		CCCP-47707	223 LO	

139

RA-47750	Antonov An-24B	79901203	CCCP-47750		Aeroflot cs
RA-47769	Antonov An-24B		CCCP-47769		
RA-47794	Antonov An-24B	09902208		223 LO	Aeroflot cs
RA-47797	Antonov An-24B		CCCP-47797	223 LO	coded 797?
RA-47798	Antonov An-24B		CCCP-47798	223 LO	coded 798?
RA-65040	Tupolev Tu-134A	49100	LY-ABC		Bashkirian Gvt
RA-65679	Tupolev Tu-134A	23249	CCCP-65679	223 LO	Aeroflot cs
RA-65680	Tupolev Tu-134A-3	49020	code 680 black	223 LO	Aeroflot cs
RA-65681	Tupolev Tu-134A-3	49760	code 681 black	223 LO	Aeroflot cs
RA-65682	Tupolev Tu-135 (Tu-134A)	62120	CCCP-65682	223 LO	
RA-65684	Tupolev Tu-135 (Tu-134A)	62205	CCCP-65684		Aeroflot cs
RA-65689	Tupolev Tu-135 (Tu-134A)	62655	CCCP-65689	223 LO	Aeroflot cs, VIP
RA-65690	Tupolev Tu-135 (Tu-134A)	62805	CCCP-65690	223 LO	Aeroflot cs, VIP
RA-65979	Tupolev Tu-135 (Tu-134A-3)	63158	CCCP-65979	223 LO	Aeroflot cs, VIP
RA-65980	Tupolev Tu-135 (Tu-134A)	63207			Aeroflot cs
RA-65984	Tupolev Tu-135 (Tu-134A-3)	63400	CCCP-65984	223 LO	Aeroflot cs
RA-65986	Tupolev Tu-135 (Tu-134A)	63475	CCCP-65986	223 LO	Aeroflot cs
RA-65987	Tupolev Tu-135 (Tu-134A-3)	63505	CCCP-65987	223 LO	Aeroflot cs, VIP
RA-65988	Tupolev Tu-135 (Tu-134A)	63550	CCCP-65988	223 LO	Aeroflot cs
RA-65989	Tupolev Tu-135 (Tu-134A)	63605	CCCP-65989	223 LO	Aeroflot cs
RA-65990	Tupolev Tu-135 (Tu-134A)	63690	CCCP-65990	223 LO	Aeroflot cs
RA-65991	Tupolev Tu-135 (Tu-134A)	63845	CCCP-65991	223 LO	Aeroflot cs
RA-65992	Tupolev Tu-135 (Tu-134A)	63850	CCCP-65992	223 LO	Aeroflot cs
RA-65996	Tupolev Tu-135 (Tu-134A-3)		CCCP-65996	223 LO	
CCCP-67571	Let 410UVP-E	861611			Aeroflot cs
RA-67574	Let 410UVP-E	861614			Aeroflot cs
CCCP-67579	Let 410UVP-E	861619			Aeroflot cs
RA-67581	Let 410UVP-E	861701			Aeroflot cs
CCCP-67586	Let 410UVP-E	861706			Aeroflot cs
CCCP-67588	Let 410UVP-E	861708			Aeroflot cs
CCCP-67589	Let 410UVP-E	861709			Aeroflot cs
RA-72905	Antonov An-72		CCCP-72905		Aeroflot cs
RA-72906	Antonov An-72		CCCP-72906		Aeroflot cs
RA-72908	Antonov An-72		CCCP-72908		Aeroflot cs
RA-72909	Antonov An-72		CCCP-72909		Aeroflot cs
RA-72910	Antonov An-72		CCCP-72910		Aeroflot cs
RA-72911	Antonov An-72		CCCP-72911		Aeroflot cs
RA-72913	Antonov An-72		CCCP-72913		Aeroflot cs
RA-72915	Antonov An-72		CCCP-72915		Aeroflot cs
RA-72916	Antonov An-72		CCCP-72916		Aeroflot cs
RA-72917	Antonov An-72		CCCP-72917		Aeroflot cs
RA-72918	Antonov An-72		CCCP-72918		Aeroflot cs
RA-72919	Antonov An-72		CCCP-72919		Aeroflot cs
RA-72922	Antonov An-72		CCCP-72922		Aeroflot cs
RA-72924	Antonov An-72		CCCP-72924		Aeroflot cs
RA-72925	Antonov An-72		CCCP-72925		Aeroflot cs
RA-72926	Antonov An-72		CCCP-72926		Aeroflot cs
RA-72928	Antonov An-72		CCCP-72928	223 LO	Aeroflot cs
RA-72929	Antonov An-72		CCCP-72929	223 LO	Aeroflot cs
RA-72930	Antonov An-72		CCCP-72930		Aeroflot cs
RA-72935	Antonov An-72		CCCP-72935		Aeroflot cs
RA-72940	Antonov An-72		CCCP-72940	223 LO	Aeroflot cs
RA-72944	Antonov An-72		CCCP-72944		Aeroflot cs
RA-72945	Antonov An-72		CCCP-72945		Aeroflot cs
RA-72952	Antonov An-72		CCCP-72952		Aeroflot cs
RA-72953	Antonov An-72		CCCP-72953		Aeroflot cs
RA-72955	Antonov An-72		CCCP-72955		Aeroflot cs
RA-72962	Antonov An-72		CCCP-72962		Aeroflot cs
RA-72963	Antonov An-72		CCCP-72963	223 LO	Aeroflot cs
RA-72964	Antonov An-72		CCCP-72964		Aeroflot cs
RA-72965	Antonov An-72		CCCP-72965		Aeroflot cs
RA-72972	Antonov An-72	36572094883	CCCP-72972		Aeroflot cs
RA-72973	Antonov An-72		CCCP-72973		Aeroflot cs
RA-72991	Antonov An-72				Aeroflot cs
RA-75411	Ilyushin Il-18D	186009205	CCCP-75411		Aeroflot cs
RA-75473	Ilyushin Il-18D				Aeroflot cs
RA-75478	Ilyushin Il-18D	189011302	CCCP-75478	223 LO	Aeroflot cs
RA-75496	Ilyushin Il-18D	189011303	CCCP-75496	223 LO	Aeroflot cs
RA-75498	Ilyushin Il-18D	187009804	CCCP-75498	223 LO	Aeroflot cs
RA-75499	Ilyushin Il-18D	188011004	CCCP-75499	223 LO	Aeroflot cs
RA-75516	Ilyushin Il-18B	183006604	CCCP-75516		Aeroflot cs
RA-75591	Ilyushin Il-18B	185008003	CCCP-75591		Aeroflot cs
RA-75602	Ilyushin Il-18V	182004203	CCCP-75602	223 LO	Aeroflot cs
RA-75606	Ilyushin Il-18V	182004405	CCCP-75606	223 LO	Aeroflot cs

Reg	Type	c/n	Prev Reg	Unit	Notes
RA-75666	Ilyushin Il-18D				Aeroflot cs
RA-75676	Ilyushin Il-18B	184007404	CCCP-75676		Aeroflot cs
75713	Ilyushin Il-18D	186009403	RA-75713		Aeroflot cs
RA-75786	Ilyushin Il-18	181003905	CCCP-75786		Aeroflot cs
RA-75804	Ilyushin Il-18	182004305	CCCP-75804		Aeroflot cs
RA-75895	Ilyushin Il-22-36 Zebra	0393607850	CCCP-75895		Cvtd Il-18, Aeroflot cs
RA-75899	Ilyushin Il-22-36 Zebra	0393607950	CCCP-75899		Cvtd Il-18, Aeroflot cs
RA-75901	Ilyushin Il-22-36 Zebra	0393609935	CCCP-75901		Cvtd Il-18, Aeroflot cs
75902	Ilyushin Il-22-36 Zebra	0393610226	CCCP-75902		Cvtd Il-18, Aeroflot cs
RA-75903	Ilyushin Il-22-36 Zebra	0393610235	CCCP-75903		Cvtd Il-18, Aeroflot cs
RA-75906	Ilyushin Il-22-36 Zebra	0393610501	CCCP-75906		Cvtd Il-18, Aeroflot cs
RA-75909	Ilyushin Il-22M-40 Bison		CCCP-75909		Cvtd Il-18, Aeroflot cs
RA-75911	Ilyushin Il-22M-40 Bison	03934011096	CCCP-75911		Cvtd Il-18, Aeroflot cs
RA-75912	Ilyushin Il-22M-40 Bison	03934011097	CCCP-75912		Cvtd Il-18, Aeroflot cs
RA-75913	Ilyushin Il-22M-40 Bison	03934011098	CCCP-75913		Cvtd Il-18, Aeroflot cs
RA-75914	Ilyushin Il-22M-40 Bison		CCCP-75914		Cvtd Il-18, Aeroflot cs
RA-75917	Ilyushin Il-22M-40 Bison		CCCP-75917		Cvtd Il-18, Aeroflot cs
CCCP-75919	Ilyushin Il-22M-40 Bison	2964009805			Cvtd Il-18, Aeroflot cs
RA-75920	Ilyushin Il-22M-40 Bison	2964017551	CCCP-75920		Cvtd Il-18, Aeroflot cs
RA-75922	Ilyushin Il-22M-40 Bison	2964017552	CCCP-75922		Cvtd Il-18, Aeroflot cs
RA-75923	Ilyushin Il-22M-40 Bison		CCCP-75923		Cvtd Il-18, Aeroflot cs
RA-75924	Ilyushin Il-22M-40 Bison		CCCP-75924		Cvtd Il-18, Aeroflot cs
RA-75925	Ilyushin Il-22M-40 Bison	2964017557	CCCP-75925		Cvtd Il-18, Aeroflot cs
CCCP-75926	Ilyushin Il-22M-40 Bison		CCCP-75476		Cvtd Il-18, Aeroflot cs
RA-75927	Ilyushin Il-22M-40 Bison	2964017558	CCCP-75927		Cvtd Il-18, Aeroflot cs
CCCP-75928	Ilyushin Il-22M-40 Bison				Cvtd Il-18, Aeroflot cs
RA-76450	Ilyushin Il-82 (Il-76VKP)	0053463900	CCCP-76450	Zhukovsky	Aeroflot cs
RA-76451	Ilyushin Il-82 (Il-76VKP)	0053464938	CCCP-76451	Zhukovsky	Aeroflot cs
CCCP-76452	Myasischev/Ilyushin Il-76/976	0053465965		Zhukovsky	Aeroflot cs
RA-76453	Myasischev/Ilyushin Il-76/976	0063466995	CCCP-76453	Zhukovsky	Aeroflot cs
CCCP-76454	Myasischev/Ilyushin Il-76/976	0063469074		Zhukovsky	Aeroflot cs
CCCP-76456	Myasischev/Ilyushin Il-76/976	0073474208		Zhukovsky	Aeroflot cs
RA-76530	Ilyushin Il-76MD	0023441180	CCCP-76530		Aeroflot cs
RA-76533	Ilyushin Il-76MD	0023442205	CCCP-76533	517 VTAP	Aeroflot cs
RA-76538	Ilyushin Il-76MD	0023442231	CCCP-76538		Aeroflot cs
RA-76542	Ilyushin Il-76MD	0033443249	CCCP-76542	334 VTAP	Std, Aeroflot cs
RA-76544	Ilyushin Il-76MD	0033443262	CCCP-76544	196 VTAP	Aeroflot cs
RA-76545	Ilyushin Il-76MD	0033443266	CCCP-76545	196 VTAP	Std, Aeroflot cs
RA-76546	Ilyushin Il-76MD	0033443272	CCCP-76546	196 VTAP	Std, Aeroflot cs
RA-76547	Ilyushin Il-76MD	0033443273	CCCP-76547	196 VTAP	Aeroflot cs
RA-76548	Ilyushin Il-76MD	0033443278	CCCP-76548	196 VTAP	Std, Aeroflot cs
RA-76549	Ilyushin Il-76MD	0033444283	CCCP-76549	196 VTAP	Aeroflot cs
RA-76550	Ilyushin Il-76MD	0033445306	CCCP-76550	196 VTAP	Std, Aeroflot cs
RA-76551	Ilyushin Il-76MD	0033445309	CCCP-76551	196 VTAP	Aeroflot cs
RA-76552	Ilyushin Il-76MD	0033445313	CCCP-76552	196 VTAP	Std, Aeroflot cs
RA-76553	Ilyushin Il-76MD	0033445318	CCCP-76553	196 VTAP	Aeroflot cs
RA-76554	Ilyushin Il-76MD	0033445324	CCCP-76554	196 VTAP	Aeroflot cs
RA-76556	Ilyushin Il-78	0033445294	CCCP-76556	230 APSZ	Std, Aeroflot cs
RA-76558	Ilyushin Il-76MD	0033446333	CCCP-76558	196 VTAP	Std, Aeroflot cs
RA-76572	Ilyushin Il-76MD	0033449434	CCCP-76572	196 VTAP	Std, Aeroflot cs
RA-76577	Ilyushin Il-76MD	0043449462	CCCP-76577	334 VTAP	Aeroflot cs
RA-76592	Ilyushin Il-76MD	0043452555	CCCP-76592	224 LO	Aeroflot cs
RA-76599	Ilyushin Il-76MD	0043453593	CCCP-76599		Std, Aeroflot cs
RA-76604	Ilyushin Il-76MD	0043454625	CCCP-76604		Aeroflot cs
RA-76605	Ilyushin Il-76MD	0043454631	CCCP-76605	196 VTAP	Std, Aeroflot cs
RA-76612	Ilyushin Il-76MD	0043455660	CCCP-76612		Std, Aeroflot cs
RA-76613	Ilyushin Il-76MD	0043455664	CCCP-76613		Aeroflot cs
RA-76615	Ilyushin Il-76MD	0043455672	CCCP-76615	196 VTAP	Aeroflot cs
RA-76616	Ilyushin Il-78	0043455676	CCCP-76616	230 APSZ	Std, Aeroflot cs
RA-76632	Ilyushin Il-78	0053459757	CCCP-76632		Std, Aeroflot cs
RA-76634	Ilyushin Il-76MD	0053459770	CCCP-76634		Aeroflot cs
RA-76635	Ilyushin Il-76MD	0053459775	CCCP-76635	223 LO	Aeroflot cs
RA-76638	Ilyushin Il-76MD	0053460802	CCCP-76638	224 LO	Aeroflot cs
RA-76639	Ilyushin Il-76MD	0053460805	CCCP-76639		Aeroflot cs
RA-76640	Ilyushin Il-76MD	0053460811	CCCP-76640		Aeroflot cs
RA-76641	Ilyushin Il-76MD	0053460813	CCCP-76641		Aeroflot cs
RA-76643	Ilyushin Il-76MD	0053460822	CCCP-76643	517 VTAP	Aeroflot cs
RA-76648	Ilyushin Il-76MD	0053461848	CCCP-76648		Aeroflot cs
RA-76649	Ilyushin Il-76MD	0053462864	CCCP-76649		Std, Aeroflot cs
RA-76650	Ilyushin Il-76MD	0053462865	CCCP-76650	224 LO	Aeroflot cs
RA-76668	Ilyushin Il-76MD	0053465946	CCCP-76668	517 VTAP	Aeroflot cs
RA-76669	Ilyushin Il-76MD	0063465949	CCCP-76669	224 LO	Aeroflot cs
CCCP-76678	Ilyushin Il-76MD	0063467011			Aeroflot cs
RA-76686	Ilyushin Il-76MD	0063468045	CCCP-76686	224 LO	Aeroflot cs

RA-76693	Ilyushin Il-76MD	0063470100	CCCP-76693		Std, Aeroflot cs
CCCP-76702	Ilyushin Il-76MD	0063471142			Aeroflot cs
RA-76713	Ilyushin Il-76MD	0063474193	CCCP-76713	224 LO	Aeroflot cs
RA-76714	Ilyushin Il-76MD	0063474198	CCCP-76714		Aeroflot cs
RA-76718	Ilyushin Il-76MD	0073474219	CCCP-76718		Std, Aeroflot cs
RA-76719	Ilyushin Il-76MD	0073474226	CCCP-76719	224 LO	Aeroflot cs
RA-76720	Ilyushin Il-76MD	0073475229	CCCP-76720		Std, Aeroflot cs
RA-76722	Ilyushin Il-76MD	0073475242	CCCP-76722		Std, Aeroflot cs
RA-76724	Ilyushin Il-76MD	0073475250	CCCP-76724		Std, Aeroflot cs
RA-76726	Ilyushin Il-76MD	0073475261	CCCP-76726		Std, Aeroflot cs
RA-76731	Ilyushin Il-76MD	0073476290	CCCP-76731	517 VTAP	Aeroflot cs
RA-76733	Ilyushin Il-76MD	0073476304	CCCP-76733	110 VTAP	Aeroflot cs
RA-76738	Ilyushin Il-76MD	0073477326	CCCP-76738	224 LO	Aeroflot cs
RA-76739	Ilyushin Il-76MD	0073477332	CCCP-76739	103 VTAP	Aeroflot cs
RA-76740	Ilyushin Il-76MD	0073477335	CCCP-76740		Std, Aeroflot cs
RA-76741	Ilyushin Il-76MD	0073478337	CCCP-76741		Aeroflot cs
RA-76743	Ilyushin Il-76MD	0073478349	CCCP-76743		Std, Aeroflot cs
RA-76745	Ilyushin Il-76MD	0073479362	CCCP-76745		Aeroflot cs
RA-76746	Ilyushin Il-76MD	0073479374	CCCP-76746		Std, Aeroflot cs
RA-76747	Ilyushin Il-76MD	0073479381	CCCP-76747		Std, Aeroflot cs
RA-76761	Ilyushin Il-76MD	0073479401	CCCP-76761	196 VTAP	Aeroflot cs
RA-76762	Ilyushin Il-76MD	0073480406	CCCP-76762	110 VTAP	Aeroflot cs
RA-76763	Ilyushin Il-76MD	0073480413	CCCP-76763	110 VTAP	Aeroflot cs
RA-76764	Ilyushin Il-76MD	0073480424	CCCP-76764	110 VTAP	Aeroflot cs
RA-76765	Ilyushin Il-76MD	0073481426	CCCP-76765		Std, Aeroflot cs
RA-76767	Ilyushin Il-76MD	0073481436	CCCP-76767	110 VTAP	Aeroflot cs
RA-76768	Ilyushin Il-76MD	0073481448	CCCP-76768		Aeroflot cs
RA-76769	Ilyushin Il-76MD	0073481452	CCCP-76769	103 VTAP	Aeroflot cs
RA-76770	Ilyushin Il-76MD	0073481456	CCCP-76770	110 VTAP	Aeroflot cs
CCCP-76771	Ilyushin Il-76MD	0083482466			Std, Aeroflot cs
RA-76772	Ilyushin Il-76MD	0083482472	CCCP-76772	103 VTAP	Aeroflot cs
RA-76773	Ilyushin Il-76MD	0083482473	CCCP-76773		Aeroflot cs
RA-76776	Ilyushin Il-76MD	0083482486	CCCP-76776	110 VTAP	Aeroflot cs
RA-76779	Ilyushin Il-76MD	0083483505	CCCP-76779		Aeroflot cs
RA-78750	Ilyushin Il-76MD	0083483510	CCCP-78750	224 LO	Aeroflot cs
RA-78762	Ilyushin Il-76MD	0083486574	CCCP-78762		Aeroflot cs
RA-78764	Ilyushin Il-76MD	0083486586	CCCP-78764	224 LO	Aeroflot cs
RA-78766	Ilyushin Il-76MD	0083486595	CCCP-78766	110 VTAP	Aeroflot cs
RA-78768	Ilyushin Il-76MD	0083487603	CCCP-78768	110 VTAP	Aeroflot cs
RA-78776	Ilyushin Il-76MD	0083489652	CCCP-78776	224 LO	Aeroflot cs
RA-78777	Ilyushin Il-76MD	0083489654	CCCP-78777	110 VTAP	Aeroflot cs
RA-78778	Ilyushin Il-76MD	0083489659	CCCP-78778	110 VTAP	Aeroflot cs
CCCP-78782	Ilyushin Il-78	0083489678		230 APSZ	Std, Aeroflot cs
RA-78784	Ilyushin Il-76MD	0083489687	CCCP-78784	110 VTAP	Aeroflot cs
RA-78788	Ilyushin Il-76MD	0083490703	CCCP-78788	224 LO	Aeroflot cs
RA-78789	Ilyushin Il-76MD	0083490706	CCCP-78789	224 LO	Std, Aeroflot cs
RA-78790	Ilyushin Il-76MD	0083490712	CCCP-78790	196 VTAP	Aeroflot cs
RA-78791	Ilyushin Il-76MD	0093490714	CCCP-78791	110 VTAP	Aeroflot cs
RA-78794	Ilyushin Il-76MD	0093490726	CCCP-78794	224 LO	Aeroflot cs
RA-78795	Ilyushin Il-76MD	0093491729	CCCP-78795	110 VTAP	Aeroflot cs
RA-78796	Ilyushin Il-76MD	0093491735	CCCP-78796	224 LO	Aeroflot cs
RA-78797	Ilyushin Il-76MD	0093491742	CCCP-78797	224 LO	Aeroflot cs
RA-78798	Ilyushin Il-78	0093491747	CCCP-78798	230 APSZ	Std, Aeroflot cs
CCCP-78800	Ilyushin Il-78M	0093491758		230 APSZ	Std, Aeroflot cs
RA-78803	Ilyushin Il-76MD	0093492774	CCCP-78803		Aeroflot cs
RA-78805	Ilyushin Il-76MD	0093492783	CCCP-78805	110 VTAP	Aeroflot cs
CCCP-78806	Ilyushin Il-78	0093492786		230 APSZ	Std, Aeroflot cs
RA-78807	Ilyushin Il-76MD	0093493791	CCCP-78807		Aeroflot cs
RA-78809	Ilyushin Il-76MD	0093493807	CCCP-78809	224 LO	Aeroflot cs
RA-78810	Ilyushin Il-76MD	0093493814	CCCP-78810		Aeroflot cs
RA-78811	Ilyushin Il-76MD	0093494823	CCCP-78811		Aeroflot cs
RA-78812	Ilyushin Il-78	0093794826	CCCP-78812	230 APSZ	Std, Aeroflot cs
RA-78813	Ilyushin Il-76MD	0093494830	CCCP-78813		Aeroflot cs
RA-78814	Ilyushin Il-78	0093494838	CCCP-78814	230 APSZ	Std, Aeroflot cs
RA-78815	Ilyushin Il-76MD	0093494842	CCCP-78815	224 LO	Aeroflot cs
RA-78816	Ilyushin Il-76MD	0093495846	CCCP-78816	224 LO	Aeroflot cs
RA-78817	Ilyushin Il-76MD	0093495851	CCCP-78817	224 LO	Aeroflot cs
RA-78818	Ilyushin Il-76MD	0093495858	CCCP-78818	224 LO	Aeroflot cs
CCCP-78822	Ilyushin Il-78M	0093495880		230 APSZ	Std, Aeroflot cs
CCCP-78823	Ilyushin Il-78M	1003496918		230 APSZ	Std, Aeroflot cs
CCCP-78824	Ilyushin Il-78M	1003497947		230 APSZ	Std, Aeroflot cs
RA-78829	Ilyushin Il-76MD	1003401006	CCCP-78829	103 VTAP	Aeroflot cs
RA-78831	Ilyushin Il-76MD	1003401017	CCCP-78831	224 LO	Aeroflot cs
RA-78833	Ilyushin Il-76MD	1003401025	CCCP-78833	224 LO	Std, Aeroflot cs

Registration	Type	Line no	Prev reg	Unit	Notes
RA-78834	Ilyushin Il-76MD	1003401032	CCCP-78834	224 LO	Aeroflot cs
RA-78835	Ilyushin Il-76MD	1003402033	CCCP-78835	224 LO	Aeroflot cs
RA-78838	Ilyushin Il-76MD	1003402044	CCCP-78838	224 LO	Aeroflot cs
RA-78840	Ilyushin Il-76MD	1003403063	CCCP-78840	224 LO	Aeroflot cs
RA-78842	Ilyushin Il-76MD	1003403069	CCCP-78842	224 LO	Aeroflot cs
RA-78844	Ilyushin Il-76MD	1003403092	CCCP-78844	224 LO	Aeroflot cs
RA-78845	Ilyushin Il-76MD	1003403095	CCCP-78845	103 VTAP	Aeroflot cs
RA-78846	Ilyushin Il-76MD	1003403115	CCCP-78846	224 LO	Aeroflot cs
RA-78847	Ilyushin Il-76MD	1003404132	CCCP-78847	224 LO	Aeroflot cs
RA-78854	Ilyushin Il-76MD	1013407220	CCCP-78854	224 LO	Aeroflot cs
RA-82006	Antonov An-124 Ruslan	19530501004	CCCP-82006		Std, Aeroflot cs
RA-82010	Antonov An-124 Ruslan	9773053616017	CCCP-82010		Std, Aeroflot cs
RA-82011	Antonov An-124 Ruslan	9773054616023	CCCP-82011		Std, Aeroflot cs
RA-82012	Antonov An-124 Ruslan	9773052732028	CCCP-82012		Std, Aeroflot cs
RA-82013	Antonov An-124 Ruslan		CCCP-82013		Std, Aeroflot cs
RA-82014	Antonov An-124 Ruslan	9773054732039	CCCP-82014		Std, Aeroflot cs
RA-82020	Antonov An-124 Ruslan	19530502001	CCCP-82020		Std, Aeroflot cs
RA-82021	Antonov An-124 Ruslan	19530502002	CCCP-82021		Std, Aeroflot cs
RA-82022	Antonov An-124 Ruslan	19530502003	CCCP-82022		Std, Aeroflot cs
RA-82023	Antonov An-124 Ruslan	19530502012	CCCP-82023		Std, Aeroflot cs
RA-82024	Antonov An-124 Ruslan	19530502035	CCCP-82024		Std, Aeroflot cs
RA-82025	Antonov An-124 Ruslan	19530502106	CCCP-82025		Aeroflot cs
RA-82028	Antonov An-124 Ruslan	19530502599	CCCP-82028	224 LO	Std, Aeroflot cs
RA-82030	Antonov An-124 Ruslan	9773054732045	CCCP-82030	224 LO	Std, Aeroflot cs
RA-82031	Antonov An-124 Ruslan	9773051832049	CCCP-82031		Std, Aeroflot cs
RA-82032	Antonov An-124 Ruslan	9773052832051	CCCP-82032	224 LO	Std, Aeroflot cs
RA-82033	Antonov An-124 Ruslan	9773052832054	code 21 black	223 LO	Aeroflot cs
RA-82034	Antonov An-124 Ruslan	9773053832057	CCCP-82034		Std, Aeroflot cs
RA-82035	Antonov An-124 Ruslan	9773054832061	CCCP-82035		Std, Aeroflot cs
RA-82036	Antonov An-124 Ruslan	9773054832068	CCCP-82036		Std, Aeroflot cs
RA-82037	Antonov An-124 Ruslan	9773052955071	CCCP-82037		Std, Aeroflot cs
RA-82039	Antonov An-124 Ruslan	9773052055082	CCCP-82039	224 LO	Aeroflot cs
RA-82040	Antonov An-124 Ruslan	9773053055086	CCCP-82040	224 LO	Aeroflot cs
RA-82041	Antonov An-124 Ruslan	9773054055089	CCCP-82041	224 LO	Aeroflot cs
RA-85360	Tupolev Tu-154B-2	79A-360	CCCP-85360	223 LO	Aeroflot cs
RA-85380	Tupolev Tu-154B-2	79A-380	CCCP-85380		Aeroflot cs
RA-85426	Tupolev Tu-154B-2	80A-426	CCCP-85426	223 LO	Aeroflot cs, HF antennas, VIP
RA-85446	Tupolev Tu-154B-2	80A-446	CCCP-85446	223 LO	Aeroflot cs
RA-85463	Tupolev Tu-154B-2	80A-463	CCCP-85463		Aeroflot cs
RA-85510	Tupolev Tu-154B-2	81A-510	CCCP-85510	223 LO	Aeroflot cs, VIP
RA-85534	Tupolev Tu-154B-2	82A-534	CCCP-85534	223 LO	Aeroflot cs
RA-85554	Tupolev Tu-154B-2	82A-554	CCCP-85554	223 LO	Aeroflot cs
RA-85555	Tupolev Tu-154B-2	82A-555	CCCP-85555	223 LO	Aeroflot cs
RA-85559	Tupolev Tu-154B-2	82A-559	CCCP-85559	223 LO	Aeroflot cs
RA-85563	Tupolev Tu-154B-2	82A-563	CCCP-85563	223 LO	Aeroflot cs
RA-85571	Tupolev Tu-154B-2	83A-571	CCCP-85571	223 LO	Aeroflot cs
RA-85572	Tupolev Tu-154B-2	83A-572	CCCP-85572	223 LO	Aeroflot cs
RA-85574	Tupolev Tu-154B-2	83A-574	CCCP-85574	223 LO	Aeroflot cs
RA-85586	Tupolev Tu-154B-2	83A-586	CCCP-85586	223 LO	Aeroflot cs
RA-85587	Tupolev Tu-154B-2	83A-587	CCCP-85587	223 LO	Aeroflot cs
RA-85594	Tupolev Tu-154B-2	84A-594	CCCP-85594	223 LO	Aeroflot cs, HF antennas, VIP
RA-85605	Tupolev Tu-154B-2	85A-605	CCCP-85605	223 LO	Aeroflot cs, HF antennas, VIP
RA-85614	Tupolev Tu-154M	86A-723	CCCP-85614	223 LO	Aeroflot cs, Far East Division
RA-85616	Tupolev Tu-154M	86A-732	CCCP-85616	223 LO	Aeroflot cs, Far East Division
RA-85655	Tupolev Tu-154M-ON	89A-798	CCCP-85655		Open Skies survey
CCCP-86020	Ilyushin Il-76M	083413403			Aeroflot cs
RA-86022	Ilyushin Il-76M	083413417	CCCP-86022		Std, Aeroflot cs
RA-86023	Ilyushin Il-76M	083413422	CCCP-86023		Std, Aeroflot cs
CCCP-86024	Ilyushin Il-76M 776	083414425			Std, Aeroflot cs
RA-86025	Ilyushin Il-76M	083414433	CCCP-86025		Std, Aeroflot cs
RA-86026	Ilyushin Il-76M	083414439	CCCP-86026		Std, Aeroflot cs
RA-86027	Ilyushin Il-76M	083415459	CCCP-86027		Std, Aeroflot cs
RA-86032	Ilyushin Il-76M	093415482	CCCP-86032		Std, Aeroflot cs
RA-86033	Ilyushin Il-76M	093416488	CCCP-86033	566 VTAP	Std, Aeroflot cs
RA-86034	Ilyushin Il-76M	093416489	CCCP-86034	334 VTAP	Std, Aeroflot cs
RA-86035	Ilyushin Il-76M	093416494	CCCP-86035	334 VTAP	Std, Aeroflot cs
RA-86037	Ilyushin Il-76M	093417511	CCCP-86037	110 VTAP	Std, Aeroflot cs
RA-86038	Ilyushin Il-76M	093417514	CCCP-86038	334 VTAP	Std, Aeroflot cs
RA-86040	Ilyushin Il-76M	093417521	CCCP-86040	334 VTAP	Std, Aeroflot cs

RA-86041	Ilyushin Il-76M	093417532	CCCP-86041	334 VTAP	Std, Aeroflot cs
RA-86042	Ilyushin Il-76M	093417535	CCCP-86042	110 VTAP	Std, Aeroflot cs
RA-86043	Ilyushin Il-76M	093418539	CCCP-86043	103 VTAP	Std, Aeroflot cs
RA-86044	Ilyushin Il-76M	093418552	CCCP-86044	110 VTAP	Std, Aeroflot cs
RA-86045	Ilyushin Il-76M	093418564	CCCP-86045		Std, Aeroflot cs
RA-86048	Ilyushin Il-76M	093419573	CCCP-86048		Std, Aeroflot cs
RA-86049	Ilyushin Il-76M	093419580	CCCP-86049	334 VTAP	Std, Aeroflot cs
RA-86146	Ilyushin Il-80 (Il-86VKU)	51483205042?	CCCP-86146		Command Post, Aeroflot cs
RA-86147	Ilyushin Il-80 (Il-86VKU)	51483205043?	CCCP-86147		Command Post, Aeroflot cs
RA-86148	Ilyushin Il-80 (Il-86VKU)	51483205046?	CCCP-86148		Command Post, Aeroflot cs
RA-86149	Ilyushin Il-80 (Il-86VKU)	51483205048?	CCCP-86149		Command Post, Aeroflot cs
RA-86495	Ilyushin Il-62M	2726628	CCCP-86495	223 LO	Aeroflot cs
RA-86496	Ilyushin Il-62M	3829859	CCCP-86496	223 LO	Aeroflot cs
RA-86538	Ilyushin Il-62M	2241158	CCCP-86538	223 LO	Aeroflot cs, HF antennas, VIP
RA-86539	Ilyushin Il-62M	2344615	CCCP-86539	223 LO	Aeroflot cs, HF antennas, VIP
RA-86555	Ilyushin Il-62M	4547315	CCCP-86555	223 LO	Aeroflot cs, HF antennas, VIP
CCCP-86556	Ilyushin Il-62	31401	SP-LAC		Aeroflot cs
RA-86557	Ilyushin Il-62	2725456	CCCP-86557		Aeroflot cs
RA-86572	Ilyushin Il-62M	3154624		223 LO	Aeroflot cs
CCCP-86601	Ilyushin Il-76	033402026			Std
RA-86625	Ilyushin Il-76	063405130	CCCP-86625	103 VTAP	Std, Aeroflot cs
RA-86628	Ilyushin Il-76	063405144	CCCP-86628		Std, Aeroflot cs
CCCP-86630	Ilyushin Il-76	063406149			Aeroflot cs
CCCP-86631	Ilyushin Il-76	063407202			Std, Aeroflot cs
CCCP-86636	Ilyushin Il-76	063408222		517 VTAP	Std, Aeroflot cs
CCCP-86637	Ilyushin Il-76	063409228	CCCP-86637	517 VTAP	Std, Aeroflot cs
RA-86642	Ilyushin Il-76	073409248	CCCP-86642	517 VTAP	Std, Aeroflot cs
RA-86647	Ilyushin Il-76	043402060	CCCP-86647	566 VTAP	Std, Aeroflot cs
CCCP-86716	Ilyushin Il-76	063406156			
CCCP-86717	Ilyushin Il-76	063406160		517 VTAP	Std, Aeroflot cs
CCCP-86721	Ilyushin Il-76 676	073410271			Telemetry station, Aeroflot cs
CCCP-86727	Ilyushin Il-76M	083413383			Aeroflot cs
RA-86731	Ilyushin Il-76M	083413391	CCCP-86731		Std, Aeroflot cs
RA-86733	Ilyushin Il-76M	083413396	CCCP-86733	566 VTAP	Std, Aeroflot cs
RA-86734	Ilyushin Il-76M	083413397	CCCP-86734		Std, Aeroflot cs
RA-86736	Ilyushin Il-76M	083411342	CCCP-86736		Std, Aeroflot cs
RA-86737	Ilyushin Il-76M	083411347	CCCP-86737		WFU
RA-86738	Ilyushin Il-76M	083411352	CCCP-86738		Std, Aeroflot cs
RA-86740	Ilyushin Il-76M	083412358	CCCP-86740		Std, Aeroflot cs
RA-86741	Ilyushin Il-76M	083412361	CCCP-86741		Std, Aeroflot cs
RA-86743	Ilyushin Il-76M	083412369	CCCP-86743		Std, Aeroflot cs
RA-86744	Ilyushin Il-76M	083412376	CCCP-86744		Std, Aeroflot cs
CCCP-86745	Ilyushin Il-76	063407162		517 VTAP	Std, Aeroflot cs
RA-86746	Ilyushin Il-76	063407165	CCCP-86746	103 VTAP	Std, Aeroflot cs
RA-86748	Ilyushin Il-76	063407175	CCCP-86748	103 VTAP	Std, Aeroflot cs
RA-86749	Ilyushin Il-76	063407179	CCCP-86749	103 VTAP	Std, Aeroflot cs
RA-86805	Ilyushin Il-76	043403073	CCCP-86805		Std, Aeroflot cs
RA-86806	Ilyushin Il-76	043403078	CCCP-86806	566 VTAP	Std, Aeroflot cs
CCCP-86807	Ilyushin Il-76	053404083			Std
CCCP-86808	Ilyushin Il-76	053404085		566 VTAP	Std
RA-86809	Ilyushin Il-76	053404091			Aeroflot cs
RA-86812	Ilyushin Il-76	053404103	CCCP-86812	566 VTAP	Std, Aeroflot cs
RA-86813	Ilyushin Il-76	053404105	CCCP-86813	566 VTAP	Std, Aeroflot cs
RA-86814	Ilyushin Il-76	053405110	CCCP-86814	566 VTAP	Std, Aeroflot cs
CCCP-86815	Ilyushin Il-76	063407183		517 VTAP	Std, Aeroflot cs
CCCP-86818	Ilyushin Il-76	063407194		517 VTAP	Std, Aeroflot cs
CCCP-86821	Ilyushin Il-76	053405114			Aeroflot cs
CCCP-86824	Ilyushin Il-76	053405128			Aeroflot cs
RA-86825	Ilyushin Il-76M	093419581	CCCP-86825	110 VTAP	Std, Aeroflot cs
RA-86826	Ilyushin Il-76M	093419588	CCCP-86826	110 VTAP	Std, Aeroflot cs
RA-86827	Ilyushin Il-76M	093419589	CCCP-86827	334 VTAP	Std, Aeroflot cs
RA-86828	Ilyushin Il-76M	093420604	CCCP-86828	334 VTAP	Std, Aeroflot cs
RA-86829	Ilyushin Il-76M	0003427798	CCCP-86829		Aeroflot cs
RA-86830	Ilyushin Il-76M	093421626	CCCP-86830	110 VTAP	Std, Aeroflot cs
CCCP-86831	Ilyushin Il-76M	093421642		334 VTAP	Std, Aeroflot cs
RA-86832	Ilyushin Il-76M	0003421646	CCCP-86832		Std, Aeroflot cs
RA-86833	Ilyushin Il-76M	0003422650	CCCP-86833	103 VTAP	Std, Aeroflot cs
RA-86835	Ilyushin Il-76M	0003422658	CCCP-86835	334 VTAP	Std, Aeroflot cs
RA-86836	Ilyushin Il-76M	0003422661	CCCP-86836		Std, Aeroflot cs
RA-86837	Ilyushin Il-76M	0003423668	CCCP-86837	110 VTAP	Std, Aeroflot cs
RA-86838	Ilyushin Il-76M	0003423669	CCCP-86838		Std, Aeroflot cs

Registration	Type	c/n	Old reg	Unit	Notes
RA-86839	Ilyushin Il-76M	0003423684	CCCP-86839	334 VTAP	Std, Aeroflot cs
RA-86841	Ilyushin Il-76M	0003423690	CCCP-86841		Std, Aeroflot cs
RA-86842	Ilyushin Il-76M	0003423693?	CCCP-86842	334 VTAP	Std, Aeroflot cs
RA-86843	Ilyushin Il-76M	0003423701	CCCP-86843	110 VTAP	Std, Aeroflot cs
RA-86844	Ilyushin Il-76M	0003424711	CCCP-86844	334 VTAP	Std, Aeroflot cs
RA-86847	Ilyushin Il-76M	0003426769	CCCP-86847	517 VTAP	Std, Aeroflot cs
RA-86849	Ilyushin Il-76M	0003426779	CCCP-86849	103 VTAP	Aeroflot cs
RA-86850	Ilyushin Il-76M	0003427782	CCCP-86850		Aeroflot cs
RA-86851	Ilyushin Il-76M	0003424715	CCCP-86851	334 VTAP	Std, Aeroflot cs
RA-86853	Ilyushin Il-76M	0003424723	CCCP-86853	334 VTAP	Std, Aeroflot cs
RA-86855	Ilyushin Il-76M	0003425734	CCCP-86855		Std, Aeroflot cs
RA-86857	Ilyushin Il-76M	0003425744	CCCP-86857		Aeroflot cs
RA-86861	Ilyushin Il-76M	0003427804	CCCP-86861		Std, Aeroflot cs
RA-86863	Ilyushin Il-76M	0003428809	CCCP-86863		Std, Aeroflot cs
CCCP-86864	Ilyushin Il-76M	0003428816		517 VTAP	Std, Aeroflot cs
RA-86865	Ilyushin Il-76M	0003428817	CCCP-86865		Aeroflot cs
RA-86866	Ilyushin Il-76M	0003428821	CCCP-86866	110 VTAP	Std, Aeroflot cs
RA-86868	Ilyushin Il-76M	0013428833	CCCP-86868	334 VTAP	Std, Aeroflot cs
RA-86869	Ilyushin Il-76M	0013428844	CCCP-86869	334 VTAP	Std, Aeroflot cs
RA-86870	Ilyushin Il-76M	0013429847	CCCP-86870	110 VTAP	Std, Aeroflot cs
RA-86872	Ilyushin Il-76MD	0013434008	CCCP-86872	196 VTAP	Aeroflot cs
RA-86873	Ilyushin Il-76M	0013429850	CCCP-86873	334 VTAP	Std, Aeroflot cs
RA-86874	Ilyushin Il-76M	0013429853	CCCP-86874	334 VTAP	Std, Aeroflot cs
CCCP-86875	Ilyushin Il-76M	0013429859		334 VTAP	Std, Aeroflot cs
RA-86876	Ilyushin Il-76M	0013429861	CCCP-86876	334 VTAP	Std, Aeroflot cs
RA-86880	Ilyushin Il-76M	0013430897	CCCP-86880		Std, Aeroflot cs
RA-86881	Ilyushin Il-76M	0013431906	CCCP-86881	110 VTAP	Std, Aeroflot cs
RA-86883	Ilyushin Il-76M	0013431921	CCCP-86883	103 VTAP	Std, Aeroflot cs
RA-86884	Ilyushin Il-76M	0013431932	CCCP-86884		Std, Aeroflot cs
RA-86885	Ilyushin Il-76M	0013431939	CCCP-86885	103 VTAP	Std, Aeroflot cs
RA-86886	Ilyushin Il-76M	0013431943	CCCP-86886		Std, Aeroflot cs
RA-86887	Ilyushin Il-76M	0013431945	CCCP-86887	110 VTAP	Std, Aeroflot cs
RA-86888	Ilyushin Il-76M	0013432966	CCCP-86888	110 VTAP	Std, Aeroflot cs
CCCP-86892	Ilyushin Il-76M	0013432969		517 VTAP	Std, Aeroflot cs
RA-86893	Ilyushin Il-76M	0013432975	CCCP-86893	103 VTAP	Aeroflot cs
RA-86894	Ilyushin Il-76M	0013432977	CCCP-86894	517 VTAP	Std, Aeroflot cs
RA-86895	Ilyushin Il-76M	0013433985	CCCP-86895	517 VTAP	Std, Aeroflot cs
RA-86897	Ilyushin Il-76MD	0013434023	CCCP-86897		Std, Aeroflot cs
RA-86898	Ilyushin Il-76MD	0023435028	CCCP-86898	517 VTAP	Aeroflot cs
86900	Ilyushin Il-76MD	0023435034	CCCP-86900	196 VTAP	Std, Aeroflot cs
RA-86901	Ilyushin Il-76MD	0023436038	CCCP-86901	196 VTAP	Std, Aeroflot cs
RA-86902	Ilyushin Il-76MD	0023436043	CCCP-86902	196 VTAP	Std, Aeroflot cs
RA-86906	Ilyushin Il-76MD	0023436064	CCCP-86906		Aeroflot cs, Hospital aircraft
RA-86907	Ilyushin Il-76MD	0023436065	CCCP-86907	196 VTAP	Std, Aeroflot cs
RA-86908	Ilyushin Il-76MD	0023437070	CCCP-86908	334 VTAP	Std, Aeroflot cs
RA-86910	Ilyushin Il-76MD	0023437077	CCCP-86910	196 VTAP	Aeroflot cs
CCCP-86911	Ilyushin Il-76MD	0023437093			Aeroflot cs
CCCP-86913	Ilyushin Il-76MD	0023438108		517 VTAP	Aeroflot cs
1711	Let 410UVP-E	861711			
1716	Let 410UVP-E	861716			
1720	Let 410UVP-E	861720			
1721	Let 410UVP-E	861721			
1722	Let 410UVP-E	861722			
1814	Let 410UVP-E3	871814			
1815	Let 410UVP-E3	871815			
1817	Let 410UVP-E3	871817			
1818	Let 410UVP-E3	871818			
1819	Let 410UVP-E3	871819			
1822	Let 410UVP-E3	871822			
1823	Let 410UVP-E3	871823			
1825	Let 410UVP-E3	871825			
1826	Let 410UVP-E3	871826			
1829	Let 410UVP-E3	871829			
1830	Let 410UVP-E3	871830			
1901	Let 410UVP-E3	871901			
1902	Let 410UVP-E3	871902			
1903	Let 410UVP-E3	871903			
1905	Let 410UVP-E3	871905			
1907	Let 410UVP-E3	871907			
1908	Let 410UVP-E3	871908			
1909	Let 410UVP-E3	871909			
1912	Let 410UVP-E3	871912			
1913	Let 410UVP-E3	871913			

1918	Let 410UVP-E3	871918
1928	Let 410UVP-E3	871928
1932	Let 410UVP-E3	871932
1933	Let 410UVP-E3	871933
1934	Let 410UVP-E3	871934
1935	Let 410UVP-E3	871935
1937	Let 410UVP-E3	871937
1940	Let 410UVP-E3	871940
2002	Let 410UVP-E3	872002
2005	Let 410UVP-E3	872005
2007	Let 410UVP-E3	872007
2013	Let 410UVP-E3	872013
2020	Let 410UVP-E3	872020
2028	Let 410UVP-E3	882028
2030	Let 410UVP-E3	882030
2034	Let 410UVP-E3	882034
2101	Let 410UVP-E3	882101
2103	Let 410UVP-E3	882103
2104	Let 410UVP-E3	882104
2105	Let 410UVP-E3	882105
2106	Let 410UVP-E3	882106
2107	Let 410UVP-E3	882107
2108	Let 410UVP-E3	882108
2109	Let 410UVP-E3	882109
2110	Let 410UVP-E3	882110
2111	Let 410UVP-E3	882111
2112	Let 410UVP-E3	882112
2113	Let 410UVP-E3	882113
2114	Let 410UVP-E3	882114
2115	Let 410UVP-E3	882115
2116	Let 410UVP-E3	882116
2117	Let 410UVP-E3	882117
2118	Let 410UVP-E3	882118
2119	Let 410UVP-E3	882119
2120	Let 410UVP-E3	882120
2121	Let 410UVP-E3	882121
2122	Let 410UVP-E3	882122
2123	Let 410UVP-E3	882123
2124	Let 410UVP-E3	882124
2125	Let 410UVP-E3	882125
2126	Let 410UVP-E3	882126
2127	Let 410UVP-E3	882127
2128	Let 410UVP-E3	882128
2129	Let 410UVP-E3	882129
2130	Let 410UVP-E3	882130
2131	Let 410UVP-E3	882131
2132	Let 410UVP-E3	882132
2133	Let 410UVP-E3	882133
2134	Let 410UVP-E3	882134
2135	Let 410UVP-E3	882135
2136	Let 410UVP-E3	882136
2137	Let 410UVP-E3	882137
2138	Let 410UVP-E3	882138
2139	Let 410UVP-E3	882139
2140	Let 410UVP-E3	882140
2201	Let 410UVP-E3	882201
2202	Let 410UVP-E3	882202
2203	Let 410UVP-E3	882203
2204	Let 410UVP-E3	882204
2205	Let 410UVP-E3	882205
2206	Let 410UVP-E3	882206
2208	Let 410UVP-E3	882208
2209	Let 410UVP-E3	882209
2210	Let 410UVP-E3	882210
2211	Let 410UVP-E3	882211
2212	Let 410UVP-E3	882212
2213	Let 410UVP-E3	882213
2217	Let 410UVP-E3	892217
2218	Let 410UVP-E3	892218
2219	Let 410UVP-E3	892219
2221	Let 410UVP-E3	892221
2222	Let 410UVP-E3	892222
2223	Let 410UVP-E3	892223
2224	Let 410UVP-E3	892224

2227	Let 410UVP-E3	892227		
2230	Let 410UVP-E3	892230		
2231	Let 410UVP-E3	892231		
2232	Let 410UVP-E3	892232		
2233	Let 410UVP-E3	892233		
2234	Let 410UVP-E3	892234		
2235	Let 410UVP-E3	892235		
2236	Let 410UVP-E3	892236		
2237	Let 410UVP-E3	892237		
2238	Let 410UVP-E3	892238		
2239	Let 410UVP-E3	892239		
2240	Let 410UVP-E3	892240		
2303	Let 410UVP-E3	892303		
2304	Let 410UVP-E3	892304		
2305	Let 410UVP-E3	892305		
2306	Let 410UVP-E3	892306		
2307 / ¯20 red	Let 410UVP-E3	892307		
2308	Let 410UVP-E3	892308		
2309	Let 410UVP-E3	892309		
2310	Let 410UVP-E3	892310		
2326	Let 410UVP-E3	892326		
2327	Let 410UVP-E3	892327		
2328	Let 410UVP-E3	892328		
2330	Let 410UVP-E3	892330		
2331	Let 410UVP-E3	892331		
2332	Let 410UVP-E3	892332		
2333	Let 410UVP-E3	892333		
2407	Let 410UVP-E3	902407		
2411	Let 410UVP-E3	902411		
2412	Let 410UVP-E3	902412		
2415	Let 410UVP-E3	902415		
2417	Let 410UVP-E3	902417		
01 blue	Antonov An-26	1605		
01 red	Antonov An-24B	99902105		
01 red	Ilyushin Il-76MD	1003401024	CCCP-78837?	517 VTAP
01 red	Tupolev Tu-134UB			
01 yellow	Antonov An-26	6708		
02 blue	Antonov An-26	4906		
02 red	Antonov An-12BP	00347602		
02 red	Antonov An-12PPS	02348206		
02 red	Tupolev Tu-134UBL	64140		
03 red	Antonov An-26	1110		
03 yellow	Antonov An-26	8309		
04 red	Antonov An-26	0809		
04 black	Antonov An-30B	0704	RA-30037	Open Skies survey
04 yellow	Antonov An-26	9108		
05 red	Antonov An-12BP	8345905		
05 red	Antonov An-24T	0204		
05 yellow	Antonov An-26	9410		
06 red	Antonov An-12PPS	01347904		
06 red	Antonov An-30	0504		
06 yellow	Antonov An-12BP	1340108		
06 yellow	Antonov An-76 (An-72P)	36576060610		
07 blue	Antonov An-26	14309		
07 red	Antonov An-12BP	8345709		
07 red	Antonov An-26	1405		
07 red	Antonov An-26	8904		
08 red	Antonov An-30	0402		
08 red	Antonov An-24T	0202		
08 yellow	Antonov An-12BP	3341304		
09 black	Antonov An-124 Ruslan	9773054955077		Std, also RA-82038 ?
09 blue	Antonov An-72	36572093875		
09 red	Antonov An-12BP	3341305		
09 red	Antonov An-12BP	9901109		
09 red	Antonov An-30	0401		
09 red	Let 410UVP-E	861728		
09 yellow	Antonov An-12BP	3341104		
10 blue	Antonov An-12BP	1340208		ELINT
10 red	Antonov An-12BP	4342001		
10 red	Antonov An-26	6501		
10 yellow	Antonov An-12BP	4342507		
11 blue	Antonov An-12BP	2401006		
11 red	Antonov An-12BP	6344302		

11 red	Antonov An-12RKR	4342604	
11 red	Antonov An-26RTR	1804	
11 red	Tupolev Tu-134UBL	64245	
11 yellow	Antonov An-12BP	4342509	
12 red	Antonov An-26	8907	
12 red	Antonov An-12BK	8345606	
12 yellow	Antonov An-12BP	402010	
14 red	Antonov An-12BP	8900701	
14 red	Antonov An-12PPS	01347805	
15 blue	Antonov An-12BP	6344005	
15 red	Antonov An-12BP	1340105	
15 red	Antonov An-26	9303	
15 yellow	Antonov An-12BP	402512	
16 blue	Antonov An-12BP	5342806	CCCP-11998
16 red	Antonov An-12BP	3340910	
16 red	Antonov An-12PPS	01347707	
17 blue	Antonov An-12BP	3341205	
17 red	Antonov An-12	5342810	
17 red	Tupolev Tu-134UBL	64753	
17 yellow	Antonov An-12BP	7344905	
18 red	Antonov An-12BP	2340701	
18 red	Antonov An-12BP	5342809	
18 yellow	Antonov An-12BP	2340407	
19 blue	Antonov An-26	1905	
19 blue	Antonov An-26	3610	
19 red	Antonov An-12BP	4342703	
20 red	Antonov An-12BP	3341007	
20 red	Ilyushin Il-20	173011502	
21 blue	Antonov An-24T	1403	
21 red	Antonov An-12BK	3341404	
21 red	Antonov An-12BP	402105	CCCP-11254
21 red	Ilyushin Il-20	173011504	
21 red	Let 410UVP-E3	871938	
21 red	Tupolev Tu-134UBL	64035	
21 yellow	Antonov An-26	13806	
22 blue	Antonov An-12BP	4341804	
22 red	Antonov An-12PPS	00347406	
22 red	Tupolev Tu-134UBL	64640	
23 blue	Antonov An-26	4602	
23 red	Tupolev Tu-134UBL	64350	
25 red	Tupolev Tu-135 (Tu-134A)	63761	
26 red	Tupolev Tu-134UBL	64392	
27 blue	Antonov An-26	6202	
27 red	Antonov An-12BP	00347605	
27 red	Tupolev Tu-134UBL	64400	
28 blue	Antonov An-12BP	9346704	
30 blue	Ilyushin Il-78M	0093498959	
30 red	Antonov An-26	0302	
30 red	Tupolev Tu-134UBL	64845	
31 blue	Ilyushin Il-78M	1003402040	
31 red	Tupolev Tu-134Sh	03551050	
31 yellow	Antonov An-12BP	5343010	
31 yellow	Antonov An-12BP	2400601	
32 blue	Ilyushin Il-78M	1003403068	
33 blue	Ilyushin Il-78M	1003403097	
33 red	Antonov An-12BP	3341308	
33 red	Antonov An-12BP	3341410	
33 red	Antonov An-26	3707	
33 yellow	Antonov An-12BP	1400203	
33 yellow	Antonov An-12BP	402208	
34 blue	Ilyushin Il-78M	1013404138	
34 red	Antonov An-12BP	5343310	
34 red	Antonov An-12BP	6344102	
34 yellow	Antonov An-12BP	2400501	
35 blue	Antonov An-12BP	2340601	
35 blue	Antonov An-12BP	3341601	
35 blue	Ilyushin Il-78M	1013405188	
36 blue	Antonov An-12BP	3341310	
36 blue	Ilyushin Il-78M	1013405197	
36 red	Antonov An-12BP	2340708	CCCP-11898
36 yellow	Antonov An-12BP	1400305	
37 red	Antonov An-12BP	8345810	
39 red	Let 410UVP-E3	871820	
40 red	Tupolev Tu-134UB	63551120	

42 red	Antonov An-12	00346908			
43 red	Antonov An-26	8105			
43 red	Tupolev Tu-134UBL	64678			
044 black	Antonov An-26	9502			
44 red	Tupolev Tu-134UBL				
46 red	Antonov An-12BP	9346306			
47 red	Antonov An-12BP	2400602			
48 red	Antonov An-12BP	02348110			
49 red ?	Ilyushin Il-76MD	0063469057			
50 blue	Antonov An-26	4902			
50 blue	Ilyushin Il-78M	1003403079		230 APSZ	
50 red	Antonov An-12PPS	02348107			
51 blue	Ilyushin Il-78M	1003403106		230 APSZ	
51 blue	Tupolev Tu-134UB	3350305			
52 blue	Ilyushin Il-78M	1003403119		230 APSZ	
52 red	Antonov An-12BP	02348109			
53 blue	Ilyushin Il-78M	1013407227		230 APSZ	
53 red	Antonov An-26	4502			
54 red	Antonov An-24	8910607			
55 blue	Antonov An-26	9703			
55 red	Antonov An-26	9602			
58 yellow	Antonov An-26	10506			
61 red	Antonov An-26	0701			
62 red	Antonov An-12BP	403113			
63 red	Antonov An-12BP	9346902			
70 black	Antonov An-12BP	3341402			
70 red	Antonov An-12BP	3341202			
72 red	Antonov An-12PPS	01347806			
74 blue	Tupolev Tu-134UB	53550550			
78 blue	Tupolev Tu-134UB	3350401			
80 red	Antonov An-12PPS	00347303			
81 red	Antonov An-12BP	5343407			
82 red	Tupolev Tu-134UB	53550650			
83 red	Antonov An-30	0803			
84 red	Antonov An-12BP	4341905			
84 red	Tupolev Tu-134UB	63550720			
86 blue	Tupolev Tu-134UB	53550580			
87 blue	Antonov An-12BP	0901407			
87 blue	Tupolev Tu-134UB	3350403			
87 red	Antonov An-30	0807			Open Skies survey
89 red	Antonov An-12BP	2340710			
90 red	Antonov An-12BKPPS	9346605			
91 red	Antonov An-12BP	4342203	CCCP-12182		
92 red	Antonov An-12BP	3341203			
92 red	Antonov An-12BP	1901507			
93 red	Antonov An-12BP	3341102			
95 red	Antonov An-12BP	4342410			
97 red	Antonov An-12BP	5343207			
98 red	Antonov An-12BP	3341507			
100 blue	Tupolev Tu-135 (Tu-134UBL)	64010			
401 black	Antonov An-26	4807	CCCP-47401		
602 black	Ilyushin Il-76	033402031	CCCP-86602	517 VTAP	Std
616 black	Ilyushin Il-76	063407185	CCCP-86816	517 VTAP	Std
626 black	Ilyushin Il-76	063405135	CCCP-86626	517 VTAP	Std
629 black	Ilyushin Il-76	063406148	CCCP-86629		
632 black	Ilyushin Il-76	073409251	CCCP-86632	103 VTAP	Std
634 black	Ilyushin Il-76	063408214	CCCP-86634	103 VTAP	Std
635 black	Ilyushin Il-76	063408217	CCCP-86635	103 VTAP	Std
637 black	Antonov An-26	0401			Calibrator
645 black	Ilyushin Il-76	043402049	CCCP-86645	103 VTAP	Std
661 black	Antonov An-12BP	5343208	CCCP-11661		
685 black	Tupolev Tu-135 (Tu-134A)	62375	CCCP-65685		
699 black	Antonov An-26		CCCP-26699		
713 black	Ilyushin Il-76	043403061	CCCP-86713		Std
719 black	Ilyushin Il-76	073409263	CCCP-86719	103 VTAP	Std
722 black	Ilyushin Il-76	073410276	CCCP-86722	566 VTAP	Std
725 black	Ilyushin Il-76	073410285	CCCP-86725	517 VTAP	Std
728 black	Ilyushin Il-76	073410322	CCCP-86728	103 VTAP	Std
811 black	Ilyushin Il-76	053404098	CCCP-86811		
819 black	Ilyushin Il-76	063407199	CCCP-86819	103 VTAP	Std
948	Antonov An-72		CCCP-72948		Aeroflot cs
949	Antonov An-72	3657209?819	CCCP-72949		Aeroflot cs
950	Antonov An-72		CCCP-72950		Aeroflot cs
976	Antonov An-72		CCCP-72976		

Voyska Protivovozdushnaya Oborona
Air Defence Aviation

UNITS/BASES	Ivanovo		A-50, A-50M	AEW
30 red	Ilyushin/Beriev A-50	0023436059		
31 red	Ilyushin/Beriev A-50	0053459777		
32 red	Ilyushin/Beriev A-50	0063466979		
33 red	Ilyushin/Beriev A-50	0043454618		
34 red	Ilyushin/Beriev A-50	0043449460		
35 red	Ilyushin/Beriev A-50	0063473178		
36 red	Ilyushin/Beriev A-50	0073475260		
37 red	Ilyushin/Beriev A-50	0083476298		
38 red	Ilyushin/Beriev A-50	0033447379		
39 red	Ilyushin/Beriev A-50	0053452537		
40 red	Ilyushin/Beriev A-50	0093481457		
41 red	Ilyushin/Beriev A-50	0083483499		
42 red	Ilyushin/Beriev A-50	0093484538		
43 red	Ilyushin/Beriev A-50	0093479377		
44 red	Ilyushin/Beriev A-50M	0093486579		
45 red	Ilyushin/Beriev A-50	0093493818		
46 red	Ilyushin/Beriev A-50	0033443258		
47 red	Ilyushin/Beriev A-50	0043453577		
48 red	Ilyushin/Beriev A-50	0053458738		
50 red	Ilyushin/Beriev A-50M	1003496899		
51 red	Ilyushin/Beriev A-50M	1003488634		
52 red	Ilyushin/Beriev A-50	1013491739		
	Ilyushin/Beriev A-50	0053451498		
	Ilyushin/Beriev A-50	0093497940		

Vozdushno-Desantnye Voyska - VDV
Airborne Troops

UNITS/BASES	Bataysk	326 OSAE	An-2	
	Belyi Klutsh	116 OVTAE	An-2	
	Ivanovo	243 OVTAE	An-2	
	Krymskaya	185 OVTAE	An-2	
	Omsk		An-2	
	Pskov	242 OVTAE	An-2	
	Ryazan	58 OVTAE	An-2	
	Tula	110 OVTAE	An-2	
01 white	Antonov/PZL-Mielec An-2T	1G237-15		
01 yellow	Antonov An-2	110147301		
01 yellow	Antonov/PZL-Mielec An-2T	1G98-43		
02 yellow	Antonov/PZL-Mielec An-2T	1G73-15		
03 white	Antonov/PZL-Mielec An-2T	1G237-17		
03 yellow	Antonov/PZL-Mielec An-2T	1G161-16		
03 yellow	Antonov/PZL-Mielec An-2T	1G85-10		
04 white	Antonov An-2	117147304		
04 yellow	Antonov/PZL-Mielec An-2T	1G108-23		
05 blue	Antonov An-2	117447308		
05 white	Antonov/PZL-Mielec An-2T	1G237-19		
05 yellow	Antonov An-2P	111647302	CCCP-05904	
05 yellow	Antonov/PZL-Mielec An-2T	1G63-27		
06 white	Antonov/PZL-Mielec An-2T	1G237-20		
07 yellow	Antonov An-2	113747304		
08 yellow	Antonov An-2T	113147306		
09 white	Antonov/PZL-Mielec An-2T	1G237-23		
09 yellow	Antonov An-2	111247308		
09 yellow	Antonov/PZL-Mielec An-2T	1G108-37		
10 yellow	Antonov An-2	117147308		
10 yellow	Antonov/PZL-Mielec An-2T	1G59-32		
100 yellow	Antonov/PZL-Mielec An-2T	1G118-10		
101 yellow	Antonov/PZL-Mielec An-2T	1G118-44		
11 red	Antonov An-2	12547302		
11 yellow	Antonov An-2	112947316		
11 yellow	Antonov/PZL-Mielec An-2T	1G63-34		
11 yellow	Antonov/PZL-Mielec An-2T	1G85-11		
12 yellow	Antonov/PZL-Mielec An-2T	1G196-15		
13 yellow	Antonov An-2	110647320		
15 yellow	Antonov/PZL-Mielec An-2T	1G108-26		
17 yellow	Antonov/PZL-Mielec An-2T	1G98-02		

17 yellow	Antonov/PZL-Mielec An-2T	1G98-42		
18 yellow	Antonov/PZL-Mielec An-2T	1G194-10		
20 red	Antonov/PZL-Mielec An-2T	1G199-44		
20 yellow	Antonov/PZL-Mielec An-2TD	1G174-27	TY-ADP	
21 white	Antonov/PZL-Mielec An-2T	1G235-46		
21 yellow	Antonov/PZL-Mielec An-2T	1G29-13		
22 yellow	Antonov/PZL-Mielec An-2T	1G108-36		
22 yellow	Antonov/PZL-Mielec An-2T	1G59-25		
23 yellow	Antonov An-2	116747308		
23 yellow	Antonov/PZL-Mielec An-2T	1G98-04		
24 black	Antonov/PZL-Mielec An-2T	1G235-58		
26 yellow	Antonov An-2	111247304		
31 yellow	Antonov/PZL-Mielec An-2T	1G59-21		
34 white	Antonov/PZL-Mielec An-2T	1G237-44		
38 white	Antonov/PZL-Mielec An-2T	1G237-48		
49 white	Antonov/PZL-Mielec An-2T	1G237-59		
52 yellow	Antonov/PZL-Mielec An-2T	1G238-02		
55 red	Antonov/PZL-Mielec An-2T	1G118-04		
58 white	Antonov/PZL-Mielec An-2T	1G238-07		
59 white	Antonov/PZL-Mielec An-2T	1G238-08		
60 white	Antonov/PZL-Mielec An-2T	1G238-09		
60 yellow	Antonov/PZL-Mielec An-2T	1G194-14		
64 white	Antonov/PZL-Mielec An-2T	1G239-34		
65 white	Antonov/PZL-Mielec An-2T	1G239-35		
65 yellow	Antonov/PZL-Mielec An-2T	1G194-20		
71 white	Antonov/PZL-Mielec An-2T	1G239-41		
73 yellow	Antonov/PZL-Mielec An-2T	1G196-11		
74 black	Antonov/PZL-Mielec An-2T	1G238-57		
75 black	Antonov/PZL-Mielec An-2T	1G238-58		
77 red	Antonov/PZL-Mielec An-2TD	1G174-28	TY-ATP	
79 black	Antonov/PZL-Mielec An-2T	1G239-43		Aeroflot cs

Aviatsiya Voenno - Morskogo Flota - AV-MF
Naval Aviation

UNITS/BASES	Ostrov, 240GvOSAP		Tu-134UBL, Il-38, An-26, Be-12, Tu-154	
	VVS SF (Northern Fleet)			
	Kilpyavr		Il-38	
	Kipelovo		Tu-142	
	Pechenga		An-12/PS, An-24, An-26	
	Severomorsk		An-12, An-24, An-26, Be-12, Il-38	
	VVS TOF (Pacific Fleet)			
	Alekseyevka		Tu-142	
	Artem		An-12, An-24, An-26, Tu-134	
	Korsakov		Il-38	
	Nikolayevka		Il-38, Be-12	
	Petropavlovsk		Be-12	
	VVS ChF (Black Sea Fleet)			
	Kacha		An-12, An-24, An-26, Be-12	
	VVS BF (Baltic Fleet)			
	Khabrov, 263 OTAP		An-12, An-24, An-26, Be-12	
RA-11358	Antonov An-12B			
RA-72914	Antonov An-72		CCCP-72914	Aeroflot cs
RA-72974	Antonov An-72		CCCP-72974	Aeroflot cs
RA-85514	Tupolev Tu-154M	86A-723	VVS TOF	Aeroflot cs
RA-85516	Tupolev Tu-154M	86A-732	VVS SF	Aeroflot cs
17 yellow	Antonov An-12PS	7344703	VVS SF	
21 red	Ilyushin Il-38	10808		
21 red	Ilyushin Il-38	081010910		
22 red	Ilyushin Il-38	11006		
46 blue	Antonov An-26	8405		
55 blue	Antonov An-26	4001		
71 red	Ilyushin Il-38	082011207		
79 red	Ilyushin Il-38	082011106		

Gosudarstvennaya transportnaya kompania Rossia
Russia State Transport Company

Aircraft carry the titles ROSSIA, ICAO code SDM, callsign Russia

UNITS/BASES   Based at Moscow-Vnukovo.

RA-64014	Tupolev Tu-204			VIP
RA-64015	Tupolev Tu-204			VIP
RA-65553	Tupolev Tu-134A-3	66300	CCCP-65553	VIP
RA-65555	Tupolev Tu-134A-3	66350	CCCP-65555	VIP
RA-65557	Tupolev Tu-134A-3	66380	CCCP-65557	VIP
RA-65904	Tupolev Tu-134A-3	63953	CCCP-65904	VIP
RA-65905	Tupolev Tu-134A-3	63965	CCCP-65905	VIP
RA-65911	Tupolev Tu-134A-3	63972	CCCP-65911	VIP
RA-65912	Tupolev Tu-134A-3	63985	CCCP-65912	VIP
RA-65916	Tupolev Tu-134A-3	66152	CCCP-65916	VIP
RA-65919	Tupolev Tu-134A-3	66168	CCCP-65919	VIP
RA-65921	Tupolev Tu-134A-3	63997	CCCP-65921	VIP
RA-65978	Tupolev Tu-134A-3	63357	CCCP-65978	VIP
RA-65994	Tupolev Tu-134A-3	66207	CCCP-65994	VIP
RA-65995	Tupolev Tu-134A-3	66400	CCCP-65995	VIP
RA-75453	Ilyushin Il-18D	187010103	CCCP-75453	
RA-75454	Ilyushin Il-18D	187010104	CCCP-75454	
RA-75464	Ilyushin Il-18D	187010401	CCCP-75464	
RA-85629	Tupolev Tu-154M	87A-758	CCCP-85629	
RA-85630	Tupolev Tu-154M	87A-759	CCCP-85630	
RA-85631	Tupolev Tu-154M	87A-760	CCCP-85631	
RA-85645	Tupolev Tu-154M	88A-782	CCCP-85645	
RA-85653	Tupolev Tu-154M	88A-795	CCCP-85653	VIP
RA-85658	Tupolev Tu-154M	89A-808	CCCP-85658	
RA-85659	Tupolev Tu-154M	89A-809	CCCP-85659	VIP
RA-85666	Tupolev Tu-154M	89A-820	CCCP-85666	HF antennas, VIP
RA-85675	Tupolev Tu-154M	90A-835	CCCP-85675	HF antennas, VIP
RA-85686	Tupolev Tu-154M	90A-854	CCCP-85686	HF antennas, VIP
RA-86466	Ilyushin Il-62M	2749316	CCCP-86466	VIP
RA-86467	Ilyushin Il-62M	3749733	CCCP-86467	
RA-86468	Ilyushin Il-62M	4749857	CCCP-86468	HF antennas, VIP
RA-86536	Ilyushin Il-62M	4445948	CCCP-86536	
RA-86537	Ilyushin Il-62M	3546733	CCCP-86537	VIP
RA-86540	Ilyushin Il-62M	3546548	CCCP-86540	VIP
RA-86553	Ilyushin Il-62M	3052657	CCCP-86553	
RA-86554	Ilyushin Il-62M	4053514	CCCP-86554	VIP
RA-86559	Ilyushin Il-62M	2153258	CCCP-86559	VIP
RA-86561	Ilyushin Il-62M	4154841	CCCP-86561	HF antennas, Presidential VIP
RA-86710	Ilyushin Il-62M	2647646	CCCP-86710	
RA-86711	Ilyushin Il-62M	4648414	CCCP-86711	VIP
RA-86712	Ilyushin Il-62M	4648339	CCCP-86712	VIP
RA-87203	Yakovlev Yak-40	9741456	CCCP-87203	VIP
RA-87334	Yakovlev Yak-40D	9510738	CCCP-87334	cvtd Yak-40
RA-87968	Yakovlev Yak-40	9831258	CCCP-87968	VIP
RA-87969	Yakovlev Yak-40	9831358	CCCP-87969	VIP
RA-87970	Yakovlev Yak-40D	9831458	CCCP-87970	cvtd Yak-40, VIP
RA-87971	Yakovlev Yak-40D	9831558	CCCP-87971	VIP
RA-87972	Yakovlev Yak-40	9831658	CCCP-87972	VIP
RA-88200	Yakovlev Yak-40	9630249	CCCP-88200	
RA-88296	Yakovlev Yak-40	9421634	VN-A445	
RA-96012	Ilyushin Il-96-300PU(M)	74393201009		Presidential VIP
RA-96014	Ilyushin Il-96-300PU(M)	74393202011		on order
RA-96016	Ilyushin Il-96-300PU(M)	74393202013		on order

Federalnaya Pogranichnaya Sluzhba
Federal Border Guards Service

The type operated in the largest quantity is reported to be the Antonov An-2, but individual details are unknown.

UNITS/BASES   Aircraft based at Moscow-Sheremetyevo Airport and are stationed in various other Border Guards Districts.

PLANS   Acquisition of the SM-92 Finist was planned to replace the An-2, status now uncertain.
The Ilyushin Il-114P and Sukhoi S-80PT were both also under review for procurement, if they enter production.

RA-72958	Antonov An-72	36572092841	CCCP-72958	Aeroflot cs
RA-72961	Antonov An-72		CCCP-72961	Aeroflot cs

RA-76780	Ilyushin Il-76T	0013430901	CCCP-76780	Aeroflot cs
RA-76781	Ilyushin Il-76TD	0023439133	CCCP-76781	Aeroflot cs
RA-76800	Ilyushin Il-76TD	0093493810	CCCP-76800	Aeroflot cs
RA-76835	Ilyushin Il-76TD	1013408244	CCCP-76835	
RA-76838	Ilyushin Il-76TD	1023411370	CCCP-76838	Aeroflot cs
RA-76839	Ilyushin Il-76TD	1023411375	CCCP-76839	Aeroflot cs

Ministerstvo po Chrezvychaynym Sitooahtsiyam Rossii - MChS Rossii
Ministry for Emergency Control - EMERCON

UNITS/EASES   Based at Moscow-Zhukovsky, ICAO code SUM.

PLANS   Seven Beriev Be-200 jet amphibians are reported to be on order.

RA-42441	Yakovlev Yak-42D	4520421402018	EP-LAN	VIP
RA-74029	Antonov An-74	36547097940		
RA-74034	Antonov An-74P	36547136012		
RA-74044	Antonov An-74-200	36547097936		
RA-74045	Antonov An-74-200	36547097938		
RA-74051	Antonov An-74			
RA-76332	Ilyushin Il-76TD	1033416533		
RA-76333	Ilyushin Il-76TD	1033417540		
RA-76420	Ilyushin Il-76TD	1023413446		
RA-76429	Ilyushin Il-76TD	1043419639		
RA-76840	Ilyushin Il-76TD	1033417553		
RA-76841	Ilyushin Il-76TD	1033418601		
RA-76845	Ilyushin Il-76TD	1043420696		
RA-86570	Ilyushin Il-62M	1356344		VIP

Ministerstvo Vnutrennykh del Rossii - MVD
Ministry of the Interior

UNITS/BASES   Aircraft based at Nizhny Novgorod

RA-76801	Ilyushin Il-76MD	0093495866	CCCP-76801	Aeroflot cs
CCCP-76802	Ilyushin Il-76MD	0093495874		STD, Aeroflot cs
RA-76803	Ilyushin Il-76MD	0093497927	CCCP-76803	Aeroflot cs
CCCP-76804	Ilyushin Il-76MD	0093497931		Aeroflot cs
RA-76825	Ilyushin Il-76MD	1003404136	CCCP-76825	Aeroflot cs
CCCP-76826	Ilyushin Il-76MD	1003404143		Aeroflot cs
CCCP-76827	Ilyushin Il-76MD	1003404151		STD, Aeroflot cs
RA-76828	Ilyushin Il-76MD	1003405164	CCCP-76828	Aeroflot cs
CCCP-76829	Ilyushin Il-76MD	1003405172		Aeroflot cs
RA-86925	Ilyushin Il-76MD	0093492766	CCCP-86925	Aeroflot cs

Kosmichesky Sily
Space and Rocket Forces

UNITS/BASES   Support aircraft are based at Chkalovskaya AB near Zvyozdnyy Gorodok (Star City)

CCCP-75481	Ilyushin Il-20RT(SIP)	173011503		Aeroflot cs, Satellite tracker
CCCP-75482	Ilyushin Il-20RT(SIP)			Aeroflot cs, Satellite tracker
CCCP-75483	Ilyushin Il-20RT(SIP)			Aeroflot cs, Satellite tracker
RA-76708	Ilyushin Il-76MD	0063473171	CCCP-76708	Aeroflot cs
RA-76725	Ilyushin Il-76MD	0073475253	CCCP-76725	Aeroflot cs
RA-76766	Ilyushin Il-76MDK	0083481431	CCCP-76766	
RA-78770	Ilyushin Il-76MDK	0083487617	CCCP-78770	Aeroflot cs
RA-78825	Ilyushin Il-76MDK	1013495871		Aeroflot cs
RA-78830	Ilyushin Il-76MD	1003401010	CCCP-78830	Aeroflot cs
RA-78850	Ilyushin Il-76MD	1013405196		Aeroflot cs

Lytono-Ispitatyelny Iinstitut - LII
Flight Research Centre

UNITS/BASES   Based at Moscow-Zhukovsky
Some aircraft are available for charter from a subsidiary, Gromov Air (ICAO code LII).

CCCP-06188	Ilyushin Il-76T	093421635	YI-AKQ	Testbed
08256	Antonov An-12BP	402207		

RA-26038	Antonov An-26	8002	CCCP-26038	
RA-64454	Tupolev Tu-134A	66140	CCCP-64454	Testbed
RA-65562	Tupolev Tu-134UB	2350104	CCCP-65562	Testbed
RA-65740	Tupolev Tu-134A	2351510	CCCP-65740	Testbed, Aeroflot cs
RA-65907	Tupolev Tu-134A	63996	CCCP-65907	
RA-65926	Tupolev Tu-134A	66101	CCCP-65926	
RA-65927	Tupolev Tu-134A	66198	CCCP-65927	VIP
RA-65939	Tupolev Tu-134A-3	1351409	LZ-TUU	
RA-75423	Ilyushin Il-18	182005601	CCCP-75423	
RA-76455	Myasischev/Ilyushin Il-76/976	0073471125	CCCP-76455	Aeroflot cs
CCCP-76492	Ilyushin Il-76MD	0043452549		Testbed, Aeroflot cs
RA-76528	Ilyushin Il-76T	073410293	CCCP-76528	Aeroflot cs
RA-76529	Ilyushin Il-76LL	073410308	CCCP-76529	Testbed
RA-76623	Ilyushin Il-76MD	0053457705	CCCP-76623	Firebomber testbed
RA-76753	Ilyushin Il-76RLSBO	0083481461	CCCP-76753	Aeroflot cs
RA-78732	Ilyushin Il-18V	181004103	CCCP-78732	
RA-78738	Ilyushin Il-76TD	0033442247	YI-ALS	Cvtd Il-76MD
RA-83962	Antonov An-12BP	402210		
RA-85317	Tupolev Tu-154M	78A-317	CCCP-85317	Cvtd Tu-154B-2, Testbed, Aeroflot cs
RA-85606	Tupolev Tu-154M	85A-701	CCCP-85606	Moscow AW titles
RA-85627	Tupolev Tu-154M	87A-756	CCCP-85627	Aeroflot cs
RA-86674	Ilyushin Il-62	80304	CCCP-86674	
RA-86891	Ilyushin Il-76M	093421628	CCCP-86891	Testbed
RA-88265	Yakovlev Yak-40	9722052	CCCP-88265	
code 43 red	Antonov An-12BP	8345902		

Respubliki Tatarstan
Government of the Tatar Republic (Tatarstan)

UNITS/BASES   Base is assumed to be the capital, Kazan. The Boeing is civil-registered in Aruban marks.

| P4-JLD | Boeing 727-193 | 19620 / 377 | VP-CWC |

RWANDA
République Rwandaise   C Africa

Rwanda became independent from Belgium in 1962 along with Burundi both formerly comprising Ruanda-Urundi. The air arm (Force Aérienne Rwandaise) was established in 1972. Internal tribal warfare through the 1990s has left the country in ruins, the Air Force being no exception with no pre-war equipment reported to have survived and no transports having been acquired since its conclusion.

SAUDI ARABIA
al-Mamlaka al-Arabiya as-Sa'udiya / Kingdom of Saudi Arabia   SW Asia

A major ally of the United States in the Middle East and probably the largest and strongest regional economy supporting one of the most up to date armed forces of the Arab states. A large detachment of US aircraft is based in the country and regular exercises and deployments take place.

SERIAL SYSTEM   Serials commence with the allocated squadron number and change if an aircraft transfers units. Government aircraft are civil registered and can combine numerical and alphabetical sequences.

al Quwwat al-Jawwiya as Sa'udiya
Royal Saudi Air Force - RSAF

UNITS/BASES	1 Sqn, King Kahlid IAP-Riyadh	Various	VIP
	4 Sqn, Prince Abdullah AB-Jeddah	C-130E/H	
	16 Sqn, Prince Sultan AB-Al Kharj	C-130E/H	
	18 Sqn, Prince Sultan AB-Al Kharj	E-3/KE-3	AEW/AAR
	19 Sqn, Prince Sultan AB-Al Kharj	KE-3, E-8B	EW
	32 Sqn, Prince Sultan AB-Al Kharj	KC-130H	AAR
	35 Sqn, King Abdullah Aziz AB-Dhahran	Jetstream	Nav Training

PLANS   Up to 24 C-130Js are required. More AEW and AAR aircraft are required, probably Boeing 767s.

HZ-105	British Aerospace 125-800B	258118	G-5-605	1 Sqn
HZ-106	Learjet 35A	35A-374		1 Sqn
HZ-107	Learjet 35A	35A-375	(YV-270CP)	1 Sqn
HZ-109	British Aerospace 125-800B	258146	G-5-703	1 Sqn

110	British Aerospace 125-800B	258148	HZ-110 (RSAF)	1 Sqn	
111	Lockheed VC-130H (L-382C-46D) Hercules	4605	102 (RSAF)	1 Sqn	VIP
112	Lockheed VC-130H (L-382C-60D) Hercules	4737		1 Sqn	VIP
118	Airtech/CASA CN235-10	SA01-C002		1 Sqn	
119	Airtech/CASA CN235-10	SA01-C003		1 Sqn	
126	Airtech/CASA CN235M-10	SA01-C004	ECT-101	1 Sqn	
127	Airtech/CASA CN235M-10	SA01-C005		1 Sqn	
HZ-130	British Aerospace 125-800B	258164	130 (RSAF)	1 Sqn	
451	Lockheed C-130E (L-382C-15B) Hercules	4076	N9258R	4 Sqn	
452	Lockheed C-130E (L-382C-15B) Hercules	4078		4 Sqn	
455	Lockheed C-130E (L-382C-3D) Hercules	4215		4 Sqn	
461	Lockheed C-130H (L-382C-39D) Hercules	4567		4 Sqn	
462	Lockheed C-130H (L-382C-46D) Hercules	4637		4 Sqn	
463	Lockheed C-130H (L-382C-46D) Hercules	4607		4 Sqn	
464	Lockheed C-130H (L-382C-46D) Hercules	4608		4 Sqn	
465	Lockheed C-130H (L-382C-46D) Hercules	4609		4 Sqn	
466	Lockheed C-130H (L-382C-60D) Hercules	4740		4 Sqn	
467	Lockheed C-130H (L-382C-60D) Hercules	4741		4 Sqn	
468	Lockheed C-130H (L-382C-60D) Hercules	4751		4 Sqn	
471	Lockheed C-130H-30 (L-382T-27F) Hercules	5211		4 Sqn	
472	Lockheed C-130H (L-382C-29F) Hercules	5234	N4099R	4 Sqn	
473	Lockheed C-130H (L-382C-29F) Hercules	5235		4 Sqn	
474	Lockheed C-130H (L-382C-29F) Hercules	5252		4 Sqn	
475	Lockheed C-130H (L-382C-30F) Hercules	5253		4 Sqn	
1601	Lockheed C-130H (L-382C-46D) Hercules	4612		16 Sqn	
1602	Lockheed C-130H (L-382C-46D) Hercules	4614		16 Sqn	
1603	Lockheed C-130H (L-382C-46D) Hercules	4618		16 Sqn	
1604	Lockheed C-130H (L-382C-46D) Hercules	4633		16 Sqn	
1605	Lockheed C-130H (L-382C-46D) Hercules	4634		16 Sqn	
1606	Lockheed C-130E (L-382C-11D) Hercules	4304		16 Sqn	
1607	Lockheed C-130E (L-382C-11D) Hercules	4306		16 Sqn	
1608	Lockheed C-130E (L-382C-11D) Hercules	4307		16 Sqn	
1609	Lockheed C-130E (L-382C-11D) Hercules	4311	N7994S	16 Sqn	
1610	Lockheed C-130H (L-382C-19D) Hercules	4396		16 Sqn	
1611	Lockheed C-130H (L-382C-19D) Hercules	4397	476 (RSAF)	16 Sqn	
1612	Lockheed C-130H (L-382C-39D) Hercules	4552		16 Sqn	
1614	Lockheed C-130H (L-382C-39D) Hercules	4560	477 (RSAF)	16 Sqn	
1615	Lockheed C-130H (L-382C-60D) Hercules	4745		16 Sqn	
1618	Lockheed C-130H (L-382C-60D) Hercules	4755		16 Sqn	
1619	Lockheed C-130H (L-382C-60D) Hercules	4758		16 Sqn	
1622	Lockheed C-130H-30 (L-382T-27F) Hercules	5212		16 Sqn	
1623	Lockheed C-130H (L-382C-30F) Hercules	5254		16 Sqn	
1624	Lockheed C-130H (L-382C-30F) Hercules	5267		16 Sqn	
1625	Lockheed C-130H (L-382C-30F) Hercules	5269		16 Sqn	
1626	Lockheed C-130H (L-382C-30F) Hercules	5270		16 Sqn	
1801	Boeing E-3A Sentry	23419 / 974	82-0068 (FMS)	18 Sqn	AEW
1802	Boeing E-3A Sentry	23418 / 973	82-0067 (FMS)	18 Sqn	AEW
1803	Boeing E-3A Sentry	23417 / 972	82-0066 (FMS)	18 Sqn	AEW
1804	Boeing E-3A Sentry	23420 / 976	82-0069 (FMS)	18 Sqn	AEW
1805	Boeing E-3A Sentry	23421 / 980	82-0070 (FMS)	18 Sqn	AEW
1811	Boeing KE-3A	23422 / 975	82-0071 (FMS)	18 Sqn	AAR
1812	Boeing KE-3A	23423 / 977	82-0072 (FMS)	18 Sqn	AAR
1813	Boeing KE-3A	23424 / 978	82-0073 (FMS)	18 Sqn	AAR
1814	Boeing KE-3A	23425 / 979	82-0074 (FMS)	18 Sqn	AAR
1815	Boeing KE-3A	23426 / 981	82-0075 (FMS)	18 Sqn	AAR
1816	Boeing KE-3A	23427 / 982	82-0076 (FMS)	18 Sqn	AAR
1818	Boeing KE-3A	23429 / 985	83-0511 (FMS)	18 Sqn	AAR
1901	Boeing KE-3A	23428 / 984	1817 (RSAF)	19 Sqn	AAR
1902	Boeing E-8B	24503 / 1001	N707UM	19 Sqn	JSTARS
2101	British Aerospace Jetstream 31	709	G-BMNS	35 Sqn	
					Nav Trainer (reserialled?)
3201	Lockheed KC-130H (L-382C-29D) Hercules	4503	456 (RSAF)	32 Sqn	AAR
3202	Lockheed KC-130H (L-382C-29D) Hercules	4511	457 (RSAF)	32 Sqn	AAR
3203	Lockheed KC-130H (L-382C-29D) Hercules	4532	458 (RSAF)	32 Sqn	AAR
3204	Lockheed KC-130H (L-382C-29D) Hercules	4539	459 (RSAF)	32 Sqn	AAR
3205	Lockheed KC-130H (L-382C-61D) Hercules	4746	1616 (RSAF)	32 Sqn	AAR
3206	Lockheed KC-130H (L-382C-61D) Hercules	4750	1617 (RSAF)	32 Sqn	AAR
3207	Lockheed KC-130H (L-382C-96D) Hercules	4873	1621 (RSAF)	32 Sqn	AAR

Saudi Arabian Airlines VIP / Special Flight Services

UNITS/BASES   All aircraft are based at Jeddah-King Abdul Aziz IAP and Riyadh-King Khalid IAP.

HZ-11<	Lockheed VC-130H (L-382C-4E) Hercules	4843	HZ-HM5	Riyadh

HZ-115	Lockheed VC-130H (L-382C-4E) Hercules	4845	HZ-HM6	Riyadh
HZ-116	Lockheed VC-130H (L-382C-26E) Hercules	4915	N4185M	Riyadh
HZ-117	Lockheed L-100-30 (L-382G-63C) Hercules	4954		Riyadh
HZ-128	Lockheed L-100-30 (L-382G-60C) Hercules	4950	HZ-MS05	Riyadh
HZ-129	Lockheed L-100-30 (L-382G-61C) Hercules	4957	HZ-MS10	Riyadh
HZ-AFA1	McDonnell Douglas MD-11	48353 / 544	HZ-HM8	Riyadh
HZ-AFA2	Bombardier Canadair CL-604 Challenger	5320	N605CC	Jeddah
HZ-AFH	Grumman G-1159 Gulfstream II	171	N17586	Jeddah
HZ-AFI	Grumman G-1159 Gulfstream IITT	201	N17585	Jeddah
HZ-AFJ	Grumman G-1159 Gulfstream IITT	203	N17587	Jeddah
HZ-AFK	Grumman G-1159 Gulfstream IITT	239	N17582	Jeddah
HZ-AFN	GAC G-1159A Gulfstream III	364	N1761D	Jeddah
HZ-AFP	Cessna 550 Citation II	550-0472/472	N12511	Jeddah
HZ-AFQ	Cessna 550 Citation II	550-0473/473	N12513	Jeddah
HZ-AFR	GAC G-1159A Gulfstream III	410	N350GA	Jeddah
HZ-AFT	Dassault Falcon 900	21	(HZ-R4A)	Jeddah
HZ-AFU	GAC Gulfstream IV	1031	N434GA	Jeddah
HZ-AFV	GAC Gulfstream IV	1035	N435GA	Jeddah
HZ-AFW	GAC Gulfstream IV	1038	N438GA	Jeddah
HZ-AFX	GAC Gulfstream IV	1143	N410GA	Jeddah
HZ-AIJ	Boeing 747SP-68	22750 / 560	N6046P	Riyadh
HZ-ATO	DeHavilland DHC-6 Twin Otter 300	836	C-GDCZ	Jeddah
HZ-HM1A	Boeing 747-3G1	23070 / 592	N1784B	Riyadh
HZ-HM1B	Boeing 747SP-68	21652 / 329	HZ-HM1	Riyadh
HZ-HM2	Boeing 707-368C	21081 / 903	HZ-HM1	Riyadh
HZ-HM3	Boeing 707-368C	21368 / 925	HZ-ACK	Riyadh
HZ-HM4	Boeing 737-268 Advanced	22050 / 622	HZ-AGT	Riyadh
HZ-HM5	Lockheed L-1011-193G TriStar 500	1250	N5129K	Riyadh
HZ-HM6	Lockheed L-1011-293A TriStar 500	1249	VR-CZZ	Riyadh
HZ-HM7	McDonnell Douglas MD-11	48352 / 532	N9093P	Riyadh
HZ-MFL	GAC Gulfstream IV	1128	N429GA	Jeddah
HZ-OCV	Boeing 727-21	19006 / 262	HZ-TFA	Riyadh
HZ-RC3	GAC G-1159A Gulfstream III	331	N17LB	Jeddah

Armed Forces Medical Services Department

UNITS/BASES   Based at Riyadh-King Khalid IAP.

HZ-HMED	Boeing 757-23A	25495 / 599	N275AW	Hospital
HZ-HM11	Douglas DC-8-72	46084 / 473	HZ-MS11	Cvtd DC-8-62
HZ-MS1	Learjet 35A	35A-467	N3796Q	Medevac
HZ-MS3	GAC G-1159A Gulfstream III	385	N1761K	Medevac
HZ-MS4	GAC Gulfstream IVSP	1365	N365GA	Medevac
HZ-MS5	GAC Gulfstream V	583	HZ-MS05	Medevac
HZ-MS6	Lockheed L-100-30 (L-382G-60C) Hercules	4952	HZ-MS06	Hospital
HZ-MS7	Lockheed C-130H (L-382C-26E) Hercules	4922	N4190M	Hospital
HZ-MS8	Lockheed C-130H-30 (L-382T-55E) Hercules	4986	N4243M	Hospital
HZ-MS09	Lockheed L-100-30 (L-382G-61C) Hercules	4956	N4255M	Hospital
HZ-MS14	Lockheed L-100-30 (L-382G-61C) Hercules	4960	N4266M	Hospital
HZ-MS19	Lockheed C-130H (L-382C-93D) Hercules	4837	N4098M	Hospital
HZ-MS21	Lockheed C-130H (L-382C-32E) Hercules	4918	N4240M	Hospital
HZ-MSD	Grumman G-1159 Gulfstream II	256	N17581	Std Riyadh

Royal Embassy of Saudi Arabia - RESA

UNITS/BASES   Based at Riyadh-King Khalid IAP.

HZ-103	GAC G-1159A Gulfstream III	453	103 (RSAF)	
HZ-108	GAC G-1159A Gulfstream III	353	HZ-BSA	
HZ-123	Boeing 707-138B	17696 / 29	N138MJ	
HZ-124	Airbus Industrie A340-211	004	F-WWBA	

SENEGAL
République du Sénégal   W Africa

Senegal became independent from France in 1958, briefly federated with Mali in 1959/60 and from 1982 until 1989 combined with the former British colony of the Gambia to form the Confederation of Senegambia although both are now independent. The Air Force is primarily transport and patrol orientated.

SERIAL SYSTEM   Civil style registrations are worn using the 6W- prefix reserved for military allocations.

Armée de l'Air du Sénégal
Senegal Air Force

UNITS/BASES   Aircraft are based at Dakar-Yoff Airport.

6W-STA	Fokker F.27 Troopship 400M	10564	PH-EXA	*'Asta'*
6W-STB	Fokker F.27 Troopship 400M	10565	PH-EXB	*'Bargny'*
6W-STC	Fokker F.27 Troopship 400M	10582	PH-EXD	*'Casamance'*
6W-STD	Fokker F.27 Troopship 400M	10583	PH-EXC	*'Djolaf'*
6W-STE	Fokker F.27 Troopship 400M	10590	PH-EXE	*'Etjalo'*
6W-STF	Fokker F.27 Troopship 400M	10591	PH-FTS	*'Fouta'*

Government of the Republic of Senegal

6V-AEF	Boeing 727-2M1 Advanced	21091 / 1134	N40104	*'Point de Sangomar'*
6V-AFF	DeHavilland Canada DHC-6 Twin Otter 300	788	C-GBOD	Fishery Patrol

SEYCHELLES
Repiblik Sesel   Indian Ocean

The Maritime Patrol and SAR functions of the Coast Guard are carried out by the Island Development Company who operate the former Seychelles Defence Force equipment from Mahé and cover the hundred plus islands that make up the chain.

SERIAL SYSTEM   Civil registrations are now worn, usually sequential but including the obvious out-of-sequence choice for the Beech 1900.

Coast Guard Air Wing - IDC Ltd

UNITS/BASES   Based at Mahé-Seychelles IAP.

S7-AAI	Reims/Cessna F406 Caravan II	F406-0051	N7148P	SAR
S7-AAL	Britten-Norman BN-2A-21 Islander	589	A2-01M	MR
S7-IDC	Raytheon Beech 1900D	UE-212	N3217U	

SIERRA LEONE
Republic of Sierra Leone   W Africa

Following a 1997 coup and military intervention by the UN and British Forces the Sierra Leone Defence Force was disbanded. Although a military force has been established by the new Government no aircraft are reported to be operated.

SINGAPORE
Republic of Singapore   SE Asia

After Singapore left the Federation of Malaysia in 1965 defence was provided by the UK and later continued by the RAAF, however foreign based units are no longer necessary, particularly with membership of ASEAN. While probably the smallest country featured in this directory at 620 sq km, Singapore has the world's biggest port and is the most important trading centre for the emerging Pacific Rim countries. The need to defend (and the means to fund its defence) result in Singapore having a small but well equipped Air Force including AEW Hawkeyes working with F-16s (the first such capabilty in the region).

Republic of Singapore Air Force - RSAF

UNITS/BASES	111 (Hawkeye) Sqn, Tengah	Hawkeye
	112 Sqn, Tengah	Stratotanker
	122 (Condor) Sqn, Paya Lebar	C-130
	121 (Gannet) Sqn, Changi	Fokker 50

PLANS   Replacement of the existing Hercules with C-130Js.
Evaluating Gulfstream IVSP and V options as a SIGINT/ELINT platform.

011	Grumman E-2C Hawkeye		Bu162793 (FMS)	111 Sqn	AEW
012	Grumman E-2C Hawkeye	A52-70	Bu162794 (FMS)	111 Sqn	AEW
014	Grumman E-2C Hawkeye		Bu162795 (FMS)	111 Sqn	AEW
015	Grumman E-2C Hawkeye		Bu162796 (FMS)	111 Sqn	AEW
710	Fokker 50UTA-B	20268	PH-LXY	121 Sqn	
711	Fokker 50UTA-B	20269	PH-LXZ	121 Sqn	
712	Fokker 50UTA-B	20294	PH-MXU	121 Sqn	

713	Fokker 50UTA-B	20295	PH-MXV	121 Sqn	
714	Fokker 50MPA Enforcer II	20267	PH-LXX	121 Sqn	MR
715	Fokker 50MPA Enforcer II	20293	PH-JCG	121 Sqn	MR
716	Fokker 50MPA Enforcer II	20305	PH-EXR	121 Sqn	MR
717	Fokker 50MPA Enforcer II	20308	PH-EXY	121 Sqn	MR
718	Fokker 50MPA Enforcer II	20311	PH-EXZ	121 Sqn	MR/SIGINT
720	Lockheed KC-130B (L-282-1B) Hercules	3519	58-0724 (USAF)	122 Sqn	AAR
721	Lockheed KC-130B (L-282-1B) Hercules	3557	58-0756 (USAF)	122 Sqn	AAR
724	Lockheed KC-130B (L-282-1B) Hercules	3611	142 (RJAF)	122 Sqn	AAR
725	Lockheed KC-130B (L-282-1B) Hercules	3620	143 (RJAF)	122 Sqn	AAR
730	Lockheed C-130H (L-382C-2E) Hercules	4842		122 Sqn	
731	Lockheed C-130H (L-382C-2E) Hercules	4844		122 Sqn	
732	Lockheed C-130H (L-382C-6E) Hercules	4846	N4108M	122 Sqn	
733	Lockheed C-130H (L-382C-6E) Hercules	4848	N4113M	122 Sqn	
734	Lockheed KC-130H (L-382C-29E) Hercules	4940	N4237M	122 Sqn	AAR
735	Lockheed C-130H (L-382C-66E) Hercules	5070	N73233	122 Sqn	
750	Boeing KC-135R Stratotanker	18626 / T0665	63-8009 (USAF)	112 Sqn	AAR, cvtd KC-135A
751	Boeing KC-135R Stratotanker	18232 / T0547	61-0325 (USAF)	112 Sqn	AAR, cvtd KC-135A
752	Boeing KC-135R Stratotanker	17942 / T0357	59-1454 (USAF)	112 Sqn	AAR, cvtd KC-135A
753	Boeing KC-135R Stratotanker	18633 / T0672	63-8016 (USAF)	112 Sqn	AAR, cvtd KC-135A
VH-PFA	Learjet 35A	35A-661	N1286G	Unicorn Intl	TT

SLOVAKIA
Slovenská Republika · C Europe

Slovakia received one third of the former Czechoslovak AF inventory on its mutual separation from the Czech Republic in 1993. Little has been changed since although the organization is now along NATO lines and membership is being pursued for 2005.

SERIAL SYSTEM The same serials used in Czechoslakian service have been retained reflecting the last four digits of the c/n.

Armady Slovenskej Republiky, Velitelstvo Vzdusnych Sil - VVS
Slovakian RepublicArmed Forces, Combat Air Force

UNITS/BASES 31 Stihaci Letecke Kridlo, Silac AB
31/4 Letka — L-410T
32 Zmiesany Doprany Kridlo, Piest'any AB
32/1 Letka — L-410M/UVP, An-24, An-26
32/1 Letka, Detachment, Trencin AB — L-410FG
Vycvikove Stredisko Letectva, Kosice — L-410

0404	Let L-410M	750404	0404 (CzechAF)	32/1 Let	
0405	Let L-410M	750405	0405 (CzechAF)	32/1 Let	Std Piest'any ?
0730	Let L-410UVP	810730	0730 (CzechAF)	32/1 Let	
0731	Let L-410UVP	810731	0731 (CzechAF)	32/1 Let	
0927	Let L-410T	820927	0927 (CzechAF)		Std Sliac
0930	Let L-410T	820930	0930 (CzechAF)	31/4 Let	
1133	Let L-410T	831133	1133 (CzechAF)	31/4 Let	
1203	Let L-410FG	841203	1203 (CzechAF)	32/1 Let	Survey
1521	Let L-410FG	851521	1521 (CzechAF)	32/1 Let	Survey
2311	Let L-410UVP-E14	892311	2311 (CzechAF)	32/1 Let	
2506	Antonov An-26	12506	2506 (CzechAF)	32/1 Let	
2903	Antonov An-24V	77302903	2903 (CzechAF)	32/1 Let	
3208	Antonov An-26Z-1	13208	3208 (CzechAF)	32/1 Let	EW
5605	Antonov An-24V	97305605	5605 (CzechAF)	32/1 Let	

Slovak Government Flying Services

UNITS/BASES Aircraft based at MR Stefanik-Bratislave Airport.

OM-BYE	Yakovlev Yak-40	9440338	OK-BYE
OM-BYL	Yakovlev Yak-40	9940560	OK-BYL
OM-BYO	Tupolev Tu-154M	89A-803	OK-BYO
OM-BYR	Tupolev Tu-154M	98A-1012	

SLOVENIA
Republika Slovenija   SE Europe

Declared independent from Yugoslavia in June 1991 without the prolonged blood letting experienced elsewhere in the former Republic. Now seeking EU and NATO membership having operated in Bosnia as part of SFOR.

SERIAL SYSTEM Each type is allocated an alphanumeric code, followed by a sequential number allotted to individual aircraft.

Slovensko Vojasko Letalstvo
Territorial Defence Force, Air Force Unit

ICAO code SIV, callsign Slovenian

UNITS/BASES   All the transports are based at Ljubljana-Brnik with 15 Brigade.

L4-01	Let L-410UVP-E	912606	S5-BAD	15 Br
L6-02	Pilatus PC-6/B2-H4 Turbo Porter	925	HB-FLQ	15 Br
L6-03	Pilatus PC-6/B2-H4 Turbo Porter	926	HB-FLR	15 Br

Government of the Republic of Slovenia

S5-BAA	Learjet 35A	35A-618	SL-BAA	Presidential Flight

SOLOMON ISLANDS
SW Pacific

Independent from Britain and Papua New Guinea from 1978 the government acquired patrol aircraft in 1997 from the USA.

SERIAL SYSTEM No details known, the civil prefix is H4-.

Government of the Solomon Islands

UNITS/BASES   Presumed based at Honiara-Henderson IAP.

Cessna O-2A Super Skymaster	M337-0164	N5151U, 68-6875
Cessna O-2A Super Skymaster	M337-0170	N6881Z, 68-6881

SOMALIA
Jamhuuriyadda Dimugradiga Somaliya / Somali Democratic Republic   E Africa

A former Italian colony reunited with the British Protectorate of Somaliland with independence in 1960, Somalia has a history of border disputes and internal civil unrest. A 1991 revolution devastated the country's infrastructure and sporadic fighting continues between various fiefdoms. The armed forces have never been reformed and what remains of the air arm (**Dayuuradaha Xooga Dalka Soma yeedis, Somali Aeronautical Corps**) is derelict at Mogadishu Airport although an An-26 is abandoned at Nairobi in Kenya.

SOUTH AFRICA
Republic of South Africa   S Africa

Having shut itself off from the rest of the world while under white minority rule through its Apartheid policy, South Africa has now emerged but still has internal problems to resolve. Mineral resources help to fund a very well developed Air Force established back in the 1920s with British colonial assistance. An indigenous manufacturing capability was developed out of necessity from the 1970s with help from Israel in particular. The armed forces have been reduced in size as the threat from Soviet backed neighbours diminished, South Africa having participated both openly and covertly in many of the Southern African conflicts.

SERIAL SYSTEM Three or four digit serials are issued in blocks by type. Most VIP aircraft carry civil registrations, sometimes in addition to the numeric serial.

South African Air Force - SAAF

UNITS/BASES	21 Sqn, Pretoria, Waterkloof AB	Citation, Falcon 50, 737BBJ
	28 Sqn, Pretoria, Waterkloof AB	C-130B, C-160
	35 Sqn, Cape Town, DF Malan AB	DC-3, DC-3TP, B200
	41 Sqn, Pretoria, Waterkloof AB	C208, B200, PC-XII
	44 Sqn, Pretoria, Waterkloof AB	DC-3TP, Aviocar
	60 Sqn, Pretoria, Waterkloof AB	707

PLANS   The Hercules are being upgraded in conjunction with Marshalls in the UK and Denel in South Africa.
Six long and ten short range MP aircraft are required to replace the C-47s that took over from the retired
Shackletons and P166s.
Up to twelve CASA 212-400s are preferred to replace the last C-47s, subject to funding.

Serial	Type	c/n	Reg/ID	Sqn	Notes
1415 / AF-615	Boeing 707-328C	19522 / 596	F-BLCH	60 Sqn	AAR
1417 / AF-617	Boeing 707-328C	19723 / 665	ZS-LSJ	60 Sqn	AAR
1419 / AF-619	Boeing 707-328C	19917 / 763	ZS-LSK	60 Sqn	ELINT/AAR
1421 / AF-621	Boeing 707-344C	20283 / 831	EL-TBA	60 Sqn	VIP
1423 / AF-623	Boeing 707-344B	19706 / 691	ZS-LSL	60 Sqn	VIP
3001	Cessna 208 Caravan 1	208-0071	ZS-LYR	41 Sqn	
3002	Cessna 208 Caravan 1	208-0080	ZS-LZS	41 Sqn	
3003	Cessna 208 Caravan 1	208-0126	ZS-MHU	41 Sqn	
3004	Cessna 208 Caravan 1	208-0130	ZS-MEF	41 Sqn	
3005	Cessna 208 Caravan 1	208-0134	ZS-MHJ	41 Sqn	
3006	Cessna 208 Caravan 1	208-0136	ZS-MEG	41 Sqn	
3007	Cessna 208 Caravan 1	208-0138	ZS-MEH	41 Sqn	
3008	Cessna 208 Caravan 1	208-0140	ZS-MHL	41 Sqn	
3009	Cessna 208 Caravan 1	208-0159	ZS-MLM	41 Sqn	
3010	Cessna 208 Caravan 1	208-0160	ZS-MLP	41 Sqn	Dam Kwazulu Feb96
3011	Cessna 208 Caravan 1	208-0161	ZS-MLT	41 Sqn	
3012	Cessna 208 Caravan 1	208-0164	ZS-MLR	41 Sqn	
331	Transall/Nord C-160Z	Z.1			Std Waterkloof AFB
332	Transall/Nord C-160Z	Z.6			Std Waterkloof AFB
333	Transall/Nord C-160Z	Z.2			Std Waterkloof AFB
334	Transall/Nord C-160Z	Z.7			Std Waterkloof AFB
335	Transall/Nord C-160Z	Z.3			Std Waterkloof AFB
336	Transall/Nord C-160Z	Z.8			Std Waterkloof AFB
338	Transall/Nord C-160Z	Z.9			Std Waterkloof AFB
339	Transall/Nord C-160Z	Z.5			Std Waterkloof AFB
401	Lockheed C-130B (L-282-11B) Hercules	3724		28 Sqn	
402	Lockheed C-130B (L-282-11B) Hercules	3749		28 Sqn	
403	Lockheed C-130B (L-282-11B) Hercules	3750		28 Sqn	
404	Lockheed C-130B (L-282-11B) Hercules	3764		28 Sqn	
405	Lockheed C-130B (L-282-11B) Hercules	3765		28 Sqn	
406	Lockheed C-130B (L-282-11B) Hercules	3767		28 Sqn	
407	Lockheed C-130B (L-282-11B) Hercules	3769		28 Sqn	
408	Lockheed C-130B (L-282-1B) Hercules	3526	58-0731 (USAF)	28 Sqn	
409	Lockheed C-130B (L-282-1B) Hercules	3530	58-0734 (USAF)	28 Sqn	
410	Lockheed C-130F (L-282-3B) Hercules	3636	Bu149787 (USN)		wfu
411	Lockheed C-130F (L-282-3B) Hercules	3660	Bu149793 (USN)		
412	Lockheed C-130F (L-282-3B) Hercules	3696	Bu149805 (USN)		Std
650 / ZS-LNT	Beech Super King Air 200C	BL-70	N6921R	35 Sqn	
651 / ZS-LXS	Beech Super King Air 200C	BL-45	N90466	35 Sqn	
652 / ZS-LAY	Beech Super King Air 200C	BL-34	N38314	35 Sqn	
653 / ZS-MHK	Beech Super King Air 300	FA-118	N3087K	41 Sqn	
6811	Douglas C-47TP	11986	FL579	35 Sqn	
6814	Douglas C-47TP	11990	FL582	44 Sqn	
6825	Douglas C-47TP	12160	FZ605	35 Sqn	
6828	Douglas C-47TP	12415	42-92597	35 Sqn	
6834	Douglas C-47TP	12590	KG478		
6837	Douglas C-47TP	13539	KG672	35 Sqn	
6839	Douglas C-47TP	13540	ZS-MRS	35 Sqn	
6840	Douglas C-47TP	13866/25311	KG767	35 Sqn	Std Ysterplaat
6845	Douglas C-47TP	14642/26087	43-48826	35 Sqn	
6847	Douglas C-47B	14670/26115	KJ941		
6852	Douglas C-47TP	15557/27002	KK220	44 Sqn	
6854	Douglas C-47BTP	15887/32635	KN327	35 Sqn	
6864	Douglas C-47ATP	12580	KG468	35 Sqn	
6870	Douglas C-47TP	16463/33211	ZS-EYN	35 Sqn	
6871	Douglas C-47TP	16965/34225	D6-CAE		
6875	Douglas C-53DTP	11746	9Q-CYI	35 Sqn	
6877	Douglas C-47ATP	11925	FL564	35 Sqn	
6882	Douglas C-47TP	15896/32644	KN334	35 Sqn	
6884	Douglas C-47ATP	12064	FL637	35 Sqn	
6887	Douglas C-47TP	12704	TN-ADS	35 Sqn	
8010	CASA 212 Aviocar srs 200	A62-1-362	TDF-362 (Transkei)	44 Sqn	
8011	CASA 212 Aviocar srs 200	A62-2-363	TDF-02 (Transkei)	44 Sqn	
8020	CASA 212 Aviocar srs 300	DD65-1-371	040 (Venda DF)	44 Sqn	
8021	CASA 212 Aviocar srs 300	DD61-1-373	T310 (Bop AF)	44 Sqn	
	CASA 212 Aviocar srs 200	A56-1-319	T301 (Bop AF)	44 Sqn	
8026	CASA/Airtech CN235	001	T330 (Bop AF)	44 Sqn	
8030	Pilatus PC-XII	145	HB-FRG	41 Sqn	VIP

ZS-CA⊏	Dassault Falcon 50	133	HZ-AKI	21 Sqn
ZS-CA⊑	Dassault Falcon 50	91	F-WZHG	21 Sqn
ZS-LIG	Cessna 550 Citation II	550-0474/474	N12514	21 Sqn
ZS-ML⌄	Cessna 551 Citation II/SP	551-0285/266	030 (Venda DF)	21 Sqn
ZS-NA⌄	Dassault Falcon 900	99	F-WWFE	21 Sqn
ZS-RS⌐	Boeing BBJ (737-7ED)	32627 / 826	N737BJ	21 Sqn

South African Police Services Air Wing

ZS-KE⊒	Cessna 402A	402A0115	ZS-IAW
ZS-LN⌐	Beech Super King Air 200	BL-71	
ZS-MH⊦	Beech Beechjet 400	RJ-59	N1559U
ZS-MS⊏	Pilatus PC6/B2-H4 Turbo Porter	866	
ZS-NIR	Pilatus PC6/B2-H4 Turbo Porter	885	
ZS-NIS	Pilatus PC6/B2-H4 Turbo Porter	886	
ZS-NI⊤	Pilatus PC6/B2-H4 Turbo Porter	896	
ZS-NIU	Pilatus PC6/B2-H4 Turbo Porter	897	
ZS-NI⌄	Pilatus PC6/B2-H4 Turbo Porter	898	
ZS-NI⌄	Pilatus PC6/B2-H4 Turbo Porter	899	
ZS-NI⌶	Pilatus PC6/B2-H4 Turbo Porter	900	
ZS-CL◗	Pilatus PC6/B2-H4 Turbo Porter	871	2070 (SAAF)

SPAIN
Reino de España   SW Europe

Spain only joined NATO in 1982 and the Air Force is not actually part of its military structure although the EdA is a regular participant in exercises. Commitment to the new EU Force is likely. Individual aircraft types receive a type and role code which is displayed as part of the serial number. Most Air Force aircraft carrying titles are marked as Fuerza Aérea Española rather than the official name.

SERIAL SYSTEM Each type is allocated an alphanumeric code which denotes role and can have additional letters in the case of a specialized use. This is displayed followed by a sequential number identifying an individual aircraft. Large codes are also worn showing the unit and an additional individual aircraft number.

Ejército del Aire Español
Spanish Air Force

ICAO code AME

UNITS/BASES   Mando Aéreo del Centro (MACEN)

Ala 12, Grupo 12, Madrid-Torrejon	Do27 (support to F/A-18/RF-4C units)
Ala 12, Grupo 43, Esc 431/432, Madrid-Torrejon	CL-215T
Ala 12, Grupo 44, CLAEX, Madrid-Torrejon	Aviocar (support to weapons test aircraft)
Ala 12, Grupo 44, Esc 408, Madrid-Torrejon	Aviocar, Falcon 20, 707
Ala 12, Grupo 45, Esc 451, Madrid-Torrejon	707, Falcon 900
Ala 12, Grupo 45, Esc 452, Madrid-Torrejon	Falcon 20, Falcon 50
Ala 35, Esc 351, Madrid-Getafe	CN235
Ala 35, Esc 352, Madrid-Getafe	CN235
Ala 37, Esc 371, Villanubla	Aviocar
Ala 37, Esc 372, Villanubla	Aviocar
Ala 37, Esc 373, Villanubla	Aviocar
Ala 48, Esc 403, Madrid-Cuatro Vientos	Aviocar, Citation V, Do27
Ala 48, Esc 803, Madrid-Cuatro Vientos	Aviocar
Grupo 74, Esc 745, Salamanca-Matacan	Aviocar
Grupo 42, Esc 421, Madrid-Getafe	Baron

Mando Aéreo de Levante (MALEV)

Ala 31, Grupo 31, Esc 311, Zaragoza	C-130H/H-30
Ala 31, Grupo 31, Esc 312, Zaragoza	C-130H/KC-130H
Ala 31, Grupo 31, Esc 801, Son San Juan, Palma de Mallorca	
	Aviocar

Mando Aéreo de Estrecho (MAEST)

Ala 14, Esc 142, Albacete-Los Llanos	Do27 (support to Mirage F1 unit)
Ala 21, Grupo 22, Esc 221, Seville-Moron	P-3A/B, Do27
Ala 23, Esc 232, Talavera	Do27 (support to F-5 units)
Ala 78, Esc 782, Granada-Armilla	Do27
Academia General del Aire	
Ala 79, Escuela de Navegación, San Javier	Aviocar, Do27

Escuela Militar de Paracaidismo

Grupo 72, Esc 721, Murcia-Alcantarilla	Aviocar

Mando Aéreo de Canarias (MACAN)
Ala 46, Esc 461, Gando, Gran Canaria   Aviocar
Ala 46, Esc 802, Gando, Gran Canaria   F.27

PLANS   Two P-3A and 5 P-3Bs are being upgraded by CASA with their Fully Integrated Tactical System (FITS) to improve
MP capability, re-deliveries from 2003.
Nine C295Ms ordered from CASA (delivery 2001-2004), with more expected.
Two A310s purchased for AAR and VIP transport, conversion to be undertaken by CASA.
30 Airbus A400Ms are required (originally 36).

D2-01 / 802-10	Fokker F.27 Friendship 200MAR	10581	PH-FTK	802 Esc	
D2-02 / 802-11	Fokker F.27 Friendship 200MAR	10585	PH-EXD	802 Esc	
D2-03 / 802-12	Fokker F.27 Friendship 200MAR	10587	PH-FTL	802 Esc	
D.3A-01	CASA 212 Aviocar srs 100	AA1-1-87	T.12B-45	801 Esc	
D.3A-02 / 803-11	CASA 212 Aviocar srs 100	AB1-1-121	T.12B-62	803 Esc	
D.3B-03	CASA 212 Aviocar srs 100	S1-1-239		801 Esc	
D.3B-04	CASA 212 Aviocar srs 100	S1-2-259		801 Esc	
D.3B-05	CASA 212 Aviocar srs 100	S1-3-260	EC-ZZX	801 Esc	
D.3A-06 / 803-12	CASA 212 Aviocar srs 100	S1-4-266		803 Esc	
D.3B-07 / 803-13	CASA 212 Aviocar srs 100	S1-5-284		803 Esc	
D.3B-08 / 22-92	CASA 212 Aviocar srs 100	S1-6-285		22 Esc	
P.3-1 / 22-20	Lockheed P-3A (L-185) Orion	5123	Bu152153 (USN)	Ala 21	
P.3-3 / 22-22	Lockheed P-3A (L-185) Orion	5115	Bu152145 (USN)	Ala 21	
P.3-8 / 22-31	Lockheed P-3B HW (L-185) Orion	5264	583 (RNorAF)	Ala 21	
P.3-9 / 22-32	Lockheed P-3B HW (L-185C) Orion	5301	599 (RNorAF)	Ala 21	
P.3-10 / 22-33	Lockheed P-3B HW (L-185C) Orion	5302	600 (RNorAF)	Ala 21	
P.3-11 / 22-34	Lockheed P-3B HW (L-185C) Orion	5303	601 (RNorAF)	Ala 21	
P.3-12 / 22-35	Lockheed P-3B HW (L-185C) Orion	5304	602 (RNorAF)	Ala 21	
TL.10-1 / 31-01	Lockheed C-130H-30 (L-382T-52E) Hercules	5003		Ala 31	
T.10-2 / 31-02	Lockheed C-130H (L-382C-31D) Hercules	4526		Ala 31	
T.10-3 / 31-03	Lockheed C-130H (L-382C-31D) Hercules	4531		Ala 31	
T.10-4 / 31-04	Lockheed C-130H (L-382C-31D) Hercules	4534		Ala 31	
TK.10-5 / 31-50	Lockheed KC-130H (L-382C-55D) Hercules	4642		Ala 31	
TK.10-6 / 31-51	Lockheed KC-130H (L-382C-55D) Hercules	4648		Ala 31	
TK.10-7 / 31-52	Lockheed KC-130H (L-382C-55D) Hercules	4652		Ala 31	
T.10-8 / 31-05	Lockheed C-130H (L-382C-92D) Hercules	4835		Ala 31	
T.10-9 / 31-06	Lockheed C-130H (L-382C-92D) Hercules	4836		Ala 31	
T.10-10 / 31-07	Lockheed C-130H (L-382C-95D) Hercules	4841		Ala 31	
TK.10-11 / 31-53	Lockheed KC-130H (L-382C-98D) Hercules	4871		Ala 31	
TK.10-12 / 31-54	Lockheed KC-130H (L-382C-98D) Hercules	4874		Ala 31	
T.11-1 / 45-02	Dassault Falcon 20E	253/486	EC-BZV	Grupo 45	EC-ZCJ
TM.11-2 / 45-03	Dassault Falcon 20D	222/471	EC-BXV	Grupo 45	
TM.11-3 / 408-11	Dassault Falcon 20D	219/470	EC-BVV	408 Esc	ECM
TM.11-4 / 408-12	Dassault Falcon 20E	332/525	EC-CTV	408 Esc	ECM
T.11-5 / 45-05	Dassault Falcon 20F	475	F-WJML	Grupo 45	EC-ZCN
XT.12A-1 / 54-10	CASA 212 Aviocar srs 100	P1		Ala 54	
TR.12A-4 / 403-02	CASA 212 Aviocar srs 100	B-2-2		403 Esc	
TR.12A-5 / 403-03	CASA 212 Aviocar srs 100	B-3-3		403 Esc	
TR.12A-6 / 403-04	CASA 212 Aviocar srs 100	B-4-4		403 Esc	
TR.12A-8 / 403-06	CASA 212 Aviocar srs 100	B-6-6		403 Esc	
TR.12B-9 / 79-91	CASA 212 Aviocar srs 100	E-1-7		Ala 79	
TE.12B-10 / 79-92	CASA 212 Aviocar srs 100	E-2-8		Ala 79	
T.12B-12 / 74-82	CASA 212 Aviocar srs 100	A1-6-16		Ala 74	
T.12B-13 / 74-70	CASA 212 Aviocar srs 100	A1-9-19		Ala 74	
T.12B-14 / 46-30	CASA 212 Aviocar srs 100	A1-2-12		Ala 46	
T.12B-15 / 37-02	CASA 212 Aviocar srs 100	A1-5-15		Ala 74	
T.12B-16 / 74-71	CASA 212 Aviocar srs 100	A1-10-20		Ala 74	
T.12B-17 / 37-03	CASA 212 Aviocar srs 100	A1-11-21		Ala 37	
T.12B-18 / 46-31	CASA 212 Aviocar srs 100	A1-12-22		Ala 46	
T.12B-19 / 46-32	CASA 212 Aviocar srs 100	A1-13-23		Ala 46	
T.12B-20 / 37-04	CASA 212 Aviocar srs 100	A1-14-24		Ala 37	
T.12B-21 / 37-05	CASA 212 Aviocar srs 100	A1-15-27		Ala 37	
T.12B-22 / 37-06	CASA 212 Aviocar srs 100	A1-16-30		Ala 37	
T.12B-23 / 72-01	CASA 212 Aviocar srs 100	A1-17-31		Ala 72	
T.12B-24 / 32-07	CASA 212 Aviocar srs 100	A1-18-40		Ala 32	
T.12B-25 / 74-72	CASA 212 Aviocar srs 100	A1-19-43		Ala 74	
T.12B-26 / 72-02	CASA 212 Aviocar srs 100	A1-20-42		Ala 72	
T.12B-27 / 46-33	CASA 212 Aviocar srs 100	A1-21-46		Ala 46	
T.12B-28 / 72-03	CASA 212 Aviocar srs 100	A1-22-48		Ala 72	
T.12B-29 / 37-08	CASA 212 Aviocar srs 100	A1-23-51		Ala 37	
T.12B-30 / 74-73	CASA 212 Aviocar srs 100	A1-24-58		Ala 74	
T.12B-31 / 46-34	CASA 212 Aviocar srs 100	A1-25-59		Ala 46	
T.12B-33 / 72-04	CASA 212 Aviocar srs 100	A1-27-66		Ala 72	
T.12B-34 / 74-74	CASA 212 Aviocar srs 100	A1-28-67		Ala 74	

T.12B-35 / 37-09	CASA 212 Aviocar srs 100	A1-29-71		Ala 37	
T.12B-36 / 37-10	CASA 212 Aviocar srs 100	A1-30-72		Ala 37	
T.12B-37 / 72-05	CASA 212 Aviocar srs 100	A1-31-73		Ala 72	
T.12B-38 / 37-10	CASA 212 Aviocar srs 100	A1-32-74		Ala 37	Std Salamanca
T.12B-39 / 74-75	CASA 212 Aviocar srs 100	A1-33-75		Ala 74	
TE.12B-40 / 79-93	CASA 212 Aviocar srs 100	E1-1-76		Ala 79	
TE.12B-41 / 79-94	CASA 212 Aviocar srs 100	E1-2-79		Ala 79	
T.12C-43 / 46-50	CASA 212 Aviocar srs 100	AV1-1-69		Ala 46	
T.12C-44 / 37-50	CASA 212 Aviocar srs 100	AV1-2-70		Ala 37	EC-ZAA
T.12B-46 / 74-76	CASA 212 Aviocar srs 100	AA1-12-88		Ala 74	
T.12B-47 / 72-06	CASA 212 Aviocar srs 100	AA1-3-94		Ala 72	
T.12B-48 / 37-11	CASA 212 Aviocar srs 100	AA1-4-99		Ala 37	
T.12B-49 / 46-36	CASA 212 Aviocar srs 100	AA1-5-100		Ala 46	
T.12B-50 / 74-77	CASA 212 Aviocar srs 100	AA1-6-102		Ala 74	Std Cuatro Vientos
T.12B-51 / 74-78	CASA 212 Aviocar srs 100	AA1-7-104		Ala 74	
T.12B-52 / 72-07	CASA 212 Aviocar srs 100	AA1-8-105		Ala 72	
T.12B-53 / 46-37	CASA 212 Aviocar srs 100	AA1-11-96		Ala 46	
T.12B-54 / 37-13	CASA 212 Aviocar srs 100	AA1-12-98		Ala 37	
T.12E-55 / 46-37	CASA 212 Aviocar srs 100	AA1-9-113		Ala 46	
T.12E-56 / 74-79	CASA 212 Aviocar srs 100	AA1-10-114		Ala 74	
T.12E-57 / 72-08	CASA 212 Aviocar srs 100	AA1-13-110		Ala 72	
T.12E-58 / 46-38	CASA 212 Aviocar srs 100	AA1-14-111		Ala 46	
T.12C-59 / 37-51	CASA 212 Aviocar srs 100	AV1-3-77		Ala 37	
T.12C-60 / 37-52	CASA 212 Aviocar srs 100	AV1-4-109		Ala 37	
T.12C-61 / 37-53	CASA 212 Aviocar srs 100	AV1-5-115		Ala 37	
T.12E-63 / 37-14	CASA 212 Aviocar srs 100	AB1-2-122		Ala 37	
T.12E-64 / 46-39	CASA 212 Aviocar srs 100	AB1-3-123		Ala 46	
T.12E-65 / 74-80	CASA 212 Aviocar srs 100	AB1-4-127		Ala 74	
T.12E-66 / 72-09	CASA 212 Aviocar srs 100	AB1-5-129		Ala 72	
T.12E-67 / 74-81	CASA 212 Aviocar srs 100	AB1-6-130		Ala 74	
T.12E-68 / 37-15	CASA 212 Aviocar srs 100	AB1-7-142		Ala 37	
T.12E-69 / 37-16	CASA 212 Aviocar srs 100	AB1-8-143		Ala 37	
T.12E-70 / 37-17	CASA 212 Aviocar srs 100	AB1-9-146		Ala 37	
T.12B-71 / 37-18	CASA 212 Aviocar srs 100	AB1-10-147		Ala 37	
TM.12D-72 / 408-01	CASA 212 Aviocar srs 200	DE1-1-313	D.3B-10	408 Esc	
TM.12D-74 / 54-11	CASA 212 Aviocar srs 200	CC49-1-301	EC-DTV	Ala 46	European Ice Research
TR.12D-75 / 403-07	CASA 212 Aviocar srs 200	CC49-2-270	EC-DUQ	403 Esc	
TR.12D-76 / 37-60	CASA 212 Aviocar srs 300	CC60-4-323	EC-FAP	Ala 37	
TR.12D-77 / 37-61	CASA 212 Aviocar srs 200	CC42-1-261	EC-FAQ	Ala 37	
TR.12D-78 / 37-62	CASA 212 Aviocar srs 200	VF25-3-311	EC-DTL	Ala 37	
TR.12D-79 / 37-63	CASA 212 Aviocar srs 200	VF25-4-359	EC-ECD	Ala 37	
TR.12D-80 / 37-64	CASA 212 Aviocar srs 200	VF25-1-178	EC-DNB	Ala 37	
TR.12D-81 / 37-65	CASA 212 Aviocar srs 200	VF25-2-247	EC-DRO	Ala 37	
T.12B-82	CASA 212 Aviocar srs 200				
T.16-1 / 45-20	Dassault Falcon 50	84	F-WZHK	Grupo 45	EC-ZCP
T.17-1 / 45-10	Boeing 707-331B (KC-137E)	20060 / 773	N275B	Grupo 45	
T.17-2 / 45-11	Boeing 707-331C (KC-137E)	18757 / 387	N792TW	Grupo 45	
T.17-3 / 45-12	Boeing 707-368C (KC-137E)	21367 / 922	N7667B	Grupo 45	
TM.17-4 / 408-21	Boeing 707-351C (KC-137E)	19164 / 508	SX-DBO	408 Esc	SIGINT
T.18-1 / 45-40	Dassault Falcon 900	38	F-WWFE	Grupo 45	
T.18-2 / 45-41	Dassault Falcon 900	90	F-WWFG	Grupo 45	
T.19A-01 / 35-60	Airtech/CASA CN235-10	C013	T.19C-01	Ala 35	
T.19A-02 / 35-61	Airtech/CASA CN235-10	C014	T.19C-02	Ala 35	
T.19B-03 / 35-21	Airtech/CASA CN235M-100	C034	EC-014	Ala 35	
T.19B-04 / 35-22	Airtech/CASA CN235M-100	C035		Ala 35	
T.19B-05 / 35-23	Airtech/CASA CN235M-100	C036		Ala 35	
T.19B-06 / 35-24	Airtech/CASA CN235M-100	C037		Ala 35	
T.19B-07 / 35-25	Airtech/CASA CN235M-100	C038		Ala 35	
T.19B-08 / 35-26	Airtech/CASA CN235M-100	C039		Ala 35	Lst Swiss AF
T.19B-09 / 35-27	Airtech/CASA CN235M-100	C040		Ala 35	
T.19B-10 / 35-28	Airtech/CASA CN235M-100	C046		Ala 35	
T.19B-11 / 35-29	Airtech/CASA CN235M-100	C047		Ala 35	
T.19B-12 / 35-30	Airtech/CASA CN235M-100	C050		Ala 35	
T.19B-13 / 35-31	Airtech/CASA CN235M-100	C054		Ala 35	
T.19B-14 / 35-32	Airtech/CASA CN235M-100	C059		Ala 35	
T.19B-15 / 35-33	Airtech/CASA CN235M-100	C060		Ala 35	
T.19B-16 / 35-34	Airtech/CASA CN235M-100	C070		Ala 35	
T.19B-17 / 35-35	Airtech/CASA CN235M-100	C074		Ala 35	
T.19B-18 / 35-36	Airtech/CASA CN235M-100	C075		Ala 35	
T.19B-19 / 35-37	Airtech/CASA CN235M-100	C076		Ala 35	
T.19B-20 / 35-38	Airtech/CASA CN235M-100	C079		Ala 35	
TR.20-01 / 403-11	Cessna 560 Citation V	560-0161	N68860	403 Esc	
TR.20-02 / 403-12	Cessna 560 Citation V	560-0193	N1282K	403 Esc	
UD.13-15 / 431-15	Canadair CL-215T	1056		Grupo 43	Cvtd CL-215

UD.13-16 / 43-16	Canadair CL-215T	1057		Grupo 43	Cvtd CL-215
UD.13-17 / 431-17	Canadair CL-215T	1061		Grupo 43	Cvtd CL-215
UD.13-19 / 431-19	Canadair CL-215T	1080		Grupo 43	Cvtd CL-215
UD.13-20 / 43-20	Canadair CL-215T	1113	C-GDRQ	Grupo 43	Cvtd CL-215
UD.13-21 / 43-21	Canadair CL-215T	1116	C-FFDN	Grupo 43	Cvtd CL-215
UD.13-22 / 43-22	Canadair CL-215T	1109	C-GBPU	Grupo 43	Cvtd CL-215
UD.13-23 / 43-23	Canadair CL-215T	1117	C-FFDO	Grupo 43	Cvtd CL-215
UD.13-24 / 43-24	Canadair CL-215T	1118		Grupo 43	Cvtd CL-215
UD.13-25 / 43-25	Canadair CL-215T	1119		Grupo 43	Cvtd CL-215
UD.13-26 / 43-26	Canadair CL-215T	1120		Grupo 43	Cvtd CL-215
UD.13-27 / 43-27	Canadair CL-215T	1121	C-FIKS	Grupo 43	Cvtd CL-215
UD.13-28 / 43-28	Canadair CL-215T	1122	C-FIKT	Grupo 43	Cvtd CL-215
UD.13-29 / 43-29	Canadair CL-215T	1124		Grupo 43	Cvtd CL-215
UD.13-30 / 43-30	Canadair CL-215T	1125		Grupo 43	Cvtd CL-215
U.9-4 / 79-112	CASA 127 (Dornier 27)	4		Ala 79	
U.9-6 / 11-01	CASA 127 (Dornier 27)	6		Ala 11	
U.9-7 / 78-92	CASA 127 (Dornier 27)	7		Ala 78	
U.9-8 / 407-70	CASA 127 (Dornier 27)	8		Esc 407	
U.9-16 / 407-26	CASA 127 (Dornier 27)	16		Esc 407	
U.9-18 / 46-90	CASA 127 (Dornier 27)	18		Ala 46	
U.9-23 / 79-114	CASA 127 (Dornier 27)	23		Ala 79	
U.9-28 / 407-28	CASA 127 (Dornier 27)	28		Esc 407	
U.9-29 / 12-90	CASA 127 (Dornier 27)	29		Ala 12	
U.9-30 / 407-24	CASA 127 (Dornier 27)	30		Esc 407	
U.9-31 / 12-02	CASA 127 (Dornier 27)	31		Ala 12	
U.9-32 / 23-40	CASA 127 (Dornier 27)	32		Ala 23	
U.9-34 / 12-95	CASA 127 (Dornier 27)	34		Ala 12	
U.9-35 / 407-13	CASA 127 (Dornier 27)	35		Esc 407	
U.9-37 / 14-03	CASA 127 (Dornier 27)	37		Ala 14	
U.9-38 / 79-115	CASA 127 (Dornier 27)	38		Ala 79	
U.9-40 / 11-90	CASA 127 (Dornier 27)	40		Ala 11	
U.9-42 / 14-95	CASA 127 (Dornier 27)	42		Ala 14	
U.9-44 / 407-20	CASA 127 (Dornier 27)	44		Esc 407	
U.9-45 / 40-13	CASA 127 (Dornier 27)	45		Grupo 40	
U.9-46 / 407-91	CASA 127 (Dornier 27)	46		Esc 407	
U.9-50 / 40-14	CASA 127 (Dornier 27)	50		Grupo 40	
U.9-52 / 12-93	Dornier 27A-4	496		Ala 12	
U.9-53 / 12-91	Dornier 27A-4	500		Ala 12	
U.9-54 / 407-11	Dornier 27A-4	504		Esc 407	
U.9-72 / 407-54	Dornier 27A-1	142		Esc 407	
U.9-74 / 12-05	Dornier 27A-5	321		Ala 12	
	Dornier 27B-1	145		Esc 407	
XT.21-01	CASA C295M			CASA	
XT.21-02	CASA C295M			CASA	
	CASA C295M				on order
	CASA C295M				on order
	CASA C295M				on order
	CASA C295M				on order
	CASA C295M				on order
	CASA C295M				on order
	CASA C295M				on order
T.22-01	Airbus Industrie A310-304	550	F-GEMP		on order 2002
T.22-02	Airbus Industrie A310-304	551	F-GEMQ		on order 2002

Arma Aérea de la Armada Española
Spanish Fleet Air Arm

UNITS/BASES	4a Escuadrilla, NAS Rota		Citation	
U.20-1 / 01-405	Cessna 550 Citation II	550-0425/424	N1218A	004 Esca
U.20-2 / 01-406	Cessna 550 Citation II	550-0446/446	N1248N	004 Esca
U.20-3 / 01-407	Cessna 550 Citation II	550-0592/592	N1302N	004 Esca

SRI LANKA
Sri Lanka prjatantrika samajawadi janarajaya   Indian Ocean

Known as Ceylon until independence from Britain in 1972, a civil war has been in progress since 1983 as the LTTE fight for their own independence as a Tamil nation. This has resulted in the loss of a number of SLAF aircraft.

SERIAL SYSTEM   A two letter prefix determines the role (CR for transports) this is followed by a three digit serial commencing with a role defining number (8** for transports) with the last two digits being batched by type.

Sri Lanka Air Force - SLAF

UNITS/BASES	1st Transport Wing, 2nd Heavy Transport Squadron, Colombo-Ratmalana			C-130, An-32, Y-8, B200, C421	
	1st Transport Wing, 8th Light Transport Squadron, Colombo-Ratmalana			Y-12	
	3rd Maritime Squadron, Trincomalee-China Bay				

PLANS	Three more An-32 are on order.
	An additional Super King Air equiped with the Hughes Integrated Surveillance and Monitoring System (HISAR) is also imminent.

Serial	Type	c/n	Prev id	Unit	Notes
CC660	Cessna 421C Golden Eagle III			2 Sqn	Survey
CR833	Hawker Siddeley HS.748-301 srs 2A (LFD)				
		1746/set228	CR832 (SLAF)	2 Sqn	
CR842	Beech Super King Air B200T	BT-30/BB-1133	CR841 (SLAF)	2 Sqn	Cvtd B200
CR853	Yunshuji/Harbin Y-12 II	0015		8 Sqn	
CR854	Yunshuji/Harbin Y-12 II	0018		8 Sqn	
CR855	Yunshuji/Harbin Y-12 II	0019		8 Sqn	
CR858	Yunshuji/Harbin Y-12 II	0022		8 Sqn	
CR859	Yunshuji/Harbin Y-12 II	0027		8 Sqn	
CR860	Antonov An-32	3501		2 Sqn	Dam 21Apr97, repaired
CR863	Antonov An-32	3508		2 Sqn	
CR864	Antonov An-32	3509		2 Sqn	
CR866	Antonov An-32	3601		2 Sqn	
CR867	Antonov An-32B	3208	UR-48007	2 Sqn	
CR868	Antonov An-32B	3410	UR-48022	2 Sqn	
CR869	Antonov An-32B	3504	UR-48025	2 Sqn	
CR873	Yunshuji/Shaanxi Y-8D	070802	4R-HVC	2 Sqn	
CR880	Lockheed C-130K (L-382-19B) Hercules	4227	XV203 (RAF)	2 Sqn	
CR881	Lockheed C-130K (L-382-19B) Hercules	4240	XV213 (RAF)	2 Sqn	
ER-AFB	Antonov An-24RV	87310810	UK-08823		Lsf Lionair
UN-46655	Antonov An-24RV	47309301	CCCP-46655		Std Ratmalana
EW-46829	Antonov An-24RV	17306706	CCCP-46829		

SUDAN
al Jamhouriyat as-Sudan al-Democratia / Democratic Republic of Sudan — NE Africa

Sudan has been enveloped in a protracted civil war between the Northern and Southern halves of this former British colony. Financial problems exacerbated by famine have left the military with a mix of former Soviet and Western types, some of which were donated by sympathetic neighbours.

SERIAL SYSTEM Three or four digit serials are worn, allocated in blocks by type in a uniform but not necessarily sequential series.

Silakh al Jawwiya as Sudaniya
Sudanese Air Force

UNITS/BASES	Details are not known but aircraft are assumed to fly from Khartoum.

Serial	Type	c/n	Prev id
700	Antonov An-12		
711	Antonov An-12		
722	Antonov An-12		
733	Antonov An-12		
744	Antonov An-12		
755	Antonov An-12		
811 / ST-AHP	DeHavilland Canada DHC-5D Buffalo	85	
822	DeHavilland Canada DHC-5D Buffalo	86	
1100	Lockheed C-130H (L-382C-76D) Hercules	4766	ST-AIF
1101	Lockheed C-130H (L-382C-76D) Hercules	4767	ST-AHN
1102	Lockheed C-130H (L-382C-76D) Hercules	4769	78-0747 (FMS)
1103	Lockheed C-130H (L-382C-76D) Hercules	4771	78-0748 (FMS)
1104	Lockheed C-130H (L-382C-76D) Hercules	4774	78-0749 (FMS)
1105	Lockheed C-130H (L-382C-76D) Hercules	4775	ST-AHO
ST-ALV	Antonov An-12BP	8345909	YI-AEP

Government of the Republic of the Sudan

Serial	Type	c/n	Prev id
ST-PRS	Dassault Falcon 20F	372	F-WRQV
ST-PSA	Dassault Falcon 900	84	F-WQBM
ST-PSR	Dassault Falcon 50	114	F-WPXM

SURINAM
Republiek van Surinam   S America

Known as Dutch Guyana until independence from the Netherlands in 1975, Surinam's Air Force is primarily tasked with patrol duties although local guerrilla worries prompted the purchase of COIN-capable equipment in the mid 1980s.

SERIAL SYSTEM   A three digit serial prefixed SAF is worn. The numbers were sequential until the receipt of the Aviocars when they took up a type-inspired series.

Suriname Defence Force

UNITS/BASES   All aircraft are based at Paramaribo-Zanderij Airport with the DF Air Element.

SAF-001	Pilatus Britten-Norman BN-2B-21 Defender	916	G-BIUA		
SAF-002	Pilatus Britten-Norman BN-2B-21 Defender	2108	G-BIXE		Std
SAF-004	Pilatus Britten-Norman BN-2B-21 Defender	2117	G-BJEB		Std
SAF-008	Cessna 310				
SAF-212	CASA 212 Aviocar srs 400	466			
SAF-214	CASA 212 Aviocar srs 400 Patrullero	467			

SWAZILAND
Umboso we Swatini / Kingdom of Swaziland   S Africa

Formerly a British Protectorate until being granted independence in 1968, Swaziland is landlocked, being bordered primarily by South Africa. The Defence Force was established in 1978 following the independence of neighbouring Mozambique and concerns over border safety. The Air Wing was created in 1979 with the delivery of the first African-operated Aravas.

SERIAL SYSTEM   Civil style registrations are used in a unique block, 3D-D**.

Umbutfo Swaziland Defence Force

UNITS/BASES   The Air Wing is based at Manzini-Matsapa Airport.

3D-DAA	IAI Arava 201	0059	4X-ICF		Camo cs
3D-DAC	IAI Arava 201	0070	4X-ICQ		White cs

SWEDEN
Konungariket Sverige / Kingdom of Sweden   N Europe

Sweden, like its Scandinavian neighbour Finland, remains neutral but at the same time has developed a major indigenous manufacturing capability. The three major services (Air Force, Army and Navy) combined their rotary wing assets in 1998/99 leaving the incongruity of the former Marine Flygtjanst Aviocar being under Helicopter Wing control !

SERIAL SYSTEM   The first two or three digits of the five or six number serial are the RSwAF type designation, the rest of the number being sequential commencing 001.

Kungliga Svenska Flygvapnet
Royal Swedish Air Force - RSweAF

ICAO code SDC, call sign Swedic

UNITS/BASES	F7 Skaraborgs Flygflottilj, Transportflydivision, Satenas	C-130H
	F7 Skaraborgs Flygflottilj, Sambandsflyggrupp, Satenas	Super King Air
	F16M Upplands Flygflottilj 16, Malflygdivision Flygenhet, Linkoping-Malmstatt	Saab 340B/Argus, G-IV
	F17 Blekinge Flygflottilj, Sambandsflyggrupp, Ronneby-Kallinge	Citation
	F21 Norrbottens Flygflottilj, Sambandsflyggrupp, Lulea-Kallax	Super King Air
	Forsvarets Materielverk (FMV), Forsokscentralen, Linkoping-Malmstatt	Sabreliner

PLANS   C-130s require an update programme rather than replacement, including a KC-130 modification.
Two S100B are Saab 340s being leased to Greece until 2004/5. The VIP Tp100 is now up for disposal.

100001 / 001	Saab 340B (Tp100A)	340B-170	SE-F70	F16M	VIP
100002 / 002	Saab 340B Argus (S100B)	340B-342	SE-C42	F16M	AEW&C
100003 / 003	Saab 340B Argus (S100B)	340B-379	SE-C79	F16M	AEW&C
100004 / 004	Saab 340B Argus (S100B)	340B-395	SE-C95		Lst Greek AF
100005 / 005	Saab 340B Argus (S100B)	340B-409	SE-B09	F16M	AEW&C
100006 / 006	Saab 340B Argus (S100B)	340B-431	SE-B31	F16M	AEW&C

10007 / 007	Saab 340B Argus (S100B)	340B-455	SE-B55	F16M	AEW&C
10102 / 012	Beech Super King Air 200 (Tp101)	BB-459	OY-BVC	F21	
10103 / 013	Beech Super King Air 200 (Tp101)	BB-619	OY-CTJ	F17	
10104 / 014	Beech Super King Air 200 (Tp101)	BB-932	SE-KKM	F7	
10201 / 021	GAC Gulfstream IV (Tp102)	1014	N779SW	F16M	VIP
10202 / 022	GAC Gulfstream IVSP Korpen (S102B)	1215	N426GA	F16M	SIGINT, 'Hugin'
10203 / 023	GAC Gulfstream IVSP Korpen (S102B)	1216	N440GA	F16M	SIGINT, 'Munin'
10204 / 024	GAC Gulfstream IVSP (Tp102C)	1274	LV-WOM	F16M	
10302 / 032	Cessna 550 Citation II (Tp103)	550-0717/717	TC-SES	F17	
84001 / 841	Lockheed C-130H (L-382-8B) Hercules (Tp84)	4039	64-0546 (FMS)	F7	Cvtd C-130E
84002 / 842	Lockheed C-130H (L-382C-16D) Hercules (Tp84)	4332		F7	Cvtd C-130E
84003 / 843	Lockheed C-130H (L-382C-56D) Hercules (Tp84)	4628		F7	
84004 / 844	Lockheed C-130H (L-382C-8E) Hercules (Tp84)	4881		F7	ECM equipped
84005 / 845	Lockheed C-130H (L-382C-8E) Hercules (Tp84)	4884		F7	
84006 / 846	Lockheed C-130H (L-382C-8E) Hercules (Tp84)	4885		F7	ECM equipped
84007 / 847	Lockheed C-130H (L-382C-8E) Hercules (Tp84)	4887		F7	
84008 / 848	Lockheed C-130H (L-382C-8E) Hercules (Tp84)	4890		F7	
86001	North American Sabreliner 40 (Tp86)	282-49	N905KB	FMV	
86002	North American Sabreliner 40 (Tp86)	282-91	N40NR	FMV	

Forsvarsmakttens Helikopterflottilj
Swedish Defence Helicopter Wing

UNITS/BASES	2.HkpBat, Ronneby-Kallinge/Berga		Aviocar		
89001 / 891	SH89 / CASA 212 Aviocar srs 200	P2-1-139	EC-DHO	2. Hkpbat	ASW

Kustbevakningen
Swedish Coast Guard

UNITS/BASES	All aircraft are based at Karlskrona.

SE-IVE	CASA 212 Aviocar srs 200	CE61-1-343	
SE-IVF	CASA 212 Aviocar srs 200	CE61-2-346	
SE-KVG	CASA 212 Aviocar srs 200	AS28-1-229	EC-502

SWITZERLAND
Schweizerische Eidgenossenschaft / Swiss Confederation   C Europe

Switzerland carefully sought neutrality in World War II and has continued this policy since. A local and capable aircraft industry has helped in this respect with major acquisitions of foreign types involved for local assembly and manufacture. As would be expected for the country's size transport requirements are limited, but expansion to support UN and disaster relief operations abroad is planned.

SERIAL SYSTEM A three or four digit number is allocated in batches by type with a role-defining letter prefix.

Kommando der Flieger und Fliegerabwehrtruppen
Swiss Air Force and Anti-Aircraft Command

ICAO code SUI, callsign Airforce Switzerland

UNITS/BASES	Fliegerbrigade 31, VIP Flight, Dübendorf	Learjet, Falcon 50
	Fliegerregiment 4, Lufttransportstaffel 7, Emmen	Turbo Porter
	(normally deployed at various locations, including Dübendorf and Alpnach)	
	Fliegerstaffel 5, Dübendorf	Dornier 27

PLANS	Two CASA C295Ms were to be ordered for delivery in 2003, although it was reported that plans were on hold in mid-2001. One CN235M or C-130H may be leased from Spain for the interim period.

T.19B-08 / 35-26	Airtech/CASA CN235M-100	C039			Lsf Spanish AF
T-781	Learjet 35A	35A-068	HB-VEM	VIP Flt	
T-783	Dassault Falcon 50	67	HB-IEP	VIP Flt	
V-601	Dornier 27H-2	2008		Fst5	Survey
V-607	Dornier 27H-2	2014	HB-HAD	Fst5	Survey
V-612	Pilatus PC-6B/H-2M Turbo Porter	624		LTSt7	Cvtd PC-6/H
V-613	Pilatus PC-6B/H-2M Turbo Porter	630		LTSt7	Cvtd PC-6/H
V-614	Pilatus PC-6B/H-2M Turbo Porter	633		LTSt7	Cvtd PC-6/H
V-615	Pilatus PC-6B/H-2M Turbo Porter	635		LTSt7	Cvtd PC-6/H
V-616	Pilatus PC-6B/H-2M Turbo Porter	639		LTSt7	Cvtd PC-6/H
V-617	Pilatus PC-6B/H-2M Turbo Porter	640		LTSt7	Cvtd PC-6/H
V-618	Pilatus PC-6B/H-2M Turbo Porter	641		LTSt7	Cvtd PC-6/H
V-619	Pilatus PC-6B/H-2M Turbo Porter	643		LTSt7	Cvtd PC-6/H

V-620	Pilatus PC-6B/H-2M Turbo Porter	644		LTSt7	Cvtd PC-6/H
V-622	Pilatus PC-6B/H-2M Turbo Porter	648		LTSt7	Cvtd PC-6/H
V-623	Pilatus PC-6B/H-2M Turbo Porter	649		LTSt7	Cvtd PC-6/H
V-631	Pilatus PC-6B/H-2M Turbo Porter	749		LTSt7	
V-632	Pilatus PC-6B/H-2M Turbo Porter	751		LTSt7	
V-633	Pilatus PC-6B/H-2M Turbo Porter	757		LTSt7	
V-634	Pilatus PC-6B/H-2M Turbo Porter	759		LTSt7	
V-635	Pilatus PC-6B/H-2M Turbo Porter	761		LTSt7	

Government of the Swiss Confederation

ICAO code SGF, callsign Stac

UNITS/BASES	Bundesamt für Landestopographie, Dübendorf				Super King Air, Twin Otter
HB-GII	Beech Super King Air 350C (B300C)	FN-1	N2758B	BfL	Survey
HB-LID	DeHavilland Canada DHC-6 Twin Otter 300	466	C-GPXO-X	BfL	Survey

SYRIA
al-Jumhouriya al-Arabiya as-Suriya — SW Asia

It was thought that with the passing of President Assad an opportunity existed for this staunchly anti-Israeli state to finalise their part in the protracted regional peace negotiations. This has not yet happened and it appears that what control Syria had over the Hizbollah guerillas is slipping away anyway. An almost entirely Soviet-procured fleet is now aging rapidly, most transports being operated under the guise of the national airline, Syrianair.

SERIAL SYSTEM While the combat aircraft wear arabic numeral serials the transports remain civil registered in the YK-A** series with each type starting a new sequence. Whether shadow military serials are also allotted requires confirmation.

al-Quwwat al-Jawwiya al-Arabiya as-Suriya
Syrian Air Force

UNITS/BASES   All transports operate from Damascus(Dimashq)-Mezze Airport.

YK-ANA	Antonov An-24B	87304203		Syrianair cs
YK-ANC	Antonov An-26	3007		Syrianair cs
YK-AND	Antonov An-26	3008		Syrianair cs
YK-ANE	Antonov An-26	3103		Syrianair cs
YK-ANF	Antonov An-26	3104		Syrianair cs
YK-ANG	Antonov An-26B	10907		Syrianair cs
YK-ANH	Antonov An-26B	11406		Syrianair cs
YK-AQA	Yakovlev Yak-40	9341932		Syrianair cs
YK-AQB	Yakovlev Yak-40	9530443		Syrianair cs
YK-AQD	Yakovlev Yak-40	9830158		Syrianair cs
YK-AQE	Yakovlev Yak-40	9830258		Syrianair cs
YK-AQF	Yakovlev Yak-40	9931859		Syrianair cs
YK-AQG	Yakovlev Yak-40K	9941959		Syrianair cs
YK-ARA	Piper PA-31-310 Navajo	31-7300942	N7556L	Syrianair titles
YK-ARB	Piper PA-31-310 Navajo	31-7300944	N7558L	Syrianair titles
YK-ASA	Dassault Falcon 20F	328	F-WMKJ	Syrianair cs
YK-ASB	Dassault Falcon 20F	331	F-WRQS	Syrianair cs
YK-ASC	Dassault Falcon 900	100	F-WWFB	Syrianair cs
YK-ATA	Ilyushin Il-76M	093421613		Syrianair titles
YK-ATB	Ilyushin Il-76M	093421619		Syrianair titles
YK-ATC	Ilyushin Il-76T	0013431911		Syrianair cs
YK-ATD	Ilyushin Il-76T	0013431915		Syrianair cs
YK-AYA	Tupolev Tu-134B-3	63992		Syrianair cs
YK-AYB	Tupolev Tu-134B-3	63994		Syrianair cs

TAIWAN
Ta Chung-Hwa Min-Kuo / Republic of China — SE Asia

Created when the Nationalist Chinese were defeated by the Communist forces in a post-World War Two civil war, the Republic of China on the island of Taiwan (formerly Formosa) still regard themselves as the true Chinese Nation. Well supported initially by the USA, assistance has gradually diminished at least publicly as the USA appeases the mainland People's Republic of China. An indigenous manufacturing capability has therefore been developed.

SERIAL SYSTEM   Four digit serials are allocated with the first two digits determining the type, the choice of numbers usually relating to the type designation in question.

Chung Kuo Kug Chuan
Republic of China Air Force - ROCAF

UNITS/BASES	Government Transport Sqn, Sungshan		737-800	
	VIP Transport Sqn, Sungshan		Boeing 727, F50, Beech 1900	
	(One Beech 1900 detached daily to the Air Force Academy at Kangshan)			
	6 TC&ASCW, 10 TG, 101 TCS, Pingtung		C-130H	
	6 TC&ASCW, 10 TG, 102 TCS, Pingtung		C-130H	
	7 TC&ASCW, 78 sqn, Pingtung		C-130H, E-2T	

| PLANS | Two additional E-2T Hawkeyes on order from the USA (upgraded ex USN E-2Cs). |
| | Selection of a Tactical transport to replace the now retired C-119s, candidates are the C-27J and CN235. |

1301	Lockheed C-130H (L-382C-69E) Hercules	5058	85-0013 (FMS)	6 TC&ASCW	
1302	Lockheed C-130H (L-382C-69E) Hercules	5059	85-0014 (FMS)	6 TC&ASCW	
1303	Lockheed C-130H (L-382C-69E) Hercules	5060	85-0015 (FMS)	6 TC&ASCW	
1304	Lockheed C-130H (L-382C-69E) Hercules	5061	85-0016 (FMS)	6 TC&ASCW	
1305	Lockheed C-130H (L-382C-69E) Hercules	5062	85-0017 (FMS)	6 TC&ASCW	
1306	Lockheed C-130H (L-382C-69E) Hercules	5063	85-0018 (FMS)	6 TC&ASCW	
1307	Lockheed C-130H (L-382C-69E) Hercules	5064	85-0019 (FMS)	6 TC&ASCW	
1308	Lockheed C-130H (L-382C-69E) Hercules	5065	85-0020 (FMS)	6 TC&ASCW	
1309	Lockheed C-130H (L-382C-69E) Hercules	5066	85-0021 (FMS)	6 TC&ASCW	
1311	Lockheed C-130H (L-382C-69E) Hercules	5068	85-0023 (FMS)	6 TC&ASCW	
1312	Lockheed C-130H (L-382C-69E) Hercules	5069	85-0024 (FMS)	6 TC&ASCW	
1313	Lockheed C-130H (L-382C-54F) Hercules	5271		6 TC&ASCW	
1314	Lockheed C-130H (L-382C-54F) Hercules	5276		6 TC&ASCW	
1315	Lockheed C-130H (L-382C-54F) Hercules	5308		6 TC&ASCW	
1316	Lockheed C-130H (L-382C-54F) Hercules	5317		6 TC&ASCW	
1317	Lockheed C-130H (L-382C-61F) Hercules	5318		6 TC&ASCW	
1318	Lockheed C-130H (L-382C-61F) Hercules	5354	97-1318 (FMS)	6 TC&ASCW	
1319	Lockheed C-130H (L-382C-61F) Hercules	5355	97-1319 (FMS)	6 TC&ASCW	
1320	Lockheed C-130H (L-382C-62F) Hercules	5358	97-1320 (FMS)	6 TC&ASCW	
1351	Lockheed C-130H (L-382C-07F) Hercules	5215	90-0176	6 TC&ASCW, 78 Sqn	ELINT
1901	Beech 1900C-1	UC-23	N3188K	6 TC&ASCW	
1902	Beech 1900C-1	UC-25	N3189F	6 TC&ASCW	
1903	Beech 1900C-1	UC-27	N31904	6 TC&ASCW	
1904	Beech 1900C-1	UC-29	N3192E	6 TC&ASCW	
1906	Beech 1900C-1	UC-6	N72423	6 TC&ASCW	
1907	Beech 1900C-1	UC-7	N72424	6 TC&ASCW	
1908	Beech 1900C-1	UC-8	N7242V	6 TC&ASCW	
1909	Beech 1900C-1	UC-34	N3206K	6 TC&ASCW	
1910	Beech 1900C-1	UC-35	N3214Z	6 TC&ASCW	
1911	Beech 1900C-1	UC-30	N3199H	6 TC&ASCW	Calibrator
1912	Beech 1900C-1	UC-32	N3206C	6 TC&ASCW	Calibrator
2501	Grumman E-2T Hawkeye		Bu151709 (USN)	6 TC&ASCW, 78 Sqn	
					Cvtd E-2B
2502	Grumman E-2T Hawkeye		Bu151710 (USN)	6 TC&ASCW, 78 Sqn	
					Cvtd E-2B
2503	Grumman E-2T Hawkeye		Bu151724 (USN)	6 TC&ASCW, 78 Sqn	
					Cvtd E-2B
2504	Grumman E-2T Hawkeye		Bu152479 (USN)	6 TC&ASCW, 78 Sqn	
					Cvtd E-2B
2721	Boeing 727-109	19399 / 380	B-1818		Std
2722	Boeing 727-109	19520 / 466	B-1820		Std
2723	Boeing 727-109C	20111 / 695	B-1822		Std Ching Chuan Kang
2724	Boeing 727-121C	19818 / 462	B-188		Std
3701	Boeing 737-8AR	30139 / 428	N1787B		
5001	Fokker 50	20229	PH-JXE	HQ	
5002	Fokker 50	20238	PH-JXH		
5003	Fokker 50	20242	PH-JXI		

Republic of China Navy - ROCN

Started operating fixed wing aircraft in July 1999 when the ROCAF transferred their S-2 Trackers.

| UNITS/BASES | S-2T based at Pinting South, not all operational from a fleet of 26 by the end of 2000. |

| PLANS | Replacement of the re-engined Trackers due to low serviceabilty, up to 12 P-3s are to be supplied from the USA. |

2203	Grumman S-2T Turbo Tracker
2205	Grumman S-2T Turbo Tracker
2206	Grumman S-2T Turbo Tracker
2207	Grumman S-2T Turbo Tracker

2208	Grumman S-2T Turbo Tracker
2209	Grumman S-2T Turbo Tracker
2210	Grumman S-2T Turbo Tracker
2211	Grumman S-2T Turbo Tracker
2212	Grumman S-2T Turbo Tracker
2213	Grumman S-2T Turbo Tracker
2214	Grumman S-2T Turbo Tracker
2215	Grumman S-2T Turbo Tracker
2216	Grumman S-2T Turbo Tracker
2217	Grumman S-2T Turbo Tracker
2218	Grumman S-2T Turbo Tracker
2221	Grumman S-2T Turbo Tracker
2222	Grumman S-2T Turbo Tracker

Republic of China Government

| B-10001 | Boeing 737-43Q | 28492 / 2837 | B-18675 | Presidential Flt | Lsd |
| B-13152 | Beech 200 Super King Air | BB-449 | N2068L | Provincial Govt | |

TAJIKISTAN
Respublika i Tojikiston   C Asia

Tajikistan is still enduring internal problems between the Government and Muslim factions, while peace keepers from Russia and Kazakhstan provide what is probably the only military air transport in the country together with attack aircraft and helicopters. An air arm is being established but the first additions are in the latter categories rather than transport.

TANZANIA
Jamhouri ya Mwungano wa Tanzania / United Republic of Tanzania   E Africa

Although independent from Britain in 1961 and a Republic since 1962, Tanganyika joined with the neighbouring island of Zanzibar (independent in 1963) following a coup there to create Tanzania in 1964. The air arm was established with West German equipment, but not assistance, in 1965 and later support came from Canada before major aid from China was forthcoming.

SERIAL SYSTEM   All serials are prefixed with the initals JW (the air arm's initials), the four digit number in the 9000 range is allocated in blocks by type.

Jeshi la Wananchi la Tanzania - JWTZ
Tanzanian People's Defence Force

UNITS/BASES   The Air Wing transports appear to be based at Dar-Es-Salaam Airport.

JW9016	Cessna 404			
JW9017	Cessna 404			
JW9018	Cessna 404			
JW9019	DeHavilland Canada DHC-5D Buffalo	91	C-GTJV	Std Dar-Es-Salaam
JW9020	DeHavilland Canada DHC-5D Buffalo	92	C-GTJW	Std Dar-Es-Salaam
JW9023	DeHavilland Canada DHC-5D Buffalo	97		Std Dar-Es-Salaam
JW9026	Cessna 402			
JW9027	Beech King Air A100	B-197	5X-UWT	
JW9028	Cessna 402			Std Dar-Es-Salaam
JW9029	Yunshuji/Harbin Y-12 II		B-580L	Std Dar-Es-Salaam
JW9030	Yunshuji/Harbin Y-12 II		B-581L	Std Dar-Es-Salaam

Government of the United Republic of Tanzania

| 5H-CCM | Fokker F.28 Fellowship 3000 | 11137 | PH-ZBS | *'Uhuru na Umoja'* |

Tanzania Police Air Wing

| 5H-MPD | Cessna U206 Super Skywagon | U206-0295 | 5Y-AEW |

THAILAND
Muang Thai   SE Asia

Unlike most of its neighbouring countries Thailand (known as Siam until 1939) is not a former European colony. Much US support was received post World War Two after Japanese occupation particularly during the support of America's Vietnamese operations. Acquisition programmes are still hindered following the 1997 Pacific Rim economic crisis. A member of ASEAN.

SERIAL SYSTEM The Air Force serial system comprises a role, sequential type and Buddhist calendar year code and an individual aircraft number. This full serial data information is incomplete in some cases below. A larger unique code is more readily displayed showing the squadron number, where known either or both means of identification are shown, but beware as this code changes when aircraft move between units. Navy serials include reference to the unit number and have changed more than once in most cases. Army serials are based on the c/n as are those of the Police but the latter's start with a two digit type code. KASET markings consist of a four digit serial the first two digits of which are a sequential type code.

Kongtap Agard Thai
Royal Thai Air Force - RTAF

UNITS/BASES 1st Air Division
Wing 2, 202 Squadron, RTAFAB Kokkathium-Lop Buri	AU-23A	COIN
Wing 6, 601 Squadron, RTAFAB, Bangkok-Don Muang	C-130H, H-30	
Wing 6, 602 Squadron, RTAFAB, Bangkok-Don Muang	A310, 737	VIP
Wing 6, 603 Squadron, RTAFAB, Bangkok-Don Muang	HS.748, G-222	
Wing 6, 605 Squadron, RTAFAB, Bangkok-Don Muang	Merlin, Nomad, Learjet, Arava	Special Mission

3rd Air Division
Wing 46, 461 Squadron, RTAFAB Phitsanulok	Nomad, BT-67	

4th Air Division
Wing 53, 531 Squadron, RTAFAB Prachuap Khiri Khan	AU-23A	COIN

PLANS CN235s on order need confirming, the last of the COIN AU-23s will be replaced by ex-Luftwaffe Alpha Jets.

Serial	Type	c/n	Code	Unit	Notes
BJH2-01/15 21304	Fairchild AU-23A Peacemaker (J.2)	2050	72-1304	531 Sqn	
BJH2-04/15 21308	Fairchild AU-23A Peacemaker (J.2)	2054	72-1308	531 Sqn	
BJH2-05/15 21310	Fairchild AU-23A Peacemaker (J.2)	2056	72-1310	531 Sqn	
BJH2-09/15 21314	Fairchild AU-23A Peacemaker (J.2)	2060	72-1314		
BJH2-10/15 21315	Fairchild AU-23A Peacemaker (J.2)	2061	72-1315	531 Sqn	
BJH2-15/19 42074	Fairchild AU-23A Peacemaker (J.2)	2074	74-2074	531 Sqn	
BJH2-16/19 42075	Fairchild AU-23A Peacemaker (J.2)	2075	74-2075	531 Sqn	
BJH2-17/19 42076	Fairchild AU-23A Peacemaker (J.2)	2076	74-2076	531 Sqn	
BJH2-18/19 42077	Fairchild AU-23A Peacemaker (J.2)	2077	74-2077	531 Sqn	
BJH2-20/19 42079	Fairchild AU-23A Peacemaker (J.2)	2079	74-2079	531 Sqn	
BJH2-21/19 42080	Fairchild AU-23A Peacemaker (J.2)	2080	74-2080	531 Sqn	
BJH2-22/19 42081	Fairchild AU-23A Peacemaker (J.2)	2081	74-2081	531 Sqn	
BJH2-23/19 42082	Fairchild AU-23A Peacemaker (J.2)	2082	74-2082	531 Sqn	
BJH2-24/19 42083	Fairchild AU-23A Peacemaker (J.2)	2083	74-2083	531 Sqn	
BJH2-26/19 42085	Fairchild AU-23A Peacemaker (J.2)	2085	74-2085	531 Sqn	
BJH2-27/19 42086	Fairchild AU-23A Peacemaker (J.2)	2086	74-2086	531 Sqn	
BJH2-28/19 42087	Fairchild AU-23A Peacemaker (J.2)	2087	74-2087	531 Sqn	
BJH2-29/19 42088	Fairchild AU-23A Peacemaker (J.2)	2088	74-2088		
BJH2-31/19 42090	Fairchild AU-23A Peacemaker (J.2)	2090	74-2090	531 Sqn	
BJH2-34/20	Fairchild AU-23A Peacemaker (J.2)	2053	72-1307		
	Fairchild AU-23A Peacemaker (J.2)		73-1699		
BL2-07/90 46151	Basler BT-67 Turbo Dakota	19572	106 (RTAF)	602 Sqn	Cvtd C-47
BL2-16/00	Basler BT-67 Turbo Dakota	14229/25674	413 (RTAF)	602 Sqn	Cvtd C-47
BL2-23/01	Basler BT-67 Turbo Dakota	13824/25269	008 (RTAF)	602 Sqn	Cvtd C-47
BL2-31/07 46152	Basler BT-67 Turbo Dakota	17024/34288	021 (RTAF)	602 Sqn	Cvtd C-47
BL2-38/14 46153	Basler BT-67 Turbo Dakota	16886/34142	883 (RTAF)	602 Sqn	Cvtd C-47
BL2-42/18	Basler BT-67 Turbo Dakota	15070/26515	254 (RTAF)	602 Sqn	Cvtd C-47
BL5-1/14 11-111	Hawker Siddeley HS.748-208 srs 2 (L.5)	1570/set48	HS-TAF	603 Sqn	
BL5-2/16 99-999	Hawker Siddeley HS.748-208 srs 2A (L.5)	1715/set198	HS-TAF	603 Sqn	
BL5-3/?? 60303	Hawker Siddeley HS.748-208 srs 2 (L.5)	1569/set39	HS-THC	603 Sqn	
BL5-4/26 60304	Hawker Siddeley HS.748-208 srs 2 (L.5)	1644/set123	HS-THD	603 Sqn	
BL5-5/26 60305	Hawker Siddeley HS.748-208 srs 2 (L.5)	1646/set138	HS-THF	603 Sqn	
BL5-6/26 60306	Hawker Siddeley HS.748-208 srs 2 LFD (L.5)	1645/set135	HS-THE	603 Sqn	
BTL6-1/22 60501	Swearingen SA.226AT Merlin IVA (L.6) AT-071		N5650M	605 Sqn	

BTL6-2/22	60502	Swearingen SA.226AT Merlin IVA (L.6)	AT-072	N5496M	605 Sqn	
BTL6-3/22	60503	Swearingen SA.226AT Merlin IVA (L.6)	AT-073	N5672M	605 Sqn	
BTL7-1/22	60509	IAI Arava srs 201 (L.7)	0056	4X-ICC	605 Sqn	
BTL7-2/22	60510	IAI Arava srs 201 (L.7)	0057	4X-ICD	605 Sqn	
BTL7-3/22	60511	IAI Arava srs 201 (L.7)	0058	4X-ICE	605 Sqn	
BL8-1/2?	60101	Lockheed C-130H (L-382C-1E) Hercules (L.8)				
			4861	79-1714 (FMS)	601 Sqn	camo cs
BL8-2/2?	60102	Lockheed C-130H (L-382C-1E) Hercules (L.8)				
			4862	79-1715 (FMS)	601 Sqn	camo cs
BL8-3/23	60103	Lockheed C-130H (L-382C-1E) Hercules (L.8)				
			4863	79-1716 (FMS)	601 Sqn	camo cs
BL8-4/??	60104	Lockheed C-130H-30 (L-382T-38E) Hercules (L.8)				
			4959	82-0666 (FMS)	601 Sqn	camo cs
BL8-5/31	60105	Lockheed C-130H-30 (L-382T-93E) Hercules (L.8)				
			5146		601 Sqn	camo cs
BL8-6/31	60106	Lockheed C-130H-30 (L-382T-93E) Hercules (L.8)				
			5148		601 Sqn	camo cs
BL8-7/33	60107	Lockheed C-130H-30 (L-382T-17F) Hercules (L.8)				
			5208		601 Sqn	camo cs
BL8-8/33	60108	Lockheed C-130H (L-382C-15F) Hercules (L.8)				
			5209		601 Sqn	camo cs
BL8-9/35	60109	Lockheed C-130H (L-382C-37F) Hercules (L.8)				
			5272		601 Sqn	white/grey cs
BL8-10/35	60110	Lockheed C-130H (L-382C-37F) Hercules (L.8)				
			5274		601 Sqn	white/grey cs
BL8-11/3?	60111	Lockheed C-130H-30 (L-382T) Hercules (L.8)	5280		601 Sqn	white/grey cs
BL8-12/3?	60112	Lockheed C-130H-30 (L-382T) Hercules (L.8)	5281		601 Sqn	white/grey cs
BL9-5/25	46131	GAF N22B Nomad Missionmaster (L.9)	137	VH-UVI	461 Sqn	
BL9-7/25	46141	GAF N22B Nomad Missionmaster (L.9)	141	VH-UVK	461 Sqn	
BL9-8/26	46113	GAF N22B Nomad Missionmaster (L.9)	145	VH-UVM	461 Sqn	
BL9-15/26	46143	GAF N22B Nomad Missionmaster (L.9)	151	VH-UZP	461 Sqn	
BL9-16/26	46144	GAF N22B Nomad Missionmaster (L.9)	153	VH-UUS	461 Sqn	
BL9-19/27	46135	GAF N22B Nomad Missionmaster (L.9)	156	VH-UUV	461 Sqn	
BL9-21/30	46116	GAF N22B Nomad Missionmaster (L.9)	152	VH-XZA	461 Sqn	
BL9-22/30	46126	GAF N22B Nomad Missionmaster (L.9)	154	VH-XZB	461 Sqn	
BL9-?/??	46111	GAF N22B Nomad Missionmaster (L.9)	109	VH-UVD	461 Sqn	
BL9-?/??	46112	GAF N22B Nomad Missionmaster (L.9)	114	VH-UVA	461 Sqn	
BL9-?/??	46114	GAF N22B Nomad Missionmaster (L.9)	146	VH-UUF	461 Sqn	
BL9-?/??	46115	GAF N22B Nomad Missionmaster (L.9)	155	VH-UUT	461 Sqn	
BL9-?/??	46121	GAF N22B Nomad Missionmaster (L.9)	133	VH-UVE	461 Sqn	
BL9-?/??	46122	GAF N22B Nomad Missionmaster (L.9)	134	VH-UVG	461 Sqn	
BL9-?/??	46123	GAF N22B Nomad Missionmaster (L.9)	147	VH-UUI	461 Sqn	
BL9-?/??	46124	GAF N22B Nomad Missionmaster (L.9)	148	VH-UUK	461 Sqn	
BL9-?/??	46125	GAF N22B Nomad Missionmaster (L.9)	157	VH-UUX	461 Sqn	
BL9-?/??	46133	GAF N22B Nomad Missionmaster (L.9)	149	VH-UUN	461 Sqn	
BL9-?/??	46134	GAF N22B Nomad Missionmaster (L.9)	150	VH-UUO	461 Sqn	
BL9-?/??	46145	GAF N22B Nomad Missionmaster (L.9)	158	VH-UUZ	461 Sqn	
BL9-?/??	46232	GAF N22B Nomad Missionmaster (L.9)	138	VH-UVJ	461 Sqn	
BL9-?/??	46242	GAF N22B Nomad Missionmaster (L.9)	144	VH-UVL	461 Sqn	
BJL9-?/??	60506	GAF N22B Nomad Missionmaster (L.9)			605 Sqn	
BJL9-?/??	60507	GAF N22B Nomad Missionmaster (L.9)			605 Sqn	
BJL9-?/??	60508	GAF N22B Nomad Missionmaster (L.9)			605 Sqn	
BL11-1/??	22-222	Boeing 737-2Z6 (L.11)	23059 / 980	N45733	602 Sqn	
BTL12-1/??	60504	Learjet 35A (L.12)	35A-623	N7260Q	605 Sqn	Survey
BTL12-2/31	60505	Learjet 35A (L.12)	35A-635	N1471B	605 Sqn	Survey
BL13-1/34	44-444	Airbus Industrie A310-324 (L.13)	591	F-WWCH	602 Sqn	c/s HS-TYQ
BL14-1/38	60307	Alenia G-222 (L.14)	4107	I-RAIT?	603 Sqn	
BL14-2/38	60308	Alenia G-222 (L.14)	4108		603 Sqn	
BL14-3/38	60309	Alenia G-222 (L.14)	4109		603 Sqn	
BL14-4/39	60310	Alenia G-222 (L.14)	4110		603 Sqn	
BL14-5/39	60311	Alenia G-222 (L.14)	4111		603 Sqn	
BL14-6/39	60312	Alenia G-222 (L.14)	4112		603 Sqn	
		Airtech/IPTN CN235-220			602 Sqn	on order
		Airtech/IPTN CN235-220			602 Sqn	on order
		Airtech/IPTN CN235-220			602 Sqn	on order
		Airtech/IPTN CN235-220			602 Sqn	on order

Kongbin Tha Han Lur Thai
Royal Thai Navy Air Division - RTN

UNITS/BASES	1 Wing, U-Tapao AB		
	101 Sqn	Do228, S-2F	
	102 Sqn	F.27-200MPA, P-3T/VP-3T	MR
	103 Sqn	C337	

	2 Wing, U-Tapao AB				
	201 sqn		F.27-400M, CL-215, Nomad		SAR
1103	Grumman S-2F Tracker	339	Bu136430	101 Sqn	
1105	Grumman S-2F Tracker	381	Bu136472	101 Sqn	
1107	Grumman S-2F Tracker	597	Bu136688	101 Sqn	
1109	Dornier 228-212	8188	121 (RTN)	101 Sqn	
1110	Dornier 228-212	8189	122 (RTN)	101 Sqn	
1111	Dornier 228-212	8190	123 (RTN)	101 Sqn	
1112	Dornier 228-212	8226	D-CBDF	101 Sqn	
1113	Dornier 228-212	8227	D-CCCP	101 Sqn	
1114	Dornier 228-212	8228	D-CBDH	101 Sqn	
1201	Fokker F.27 Friendship 200MAR	10666	10666 (RTN)	102 Sqn	
1202	Fokker F.27 Friendship 200MAR	10663	10663 (RTN)	102 Sqn	
1203	Fokker F.27 Friendship 200MAR	10676	10676 (RTN)	102 Sqn	
1204	Lockheed P-3T (L-185) Orion	5112	1202 (RTN)	102 Sqn	Cvtd P-3A
1205	Lockheed P-3T (L-185) Orion	5113	1204 (RTN)	102 Sqn	Cvtd P-3A
1206	Lockheed VP-3T (L-185) Orion	5154	Bu152184 (USN)	102 Sqn	Cvtd P-3A
1310	Summit Sentry O2-337	33701924	327 (RTN)	103 Sqn	Cvtd Cessna 337H
1311	Summit Sentry O2-337	33701925	328 (RTN)	103 Sqn	Cvtd Cessna 337H
	Summit Sentry O2-337	33701926	329 (RTN)	103 Sqn	Cvtd Cessna 337H
1313	Summit Sentry O2-337	33701927	330 (RTN)	103 Sqn	Cvtd Cessna 337H
1314	Summit Sentry O2-337	33701951	331 (RTN)	103 Sqn	Cvtd Cessna 337H
1315	Summit Sentry O2-337			103 Sqn	Cvtd Cessna 337H
1316	Summit Sentry O2-337			103 Sqn	Cvtd Cessna 337H
1317	Summit Sentry O2-337		336 (RTN)	103 Sqn	Cvtd Cessna 337H
1318	Summit Sentry O2-337		337 (RTN)	103 Sqn	Cvtd Cessna 337H
1319	Summit Sentry O2-337	33701813	332 (RTN)	103 Sqn	Cvtd Cessna 337H
1320	Summit Sentry O2-337	33701833	333 (RTN)	103 Sqn	Cvtd Cessna 337H
2105	GAF N24A Nomad Searchmaster L	120	211 (RTN)	201 Sqn	
2107	GAF N24A Nomad Searchmaster L	123	213 (RTN)	201 Sqn	
2108	GAF N24A Nomad Searchmaster L	127	214 (RTN)	201 Sqn	
2109	GAF N24A Nomad Searchmaster L	129	215 (RTN)	201 Sqn	
2110	Fokker F.27 Troopship 400M	10650	2211 (RTN)	202 Sqn	
2111	Fokker F.27 Troopship 400M	10651	2212 (RTN)	202 Sqn	
2204	Canadair CL-215	1058	231 (RTN)	201 Sqn	
2205	Canadair CL-215	1059	232 (RTN)	201 Sqn	

Korbin Tha Han Bo
Royal Thai Army Air Division - RTAAD

UNITS/BASES   The Army Aviation Battalion is based at Kokkathium-Lop Buri but deploys as required.

PLANS   Up to 38 utility aircraft are required (Cessna Caravan, PC-6B, Islander or Caravan II shortlisted).

0169	Beech 1900C-1	UC-169	N8181E	
0170	Beech 1900C-1	UC-170	N8265K	
0342	Beech Super King Air 200	BB-342	N23794	Survey
348	Swearingen SA.226T Merlin	T-348	N1009G	
446	CASA 212-300 Aviocar	A83-1-446	EC-144	
447	CASA 212-300 Aviocar	A83-2-447		
1165	Beech Super King Air B200	BB-1165	N6922P	VIP
3102	Shorts 330-UTT	SH.3102	G-BLLL	
41060	British Aerospace Jetstream 41	41060	G-BWGW	VIP
41094	British Aerospace Jetstream 41	41094	G-BWTZ	VIP

Royal Thai Border Police - RTP

UNITS/BASES   Fixed Wing aircraft are based at Bangkok-Don Muang with 3 Division.

PLANS   Additional CN.235s are being considered, subject to funding.

1601	Pilatus/Fairchild PC-6/B2-H2 Turbo Porter	2030	
1604	Pilatus/Fairchild PC-6/B2-H2 Turbo Porter	2043	
1605	Pilatus/Fairchild PC-6/B2-H2 Turbo Porter	2063	
1606	Pilatus/Fairchild PC-6/B2-H2 Turbo Porter	2064	
1608	Pilatus/Fairchild PC-6/B2-H2 Turbo Porter	2066	
1613	Pilatus/Fairchild PC-6/B2-H2 Turbo Porter		
21897	Shorts SC.7 Skyvan srs 3M-400	SH.1897	G-AZKL
21902	Shorts SC.7 Skyvan srs 3M-400	SH.1902	G-AZSR
21919	Shorts SC.7 Skyvan srs 3M-400	SH.1919	G-BBFA
25099	Shorts 330-UTT	SH.3099	G-BLJB

25105	Shorts 330-UTT	SH.3105	G-BLRR
27228	Fokker 50	20228	PH-JXD
28053	Airtech/CASA CN235M-200	C053	EC-235

Royal Thai Survey Department - RTSD

UNITS/BASES   Aircraft are based at Bangkok-Don Muang.

00923	Beech King Air E90	LW-26	N1769W	RTSD	Std Don Muang
code 81491	Rockwell Commander 690A	11340	HS-TFA	RTSD	Survey
code 93303	Beech Super King Air B200	BB-1436	N1564M	RTSD	Survey
code 93304	Beech Super King Air B200	BB-1441	N56385	RTSD	Survey
code 93305	Beech Super King Air B200	BB-1443	N56379	RTSD	Survey

KASET
Royal Thai Agricultural Aviation Division

UNITS/BASES   Aircraft are based at Nakhon Sawan-Takhli and deployed as required.

PLANS   The Aviocars are to be replaced with Super King Airs, timescale not known.

501	UU110201	Britten-Norman BN-2 Islander	26	HS-SKB	
1112		Cessna U206G Turbo Stationair II	U206-04615	N9965M	
1113	UU111036	Cessna U206G Turbo Stationair II	U206-04618	N9968M	
1114	UU111037	Cessna U206G Turbo Stationair 6 II	U206-06414	N9348Z	
1311		Pilatus PC-6/B1-H2 Turbo Porter	753	HB-FGH	
1312		Pilatus PC-6/B1-H2 Turbo Porter	754	HB-FGL	
1314		Pilatus PC-6/B1-H2 Turbo Porter	768	HB-FGP	
1315		Pilatus PC-6/B1-H2 Turbo Porter	782	HB-FGS	
1316		Pilatus PC-6/B1-H2 Turbo Porter	783	HB-FGT	
1317		Pilatus PC-6/B1-H2 Turbo Porter	784	HB-FGR	
1511	UU110208	CASA/IPTN NC212 Aviocar srs 100	A4-8-85/N11	PK-XCJ	Std?
1512	UU110205	CASA/IPTN NC212 Aviocar srs 100	A4-9-86/N12	PK-XCK	
1513	UU110206	CASA/IPTN NC212 Aviocar srs 100	A4-22-148/N25	PK-XCX	
1514	UU110207	CASA/IPTN NC212 Aviocar srs 100	A4-24-157/N27	PK-XCZ	
1521	UU110204	CASA/IPTN NC212 Aviocar srs 100	CC4-3-211/N51	PK-XAY	
1531		CASA 212 Aviocar srs 300	AA72-1-395		
1532		CASA 212 Aviocar srs 300	AA72-2-396		
1533		CASA 212 Aviocar srs 300	AA73-1-444		
1534		CASA 212 Aviocar srs 300	AA73-2-451	EC-149	
1536		CASA 212 Aviocar srs 300	AA73-3-452	EC-147	
1537		CASA 212 Aviocar srs 300	AA73-4-453	EC-148	
1911		Cessna 208 Caravan 1	208-00204	N9788F	
1912		Cessna 208 Caravan 1	208-00205	N9789F	
1913		Cessna 208 Caravan 1	208-00206	N9790F	
1914		Cessna 208 Caravan 1	208-00263	N1229Q	
1915		Cessna 208 Caravan 1	208-00265	N1240T	
1916		Cessna 208 Caravan 1	208-00266	N1240Z	
1917		Cessna 208 Caravan 1	208-00267	N12408	
1918		Cessna 208 Caravan 1			
2011		Raytheon Beech Super King Air 350 (B300)	FL-146	N3268Z	
2012		Raytheon Beech Super King Air 350 (B300)	FL-147	N3269W	
2221		Airtech/IPTN CN235-220S	N041		Cloud seeder
2222		Airtech/IPTN CN235-220S	N042		Cloud seeder
		Airtech/IPTN CN235-220S			on order
		Airtech/IPTN CN235-220S			on order
		Airtech/IPTN CN235-220S			on order
		Airtech/IPTN CN235-220S			on order
		Airtech/IPTN CN235-220S			on order

The last Caravan is believed to be c/n 208-00268 ex N1241A

TOGO
République Togolaise   W Africa

Following independence from France in 1964, the former colonial power helped establish the Air Force in 1964. Support from France is still apparent in the form of training and maintenance and this is evident by its continued effective operation made financially possible by mining and food processing industries.

SERIAL SYSTEM   Civil style registrations are allocated in the 5V-M** block.

Force Aérienne Togolaise
Togolese Air Force

UNITS/BASES   The transport types are based at Lome-Tokoin Airport.

5V-MAD	Cessna 337D Super Skymaster	33701128	N86244	
5V-MAE	Reims F337E Super Skymaster	F33700016/ 01283		
5V-MAG	DeHavilland Canada DHC-5D Buffalo	62		Sold?
5V-MAI	Dornier 27A-5	433	57+07 (WGAF)	
5V-MCG	Beech Super King Air 200	BB-857	YV-423CP	
5V-MCH	Beech Super King Air 200	BB-858	C-GCMU	

Government of the Togolese Republic

5V-TAI	Fokker F.28 Fellowship 1000	11079	5V-MAB	Opf Air Togo
5V-TGE	Boeing 707-3L6B	21049 / 896	P4-TBN	

TONGA
Pule'anga Tonga   S Pacific

This Polynesian Kingdom, formerly the Friendly Islands, became independent in 1970 and established a Defence Service in 1986. The Beech 18 operates patrol and SAR services around the 158 coral and volcanic islands. The serial allocation speaks for itself.

Tonga Defence Services - Air Wing

UNITS/BASES   Operates from Fua'amotu Airport.

AW-C1	Beech G18S	BA-483	N9644R	MR

TRINIDAD & TOBAGO
W Indies

Independent from Britain since 1962 and a joint Republic since 1976, Trinidad and Tobago formed their Defence Force Air Wing in 1977. Tasked mainly with patrol, recent US acquisitions are presumably to enable counter drug operations given the islands' proximity to the South American coast.

SERIAL SYSTEM   Serials appear sequential in the 2** series, but little is known as yet of the most recent additions.

Trinidad & Tobago Defence Force - TTDF

UNITS/BASES   All Air Wing aircraft are based at Port of Spain-Piarco International Airport.

201	Cessna 401B	TTDF-1	
	Cessna 310R		
204	Piper PA-31-350 Navajo Chieftain		Colemill Panther II conv?
	Piper PA-31-350 Navajo Chieftain		
	Fairchild C-26B Metro (SA.227AC)	ex USAF	
	Fairchild C-26B Metro (SA.227AC)	ex USAF	

TUNISIA
al-Jumhouriya at-Tunisiyah   N Africa

Independent from France since 1954, Tunisia has kept a low profile compared with the other North African countries despite their efforts to involve it in Middle Eastern crises, the Israeli bombing of the PLO's former HQ near Tunis coming closest to. US assistance in a modernisation programme should be noted, with other acquisitions from Europe.

SERIAL SYSTEM   The transport types' serials all begin with the letter Z (combat types Y etc), followed by a two digit numerical type designator and then a sequential three digit number. Most types also wear civil style registrations as call signs.

al-Quwwat al Jawwiya al Jamahiriyah at'Tunisia
Tunisian Republican Air Force

UNITS/BASES   21 Sqn, Bizerte-Sidi Ahmed   C-130H/B, L-410

PLANS   Three more ex AMI G222TCMs are expected.

Z21011 / TS-MTA	Lockheed C-130H (L-382C-65E) Hercules	5020	N4249Y	21 Sqn
Z21012 / TS-MTB	Lockheed C-130H (L-382C-65E) Hercules	5021	N4103D	21 Sqn
Z21113 / TS-MTC	Lockheed C-130B (L-282-1B) Hercules	3625	61-0949 (USAF)	21 Sqn
Z21114 / TS-MTD	Lockheed C-130B (L-282-1B) Hercules	3586	59-1533 (USAF)	21 Sqn
Z21115 / TS-MTE	Lockheed C-130B (L-282-1B) Hercules	3550	58-0751 (USAF)	21 Sqn
Z21116 / TS-MTF	Lockheed C-130B (L-282-1B) Hercules	3523	58-0728 (USAF)	21 Sqn
Z21117 / TS-MTG	Lockheed C-130B (L-282-1B) Hercules	3571	59-1528 (USAF)	21 Sqn
Z21118 / TS-MTH	Lockheed C-130B (L-282-1B) Hercules	3721	62-3495 (USAF)	21 Sqn
Z21119 / TS-MTI	Lockheed C-130B (L-282-1B) Hercules	3603	60-0299 (USAF)	21 Sqn
	Lockheed C-130B (L-282-1B) Hercules	3510	58-0715 (USAF)	21 Sqn
Z94041 / TS-OTA	Let 410UVP-E20G	942705	OK-ZDF	21 Sqn
Z94042 / TS-OTC	Let 410UVP-E20G	942706	OK-ZDA	21 Sqn
Z94043 / TS-OTE	Let 410UVP-E20G	942707	OK-ZDB	21 Sqn
TS-OTG	Let 410UVP-E20G	922708	OK-AND	21 Sqn
TS-OTI	Let 410UVP-E20G	922709	OK-BDH	21 Sqn
	Aeritalia G-222TCM	4020	MM62115 (AMI)	
	Aeritalia G-222TCM	4046	MM62133 (AMI)	

Government of the Republic of Tunisia

| TS-IOO | Boeing BBJ (737-7H3) | 29149 / 348 | N5573L | VIP |

TURKEY
Türkiye Cumhuriyeti   SE Europe

Turkey sits between Europe and Asia and represented an important strategic point for NATO (joining in 1952) during the 'cold war' period. Reconciliation with their traditional enemies in Greece is being pursued and participation in joint NATO exercises has taken place, rejected membership of the EU however may set this process back. A developing manufacturing capability is being built around TAI (TUSAS Aerospace Industries).

SERIAL SYSTEM No universal system is in use, usually the serial is derived from the c/n or previous identity.

Türk Hava Kuvvetleri - THK
Turkish Air Force

UNITS/BASES	1ci Taktik Hava Kuvveti		
	HQ Flight, Eskisehir	CN235	
	2ci Taktik Hava Kuvveti		
	HQ Flight, Diyarbakir	CN235	
	Hava Ulastirma Komutanligi		
	12 Ana Us, 221 Filo 'Esen', Erkilet-Kayseri	C-160	
	12 Ana Us, 222 Filo 'Alev', Erkilet-Kayseri	C-130	
	12 Ana Us, 223 Filo 'Gezgin', Ankara-Etimesgut	CN235	
	12 Ana Us, 224 Ozel Filo 'Dogan', Ankara-Etimesgut	CN235, Citation	Calibration, VIP
	12 Ana Us, Tanker Filo, Incirlik	KC-135R	AAR
	Hava Okullari Komutanligi		
	HQ Flight, Gaziemir		
	BLTS, Izmir-Cigli		
	Hava Harp Okulu, Flying Unit, Istanbul-Yesilköy	CN235	

PLANS — Six AEW&C 737s have been selected (another one on option) for delivery from 2005 but the program has recently been reported as delayed.
The KC-135Rs are being modified on the PACER CRAG programme to match the USAF standard.
20 Airbus A400Ms are to be ordered and seven C-130Es to be upgraded, interest in ex RAAF C-130Es is also reported.

051	Airtech/CASA/TAI CN235M-100	C051		Medevac
052	Airtech/CASA/TAI CN235M-100	C052		Medevac
055	Airtech/CASA/TAI CN235M-100	C055		
056	Airtech/CASA/TAI CN235M-100	C056		
057	Airtech/CASA/TAI CN235M-100	C057		
058	Airtech/CASA/TAI CN235M-100	C058		
061	Airtech/CASA/TAI CN235M-100	C061		
064	Airtech/CASA/TAI CN235M-100	C064	224 Filo	VIP
067	Airtech/CASA/TAI CN235M-100	C067	224 Filo	VIP
068	Airtech/CASA/TAI CN235M-100	C068		VIP
069	Airtech/CASA/TAI CN235M-100	C069/TK201		VIP
073	Airtech/CASA/TAI CN235M-100	C073/TK202		VIP
077	Airtech/CASA/TAI CN235M-100	C077/TK203		VIP
080	Airtech/CASA/TAI CN235M-100	C080/TK108		
083	Airtech/CASA/TAI CN235M-100	C083/TK109		

086	Airtech/CASA/TAI CN235M-100	C086/TK-110			
089	Airtech/CASA/TAI CN235M-100	C089/TK111			
091	Airtech/CASA/TAI CN235M-100	C091/TK112			
093	Airtech/CASA/TAI CN235M-100	C093			
095	Airtech/CASA/TAI CN235M-100	C095			
099	Airtech/CASA/TAI CN235M-100	C099			
101	Airtech/CASA/TAI CN235M-100	C101			
103	Airtech/CASA/TAI CN235M-100	C103/TK118			
104	Airtech/CASA/TAI CN235M-100	C104/TK119			
106	Airtech/CASA/TAI CN235M-100	C106/TK120			
108	Airtech/CASA/TAI CN235M-100	C108/TK121			
110	Airtech/CASA/TAI CN235M-100	C110/TK122			
112	Airtech/CASA/TAI CN235M-100	C112/TK123			
113	Airtech/CASA/TAI CN235M-100	C113			
117	Airtech/CASA/TAI CN235M-100	C117/TK124			
119	Airtech/CASA/TAI CN235M-100	C119			
122	Airtech/CASA/TAI CN235M-100	C122			
124	Airtech/CASA/TAI CN235M-100	C124			
125	Airtech/CASA/TAI CN235M-100	C125			
126	Airtech/CASA/TAI CN235M-100	C126			
127	Airtech/CASA/TAI CN235M-100	C127			
131	Airtech/CASA/TAI CN235M-100	C131			
132	Airtech/CASA/TAI CN235M-100	C132			
133	Airtech/CASA/TAI CN235M-100	C133			
134	Airtech/CASA/TAI CN235M-100	C134			
136	Airtech/CASA/TAI CN235M-100	C136			
138	Airtech/CASA/TAI CN235M-100	C137			
140 / 95-140	Airtech/CASA/TAI CN235M-100	C140			Medevac
142	Airtech/CASA/TAI CN235M-100	C142			
144	Airtech/CASA/TAI CN235M-100	C144			
146	Airtech/CASA/TAI CN235M-100	C146			
148	Airtech/CASA/TAI CN235M-100	C148			
149	Airtech/CASA/TAI CN235M-100	C149			
4005	Beech Super King Air B200	BB-1434	N81148		
4006	Beech Super King Air B200	BB-1375	M-1375		
10010	Beech Super King Air B200	BB-1409			
10012	Beech Super King Air B200	BB-1413			
10013	Beech Super King Air B200	BB-1414			
10014	Beech Super King Air B200	BB-1415			
00325	Boeing KC-135R Stratotanker	18100 / T0439	60-0325 (USAF)		Cvtd KC-135A
00326	Boeing KC-135R Stratotanker	18101 / T0440	60-0326 (USAF)		Cvtd KC-135A
23512	Boeing KC-135R Stratotanker	18495 / T0563	62-3512 (USAF)		Cvtd KC-135A
23539	Boeing KC-135R Stratotanker	18522 / T0590	62-3539 (USAF)		Cvtd KC-135A
23563	Boeing KC-135R Stratotanker	18546 / T0614	62-3563 (USAF)		Cvtd KC-135A
23567	Boeing KC-135R Stratotanker	18550 / T0618	62-3567 (USAF)		Cvtd KC-135A
23568	Boeing KC-135R Stratotanker	18551 / T0619	62-3568 (USAF)		Cvtd KC-135A
72609	Boeing KC-135R Stratotanker	17745 / T0215	57-2609 (USAF)		Cvtd KC-135A
80110	Boeing KC-135R Stratotanker	17855 / T0325	58-0110 (USAF)		Cvtd KC-135A
12-001	Cessna 550 Citation II	550-0502/502	N1255D	224 Filo	
12-002	Cessna 550 Citation II	550-0503/503	N1255G	224 Filo	
93-702 / ETI-024	Cessna 670 Citation VII	670-7024	N1262Z	224 Filo	Re-coded 004 ?
93-702 / ETI-026	Cessna 670 Citation VII	670-7026	N1263G	224 Filo	Re-coded 005 ?
12-003	GAC Gulfstream IV	1163	N458GA	224 Filo	
00991 / 12-991	Lockheed C-130E (L-382C-15D) Hercules	4524	73-0991 (FMS)	222 Filo	
01468 / 12-468	Lockheed C-130E (L-382C-15D) Hercules	4514	71-1468 (FMS)	222 Filo	
01947 / 12-947	Lockheed C-130E (L-382C-15D) Hercules	4427	70-1947 (FMS)	222 Filo	
10960	Lockheed C-130B (L-282-1B) Hercules	3643	61-0960 (USAF)	222 Filo	
10963	Lockheed C-130B (L-282-1B) Hercules	3648	61-0963 (USAF)	222 Filo	
12643	Lockheed C-130B (L-282-1B) Hercules	3670	61-2643 (USAF)	222 Filo	
13186 / 12-186	Lockheed C-130E (L-382-13B) Hercules	4011	63-13186 (FMS)	222 Filo	
13187 / 12-187	Lockheed C-130E (L-382-13B) Hercules	4012	63-13187 (FMS)	222 Filo	Turkish Stars c/s
13188 / 12-188	Lockheed C-130E (L-382-13B) Hercules	4015	63-13188 (FMS)	222 Filo	
13189 / 12-189	Lockheed C-130E (L-382-13B) Hercules	4016	63-13189 (FMS)	222 Filo	
23496	Lockheed C-130E (L-382-1B) Hercules	3722	62-3496 (USAF)	222 Filo	
70527	Lockheed C-130B (L-282-1B) Hercules	3503	57-0527 (USAF)	222 Filo	
80736	Lockheed C-130B (L-282-1B) Hercules	3532	58-0736 (USAF)	222 Filo	
019 / 12-019	Transall/VFW C-160D	D019	50+11 (WGAF)	221 Filo	
020 / 12-020	Transall/MBB C-160D	D020	50+12 (WGAF)	221 Filo	
021 / 12-021	Transall/Nord C-160D	D021	50+13 (WGAF)	221 Filo	
022 / 12-022	Transall/VFW C-160D	D022	50+14 (WGAF)	221 Filo	
023 / 12-023	Transall/MBB C-160D	D023	50+15 (WGAF)	221 Filo	
024 / 12-024	Transall/Nord C-160D	D024	50+16 (WGAF)	221 Filo	
025 / 12-025	Transall/VFW C-160D	D025	50+17 (WGAF)	221 Filo	
026 / 12-026	Transall/MBB C-160D	D026	50+18 (WGAF)	221 Filo	

027 / 12-027	Transall/Nord C-160D	D027	50+19 (WGAF)	221 Filo
028 / 12-028	Transall/VFW C-160D	D028	50+20 (WGAF)	221 Filo
029 / 12-029	Transall/MBB C-160D	D029	50+21 (WGAF)	221 Filo
031 / 12-031	Transall/VFW C-160D	D031	50+23 (WGAF)	221 Filo
032 / 12-032	Transall/MBB C-160D	D032	50+24 (WGAF)	221 Filo
033 / 12-033	Transall/Nord C-160D	D033	50+25 (WGAF)	221 Filo
034 / 12-034	Transall/VFW C-160D	D034	50+26 (WGAF)	221 Filo
035 / 12-035	Transall/MBB C-160D	D035	50+27 (WGAF)	221 Filo
036 / 12-036	Transall/Nord C-160D	D036	50+28 (WGAF)	221 Filo
037 / 12-037	Transall/VFW C-160D	D037	50+29 (WGAF)	221 Filo
038 / 12-038	Transall/MBB C-160D	D038	50+30 (WGAF)	221 Filo
039 / 12-039	Transall/VFW C-160D	D039	50+31 (WGAF)	221 Filo
040 / 12-040	Transall/MBB C-160D	D040	50+32 (WGAF)	221 Filo

Türk Donanma Havaciligi - TDH
Turkish Naval Aviation

UNITS/BASES	Türk Cumhuriyet Bahriye Havaciligi	
	301 Deniz Hava Filosu, NAS Topel	CN235

PLANS	A further 10 CN235MPA-300 are on option for an Integrated Maritime Surveillance System project termed Long Horizon.

Airtech/CASA/TAI CN.235MPA-300	on order
Airtech/CASA/TAI CN.235MPA-300	on order
Airtech/CASA/TAI CN.235MPA-300	on order
Airtech/CASA/TAI CN.235MPA-300	on order
Airtech/CASA/TAI CN.235MPA-300	on order
Airtech/CASA/TAI CN.235MPA-300	on order

Türk Kara Kuvvetleri - TKK
Turkish Land Forces

UNITS/BASES	Türk Kara Ucak Komutanligi	
	Kara Havacilik Okulu, Güvernçinlik	T-42, Do28D, Super King Air, C421B/C

PLANS	Two CN235s to be acquired as replacements for the ELINT Do28s.

0884	Cessna U206B Super Skywagon	U206-0884		
0885	Cessna U206B Super Skywagon	U206-0885		
0886	Cessna U206B Super Skywagon	U206-0886		
0887	Cessna U206B Super Skywagon	U206-0887		
1129	Cessna U206C Super Skywagon	U206-1129		
1130	Cessna U206C Super Skywagon	U206-1130		
1155	Cessna U206C Super Skywagon	U206-1155		
1191	Cessna U206C Super Skywagon	U206-1191		
10025	Cessna 421B Golden Eagle	421B0882	N5423J	
10026	Cessna 421B Golden Eagle	421B0896	N5437J	
10027	Cessna 421B Golden Eagle	421B0902	N5444J	
10032	Cessna 421B Golden Eagle			
10035	Cessna 421B Golden Eagle			
10037	Cessna 421B Golden Eagle			
10291	Dornier 27B-1	226	55+79 (WGAF)	
10292	Dornier 27B-1	248	55+90 (WGAF)	
10293	Dornier 27H-2	2141	D-EFCI	
10017	Dornier 28D-2 Skyservant		(WGAF)	
10018	Dornier 28D-2 Skyservant		(WGAF)	
10019	Dornier 28D-2 Skyservant		(WGAF)	
10021	Dornier 28D-1 Skyservant	4022	D-IBBB	
10023	Dornier 28D-2 Skyservant		(WGAF)	
10027	Dornier 28D-2 Skyservant		(WGAF)	
10028	Dornier 28D-2 Skyservant	4307		
10030	Dornier 28D-2 Skyservant		(WGAF)	
10040	Dornier 28D-2 Skyservant		(WGAF)	
10041	Dornier 28D-2 Skyservant		(WGAF)	
10070	Dornier 28D-2 Skyservant		(WGAF)	
10071	Dornier 28D-2 Skyservant		(WGAF)	SIGINT

(Unidentified Dornier 28Ds from West German Air Force stocks included c/ns 4085, 4088, 4091, 4096, 4115, 4118, 4126, 4132, 4139, 4150, 4168, 4171, 4172 and 4181)

Türk Cumhuriyet Sahil Güvenlik - TCSG
Turkish Coast Guard

UNITS/BASES	NAS Topel		CN235		
551	Airtech/CASA/TAI CN235MSA-300				
553	Airtech/CASA/TAI CN235MSA-300				
	Airtech/CASA/TAI CN235MSA-300				on order

Government of the Republic of Turkey

TC-ATA	GAC Gulfstream IV	1043	TC-ANA	Office of the PM
TC-GAP / 001	GAC Gulfstream IV	1027	N1761B	

TURKMENISTAN
Turkmenostan Respublikasy   C Asia

Despite having a petroleum industry Turkmenistan has been hard pressed financially since the mid 1990s. A large number of aircraft were left behind when the Russian Forces left following independence in 1991 but little is probably now serviceable and attempts have been made to trade what they have.

SERIAL SYSTEM The few military aircraft retain Soviet style two digit tactical codes while the Government aircraft are civil registered.

Voyenno-Vozdushnyye Sily - VVS
(Turkmenistan) Air Force

UNITS-BASES	Aircraft based at Ashkhabad.	
01 yellow	Antonov/PZL-Mielec An-2T	1G108-01
	Antonov An-12	
	Antonov An-12	
	Antonov An-12	
	Antonov An-24	

Government of the Republic of Turkmenistan

EZ-A001	Boeing 737-341	26855 / 2305	EK-A001
EZ-A010	Boeing 757-23A	25345 / 412	N58AW
EZ-B021	British Aerospace 125-1000B	259029	G-5-751

UGANDA
Jamhouriya Uganda   E Africa

A former British colony independent in 1962, Uganda has suffered dictatorship and three successful coups between 1971 and 1985, together with the effects of instability of neighbours in the Congo and Ruanda. Serviceabilty in the Air Force has suffered greatly, despite offers and token support from several countries, and no fixed wing transports are currently operated. The Government owned VIP aircraft is based at Entebbe Airport in civil marks.

Government of the Republic of Uganda

5X-UEF	GAC Gulfstream IVSP	1413	N413GA

UKRAINE
Ukrainia   E Europe

Ukraine gained a large quantity of Soviet equipment with the formation of the CIS. Some of it has been traded back to Russia but the Air Force is still the second largest in the CIS, having been officially formed in March 1992.

SERIAL SYSTEM Markings are either displayed as the former Soviet civil registration with or without the civil UR- prefix or as a Soviet style two digit tactical code. Recently Western style all letter UR- registrations have begun to be allocated to the commercially operated Il-76s.

Zbroyni Sily Ukrainy - Viys'Kovo Povitryani Syly
Ukrainian Armed Forces - Air Force

ICAO code UTF

UNITS/BASES	Kiev-Borispol, 1 OTAP, 10 OAE		Tu-134, Il-76, An-30, An-26, An-24, An-12
	Kiev-Zhulyany, 223 OTAE		An-24, An-26
	Krivoy Rog, 16 AvB		Il-76
	Melitpol, 25 VTAP		Il-76, An-12 (red codes)
	Nezhin, 18 ODRAE		An-24 (support to Tu-22)
	Nikolayev, 316 OPLAE		Be-12, Tu-134UBK
	Lvov-Snilow, 243 OSAP		An-12, An-26, An-24
	Odessa-Tsentralny, 2 OSAP		An-12, An-26
	Priluki, 184 TBAP		Tu-134UBL
	Uzin, 409 APSZ		Il-78
	Vinnitsa, 456 OSAP		An-12, An-26, An-24, Il-22
	Zaparozhye, 338 VTAP		Il-76

The Il-76 fleet, second only in size to Russia's, is for the most part leased to commercial operators, recent details being reflected below. The operators are listed by ICAO code as follows:
ASG (Ukraine Airservice Airlines), ATG (Atlant SV Aviation), AZV (Azov Avia), BEK (Belbek), BSL (BSL Airline), BUA (Busol Air Company), HOS (Hoseba), KHO (Khors Air), LON (Avilond), OTL (South Airlines) RKS (Lana Air Company), TII (ATI Airlines), UKC (Air Ukraine Cargo), UKS (Ukraine Cargo Airways), UKW (Lvov Airlines), UMK (Yuzhmashavia), VPB (Veteran Airlines), VRE (Volare Aviation Enterprise).

PLANS   65 Antonov An-70 to be procured from Aviant by 2018, the first five were confirmed ordered in April 2001.

UR-11314	Antonov An-12BK	8345604	87		
UR-11315	Antonov An-12				
UR-11352	Antonov An-12BP				Radar fairings
UR-13332	Antonov An-12BP				
63957	Tupolev Tu-135 (Tu-134A-3)	63957	01 yellow	1 OTAP	
63982	Tupolev Tu-135 (Tu-134A-3)	63982	03 yellow		
UR-71488	Antonov An-26				
UR-71815	Antonov An-26				
UR-72959	Antonov An-72		CCCP-72959		
UR-72984	Antonov An-72				
UR-75896	Ilyushin Il-22-36 Zebra	0393607150	75896 (Uk AF)		Cvtd Il-18
75918	Ilyushin Il-22M-40 Bison		CCCP-75918	456 OSAP	
UR-76316	Ilyushin Il-76MD	0043454633	CCCP-76606	16AvB	Lst RKS
UR-76317	Ilyushin Il-76MD	0053458733	CCCP-76627	25 VTAP	Lst ATG
UR-76318	Ilyushin Il-76MD	0023438127	CCCP-86918	16 AvB	Lst ATG
UR-76319	Ilyushin Il-76MD	0023438129	CCCP-86919	16 AvB	Lst ATG
UR-76321	Ilyushin Il-76MD	0053457713	CCCP-76625	25 VTAP	Lst ATG
UR-76322	Ilyushin Il-76MD	0053462873	CCCP-76652	25 VTAP	Lst ATG
UR-76323	Ilyushin Il-76MD	0063466988	CCCP-76673	25 VTAP	
UR-76390	Ilyushin Il-76MD	0043453562	CCCP-76593	25 VTAP	Lst ATG
UR-76391	Ilyushin Il-76MD	0043453568	CCCP-76391	25 VTAP	Lst ATG
UR-76392	Ilyushin Il-76MD	0043454602	CCCP-76600	25 VTAP	Lst ATG
UR-76393	Ilyushin Il-76MD	0043455653	CCCP-76393	25 VTAP	Lst ATG
UR-76394	Ilyushin Il-76MD	0063466989	CCCP-76674	25 VTAP	Lst ATG
UR-76395	Ilyushin Il-76MD	0033443255	CCCP-76543	338 VTAP	Lst KHO
UR-76396	Ilyushin Il-76MD	0043451508	CCCP-76586	338 VTAP	Lst KHO
UR-76408	Ilyushin Il-76MD	0053460820	CCCP-76642	25 VTAP	Lst ASG
76413	Ilyushin Il-76MD	1013407215	UR-76413	409 APSZ	
UR-76415	Ilyushin Il-76MD	0083481440	CCCP-76715		
UR-76423	Ilyushin Il-76MD	0053457720	RA-76423	25 VTAP	Lst ATG
UR-76433	Ilyushin Il-76MD	0053460827	CCCP-76644	25 VTAP	Lst ATG
UR-76443	Ilyushin Il-76MD	0043452534	CCCP-76443	25 VTAP	Lst ATG
76520	Ilyushin Il-76T	093420605	RA-76520		Std Tashkent
76531	Ilyushin Il-76MD	0023441181	CCCP-76531	338 VTAP	
UR-76532	Ilyushin Il-76MD	0023441201	CCCP-76532	338 VTAP	Lst HOS
UR-76534	Ilyushin Il-76MD	0023442210	CCCP-76534	338 VTAP	Lst HOS
UR-76535	Ilyushin Il-76MD	0023442213	CCCP-76535	338 VTAP	Lst HOS
UR-76537	Ilyushin Il-76MD	0023442225	CCCP-76537	338 VTAP	
UR-76541	Ilyushin Il-76MD	0033442241	CCCP-76541	338 VTAP	
UR-76555	Ilyushin Il-76MD	0033446325	CCCP-76555	16 AvB	Lst UKC
76557	Ilyushin Il-76MD	0033446329	CCCP-76557	16 AvB	
76559	Ilyushin Il-76MD	0033446340	CCCP-76559	16 AvB	
UR-76560	Ilyushin Il-76MD	0033446341	CCCP-76560	16 AvB	
UR-76561	Ilyushin Il-76MD	0033447364	CCCP-76561	16 AvB	Lst UKC
76562	Ilyushin Il-76MD	0033447365	CCCP-76562	16 AvB	
UR-76563	Ilyushin Il-76MD	0033447372	CCCP-76563	16 AvB	Lst UKC
76564	Ilyushin Il-76MD	0033448373	CCCP-76564	16 AvB	
76565	Ilyushin Il-76MD	0033448382	CCCP-76565	16 AvB	
76566	Ilyushin Il-76MD	0033448385	CCCP-76566	16 AvB	
76567	Ilyushin Il-76MD	0033448390	CCCP-76567	16 AvB	
UR-76568	Ilyushin Il-76MD	0033448420	CCCP-76568		
UR-76570	Ilyushin Il-76MD	0033448427	CCCP-76570		

UR-76571	Ilyushin Il-76MD	0033448429	CCCP-76571		Lst BEK
UR-76573	Ilyushin Il-76MD	0033449437	CCCP-76573		
UR-76574	Ilyushin Il-76MD	0033449441	CCCP-76574	16 AvB	Lst RKS
UR-76576	Ilyushin Il-76MD	0043449449	CCCP-76576	16 AvB	
UR-76578	Ilyushin Il-76MD	0043449468	CCCP-76578		Lst ATG
UR-76579	Ilyushin Il-76MD	0043449471	CCCP-76579		
UR-76580	Ilyushin Il-76MD	0043450476	CCCP-76580		Lst BEK
UR-76581	Ilyushin Il-76MD	0043450484	CCCP-76581		
UR-76582	Ilyushin Il-76MD	0043450487	CCCP-76582		Lst Centre
UR-76583	Ilyushin Il-76MD	0043450491	CCCP-76583		Lst ATG
UR-76584	Ilyushin Il-76MD	0043450493	CCCP-76584	16 AvB	Lst TII
76585	Ilyushin Il-76MD	0043451503	CCCP-76585		Aeroflot cs
UR-76590	Ilyushin Il-76MD	0043452544	CCCP-76590	16 AvB	Aeroflot cs
UR-76595	Ilyushin Il-76MD	0043453571	CCCP-76595	25 VTAP	Lst ATG
76596	Ilyushin Il-76MD	0043453583	CCCP-76596	25 VTAP	Aeroflot cs
76597	Ilyushin Il-76MD	0043453585	CCCP-76597	25 VTAP	
76598	Ilyushin Il-76MD	0043453591	CCCP-76598	25 VTAP	
UR-76601	Ilyushin Il-76MD	0043454606	CCCP-76601	16 AvB	Lst Centre
UR-76603	Ilyushin Il-76MD	0043454623	CCCP-76603	25 VTAP	Lst ASG
76609	Ilyushin Il-76MD	0043453597	UR-76609	409 APSZ	Lst BUA, cvtd Il-78
UR-76610	Ilyushin Il-76MD	0043454640	CCCP-76610	409 APSZ	Lst BSL, cvtd Il-78
UR-76614	Ilyushin Il-76MD	0043455665	CCCP-76614	25 VTAP	Aeroflot cs
UR-76618	Ilyushin Il-76MD	0043455682	CCCP-76618	16 AvB	Lst RKS
UR-76622	Ilyushin Il-76MD	0053457702	CCCP-76622	25 VTAP	Lst ASG
UR-76624	Ilyushin Il-76MD	0053457710	CCCP-76624	25 VTAP	
UR-76628	Ilyushin Il-76MD	0053458741	CCCP-76628	16 AvB	Lst VRE
UR-76629	Ilyushin Il-76MD	0053458745	CCCP-76629	16 AvB	Lst TII
UR-76631	Ilyushin Il-76MD	0053458756	CCCP-76631	25 VTAP	Lst ATG
UR-76633	Ilyushin Il-76MD	0053459764	76633 (Uk AF)	25 VTAP	Lst ASG
UR-76636	Ilyushin Il-76MD	0053459781	CCCP-76636		Lst VRE
UR-76637	Ilyushin Il-76MD	0053460797	CCCP-76637	25 VTAP	Lst ATG
76645	Ilyushin Il-76MD	0053461834	CCCP-76645	25 VTAP	
UR-76646	Ilyushin Il-78	0053461837	CCCP-76646	409 APSZ	Aeroflot cs
UR-76647	Ilyushin Il-76MD	0053461843	CCCP-76647		
UR-76651	Ilyushin Il-76MD	0053462872	CCCP-76651	25 VTAP	Lst KHO
76653	Ilyushin Il-78	0053462879	CCCP-76653	409 APSZ	AAR
UR-76654	Ilyushin Il-76MD	0053462884	CCCP-76654		Lst LON
UR-76655	Ilyushin Il-76MD	0053463885	CCCP-76655	25 VTAP	
UR-76656	Ilyushin Il-76MD	0053463891	CCCP-76656	25 VTAP	Lst AZV
76657	Ilyushin Il-76MD	0053463896	CCCP-76657	25 VTAP	Aeroflot cs
UR-76658	Ilyushin Il-76MD	0053463902	CCCP-76658	25 VTAP	Lst ASG
76660	Ilyushin Il-76MD	0053463910	CCCP-76660	25 VTAP	
76661	Ilyushin Il-76MD	0053463913	CCCP-76661	25 VTAP	
UR-76662	Ilyushin Il-76MD	0053464919	CCCP-76662	409 APSZ	Lst BSL, cvtd Il-78
UR-76663	Ilyushin Il-76MD	0053464922	CCCP-76663	25 VTAP	
UR-76664	Ilyushin Il-76MD	0053464926	CCCP-76664	25 VTAP	Lst KHO
UR-76667	Ilyushin Il-76MD	0053465941	CCCP-76667		
UR-76670	Ilyushin Il-76MD	0063465958	CCCP-76670	409 APSZ	Lst BSL, cvtd Il-78
UR-76671	Ilyushin Il-76MD	0063465963	CCCP-76671		
76675	Ilyushin Il-78	0063466998	CCCP-76675	409 APSZ	AAR
UR-76677	Ilyushin Il-76MD	0063467005	4K-76677	25 VTAP	Lst ASG
UR-76680	Ilyushin Il-76MD	0063467020	CCCP-76680		Lst BUA
UR-76681	Ilyushin Il-76MD	0063467021	CCCP-76681		Std Kiev-Borispol?
UR-76682	Ilyushin Il-76MD	0063467027	CCCP-76682	409 APSZ	Lst BUA, cvtd Il-78
UR-76683	Ilyushin Il-76MD	0063468029	CCCP-76683		
UR-76684	Ilyushin Il-76MD	0063468036	CCCP-76684		Lst ATG
UR-76687	Ilyushin Il-76MD	0063469051	CCCP-76687		Lst VRE
UR-76688	Ilyushin Il-76MD	0063469062	CCCP-76688		Std Kiev-Borispol?
UR-76689	Ilyushin Il-76MD	0063469066	CCCP-76689		Lst BSL, cvtd Il-78
UR-76690	Ilyushin Il-76MD	0063469080	CCCP-76690		Lst BSL, cvtd Il-78
UR-76694	Ilyushin Il-76MD	0063470107	CCCP-76694		
UR-76697	Ilyushin Il-76MD	0063470118	CCCP-76697	16 AvB	
UR-76698	Ilyushin Il-76MD	0063471123	CCCP-76698		
UR-76700	Ilyushin Il-76MD	0063471134	CCCP-76700		Lst TII
76703	Ilyushin Il-76MD	0063471147	CCCP-76703	25 VTAP	Aeroflot cs
UR-76704	Ilyushin Il-76MD	0063471150	CCCP-76704		Lst VRE
UR-76705	Ilyushin Il-76MD	0063472158	CCCP-76705	243 OSAP	Lst UKR
UR-76706	Ilyushin Il-76MD	0083472163	CCCP-76706	25 VTAP	Lst ANTAU
UR-76716	Ilyushin Il-76MD	0073474211	CCCP-76716	16 AvB	Lst TII
UR-76717	Ilyushin Il-76MD	0073474216	CCCP-76717		Lst UKW
UR-76721	Ilyushin Il-76MD	0073475239	CCCP-76721	409 APSZ	Lst BSL, cvtd Il-78
UR-76727	Ilyushin Il-76MD	0073475268	CCCP-76727		Lst VRE
UR-76730	Ilyushin Il-76MD	0073476277	CCCP-76730	409 APSZ	Lst BSL, cvtd Il-78
UR-76732	Ilyushin Il-76MD	0073476296	CCCP-76732	25 VTAP	Lst ASG

76736	Ilyushin Il-78	0073476317	CCCP-76736	409 APSZ	AAR
UR-76742	Ilyushin Il-76MD	0073478346	CCCP-76742	409 APSZ	Lst BSL, cvtd Il-78
UR-76744	Ilyushin Il-76MD	0073478359	CCCP-76744	409 APSZ	Lst BSL, cvtd Il-78
UR-76748	Ilyushin Il-76MD	0073479386	76748 (Uk AF)	16 AvB	Std Kiev-Borispol?
76749	Ilyushin Il-76MD	0073479392	CCCP-76749	25 VTAP	
UR-76759	Ilyushin Il-78	0083485558	CCCP-78759	409 APSZ	Lst TII
UR-76760	Ilyushin Il-76MD	0073479400	CCCP-76760	409 APSZ	Lst BSL, cvtd Il-78
UR-76777	Ilyushin Il-76MD	0083482490	CCCP-76777	25 VTAP	Lst TII
UR-76778	Ilyushin Il-76MD	0083482502	CCCP-76778	243 OSAP	Lst UKW
UR-78752	Ilyushin Il-76MD	0083483519	CCCP-78752	338 VTAP	Lst TII
UR-78758	Ilyushin Il-76MD	0083484551	CCCP-78758	16 AvB	Lst TII
UR-78767	Ilyushin Il-78	0083487598	CCCP-78767	409 APSZ	Lst TII
UR-78772	Ilyushin Il-76MD	0083487627	CCCP-78772	16 AvB	Lst TII
UR-78785	Ilyushin Il-76MD	0083489691	CCCP-78785	16 AvB	Lst UMK
UR-78786	Ilyushin Il-76MD	9069489692	CCCP-78786	16 AvB	Lst UMK
78820	Ilyushin Il-76MD	0093496907	UR-78820	25 VTAP	
UR-78821	Ilyushin Il-76MD	0093496914	CCCP-78821	16 AvB	Lst OTL, damaged 18Apr01
UR-85445	Tupolev Tu-154B-2	80A-445	CCCP-85445		
86028	Ilyushin Il-76M	083415464	CCCP-86028		
86029	Ilyushin Il-76M	083415465	CCCP-86029		
86030	Ilyushin Il-76M	083415475	CCCP-86030		
86612	Ilyushin Il-62	41804	CCCP-86612		
86633	Ilyushin Il-76	073409256	CCCP-86633		
86639	Ilyushin Il-76	073409235	CCCP-86639		Aeroflot cs
86648	Ilyushin Il-62		CCCP-86648		
CCCP-86914	Ilyushin Il-76MD	0023438111			Std Biela, Aeroflot cs
CCCP-86917	Ilyushin Il-76MD	0023438122			Std Biela, Aeroflot cs
86915	Ilyushin Il-76MD	0023438116	CCCP-86915	16 AvB	
UR-86920	Ilyushin Il-76MD	0023440152	CCCP-86920	16 AvB	Lst RKS
UR-86921	Ilyushin Il-76MD	0023440161	CCCP-86921	338 VTAP	
86922	Ilyushin Il-76MD	0023440168	CCCP-86922		Lst HOS
86923	Ilyushin Il-76MD	0023441169	CCCP-86923	338 VTAP	
UR-86924	Ilyushin Il-76MD	0023441174	CCCP-86924	338 VTAP	Lst ASG
UR-UCA	Ilyushin Il-76MD	0073479394	UR-76715	25 VTAP	Lst UKS
UR-UCB	Ilyushin Il-76MD	0063467003	UR-76676		Lst United Nations
UR-UCC	Ilyushin Il-76MD	0083489647	UR-78775	338 VTAP	Lst United Nations
UR-UCD	Ilyushin Il-76MD	0083488643	UR-78774	338 VTAP	Lst UKS
UR-UCE	Ilyushin Il-76MD	0083484522	UR-76398	338 VTAP	Lst UKS
UR-UCF	Ilyushin Il-76MD	0083488638	UR-76412	409 APSZ	Lst UKS, Cvtd Il-78
UR-UCG	Ilyushin Il-76MD	0083482478	UR-76414	409 APSZ	Lst UKS, Cvtd Il-78
UR-UCH	Ilyushin Il-76MD	0083484536	UR-78756	338 VTAP	Lst UKS
UR-UCJ	Ilyushin Il-76MD	0083484531	UR-78755	338 VTAP	Lst UKS/KHO
UR-UCL	Ilyushin Il-76MD	0043456692	UR-76620	16 AvB	Lst UKS
UR-UCO	Ilyushin Il-76MD	0053458749	UR-76630	25 VTAP	Lst United Nations
UR-UCR	Ilyushin Il-76MD	0073475270	UR-76728		Lst United Nations
UR-UCS	Ilyushin Il-76MD	0063470113	UR-76444	25 VTAP	Lst UKS
UR-UCT	Ilyushin Il-76MD	0063470089	UR-76691		Lst AZV
UR-UCU	Ilyushin Il-76MD	0073476275	UR-76729		Lst AZV
UR-UCV	Ilyushin Il-76MD	0043451517	UR-76397	338 VTAP	Lst UKS
UR-UCX	Ilyushin Il-76MD	0063470112	UR-76695	25 VTAP	Lst United Nations
UR-UCY	Ilyushin Il-76MD	0083485566	UR-76399	338 VTAP	Lst UKS
UR-UDB	Ilyushin Il-76MD	0043455686	UR-76320	16 AvB	Lst UKS
002 black	Antonov An-72				
01 blue	Antonov An-26	2005			
01 red	Antonov An-26	4209			
01 yellow	Antonov An-26	4706			
02 blue	Antonov An-26	8206			
02 blue	Antonov An-24T	8910708			
02 red	Antonov An-76 (An-72P)	36576097927			
02 yellow	Tupolev Tu-135 (Tu-134A-3)	63960			
03 blue	Antonov An-30	0303			
03 blue	Antonov An-12BP	8346106			
04 black	Tupolev Tu-134				
05 blue	Antonov An-26	0808			
05 red	Antonov An-26				
05 red	Antonov An-12BK	00346907			
06 blue	Antonov An-26				
06 yellow	Antonov An-76 (An-72P)				
07 red	Antonov An-76 (An-72P)	36576096915			
07 red	Antonov An-72				
08 red	Antonov An-26	4101			

09 red	Ilyushin Il-20	011409			
10 blue	Antonov An-26				
10 red	Antonov An-26	4002			
11 green	Antonov An-26				
12 yellow	Antonov/PZL-Mielec An-2T	1G160-30			
14 yellow	Antonov/PZL-Mielec An-2T	1G160-33			
16 yellow	Antonov/PZL-Mielec An-2T	1G160-36			
17 yellow	Antonov/PZL-Mielec An-2T	1G160-44			
18 yellow	Antonov/PZL-Mielec An-2T	1G160-51			
20 black	Antonov/PZL-Mielec An-2T	1G235-54			
20 yellow	Antonov/PZL-Mielec An-2T	1G160-56			
21 blue	Antonov An-12BP	7345208			
22 blue	Antonov An-26B	11607			
23 blue	Antonov An-12BK	1400304			
23 blue	Antonov An-24T	8911405			
23 yellow	Antonov/PZL-Mielec An-2T	1G160-24			
25 red	Antonov An-26	4210			
25 red	Antonov/PZL-Mielec An-2T	1G235-50			
32 red	Antonov An-26	5106			
34	Antonov/PZL-Mielec An-2T	1G194-26			
35	Antonov/PZL-Mielec An-2T	1G194-37			
35 red	Antonov An-26	5801			
38 red	Antonov/PZL-Mielec An-2T	1G236-13			
39 red	Antonov An-26	5508			
40 black	Antonov An-24B	87304706			
41 red	Antonov An-26	6709			
41 red	Tupolev Tu-134UBL				
42 blue	Antonov An-24T	9911209			
42 red	Tupolev Tu-134UBL	64670			
43 red	Tupolev Tu-134UBL				
44 blue	Antonov An-26				
45 blue	Antonov An-26				
45 red	Tupolev Tu-134UBL				
46 red	Antonov An-26	5609			
48 red	Antonov/PZL-Mielec An-2T	1G236-23			
49 yellow	Antonov/PZL-Mielec An-2T	1G194-51			
50 red	Antonov An-12	4342306			
53 yellow	Antonov/PZL-Mielec An-2T	1G195-51			
56 yellow	Antonov/PZL-Mielec An-2T	1G195-54			
57 blue	Antonov An-12BK	00347006			
60	Antonov/PZL-Mielec An-2T	1G195-58			
61 blue	Antonov An-12BP	4341710			
61 red	Antonov An-12	4342308			
69 red	Antonov An-12BP	3341610			
69 yellow	Antonov/PZL-Mielec An-2T	1G196-24			
71 blue	Tupolev Tu-134UB				
77 red	Antonov An-12	4342007			
78 red	Antonov An-12	3341301			
79 red	Antonov An-12	4342106			
80 yellow	Antonov An-30	0608	10 OAE	Open Skies survey	
81 yellow	Antonov An-30	0609	10 OAE	Open Skies survey	
82 blue	Antonov An-26	8402	10 OAE	Open Skies support	
82 yellow	Antonov/PZL-Mielec An-2T	1G196-20			
83 blue	Antonov An-26	8010			
83 blue	Antonov An-12BP	1400301			
83 red	Antonov An-12	4342110			
84 yellow	Antonov An-26				
86 blue	Antonov An-30	0602			
86 blue	Antonov An-12	6344607			
86 red	Antonov An-12	9346607			
87 blue	Antonov An-30				
87 red	Antonov An-12BP	9346809			
328	Antonov An-24				
777 blue	Antonov An-24	47301504	UR-46777	CinC	VIP

Aviatsiia Voienno-Morsk'Kykh Syl - AVMS
Naval Aviation

UNITS/BASES	Donuzlav Lake-Evapatoriya, Crimea, 318 OMPAP	Be-12	
	Kacha, Crimea, 17 OMTAP	An-12, An-26, An-72P	
09 blue	Antonov An-26	3605	

Tovaristo Spriyanniya Oboroni Ukrayini - TSOU
Society for the Support of the Defence of the Ukraine, (formerly the Soviet DOSAAF)

UNITS/BASES	Krasilov	An-2	
	Simferopol	An-2	
UR-BAP	Antonov/PZL-Mielec An-2T	1G237-16	
UR-BAQ	Antonov/PZL-Mielec An-2T	1G196-09	TSOU
UR-BBV	Antonov/PZL-Mielec An-2T	1G160-29	TSOU
UR-BBW	Antonov/PZL-Mielec An-2T	1G236-22	TSOU
UR-BEQ	Antonov/PZL-Mielec An-2T	1G236-21	TSOU
UR-BJD	Antonov An-2		TSOU
UR-BJE	Antonov An-2	113947315	TSOU
UR-BJM	Antonov An-2		TSOU
UR-BJV	Antonov/PZL-Mielec An-2T	1G160-60	TSOU
UR-BKU	Antonov/PZL-Mielec An-2T	1G236-28	TSOU
UR-BMG	Antonov/PZL-Mielec An-2T	1G98-46	TSOU
UR-BMH	Antonov/PZL-Mielec An-2T	1G235-30	TSOU
UR-BMI	Antonov/PZL-Mielec An-2T	1G239-40	TSOU
UR-BPI	Antonov/PZL-Mielec An-2T	1G63-08	TSOU
UR-BRT	Antonov An-2	14847320	TSOU
UR-BSK / 62	Antonov/PZL-Mielec An-2T	1G195-60	TSOU
UR-BSL	Antonov/PZL-Mielec An-2R	1G136-14	TSOU
UR-BSM	Antonov/PZL-Mielec An-2T	1G237-47	TSOU
UR-BSO	Antonov/PZL-Mielec An-2T	1G235-59	TSOU
UR-BTK	Antonov/PZL-Mielec An-2T	1G236-10	TSOU
UR-BWL	Antonov An-2		TSOU
UR-BWR	Antonov/PZL-Mielec An-2T	1G159-57	TSOU
UR-BWS	Antonov/PZL-Mielec An-2T	1G160-25	TSOU

Government of the Republic of the Ukraine

UR-65556	Tupolev Tu-134A-3	66372	CCCP-65556
UR-65718	Tupolev Tu-134A-3	63668	CCCP-65718
UR-65782	Tupolev Tu-134A-3	62672	CCCP-65782
UR-86527	Ilyushin Il-62M	4037758	86527 (Uk AF)
UR-86528	Ilyushin Il-62M	4038111	86528 (Uk AF)
UR-87964	Yakovlev Yak-40	9820758	CCCP-87964

UNITED ARAB EMIRATES
al-Imarat al-Arabiya al-Muttahida   SW Asia

The UAE was formed in 1971 by the seven former Trucial States of Abu Dhabi, Ajman, Dubai, Al Fujayrah, Ra's al Khaimah, Sharjah and Umm-al-Quaywayn. Defence is handled mutually but some of the states fly their own VIP operation. Abu Dhabi and Dubai contribute the military aircraft to the UAEAF and while they should operate as a unified force, in practice they fly as independent forces with a common aim. Sharjah's transports were taken over by Dubai in 1995.

SERIAL SYSTEM Serials are displayed in arabic and western style beginning with 1and 3 for Dubai and either 8 or 12 for the Abu Dhabi procured types.

United Arab Emirates Air Force - UAE AF

UNITS/BASES	Western Air Command (Abu Dhabi Air Force)		
	Bateen, Abu Dhabi	Aviocar, CN235M, C-130H, Super King Air	
	Central Air Command (Dubai Air Force)		
	al-Mindhat-Dubai	C-130H, PC-6B, Skyvan, Shorts 330	
PLANS	The CASA C295 Persuader was selected in March 2001 for delivery in 2004 (4 aircraft) in place of a stalled order for IPTN built CN235MPAs.		

121	Shorts SC.7 Skyvan srs 3	SH.1981	G-BMHH	Dubai
311	Lockheed C-130H (L-382C-54E) Hercules	4834	N4085M	Dubai
312	Lockheed C-130H-30 (L-382T-39E) Hercules	4961		Dubai
321	Pilatus PC-6/B2-H4 Turbo Porter	863	HB-FKI	Dubai
322	Pilatus PC-6/B2-H4 Turbo Porter	864	HB-FKK	Dubai
331	Shorts 330UTT	SH.3121	131 (UAEAF)	Dubai
800	Learjet 35A	35A-429	G-ZENO	Dubai
801	Raytheon Beech Super King Air 350 (B300)	FL-131	A6-MHH	Abu Dhabi
805	CASA 212 Aviocar srs 200	A36-1-230		Abu Dhabi
806	CASA 212 Aviocar srs 200	A36-2-233		Abu Dhabi
807	CASA 212 Aviocar srs 200	A36-3-244		Abu Dhabi

808	CASA 212 Aviocar srs 200		A36-4-246		Abu Dhabi	
810	Airtech/IPTN CN235M-100		N026	PK-XNA	Abu Dhabi	
811	Airtech/IPTN CN235M-100		N027	AX-2308	Abu Dhabi	
812	Airtech/IPTN CN235M-100		N028	AX-2309	Abu Dhabi	
813	Airtech/IPTN CN235M-100		N029	AX-2310	Abu Dhabi	
814	Airtech/IPTN CN235M-100		N030	AX-2311	Abu Dhabi	
815	Airtech/IPTN CN235M-100		N031		Abu Dhabi	
816	Airtech/IPTN CN235M-100		N032		Abu Dhabi	
825	Raytheon Beech Super King Air 350 (B300)		FL-132	A6-KHZ	Abu Dhabi	
1211	Lockheed C-130H (L-382C-54E) Hercules		4983	N4161T	Abu Dhabi	Std?
1212	Lockheed C-130H (L-382C-54E) Hercules		4985	N4249Y	Abu Dhabi	
1213	Lockheed C-130H (L-382C-14E) Hercules		4879	N4140M	Abu Dhabi	
1214	Lockheed C-130H (L-382C-14E) Hercules		4882	N4147M	Abu Dhabi	
1215	Lockheed L-100-30 (L-382G-65C) Hercules		5024	G-52-23	Abu Dhabi	

Abu Dhabi Amiri Flight

ICAO code AUH or MO, callsign Sultan, based at Abu Dhabi IAP.

A6-AIN	Boeing BBJ (737-7Z5)	29268 / 280	N1786B	
A6-AUH	Dassault Falcon 900	84	F-WWFD	
A6-DAS	Boeing BBJ (737-7Z5)	29858 / 530	N1786B	
A6-LIW	Boeing BBJ (737-7Z5)	29857 / 445	N1795B	
A6-SHZ	Airbus Industrie A300-620	354	F-ODRM	
A6-SIR	Boeing BBJ (737-7Z5)	29269 / 432	N1786B	Damaged Aug01
A6-SUL	Boeing 767-341ER	30341 / 768	N60659	
A6-YAS	Boeing 747-4F6	28961 / 1174	N1794B	
A6-ZSN	Boeing 747SP-Z5	23610 / 676	N60697	

Dubai Air Wing

ICAO code DUB, callsign Dubai, Based at Dubai IAP.

A6-GDP	Boeing 747-2B4B(F) SCD	21098 / 263	N712CK
A6-HHH	GAC Gulfstream IV	1011	N17581
A6-HRS	Boeing BBJ (737-7E0)	29251 / 150	
A6-MRM	Boeing BBJ2 (737-8E0)	32450 / 787	N1787B
A6-SMM	Boeing 747SP-31	21963 / 441	
A6-SMR	Boeing 747SP-31	21961 / 415	

Sharjah Ruler's Flight

ICAO code SHJ, callsign Sharjah, Based at Sharjah IAP.

A6-ESH	Airbus Industrie A319-133X (CJ)	910	D-AWFR

UNITED KINGDOM
of Great Britain & Northern Ireland   W Europe

While no longer possessing the extensive empire that made necessary the large and separate Transport Command which was operated after the end of World War Two, the modern British Armed Forces are still among the best trained and equipped in the world. Recent emphasis has been placed on developing a rapid reaction force capable of moving relevant units anywhere on the globe to support NATO or UN requirements. Involvement in a similar joint European force is also being reviewed.

SERIAL SYSTEM   A universal system is employed for all air arms consisting of a two letter and three digit sequence. Although usually sequential, blocks are omitted deliberately and out of sequence allocations are sometimes made, as with the C-17s. Codes are common, usually for transports consisting of the three serial digits in larger presentation on the tail, although letter codes are also used.

Royal Air Force

ICAO codes: RFR (callsign Rafair), RRR (Transports, callsign Ascot), CWL (Cranwell FTS, callsign Cranwell).

UNITS-BASES   Strike Command
No 2 Group

8 Sqn, RAF Waddington	Sentry	AEW (aircraft pooled with 23 Sqn)
10 Sqn, RAF Brize Norton	VC-10 C.1K	AAR/Transport
23 Sqn, RAF Waddington	Sentry	AEW (aircraft pooled with 8 Sqn)
24 Sqn, RAF Lyneham	C-130J	(pooled aircraft/LTW)
30 Sqn, RAF Lyneham	C-130J (converting from Feb2001)	
32 (The Royal) Sqn, RAF Northolt	BAe146, BAe125	VIP

47 Sqn, RAF Lyneham	C-130K	(pooled aircraft/LTW)	
51 Sqn, RAF Waddington	Nimrod	EW	
57 (Reserve) Sqn, RAF Lyneham	C-130K	(pooled aircraft/LTW)	
70 Sqn, RAF Lyneham	C-130K	(pooled aircraft/LTW)	
99 Sqn, RAF Brize Norton	C-17 (from late 2001)		
101 Sqn, RAF Brize Norton	VC-10	AAR	
216 Sqn, RAF Brize Norton	TriStar	AAR/Transport	
Hercules Operational Evaluation Unit (HOEU), RAF Lyneham	C-130K		
Northolt Station Flight	Islander	Communications & Surveillance	

No 3 Group

42 (Reserve) Sqn, RAF Kinloss	Nimrod	(pooled aircraft/KW)
120 Sqn, RAF Kinloss	Nimrod	(pooled aircraft/KW)
201 Sqn, RAF Kinloss	Nimrod	(pooled aircraft/KW)
206 Sqn, RAF Kinloss	Nimrod	(pooled aircraft/KW)

1312 Flt, RAF Mount Pleasant, Falkland Islands	C-130, VC-10	Tanker/Transport/MR

Pooled aircraft come from the Lyneham Transport Wing (LTW) and Kinloss Wing (KW)

Personnel & Training Command
3 Flying Training School, RAF Cranwell

45 (Reserve) Sqn	Jetstream	Multi engine Training
55 (Reserve) Sqn	Dominie	Navigation Training

Civilian Contractors - FR Aviation, Bournemouth-Hurn	Falcon 20	Training, (see RN for listing)
Civilian Contractors - Hunting Contract Services	Andover	Calibration
Civilian Contractors - Hunting Contract Services	Skyvan	Parachute Training

PLANS   The largest programme is the Future Strategic Tanker Aircraft (FSTA) to replace the VC-10 and TriStar fleet, which will involve up to 30 aircraft (A330-200, 767-300) depending on which bidder obtains the contract set for award in October 2002, with service entry from 2007/9. The aircraft will be leased rather than owned.
21 Nimrod MR Mk.2 are being rebuilt by BAE Systems at Woodford as MRA.4s, work includes building new wings and re-engining with BMW/RR BR710. Service entry looks like 2005 at the earliest at present.
Raytheon Systems Ltd will configure 5 Bomardier Global Express airframes for the Airborne Stand-Off RADAR (ASTOR) battlefield surveillance programme, service entry of 2005 is planned based at RAF Waddington.
Four Boeing C-17As have been leased from 2001 for an initial 7 years to cover until the first of 25 Airbus Industrie A400M are delivered from 2005. The acquisition of two further aircraft is being evaluated.

XR807	Vickers 1106 VC-10 C.1K	827		10 Sqn	'Thomas Grey VC'	
XR808	Vickers 1106 VC-10 C.1K	828		10 Sqn	'Kenneth Campbell VC'	
XR810	Vickers 1106 VC-10 C.1K	830		10 Sqn	'David Lord VC'	
XS709 / M	Hawker Siddeley Dominie T.1	25011	G-37-65	55(R) Sqn		
XS711 / L	Hawker Siddeley Dominie T.1	25024		55(R) Sqn		
XS712 / A	Hawker Siddeley Dominie T.1	25040		55(R) Sqn		
XS713 / C	Hawker Siddeley Dominie T.1	25041		55(R) Sqn		
XS727 / D	Hawker Siddeley Dominie T.1	25045		55(R) Sqn		
XS730 / H	Hawker Siddeley Dominie T.1	25050		55(R) Sqn		
XS731 / J	Hawker Siddeley Dominie T.1	25055		55(R) Sqn		
XS736 / S	Hawker Siddeley Dominie T.1	25072		55(R) Sqn		
XS737 / K	Hawker Siddeley Dominie T.1	25076		55(R) Sqn		
XS739 / F	Hawker Siddeley Dominie T.1	25081		55(R) Sqn		
XV101	Vickers 1106 VC-10 C.1K	831		10 Sqn	'Lanoe Hawker VC'	
XV102	Vickers 1106 VC-10 C.1K	832		10 Sqn	'Guy Gibson VC'	
XV104	Vickers 1106 VC-10 C.1K	834		10 Sqn	'James McCudden VC'	
XV105	Vickers 1106 VC-10 C.1K	835		10 Sqn	'Albert Ball VC'	
XV106	Vickers 1106 VC-10 C.1K	836		10 Sqn	'Thomas Mottershead VC'	
XV107	Vickers 1106 VC-10 C.1K	837		10 Sqn	'James Nicholson VC'	
XV108	Vickers 1106 VC-10 C.1K	838		10 Sqn	'W Rhodes-Moorhouse VC'	
XV109	Vickers 1106 VC-10 C.1K	839		10 Sqn	'Arthur Scarfe VC'	
XV177	Lockheed C-130K (L-382-19B) Hercules C.3P	4182	65-13022 (FMS)	LTW	Cvtd C.1	
XV179	Lockheed C-130K (L-382-19B) Hercules C.1P	4195	65-13024 (FMS)	LTW	Cvtd C.1	
XV181	Lockheed C-130K (L-382-19B) Hercules C.1P	4198	65-13026 (FMS)		Std Lyneham	
XV183	Lockheed C-130K (L-382-19B) Hercules C.3P	4200	65-13028 (FMS)	LTW	Cvtd C.1	
XV184	Lockheed C-130K (L-382-19B) Hercules C.3P	4201	65-13029 (FMS)	LTW	Cvtd C.1	
XV188	Lockheed C-130K (L-382-19B) Hercules C.1P	4206	65-13033 (FMS)	LTW	Cvtd C.1	
XV190	Lockheed C-130K (L-382-19B) Hercules C.3P	4210	65-13035 (FMS)	LTW	Cvtd C.1	
XV196	Lockheed C-130K (L-382-19B) Hercules C.1P	4217	65-13041 (FMS)	LTW	Cvtd C.1	
XV197	Lockheed C-130K (L-382-19B) Hercules C.3P	4218	65-13042 (FMS)	LTW	Cvtd C.1	
XV199	Lockheed C-130K (L-382-19B) Hercules C.3P	4220	65-13044 (FMS)	LTW	Cvtd C.1	
XV200	Lockheed C-130K (L-382-19B) Hercules C.1P	4223	66-8850 (FMS)	LTW	Cvtd C.1	
XV202	Lockheed C-130K (L-382-19B) Hercules C.3P	4226	66-8852 (FMS)	LTW	Cvtd C.1	
XV205	Lockheed C-130K (L-382-19B) Hercules C.1P	4230	66-8855 (FMS)		Std Cambridge	
XV206	Lockheed C-130K (L-382-19B) Hercules C.1P	4231	66-8856 (FMS)	LTW	Cvtd C.1	

XV209	Lockheed C-130K (L-382-19B) Hercules C.3P	4235	66-8859 (FMS)	LTW	Cvtd C.1
XV212	Lockheed C-130K (L-382-19B) Hercules C.3P	4238	66-8862 (FMS)	LTW	Cvtd C.1
XV214	Lockheed C-130K (L-382-19B) Hercules C.3P	4241	66-8864 (FMS)	LTW	Cvtd C.1
XV217	Lockheed C-130K (L-382-19B) Hercules C.3P	4244	66-8867 (FMS)	LTW	Cvtd C.1
XV220	Lockheed C-130K (L-382-19B) Hercules C.3P	4247	66-8870 (FMS)	LTW	Cvtd C.1
XV221	Lockheed C-130K (L-382-19B) Hercules C.3P	4251	66-8871 (FMS)	LTW	Cvtd C.1
XV222	Lockheed C-130K (L-382-19B) Hercules C.3P	4252	66-8872 (FMS)	LTW	Cvtd C.1
XV226	Hawker Siddeley 802 Nimrod MR.2	8001		120 Sqn	Cvtd MR.1
XV227	Hawker Siddeley 802 Nimrod MR.2	8002		42(R) Sqn	Cvtd MR.1
XV228	Hawker Siddeley 802 Nimrod MR.2	8003		42(R) Sqn	Cvtd MR.1
XV229	Hawker Siddeley 802 Nimrod MR.2	8004		206 Sqn	Cvtd MR.1
XV230	Hawker Siddeley 802 Nimrod MR.2	8005		201 Sqn	Cvtd MR.1
XV231	Hawker Siddeley 802 Nimrod MR.2	8006		206 Sqn	Cvtd MR.1
XV232	Hawker Siddeley 802 Nimrod MR.2	8007		201 Sqn	Cvtd MR.1
XV235	Hawker Siddeley 802 Nimrod MR.2	8010		120 Sqn	Cvtd MR.1
XV236	Hawker Siddeley 802 Nimrod MR.2	8011		42(R) Sqn	Cvtd MR.1
XV240	Hawker Siddeley 802 Nimrod MR.2	8015		120 Sqn	Cvtd MR.1
XV241	Hawker Siddeley 802 Nimrod MR.2	8016			Cvtd MR.1
XV243	Hawker Siddeley 802 Nimrod MR.2	8018		120 Sqn	Cvtd MR.1
XV244	Hawker Siddeley 802 Nimrod MR.2	8019		201 Sqn	Cvtd MR.1
XV245	Hawker Siddeley 802 Nimrod MR.2	8020		201 Sqn	Cvtd MR.1
XV246	Hawker Siddeley 802 Nimrod MR.2	8021		201 Sqn	Cvtd MR.1
XV248	Hawker Siddeley 802 Nimrod MR.2	8023		206 Sqn	Cvtd MR.1
XV249	Hawker Siddeley 802 Nimrod R.1	8024		51 Sqn	Cvtd MR.1/2
XV250	Hawker Siddeley 802 Nimrod MR.2	8025		120 Sqn	Cvtd MR.1
XV252	Hawker Siddeley 802 Nimrod MR.2	8027		201 Sqn	Cvtd MR.1
XV254	Hawker Siddeley 802 Nimrod MR.2	8029		201 Sqn	Cvtd MR.1
XV255	Hawker Siddeley 802 Nimrod MR.2	8030		Kinloss MR Wing	Cvtd MR.1
XV260	Hawker Siddeley 802 Nimrod MR.2P	8035		120 Sqn	Cvtd MR.1
XV290	Lockheed C-130K (L-382-19B) Hercules C.3P	4254	66-13533 (FMS)	LTW	Cvtd C.1
XV291	Lockheed C-130K (L-382-19B) Hercules C.1P	4256	66-13534 (FMS)		Std Lyneham
XV292	Lockheed C-130K (L-382-19B) Hercules C.1P	4257	66-13535 (FMS)		Std Lyneham
XV294	Lockheed C-130K (L-382-19B) Hercules C.3P	4259	66-13537 (FMS)	LTW	Cvtd C.1
XV295	Lockheed C-130K (L-382-19B) Hercules C.1P	4261	66-13538 (FMS)	LTW	Cvtd C.1
XV296	Lockheed C-130K (L-382-19B) Hercules C.1K	4262	66-13539 (FMS)		Std Cambridge
XV299	Lockheed C-130K (L-382-19B) Hercules C.3P	4266	66-13542 (FMS)	LTW	Cvtd C.1
XV301	Lockheed C-130K (L-382-19B) Hercules C.3P	4268	66-13544 (FMS)	LTW	Cvtd C.1
XV302	Lockheed C-130K (L-382-19B) Hercules C.3P	4270	66-13545 (FMS)	LTW	Cvtd C.1
XV303	Lockheed C-130K (L-382-19B) Hercules C.3P	4271	66-13546 (FMS)	LTW	Cvtd C.1
XV304	Lockheed C-130K (L-382-19B) Hercules C.3P	4272	66-13547 (FMS)	LTW	Cvtd C.1
XV305	Lockheed C-130K (L-382-19B) Hercules C.3P	4273	66-13548 (FMS)	LTW	Cvtd C.1
XV307	Lockheed C-130K (L-382-19B) Hercules C.3P	4275	66-13550 (FMS)	LTW	Cvtd C.1
XW664	Hawker Siddeley 802 Nimrod R.1	8039		51 Sqn	
XW665	Hawker Siddeley 802 Nimrod R.1	8040		51 Sqn	
XX482 / J	Scottish Aviation Jetstream T.1	263		45(R) Sqn	
XX491 / K	Scottish Aviation Jetstream T.1	275		45(R) Sqn	
XX492 / A	Scottish Aviation Jetstream T.1	274		45(R) Sqn	
XX493 / L	Scottish Aviation Jetstream T.1	278		45(R) Sqn	
XX494 / B	Scottish Aviation Jetstream T.1	422		45(R) Sqn	
XX495 / C	Scottish Aviation Jetstream T.1	423		45(R) Sqn	
XX496 / D	Scottish Aviation Jetstream T.1	276		45(R) Sqn	
XX497 / E	Scottish Aviation Jetstream T.1	280		45(R) Sqn	
XX498 / F	Scottish Aviation Jetstream T.1	424		45(R) Sqn	
XX499 / G	Scottish Aviation Jetstream T.1	425		45(R) Sqn	
XX500 / H	Scottish Aviation Jetstream T.1	426		45(R) Sqn	
ZA147 / F	BAC 1154 VC-10 K.3	882	5H-MMT	101 Sqn	
ZA148 / G	BAC 1154 VC-10 K.3	883	5Y-ADA	101 Sqn	
ZA149 / H	BAC 1154 VC-10 K.3	884	5X-UVJ	101 Sqn	
ZA150 / J	BAC 1154 VC-10 K.3	885	5H-MOG	101 Sqn	
ZD230 / K	BAC 1151 Super VC-10 K.4	851	G-ASGA	101 Sqn	
ZD235 / L	BAC 1151 Super VC-10 K.4	857	G-ASGG	101 Sqn	
ZD240 / M	BAC 1151 Super VC-10 K.4	862	G-ASGL	101 Sqn	
ZD241 / N	BAC 1151 Super VC-10 K.4	863	G-ASGM	101 Sqn	
ZD242 / P	BAC 1151 Super VC-10 K.4	866	G-ASGP	101 Sqn	
ZD620	British Aerospace 125-700B CC.3	257181		32 Sqn	
ZD621	British Aerospace 125-700B CC.3	257190		32 Sqn	
ZD703	British Aerospace 125-700B CC.3	257183		32 Sqn	
ZD704	British Aerospace 125-700B CC.3	257194		32 Sqn	
ZD948	Lockheed L-1011-193V TriStar KC.1 (TriStar 500)	1157	G-BFCA	216 Sqn	AAR
ZD949	Lockheed L-1011-193V TriStar K.1 (TriStar 500)	1159	G-BFCB	216 Sqn	AAR
ZD950	Lockheed L-1011-193V TriStar KC.1 (TriStar 500)	1164	G-BFCC	216 Sqn	AAR
ZD951	Lockheed L-1011-193V TriStar K.1 (TriStar 500)	1165	G-BFCD	216 Sqn	AAR
ZD952	Lockheed L-1011-193V TriStar KC.1 (TriStar 500)	1168	G-BFCE	216 Sqn	AAR
ZD953	Lockheed L-1011-193V TriStar KC.1 (TriStar 500)	1174	G-BFCF	216 Sqn	AAR

ZE395	British Aerospace 125-700B CC.3	257205		32 Sqn	
ZE396	British Aerospace 125-700B CC.3	257211		32 Sqn	
ZE700	British Aerospace 146-100 CC.2	E.1021		32 Sqn	
ZE701	British Aerospace 146-100 CC.2	E.1029		32 Sqn	
ZE702	British Aerospace 146-100 CC.2	E.1124		32 Sqn	
ZE704	Lockheed L-1011-193Y TriStar C.2 (TriStar 500)	1186	N508PA	216 Sqn	
ZE705	Lockheed L-1011-193Y TriStar C.2 (TriStar 500)	1188	N509PA	216 Sqn	
ZE706	Lockheed L-1011-193Y TriStar C.2A (TriStar 500)	1177	N503PA	216 Sqn	
ZF573	Pilatus Britten-Norman BN-2T Islander CC.2A	2034	G-SRAY	RAF Northolt Station Flt	
ZH101	Boeing E-3D Sentry AEW.1	24109 / 993		8Sqn/23Sqn	
ZH102	Boeing E-3D Sentry AEW.1	24110 / 996		8Sqn/23Sqn	
ZH103	Boeing E-3D Sentry AEW.1	24111 / 1004		8Sqn/23Sqn	
ZH104	Boeing E-3D Sentry AEW.1	24112 / 1007		8Sqn/23Sqn	
ZH105	Boeing E-3D Sentry AEW.1	24113 / 1010		8Sqn/23Sqn	
ZH106	Boeing E-3D Sentry AEW.1	24114 / 1011		8Sqn/23Sqn	
ZH107	Boeing E-3D Sentry AEW.1	24499 / 1012		8Sqn/23Sqn	
ZH536	Pilatus Britten-Norman BN-2T Islander CC.2	2235	G-BSAH	RAF Northolt Station Flt	
ZH865	Lockheed Martin C-130J-30 (L-382V-49F) Hercules C.4	5408	N130JA	LTW	
ZH866	Lockheed Martin C-130J-30 (L-382V-49F) Hercules C.4	5414	N130JE	LTW	
ZH867	Lockheed Martin C-130J-30 (L-382V-49F) Hercules C.4	5416	N130JJ	LTW	
ZH868	Lockheed Martin C-130J-30 (L-382V-49F) Hercules C.4	5443	N130JN	LTW	
ZH869	Lockheed Martin C-130J-30 (L-382V-49F) Hercules C.4	5444	N130JV	LTW	
ZH870	Lockheed Martin C-130J-30 (L-382V-49F) Hercules C.4	5445	N78235	LTW	
ZH871	Lockheed Martin C-130J-30 (L-382V-49F) Hercules C.4	5446	N73238	LTW	
ZH872	Lockheed Martin C-130J-30 (L-382V-49F) Hercules C.4	5456	N4249Y	LTW	
ZH873	Lockheed Martin C-130J-30 (L-382V-49F) Hercules C.4	5457	N4242N	LTW	
ZH874	Lockheed Martin C-130J-30 (L-382V-49F) Hercules C.4	5458	N41030	LTW	
ZH875	Lockheed Martin C-130J-30 (L-382V-49F) Hercules C.4	5459	N4099R	LTW	
ZH876	Lockheed Martin C-130J-30 (L-382V-49F) Hercules C.4	5460	N4080M	LTW	
ZH877	Lockheed Martin C-130J-30 (L-382V-49F) Hercules C.4	5461	N4081M	LTW	
ZH878	Lockheed Martin C-130J-30 (L-382V-05J) Hercules C.4	5462	N73232	LTW	
ZH879	Lockheed Martin C-130J-30 (L-382V-05J) Hercules C.4	5463		LTW	
ZH880	Lockheed Martin C-130J (L-382U-06J) Hercules C.5	5478	N73238	DERA,Boscombe Down	
ZH881	Lockheed Martin C-130J (L-382U-06J) Hercules C.5	5479	N4249Y	LTW	
ZH882	Lockheed Martin C-130J (L-382U-06J) Hercules C.5	5480	N4081M	LTW	
ZH883	Lockheed Martin C-130J (L-382U-06J) Hercules C.5	5481	N4242N	LTW	
ZH884	Lockheed Martin C-130J (L-382U-06J) Hercules C.5	5482	N4249Y	LTW	
ZH885	Lockheed Martin C-130J (L-382U-06J) Hercules C.5	5483	N41030	LTW	
ZH886	Lockheed Martin C-130J (L-382U-06J) Hercules C.5	5484	N73235	LTW	
ZH887	Lockheed Martin C-130J (L-382U-06J) Hercules C.5	5485	N4187W	LTW	
ZH888	Lockheed Martin C-130J (L-382U-06J) Hercules C.5	5496	N4187	LTW	
ZH889	Lockheed Martin C-130J (L-382U-06J) Hercules C.5	5500	N4099R	LTW	
ZJ514	British Aerospace Nimrod MRA.4	PA-4	XV251	BAE Systems	Cvtd MR.2
ZJ515	British Aerospace Nimrod MRA.4	PA-5	XV258	BAE Systems	Cvtd MR.2
ZJ516	British Aerospace Nimrod MRA.4	PA-1	XV247	BAE Systems	Cvtd MR.2
ZJ517	British Aerospace Nimrod MRA.4	PA-3	XV242	BAE Systems	Cvtd MR.2
ZJ518	British Aerospace Nimrod MRA.4	PA-2	XV234	BAE Systems	Cvtd MR.2
ZJ519	British Aerospace Nimrod MRA.4	PA-6	XZ284	BAE Systems	Cvtd MR.2
ZJ520	British Aerospace Nimrod MRA.4	PA-7	XV233	BAE Systems	Cvtd MR.2

ZZ171	Boeing C-17A Globemaster III	UK-1	N171UK	99 Sqn	Lsf Boeing
ZZ172	Boeing C-17A Globemaster III	UK-2	N172UK	99 Sqn	Lsf Boeing
ZZ173	Boeing C-17A Globemaster III	UK-3	N173UK	99 Sqn	Lsf Boeing
ZZ174	Boeing C-17A Globemaster III	UK-4	N174UK	99 Sqn	Lsf Boeing
	British Aerospace Nimrod MRA.4	PA-8	XV253	BAE Systems	Cvtd MR.2
G-BVXA	Shorts SC.7 Skyvan srs 3M-100	SH.1889	LX-DEF	Hunting	
G-PIGY	Shorts SC.7 Skyvan srs 3M-100	SH.1943	LX-JUL	Hunting	

Royal Navy

ICAO code NVY, callsign Navy

UNITS/BASES	Fleet Air Arm				
	750 Sqn, RNAS Culdrose/HMS Seahawk			Jetstream	Observer Training
	Heron Flight, RNAS Yeovilton/HMS Heron			Jetstream	Communications
	Civilian Contractors - FR Aviation, Bournemouth-Hurn & Teeside			Falcon 20	Training
XX476 / CU561	Scottish Aviation Jetstream T.2	216	N1037S	750 Sqn	Cvtd T.1
XX478 / CU564	Scottish Aviation Jetstream T.2	261	G-AXXT	750 Sqn	Cvtd T.1
XX481 / CU560	Scottish Aviation Jetstream T.2	251	G-AXUP	750 Sqn	Cvtd T.1
XX484 / CU566	Scottish Aviation Jetstream T.2	266		750 Sqn	Cvtd T.1
XX486 / CU569	Scottish Aviation Jetstream T.2	265		750 Sqn	Cvtd T.1
XX487 / CU568	Scottish Aviation Jetstream T.2	269		750 Sqn	Cvtd T.1
XX488 / CU562	Scottish Aviation Jetstream T.2	267		750 Sqn	Cvtd T.1
ZA110 / CU573	Handley Page Jetstream T.2	248	F-BTMI	750 Sqn	
ZA111 / CU565	Handley Page Jetstream T.2	211	9Q-CTC	750 Sqn	
ZE438 / CU576	British Aerospace Jetstream T.3 (Jetstream 31)	647	G-31-647	Heron Flt	
ZE439 / CU577	British Aerospace Jetstream T.3 (Jetstream 31)	656	G-31-656	Heron Flt	Std Shawbury
ZE440 / CU578	British Aerospace Jetstream T.3 (Jetstream 31)	659	G-31-659	Heron Flt	
ZE441 / CU579	British Aerospace Jetstream T.3 (Jetstream 31)	667	G-31-667	Heron Flt	
G-AZXA	Beech Baron C55	TE-72	SE-EXZ	FR Aviation	TT
G-FRBY	Beech Baron E55	TE-868	N78PS	FR Aviation	TT
G-MAFF	Pilatus Britten-Norman BN-2T Turbine Islander	2119	G-BJED	FR Aviation	Surveyer
G-FPLC	Cessna 441 Conquest	441-0207	G-FRAX	FR Aviation	
G-FRAZ	Cessna 441 Conquest	441-0035	SE-GYC	FR Aviation	TT
G-MAFE	Dornier 228-202K	8009	G-OALF	FR Aviation	Surveyer
G-MAFI	Dornier 228-200	8115	D-CAAE	FR Aviation	Surveyer
G-OMAF	Dornier 228-200	8112	D-CAAD	FR Aviation	Surveyer
G-FFRA	Dassault Falcon 20DC	132	N902FR	FR Aviation	TS Trainer
G-FRAE	Dassault Falcon 20E	280	N910FR	FR Aviation	TT
G-FRAF	Dassault Falcon 20E	295	N911FR	FR Aviation	TT
G-FRAH	Dassault Falcon 20DC	223	N900FR	FR Aviation	TS Trainer
G-FRAI	Dassault Falcon 20DC	270	N901FR	FR Aviation	TS Trainer
G-FRAJ	Dassault Falcon 20DC	20	N903FR	FR Aviation	TS Trainer
G-FRAK	Dassault Falcon 20DC	213	N905FR	FR Aviation	TS Trainer
G-FRAL	Dassault Falcon 20DC	151	N904FR	FR Aviation	TS Trainer
G-FRAN	Dassault Falcon 20DC	224	N907FR	FR Aviation	EW Trainer
G-FRAO	Dassault Falcon 20DC	214	N906FR	FR Aviation	TS Trainer
G-FRAP	Dassault Falcon 20DC	207	N908FR	FR Aviation	EW Trainer
G-FRAR	Dassault Falcon 20DC	209	N909FR	FR Aviation	EW Trainer
G-FRAS	Dassault Falcon 20C	82	117501 (CAF)	FR Aviation	Trainer
G-FRAT	Dassault Falcon 20C	87	117502 (CAF)	FR Aviation	Trainer
G-FRAU	Dassault Falcon 20C	97	117504 (CAF)	FR Aviation	Trainer
G-FRAW	Dassault Falcon 20C	114	117507 (CAF)	FR Aviation	Trainer
G-FRBA	Dassault Falcon 20C	178	OH-FFA	FR Aviation	TT

British Army, Army Air Corps - AAC

ICAO code AAC, callsign Armyair

UNITS/BASES	2 (Training) Regiment/School of Army Aviation				
	Advanced Fixed Wing Flight, Middle Wallop		Islander	Training	
	5 Regiment				
	No 1 Flight, Aldergrove		Islander	Recon & Surveillance	
ZG844	Pilatus Britten-Norman BN-2T Islander AL.1	2184	G-BLNE	AAC No1 Flt, Aldergrove	
ZG845	Pilatus Britten-Norman BN-2T Islander AL.1	2194	G-BLNT	AAC AFWF	
ZG846	Pilatus Britten-Norman BN-2T Islander AL.1	2195	G-BLNU	AAC No1 Flt, Aldergrove	
ZG847	Pilatus Britten-Norman BN-2T Islander AL.1	2196	G-BLNV	AAC No1 Flt, Aldergrove	
ZG848	Pilatus Britten-Norman BN-2T Islander AL.1	2199	G-BLNY	AAC No1 Flt, Aldergrove	
ZG993	Pilatus Britten-Norman BN-2T Islander AL.1	2202	G-BOMD	AAC	

Defence Evaluation & Research Agency - DERA

ICAO code: BDN (MOD/PE Boscombe Down callsign Gauntlet), ETP (ETPS, callsign Tester)

DERA was partially privatised in July 2001 under the new name 'QinetiQ'. The remaining 25% staying under Government control will be known as the Defence Science Technology Laboratory (DSTL). The distribution of aircraft had not been announced as this edition went to press.

UNITS/BASES	Aircraft Test & Evaluation Sector, Boscombe Down	
	Heavy Test Wing	Various
	Empire Test Pilots School (ETPS)	Various
	Meteorological Research Flight, Boscombe Down	C-130K (Std Mar01)
	Air and Sea Capabilities Sector, West Freugh	Jetstream

PLANS   The prototype BAe146 (now a series 300) is being converted for use in a Meteorological Research role replacing the retired C-130K W.2.

XS596	Hawker Siddeley Andover C.1PR	1574/set 3		AETS	Cvtd C.1
XS646	Hawker Siddeley Andover C.1	set30		DRA	
XS728 / E	Hawker Siddeley Dominie T.2	25048		HATS	DTEO Boscombe Down
XS743	Beagle 206Z-2 Bassett CC.1	B.004		ETPS	DTEO Boscombe Down
XV208	Lockheed C-130K (L-382-19B) Hercules W.2	4233	66-8858 (FMS)		Std, Cvtd C.1
XW750	Hawker Siddeley HS.748-107 Srs 1	1559/set29	G-ASJT	HTW	DTEO Boscombe Down
XX105	BAC One Eleven 201AC	008	G-ASJD		
XX475	Scottish Aviation Jetstream T.2	206	N1036S	A&SCS	Std Boscombe Down
XX479	Scottish Aviation Jetstream T.2	259	G-AXUR		DTEO Predanneck
ZE432	BAC One Eleven 479FU	250	DQ-FBV		
ZE433	BAC One Eleven 479FU	245	DQ-FBQ		
ZF130	British Aerospace 125-600B	256059	G-BLUW		BAe Dunsfold
ZF521	Piper PA-31-350 Navajo Chieftain	31-7852032			DTEO Llanbedr
ZF622	Piper PA-31-350 Navajo Chieftain	31-8052033			DTEO Boscombe Down
ZG989	Pilatus Britten-Norman BN-2T Islander (ASTOR)	2140	G-DLRA	MoD(PE), PBN	
ZH763	BAC One Eleven 539GL	263	G-BGKE	HTW	DTEO Boscombe Down

UNITED STATES OF AMERICA
N America

Since the collapse of the Soviet Union the USA has become the leading global power particularly when it comes to providing hardware and sustained military power. The backbone of NATO and economically the wealthiest of its members, America has taken on a role of providing support for peacekeeping actions worldwide, sometimes with criticism. The size and strength of US capabilities is reflected below, whether this can continue to be justified remains to be seen.

SERIAL SYSTEM   The USAF and US Army serial system is straightforward but the presentation on the aircraft is not uniform and is sometimes confusing. A two digit fiscal year (FY, indicating the year that the acquisition was funded) is followed by what is now a sequential four digit number (but in past years has run to five digits, particularly during the 1960s). A new sequence is begun each FY at 0001.

For example: 63-8004 is a Boeing KC-135R, '63' refers to the FY and '8004' shows it was the eight thousand and fourth aircraft procured in that year. This is usually presented as 38004 on a transport type. A combat type may show just 63-004 with a two letter tail code and this style is sometimes adopted on transport and special mission types.

Although now grouped with the USAF purchases, the US Army (until 1985) was allocating a five digit number prefixed by the FY without re-starting the sequence each new year.

The USN and USMC serials are allocated sequentially by the Navy Bureau of Aeronautics and are known colloquially as Bu Numbers. They currently run in the 165000 series, purchases being allocated blocks according to which FY they were bought.

USCG aircraft wear (with one exception) four digit numbers, the first two digits of which are unique to type. The exceptions are the VIP aircraft which are marked 01, 02 etc numbers, are usually re-allocated when the aircraft is replaced.

Customs Service and NASA equipment bear civilian 'N' registrations, usually with common identifying suffix letters.

Transfers between US air arms used to involve re-serialling but more commonly now the presentation is simply changed to conform to the style normally allocated.

Civil aircraft taken on charge (sometimes temporarily) can just have their c/n prefixed with an appropriate (or deliberately confusing) FY !

United States Air Force - USAF

*UNITS*BASES:*

Air Combat Command - ACC

tail code/band colour

41st RW, 71st RQS, 'Kings' Moody AFB, GA	MY	HC-130P (was 347 W until Apr01)
53rd Wg, 82nd ATRS, Eglin AFB, FL	WE	E-9A, 707 (uncoded)
55th Wg, 1st ACCS, Offutt AFB, NB	OF	E-4B
55th Wg, 38th RS, 'Fighting Hellcats', Offutt AFB, NB	OF, green	RC-135U/V/W
55th Wg, 45th RS, 'Sylvester', Offutt AFB, NB	OF, black	OC-135B, WC-135W, RC-135S, TC-135B/S
55th Wg, 82nd RS, Kadena AB, Japan		RC-135U/V/W
55th Wg, 95th RS, RAF Mildenhall, United Kingdom		RC-135V/W
93rd ACW, 12th ACCS, Robins AFB, GA	WR, green	E-8C
93rd ACW, 16th ACCS, Robins AFB, GA	WR, red	E-8C
93rd ACW, 93rd TRS, Robins AFB, GA	WR, yellow	TE-8C
355th Wg, 41st ECS, 'Scorpions', Davis-Montham AFB, AZ	DM, blue	EC-130H
355th Wg, 42nd ACCS, 'Axe', Davis-Montham AFB, AZ	DM, grey	EC-130E
355th Wg, 43rd ECS, 'Bats', Davis-Montham AFB, AZ	DM, red	EC-130H
363rd AEW, 9th EAS, Prince Sultan AB-Al Kahrj, Saudi Arabia		C-130E/H
363rd AEW, 9th ERQS, Prince Sultan AB-Al Kahrj, Saudi Arabia		HC-130P
363rd AEW, 363rd EAACS, Prince Sultan AB-Al Kahrj, Saudi Arabia		E-3B/C
363rd AEW, 363rd EARS, Prince Sultan AB-Al Kahrj, Saudi Arabia		KC-135E/R
363rd AEW, 363rd EAS, Prince Sultan AB-Al Kahrj, Saudi Arabia		C-130E/H
363rd AEW, 763rd EARS, Prince Sultan AB-Al Kahrj, Saudi Arabia		KC-135E/R
363rd AEW, 763rd EAS, Prince Sultan AB-Al Kahrj, Saudi Arabia		C-130E/H
363rd AEW, 763rd ERS, Prince Sultan AB-Al Kahrj, Saudi Arabia		RC-135V/W
366th Wg, 22nd ARS, 'Mules', Mountain Home AFB, ID	MO	KC-135R
552nd ACW, 960th AACS 'Viking Warriors', Tinker AFB, OK	OK	E-3B/C
552nd ACW, 963rd AACS, 'Blue Knights', Tinker AFB, OK	OK, black	E-3B/C
552nd ACW, 964th AACS, Tinker AFB, OK	OK, purple	E-3B/C
552nd ACW, 965th AACS, Tinker AFB, OK	OK, yellow	E-3B/C
552nd ACW, 966th AACS, Tinker AFB, OK	OK, blue	E-3B/C, TC-18E

Air Education & Training Command - AETC

81st TW, 45th AS, Keesler AFB, MS	KS	C-21A
Inter-American Air Forces Academy, Kelly AFB, TX		Various GIA
82nd TW, Sheppard AFB, TX	ST	Various GIA
12th FTW, 99th FTS 'Panthers', Randolph AFB, TX	RA, yellow	T-1A
12th FTW, 559nd FTS 'Billy Goats', Randolph AFB, TX	RA, blue	T-1A
12th FTW, 562nd FTS 'Gators', Randolph AFB, TX	RA, blue	T-43A
14th FTW, 48th FTS 'Alley Cats', Columbus AFB, MS	CB	T-1A
47th FTW, 86th FTS 'Rio Lobos', Laughlin AFB, TX	XL, black-white	T-1A
58th SOW, 550th SOS 'Wolf Pack', Kirtland AFB, NM		MC-130H/P
71st FTW, 32nd FTS 'Liberty', Vance AFB, OK	VN, red-blue-yellow	T-1A
97th AMW, 54th ARS 'Masters', Altus AFB, OK		KC-135R, no assigned aircraft
97th AMW, 55th ARS, Altus AFB, OK		KC-135R
97th AMW, 56th AS, Altus AFB, OK		C-5A
97th AMW, 58th AS, Altus AFB, OK		C-17A
314th AW, 53rd AS 'Black Jacks', Little Rock AFB, AR	black	C-130E
314th AW, 62nd AS 'Blue Barons', Little Rock AFB, AR	blue	C-130E

Air Force Material Command - AFMC

645th MATS, Palmdale Airport, CA		NC-130E, EC-130H
646 MATS, det 2, Majors Field, Greenville, TX		WC-135W
46th TW, 40th FLTS, Duke Field, FL	ET	NC-130A
46th TW, 586th FLTS, Holloman AFB, NM	HT	C-12J (support for AT-38A)
486th FLTS, Wright Patterson AFB, OH		C-22C, 707
412th TW, 412th FLTS, Edwards AFB, CA		C-135C
412th TW, 418th FLTS, Edwards AFB, CA	ED	Various
412th TW, 452nd FLTS, Edwards AFB, CA		EC-18B, KC-135R, NKC-135E
412th TW, 452nd FLTS, det 2, Kirtland AFB, NM		NKC-135B/E, C-135E
Aerospace Maintenance & Regeneration Centre, Davis-Monthan AFB, AZ		Various

Air Force Special Operations Command - AFSOC

16th SOW, 4th SOS, 'Ghostriders', Hurlbert Field, FL		AC-130U
16th SOW, 6th SOS, 'Commandos', Hurlbert Field, FL		CASA 212
16th SOW, 8th SOS, 'Blackbirds', Hurlbert Field/Duke Field, FL		MC-130E, C-130E
16th SOW, 9th SOS, 'Night Wings', Eglin AFB, FL		MC-130P
16th SOW, 15th SOS, Eglin AFB, FL		MC-130H
16th SOW, 16th SOS 'Spectre', Eglin AFB, FL		AC-130H

352nd SOG, 7th SOS, RAF Mildenhall, United Kingdom		MC-130H
352nd SOG, 67th SOS, RAF Mildenhall, United Kingdom		MC-130P, C-130E
353rd SOG, 1st SOS, Kadena AB, Japan		MC-130H
353rd SOG, 17th SOS, Kadena AB, Japan		MC-130P, C-130E
427th SOS, Pope AFB, NC		CASA 212, UV-20A

Air Mobility Command - AMC

6th ARW, 91st ARS, MacDill AFB, FL	blue	KC-135R
6th ARW, 310th AS, MacDill AFB, FL (CinCENTCOM)		C-37A
19th ARG, 99th ARS, Robins AFB, GA	blue	KC-135R
22nd ARW, 344th ARS 'Ravens', McConnell AFB, KS		KC-135R/T
22nd ARW, 349th ARS 'Blue Knights', McConnell AFB, KS		KC-135R
22nd ARW, 350th ARS 'Red Falcons', McConnell AFB, KS		KC-135R
22nd ARW, 384th ARS 'Square Patches', McConnell AFB, KS		KC-135R
43rd AW, 2nd AS 'Lancers', Pope AFB, NC	blue	C-130E
43rd AW, 41st AS 'Black Cats', Pope AFB, NC	green	C-130E
60th AMW, 6th ARS, Travis AFB, CA	blue	KC-10A
60th AMW, 9th ARS 'Universal', Travis AFB, CA	red	KC-10A
60th AMW, 21st AS 'Beeliners', Travis AFB, CA	blue	C-5A/B/C
60th AMW, 22nd AS, Travis AFB, CA	gold	C-5A/B
62nd AW, 4th AS 'Fightin'Fourth', McChord AFB, WA	green/red	C-141B (to replace with C-17A)
62nd AW, 7th AS 'Willing and able', McChord AFB, WA	green/blue	C-17A
62nd AW, 8th AS 'Soarin' Eagles', McChord AFB, WA	green/silver	C-141B (to replace with C-17A)
89th AW, Presidential Flight, Andrews AFB, MD		VC-25A
89th AW, 1st AS, Andrews AFB, MD		C-137C, C-32A (C-40B from 2002)
89th AW, 99th AS, Andrews AFB, MD		VC-9C, C-37A, C-20B/C/H, C-21A
92nd ARW, 92nd ARS, Fairchild AFB, WA	black	KC-135R/T
92nd ARW, 93rd ARS, Fairchild AFB, WA	blue	KC-135R/T
92nd ARW, 96th ARS 'Screamin' Eagles', Fairchild AFB, WA	green	KC-135R/T
92nd ARW, 97th ARS, Fairchild AFB, WA	gold	KC-135R/T
305th AMW, 2nd ARS 'Second to None', McGuire AFB, NJ	red	KC-10A
305th AMW, 6th AS 'Bully Beef Express', McGuire AFB, NJ	blue	C-141B (SOLL II)
		under AFSOC authority
305th AMW, 13th AS, McGuire AFB, NJ	red	C-141B
305th AMW, 32nd ARS, McGuire AFB, NJ	blue	KC-10A
317th AG, 39th AS 'Trailblazers', Dyess AFB, TX		C-130H
317th AG, 40th AS, Dyess AFB, TX		C-130H
319th ARW, 905th ARS, Grand Forks, ND	blue	KC-135R
319th ARW, 906th ARS, Grand Forks, ND	yellow	KC-135R
319th ARW, 911th ARS, Grand Forks, ND	red	KC-135R
319th ARW, 912th ARS, Grand Forks, ND	white	KC-135R
375th AW, 11th AS, Scott AFB, IL		C-9A
375th AW, 457th AS, Andrews AFB, MD		C-21A
375th AW, 12th ALF, Langley AFB, VA		C-21A
375th AW, 47th ALF, Wright Patterson AFB, OH		C-21A
375th AW, 54th ALF, Maxwell AFB, AL		C-21A
375th AW, 458th AS, Scott AFB, IL		C-21A
375th AW, 84th ALF, Peterson AFB, CO		C-21A
375th AW, 311th ALF, Offutt AFB, NE	OF	C-21A
375th AW, 332nd ALF, Randolph AFB, TX		C-21A
436th AW, 3rd AS, Dover AFB, DE		C-5A/B
436th AW, 9th AS 'Pelicans', Dover AFB, DE		C-5A/B
437th AW, 14th AS, Charleston AFB, SC		C-17A
437th AW, 15th AS 'Global Eagles', Charleston AFB, SC		C-17A
437th AW, 16th AS, Charleston AFB, SC (currently deactivated)		C-17A SOLL (from Oct2003)
437th AW, 17th AS, Charleston AFB, SC		C-17A
463rd AG, 50th AS 'Red Devils', Little Rock AFB, AL	red	C-130H
463rd AG, 61st AS 'Green Hornets', Little Rock AFB, AL	green	C-130H

Pacific Air Forces - PACAF

3rd Wg, 517th AS 'Firebirds', Elmendorf AFB, AK	AK	C-130H
3rd Wg, 517th AS det 1, Elmendorf AFB, AK	AK	C-12F,/J
3rd Wg, 962nd AACS 'Eye of the Eagle', Elmendorf AFB, AK	AK	E-3B/C
15th ABW, 65th AS, Hickam AFB, HI		C-135C/E (C-37A due to replace)
18th Wg, 909th ARS 'Shoguns', Kadena AB, Japan	ZZ	KC-135R
18th Wg, 909th ARS, det 1, Anderson AFB, Guam	ZZ	KC-135R
18th Wg, 961st AACS 'Eyes of the Pacific', Kadena AB, Japan	ZZ	E-3B/C
51st FW, 55th ALF 'Double Nickel', Osan, Republic of Korea	OS	C-12J (supporting A-10 and F-16)
374th AW, 30th AS, Yokota AB, Japan		C-9A
374th AW, 36th AS 'Eagle Airlifters', Yokota AB, Japan	YJ	C-130E
374th AW, 459th AS 'Orient Express', Yokota AB, Japan		C-21A

US Air Forces in Europe - USAFE

Unit	Code	Aircraft	
86th AW, 37th AS 'Bluetail Flies', Ramstein AB, Germany	RS	C-130E	
86th AW, 75th AS, Ramstein AB, Germany	RS	C-9A	c/s Spar**
86th AW, 75th AS, det. at SHAPE at Cheives AB, Belgium		C-37A	
86th AW, 76th AS, Ramstein AB, Germany		C-20A. C-21A, C-37A	c/s Spar**
86th AW, 7005th ABS, Echterdingen AB, Germany (for USEUCOM)		C-21A	c/s Clue**
100th ARW, 351st ARS, RAF Mildenhall, United Kingdom	D	KC-135R	

Air Force Reserve Command - AFRC
Associate units with no assigned aircraft are not listed

Unit	Color	Aircraft
94th AW, 700th AS, Dobbins ARB-Marietta, GA	black	C-130H
302nd AW, 731st AS, Peterson AFB, CO	green	C-130H
403rd Wg, 53rd WRS 'Hurricane Hunters', Keesler AFB, MS	blue	WC-130H converting to WC-130J
403rd Wg, 815th AS 'Jennies', Keesler AFB, MS	red	C-130E converting to C-130J
433th AW, 68th AS, Kelly AFB, TX		C-5A
434th ARW, 72nd ARS, Grissom ARB, IN	blue	KC-135R
434th ARW, 74th ARS, Grissom ARB, IN	red	KC-135R
439th AW, 337th AS, Patriot Wing-Westover ARB, MA	red	C-5A
440th AW, 95th AS 'Badgers', General Mitchell IAP-Milwaukee, WI	yellow	C-130H
445th AW, 89th AS 'Rhinos', Wright-Patterson AFB, OH		C-141C
445th AW, 356th AS, Wright-Patterson AFB, OH		C-141C
452nd AW, 336th ARS 'Rrats', March ARB, CA	yellow	KC-135R
452nd AW, 729th AS 'Pegasus', March ARB, CA		C-141C
452nd AW, 730th AS, March ARB, CA		C-141C
459th AW, 756th AS, Andrews AFB, MD		C-141C
507th ARW, 465th ARS 'Okies', Tinker AFB, OK	blue	KC-135R/T
908th AW, 357th AS, Maxwell AFB, AL	blue	C-130H
910th AW, 757th AS 'Blue Tigers', Youngstown-Warren RAP OH	blue	C-130H
910th AW, 773th AS 'Quiet Professionals', Youngstown-Warren RAP OH	red	C-130H
911th AW, 758th AS, Greater Pittsburgh IAP, PA	black	C-130H
913th AW, 327th AS, NAS Willow Grove JRB, PA		C-130H
914th AW, 328th AS, Niagara Falls IAP, NY	green	C-130H
916th ARW, 77th ARS, Seymour Johnson AFB, SC		KC-135R
919th SOW, 5th SOS, Eglin AFB, FL		MC-130P
927th ARW, 63rd ARS, Selfridge ANGB, MI	purple	KC-135R
934th AW, 96th AS 'Flying Vikings', Minneapolis-St Paul IAP, MN	purple	C-130E
939th RW*, 303rd RQS, Portland IAP, OR	PD	HC-130P, C-130E
939th RW, 920th RQG/39th RQS, Patrick AFB, FL	FL	HC-130P
* to be re-designated as the 939th ARW and take KC-135Rs in 2002.		
940th ARW, 314th ARS 'Warhawks', Beale AFB, CA	red	KC-135E

Air National Guard - ANG

Unit	Code	Aircraft
101st ARW, 132nd ARS 'Maineacs', Bangor IAP, ME		KC-135E
105th AW, 137th AS 'Fearless Ones', Stewart IAP-Newburgh, NY		C-5A
106th RW, 102nd RQS, Frances K Gabreski ANGB, Long Island, NY	LI	HC-130N/P
107th ARW, 136th ARS 'New York's Finest', Niagara Falls ARB, NY		KC-135R
108th ARW, 141st ARS 'Tigers', McGuire AFB, NJ		C-135B, KC-135E
108th ARW, 150th ARS, McGuire AFB, NJ		KC-135E
109th AW, 139th AS, Stratton ANGB-Schenectady County Airport, NY		C-130H/LC-130H, C-26B
111th FW, 103rd FS, NAS Willow Grove JRB, PA		C-26A (support to A-10)
113th Wg, 201st AS, Andrews AFB, MD		C-21A, C-22B, C-38A (replacing C-22B)
115th FW, 176th FS, 'Badgers', Truax Field-Madison, WI		C-26B (support to F-16)
117th ARW, 106th ARS 'Rebels', Sumter Smith ANGB-Birmingham MAP, AL		KC-135R
118th AW, 105th AS 'Old Hickory', Nashville Metro Airport, TN		C-130H
121st ARW, 145th ARS 'Tazz', Rickenbacker IAP, OH		KC-135R
121st ARW, 166th ARS 'Sluff', Rickenbacker IAP, OH		KC-135R
123rd AW, 165th AS, Standiford Field-Louisville IAP, KY		C-130H
124th Wg, 189th AS, Boise Air Terminal, Boise, ID	ID	C-130E
125th FW, 159th FS, 'Jaguars', Jacksonville, IAP, FL	FL	C-26B (support to F-15)
126th ARW, 108th ARS, Scott AFB, IL		KC-135E
127th AG, 171st AS 'Red Devils', Selfridge ANGB, MI	yellow/black	C-130E
128th ARW, 126th ARS, General Mitchell IAP-Milwaukee, WI		KC-135R
129th RW, 129th RQS, Moffett Federal ANGB, CA	CA	H/MC-130P
130th AW, 130th AS 'Mountaineers', Yeager Airport-Charleston, WV	WV	C-130H

133rd AW, 109th AS, Minneapolis-St Paul IAP, MN	MN	C-130H
134th ARW, 151st ARS, McGhee Tyson ANGB, TN		KC-135E
136th AW, 181st AS, NAS Fort Worth-Carswell JRB, TX	TX	C-130H
137th AW, 185th AS, Will Rogers World IAP, OK	OK	C-130H
139th AW, 180th AS, Rosecrans Memorial Airport-St Joseph, MO	XP	C-130H
140th Wg, 200th AS, Buckley ANGB, CO		C-21A, C-26B
141st ARW, 116th ARS, Fairchild AFB, WA		KC-135E, C-26B
142nd FW, 123rd FS, Portland IAP, OR		C-26A (support to F-15)
143rd AW, 143rd AS, Quonset State Airport-Providence, RI	RI, red	C-130E
		(to get C-130J-30 from Nov2001)
144th FW, 194th FS, 'Griffins', Fresno-Yosemite ANGB, CA		C-26B (support to F-16)
145th AW, 156th AS, Charlotte-Douglas IAP, NC	NC, blue	C-130H
146th AW, 115th AS, Channel Islands ANGB-Point Mugu, CA		C-130E
147th FW, 111th FS, 'Ace in the Hole', Ellington ANGB, TX		C-26B (support to F-16)
150th FW, 188th FS 'Tacos', Kirtland AFB, NM		C-26B (support to F-16)
151st ARW, 191st ARS 'Salty Guard', Salt Lake City IAP, UT		KC-135E
152nd AW, 192nd AS 'High Rollers', May ANGB/		
Reno-Tahoe Intl, NV		C-130H replacing C-130E
153rd AW, 187th AS, Cheyenne MAP, WY	WY	C-130H
154th Wg, 203rd ARS, Hickam Field, HI	HH	KC-135R
154th AW, 204th AS, Hickam Field, HI		C-130H
155th ARW, 173rd ARS 'Huskers', Lincoln ANGB, NE		KC-135R
156th AW, 198th AS 'Buccaneros',		
Luis Munoz Marin ANGB, PR		C-130E
157th ARW, 133rd ARS, Pease ANGB, NH		KC-135R
159 FW, 122 FS, New Orleans JRB, LA	JZ	C-130H (support to F-15)
161st ARW, 197th ARS 'Copperheads',		
Phoenix-Sky Harbour IAP, AZ		KC-135E
162nd FW, 148th FS, Tucson IAP, AZ		C-26B (support to F-16)
163rd ARW, 196th ARS, March ARB, CA		KC-135R
164th AW, 155th AS, Memphis IAP, TN		C-141C
165th AW, 158th AS, Savannah IAP, GA	red	C-130H
166th AW, 142nd AS, New Castle County Airport, DE	DE, grey	C-130H
167th AW, 167th AS, Shepherd Field ANGB, WV	WV, black	C-130H
168th ARW, 168th ARS, Eielson AFB, AK		KC-135R
169th FW ,157th FS, 'Swamp Foxes',		
Columbia-McEntire ANGB, SC	SC	C-130H (support to F-16)
171st ARW, 146th ARS, Greater Pittsburgh IAP, PA	black	KC-135E
171st ARW, 147th ARS, Greater Pittsburgh IAP, PA	yellow	KC-135E
172nd AW, 183rd AS, Thompson ANGB-Jackson IAP, MS	MS	C-141C
175th AW, 135th AS, Baltimore-Martin State Airport, MD		C-130J
176th Wg, 144th AS, Anchorage IAP, AK	AK	C-130H
176th Wg, 210th RQS, Anchorage IAP, AK	AK	HC-130H/P
179th AW, 164th AS, Mansfield Lahm Airport, OH	OH	C-130H
182nd AW, 169th AS, Greater Peoria Regional Airport, IL	IL	C-130E
186th ARW, 153rd ARS 'Magnolia Militia',		
Key Field ANGB-Meridian, MS		KC-135R, C-26B
187th FW, 160th FS, 'Snakes', Dannelly Field-Montgomery, AL		C-26B (support to F-16)
189th AW, 154th TS 'Razorbacks', Little Rock AFB, AR		C-130E
190th ARW, 117th ARS 'Coyotes', Forbes Field-Topeka, KS		KC-135D/E
193rd SOW, 193rd SOS, Harrisburg IAP, PA		EC-130E(CL/RR)

US Air Force Academy

34th TW, 94th FTS, AFA Colorado Springs, CO	UV-18A
34th TW, 98th FTS, AFA Colorado Springs, CO	UV-18B

US Embassies with aircraft assigned

Abidjan, Ivory Coast	C-12A
Ankara, Turkey	C-12A
Athens, Greece	C-12A
Bangkok, Thailand	C-12A
Bogota, Colombia	C-12A
Buenos Aires, Argentina	C-12A
Canberra, Australia	C-12A
Islamabad, Pakistan	C-12A
Jakarta, Indonesia	C-12A
Kinshasa, Congo	C-12A
Manila, Philippines	C-12A
Rabat, Morocco	C-12A
Riaydh, Saudi Arabia	C-12A
Tegucigalpa, Honduras	C-12A

Civilian Contractors:

Aviation Development Corp, Montgomery, AL	OT-47B
EG&G Special Projects, Las Vegas-McCarran Airport, NV (c/s Janet)	B200, B1900, 737/CT-43

PLANS   Up to 180 C-17s are now being planned for acquisition.
Re-engining the C-5Bs (with GE CF-6-80) rather than replacement, current serviceability hovers between 50 and 60%.
544 KC-135 are being upgraded as part of the PACER CRAG (Compass, Radar And GPS) programme, a replacement has been suggested in the form of 100 new Boeing 767s on a lease/purchase basis.
A requirement for up to 168 C-130Js is declared but funding is a problem with the C-17 taking most of what is allocated at present and orders only slowly being placed.
While EC-130Js are on order the EC-130Es may be replaced by a 767-300 fleet offering more capabilty and flexibility.
Following the Navy's lead, seven 737-700s have been ordered for delivery from 2002 as the C-40B, some are destined for the ANG as C-22 replacements.

54-1627	Lockheed AC-130A (L-182-1A) Hercules	3014		Std AMARC [CF015]
54-1628	Lockheed AC-130A (L-182-1A) Hercules	3015		Std AMARC [CF178]
54-1632	Lockheed C-130A (L-182-1A) Hercules	3019		Std AMARC [CF017]
54-1634	Lockheed C-130A (L-182-1A) Hercules	3021		Std AMARC [CF189]
55-0004	Lockheed C-130A (L-182-1A) Hercules	3031		Std AMARC [CF085]
55-0011	Lockheed AC-130A (L-182-1A) Hercules	3038		Std AMARC [CF168]
55-0022	Lockheed NC-130A (L-182-1A) Hercules	3049	46TW	
55-0026	Lockheed C-130A (L-182-1A) Hercules	3053		Std AMARC [CF152]
55-0029	Lockheed AC-130A (L-182-1A) Hercules	3056		Std AMARC [CF167]
55-0033	Lockheed C-130A (L-182-1A) Hercules	3060		Std AMARC [CF077]
55-0036	Lockheed C-130A (L-182-1A) Hercules	3063		Std AMARC [CF073]
55-0040	Lockheed AC-130A (L-182-1A) Hercules	3067		Std AMARC [CF018]
55-0041	Lockheed C-130A (L-182-1A) Hercules	3068		Std AMARC [CF068]
55-0046	Lockheed AC-130A (L-182-1A) Hercules	3073		Std AMARC [CF166]
55-3119 / OF	Boeing NKC-135A Stratotanker	17235 /T0002		Std AMARC [CA067]
55-3120	Boeing NKC-135A Stratotanker	17236 /T0003		Std AMARC [CA095]
55-3122	Boeing NKC-135A Stratotanker	17238 /T0005		Std AMARC [CA094]
55-3125	Boeing EC-135Y	17241 /T0008		Std AMARC [CA126]
55-3127	Boeing NKC-135A Stratotanker	17243 /T0010		Std AMARC [CA040]
55-3128	Boeing NKC-135A Stratotanker	17244 /T0011		Std AMARC [CA106]
55-3129 / FF	Boeing EC-135P	17245 /T0012		Std AMARC [CA008]
55-3131	Boeing NKC-135A Stratotanker	17247 /T0014		Std AMARC [CA053]
55-3132	Boeing NKC-135E Stratotanker	17248 /T0015	412TW	
55-3135	Boeing NKC-135E Stratotanker	17251 /T0018	412TW	
55-3136 / DY	Boeing KC-135A Stratotanker	17252 /T0019		Std AMARC [CA062]
55-3137	Boeing KC-135A Stratotanker	17253 /T0020		Std AMARC [CA070]
55-3142	Boeing KC-135A Stratotanker	17258 /T0025		Std AMARC [CA104]
55-3143	Boeing KC-135E Stratotanker	17259 /T0026	161ARW AZ ANG	
55-3145	Boeing KC-135E Stratotanker	17261 /T0028	940ARW	
55-3146	Boeing KC-135E Stratotanker	17262 /T0029	108ARW/NJ ANG	
56-0470	Lockheed C-130A (L-182-1A) Hercules	3078		Std AMARC [CF071]
56-0471	Lockheed C-130A (L-182-1A) Hercules	3079		Std AMARC [CF087]
56-0481	Lockheed C-130A (L-182-1A) Hercules	3089		Std AMARC [CF069]
56-0494	Lockheed C-130A (L-182-1A) Hercules	3102		Std AMARC [CF100]
56-0495	Lockheed C-130A (L-182-1A) Hercules	3103		Std AMARC [CF097]
56-0503	Lockheed C-130A (L-182-1A) Hercules	3111		Std AMARC [CF101]
56-0523	Lockheed C-130A (L-182-1A) Hercules	3131		Std AMARC [CF082]
56-0527	Lockheed DC-130A (L-182-1A) Hercules	3135		Std AMARC [CF051]
56-0529	Lockheed C-130A (L-182-1A) Hercules	3137		Std AMARC [CF091]
56-0544	Lockheed C-130A (L-182-1A) Hercules	3152		Std AMARC [CF084]
56-3551	Boeing KC-135A Stratotanker	17340 /T0030		Std AMARC [CA074]
56-3553	Boeing KC-135E Stratotanker	17342 /T0032	108ARW/NJ ANG	
56-3554	Boeing KC-135A Stratotanker	17343 /T0033		Std AMARC [CA047]
56-3610	Boeing KC-135A Stratotanker	17349 /T0039		Std AMARC [CA059]
56-3611	Boeing KC-135A Stratotanker	17350 /T0040		Std AMARC [CA072]
56-3613	Boeing KC-135A Stratotanker	17352 /T0042		Std AMARC [CA029]
56-3614	Boeing KC-135E Stratotanker	17353 /T0043	108ARW/NJ ANG	
56-3606	Boeing KC-135E Stratotanker	17355 /T0045	101ARW/ME ANG	
56-3607	Boeing KC-135E Stratotanker	17356 /T0046	134ARW TN ANG	
56-3608	Boeing KC-135E Stratotanker	17357 /T0047		Std AMARC [CA030]
56-3609	Boeing KC-135E Stratotanker	17358 /T0048	134ARW TN ANG	
56-3610	Boeing KC-135A Stratotanker	17359 /T0049		Std AMARC [CA055]
56-3611	Boeing KC-135E Stratotanker	17360 /T0050	171ARW/PA ANG	
56-3612	Boeing KC-135E Stratotanker	17361 /T0051	171ARW/PA ANG	
56-3614	Boeing KC-135A Stratotanker	17363 /T0053		Std AMARC [CA064]
56-3615	Boeing KC-135A Stratotanker	17364 /T0054		Std AMARC [CA032]
56-3619	Boeing KC-135A Stratotanker	17368 /T0058		Std AMARC [CA051]

56-3620	Boeing KC-135A Stratotanker	17369 /T0059	Std AMARC [CA096]
56-3621	Boeing KC-135A Stratotanker	17370 /T0060	Std AMARC [CA102]
56-3622	Boeing KC-135E Stratotanker	17371 /T0061	101ARW/ME ANG
56-3623	Boeing GKC-135E Stratotanker	17372 /T0062	82TW
56-3624	Boeing KC-135A Stratotanker	17373 /T0063	Std AMARC [CA103]
56-3625 / DY	Boeing KC-135A Stratotanker	17374 /T0064	Std AMARC [CA063]
56-3626	Boeing KC-135E Stratotanker	17375 /T0065	171ARW/PA ANG
56-3627	Boeing KC-135A Stratotanker	17376 /T0066	Std AMARC [CA054]
56-3630	Boeing KC-135E Stratotanker	17379 /T0069	171ARW/PA ANG
56-3631	Boeing KC-135E Stratotanker	17380 /T0070	151ARW/UT ANG
56-3633	Boeing KC-135A Stratotanker	17382 /T0072	Std AMARC [CA037]
56-3634	Boeing KC-135A Stratotanker	17383 /T0073	Std AMARC [CA049]
56-3635 / DY	Boeing KC-135A Stratotanker	17384 /T0074	Std AMARC [CA038]
56-3636	Boeing KC-135A Stratotanker	17385 /T0075	Std AMARC [CA031]
56-3637	Boeing KC-135A Stratotanker	17386 /T0076	Std AMARC [CA033]
56-3638	Boeing KC-135E Stratotanker	17387 /T0077	161ARW/AZ ANG
56-3640	Boeing KC-135E Stratotanker	17389 /T0079	101ARW/ME ANG
56-3641	Boeing KC-135E Stratotanker	17390 /T0080	190ARW/KS ANG
56-3642	Boeing KC-135A Stratotanker	17391 /T0081	Std AMARC [CA078]
56-3643	Boeing KC-135E Stratotanker	17392 /T0082	134ARW TN ANG
56-3644	Boeing KC-135A Stratotanker	17393 /T0083	Std AMARC [CA028]
56-3645	Boeing GKC-135E Stratotanker	17394 /T0084	82TW
56-3646 / DY	Boeing KC-135A Stratotanker	17395 /T0085	Std AMARC [CA034]
56-3647	Boeing KC-135A Stratotanker	17396 /T0086	Std AMARC [CA044]
56-3648	Boeing KC-135E Stratotanker	17397 /T0087	171ARW/PA ANG
56-3649	Boeing KC-135A Stratotanker	17398 /T0088	Std AMARC [CA065]
56-3650	Boeing KC-135E Stratotanker	17399 /T0089	141ARW/WA ANG
56-3651	Boeing KC-135A Stratotanker	17400 /T0090	Std AMARC [CA041]
56-3652	Boeing KC-135A Stratotanker	17401 /T0091	Std AMARC [CA077]
56-3653	Boeing KC-135A Stratotanker	17402 /T0092	Std AMARC [CA025]
56-3654	Boeing KC-135E Stratotanker	17403 /T0093	101ARW/ME ANG
56-3658	Boeing KC-135E Stratotanker	17407 /T0097	190ARW/KS ANG
57-0458	Lockheed C-130A (L-182-1A) Hercules	3165	Std AMARC [CF074]
57-0488	Lockheed C-130D (L-182-1A) Hercules	3195	Std AMARC [CF016]
57-0492	Lockheed C-130D (L-182-1A) Hercules	3199	Std AMARC [CF046]
57-0494	Lockheed C-130A (L-182-1A) Hercules	3201	Std AMARC [CF040]
57-1419	Boeing KC-135R Stratotanker	17490 /T0099	19ARG
57-1420	Boeing KC-135A Stratotanker	17491 /T0100	Std AMARC [CA046]
57-1421	Boeing KC-135E Stratotanker	17492 /T0101	141ARW/WA ANG
57-1422	Boeing KC-135E Stratotanker	17493 /T0102	927ARW
57-1423	Boeing KC-135E Stratotanker	17494 /T0103	171ARW/PA ANG
57-1425	Boeing KC-135E Stratotanker	17496 /T0105	134ARW/TN ANG
57-1426	Boeing KC-135E Stratotanker	17497 /T0106	161ARW/AZ ANG
57-1427	Boeing KC-135R Stratotanker	17498 /T0107	121ARW/OH ANG
57-1428	Boeing KC-135E Stratotanker	17499 /T0108	163ARW/CA ANG
57-1429	Boeing KC-135E Stratotanker	17500 /T0109	190ARW/KS ANG
57-1430	Boeing KC-135R Stratotanker	17501 /T0110	157ARW/NH ANG
57-1431	Boeing KC-135E Stratotanker	17502 /T0111	108ARW/NJ ANG
57-1432	Boeing KC-135R Stratotanker	17503 /T0112	117ARW/AL ANG
57-1433	Boeing KC-135E Stratotanker	17504 /T0113	161ARW/AZ ANG
57-1434	Boeing KC-135E Stratotanker	17505 /T0114	141ARW/WA ANG
57-1435 / ZZ	Boeing KC-135R Stratotanker	17506 /T0115	18Wg
57-1436	Boeing KC-135R Stratotanker	17507 /T0116	163ARW/CA ANG
57-1437	Boeing KC-135R Stratotanker	17508 /T0117	916ARW
57-1438	Boeing KC-135E Stratotanker	17509 /T0118	927ARW
57-1439	Boeing KC-135R Stratotanker	17510 /T0119	6ARW
57-1440	Boeing KC-135E Stratotanker	17511 /T0120	319ARW
57-1441	Boeing KC-135E Stratotanker	17512 /T0121	126ARW/IL ANG
57-1443	Boeing KC-135E Stratotanker	17514 /T0123	101ARW/ME ANG
57-1445	Boeing KC-135E Stratotanker	17516 /T0125	108ARW/NJ ANG
57-1447	Boeing KC-135E Stratotanker	17518 /T0127	171ARW/PA ANG
57-1448	Boeing KC-135E Stratotanker	17519 /T0128	101ARW/ME ANG
57-1450	Boeing KC-135E Stratotanker	17521 /T0130	101ARW/ME ANG
57-1451	Boeing KC-135E Stratotanker	17522 /T0131	141ARW/WA ANG
57-1452	Boeing KC-135E Stratotanker	17523 /T0132	161ARW/AZ ANG
57-1453	Boeing KC-135R Stratotanker	17524 /T0133	117ARW/AL ANG
57-1454	Boeing KC-135R Stratotanker	17525 /T0134	319ARW
57-1455	Boeing KC-135R Stratotanker	17526 /T0135	134ARW/TN ANG
57-1456 / ZZ	Boeing KC-135R Stratotanker	17527 /T0136	18Wg
57-1458	Boeing KC-135E Stratotanker	17529 /T0138	126ARW/IL ANG
57-1459	Boeing KC-135E Stratotanker	17530 /T0139	163ARW/CA ANG
57-1460	Boeing KC-135E Stratotanker	17531 /T0140	190ARW/KS ANG
57-1461	Boeing KC-135R Stratotanker	17532 /T0141	155ARW/NE ANG
57-1462	Boeing KC-135R Stratotanker	17533 /T0142	121ARW/OH ANG

57-1463	Boeing KC-135E Stratotanker	17534 /T0143	190ARW/KS ANG
57-1464	Boeing KC-135E Stratotanker	17535 /T0144	108ARW/NJ ANG
57-1465	Boeing KC-135E Stratotanker	17536 /T0145	134ARW/TN ANG
57-1467	Boeing KC-135A Stratotanker	17538 /T0147	Std AMARC [CA039]
57-1468	Boeing KC-135E Stratotanker	17539 /T0148	452AMW
57-1469	Boeing KC-135R Stratotanker	17540 /T0149	121ARW/OH ANG
57-1471	Boeing KC-135E Stratotanker	17542 /T0151	101ARW/ME ANG
57-1472	Boeing KC-135R Stratotanker	17543 /T0152	434ARW
57-1473	Boeing KC-135R Stratotanker	17544 /T0153	22ARW
57-1474	Boeing KC-135R Stratotanker	17545 /T0154	
57-1475	Boeing KC-135E Stratotanker	17546 /T0155	161ARW/AZ ANG
57-1476	Boeing KC-135A Stratotanker	17547 /T0156	Std AMARC [CA035]
57-1477	Boeing KC-135A Stratotanker	17548 /T0157	Std AMARC [CA036]
57-1479	Boeing KC-135E Stratotanker	17550 /T0159	452AMW
57-1480	Boeing KC-135E Stratotanker	17551 /T0160	126ARW/IL ANG
57-1482	Boeing KC-135E Stratotanker	17553 /T0162	190ARW/KS ANG
57-1483	Boeing KC-135R Stratotanker	17554 /T0163	92ARW
57-1484	Boeing KC-135E Stratotanker	17555 /T0164	161ARW/AZ ANG
57-1485	Boeing KC-135E Stratotanker	17556 /T0165	134ARW/TN ANG
57-1486	Boeing KC-135R Stratotanker	17557 /T0166	92ARW
57-1487	Boeing KC-135R Stratotanker	17558 /T0167	434ARW
57-1488 / ZZ	Boeing KC-135R Stratotanker	17559 /T0168	18Wg
57-1490	Boeing KC-135A Stratotanker	17561 /T0170	Std AMARC [CA050]
57-1491	Boeing KC-135E Stratotanker	17562 /T0171	101ARW/ME ANG
57-1492	Boeing KC-135E Stratotanker	17563 /T0172	134ARW/TN ANG
57-1493	Boeing KC-135R Stratotanker	17564 /T0173	22ARW
57-1494	Boeing KC-135E Stratotanker	17565 /T0174	126ARW/IL ANG
57-1495	Boeing KC-135E Stratotanker	17566 /T0175	161ARW/AZ ANG
57-1496	Boeing KC-135E Stratotanker	17567 /T0176	161ARW/AZ ANG
57-1497	Boeing KC-135E Stratotanker	17568 /T0177	151ARW/UT ANG
57-1499	Boeing KC-135R Stratotanker	17570 /T0179	92ARW
57-1501	Boeing KC-135E Stratotanker	17572 /T0181	141ARW/WA ANG
57-1502	Boeing KC-135R Stratotanker	17573 /T0182	319ARW
57-1503	Boeing KC-135E Stratotanker	17574 /T0183	134ARW/TN ANG
57-1504	Boeing KC-135E Stratotanker	17575 /T0184	927ARW
57-1505	Boeing KC-135E Stratotanker	17576 /T0185	101ARW/ME ANG
57-1506	Boeing KC-135R Stratotanker	17577 /T0186	319ARW
57-1507	Boeing KC-135E Stratotanker	17578 /T0187	108ARW/NJ ANG
57-1508	Boeing KC-135R Stratotanker	17579 /T0188	154Wg/HI ANG
57-1509	Boeing KC-135E Stratotanker	17580 /T0189	171ARW/PA ANG
57-1510	Boeing KC-135E Stratotanker	17581 /T0190	151ARW/UT ANG
57-1511	Boeing KC-135E Stratotanker	17582 /T0191	940ARW
57-1512	Boeing KC-135E Stratotanker	17583 /T0192	452AMW
57-1514	Boeing KC-135R Stratotanker	17585 /T0194	128ARW/WI ANG
57-2539 / OF	Boeing KC-135R Stratotanker	17725 /T0195	15BW
57-2530	Boeing KC-135A Stratotanker	17726 /T0196	Std AMARC [CA042]
57-2531	Boeing KC-135A Stratotanker	17727 /T0197	Std AMARC [CA060]
57-2532	Boeing KC-135A Stratotanker	17728 /T0198	Std AMARC [CA066]
57-2533	Boeing KC-135R Stratotanker	17729 /T0199	121ARW/OH ANG
57-2534	Boeing KC-135E Stratotanker	17730 /T0200	126ARW/IL ANG
57-2535	Boeing KC-135E Stratotanker	17731 /T0201	171ARW/PA ANG
57-2596	Boeing KC-135A Stratotanker	17732 /T0202	Std AMARC [CA061]
57-2597	Boeing KC-135E Stratotanker	17733 /T0203	186ARW/MS ANG
57-2598	Boeing KC-135E Stratotanker	17734 /T0204	452AMW
57-2599	Boeing KC-135R Stratotanker	17735 /T0205	916ARW
57-2600	Boeing KC-135E Stratotanker	17736 /T0206	141ARW/WA ANG
57-2601	Boeing KC-135E Stratotanker	17737 /T0207	134ARW/TN ANG
57-2602	Boeing KC-135E Stratotanker	17738 /T0208	108ARW/NJ ANG
57-2603	Boeing KC-135E Stratotanker	17739 /T0209	452AMW
57-2604	Boeing KC-135E Stratotanker	17740 /T0210	171ARW/PA ANG
57-2605 / D	Boeing KC-135R Stratotanker	17741 /T0211	100ARW
57-2606	Boeing KC-135E Stratotanker	17742 /T0212	108ARW/NJ ANG
57-2607	Boeing KC-135E Stratotanker	17743 /T0213	171ARW/PA ANG
57-2608	Boeing KC-135E Stratotanker	17744 /T0214	171ARW/PA ANG
58-0001	Boeing KC-135R Stratotanker	17746 /T0216	22ARW
58-0003	Boeing KC-135E Stratotanker	17748 /T0218	126ARW/IL ANG
58-0004	Boeing KC-135R Stratotanker	17749 /T0219	186ARW/MS ANG
58-0005	Boeing KC-135E Stratotanker	17750 /T0220	190ARW/KS ANG
58-0006	Boeing KC-135E Stratotanker	17751 /T0221	151ARW/UT ANG
58-0008	Boeing KC-135E Stratotanker	17753 /T0223	157ARW/NH ANG
58-0009	Boeing KC-135E Stratotanker	17754 /T0224	128ARW/WI ANG
58-0010	Boeing KC-135R Stratotanker	17755 /T0225	186ARW/MS ANG
58-0011	Boeing KC-135R(RT) Stratotanker	17756 /T0226	22ARW
58-0012	Boeing KC-135E Stratotanker	17757 /T0227	151ARW/UT ANG

58-0013	Boeing KC-135E Stratotanker	17758 /T0228	927ARW
58-0014	Boeing KC-135E Stratotanker	17759 /T0229	126ARW/IL ANG
58-0015	Boeing KC-135R Stratotanker	17760 /T0230	434ARW
58-0016 / ZZ	Boeing KC-135R Stratotanker	17761 /T0231	18Wg
58-0017	Boeing KC-135E Stratotanker	17762 /T0232	171ARW/PA ANG
58-0018	Boeing KC-135R(RT) Stratotanker	17763 /T0233	22ARW
58-0019 / FF	Boeing EC-135P Stratotanker	17764 /T0234	Std AMARC [CA009]
58-0020	Boeing KC-135E Stratotanker	17765 /T0235	141ARW/WA ANG
58-0021	Boeing KC-135R Stratotanker	17766 /T0236	128ARW/WI ANG
58-0022 / FF	Boeing EC-135P Stratotanker	17767 /T0237	Std AMARC [CA011]
58-0023	Boeing KC-135R Stratotanker	17768 /T0238	107ARW/NY ANG
58-0024	Boeing KC-135E Stratotanker	17769 /T0239	171ARW/PA ANG
58-0025	Boeing KC-135A Stratotanker	17770 /T0240	Std AMARC [CA075]
58-0027	Boeing KC-135R Stratotanker	17772 /T0242	22ARW
58-0028	Boeing KC-135A Stratotanker	17773 /T0243	Std AMARC [CA058]
58-0029	Boeing KC-135A Stratotanker	17774 /T0244	Std AMARC [CA056]
58-0030	Boeing KC-135R Stratotanker	17775 /T0245	117ARW/AL ANG
58-0032	Boeing KC-135E Stratotanker	17777 /T0247	108ARW/NJ ANG
58-0033	Boeing KC-135A Stratotanker	17778 /T0248	Std AMARC [CA026]
58-0034	Boeing KC-135R Stratotanker	17779 /T0249	319ARW
58-0035	Boeing KC-135R Stratotanker	17780 /T0250	22ARW
58-0036 / ZZ	Boeing KC-135R Stratotanker	17781 /T0251	18Wg
58-0037	Boeing KC-135E Stratotanker	17782 /T0252	171ARW/PA ANG
58-0038	Boeing KC-135R Stratotanker	17783 /T0253	916ARW
58-0040	Boeing KC-135E Stratotanker	17785 /T0255	108ARW/NJ ANG
58-0041	Boeing KC-135E Stratotanker	17786 /T0256	927ARW
58-0042	Boeing KC-135T Stratotanker	17787 /T0257	319ARW
58-0043	Boeing KC-135E Stratotanker	17788 /T0258	151ARW/UT ANG
58-0044	Boeing KC-135E Stratotanker	17789 /T0259	108ARW/NJ ANG
58-0045	Boeing KC-135T Stratotanker	17790 /T0260	92ARW
58-0046	Boeing KC-135T Stratotanker	17791 /T0261	92ARW
58-0047	Boeing KC-135T Stratotanker	17792 /T0262	319ARW
58-0049	Boeing KC-135T Stratotanker	17794 /T0264	92ARW
58-0050	Boeing KC-135T Stratotanker	17795 /T0265	92ARW
58-0051	Boeing KC-135R Stratotanker	17796 /T0266	507ARW
58-0052	Boeing KC-135E Stratotanker	17797 /T0267	452AMW
58-0053	Boeing KC-135E Stratotanker	17798 /T0268	940ARW
58-0054	Boeing KC-135T Stratotanker	17799 /T0269	92ARW
58-0055	Boeing KC-135T Stratotanker	17800 /T0270	92ARW
58-0056	Boeing KC-135R Stratotanker	17801 /T0271	186ARW/MS ANG
58-0057	Boeing KC-135E Stratotanker	17802 /T0272	126ARW/IL ANG
58-0058	Boeing KC-135R Stratotanker	17803 /T0273	507ARW
58-0059	Boeing KC-135R Stratotanker	17804 /T0274	186ARW/MS ANG
58-0060	Boeing KC-135T Stratotanker	17805 /T0275	92ARW
58-0061	Boeing KC-135T Stratotanker	17806 /T0276	319ARW
58-0062	Boeing KC-135T Stratotanker	17807 /T0277	92ARW
58-0063	Boeing KC-135R Stratotanker	17808 /T0278	507ARW
58-0064	Boeing KC-135E Stratotanker	17809 /T0279	940ARW
58-0065	Boeing KC-135T Stratotanker	17810 /T0280	92ARW
58-0066	Boeing KC-135R Stratotanker	17811 /T0281	507ARW
58-0067	Boeing KC-135E Stratotanker	17812 /T0282	126ARW/IL ANG
58-0068	Boeing KC-135E Stratotanker	17813 /T0283	126ARW/IL ANG
58-0069	Boeing KC-135T Stratotanker	17814 /T0284	92ARW
58-0071	Boeing KC-135T Stratotanker	17816 /T0286	22ARW
58-0072	Boeing KC-135T Stratotanker	17817 /T0287	92ARW
58-0073	Boeing KC-135R Stratotanker	17818 /T0288	117ARW/AL ANG
58-0074	Boeing KC-135T Stratotanker	17819 /T0289	92ARW
58-0075	Boeing KC-135R Stratotanker	17820 /T0290	434ARW
58-0076	Boeing KC-135R Stratotanker	17821 /T0291	434ARW
58-0077	Boeing KC-135T Stratotanker	17822 /T0292	92ARW
58-0078	Boeing KC-135E Stratotanker	17823 /T0293	108ARW/NJ ANG
58-0079	Boeing KC-135R Stratotanker	17824 /T0294	507ARW
58-0080	Boeing KC-135E Stratotanker	17825 /T0295	151ARW/UT ANG
58-0081	Boeing KC-135A Stratotanker	17826 /T0296	Std AMARC [CA052]
58-0082	Boeing KC-135E Stratotanker	17827 /T0297	141ARW/WA ANG
58-0083	Boeing KC-135R Stratotanker	17828 /T0298	121ARW/OH ANG
58-0084	Boeing KC-135T Stratotanker	17829 /T0299	92ARW
58-0085	Boeing KC-135T Stratotanker	17830 /T0300	452AMW
58-0086	Boeing KC-135T Stratotanker	17831 /T0301	92ARW
58-0087	Boeing KC-135E Stratotanker	17832 /T0302	108ARW/NJ ANG
58-0088	Boeing KC-135T Stratotanker	17833 /T0303	22ARW
58-0089	Boeing KC-135T Stratotanker	17834 /T0304	22ARW
58-0090	Boeing KC-135E Stratotanker	17835 /T0305	940ARW
58-0091	Boeing KC-135A Stratotanker	17836 /T0306	Std AMARC [CA079]

58-0092	Boeing KC-135R Stratotanker	17837 /T0307	157ARW/NH ANG
58-0093	Boeing KC-135R Stratotanker	17838 /T0308	319ARW
58-0094	Boeing KC-135T Stratotanker	17839 /T0309	92ARW
58-0095	Boeing KC-135T Stratotanker	17840 /T0310	22ARW
58-0096	Boeing KC-135E Stratotanker	17841 /T0311	940ARW
58-0097	Boeing KC-135A Stratotanker	17842 /T0312	Std AMARC [CA043]
58-0098	Boeing KC-135R Stratotanker	17843 /T0313	157ARW/NH ANG
58-0099	Boeing KC-135T Stratotanker	17844 /T0314	92ARW
58-0100	Boeing KC-135R Stratotanker	17845 /T0315	22ARW
58-0102	Boeing KC-135R Stratotanker	17847 /T0317	434ARW
58-0103	Boeing KC-135T Stratotanker	17848 /T0318	92ARW
58-0104	Boeing KC-135R Stratotanker	17849 /T0319	107ARW/NY ANG
58-0105	Boeing KC-135A Stratotanker	17850 /T0320	Std AMARC [CA080]
58-0106	Boeing KC-135R Stratotanker	17851 /T0321	117ARW/AL ANG
58-0107	Boeing KC-135E Stratotanker	17852 /T0322	151ARW/UT ANG
58-0108	Boeing KC-135E Stratotanker	17853 /T0323	940ARW
58-0109	Boeing KC-135R Stratotanker	17854 /T0324	186ARW/MS ANG
58-0111	Boeing KC-135E Stratotanker	17856 /T0326	108ARW/NJ ANG
58-0112	Boeing KC-135T Stratotanker	17857 /T0326	92ARW
58-0113	Boeing KC-135R Stratotanker	17858 /T0327	319ARW
58-0114	Boeing KC-135R Stratotanker	17859 /T0328	18Wg
58-0115	Boeing KC-135E Stratotanker	17860 /T0329	108ARW/NJ ANG
58-0116	Boeing KC-135E Stratotanker	17861 /T0330	161ARW/AZ ANG
58-0117	Boeing KC-135T Stratotanker	17862 /T0331	92ARW
58-0118 / ZZ	Boeing KC-135R Stratotanker	17863 /T0332	18Wg
58-0119 / ZZ	Boeing KC-135R Stratotanker	17864 /T0333	18Wg
58-0120	Boeing KC-135R Stratotanker	17865 /T0334	97AMW
58-0121	Boeing KC-135R Stratotanker	17866 /T0335	507ARW
58-0122	Boeing KC-135R Stratotanker	17867 /T0336	168ARW/AK ANG
58-0123	Boeing KC-135R Stratotanker	17868 /T0337	22ARW
58-0124	Boeing KC-135R(RT) Stratotanker	17869 /T0338	22ARW
58-0125	Boeing KC-135T Stratotanker	17870 /T0339	92ARW
58-0126	Boeing KC-135R(RT) Stratotanker	17871 /T0340	22ARW
58-0128	Boeing KC-135R Stratotanker	17873 /T0342	6ARW
58-0129	Boeing KC-135T Stratotanker	17874 /T0344	92ARW
58-0130	Boeing KC-135R Stratotanker	17875 /T0345	128ARW/WI ANG
58-0713	Lockheed C-130B (L-282-1B) Hercules	3508	Std AMARC [CF096]
58-0714	Lockheed C-130B (L-282-1B) Hercules	3509	Std AMARC [CF098]
58-0716	Lockheed NC-130B (L-282-1B) Hercules	3511	Std AMARC [CF162]
58-0750	Lockheed C-130B (L-282-1B) Hercules	3549	Std AMARC [CF123]
58-0757	Lockheed C-130B (L-282-1B) Hercules	3558	Std AMARC [CF121]
58-6972	Boeing C-137B (707-153B)	17927 / 47	Std McConnell AFB
59-1444	Boeing KC-135R Stratotanker	17932 /T0347	121ARW/OH ANG
59-1445	Boeing KC-135E Stratotanker	17933 /T0348	141ARW/WA ANG
59-1446	Boeing KC-135R Stratotanker	17934 /T0349	186ARW/MS ANG
59-1447	Boeing KC-135E Stratotanker	17935 /T0350	927ARW
59-1448	Boeing KC-135E Stratotanker	17936 /T0351	163ARW/CA ANG
59-1449	Boeing KC-135A Stratotanker	17937 /T0352	Std AMARC [CA082]
59-1450	Boeing KC-135E Stratotanker	17938 /T0353	163ARW/CA ANG
59-1451	Boeing KC-135E Stratotanker	17939 /T0354	927ARW
59-1453	Boeing KC-135R Stratotanker	17941 /T0356	163ARW/CA ANG
59-1455	Boeing KC-135R Stratotanker	17943 /T0358	186ARW/MS ANG
59-1456	Boeing KC-135E Stratotanker	17944 /T0359	108ARW/NJ ANG
59-1457	Boeing KC-135E Stratotanker	17945 /T0360	171ARW/PA ANG
59-1458	Boeing KC-135R Stratotanker	17946 /T0361	121ARW/OH ANG
59-1459 / D	Boeing KC-135R Stratotanker	17947 /T0362	100ARW
59-1460	Boeing KC-135T Stratotanker	17948 /T0363	92ARW
59-1461	Boeing KC-135R Stratotanker	17949 /T0364	168ARW/AK ANG
59-1462	Boeing KC-135T Stratotanker	17950 /T0365	319ARW
59-1463	Boeing KC-135R Stratotanker	17951 /T0366	155ARW/NE ANG
59-1464	Boeing KC-135T Stratotanker	17952 /T0367	92ARW
59-1466	Boeing KC-135R Stratotanker	17954 /T0369	107ARW/NY ANG
59-1467	Boeing KC-135T Stratotanker	17955 /T0370	92ARW
59-1468	Boeing KC-135T Stratotanker	17956 /T0371	92ARW
59-1469	Boeing KC-135R Stratotanker	17957 /T0372	916ARW
59-1470	Boeing KC-135T Stratotanker	17958 /T0373	92ARW
59-1471	Boeing KC-135T Stratotanker	17959 /T0374	92ARW
59-1472	Boeing KC-135R Stratotanker	17960 /T0375	154Wg/HI ANG
59-1473	Boeing KC-135E Stratotanker	17961 /T0376	151ARW/UT ANG
59-1474	Boeing KC-135T Stratotanker	17962 /T0377	92ARW
59-1475	Boeing KC-135R Stratotanker	17963 /T0378	319ARW
59-1476	Boeing KC-135R Stratotanker	17964 /T0379	22ARW
59-1477	Boeing KC-135E Stratotanker	17965 /T0380	927ARW
59-1478	Boeing KC-135R Stratotanker	17966 /T0381	186ARW/MS ANG

59-1479	Boeing KC-135E Stratotanker	17967 /T0382		171ARW/PA ANG
59-1480	Boeing KC-135T Stratotanker	17968 /T0383		92ARW
59-1482 / D	Boeing KC-135R Stratotanker	17970 /T0385		319ARW
59-1483	Boeing KC-135R Stratotanker	17971 /T0386		121ARW/OH ANG
59-1484	Boeing KC-135E Stratotanker	17972 /T0387		171ARW/PA ANG
59-1485	Boeing KC-135R Stratotanker	17973 /T0388		108ARW/NJ ANG
59-1486	Boeing KC-135R Stratotanker	17974 /T0389		22ARW
59-1487	Boeing KC-135E Stratotanker	17975 /T0390		126ARW/IL ANG
59-1488 / ZZ	Boeing KC-135R Stratotanker	17976 /T0391		18Wg
59-1489	Boeing KC-135E Stratotanker	17977 /T0392		151ARW/UT ANG
59-1490	Boeing KC-135T Stratotanker	17978 /T0393		92ARW
59-1492 / ZZ	Boeing KC-135R Stratotanker	17980 /T0395		18Wg
59-1493	Boeing KC-135E Stratotanker	17981 /T0396		101ARW/ME ANG
59-1495	Boeing KC-135R Stratotanker	17983 /T0398		155ARW/NE ANG
59-1496	Boeing KC-135E Stratotanker	17984 /T0399		171ARW/PA ANG
59-1497	Boeing KC-135E Stratotanker	17985 /T0400		108ARW/NJ ANG
59-1498 / MO	Boeing KC-135R Stratotanker	17986 /T0401		366Wg
59-1499	Boeing KC-135E Stratotanker	17987 /T0402		163ARW/CA ANG
59-1500	Boeing KC-135R Stratotanker	17988 /T0403		22ARW
59-1501 / ZZ	Boeing KC-135R Stratotanker	17989 /T0404		18Wg
59-1502	Boeing KC-135R Stratotanker	17990 /T0405		22ARW
59-1503	Boeing KC-135E Stratotanker	17991 /T0406		108ARW/NJ ANG
59-1504	Boeing KC-135T Stratotanker	17992 /T0407		92ARW
59-1505	Boeing KC-135E Stratotanker	17993 /T0408		163ARW/CA ANG
59-1506	Boeing KC-135E Stratotanker	17994 /T0409		171ARW/PA ANG
59-1507	Boeing KC-135R Stratotanker	17995 /T0410		22ARW
59-1508	Boeing KC-135R Stratotanker	17996 /T0411		319ARW
59-1509	Boeing KC-135E Stratotanker	17997 /T0412		163ARW/CA ANG
59-1510	Boeing KC-135T Stratotanker	17998 /T0413		319ARW
59-1511	Boeing KC-135R Stratotanker	17999 /T0414		22ARW
59-1512	Boeing KC-135T Stratotanker	18000 /T0415		92ARW
59-1513	Boeing KC-135T Stratotanker	18001 /T0416		92ARW
59-1514 / OF	Boeing KC-135E(RT) Stratotanker	18002 /T0417		55Wg
59-1515 / ZZ	Boeing KC-135R Stratotanker	18003 /T0418		18Wg
59-1516	Boeing KC-135E Stratotanker	18004 /T0419		163ARW/CA ANG
59-1517	Boeing KC-135R Stratotanker	18005 /T0420		22ARW
59-1518	Boeing EC-135K	18006 /T0421	N96	15BW
59-1519	Boeing KC-135E Stratotanker	18007 /T0422		171ARW/PA ANG
59-1520	Boeing KC-135T Stratotanker	18008 /T0423		92ARW
59-1521	Boeing KC-135R Stratotanker	18009 /T0424		168ARW/AK ANG
59-1522	Boeing KC-135R Stratotanker	18010 /T0425		107ARW/NY ANG
59-1523	Boeing KC-135T Stratotanker	18011 /T0426		92ARW
59-1525	Lockheed C-130B (L-282-1B) Hercules	3561		Std AMARC [CF099]
59-1529	Lockheed C-130B (L-282-1B) Hercules	3569		Std AMARC [CF108]
59-2870 / ED	North American NT-39A Sabreliner	265-3		412TW
59-2872	North American CT-39A Sabreliner	265-5		Std AMARC [TG015]
59-2873	North American CT-39B Sabreliner	270-1		412TW
59-2874	North American T-39B Sabreliner	270-2		Std AMARC [TG103]
59-5957	Lockheed C-130B (L-282-1B) Hercules	3584		Std AMARC [CF132]
60-0313	Boeing KC-135R Stratotanker	18088 /T0429		22ARW
60-0314	Boeing KC-135R Stratotanker	18089 /T0428		434ARW
60-0315	Boeing KC-135R Stratotanker	18090 /T0435		128ARW/WI ANG
60-0316	Boeing KC-135E Stratotanker	18091 /T0430		141ARW/WA ANG
60-0318	Boeing KC-135R Stratotanker	18093 /T0432		154ARW/HI ANG
60-0319	Boeing KC-135R Stratotanker	18094 /T0433		319ARW
60-0320	Boeing KC-135R Stratotanker	18095 /T0434		319ARW
60-0321	Boeing KC-135R Stratotanker	18096 /T0441		97AMW
60-0322	Boeing KC-135R Stratotanker	18097 /T0436		434ARW
60-0323	Boeing KC-135R Stratotanker	18098 /T0437		154ARW/HI ANG
60-0324	Boeing KC-135R Stratotanker	18099 /T0438		319ARW
60-0327	Boeing KC-135E Stratotanker	18102 /T0447		151ARW/UT ANG
60-0328	Boeing KC-135R Stratotanker	18103 /T0442		22ARW
60-0329 / HH	Boeing KC-135R Stratotanker	18104 /T0443		154ARW/HI ANG
60-0331	Boeing KC-135R Stratotanker	18106 /T0445		97AMW
60-0332	Boeing KC-135R Stratotanker	18107 /T0446		6ARW
60-0333	Boeing KC-135R Stratotanker	18108 /T0427		97AMW
60-0334	Boeing KC-135R Stratotanker	18109 /T0448		168ARW/AK ANG
60-0335	Boeing KC-135T Stratotanker	18110 /T0449		22ARW
60-0336	Boeing KC-135T Stratotanker	18111 /T0450		92ARW
60-0337	Boeing KC-135T Stratotanker	18112 /T0451		92ARW
60-0339	Boeing KC-135T Stratotanker	18114 /T0453		92ARW
60-0341	Boeing KC-135T Stratotanker	18116 /T0455		121ARW/OH ANG
60-0342	Boeing KC-135T Stratotanker	18117 /T0456		319ARW
60-0343	Boeing KC-135T Stratotanker	18118 /T0457		319ARW

60-0344	Boeing KC-135T Stratotanker	18119 /T0458	22ARW
60-0345	Boeing KC-135T Stratotanker	18120 /T0459	92ARW
60-0346	Boeing KC-135T Stratotanker	18121 /T0460	92ARW
60-0347	Boeing KC-135R Stratotanker	18122 /T0461	121ARW/OH ANG
60-0348	Boeing KC-135R Stratotanker	18123 /T0462	319ARW
60-0349	Boeing KC-135R Stratotanker	18124 /T0463	916ARW
60-0350	Boeing KC-135R Stratotanker	18125 /T0464	22ARW
60-0351	Boeing KC-135R Stratotanker	18126 /T0465	22ARW
60-0353	Boeing KC-135R Stratotanker	18128 /T0467	22ARW
60-0355	Boeing KC-135R Stratotanker	18130 /T0469	319ARW
60-0356	Boeing KC-135R(RT) Stratotanker	18131 /T0470	22ARW
60-0357	Boeing KC-135R(RT) Stratotanker	18132 /T0471	22ARW
60-0358	Boeing KC-135R Stratotanker	18133 /T0472	107ARW/NY ANG
60-0359	Boeing KC-135R Stratotanker	18134 /T0473	434ARW
60-0360 / D	Boeing KC-135R Stratotanker	18135 /T0474	100ARW
60-0362	Boeing KC-135R(RT) Stratotanker	18137 /T0476	22ARW
60-0363	Boeing KC-135R Stratotanker	18138 /T0477	434ARW
60-0364	Boeing KC-135R(RT) Stratotanker	18139 /T0478	434ARW
60-0365 / MO	Boeing KC-135R Stratotanker	18140 /T0484	366Wg
60-0366	Boeing KC-135R Stratotanker	18141 /T0480	19ARG
60-0367	Boeing KC-135R Stratotanker	18142 /T0481	121ARW/OH ANG
60-0372	Boeing C-135E Stratolifter	18147 /C3004	412TW
60-0375	Boeing C-135E Stratolifter	18150 /C3007	Std AMARC [CA129]
60-0376	Boeing C-135E Stratolifter	18151 /C3008	15BW
60-0378 / OF	Boeing C-135A Stratolifter	18153 /C3010	Std Tinker AFB, OK
60-3474	North American CT-39B Sabreliner	270-3	4950TW
60-3475	North American T-39B Sabreliner	270-4	Std AMARC [TG098]
60-3476	North American T-39B Sabreliner	270-5	Std AMARC [TG102]
60-3477	North American T-39B Sabreliner	270-6	Std AMARC [TG101]
60-3478 / ED	North American NT-39A Sabreliner	265-6	412TW
61-0261	Boeing EC-135L	18168 /T0483	Std AMARC [CA020]
61-0263	Boeing EC-135L	18170 /T0485	Std AMARC [CA015]
61-0264	Boeing KC-135R Stratotanker	18171 /T0486	121ARW/OH ANG
61-0266	Boeing KC-135R Stratotanker	18173 /T0488	155ARW/NE ANG
61-0267	Boeing KC-135R Stratotanker	18174 /T0489	
61-0268	Boeing KC-135E Stratotanker	18175 /T0490	940ARW
61-0270	Boeing KC-135E Stratotanker	18177 /T0492	927ARW
61-0271	Boeing KC-135E Stratotanker	18178 /T0493	927ARW
61-0272	Boeing KC-135R Stratotanker	18179 /T0494	434ARW
61-0274 / FF	Boeing EC-135P	18181 /T0496	Std AMARC [CA010]
61-0275	Boeing KC-135R Stratotanker	18182 /T0497	6ARW
61-0276	Boeing KC-135R Stratotanker	18183 /T0498	155ARW/NE ANG
61-0277 / MO	Boeing KC-135R Stratotanker	18184 /T0499	366Wg
61-0278	Boeing EC-135A	18185 /T0500	Std AMARC [CA048]
61-0279	Boeing EC-135L	18186 /T0501	Std AMARC [CA018]
61-0280	Boeing KC-135E Stratotanker	18187 /T0502	452AMW
61-0281	Boeing KC-135E(RT) Stratotanker	18188 /T0503	
61-0283	Boeing EC-135L	18190 /T0505	Std AMARC [CA016]
61-0284	Boeing KC-135R Stratotanker	18191 /T0506	
61-0285	Boeing EC-135H	18192 /T0507	Std AMARC [CA012]
61-0286	Boeing GEC-135H	18193 /T0508	82TRW
61-0288	Boeing KC-135R(RT) Stratotanker	18195 /T0510	
61-0289	Boeing EC-135A	18196 /T0511	Std AMARC [CA022]
61-0290	Boeing KC-135R Stratotanker	18197 /T0512	154ARW/HI ANG
61-0292	Boeing KC-135R Stratotanker	18199 /T0514	6ARW
61-0293	Boeing KC-135R(RT) Stratotanker	18200 /T0515	22ARW
61-0294	Boeing KC-135R Stratotanker	18201 /T0516	6ARW
61-0295	Boeing KC-135R Stratotanker	18202 /T0517	6ARW
61-0297	Boeing EC-135A	18204 /T0519	Std AMARC [CA021]
61-0298	Boeing KC-135R Stratotanker	18205 /T0520	128ARW/WI ANG
61-0299	Boeing KC-135R Stratotanker	18206 /T0521	92ARW
61-0300	Boeing KC-135R Stratotanker	18207 /T0522	6ARW
61-0302	Boeing KC-135R(RT) Stratotanker	18209 /T0524	100ARW
61-0303	Boeing KC-135E Stratotanker	18210 /T0525	940ARW
61-0304	Boeing KC-135R Stratotanker	18211 /T0526	319ARW
61-0305	Boeing KC-135R Stratotanker	18212 /T0527	92ARW
61-0306	Boeing KC-135R Stratotanker	18213 /T0528	22ARW
61-0307	Boeing KC-135R Stratotanker	18214 /T0529	434ARW
61-0308	Boeing KC-135R Stratotanker	18215 /T0530	97AMW
61-0309	Boeing KC-135R Stratotanker	18216 /T0531	128ARW/WI ANG
61-0310	Boeing KC-135R Stratotanker	18217 /T0532	157ARW/NH ANG
61-0311	Boeing KC-135R Stratotanker	18218 /T0533	22ARW
61-0312	Boeing KC-135R Stratotanker	18219 /T0534	
61-0313	Boeing KC-135R Stratotanker	18220 /T0535	916ARW

61-0314	Boeing KC-135R Stratotanker	18221 /T0536	97AMW
61-0315	Boeing KC-135R Stratotanker	18222 /T0537	97AMW
61-0317 / ZZ	Boeing KC-135R Stratotanker	18224 /T0539	18Wg
61-0318	Boeing KC-135R Stratotanker	18225 /T0540	6ARW
61-0320	Boeing KC-135R Stratotanker	18227 /T0542	
61-0321	Boeing KC-135R Stratotanker	18228 /T0543	92ARW
61-0323	Boeing KC-135R Stratotanker	18230 /T0545	6ARW
61-0324	Boeing KC-135R Stratotanker	18231 /T0546	452AMW
61-0326	Boeing EC-135E	18233 /C3011	Std AMARC [CA122]
61-0327	Boeing EC-135Y	18234 /C3012	Std
61-0330	Boeing EC-135E	18237 /C3015	Std
61-0670	North American CT-39A Sabreliner	265-73	375AW
61-0951	Lockheed C-130B (L-282-1B) Hercules	3628	Lockheed Martin
61-0952	Lockheed C-130B (L-282-1B) Hercules	3629	Std AMARC [CF120]
61-0958	Lockheed C-130B (L-282-1B) Hercules	3639	Std AMARC [CF109]
61-0959	Lockheed C-130B (L-282-1B) Hercules	3642	Std AMARC [CF093]
61-2358	Lockheed C-130E (L-382-4B) Hercules	3609	127Wg/MI ANG
61-2359	Lockheed C-130E (L-382-4B) Hercules	3651	146AW/CA ANG
61-2360	Lockheed C-130E (L-382-4B) Hercules	3659	Std AMARC [CF143]
61-2361	Lockheed C-130E (L-382-4B) Hercules	3662	152AW/NV ANG
61-2366	Lockheed WC-130E (L-382-4B) Hercules	3706	Std AMARC [CF146]
61-2367	Lockheed C-130E (L-382-4B) Hercules	3712	146AW/CA ANG
61-2369	Lockheed C-130E (L-382-4B) Hercules	3714	156AW/PR ANG
61-2370	Lockheed C-130E (L-382-4B) Hercules	3715	127Wg/MI ANG
61-2371	Lockheed C-130E (L-382-4B) Hercules	3716	127Wg/MI ANG
61-2372 / CI	Lockheed C-130E (L-382-4B) Hercules	3717	146AW/CA ANG
61-2643	Lockheed C-130B (L-282-1B) Hercules	3679	Std AMARC [CF127]
61-2662 / OF	Boeing RC-135S	18292 /C3018	55Wg
61-2663 / OF	Boeing RC-135S	18333 /C3019	55Wg
61-2665 / OF	Boeing WC-135B	18341 /C3021	Std AMARC [CA107]
61-2666	Boeing WC-135W	18342 /C3022	
61-2667 / OF	Boeing TC-135B	18343 /C3023	55Wg
61-2668	Boeing C-135C Stratolifter	18344 /C3024	15BW
61-2669 / ED	Boeing C-135C Stratolifter	18345 /C3025	412TW
61-2670 / OF	Boeing OC-135B	18346 /C3026	55Wg
61-2672	Boeing OC-135B	18348 /C3028	55Wg
61-2673	Boeing WC-135B	18349 /C3029	Std AMARC [CA090]
61-2674	Boeing OC-135B	18350 /C3030	Std AMARC [CA115]
61-2776	Lockheed NC-141A Starlifter	300-6002	Std AMARC [CR055]
61-2777	Lockheed NC-141A Starlifter	300-6003	Std AMARC [CR010]
61-2778	Lockheed C-141C Starlifter	300-6004	164AW/TN ANG
62-1784 / 84	Lockheed C-130E (L-382-4B) Hercules	3729	189AW/AR ANG
62-1786	Lockheed C-130E (L-382-4B) Hercules	3731	124Wg/ID ANG
62-1788 / 88	Lockheed C-130E (L-382-4B) Hercules	3735	189AW/AR ANG
62-1789	Lockheed C-130E (L-382-4B) Hercules	3736	314AW
62-1790 / 90	Lockheed C-130E (L-382-4B) Hercules	3737	189AW/AR ANG
62-1791 / DM	Lockheed EC-130E (L-382-4B) Hercules	3738	355Wg
62-1792	Lockheed C-130E (L-382-4B) Hercules	3739	146AW/CA ANG
62-1793	Lockheed C-130E (L-382-4B) Hercules	3743	146AW/CA ANG
62-1795 / 95	Lockheed C-130E (L-382-4B) Hercules	3746	189AW/AR ANG
62-1798 / 98	Lockheed C-130E (L-382-4B) Hercules	3752	189AW/AR ANG
62-1799	Lockheed C-130E (L-382-4B) Hercules	3753	146AW/CA ANG
62-1801 / CI	Lockheed C-130E (L-382-4B) Hercules	3755	146AW/CA ANG
62-1803	Lockheed C-130E (L-382-4B) Hercules	3757	Std AMARC [CF159]
62-1804 / 04	Lockheed C-130E (L-382-4B) Hercules	3758	189AW/AR ANG
62-1806	Lockheed C-130E (L-382-4B) Hercules	3760	934AW
62-1808	Lockheed C-130E (L-382-4B) Hercules	3762	314AW
62-1810	Lockheed C-130E (L-382-4B) Hercules	3771	314AW
62-1811 / CI	Lockheed C-130E (L-382-4B) Hercules	3772	146AW/CA ANG
62-1812	Lockheed C-130E (L-382-4B) Hercules	3774	152AW/NV ANG
62-1816 / LK	Lockheed C-130E (L-382-8B) Hercules	3778	314AW
62-1817 / ID	Lockheed C-130E (L-382-8B) Hercules	3779	124Wg/ID ANG
62-1818 / DM	Lockheed EC-130E (L-382-8B) Hercules	3780	355Wg
62-1819	Lockheed C-130B (L-382-4B) Hercules	3782	Std AMARC [CF187]
62-1820	Lockheed C-130B (L-382-4B) Hercules	3783	127Wg/MI ANG
62-1821	Lockheed C-130B (L-382-4B) Hercules	3784	Std AMARC [CF180]
62-1822	Lockheed C-130B (L-382-4B) Hercules	3785	Std AMARC [CF182]
62-1823	Lockheed C-130E (L-382-8B) Hercules	3786	934AW
62-1824 / 24	Lockheed C-130E (L-382-8B) Hercules	3787	189AW/AR ANG
62-1825 / DM	Lockheed EC-130E (L-382-8B) Hercules	3788	355Wg
62-1826	Lockheed C-130E (L-382-8B) Hercules	3789	146AW/CA ANG
62-1827	Lockheed C-130B (L-382-4B) Hercules	3790	Std AMARC [CF181]
62-1828	Lockheed C-130B (L-382-4B) Hercules	3791	Std AMARC [CF188]
62-1829	Lockheed C-130B (L-382-4B) Hercules	3792	152AW/NV ANG

62-1332 / DM	Lockheed EC-130E (L-382-8B) Hercules	3795	355Wg
62-1333 / CI	Lockheed C-130E (L-382-8B) Hercules	3796	146AW/CA ANG
62-1334 / YJ	Lockheed C-130E (L-382-8B) Hercules	3797	374AW
62-1335	Lockheed C-130E (L-382-8B) Hercules	3798	934AW
62-1336 / DM	Lockheed EC-130E (L-382-8B) Hercules	3799	355Wg
62-1337 / ID	Lockheed C-130B (L-382-4B) Hercules	3800	124Wg/ID ANG
62-1339	Lockheed C-130B (L-382-4B) Hercules	3802	934AW
62-1342	Lockheed C-130E (L-382-8B) Hercules	3805	127Wg/MI ANG
62-1344	Lockheed C-130E (L-382-8B) Hercules	3807	934AW
62-1346 / ID	Lockheed C-130E (L-382-8B) Hercules	3809	124Wg/ID ANG
62-1347	Lockheed C-130E (L-382-4B) Hercules	3810	934AW
62-1348	Lockheed C-130E (L-382-4B) Hercules	3811	934AW
62-1349 / KT	Lockheed C-130E (L-382-4B) Hercules	3812	403Wg
62-1850	Lockheed C-130E (L-382-4B) Hercules	3814	314AW
62-1851	Lockheed C-130E (L-382-4B) Hercules	3815	146AW/CA ANG
62-1852	Lockheed C-130E (L-382-8B) Hercules	3816	934AW
62-1855	Lockheed C-130E (L-382-8B) Hercules	3819	374AW
62-1856 / RI	Lockheed C-130E (L-382-8B) Hercules	3820	143AW/RI ANG
62-1857 / DM	Lockheed EC-130E (L-382-8B) Hercules	3821	355Wg
62-1858	Lockheed C-130E (L-382-8B) Hercules	3822	127AG/MI ANG
62-1859	Lockheed C-130E (L-382-8B) Hercules	3823	159FW
62-1862 / CI	Lockheed C-130E (L-382-8B) Hercules	3826	146AW/CA ANG
62-1863 / DM	Lockheed EC-130E (L-382-8B) Hercules	3827	355Wg
62-1864 / ID	Lockheed C-130E (L-382-8B) Hercules	3828	124Wg/ID ANG
62-1866	Lockheed C-130E (L-382-8B) Hercules	3830	314AW
62-3498	Boeing KC-135R Stratotanker	18481 /T0549	
62-3499	Boeing KC-135R Stratotanker	18482 /T0550	22ARW
62-3500	Boeing KC-135R Stratotanker	18483 /T0551	128ARW/WI ANG
62-3501	Boeing KC-135A Stratotanker	18484 /T0552	Std AMARC [CA068]
62-3502	Boeing KC-135R Stratotanker	18485 /T0553	319ARW
62-3503 / ZZ	Boeing KC-135R Stratotanker	18486 /T0554	18Wg
62-3504	Boeing KC-135R Stratotanker	18487 /T0555	6ARW
62-3505	Boeing KC-135R Stratotanker	18488 /T0556	22ARW
62-3506	Boeing KC-135R Stratotanker	18489 /T0557	157ARW/NH ANG
62-3507 / ZZ	Boeing KC-135R Stratotanker	18490 /T0558	18Wg
62-3508	Boeing KC-135R Stratotanker	18491 /T0559	19ARG
62-3509	Boeing KC-135R Stratotanker	18492 /T0560	916ARW
62-3510	Boeing KC-135R Stratotanker	18493 /T0561	434ARW
62-3511	Boeing KC-135R Stratotanker	18494 /T0562	121ARW/OH ANG
62-3513 / MO	Boeing KC-135R Stratotanker	18496 /T0564	366Wg
62-3514 / HH	Boeing KC-135R Stratotanker	18497 /T0565	154Wg/HI ANG
62-3515	Boeing KC-135R Stratotanker	18498 /T0566	157ARW/NH ANG
62-3516	Boeing KC-135R Stratotanker	18499 /T0567	319ARW
62-3517	Boeing KC-135R Stratotanker	18500 /T0568	22ARW
62-3518	Boeing KC-135R Stratotanker	18501 /T0569	434ARW
62-3519	Boeing KC-135R Stratotanker	18502 /T0570	319ARW
62-3520	Boeing KC-135R Stratotanker	18503 /T0571	6ARW
62-3521	Boeing KC-135R Stratotanker	18504 /T0572	434ARW
62-3523	Boeing KC-135R Stratotanker	18506 /T0574	19ARG
62-3524	Boeing KC-135R Stratotanker	18507 /T0575	117ARW/AL ANG
62-3526	Boeing KC-135R Stratotanker	18509 /T0577	155ARW/NE ANG
62-3527	Boeing KC-135E Stratotanker	18510 /T0578	108ARW/NJ ANG
62-3528	Boeing KC-135R Stratotanker	18511 /T0579	
62-3529	Boeing KC-135R Stratotanker	18512 /T0580	97AMW
62-3530	Boeing KC-135R Stratotanker	18513 /T0581	434ARW
62-3531	Boeing KC-135R Stratotanker	18514 /T0582	121ARW/OH ANG
62-3532 / DY	Boeing KC-135A Stratotanker	18515 /T0583	Std AMARC [CA076]
62-3533	Boeing KC-135R Stratotanker	18516 /T0584	
62-3534	Boeing KC-135R Stratotanker	18517 /T0585	22ARW
62-3537	Boeing KC-135R Stratotanker	18520 /T0588	22ARW
62-3538	Boeing KC-135R Stratotanker	18521 /T0589	
62-3540	Boeing KC-135R Stratotanker	18523 /T0591	92ARW
62-3541	Boeing KC-135R Stratotanker	18524 /T0592	22ARW
62-3542	Boeing KC-135R Stratotanker	18525 /T0593	916ARW
62-3543	Boeing KC-135R Stratotanker	18526 /T0594	434ARW
62-3544	Boeing KC-135R Stratotanker	18527 /T0595	19ARG
62-3545	Boeing KC-135R Stratotanker	18528 /T0596	22ARW
62-3546	Boeing KC-135R Stratotanker	18529 /T0597	97AMW
62-3547	Boeing KC-135R Stratotanker	18530 /T0598	157ARW/NH ANG
62-3548 / ZZ	Boeing KC-135R Stratotanker	18531 /T0599	18Wg
62-3549	Boeing KC-135R Stratotanker	18532 /T0600	319ARW
62-3550	Boeing KC-135R Stratotanker	18533 /T0601	97AMW
62-3551	Boeing KC-135R Stratotanker	18534 /T0602	100ARW
62-3552	Boeing KC-135R Stratotanker	18535 /T0603	319ARW

62-3553	Boeing KC-135R Stratotanker	18536 /T0604	22ARW	
62-3554	Boeing KC-135R Stratotanker	18537 /T0605	19ARG	
62-3555	Boeing KC-135A Stratotanker	18538 /T0606		Std AMARC [CA087]
62-3556	Boeing KC-135R Stratotanker	18539 /T0607	916ARW	
62-3557 / ZZ	Boeing KC-135R Stratotanker	18540 /T0608	18Wg	
62-3558	Boeing KC-135R Stratotanker	18541 /T0609	22ARW	
62-3559	Boeing KC-135R Stratotanker	18542 /T0610	22ARW	
62-3560	Boeing KC-135A Stratotanker	18543 /T0611		Std AMARC [CA101]
62-3561	Boeing KC-135R Stratotanker	18544 /T0612		
62-3562	Boeing KC-135R Stratotanker	18545 /T0613	319ARW	
62-3564	Boeing KC-135R Stratotanker	18547 /T0615		
62-3565	Boeing KC-135R Stratotanker	18548 /T0616	22ARW	
62-3566	Boeing KC-135E Stratotanker	18549 /T0617	101ARW/ME ANG	
62-3569	Boeing KC-135R Stratotanker	18552 /T0620	19ARG	
62-3570	Boeing EC-135G	18553 /T0621		Std AMARC [CA024]
62-3571	Boeing KC-135R Stratotanker	18554 /T0622	168ARW/AK ANG	
62-3572	Boeing KC-135R Stratotanker	18555 /T0623		Std AMARC
62-3573	Boeing KC-135R Stratotanker	18556 /T0624	22ARW	
62-3575	Boeing KC-135R Stratotanker	18558 /T0626	22ARW	
62-3576	Boeing KC-135R Stratotanker	18559 /T0627	157ARW/NH ANG	
62-3577	Boeing KC-135R Stratotanker	18560 /T0628	916ARW	
62-3578	Boeing KC-135R Stratotanker	18561 /T0629		
62-3579	Boeing KC-135A Stratotanker	18562 /T0630		Std AMARC [CA023]
62-3580	Boeing KC-135R Stratotanker	18563 /T0631	97AMW	
62-3581 / OF	Boeing EC-135C	18564 /C2101		Std AMARC [CA127]
62-3582 / OF	Boeing EC-135C	18565 /C2102	55Wg	
62-3583 / OF	Boeing EC-135C	18566 /C2103		Std AMARC [CA019]
62-3585 / OF	Boeing EC-135C	18568 /C2105		Std AMARC [CA123]
62-4125	Boeing C-135B Stratolifter	18465 /C3031		
62-4126	Boeing C-135B Stratolifter	18466 /C3032	108ARW/NJ ANG	
62-4127	Boeing C-135C Stratolifter	18467 /C3033		
62-4128 / OF	Boeing RC-135X	18468 /C3034		Std Greenville TX
62-4129 / OF	Boeing TC-135W	18469 /C3035	55Wg	
62-4130 / OF	Boeing C-135B Stratolifter	18470 /C3036		
62-4131 / OF	Boeing RC-135W	18471 /C3037	55Wg	
62-4132 / OF	Boeing RC-135W	18472 /C3038	55Wg	
62-4133 / OF	Boeing TC-135W	18473 /C3039	55Wg	
62-4134 / OF	Boeing RC-135W	18474 /C3040	55Wg	
62-4135 / OF	Boeing RC-135W	18475 /C3041	55Wg	
62-4138 / OF	Boeing RC-135W	18478 /C3044	55Wg	CFM56 engined
62-4139 / OF	Boeing RC-135W	18479 /C3045	55Wg	
62-4454	North American CT-39A Sabreliner	276-7		Std AMARC [TG018]
62-4457	North American CT-39A Sabreliner	276-10		Std AMARC [TG002]
62-4462	North American CT-39A Sabreliner	276-15		Std AMARC [TG046]
62-4463	North American CT-39A Sabreliner	276-16		Std AMARC [TG100]
62-4476	North American T-39A Sabreliner	276-29		Std AMARC [TG099]
62-4488	North American CT-39A Sabreliner	276-41	HQ ANG	
63-7764 / KT	Lockheed C-130E (L-382-8B) Hercules	3813	403Wg	
63-7765	Lockheed C-130E (L-382-8B) Hercules	3831	314AW	
63-7767	Lockheed C-130E (L-382-8B) Hercules	3833	314AW	
63-7768	Lockheed C-130E (L-382-8B) Hercules	3834	314AW	
63-7769	Lockheed C-130E (L-382-8B) Hercules	3835	913AW	
63-7770	Lockheed C-130E (L-382-8B) Hercules	3836	934AW	
63-7771	Lockheed C-130E (L-382-8B) Hercules	3837		Std AMARC [CF176]
63-7773	Lockheed EC-130E (L-382-8B) Hercules	3839	193SOW/PA ANG	
63-7776	Lockheed C-130E (L-382-8B) Hercules	3842	913AW	
63-7777	Lockheed C-130E (L-382-8B) Hercules	3843	152AW/NV ANG	
63-7778	Lockheed C-130E (L-382-8B) Hercules	3844	314AW	
63-7781	Lockheed C-130E (L-382-8B) Hercules	3847	463AG	
63-7782 / RI	Lockheed C-130E (L-382-4B) Hercules	3848	143AW/RI ANG	
63-7783	Lockheed EC-130E (L-382-4B) Hercules	3850		
63-7784	Lockheed C-130E (L-382-4B) Hercules	3851	314AW	
63-7786	Lockheed C-130E (L-382-4B) Hercules	3853	127Wg/MI ANG	
63-7788	Lockheed C-130E (L-382-4B) Hercules	3855	143AW/RI ANG	
63-7790 / YJ	Lockheed C-130E (L-382-4B) Hercules	3857	374AW	
63-7791	Lockheed C-130E (L-382-4B) Hercules	3859	314AW	
63-7792 / IL	Lockheed C-130E (L-382-4B) Hercules	3860	182AW/IL ANG	
63-7793	Lockheed C-130E (L-382-4B) Hercules	3872		Std AMARC [CF174]
63-7794	Lockheed C-130E (L-382-4B) Hercules	3873		Std AMARC [CF184]
63-7796	Lockheed C-130E (L-382-8B) Hercules	3862	314AW	
63-7799	Lockheed C-130E (L-382-8B) Hercules	3865	314AW	
63-7800 / IL	Lockheed C-130E (L-382-8B) Hercules	3866	182AW/IL ANG	
63-7804	Lockheed C-130E (L-382-8B) Hercules	3870	314AW	
63-7805	Lockheed C-130E (L-382-4B) Hercules	3874	913AW	

63-7806	Lockheed C-130E (L-382-4B) Hercules	3875	Std AMARC [CF164]
63-7807	Lockheed C-130E (L-382-4B) Hercules	3876	Std AMARC [CF165]
63-7808	Lockheed C-130E (L-382-4B) Hercules	3877	463AG
63-7809	Lockheed C-130E (L-382-4B) Hercules	3879	463AG
63-7811 / RI	Lockheed C-130E (L-382-4B) Hercules	3881	143AW/RI ANG
63-7812	Lockheed C-130E (L-382-4B) Hercules	3882	182AW/IL ANG
63-7813	Lockheed GC-130E (L-382-4B) Hercules	3883	82TRW
63-7814	Lockheed C-130E (L-382-4B) Hercules	3888	352SOG
63-7815	Lockheed EC-130E (L-382-4B) Hercules	3889	193SOW/PA ANG
63-7816	Lockheed EC-130E (L-382-4B) Hercules	3894	193SOW/PA ANG
63-7817	Lockheed C-130E (L-382-4B) Hercules	3895	403Wg
63-7818 / IL	Lockheed C-130E (L-382-8B) Hercules	3884	182AW/IL ANG
63-7819 / YJ	Lockheed C-130E (L-382-8B) Hercules	3885	374AW
63-7821 / YJ	Lockheed C-130E (L-382-8B) Hercules	3887	374AW
63-7822	Lockheed C-130E (L-382-8B) Hercules	3890	934AW
63-7823	Lockheed C-130E (L-382-8B) Hercules	3891	913AW
63-7824	Lockheed C-130E (L-382-8B) Hercules	3892	143AW/RI ANG
63-7825	Lockheed C-130E (L-382-8B) Hercules	3893	182AW/IL ANG
63-7826	Lockheed C-130E (L-382-8B) Hercules	3903	913AW
63-7828	Lockheed EC-130E (L-382-4B) Hercules	3896	193SOW/PA ANG
63-7829	Lockheed C-130E (L-382-4B) Hercules	3897	463AG
63-7830	Lockheed C-130E (L-382-4B) Hercules	3898	314AW
63-7831	Lockheed C-130E (L-382-4B) Hercules	3899	146AW/CA ANG
63-7832	Lockheed C-130E (L-382-4B) Hercules	3900	913AW
63-7833	Lockheed C-130E (L-382-4B) Hercules	3901	913AW
63-7834	Lockheed C-130E (L-382-4B) Hercules	3902	913AW
63-7835	Lockheed C-130E (L-382-4B) Hercules	3905	314AW
63-7836	Lockheed C-130E (L-382-4B) Hercules	3906	Std AMARC [CF163]
63-7837 / YJ	Lockheed C-130E (L-382-4B) Hercules	3907	374AW
63-7838	Lockheed C-130E (L-382-8B) Hercules	3908	314AW
63-7839	Lockheed C-130E (L-382-8B) Hercules	3909	463AG
63-7840 / RI	Lockheed C-130E (L-382-8B) Hercules	3910	143AW/RI ANG
63-7841	Lockheed C-130E (L-382-8B) Hercules	3911	156AW/PR ANG
63-7842	Lockheed C-130E (L-382-8B) Hercules	3912	939RQW
63-7845	Lockheed C-130E (L-382-4B) Hercules	3915	314AW
63-7846	Lockheed C-130E (L-382-4B) Hercules	3916	314AW
63-7847 / 47	Lockheed C-130E (L-382-4B) Hercules	3917	189AW/AR ANG
63-7848	Lockheed C-130E (L-382-4B) Hercules	3918	913AW
63-7849	Lockheed C-130E (L-382-4B) Hercules	3919	314AW
63-7850 / YJ	Lockheed C-130E (L-382-4B) Hercules	3920	463AG
63-7851	Lockheed C-130E (L-382-4B) Hercules	3921	152AW/NV ANG
63-7852	Lockheed C-130E (L-382-4B) Hercules	3922	463AG
63-7853 / WG	Lockheed C-130E (L-382-4B) Hercules	3923	913AW
63-7854	Lockheed C-130E (L-382-4B) Hercules	3924	Std AMARC [CF194]
63-7856	Lockheed C-130E (L-382-4B) Hercules	3926	403Wg
63-7857	Lockheed C-130E (L-382-8B) Hercules	3927	463AG
63-7858	Lockheed C-130E (L-382-8B) Hercules	3928	182AW/IL ANG
63-7859	Lockheed C-130E (L-382-8B) Hercules	3929	143AW/RI ANG
63-7860	Lockheed C-130E (L-382-8B) Hercules	3930	314AW
63-7861	Lockheed C-130E (L-382-8B) Hercules	3931	152AW/NV ANG
63-7864	Lockheed C-130E (L-382-8B) Hercules	3934	314AW
63-7865 / YJ	Lockheed C-130E (L-382-8B) Hercules	3935	374AW
63-7866 / LK	Lockheed C-130E (L-382-8B) Hercules	3936	314AW
63-7867	Lockheed C-130E (L-382-8B) Hercules	3937	913AW
63-7868 / RI	Lockheed C-130E (L-382-8B) Hercules	3938	143AW/RI ANG
63-7869	Lockheed EC-130E (L-382-4B) Hercules	3939	193SOW/PA ANG
63-7871	Lockheed C-130E (L-382-4B) Hercules	3941	374AW
63-7872 / IL	Lockheed C-130E (L-382-4B) Hercules	3942	182AW/IL ANG
63-7874	Lockheed C-130E (L-382-4B) Hercules	3944	314AW
63-7876	Lockheed C-130E (L-382-8B) Hercules	3947	463AG
63-7877 / IL	Lockheed C-130E (L-382-8B) Hercules	3948	182AW/IL ANG
63-7879 / YJ	Lockheed C-130E (L-382-8B) Hercules	3950	374AW
63-7880	Lockheed C-130E (L-382-8B) Hercules	3951	314AW
63-7882	Lockheed C-130E (L-382-4B) Hercules	3953	314AW
63-7883 / WG	Lockheed C-130E (L-382-4B) Hercules	3954	913AW
63-7884	Lockheed C-130E (L-382-8B) Hercules	3955	463AG
63-7885	Lockheed C-130E (L-382-8B) Hercules	3956	86AW
63-7887 / RS	Lockheed C-130E (L-382-8B) Hercules	3958	86AW
63-7888	Lockheed C-130E (L-382-4B) Hercules	3959	463AG
63-7889 / RI	Lockheed C-130E (L-382-4B) Hercules	3960	143AW/RI ANG
63-7890	Lockheed C-130E (L-382-4B) Hercules	3961	314AW
63-7891	Lockheed C-130E (L-382-4B) Hercules	3962	Std AMARC [CF173]
63-7892 / WG	Lockheed C-130E (L-382-4B) Hercules	3963	913AW
63-7893 / LK	Lockheed C-130E (L-382-4B) Hercules	3964	314AW

63-7894	Lockheed C-130E (L-382-4B) Hercules	3965	463AG
63-7895	Lockheed C-130E (L-382-8B) Hercules	3966	127Wg/MI ANG
63-7896	Lockheed C-130E (L-382-8B) Hercules	3967	314AW
63-7897 / IL	Lockheed C-130E (L-382-8B) Hercules	3968	182AW/IL ANG
63-7898	Lockheed C-130E (L-382-8B) Hercules	3969	16SOW
63-7899 / LK	Lockheed C-130E (L-382-8B) Hercules	3970	314AW
63-7976	Boeing KC-135R Stratotanker	18593 /T0632	6ARW
63-7977	Boeing KC-135R Stratotanker	18594 /T0633	6ARW
63-7978	Boeing KC-135R Stratotanker	18595 /T0634	100ARW
63-7979	Boeing KC-135R Stratotanker	18596 /T0635	
63-7980	Boeing KC-135R Stratotanker	18597 /T0636	100ARW
63-7981	Boeing KC-135R Stratotanker	18598 /T0637	107ARW/NY ANG
63-7982	Boeing KC-135R Stratotanker	18599 /T0638	319ARW
63-7984	Boeing KC-135R Stratotanker	18601 /T0640	117ARW/AL ANG
63-7985	Boeing KC-135R Stratotanker	18602 /T0641	507ARW
63-7986	Boeing KC-135A Stratotanker	18603 /T0642	Std AMARC [CA086]
63-7987	Boeing KC-135R Stratotanker	18604 /T0643	319ARW
63-7988	Boeing KC-135R Stratotanker	18605 /T0644	155ARW/NE ANG
63-7991	Boeing KC-135R Stratotanker	18608 /T0647	155ARW/NE ANG
63-7992	Boeing KC-135R Stratotanker	18609 /T0648	163ARW/CA ANG
63-7993	Boeing KC-135R Stratotanker	18610 /T0649	121ARW/OH ANG
63-7994	Boeing EC-135G	18611 /T0650	Std AMARC [CA045]
63-7995	Boeing KC-135R Stratotanker	18612 /T0651	22ARW
63-7996	Boeing KC-135R Stratotanker	18613 /T0652	434ARW
63-7997	Boeing KC-135R Stratotanker	18614 /T0653	19ARG
63-7999	Boeing KC-135R Stratotanker	18616 /T0655	97AMW
63-8000	Boeing KC-135R Stratotanker	18617 /T0656	22ARW
63-8001	Boeing EC-135G	18618 /T0657	Std AMARC [CA017]
63-8002	Boeing KC-135R Stratotanker	18619 /T0658	19ARG
63-8003	Boeing KC-135R Stratotanker	18620 /T0659	22ARW
63-8004 / MO	Boeing KC-135R Stratotanker	18621 /T0660	366Wg
63-8006	Boeing KC-135R Stratotanker	18623 /T0662	19ARG
63-8007	Boeing KC-135R Stratotanker	18624 /T0663	117ARW/AL ANG
63-8008	Boeing KC-135R Stratotanker	18625 /T0664	100ARW
63-8011	Boeing KC-135R Stratotanker	18628 /T0667	92ARW
63-8012	Boeing KC-135R Stratotanker	18629 /T0668	100ARW
63-8013	Boeing KC-135R Stratotanker	18630 /T0669	121ARW/OH ANG
63-8014	Boeing KC-135R Stratotanker	18631 /T0670	92ARW
63-8015	Boeing KC-135R Stratotanker	18632 /T0671	168ARW/AK ANG
63-8017	Boeing KC-135R Stratotanker	18634 /T0673	
63-8018	Boeing KC-135R Stratotanker	18635 /T0674	155ARW/NE ANG
63-8019	Boeing KC-135R Stratotanker	18636 /T0675	22ARW
63-8020	Boeing KC-135R Stratotanker	18637 /T0676	319ARW
63-8021 / ZZ	Boeing KC-135R Stratotanker	18638 /T0677	18Wg
63-8022	Boeing KC-135R Stratotanker	18639 /T0678	22ARW
63-8023	Boeing KC-135R Stratotanker	18640 /T0679	22ARW
63-8024	Boeing KC-135R Stratotanker	18641 /T0680	452AMW
63-8025	Boeing KC-135R Stratotanker	18642 /T0681	100ARW
63-8026	Boeing KC-135R Stratotanker	18643 /T0682	319ARW
63-8027	Boeing KC-135R Stratotanker	18644 /T0683	92ARW
63-8028	Boeing KC-135R Stratotanker	18645 /T0684	168ARW/AK ANG
63-8029	Boeing KC-135R Stratotanker	18646 /T0685	128ARW/WI ANG
63-8030	Boeing KC-135R Stratotanker	18647 /T0686	154Wg/HI ANG
63-8031	Boeing KC-135R Stratotanker	18648 /T0687	19ARG
63-8032	Boeing KC-135R Stratotanker	18649 /T0688	434ARW
63-8033	Boeing KC-135R Stratotanker	18650 /T0689	92ARW
63-8034	Boeing KC-135R Stratotanker	18651 /T0690	97AMW
63-8035	Boeing KC-135R Stratotanker	18652 /T0691	117ARW/AL ANG
63-8036	Boeing KC-135R Stratotanker	18653 /T0692	107ARW/NY ANG
63-8037	Boeing KC-135R Stratotanker	18654 /T0693	97AMW
63-8038	Boeing KC-135R Stratotanker	18655 /T0694	157ARW/NH ANG
63-8039	Boeing KC-135R Stratotanker	18656 /T0695	507ARW
63-8040	Boeing KC-135R Stratotanker	18657 /T0696	22ARW
63-8041	Boeing KC-135R Stratotanker	18658 /T0697	319ARW
63-8043	Boeing KC-135R Stratotanker	18660 /T0699	168ARW/AK ANG
63-8044 / ZZ	Boeing KC-135R Stratotanker	18661 /T0700	18Wg
63-8045	Boeing KC-135R Stratotanker	18662 /T0701	97AMW
63-8046 / OF	Boeing EC-135C	18663 /C2106	Std AMARC [CA124]
63-8047 / OF	Boeing EC-135C	18664 /C2107	Std AMARC [CA093]
63-8048 / OF	Boeing EC-135C	18665 /C2108	Std AMARC [CA128]
63-8050 / OF	Boeing EC-135C	18667 /C2110	412TW
63-8051	Boeing EC-135C	18668 /C2111	Std AMARC [CA027]
63-8052 / OF	Boeing EC-135C	18669 /C2112	Std AMARC [CA117]
63-8053	Boeing EC-135C	18701 /C2113	Std Pope AFB

63-8054	Boeing EC-135C	18702 /C2114	Std AMARC [CA125]
63-8055	Boeing EC-135J	18703 /C2115	Std AMARC [CA092]
63-8056	Boeing EC-135J	18704 /C2116	Std AMARC [CA013]
63-8058	Boeing KC-135D Stratotanker	18670 /C2201	190ARW/KS ANG
63-8059	Boeing KC-135D Stratotanker	18671 /C2202	190ARW/KS ANG
63-8060	Boeing KC-135D Stratotanker	18672 /C2203	190ARW/KS ANG
63-8061	Boeing KC-135D Stratotanker	18673 /C2204	190ARW/KS ANG
63-8076	Lockheed C-141B Starlifter	300-6007	62AW
63-8078	Lockheed C-141B Starlifter	300-6009	Std AMARC [CR015]
63-8080	Lockheed C-141C Starlifter	300-6011	164AW/TN ANG
63-8081	Lockheed C-141B Starlifter	300-6012	Std AMARC [CR104]
63-8082	Lockheed C-141B Starlifter	300-6013	62AW
63-8083	Lockheed C-141B Starlifter	300-6014	Std AMARC [CR022]
63-8084	Lockheed C-141C Starlifter	300-6015	452AMW
63-8085	Lockheed C-141C Starlifter	300-6016	452AMW
63-8086	Lockheed C-141B Starlifter	300-6017	Std AMARC [CR048]
63-8087	Lockheed C-141B Starlifter	300-6018	Std AMARC [CR069]
63-8088	Lockheed C-141B Starlifter	300-6019	60AMW
63-8089	Lockheed C-141B Starlifter	300-6020	Std AMARC [CR028]
63-8090	Lockheed C-141B Starlifter	300-6021	Std AMARC [CR027]
63-8871 / ZZ	Boeing KC-135R Stratotanker	18719 /T0702	18Wg
63-8872	Boeing KC-135R Stratotanker	18720 /T0703	107ARW/NY ANG
63-8873	Boeing KC-135R Stratotanker	18721 /T0704	6ARW
63-8874	Boeing KC-135R Stratotanker	18722 /T0705	
63-8875 / MO	Boeing KC-135R Stratotanker	18723 /T0706	366Wg
63-8876	Boeing KC-135R Stratotanker	18724 /T0707	168ARW/AK ANG
63-8877	Boeing KC-135R Stratotanker	18725 /T0708	97AMW
63-8878	Boeing KC-135R Stratotanker	18726 /T0709	97AMW
63-8879	Boeing KC-135R Stratotanker	18727 /T0710	100ARW
63-8880	Boeing KC-135R Stratotanker	18728 /T0711	
63-8881	Boeing KC-135R Stratotanker	18729 /T0712	97AMW
63-8883	Boeing KC-135R Stratotanker	18731 /T0714	319ARW
63-8884	Boeing KC-135R Stratotanker	18732 /T0715	22ARW
63-8885	Boeing KC-135R Stratotanker	18733 /T0716	319ARW
63-8886	Boeing KC-135R Stratotanker	18734 /T0717	97AMW
63-8887	Boeing KC-135R Stratotanker	18735 /T0718	100ARW
63-8888	Boeing KC-135R Stratotanker	18736 /T0719	319ARW
63-9792 / OF	Boeing RC-135V	18706 /C2301	55Wg — CFM56 engined
63-9810 / MY	Lockheed C-130E (L-382-8B) Hercules	3971	347Wg
63-9811 / LK	Lockheed C-130E (L-382-8B) Hercules	3972	Std AMARC [CF171]
63-9812	Lockheed C-130E (L-382-8B) Hercules	3973	314AW
63-9813	Lockheed C-130E (L-382-4B) Hercules	3974	127Wg/MI ANG
63-9814	Lockheed C-130E (L-382-4B) Hercules	3975	62AW
63-9815	Lockheed C-130E (L-382-4B) Hercules	3976	156AW/MI ANG
63-9816	Lockheed EC-130E (L-382-8B) Hercules	3977	193SOW/PA ANG
63-9817	Lockheed EC-130E (L-382-8B) Hercules	3978	193SOW/PA ANG
64-0495	Lockheed C-130E (L-382-8B) Hercules	3979	43AW
64-0496	Lockheed C-130E (L-382-8B) Hercules	3980	43AW
64-0497 / YJ	Lockheed C-130E (L-382-8B) Hercules	3981	Std AMARC [CF134]
64-0498	Lockheed C-130E (L-382-8B) Hercules	3982	43AW
64-0499	Lockheed C-130E (L-382-8B) Hercules	3983	43AW
64-0502	Lockheed C-130E (L-382-8B) Hercules	3986	86AW
64-0503	Lockheed C-130E (L-382-8B) Hercules	3987	Std AMARC [CF139]
64-0504	Lockheed C-130E (L-382-8B) Hercules	3988	43AW
64-0510	Lockheed C-130E (L-382-8B) Hercules	3994	156AW/PR ANG
64-0512 / 12	Lockheed C-130E (L-382-8B) Hercules	3996	189AW/AR ANG
64-0513 / LK	Lockheed C-130E (L-382-8B) Hercules	3997	Std AMARC [CF175]
64-0514 / MD	Lockheed C-130E (L-382-8B) Hercules	3998	175Wg/MD ANG
64-0515	Lockheed C-130E (L-382-8B) Hercules	3999	156AW
64-0517 / FT	Lockheed C-130E (L-382-8B) Hercules	4001	43AW
64-0518	Lockheed C-130E (L-382-8B) Hercules	4002	463AG
64-0519 / LK	Lockheed C-130E (L-382-8B) Hercules	4003	314AW
64-0520	Lockheed C-130E (L-382-8B) Hercules	4004	169FW
64-0521	Lockheed C-130E (L-382-8B) Hercules	4005	125FW
64-0523	Lockheed MC-130E (L-382-8B) Hercules	4007	919SOW
64-0525	Lockheed C-130E (L-382-8B) Hercules	4009	43AW
64-0526	Lockheed C-130E (L-382-8B) Hercules	4010	175Wg/MD ANG
64-0527	Lockheed C-130E (L-382-8B) Hercules	4013	86AW
64-0529 / FT	Lockheed C-130E (L-382-8B) Hercules	4017	43AW
64-0530	Lockheed C-130E (L-382-8B) Hercules	4018	Std AMARC [CF151]
64-0531	Lockheed C-130E (L-382-8B) Hercules	4019	43AW
64-0533 / RS	Lockheed C-130E (L-382-8B) Hercules	4022	86AW
64-0535	Lockheed GC-130E (L-382-8B) Hercules	4024	82TRW
64-0537	Lockheed C-130E (L-382-8B) Hercules	4027	43AW

64-0538	Lockheed C-130E (L-382-8B) Hercules	4028	314AW
64-0539	Lockheed C-130E (L-382-8B) Hercules	4029	43AW
64-0540	Lockheed C-130E (L-382-8B) Hercules	4030	43AW
64-0541	Lockheed C-130E (L-382-8B) Hercules	4031	314AW
64-0542	Lockheed C-130E (L-382-8B) Hercules	4032	314AW
64-0544	Lockheed C-130E (L-382-8B) Hercules	4034	175Wg/MD ANG MD ANG
64-0550 / RS	Lockheed C-130E (L-382-8B) Hercules	4045	86AW
64-0551	Lockheed MC-130E (L-382-8B) Hercules	4046	919SOW
64-0553	Lockheed C-130E (L-382-8B) Hercules	4048	Std AMARC [CF145]
64-0554	Lockheed WC-130E (L-382-8B) Hercules	4049	Std AMARC [CF136]
64-0555	Lockheed MC-130E (L-382-8B) Hercules	4056	919SOW
64-0557	Lockheed GC-130E (L-382-8B) Hercules	4058	82TRW
64-0559	Lockheed MC-130E (L-382-8B) Hercules	4062	919SOW
64-0560 / LK	Lockheed C-130E (L-382-8B) Hercules	4063	Std AMARC [CF169]
64-0561	Lockheed MC-130E (L-382-8B) Hercules	4065	919SOW
64-0562	Lockheed MC-130E (L-382-8B) Hercules	4068	919SOW
64-0565	Lockheed MC-130E (L-382-8B) Hercules	4077	919SOW
64-0566	Lockheed MC-130E (L-382-8B) Hercules	4080	919SOW
64-0567	Lockheed MC-130E (L-382-8B) Hercules	4083	919SOW
64-0568	Lockheed MC-130E (L-382-8B) Hercules	4086	919SOW
64-0570	Lockheed C-130E (L-382-4B) Hercules	4085	43AW
64-0571	Lockheed MC-130E (L-382-4B) Hercules	4087	919SOW
64-0572	Lockheed MC-130E (L-382-4B) Hercules	4090	919SOW
64-0609	Lockheed C-141B Starlifter	300-6022	Std AMARC [CR038]
64-0610	Lockheed C-141B Starlifter	300-6023	Std AMARC [CR065]
64-0611	Lockheed C-141B Starlifter	300-6024	62AW
64-0612	Lockheed C-141B Starlifter	300-6025	Std AMARC [CR082]
64-0613	Lockheed C-141B Starlifter	300-6026	Std AMARC [CR044]
64-0614	Lockheed C-141C Starlifter	300-6027	172AW/MS ANG
64-0615	Lockheed C-141B Starlifter	300-6028	Std AMARC [CR083]
64-0616	Lockheed C-141B Starlifter	300-6029	Std AMARC [CR110]
64-0617	Lockheed C-141B Starlifter	300-6030	Std AMARC [CR019]
64-0618	Lockheed C-141B Starlifter	300-6031	Std AMARC [CR122]
64-0619	Lockheed C-141B Starlifter	300-6032	305AMW
64-0620	Lockheed C-141C Starlifter	300-6033	459AW
64-0621	Lockheed C-141B Starlifter	300-6034	Std AMARC [CR091]
64-0622	Lockheed C-141C Starlifter	300-6035	172AW/MS ANG
64-0623	Lockheed C-141B Starlifter	300-6036	Std AMARC [CR075]
64-0625	Lockheed C-141B Starlifter	300-6038	Std AMARC [CR041]
64-0627	Lockheed C-141C Starlifter	300-6040	164AW/TN ANG
64-0628	Lockheed C-141B Starlifter	300-6041	Std AMARC [CR112]
64-0629	Lockheed C-141B Starlifter	300-6042	Std AMARC [CR071]
64-0630	Lockheed C-141B Starlifter	300-6043	Std AMARC [CR111]
64-0631	Lockheed C-141B Starlifter	300-6044	Std AMARC [CR113]
64-0632	Lockheed C-141B Starlifter	300-6045	172AW/MS ANG
64-0633	Lockheed C-141B Starlifter	300-6046	62AW
64-0634	Lockheed C-141B Starlifter	300-6047	Std AMARC [CR025]
64-0635	Lockheed C-141B Starlifter	300-6048	Std AMARC [CR036]
64-0636	Lockheed C-141B Starlifter	300-6049	Std AMARC [CR004]
64-0637	Lockheed C-141B Starlifter	300-6050	459AW
64-0638	Lockheed C-141B Starlifter	300-6051	62AW
64-0639	Lockheed C-141B Starlifter	300-6052	Std AMARC [CR037]
64-0640	Lockheed C-141C Starlifter	300-6053	172AW/MS ANG
64-0642	Lockheed C-141B Starlifter	300-6055	97AMW
64-0643	Lockheed C-141B Starlifter	300-6056	Std AMARC [CR109]
64-0645	Lockheed C-141C Starlifter	300-6058	459AW
64-0646	Lockheed C-141B Starlifter	300-6059	Std AMARC [CR086]
64-0648	Lockheed C-141B Starlifter	300-6061	Std AMARC [CR005]
64-0649	Lockheed C-141B Starlifter	300-6062	Std AMARC [CR107]
64-0650	Lockheed C-141B Starlifter	300-6063	Std AMARC [CR012]
64-0651	Lockheed C-141B Starlifter	300-6064	Std AMARC [CR029]
64-0653	Lockheed C-141B Starlifter	300-6066	Std AMARC [CR034]
64-14828	Boeing KC-135R Stratotanker	18768 /T0720	22ARW
64-14829	Boeing KC-135R Stratotanker	18769 /T0721	100ARW
64-14830	Boeing KC-135R Stratotanker	18770 /T0722	6ARW
64-14831	Boeing KC-135R Stratotanker	18771 /T0723	22ARW
64-14832	Boeing KC-135R Stratotanker	18772 /T0724	154Wg/HI ANG
64-14833	Boeing KC-135R Stratotanker	18773 /T0725	6ARW
64-14834	Boeing KC-135R Stratotanker	18774 /T0726	434ARW
64-14835	Boeing KC-135R Stratotanker	18775 /T0727	100ARW
64-14836	Boeing KC-135R Stratotanker	18776 /T0728	319ARW
64-14837	Boeing KC-135R Stratotanker	18777 /T0729	6ARW
64-14838	Boeing KC-135R Stratotanker	18778 /T0730	100ARW
64-14839	Boeing KC-135R Stratotanker	18779 /T0731	107ARW/NY ANG

64-14840	Boeing KC-135R Stratotanker	18780 /T0732	121ARW/OH ANG
64-14841 / OF	Boeing RC-135V	18781 /C2302	55Wg
64-14842 / OF	Boeing RC-135V	18782 /C2303	55Wg
64-14843 / OF	Boeing RC-135V	18783 /C2304	55Wg CFM56 engined
64-14844 / OF	Boeing RC-135V	18784 /C2305	55Wg
64-14845 / OF	Boeing RC-135V	18785 /C2306	55Wg
64-14846 / OF	Boeing RC-135V	18786 /C2307	55Wg
64-14847 / OF	Boeing RC-135U	18787 /C2308	55Wg
64-14848 / OF	Boeing RC-135V(R)	18788 /C2309	55Wg
64-14849	Boeing RC-135U	18789 /C2310	55Wg
64-14852 / MY	Lockheed HC-130P (L-382-12B) Hercules	4036	347Wg
64-14853 / MY	Lockheed HC-130P (L-382-12B) Hercules	4037	347Wg
64-14854	Lockheed MC-130H (L-382-12B) Hercules	4038	16SOW
64-14855 / PD	Lockheed HC-130P (L-382-12B) Hercules	4055	939RQW
64-14857	Lockheed HC-130H (L-382-12B) Hercules	4073	514TS
64-14858	Lockheed MC-130P (L-382-12B) Hercules	4081	58SOW
64-14859	Lockheed C-130E (L-382-12B) Hercules	4082	16SOW
64-14860 / PD	Lockheed HC-130P (L-382-12B) Hercules	4084	939RQW
64-14861	Lockheed WC-130H (L-382-12B) Hercules	4088	403Wg
64-14862 / D4	Lockheed EC-130H (L-382-12B) Hercules	4089	645MATS
64-14863	Lockheed HC-130P (L-382-12B) Hercules	4094	347Wg
64-14864	Lockheed HC-130H (L-382-12B) Hercules	4097	939RQW
64-14865 / MY	Lockheed HC-130H (L-382-12B) Hercules	4098	347Wg
64-14866	Lockheed WC-130H (L-382-12B) Hercules	4099	403Wg
64-17680	Lockheed C-130E (L-382-8B) Hercules	4064	314AW
64-17681 / RS	Lockheed C-130E (L-382-8B) Hercules	4069	86AW
64-18240 / RS	Lockheed C-130E (L-382-8B) Hercules	4105	86AW
65-0216	Lockheed C-141C Starlifter	300-6067	445AW
65-0217	Lockheed C-141B Starlifter	300-6068	Std AMARC [CR136]
65-0218	Lockheed C-141B Starlifter	300-6069	62AW
65-0219	Lockheed C-141B Starlifter	300-6070	Std AMARC [CR137]
65-0220	Lockheed C-141B Starlifter	300-6071	Std AMARC [CR135]
65-0221	Lockheed C-141B Starlifter	300-6072	62AW
65-0222	Lockheed C-141C Starlifter	300-6073	164AW/TN ANG
65-0223	Lockheed C-141B Starlifter	300-6074	
65-0224	Lockheed C-141B Starlifter SOLL II	300-6075	305AMW
65-0225	Lockheed C-141C Starlifter	300-6076	452AMW
65-0226	Lockheed C-141C Starlifter	300-6077	459AW
65-0227	Lockheed C-141B Starlifter	300-6078	
65-0229	Lockheed C-141C Starlifter	300-6080	452AMW
65-0230	Lockheed C-141B Starlifter	300-6081	Std AMARC [CR095]
65-0231	Lockheed C-141B Starlifter	300-6082	Std AMARC [CR123]
65-0232	Lockheed C-141C Starlifter	300-6083	445AW
65-0233	Lockheed C-141B Starlifter	300-6084	Std AMARC [ZH001]
65-0234	Lockheed C-141B Starlifter	300-6085	Std AMARC [CR066]
65-0235	Lockheed C-141B Starlifter	300-6086	Std AMARC [CR133]
65-0237	Lockheed C-141C Starlifter	300-6088	445AW
65-0238	Lockheed C-141B Starlifter	300-6089	Std AMARC [CR081]
65-0239	Lockheed C-141B Starlifter	300-6090	Std AMARC [CR097]
65-0240	Lockheed C-141B Starlifter	300-6091	62AW
65-0241	Lockheed C-141B Starlifter	300-6092	Std AMARC [CR084]
65-0242	Lockheed C-141B Starlifter	300-6093	Std AMARC [CR067]
65-0243	Lockheed C-141B Starlifter	300-6094	Std AMARC [CR068]
65-0244	Lockheed C-141B Starlifter	300-6095	Std AMARC [CR096]
65-0245	Lockheed C-141C Starlifter	300-6096	452AMW
65-0247	Lockheed C-141B Starlifter	300-6098	Std AMARC [CR011]
65-0248	Lockheed C-141C Starlifter	300-6099	452AMW
65-0249	Lockheed C-141C Starlifter	300-6100	445AW
65-0250	Lockheed C-141C Starlifter	300-6101	445AW
65-0251	Lockheed C-141B Starlifter	300-6102	Std AMARC [CR121]
65-0252	Lockheed C-141B Starlifter	300-6103	
65-0254	Lockheed C-141B Starlifter	300-6105	Std AMARC [CR103]
65-0256	Lockheed C-141C Starlifter	300-6107	445AW
65-0257	Lockheed C-141C Starlifter	300-6108	452AMW
65-0258	Lockheed C-141B Starlifter	300-6109	445AW
65-0259	Lockheed C-141B Starlifter	300-6111	Std AMARC [CR118]
65-0260	Lockheed C-141B Starlifter	300-6112	Std AMARC [CR073]
65-0261	Lockheed C-141C Starlifter	300-6113	445AW
65-0262	Lockheed C-141B Starlifter	300-6114	Std AMARC [CR007]
65-0263	Lockheed C-141B Starlifter	300-6115	Std AMARC [CR064]
65-0264	Lockheed C-141B Starlifter	300-6116	Std AMARC [CR020]
65-0265	Lockheed C-141B Starlifter	300-6117	Std AMARC [CR026]
65-0266	Lockheed C-141B Starlifter	300-6118	Std AMARC [CR101]
65-0267	Lockheed C-141B Starlifter	300-6119	62AW

65-0268	Lockheed C-141B Starlifter	300-6120		Std AMARC [CR035]
65-0269	Lockheed C-141B Starlifter	300-6121		Std AMARC [CR098]
65-0270	Lockheed C-141B Starlifter	300-6122		Std AMARC [CR042]
65-0271	Lockheed C-141C Starlifter	300-6123	459AW	
65-0272	Lockheed C-141B Starlifter	300-6124		
65-0273	Lockheed C-141B Starlifter	300-6125	305AMW	
65-0275	Lockheed C-141B Starlifter	300-6127		
65-0276	Lockheed C-141B Starlifter	300-6128		Std AMARC [CR102]
65-0278	Lockheed C-141B Starlifter	300-6130		Std AMARC [CR016]
65-0279	Lockheed C-141B Starlifter	300-6131	305AMW	
65-0280	Lockheed C-141B Starlifter	300-6132		Std AMARC [CR094]
65-0962 / DM	Lockheed EC-130H (L-382-12B) Hercules	4102	355Wg	
65-0963	Lockheed WC-130H (L-382-12B) Hercules	4103	403Wg	
65-0964	Lockheed HC-130P (L-382-12B) Hercules	4104	58SOW	
65-0966	Lockheed WC-130H (L-382-12B) Hercules	4107	403Wg	
65-0967	Lockheed WC-130H (L-382-12B) Hercules	4108	403Wg	
65-0968	Lockheed WC-130H (L-382-12B) Hercules	4110	403Wg	
65-0970 / PD	Lockheed HC-130P (L-382-12B) Hercules	4112	939RQW	
65-0971	Lockheed MC-130P (L-382-12B) Hercules	4116	58SOW	
65-0972	Lockheed C-130E (L-382-12B) Hercules	4120		Std AMARC [CF183]
65-0973 / MY	Lockheed HC-130P (L-382-12B) Hercules	4121	347Wg	
65-0974	Lockheed HC-130P (L-382-12B) Hercules	4123	106RQW/NY ANG	
65-0975	Lockheed MC-130P (L382-12B) Hercules	4125	58SOW	
65-0976	Lockheed HC-130P (L-382-12B) Hercules	4126	939RQW	
65-0977	Lockheed WC-130H (L-382-12B) Hercules	4127	403Wg	
65-0978	Lockheed HC-130P (L-382-12B) Hercules	4130	106RQW/NY ANG	NY ANG
65-0979	Lockheed NC-130H (L-382-12B) Hercules	4131	412TW	
65-0980	Lockheed WC-130H (L-382-12B) Hercules	4132	403Wg	
65-0981 / MY	Lockheed HC-130P (L-382-12B) Hercules	4133	347Wg	
65-0982 / MY	Lockheed HC-130P (L-382-12B) Hercules	4135	347Wg	
65-0983	Lockheed HC-130H (L-382-12B) Hercules	4138	347Wg	
65-0984	Lockheed WC-130H (L-382-12B) Hercules	4139	403Wg	
65-0985	Lockheed WC-130H (L-382-12B) Hercules	4140	403Wg	
65-0986 / MY	Lockheed HC-130H (L-382-12B) Hercules	4141	347Wg	
65-0987 / MY	Lockheed HC-130P (L-382-12B) Hercules	4142	347Wg	
65-0988 / MY	Lockheed HC-130P (L-382-12B) Hercules	4143	347Wg	
65-0989 / DM	Lockheed EC-130H (L382-12B) Hercules	4150	355Wg	
65-0991	Lockheed MC-130P (L-382-12B) Hercules	4152	16SOW	
65-0992	Lockheed MC-130P (L-382-12B) Hercules	4155	353SOG	
65-0993	Lockheed MC-130P (L-382-12B) Hercules	4156	353SOG	
65-0994	Lockheed MC-130P (L-382-12B) Hercules	4157	353SOG	
65-9397	Lockheed C-141B Starlifter	300-6134		Std AMARC [CR021]
65-9398	Lockheed C-141B Starlifter	300-6135		Std AMARC [CR002]
65-9399	Lockheed C-141B Starlifter	300-6136		Std AMARC [CR014]
65-9400	Lockheed C-141B Starlifter	300-6137	97AMW	Std
65-9401	Lockheed C-141B Starlifter	300-6138	305AMW	
65-9402	Lockheed C-141B Starlifter	300-6139		Std AMARC [CR018]
65-9403	Lockheed C-141B Starlifter	300-6140		Std AMARC [CR100]
65-9404	Lockheed C-141B Starlifter	300-6141		Std AMARC [CR047]
65-9405	Lockheed C-141B Starlifter	300-6142		Std AMARC [CR120]
65-9408	Lockheed C-141B Starlifter	300-6145	305AMW	
65-9409	Lockheed C-141C Starlifter	300-6146	445AW	
65-9410	Lockheed C-141B Starlifter	300-6147		Std AMARC [CR003]
65-9411	Lockheed C-141B Starlifter	300-6148		Std AMARC [CR124]
65-9412	Lockheed C-141C Starlifter	300-6149	445AW	
65-9413	Lockheed C-141B Starlifter	300-6150		Std AMARC [CR119]
65-9414	Lockheed C-141C Starlifter	300-6151	452AMW	
66-0128	Lockheed C-141B Starlifter	300-6154		
66-0129	Lockheed C-141B Starlifter	300-6155		Std AMARC [CR023]
66-0130	Lockheed C-141C Starlifter	300-6156	172AW/MS ANG	
66-0131	Lockheed C-141B Starlifter	300-6157	305AMW	
66-0132	Lockheed C-141C Starlifter	300-6158	445AW	
66-0133	Lockheed C-141B Starlifter	300-6159	305AMW	
66-0134	Lockheed C-141C Starlifter	300-6160	445AW	
66-0135	Lockheed C-141B Starlifter	300-6161		Std AMARC [CR049]
66-0136	Lockheed C-141C Starlifter	300-6162	452AMW	
66-0137	Lockheed C-141B Starlifter	300-6163		Std AMARC [CR115]
66-0138	Lockheed C-141B Starlifter	300-6164		Std AMARC [CR017]
66-0139	Lockheed C-141C Starlifter	300-6165	164AW/TN ANG	
66-0140	Lockheed C-141B Starlifter	300-6166	62AW	
66-0141	Lockheed C-141B Starlifter	300-6167		Std AMARC [CR046]
66-0143	Lockheed C-141B Starlifter	300-6169		Std AMARC [CR001]
66-0144	Lockheed C-141B Starlifter	300-6170	62AW	
66-0145	Lockheed C-141B Starlifter	300-6171		Std AMARC [CR030]

66-0146	Lockheed C-141B Starlifter	300-6172	Std AMARC [CR108]
66-0147	Lockheed C-141B Starlifter	300-6173	62AW
66-0148	Lockheed C-141C Starlifter	300-6174	445AW
66-0149	Lockheed C-141B Starlifter	300-6175	62AW
66-0151	Lockheed C-141C Starlifter	300-6177	452AMW
66-0152	Lockheed C-141C Starlifter	300-6178	452AMW
66-0153	Lockheed C-141B Starlifter	300-6179	Std AMARC [CR093]
66-0154	Lockheed C-141B Starlifter	300-6180	97AMW Std
66-0155	Lockheed C-141B Starlifter SOLL II	300-6181	Std AMARC [CR125]
66-0156	Lockheed C-141B Starlifter	300-6182	62AW
66-0157	Lockheed C-141C Starlifter	300-6183	164AW/TN ANG
66-0158	Lockheed C-141B Starlifter	300-6184	62AW
66-0160	Lockheed C-141B Starlifter	300-6186	62AW
66-0161	Lockheed C-141B Starlifter	300-6187	97AMW
66-0162	Lockheed C-141B Starlifter	300-6188	Std AMARC [CR126]
66-0163	Lockheed C-141B Starlifter	300-6189	Std AMARC [CR127]
66-0164	Lockheed C-141C Starlifter	300-6190	172AW
66-0165	Lockheed C-141B Starlifter	300-6191	62AW
66-0166	Lockheed C-141B Starlifter	300-6192	62AW
66-0167	Lockheed C-141C Starlifter	300-6193	452AMW
66-0168	Lockheed C-141B Starlifter	300-6194	305AMW
66-0169	Lockheed C-141B Starlifter	300-6195	305AMW
66-0170	Lockheed C-141B Starlifter	300-6196	Std AMARC [CR006]
66-0171	Lockheed C-141B Starlifter	300-6197	62AW
66-0173	Lockheed C-141B Starlifter	300-6198	
66-0174	Lockheed C-141C Starlifter	300-6200	459AW
66-0175	Lockheed C-141B Starlifter	300-6201	62AW
66-0177	Lockheed C-141C Starlifter	300-6203	445AW
66-0178	Lockheed C-141B Starlifter	300-6204	
66-0179	Lockheed C-141B Starlifter	300-6205	Std AMARC [CR039]
66-0181	Lockheed C-141C Starlifter	300-6207	452AMW
66-0182	Lockheed C-141C Starlifter	300-6208	452AMW
66-0183	Lockheed C-141B Starlifter	300-6209	305AMW
66-0184	Lockheed C-141B Starlifter	300-6210	62AW
66-0185	Lockheed C-141C Starlifter	300-6211	172AW/MS ANG
66-0186	Lockheed C-141B Starlifter	300-6212	Std Atlus AFB
66-0187	Lockheed C-141B Starlifter	300-6213	Std AMARC [CR089]
66-0188	Lockheed C-141B Starlifter	300-6214	Std AMARC [CR008]
66-0190	Lockheed C-141C Starlifter	300-6216	172AW/MS ANG
66-0191	Lockheed C-141C Starlifter	300-6217	172AW/MS ANG
66-0192	Lockheed C-141B Starlifter SOLL II	300-6218	305AMW
66-0193	Lockheed C-141C Starlifter	300-6219	445AW
66-0194	Lockheed C-141B Starlifter	300-6220	Std AMARC [CR088]
66-0195	Lockheed C-141B Starlifter	300-6221	Std AMARC [CR090]
66-0196	Lockheed C-141B Starlifter	300-6222	305AMW
66-0197	Lockheed C-141B Starlifter	300-6223	Std AMARC [CR114]
66-0198	Lockheed C-141B Starlifter	300-6224	Std AMARC [CR077]
66-0199	Lockheed C-141B Starlifter	300-6225	Std AMARC [CR092]
66-0200	Lockheed C-141B Starlifter	300-6226	
66-0201	Lockheed C-141C Starlifter	300-6227	452AMW
66-0202	Lockheed C-141B Starlifter	300-6228	Std AMARC [CR085]
66-0203	Lockheed C-141B Starlifter	300-6229	Std AMARC [CR050]
66-0204	Lockheed C-141B Starlifter	300-6230	Std AMARC [CR045]
66-0205	Lockheed C-141B Starlifter	300-6231	Std AMARC [CR031]
66-0206	Lockheed C-141B Starlifter	300-6232	Std AMARC [CR138]
66-0207	Lockheed C-141B Starlifter	300-6233	Std AMARC [CR040]
66-0208	Lockheed C-141B Starlifter	300-6234	Std AMARC [CR034]
66-0209	Lockheed C-141B Starlifter	300-6235	Std AMARC [CR087]
66-0212	Lockheed MC-130P (L-382C-12B) Hercules	4162	129RQW/CA ANG
66-0213	Lockheed MC-130P (L-382C-12B) Hercules	4163	16SOW
66-0215	Lockheed MC-130P (L-382C-12B) Hercules	4165	353SOG
66-0216	Lockheed MC-130P (L-382C-12B) Hercules	4166	919SOW
66-0217	Lockheed MC-130P (L-382C-12B) Hercules	4173	16SOW
66-0219	Lockheed MC-130P (L-382C-12B) Hercules	4175	129RQW/CA ANG
66-0220	Lockheed MC-130P (L-382C-12B) Hercules	4179	353SOG
66-0221	Lockheed HC-130P (L-382C-12B) Hercules	4183	129RQW/CA ANG
66-0222 / LI	Lockheed HC-130P (L-382C-12B) Hercules	4184	106RQW/NY ANG
66-0223	Lockheed MC-130P (L-382C-12B) Hercules	4185	16SOW
66-0224	Lockheed HC-130P (L-382C-12B) Hercules	4186	129RQW/CA ANG
66-0225	Lockheed MC-130P (L-382C-12B) Hercules	4187	16SOW
66-7944	Lockheed C-141B Starlifter	300-6236	62AW
66-7945	Lockheed C-141B Starlifter	300-6237	Std AMARC [CR024]
66-7946	Lockheed C-141B Starlifter	300-6238	Std AMARC [CR072]
66-7947	Lockheed C-141B Starlifter	300-6239	305AMW

66-7948	Lockheed C-141B Starlifter	300-6240		305AMW	
66-7949	Lockheed C-141B Starlifter	300-6241			Std AMARC [CR070]
66-7950	Lockheed C-141C Starlifter	300-6242		445AW	
66-7951	Lockheed C-141B Starlifter	300-6243			Std AMARC [CR078]
66-7952	Lockheed C-141C Starlifter	300-6244		452AMW	
66-7953	Lockheed C-141C Starlifter	300-6245		445AW	
66-7954	Lockheed C-141C Starlifter	300-6246		445AW	
66-7955	Lockheed C-141B Starlifter	300-6247		62AW	
66-7956	Lockheed C-141B Starlifter	300-6248		62AW	
66-7957	Lockheed C-141C Starlifter	300-6249		452AMW	
66-7958	Lockheed C-141B Starlifter	300-6250			Std AMARC [CR051]
66-7959	Lockheed C-141B Starlifter	300-6251		445AW	
66-8304	Lockheed C-5A Galaxy	500-0002		439AW	
66-8305	Lockheed C-5A Galaxy	500-0003		433AW	
66-8306	Lockheed C-5A Galaxy	500-0004		433AW	
66-8307	Lockheed C-5A Galaxy	500-0005		433AW	
67-0001	Lockheed C-141B Starlifter	300-6252			Std AMARC [CR080]
67-0002	Lockheed C-141B Starlifter	300-6253		62AW	
67-0003	Lockheed C-141B Starlifter SOLL II	300-6254		305AMW	
67-0004	Lockheed C-141B Starlifter SOLL II	300-6255		305AMW	
67-0005	Lockheed C-141B Starlifter	300-6256			Std AMARC [CR043]
67-0007	Lockheed C-141B Starlifter	300-6258			Std AMARC [CR076]
67-0009	Lockheed C-141B Starlifter	300-6260			Std AMARC [CR054]
67-0010	Lockheed C-141B Starlifter SOLL II	300-6261		305AMW	
67-0011	Lockheed C-141B Starlifter	300-6262		305AMW	
67-0012	Lockheed C-141B Starlifter	300-6263		305AMW	
67-0013	Lockheed C-141B Starlifter	300-6264			Std AMARC [CR105]
67-0014	Lockheed C-141B Starlifter SOLL II	300-6265		305AMW	
67-0015	Lockheed C-141C Starlifter	300-6266		452AMW	
67-0016	Lockheed C-141B Starlifter	300-6267			Std AMARC [CR134]
67-0018	Lockheed C-141B Starlifter	300-6269			Std AMARC [CR116]
67-0019	Lockheed C-141B Starlifter	300-6270		62AW	
67-0020	Lockheed C-141B Starlifter	300-6271			Std AMARC [CR106]
67-0021	Lockheed C-141B Starlifter	300-6272		164AW/TN ANG	
67-0022	Lockheed C-141B Starlifter	300-6273			Std AMARC [CR099]
67-0023	Lockheed C-141B Starlifter	300-6274			Std AMARC [CR013]
67-0024	Lockheed C-141C Starlifter	300-6275		164AW/TN ANG	
67-0025	Lockheed C-141B Starlifter	300-6276			Std AMARC [CR033]
67-0026	Lockheed C-141B Starlifter	300-6277			Std AMARC [CR074]
67-0027	Lockheed C-141C Starlifter	300-6278		459AW	
67-0028	Lockheed C-141B Starlifter	300-6279		62AW	
67-0029	Lockheed C-141C Starlifter	300-6280		164AW/TN ANG	
67-0031	Lockheed C-141C Starlifter	300-6282		445AW	
67-0164	Lockheed C-141B Starlifter	300-6283			Std AMARC [CR060]
67-0165	Lockheed C-141B Starlifter	300-6284		305AMW	
67-0166	Lockheed C-141B Starlifter	300-6285		305AMW	VIP
67-0167	Lockheed C-5A Galaxy	500-0006		439AW	
67-0168	Lockheed C-5A Galaxy	500-0007		433AW	
67-0169	Lockheed C-5A Galaxy	500-0008		105AW/NY ANG	
67-0170	Lockheed C-5A Galaxy	500-0009		105AW/NY ANG	
67-0171	Lockheed C-5A Galaxy	500-0010		433AW	
67-0173	Lockheed C-5A Galaxy	500-0012		105AW/NY ANG	
67-0174	Lockheed C-5A Galaxy	500-0013		105AW/NY ANG	
67-19417	Boeing EC-137D (707-355C)	19417 / 582	N707HL	6ARW	
67-21303	Cessna O-2A Super Skymaster	M337-0009			Std AMARC [HV178]
67-21313	Cessna O-2A Super Skymaster	M337-0019			Std AMARC [HV120]
67-21321	Cessna O-2A Super Skymaster	M337-0027			Std AMARC [HV179]
67-21345	Cessna O-2A Super Skymaster	M337-0051			Std AMARC [HV216]
67-21346	Cessna O-2A Super Skymaster	M337-0052			Std AMARC [HV127]
67-21355	Cessna O-2A Super Skymaster	M337-0061			Std AMARC [HV164]
67-21360	Cessna O-2A Super Skymaster	M337-0066			Std AMARC [HV115]
67-21366	Cessna O-2A Super Skymaster	M337-0072			Std AMARC [HV176]
67-21371	Cessna O-2A Super Skymaster	M337-0077			Std AMARC [HV177]
67-21392	Cessna O-2A Super Skymaster	M337-0098			Std AMARC [HV180]
67-21397	Cessna O-2A Super Skymaster	M337-0103			Std AMARC [HV183]
67-21417	Cessna O-2A Super Skymaster	M337-0123			Std AMARC [HV173]
67-22583	McDonnell Douglas C-9A Nightingale (DC-9-32F)				
		47241 / 281		374AW	
67-22584	McDonnell Douglas C-9A Nightingale (DC-9-32F)				
		47242 / 304		375AW	
67-22585	McDonnell Douglas C-9A Nightingale (DC-9-32F)				
		47295 / 340		86AW	
67-7183	Lockheed C-130H (L-382C-12B) Hercules	4255	1452 (USCG)		Std AMARC [CF119]
67-7184	Lockheed C-130H (L-382C-12B) Hercules	4260	1453 (USCG)	24Wg	

68-02	Lockheed C-5A Galaxy	500-0014	439AW
68-02 2	Lockheed C-5A Galaxy	500-0015	105AW/NY ANG
68-02 3	Lockheed C-5A Galaxy	500-0016	60AMW
68-02 4	Lockheed C-5A Galaxy	500-0017	436AW
68-02 5	Lockheed C-5A Galaxy	500-0018	439AW
68-02 6	Lockheed C-5A Galaxy	500-0019	60AMW
68-02 7	Lockheed C-5A Galaxy	500-0020	97AMW
68-02 9	Lockheed C-5A Galaxy	500-0022	439AW
68-0220	Lockheed C-5A Galaxy	500-0023	433AW
68-0221	Lockheed C-5A Galaxy	500-0024	433AW
68-0222	Lockheed C-5A Galaxy	500-0025	439AW
68-0223	Lockheed C-5A Galaxy	500-0026	433AW
68-022	Lockheed C-5A Galaxy	500-0027	105AW/NY ANG
68-0225	Lockheed C-5A Galaxy	500-0028	439AW
68-0226	Lockheed C-5A Galaxy	500-0029	105AW/NY ANG
68-10534	Lockheed C-130E (L-382C-15D) Hercules	4314	43AW
68-10535 / RS	Lockheed C-130E (L-382C-15D) Hercules	4315	86AW
68-10537	Lockheed C-130E (L-382C-15D) Hercules	4317	43AW
68-10538 / RS	Lockheed C-130E (L-382C-15D) Hercules	4318	86AW
68-10539	Lockheed C-130E (L-382C-15D) Hercules	4319	43AW
68-10540	Lockheed C-130E (L-382C-15D) Hercules	4320	43AW
68-10541	Lockheed C-130E (L-382C-15D) Hercules	4321	43AW
68-10542	Lockheed C-130E (L-382C-15D) Hercules	4322	43AW
68-10543 / RS	Lockheed C-130E (L-382C-15D) Hercules	4323	86AW
68-10547 / RS	Lockheed C-130E (L-382C-15D) Hercules	4327	86AW
68-10548	Lockheed C-130E (L-382C-15D) Hercules	4328	314AW
68-10958	McDonnell Douglas C-9A Nightingale (DC-9-32F)		
		47366 / 530	375AW
68-10959	McDonnell Douglas C-9A Nightingale (DC-9-32F)		
		47367 / 539	375AW
68-10960	McDonnell Douglas C-9A Nightingale (DC-9-32F)		
		47448 / 548	375AW
68-10961	McDonnell Douglas C-9A Nightingale (DC-9-32F)		
		47449 / 552	375AW
68-10967	Cessna O-2A Super Skymaster	M337-0243	Std AMARC [HV165]
68-10977	Cessna O-2A Super Skymaster	M337-0253	Std AMARC [HV171]
68-10989	Cessna O-2A Super Skymaster	M337-0265	Std AMARC [HV181]
68-11033	Cessna O-2A Super Skymaster	M337-0304	Std AMARC [HV184]
68-11171	Cessna O-2A Super Skymaster	M337-0396	Std AMARC [HV198]
68-11173	Cessna O-2A Super Skymaster	M337-0398	Std AMARC [HV193]
68-6874	Cessna O-2A Super Skymaster	M337-0163	Std AMARC [HV186]
68-6875	Cessna O-2A Super Skymaster	M337-0165	Std AMARC [HV147]
68-6895	Cessna O-2A Super Skymaster	M337-0184	Std AMARC [HV140]
68-8932	McDonnell Douglas C-9A Nightingale (DC-9-32F)		
		47297 / 377	375AW
68-8933	McDonnell Douglas C-9A Nightingale (DC-9-32F)		
		47298 / 399	375AW
68-8934	McDonnell Douglas C-9A Nightingale (DC-9-32F)		
		47299 / 421	375AW
68-8935	McDonnell Douglas C-9A Nightingale (DC-9-32F)		
		47300 / 438	375AW
69-0001	Lockheed C-5A Galaxy	500-0032	60AMW
69-0002	Lockheed C-5A Galaxy	500-0033	439AW
69-0003	Lockheed C-5A Galaxy	500-0034	439AW
69-0004	Lockheed C-5A Galaxy	500-0035	433AW
69-0005	Lockheed C-5A Galaxy	500-0036	439AW
69-0006	Lockheed C-5A Galaxy	500-0037	433AW
69-0007	Lockheed C-5A Galaxy	500-0038	433AW
69-0008	Lockheed C-5A Galaxy	500-0039	105AW/NY ANG
69-0009	Lockheed C-5A Galaxy	500-0040	105AW/NY ANG
69-0010	Lockheed C-5A Galaxy	500-0041	60AMW
69-0011	Lockheed C-5A Galaxy	500-0042	439AW
69-0012	Lockheed C-5A Galaxy	500-0043	105AW/NY ANG
69-0013	Lockheed C-5A Galaxy	500-0044	439AW
69-0014	Lockheed C-5A Galaxy	500-0045	97AMW
69-0015	Lockheed C-5A Galaxy	500-0046	105AW/NY ANG
69-0016	Lockheed C-5A Galaxy	500-0047	433AW
69-0017	Lockheed C-5A Galaxy	500-0048	439AW
69-0018	Lockheed C-5A Galaxy	500-0049	97AMW
69-0019	Lockheed C-5A Galaxy	500-0050	439AW
69-0020	Lockheed C-5A Galaxy	500-0051	439AW
69-0021	Lockheed C-5A Galaxy	500-0052	105AW/NY ANG
69-0022	Lockheed C-5A Galaxy	500-0053	439AW
69-0023	Lockheed C-5A Galaxy	500-0054	60AMW

69-0024	Lockheed C-5A Galaxy	500-0055	97AMW	
69-0025	Lockheed C-5A Galaxy	500-0056	60AMW	
69-0026	Lockheed C-5A Galaxy	500-0057	60AMW	
69-0027	Lockheed C-5A Galaxy	500-0058	436AW	
69-5819	Lockheed MC-130P (L-382-20B) Hercules	4363	16SOW	
69-5820	Lockheed MC-130P (L-382-20B) Hercules	4367	16SOW	
69-5821	Lockheed MC-130P (L-382-20B) Hercules	4368	58SOW	
69-5822	Lockheed MC-130P (L-382-20B) Hercules	4370	16SOW	
69-5823	Lockheed MC-130P (L-382-20B) Hercules	4371	352SOG	
69-5824 / FL	Lockheed HC-130N (L-382-20B) Hercules	4372	939RW	
69-5825	Lockheed MC-130P (L-382-20B) Hercules	4374	16SOW	
69-5826	Lockheed MC-130P (L-382-20B) Hercules	4375	352SOG	
69-5827	Lockheed MC-130P (L-382-20B) Hercules	4376	919SOW	
69-5828	Lockheed MC-130P (L-382-20B) Hercules	4377	352SOG	
69-5829 / FL	Lockheed HC-130N (L-382-20B) Hercules	4378	939RW	
69-5830 / FL	Lockheed HC-130N (L-382-20B) Hercules	4379	939RW	
69-5831	Lockheed MC-130P (L-382-20B) Hercules	4380	352SOG	*'Night Owl on the Prowl'*
69-5832	Lockheed MC-130P (L-382-20B) Hercules	4381	352SOG	
69-5833 / FL	Lockheed HC-130N (L-382-20B) Hercules	4382	939RW	
69-6566 / RS	Lockheed C-130E (L-382C-15D) Hercules	4340	86AW	
69-6568	Lockheed AC-130H (L-382C-15D) Hercules	4342	16SOW	
69-6569	Lockheed AC-130H (L-382C-15D) Hercules	4343	16SOW	
69-6570	Lockheed AC-130H (L-382C-15D) Hercules	4344	16SOW	
69-6572	Lockheed AC-130H (L-382C-15D) Hercules	4346	16SOW	
69-6573	Lockheed AC-130H (L-382C-15D) Hercules	4347	16SOW	
69-6574	Lockheed AC-130H (L-382C-15D) Hercules	4348	16SOW	
69-6575	Lockheed AC-130H (L-382C-15D) Hercules	4349	16SOW	
69-6577	Lockheed AC-130H (L-382C-15D) Hercules	4352	16SOW	
69-6580	Lockheed C-130E (L-382C-15D) Hercules	4356	43AW	
69-6582	Lockheed C-130E (L-382C-15D) Hercules	4359	86AW	
69-6583	Lockheed C-130E (L-382C-15D) Hercules	4360	86AW	
69-7606	Cessna O-2A Super Skymaster	M337-0404		Std AMARC [HV252]
69-7607	Cessna O-2A Super Skymaster	M337-0405		Std AMARC [HV244]
69-7611	Cessna O-2A Super Skymaster	M337-0409		Std AMARC [HV232]
69-7624	Cessna O-2A Super Skymaster	M337-0422		Std AMARC [HV234]
69-7626	Cessna O-2A Super Skymaster	M337-0424		Std AMARC [HV239]
69-7631	Cessna O-2A Super Skymaster	M337-0429		Std AMARC [HV175]
69-7636	Cessna O-2A Super Skymaster	M337-0434		Std AMARC [HV257]
69-7637	Cessna O-2A Super Skymaster	M337-0435		Std AMARC [HV182]
69-7643	Cessna O-2A Super Skymaster	M337-0441		Std AMARC [HV235]
69-7649	Cessna O-2A Super Skymaster	M337-0447		Std AMARC [HV236]
69-7665	Cessna O-2A Super Skymaster	M337-0463		Std AMARC [HV233]
70-0445	Lockheed C-5A Galaxy	500-0059	433AW	
70-0446	Lockheed C-5A Galaxy	500-0060	433AW	
70-0447	Lockheed C-5A Galaxy	500-0061	436AW	
70-0448	Lockheed C-5A Galaxy	500-0062	439AW	
70-0449	Lockheed C-5A Galaxy	500-0063	97AMW	
70-0450	Lockheed C-5A Galaxy	500-0064	60AMW	
70-0451	Lockheed C-5A Galaxy	500-0065	97AMW	
70-0452	Lockheed C-5A Galaxy	500-0066	97AMW	
70-0453	Lockheed C-5A Galaxy	500-0067	436AW	
70-0454	Lockheed C-5A Galaxy	500-0068	97AMW	
70-0455	Lockheed C-5A Galaxy	500-0069	97AMW	
70-0456	Lockheed C-5A Galaxy	500-0070	60AMW	
70-0457	Lockheed C-5A Galaxy	500-0071	60AMW	
70-0458	Lockheed C-5A Galaxy	500-0072	433AW	
70-0459	Lockheed C-5A Galaxy	500-0073	60thAMW	
70-0460	Lockheed C-5A Galaxy	500-0074	105AW/NY ANG	
70-0461	Lockheed C-5A Galaxy	500-0075	436AW	
70-0462	Lockheed C-5A Galaxy	500-0076	97AMW	
70-0463	Lockheed C-5A Galaxy	500-0077	436AW	
70-0464	Lockheed C-5A Galaxy	500-0078	60AMW	
70-0465	Lockheed C-5A Galaxy	500-0079	436AW	
70-0466	Lockheed C-5A Galaxy	500-0080	97AMW	
70-0467	Lockheed C-5A Galaxy	500-0081	436AW	
70-1259	Lockheed C-130E (L-382C-15D) Hercules	4404	43AW	
70-1260	Lockheed C-130E (L-382C-15D) Hercules	4410	86AW	
70-1261	Lockheed C-130E (L-382C-15D) Hercules	4413	43AW	
70-1262	Lockheed C-130E (L-382C-15D) Hercules	4414	43AW	
70-1263	Lockheed C-130E (L-382C-15D) Hercules	4415	43AW	
70-1264 / RS	Lockheed C-130E (L-382C-15D) Hercules	4417	86AW	
70-1265	Lockheed C-130E (L-382C-15D) Hercules	4418	43AW	
70-1266	Lockheed C-130E (L-382C-15D) Hercules	4419	43AW	
70-1267	Lockheed C-130E (L-382C-15D) Hercules	4420	43AW	

Serial	Type	C/n	Unit	Name
70-1268	Lockheed C-130E (L-382C-15D) Hercules	4421	43AW	
70-1270	Lockheed C-130E (L-382C-15D) Hercules	4424	43AW	
70-1271 / RS	Lockheed C-130E (L-382C-15D) Hercules	4425	86AW	
70-1272	Lockheed C-130E (L-382C-15D) Hercules	4426	43AW	
70-1273	Lockheed C-130E (L-382C-15D) Hercules	4428	43AW	
70-1274 / RS	Lockheed C-130E (L-382C-15D) Hercules	4429	86AW	
70-1275	Lockheed C-130E (L-382C-15D) Hercules	4434	43AW	
70-1276	Lockheed C-130E (L-382C-15D) Hercules	4435	43AW	
71-0874	McDonnell Douglas C-9A Nightingale (DC-9-32F) 47467 / 647		374AW	
71-0875	McDonnell Douglas C-9A Nightingale (DC-9-32F) 47471 / 650		374AW	
71-0876	McDonnell Douglas C-9A Nightingale (DC-9-32F) 47475 / 653		86AW	
71-0877	McDonnell Douglas C-9A Nightingale (DC-9-32F) 47495 / 656		374AW	
71-0878	McDonnell Douglas C-9A Nightingale (DC-9-32F) 47536 / 659		375AW	
71-0879	McDonnell Douglas C-9A Nightingale (DC-9-32F) 47537 / 662		86AW	
71-0880	McDonnell Douglas C-9A Nightingale (DC-9-32F) 47538 / 665		86AW	
71-0881	McDonnell Douglas C-9A Nightingale (DC-9-32F) 47540 / 668		86AW	
71-0882	McDonnell Douglas C-9A Nightingale (DC-9-32F) 47541 / 670		86AW	
71-1403 / RA	Boeing T-43A (737-200)	20685 / 317	12FTW	
71-1404 / RA	Boeing T-43A (737-200)	20686 / 326	12FTW	
71-1405 / RA	Boeing T-43A (737-200)	20687 / 329	12FTW	
71-1406 / RA	Boeing T-43A (737-200)	20688 / 330	12FTW	
71-1407 / OK	Boeing E-3B Sentry (707)	20518 / 898	552ACW	
71-1408 / OK	Boeing E-3B Sentry (707)	20519 / 920	552ACW	
72-0283	Boeing CT-43A (737-200)	20690 / 336	6ARW	
72-0288 / RA	Boeing T-43A (737-200)	20695 / 345	12FTW	
72-1288 / YJ	Lockheed C-130E (L-382C-15D) Hercules	4499	374AW	
72-1289 / YJ	Lockheed C-130E (L-382C-15D) Hercules	4500	374AW	
72-1290 / YJ	Lockheed C-130E (L-382C-15D) Hercules	4502	374AW	
72-1291 / LK	Lockheed C-130E (L-382C-15D) Hercules	4504	314AW	
72-1292 / LK	Lockheed C-130E (L-382C-15D) Hercules	4505	463AG	
72-1293 / LK	Lockheed C-130E (L-382C-15D) Hercules	4506	463AG	
72-1294 / LK	Lockheed C-130E (L-382C-15D) Hercules	4509	463AG	
72-1295	Lockheed C-130E (L-382C-15D) Hercules	4510	314AW	
72-1296	Lockheed C-130E (L-382C-15D) Hercules	4517	314AW	
72-1299 / YJ	Lockheed C-130E (L-382C-15D) Hercules	4527	374AW	
73-1150 / RA	Boeing T-43A (737-200)	20697 / 349	12FTW	
73-1151 / RA	Boeing T-43A (737-200)	20698 / 350	12FTW	
73-1152 / RA	Boeing T-43A (737-200)	20699 / 355	12FTW	
73-1153 / RA	Boeing T-43A (737-200)	20700 / 357	12FTW	'Spirit of San Antonio'
73-1154 / RA	Boeing T-43A (737-200)	20701 / 359	12FTW	
73-1155	Boeing T-43A (737-200)	20702 / 362		Ogden ALC
73-1156 / RA	Boeing T-43A (737-200)	20703 / 363	12FTW	
73-1206	Beech C-12C (Super King Air 200)	BD-2		US Embassy - Kinshasa
73-1208	Beech C-12C (Super King Air 200)	BD-4	81TRW	
73-1210	Beech C-12C (Super King Air 200)	BD-6	81TRW	
73-1214	Beech C-12C (Super King Air 200)	BD-10		US Embassy - Bangkok
73-1215 / ED	Beech C-12C (Super King Air 200)	BD-11	412TW	
73-1216	Beech C-12C (Super King Air 200)	BD-12		US Embassy - Ankara
73-1217	Beech C-12C (Super King Air 200)	BD-13		US Embassy - Manila
73-1218	Beech C-12C (Super King Air 200)	BD-14		US Embassy - Athens
73-1580 / DM	Lockheed EC-130H (L-382C-33D) Hercules	4542	355Wg	
73-1581 / DM	Lockheed EC-130H (L-382C-33D) Hercules	4543	355Wg	
73-1582	Lockheed C-130H (L-382C-33D) Hercules	4544	317AG	
73-1583 / DM	Lockheed EC-130H (L-382C-33D) Hercules	4545	355Wg	
73-1584 / DM	Lockheed EC-130H (L-382C-33D) Hercules	4546	355Wg	
73-1585 / DM	Lockheed EC-130H (L-382C-33D) Hercules	4547	355Wg	
73-1586 / DM	Lockheed EC-130H (L-382C-33D) Hercules	4548	355Wg	
73-1587 / DM	Lockheed EC-130H (L-382C-33D) Hercules	4549	355Wg	
73-1588 / DM	Lockheed EC-130H (L-382C-33D) Hercules	4550	355Wg	
73-1590 / DM	Lockheed EC-130H (L-382C-33D) Hercules	4554	355Wg	
73-1592 / DM	Lockheed EC-130H (L-382C-33D) Hercules	4557	355Wg	
73-1594 / DM	Lockheed EC-130H (L-382C-33D) Hercules	4563	355Wg	
73-1595 / DM	Lockheed EC-130H (L-382C-33D) Hercules	4564	355Wg	
73-1597	Lockheed C-130H (L-382C-33D) Hercules	4571	317AG	
73-1598 / YJ	Lockheed C-130H (L-382C-33D) Hercules	4573	374AW	

73-1674	Boeing E-3C Sentry (707)	21046 / 901			
73-1675 / OK	Boeing E-3B Sentry (707)	21185 / 904		552ACW	
73-1676	Boeing E-4B (747-200B)	20682 / 202		55Wg	Command Post
73-1677	Boeing E-4B (747-200B)	20683 / 204		55Wg	Command Post
73-1681	McDonnell Douglas VC-9C (DC-9-32)	47668 / 765		89AW	
73-1682	McDonnell Douglas VC-9C (DC-9-32)	47670 / 769		89AW	
73-1683	McDonnell Douglas VC-9C (DC-9-32)	47671 / 774		89AW	
73-3300	Lockheed LC-130H (L-382C-26D) Hercules	4508	Bu159129 (USN)	109AW	Cvtd LC-130R
74-0787	Boeing E-4B (747-200B)	20684 / 232		55Wg	Command Post
74-1658 / AK	Lockheed C-130H (L-382C-41D) Hercules	4579		3rdWg	
74-1659 / AK	Lockheed C-130H (L-382C-41D) Hercules	4585		3rdWg	
74-1660 / AK	Lockheed C-130H (L-382C-41D) Hercules	4592		3Wg	
74-1661 / AK	Lockheed C-130H (L-382C-41D) Hercules	4596		3Wg	
74-1663 / DY	Lockheed C-130H (L-382C-41D) Hercules	4598		317AG	
74-1664 / AK	Lockheed C-130H (L-382C-41D) Hercules	4603		3Wg	
74-1665	Lockheed C-130H (L-382C-41D) Hercules	4604		317AG	
74-1666	Lockheed C-130H (L-382C-41D) Hercules	4611		317AG	
74-1667	Lockheed C-130H (L-382C-41D) Hercules	4613		317AG	
74-1668 / AK	Lockheed C-130H (L-382C-41D) Hercules	4616		3Wg	
74-1669	Lockheed C-130H (L-382C-41D) Hercules	4617		317AG	
74-1670	Lockheed C-130H (L-382C-41D) Hercules	4620		317AG	
74-1671	Lockheed C-130H (L-382C-41D) Hercules	4621		317AG	
74-1673	Lockheed C-130H (L-382C-41D) Hercules	4627		317AG	
74-1674	Lockheed C-130H (L-382C-41D) Hercules	4631		317AG	
74-1675	Lockheed C-130H (L-382C-41D) Hercules	4640		317AG	
74-1676 / AK	Lockheed C-130H (L-382C-41D) Hercules	4641		3Wg	
74-1677	Lockheed C-130H (L-382C-41D) Hercules	4643		317AG	
74-1679 / DY	Lockheed C-130H (L-382C-41D) Hercules	4646		317AG	
74-1680	Lockheed C-130H (L-382C-41D) Hercules	4651		317AG	
74-1682 / AK	Lockheed C-130H (L-382C-41D) Hercules	4657		3Wg	
74-1684 / AK	Lockheed C-130H (L-382C-41D) Hercules	4663		3Wg	
74-1685 / AK	Lockheed C-130H (L-382C-41D) Hercules	4666		3Wg	
74-1687	Lockheed C-130H (L-382C-41D) Hercules	4670		317AG	
74-1688	Lockheed C-130H (L-382C-41D) Hercules	4675		317AG	
74-1689	Lockheed C-130H (L-382C-41D) Hercules	4681		317AG	
74-1690 / AK	Lockheed C-130H (L-382C-41D) Hercules	4682		3Wg	
74-1691	Lockheed C-130H (L-382C-41D) Hercules	4687		317AG	
74-1692 / AK	Lockheed C-130H (L-382C-41D) Hercules	4688		3Wg	
74-2061	Lockheed C-130H (L-382C-41D) Hercules	4644		317AG	
74-2062 / AK	Lockheed C-130H (L-382C-41D) Hercules	4647		3Wg	
74-2063	Lockheed C-130H (L-382C-41D) Hercules	4655		317AG	
74-2065	Lockheed C-130H (L-382C-41D) Hercules	4667		317AG	
74-2066 / AK	Lockheed C-130H (L-382C-41D) Hercules	4671		3Wg	
74-2067	Lockheed C-130H (L-382C-41D) Hercules	4678		317AG	
74-2069	Lockheed C-130H (L-382C-41D) Hercules	4699		317AG	
74-2070 / AK	Lockheed C-130H (L-382C-41D) Hercules	4700		3Wg	
74-2071 / AK	Lockheed C-130H (L-382C-41D) Hercules	4703		3Wg	
74-2072	Lockheed C-130H (L-382C-41D) Hercules	4705		317AG	
74-2130	Lockheed C-130H (L-382C-41D) Hercules	4711		317AG	
74-2131 / AK	Lockheed C-130H (L-382C-41D) Hercules	4718		3Wg	
74-2132 / DY	Lockheed C-130H (L-382C-41D) Hercules	4722		317AG	
74-2133 / AK	Lockheed C-130H (L-382C-41D) Hercules	4730		3Wg	
74-2134	Lockheed C-130H (L-382C-41D) Hercules	4735		317AG	
75-0125	Boeing E-4B (747-200B)	20949 / 257		55Wg	Command Post
75-0556 / ZZ	Boeing E-3B Sentry (707)	21047 / 902		18Wg	
75-0557 / AK	Boeing E-3B Sentry (707)	21207 / 907		3Wg	
75-0558 / OK	Boeing E-3B Sentry (707)	21208 / 908		552ACW	
75-0559 / OK	Boeing E-3B Sentry (707)	21209 / 913		552ACW	
75-0560 / OK	Boeing E-3B Sentry (707)	21250 / 916		552ACW	
76-0158	Beech C-12C (Super King Air 200)	BD-15			US Embassy - Jakarta
76-0160	Beech C-12C (Super King Air 200)	BD-17			US Embassy - Riyadh
76-0161 / ED	Beech C-12C (Super King Air 200)	BD-18		418FLTS	
76-0163	Beech C-12C (Super King Air 200)	BD-20			US Embassy - Canberra
76-0164	Beech C-12C (Super King Air 200)	BD-21			USMTM, Dhahran
76-0165	Beech C-12C (Super King Air 200)	BD-22			US Embassy - Tegucigalpa
76-0166	Beech C-12C (Super King Air 200)	BD-23			US Embassy - Islamabad
76-0168	Beech C-12C (Super King Air 200)	BD-25			US Embassy - Abidjan
76-0170	Beech C-12C (Super King Air 200)	BD-27			Std AMARC [CE004]
76-0171	Beech C-12C (Super King Air 200)	BD-28			US Embassy - Rabat
76-0172	Beech C-12C (Super King Air 200)	BD-29			US Embassy - Manila
76-0173	Beech C-12C (Super King Air 200)	BD-30			US Embassy - Ankara
76-1604 / OK	Boeing E-3B Sentry (707)	21434 / 921		552ACW	
76-1605 / ZZ	Boeing E-3B Sentry (707)	21435 / 924		18Wg	
76-1606 / OK	Boeing E-3B Sentry (707)	21436 / 926		552ACW	

76-1607 / OK	Boeing E-3B Sentry (707)	21437 / 927		552ACW
76-3239	Beech C-12C (Super King Air 200)	BD-24	76-0167	US Embassy - Jakarta
76-3301	Lockheed LC-130R (L-382C-65D) Hercules	4725	Bu160740 (USN)	109AW/NY ANG
76-3302	Lockheed LC-130R (L-382C-65D) Hercules	4731	Bu160741 (USN)	Std AMARC [CF179]
77-0351 / OK	Boeing E-3B Sentry (707)	21551 / 930		552ACW
77-0352 / OK	Boeing E-3B Sentry (707)	21552 / 931		552ACW
77-0353 / OK	Boeing E-3B Sentry (707)	21553 / 932		552ACW
77-0355 / OK	Boeing E-3B Sentry (707)	21555 / 934		552ACW
77-0356 / OK	Boeing E-3B Sentry (707)	21556 / 935		552ACW
77-0464	DeHavilland Canada UV-18B Twin Otter (DHC-6)	554		94ATS Also wears N70464
77-0465	DeHavilland Canada UV-18B Twin Otter (DHC-6)	555		94ATS Also wears N70465
78-0576 / ZZ	Boeing E-3B Sentry (707)	21752 / 937		18Wg
78-0577 / OK	Boeing E-3B Sentry (707)	21753 / 939		552ACW
78-0578 / OK	Boeing E-3B Sentry (707)	21754 / 940		552ACW
78-0806	Lockheed C-130H (L-382C-80D) Hercules	4815		137AW/OK ANG
78-0807 / OK	Lockheed C-130H (L-382C-80D) Hercules	4817		137AW/OK ANG
78-0808 / OK	Lockheed C-130H (L-382C-80D) Hercules	4818		137AW/OK ANG
78-0809	Lockheed C-130H (L-382C-80D) Hercules	4819		137AW/OK ANG
78-0810	Lockheed C-130H (L-382C-80D) Hercules	4820		137AW/OK ANG
78-0811 / OK	Lockheed C-130H (L-382C-80D) Hercules	4821		137AW/OK ANG
78-0812 / OK	Lockheed C-130H (L-382C-80D) Hercules	4822		137AW/OK ANG
78-0813 / OK	Lockheed C-130H (L-382C-80D) Hercules	4823		137AW/OK ANG
79-0001 / ZZ	Boeing E-3B Sentry (707)	21755 / 942		18Wg
79-0002 / OK	Boeing E-3C Sentry (707)	21756 / 943		552ACW
79-0003 / OK	Boeing E-3C Sentry (707)	21757 / 944		552ACW
79-0433	McDonnell Douglas KC-10A Extender (DC-10-30)	48200 / 311	N110KC	305AMW
79-0434	McDonnell Douglas KC-10A Extender (DC-10-30)	48201 / 333	N434KC	305AMW
79-0473	Lockheed C-130H (L-382C-88D) Hercules	4852		152AW/NV ANG
79-0474	Lockheed C-130H (L-382C-88D) Hercules	4854		137AW/OK ANG
79-0475	Lockheed C-130H (L-382C-88D) Hercules	4855		152AW/NV ANG
79-0476 / SC	Lockheed C-130H (L-382C-88D) Hercules	4856		169FW/SC ANG
79-0477	Lockheed C-130H (L-382C-88D) Hercules	4857		152AW/NV ANG
79-0478	Lockheed C-130H (L-382C-88D) Hercules	4858		152AW/NV ANG
79-0479	Lockheed C-130H (L-382C-88D) Hercules	4859		152AW/NV ANG
79-0480	Lockheed C-130H (L-382C-88D) Hercules	4860		152AW/NV ANG
79-1710	McDonnell Douglas KC-10A Extender (DC-10-30)	48202 / 359		305AMW
79-1711	McDonnell Douglas KC-10A Extender (DC-10-30)	48203 / 360		305AMW
79-1712	McDonnell Douglas KC-10A Extender (DC-10-30)	48204 / 361		305AMW
79-1713	McDonnell Douglas KC-10A Extender (DC-10-30)	48205 / 363		305AMW
79-1946	McDonnell Douglas KC-10A Extender (DC-10-30)	48206 / 373		60AMW
79-1947	McDonnell Douglas KC-10A Extender (DC-10-30)	48207 / 375		305AMW
79-1948	McDonnell Douglas KC-10A Extender (DC-10-30)	48208 / 376		60AMW
79-1949	McDonnell Douglas KC-10A Extender (DC-10-30)	48209 / 377		305AMW
79-1950	McDonnell Douglas KC-10A Extender (DC-10-30)	48210 / 378		60AMW
79-1951	McDonnell Douglas KC-10A Extender (DC-10-30)	48211 / 380		60AMW
80-0137 / OK	Boeing E-3C Sentry (707)	22829 / 946		552ACW
80-0138 / OK	Boeing E-3C Sentry (707)	22830 / 948		552ACW
80-0139 / OK	Boeing E-3C Sentry (707)	22831 / 950		552ACW
80-0320	Lockheed C-130H (L-382C-5E) Hercules	4900		165AW/GA ANG
80-0321	Lockheed C-130H (L-382C-5E) Hercules	4902		165AW/GA ANG
80-0322	Lockheed C-130H (L-382C-5E) Hercules	4903		165AW/GA ANG
80-0323	Lockheed C-130H (L-382C-5E) Hercules	4905		165AW/GA ANG
80-0324	Lockheed C-130H (L-382C-5E) Hercules	4906		165AW/GA ANG
80-0325	Lockheed C-130H (L-382C-5E) Hercules	4908		165AW/GA ANG
80-0326	Lockheed C-130H (L-382C-5E) Hercules	4910		165AW/GA ANG
80-0332	Lockheed C-130H (L-382C-18E) Hercules	4943		165AW/GA ANG
81-0004 / OK	Boeing E-3C Sentry (707)	22832 / 951		552ACW
81-0005 / ZZ	Boeing E-3C Sentry (707)	22833 / 952		18Wg
81-0626	Lockheed C-130H (L-382C-18E) Hercules	4939		94AW
81-0627	Lockheed C-130H (L-382C-18E) Hercules	4941		94AW
81-0628	Lockheed C-130H (L-382C-18E) Hercules	4942		94AW
81-0629	Lockheed C-130H (L-382C-18E) Hercules	4944		94AW

81-0630 / DB	Lockheed C-130H (L-382C-18E) Hercules	4945		94AW	
81-0631	Lockheed C-130H (L-382C-18E) Hercules	4946		94AW	
81-0891	Boeing EC-18B (707-323C)	19518 / 616	N7598A	412TW	
81-0892	Boeing EC-18B (707-323C)	19382 / 627	N7567A	412TW	
81-0893 / OK	Boeing EC-18D (707-323C)	19384 / 647	N7569A	552ACW	
81-0894	Boeing EC-18D (707-323C)	19583 / 650	N8403	412TW	
81-0895	Boeing EC-18D (707-323C)	19381 / 610	N7566A	412TW	
81-0896	Boeing EC-18D (707-323C)	19581 / 638	N8401	412TW	
81-0898	Boeing C-18A (707-323C)	19380 / 525	N7565A	412TW	
82-0006 / OK	Boeing E-3C Sentry (707)	22834 / 958		552ACW	
82-0007 / OK	Boeing E-3C Sentry (707)	22835 / 960		552ACW	
82-0054 / AK	Lockheed C-130H (L-382C-35E) Hercules	4968		176Wg/AK ANG	
82-0055	Lockheed C-130H (L-382C-35E) Hercules	4970		176Wg/AK ANG	
82-0056	Lockheed C-130H (L-382C-35E) Hercules	4971		176Wg/AK ANG	
82-0057 / AK	Lockheed C-130H (L-382C-35E) Hercules	4973		176Wg/AK ANG	
82-0058 / AK	Lockheed C-130H (L-382C-35E) Hercules	4975		176Wg/AK ANG	
82-0059	Lockheed C-130H (L-382C-35E) Hercules	4977		176Wg/AK ANG	
82-0060	Lockheed C-130H (L-382C-35E) Hercules	4979		176Wg/AK ANG	
82-0061	Lockheed C-130H (L-382C-35E) Hercules	4982		176Wg/AK ANG	
82-0191	McDonnell Douglas KC-10A Extender (DC-10-30)	48213 / 383		60AMW	
82-0192	McDonnell Douglas KC-10A Extender (DC-10-30)	48214 / 384		60AMW	
82-0193	McDonnell Douglas KC-10A Extender (DC-10-30)	48215 / 385		60AMW	
82-8000	Boeing VC-25A (747-2G4B)	23824 / 679	N6005C	89AW	Presidential Aircraft
83-0008 / OK	Boeing E-3C Sentry (707)	22836 / 962		552ACW	
83-0009 / OK	Boeing E-3C Sentry (707)	22837 / 965		552ACW	
83-0075	McDonnell Douglas KC-10A Extender (DC-10-30)	48216 / 386		60AMW	
83-0076	McDonnell Douglas KC-10A Extender (DC-10-30)	48217 / 387		60AMW	
83-0077	McDonnell Douglas KC-10A Extender (DC-10-30)	48218 / 388		60AMW	
83-0078	McDonnell Douglas KC-10A Extender (DC-10-30)	48219 / 389		60AMW	
83-0079	McDonnell Douglas KC-10A Extender (DC-10-30)	48220 / 390		305AMW	
83-0080	McDonnell Douglas KC-10A Extender (DC-10-30)	48221 / 391		60AMW	
83-0081	McDonnell Douglas KC-10A Extender (DC-10-30)	48222 / 392		305AMW	
83-0082	McDonnell Douglas KC-10A Extender (DC-10-30)	48223 / 393		305AMW	
83-0486	Lockheed C-130H (L-382C-46E) Hercules	5008		109AW/NY ANG	
83-0487	Lockheed C-130H (L-382C-46E) Hercules	5012		109AW/NY ANG	
83-0488	Lockheed C-130H (L-382C-46E) Hercules	5014		109AW/NY ANG	
83-0489	Lockheed C-130H (L-382C-46E) Hercules	5018		109AW/NY ANG	
83-0490	Lockheed LC-130H (L-382C-47E) Hercules	5007		109AW/NY ANG	
83-0491	Lockheed LC-130H (L-382C-47E) Hercules	5010		109AW/NY ANG	
83-0492	Lockheed LC-130H (L-382C-47E) Hercules	5013		109AW/NY ANG	
83-0493	Lockheed LC-130H (L-382C-47E) Hercules	5016		109AW/NY ANG	
83-0494	Beech C-12D Huron (Super King Air 200)	BP-40			US Embassy-Abidjan
83-0495	Beech C-12D Huron (Super King Air 200)	BP-41			US Embassy-Budapest
83-0496	Beech C-12D Huron (Super King Air 200)	BP-42		89AW	
83-0497	Beech C-12D Huron (Super King Air 200)	BP-43			US Embassy-Buenos Aires
83-0498	Beech C-12D Huron (Super King Air 200)	BP-44		89AW	
83-0499	Beech C-12D Huron (Super King Air 200)	BP-45			US Embassy-La Paz
83-0500	GAC C-20A (G-1159A Gulfstream III)	382	N305GA	89AW	
83-0501	GAC C-20A (G-1159A Gulfstream III)	383	N308GA	89AW	
83-0502	GAC C-20A (G-1159A Gulfstream III)	389	N310GA	89AW	
83-1212	Lockheed MC-130H (L-382C-49E) Hercules	5004		16SOW	
83-1285	Lockheed C-5B Galaxy	500-0082		436AW	
83-4610	Boeing C-22B (727-35)	18811 / 85	N4610	113Wg	
83-4615	Boeing C-22B (727-35)	18816 / 112	N4615	113Wg	
83-4616	Boeing C-22B (727-35)	18817 / 118	N4616	113Wg	
83-4618	Boeing C-22C (727-212 Advanced)	21946 / 1504	N48054		Std AMARC [CU003]
84-0047 / WE	DeHavilland Canada E-9A (Dash 8)	37	N801AP	475WEG	
84-0048 / WE	DeHavilland Canada E-9A (Dash 8)	45	N802AP	475WEG	
84-0059	Lockheed C-5B Galaxy	500-0083		436AW	
84-0060	Lockheed C-5B Galaxy	500-0084		60AMW	
84-0061	Lockheed C-5B Galaxy	500-0085		436AW	
84-0062	Lockheed C-5B Galaxy	500-0086		60AMW	
84-0064	Gates C-21A Learjet	35A-510	N7263D	375AW	

84-0065	Gates C-21A Learjet	35A-511	N7263E	375AW
84-0066	Gates C-21A Learjet	35A-512	N7263F	375AW
84-0068	Gates C-21A Learjet	35A-514	N7263K	HQ USEUCOM
84-0069 / KS	Gates C-21A Learjet	35A-515	N7263L	81TRW
84-0070 / KS	Gates C-21A Learjet	35A-516	N7263N	81TRW
84-0071 / KS	Gates C-21A Learjet	35A-517	N7263R	81TRW
84-0072 / KS	Gates C-21A Learjet	35A-518	N7263X	81TRW
84-0073	Gates C-21A Learjet	35A-519	N400AD	375AW
84-0074	Gates C-21A Learjet	35A-520	N400AK	375AW
84-0075	Gates C-21A Learjet	35A-521	N400AN	375AW
84-0076	Gates C-21A Learjet	35A-522	N400AP	375AW
84-0077	Gates C-21A Learjet	35A-523	N400AQ	375AW
84-0078	Gates C-21A Learjet	35A-524	N400AS	375AW
84-0079	Gates C-21A Learjet	35A-525	N400AT	375AW
84-0080	Gates C-21A Learjet	35A-526	N400AU	375AW
84-0081	Gates C-21A Learjet	35A-527	N400AX	HQ USEUCOM
84-0082	Gates C-21A Learjet	35A-528	N400AY	HQ USEUCOM
84-0083	Gates C-21A Learjet	35A-529	N400AZ	HQ USEUCOM
84-0084	Gates C-21A Learjet	35A-530	N400BA	86AW
84-0085	Gates C-21A Learjet	35A-531	N400FY	86AW
84-0086	Gates C-21A Learjet	35A-532	N400BN	86AW
84-0087 / OF	Gates C-21A Learjet	35A-533	N400BQ	86AW
84-0088 / OF	Gates C-21A Learjet	35A-534	N400BU	375AW
84-0090 / OF	Gates C-21A Learjet	35A-536	N400BZ	375AW
84-0091 / OF	Gates C-21A Learjet	35A-537	N400CD	375AW
84-0092 / OF	Gates C-21A Learjet	35A-538	N400CG	375AW
84-0093 / OF	Gates C-21A Learjet	35A-539	N400CJ	375AW
84-0094 / OF	Gates C-21A Learjet	35A-540	N400CK	375AW
84-0095 / OF	Gates C-21A Learjet	35A-541	N400CQ	375AW
84-0096	Gates C-21A Learjet	35A-542	N400CR	375AW
84-0097	Gates C-21A Learjet	35A-543	N400CU	375AW
84-0098	Gates C-21A Learjet	35A-544	N400CV	375AW
84-0099	Gates C-21A Learjet	35A-545	N400CX	375AW
84-0100	Gates C-21A Learjet	35A-546	N400CY	375AW
84-0101	Gates C-21A Learjet	35A-547	N400CZ	374AW
84-0102	Gates C-21A Learjet	35A-548	N400DD	374AW
84-0103 / CS	Gates C-21A Learjet	35A-549	N400DJ	375AW
84-0104 / CS	Gates C-21A Learjet	35A-550	N400DL	375AW
84-0105 / CS	Gates C-21A Learjet	35A-551	N400DN	375AW
84-0106 / CS	Gates C-21A Learjet	35A-552	N400DQ	81TRW
84-0107 / CS	Gates C-21A Learjet	35A-553	N400DR	375AW
84-0108	Gates C-21A Learjet	35A-554	N400DU	86AW
84-0109	Gates C-21A Learjet	35A-555	N400DV	86AW
84-0110	Gates C-21A Learjet	35A-556	N400DX	86AW
84-0111	Gates C-21A Learjet	35A-557	N400DY	86AW
84-0112	Gates C-21A Learjet	35A-558	N400DZ	86AW
84-0113 / FF	Gates C-21A Learjet	35A-559	N400EC	375AW
84-0114 / FF	Gates C-21A Learjet	35A-560	N400EE	375AW
84-0115 / FF	Gates C-21A Learjet	35A-561	N400EF	375AW
84-0116 / FF	Gates C-21A Learjet	35A-562	N400EG	375AW
84-0117 / FF	Gates C-21A Learjet	35A-563	N400EJ	375AW
84-0118	Gates C-21A Learjet	35A-564	N400EK	375AW
84-0119	Gates C-21A Learjet	35A-565	N400EL	375AW
84-0120	Gates C-21A Learjet	35A-566	N400EM	375AW
84-0122 / AU	Gates C-21A Learjet	35A-568	N400EQ	375AW
84-0123 / AU	Gates C-21A Learjet	35A-569	N400ER	375AW
84-0124 / AU	Gates C-21A Learjet	35A-570	N400ES	375AW
84-0125 / AU	Gates C-21A Learjet	35A-571	N400ET	375AW
84-0126 / RA	Gates C-21A Learjet	35A-572	N400EU	375AW
84-0127	Gates C-21A Learjet	35A-573	N400EV	375AW
84-0128 / RA	Gates C-21A Learjet	35A-575	N400EY	375AW
84-0129	Gates C-21A Learjet	35A-576	N400EZ	375AW
84-0130	Gates C-21A Learjet	35A-577	N400FE	375AW
84-0131	Gates C-21A Learjet	35A-578	N400FG	375AW
84-0132	Gates C-21A Learjet	35A-579	N400FH	375AW
84-0133	Gates C-21A Learjet	35A-580	N400FK	375AW
84-0134 / RA	Gates C-21A Learjet	35A-581	N400FM	375AW
84-0135 / RA	Gates C-21A Learjet	35A-582	N400FN	375AW
84-0137 / CS	Gates C-21A Learjet	35A-585	N400FR	375AW
84-0138 / RA	Gates C-21A Learjet	35A-574	N400EX	375AW
84-0139	Gates C-21A Learjet	35A-587	N400FU	332AF
84-0140	Gates C-21A Learjet	35A-588	N400FV	375AW
84-0141 / RA	Gates C-21A Learjet	35A-584	N400FQ	375AW
84-0142	Gates C-21A Learjet	35A-586	N400FT	375AW

84-0147 / AK	Beech C-12F Huron (Super King Air 200)	BL-77		3Wg
84-0148 / AK	Beech C-12F Huron (Super King Air 200)	BL-78		3Wg
84-0185	McDonnell Douglas KC-10A Extender (DC-10-30)			
		48224 / 394		60AMW
84-0186	McDonnell Douglas KC-10A Extender (DC-10-30)			
		48225 / 395		305AMW
84-0187	McDonnell Douglas KC-10A Extender (DC-10-30)			
		48226 / 396		60AMW
84-0188	McDonnell Douglas KC-10A Extender (DC-10-30)			
		48227 / 397		305AMW
84-0189	McDonnell Douglas KC-10A Extender (DC-10-30)			
		48228 / 398		60AMW
84-0190	McDonnell Douglas KC-10A Extender (DC-10-30)			
		48229 / 399		305AMW
84-0191	McDonnell Douglas KC-10A Extender (DC-10-30)			
		48230 / 400		60AMW
84-0192	McDonnell Douglas KC-10A Extender (DC-10-30)			
		48231 / 401		305AMW
84-0193	Boeing C-22A (727-30)	18362 / 33	N78	Std AMARC [CU002]
84-0204	Lockheed C-130H (L-382C-60E) Hercules	5038		94AW
84-0205	Lockheed C-130H (L-382C-60E) Hercules	5039		94AW
84-0206 / DE	Lockheed C-130H (L-382C-60E) Hercules	5043		166AW/DE ANG
84-0207 / DE	Lockheed C-130H (L-382C-60E) Hercules	5044		166AW/DE ANG
84-0208 / DE	Lockheed C-130H (L-382C-60E) Hercules	5046		166AW/DE ANG
84-0209 / DE	Lockheed C-130H (L-382C-60E) Hercules	5047		166AW/DE ANG
84-0210 / DE	Lockheed C-130H (L-382C-60E) Hercules	5049		166AW/DE ANG
84-0211 / DE	Lockheed C-130H (L-382C-60E) Hercules	5050		166AW/DE ANG
84-0212 / DE	Lockheed C-130H (L-382C-60E) Hercules	5051		166AW/DE ANG
84-0213 / DE	Lockheed C-130H (L-382C-60E) Hercules	5052		166AW/DE ANG
84-0458	Shorts C-23A Sherpa (330UTT)	SH.3103		Std AMARC [CD002]
84-0475	Lockheed MC-130H (L-382C-59E) Hercules	5041		16SOW
84-0476	Lockheed MC-130H (L-382C-59E) Hercules	5042		352SOG
84-1398 / OK	Boeing TC-18E (707-331C)	18713 / 378	N131EA	552ACW
84-1399 / OK	Boeing TC-18E (707-331C)	19566 / 717	N132EA	552ACW
85-0001	Lockheed C-5B Galaxy	500-0087		436AW
85-0002	Lockheed C-5B Galaxy	500-0088		60AMW
85-0003	Lockheed C-5B Galaxy	500-0089		436AW
85-0004	Lockheed C-5B Galaxy	500-0090		60AMW
85-0005	Lockheed C-5B Galaxy	500-0091		436AW
85-0006	Lockheed C-5B Galaxy	500-0092		60AMW
85-0007	Lockheed C-5B Galaxy	500-0093		436AW
85-0008	Lockheed C-5B Galaxy	500-0094		60AMW
85-0009	Lockheed C-5B Galaxy	500-0095		436AW
85-0010	Lockheed C-5B Galaxy	500-0096		60AMW
85-0011	Lockheed MC-130H (L-382C-59E) Hercules	5053		58SOW
85-0012	Lockheed MC-130H (L-382C-59E) Hercules	5054		16SOW
85-0027	McDonnell Douglas KC-10A Extender (DC-10-30)			
		48232 / 402		305AMW
85-0028	McDonnell Douglas KC-10A Extender (DC-10-30)			
		48233 / 403		305AMW
85-0029	McDonnell Douglas KC-10A Extender (DC-10-30)			
		48234 / 404		60AMW
85-0030	McDonnell Douglas KC-10A Extender (DC-10-30)			
		48235 / 405		305AMW
85-0031	McDonnell Douglas KC-10A Extender (DC-10-30)			
		48236 / 406		305AMW
85-0032	McDonnell Douglas KC-10A Extender (DC-10-30)			
		48237 / 407		305AMW
85-0033	McDonnell Douglas KC-10A Extender (DC-10-30)			
		48238 / 408		305AMW
85-0034	McDonnell Douglas KC-10A Extender (DC-10-30)			
		48239 / 410		305AMW
85-0035	Lockheed C-130H (L-382C-71E) Hercules	5073		908AW
85-0036	Lockheed C-130H (L-382C-71E) Hercules	5074		908AW
85-0037	Lockheed C-130H (L-382C-71E) Hercules	5077		908AW
85-0038	Lockheed C-130H (L-382C-71E) Hercules	5079		908AW
85-0039	Lockheed C-130H (L-382C-71E) Hercules	5080		908AW
85-0040	Lockheed C-130H (L-382C-71E) Hercules	5083		908AW
85-0041	Lockheed C-130H (L-382C-71E) Hercules	5086		908AW
85-0042	Lockheed C-130H (L-382C-71E) Hercules	5089		908AW
85-0049	GAC C-20C (G-1159A Gulfstream III)	456	N336GA	89AW
85-0050	GAC C-20C (G-1159A Gulfstream III)	458	N338GA	89AW
85-1361 / TX	Lockheed C-130H (L-382C-71E) Hercules	5071		136AW/TX ANG
85-1362 / TX	Lockheed C-130H (L-382C-71E) Hercules	5072		136AW/TX ANG

Serial	Type	C/N	Reg	Unit	Notes
85-1363 / TX	Lockheed C-130H (L-382C-71E) Hercules	5075		136AW/TX ANG	
85-1364 / TX	Lockheed C-130H (L-382C-71E) Hercules	5076		136AW/TX ANG	
85-1365 / TX	Lockheed C-130H (L-382C-71E) Hercules	5078		136AW/TX ANG	
85-1366 / TX	Lockheed C-130H (L-382C-71E) Hercules	5081		136AW/TX ANG	
85-1367 / TX	Lockheed C-130H (L-382C-71E) Hercules	5082		136AW/TX ANG	
85-1368	Lockheed C-130H (L-382C-71E) Hercules	5084		136AW/TX ANG	
85-1603	Piper PA-31T Cheyenne II	31T-7720051			
85-6039	Pilatus UV-20A Turbo Porter (PC-6B)			427SOS	
85-6973	Boeing VC-137C (707-396C)	20043 / 786	OE-IDA	89AW	
85-6974	Boeing C-137C (707-382B)	20297 / 836	N105BV		Std McConnell AFB
86-0011	Lockheed C-5B Galaxy	500-0097		436AW	
86-0012	Lockheed C-5B Galaxy	500-0098		60AMW	
86-0013	Lockheed C-5B Galaxy	500-0099		436AW	
86-0014	Lockheed C-5B Galaxy	500-0100		60AMW	
86-0015	Lockheed C-5B Galaxy	500-0101		436AW	
86-0016	Lockheed C-5B Galaxy	500-0102		60AMW	
86-0017	Lockheed C-5B Galaxy	500-0103		436AW	
86-0018	Lockheed C-5B Galaxy	500-0104		60AMW	
86-0019	Lockheed C-5B Galaxy	500-0105		436AW	
86-0020	Lockheed C-5B Galaxy	500-0106		436AW	
86-0021	Lockheed C-5B Galaxy	500-0107		60AMW	
86-0022	Lockheed C-5B Galaxy	500-0108		60AMW	
86-0023	Lockheed C-5B Galaxy	500-0109		436AW	
86-0024	Lockheed C-5B Galaxy	500-0110		60AMW	
86-0025	Lockheed C-5B Galaxy	500-0111		436AW	
86-0026	Lockheed C-5B Galaxy	500-0112		60AMW	
86-0027	McDonnell Douglas KC-10A Extender (DC-10-30)	48240 / 411		305AMW	
86-0028	McDonnell Douglas KC-10A Extender (DC-10-30)	48241 / 413		305AMW	
86-0029	McDonnell Douglas KC-10A Extender (DC-10-30)	48242 / 414		60AMW	
86-0030	McDonnell Douglas KC-10A Extender (DC-10-30)	48243 / 415		305AMW	
86-0031	McDonnell Douglas KC-10A Extender (DC-10-30)	48244 / 417		60AMW	
86-0032	McDonnell Douglas KC-10A Extender (DC-10-30)	48245 / 418		60AMW	
86-0033	McDonnell Douglas KC-10A Extender (DC-10-30)	48246 / 420		60AMW	
86-0034	McDonnell Douglas KC-10A Extender (DC-10-30)	48247 / 421		60AMW	
86-0035	McDonnell Douglas KC-10A Extender (DC-10-30)	48248 / 423		305AMW	
86-0036	McDonnell Douglas KC-10A Extender (DC-10-30)	48249 / 424		305AMW	
86-0037	McDonnell Douglas KC-10A Extender (DC-10-30)	48250 / 425		60AMW	
86-0038	McDonnell Douglas KC-10A Extender (DC-10-30)	48251 / 426		60AMW	
86-0078 / OS	Beech C-12J Huron (B1900)	UC-1		51FW	
86-0080	Beech C-12J Huron (B1900)	UC-3		46TW	
86-0081	Beech C-12J Huron (B1900)	UC-4		51FW	
86-0083 / OS	Beech C-12J Huron (B1900)	UC-6		51FW	
86-0201	GAC C-20B (G-1159A Gulfstream III)	470	N344GA	89AW	
86-0202	GAC C-20B (G-1159A Gulfstream III)	468	N342GA	89AW	
86-0203	GAC C-20B (G-1159A Gulfstream III)	475	N312GA	89AW	
86-0204	GAC C-20B (G-1159A Gulfstream III)	476	N314GA	89AW	
86-0206	GAC C-20B (G-1159A Gulfstream III)	478	N318GA	89AW	
86-0374	Gates C-21A Learjet	35A-624	N39404	140Wg/CO ANG	
86-0377	Gates C-21A Learjet	35A-629	N40144	140Wg/CO ANG	
86-0403	GAC C-20C (G-1159A Gulfstream III)	473	N326GA	89AW	
86-0410	Lockheed C-130H (L-382C-74E) Hercules	5094		911AW	
86-0411	Lockheed C-130H (L-382C-74E) Hercules	5097		911AW	
86-0412	Lockheed C-130H (L-382C-74E) Hercules	5098		911AW	
86-0413	Lockheed C-130H (L-382C-74E) Hercules	5100		911AW	
86-0414	Lockheed C-130H (L-382C-74E) Hercules	5102		911AW	
86-0415 / PI	Lockheed C-130H (L-382C-74E) Hercules	5105		911AW	
86-0417	Boeing E-8A J-Stars (707-323C)	19574 / 710	N8411	93ACW	
86-0418	Lockheed C-130H (L-382C-74E) Hercules	5110		911AW	
86-0419	Lockheed C-130H (L-382C-74E) Hercules	5113		911AW	
86-0451	Fairchild C-26A Metro III (SA227AC)	AC-737B			Std Rickenbacker ANGB
86-0453	Fairchild C-26A Metro III (SA227AC)	AC-742B			Std Rickenbacker ANGB
86-0454	Fairchild C-26A Metro III (SA227AC)	AC-743B			Std Rickenbacker ANGB

86-0456	Fairchild C-26A Metro III (SA227AC)	AC-747B			Fairchild
86-0457	Fairchild C-26A Metro III (SA227AC)	AC-749B			Fairchild
86-0458	Fairchild C-26A Metro III (SA227AC)	AC-751B			Fairchild
86-0459	Fairchild C-26A Metro III (SA227AC)	AC-753B			Fairchild
86-1391 / XP	Lockheed C-130H (L-382C-74E) Hercules	5093		139AW/MO ANG	
86-1392	Lockheed C-130H (L-382C-74E) Hercules	5095		139AW/MO ANG	
86-1393 / XP	Lockheed C-130H (L-382C-74E) Hercules	5096		139AW/MO ANG	
86-1394 / XP	Lockheed C-130H (L-382C-74E) Hercules	5099		139AW/MO ANG	
86-1395 / XP	Lockheed C-130H (L-382C-74E) Hercules	5101		139AW/MO ANG	
86-1396 / XP	Lockheed C-130H (L-382C-74E) Hercules	5103		139AW/MO ANG	
86-1397 / XP	Lockheed C-130H (L-382C-74E) Hercules	5111		139AW/MO ANG	
86-1398 / XP	Lockheed C-130H (L-382C-74E) Hercules	5112		139AW/MO ANG	
86-1683	Beech King Air A90	LJ-129			
86-1699	Lockheed MC-130H (L-382C-73E) Hercules	5026	N4278M	352SOG	*'Merlin's Magic'*
87-0023	Lockheed MC-130H (L-382C-77E) Hercules	5091		352SOG	
87-0024	Lockheed MC-130H (L-382C-77E) Hercules	5092		16SOW	
87-0025	McDonnell Douglas C-17A Globemaster III	T-1		412TW	
87-0027	Lockheed C-5B Galaxy	500-0113		436AW	
87-0028	Lockheed C-5B Galaxy	500-0114		60AMW	
87-0029	Lockheed C-5B Galaxy	500-0115		436AW	
87-0030	Lockheed C-5B Galaxy	500-0116		60AMW	
87-0031	Lockheed C-5B Galaxy	500-0117		436AW	
87-0032	Lockheed C-5B Galaxy	500-0118		60AMW	
87-0033	Lockheed C-5B Galaxy	500-0119		436AW	
87-0034	Lockheed C-5B Galaxy	500-0120		60AMW	
87-0035	Lockheed C-5B Galaxy	500-0121		436AW	
87-0036	Lockheed C-5B Galaxy	500-0122		60AMW	
87-0037	Lockheed C-5B Galaxy	500-0123		436AW	
87-0038	Lockheed C-5B Galaxy	500-0124		60AMW	
87-0039	Lockheed C-5B Galaxy	500-0125		436AW	
87-0040	Lockheed C-5B Galaxy	500-0126		60AMW	
87-0041	Lockheed C-5B Galaxy	500-0127		436AW	
87-0042	Lockheed C-5B Galaxy	500-0128		60AMW	
87-0043	Lockheed C-5B Galaxy	500-0129		436AW	
87-0044	Lockheed C-5B Galaxy	500-0130		60AMW	
87-0045	Lockheed C-5B Galaxy	500-0131		436AW	
87-0117	McDonnell Douglas KC-10A Extender (DC-10-30)				
		48303 / 427		60AMW	
87-0118	McDonnell Douglas KC-10A Extender (DC-10-30)				
		48304 / 428		60AMW	
87-0119	McDonnell Douglas KC-10A Extender (DC-10-30)				
		48305 / 429		60AMW	
87-0120	McDonnell Douglas KC-10A Extender (DC-10-30)				
		48306 / 430		305AMW	
87-0121	McDonnell Douglas KC-10A Extender (DC-10-30)				
		48307 / 431		305AMW	
87-0122	McDonnell Douglas KC-10A Extender (DC-10-30)				
		48308 / 432		305AMW	
87-0123	McDonnell Douglas KC-10A Extender (DC-10-30)				
		48309 / 439		305AMW	
87-0124	McDonnell Douglas KC-10A Extender (DC-10-30)				
		48310 / 441	N6204N	305AMW	
87-0125	Lockheed MC-130H (L-382C-77E) Hercules	5115		58SOW	
87-0126	Lockheed MC-130H (L-382C-77E) Hercules	5117		58SOW	
87-0127	Lockheed MC-130H (L-382C-77E) Hercules	5118		58SOW	
87-0128	Lockheed AC-130U (L-382C-86E) Hercules	5139		16SOW	
87-0142	Beech 65 Queen Air				
87-0159	CASA 212 Aviocar srs 200	CC60-4-328	N215TA	427SOS	
87-9281	Lockheed C-130H (L-382C-81E) Hercules	5122		440AW	
87-9282	Lockheed C-130H (L-382C-81E) Hercules	5123		440AW	
87-9283	Lockheed C-130H (L-382C-81E) Hercules	5124		440AW	
87-9284	Lockheed C-130H (L-382C-81E) Hercules	5125		94AW	
87-9285 / MK	Lockheed C-130H (L-382C-81E) Hercules	5126		440AW	
87-9286	Lockheed C-130H (L-382C-81E) Hercules	5127		908AW	
87-9287	Lockheed C-130H (L-382C-81E) Hercules	5128		440AW	
87-9288	Lockheed C-130H (L-382C-81E) Hercules	5129		911AW	
88-0191	Lockheed MC-130H (L-382C-87E) Hercules	5130		353SOG	
88-0192	Lockheed MC-130H (L-382C-87E) Hercules	5131		353SOG	
88-0193	Lockheed MC-130H (L-382C-87E) Hercules	5132		352SOG	
88-0194	Lockheed MC-130H (L-382C-87E) Hercules	5133		352SOG	
88-0195	Lockheed MC-130H (L-382C-87E) Hercules	5134		353SOG	
88-0264	Lockheed MC-130H (L-382C-87E) Hercules	5135		353SOG	
88-0265	McDonnell Douglas C-17A Globemaster III	P-1		437AMW	
88-0266	McDonnell Douglas C-17A Globemaster III	P-2		437AMW	

88-1301 / WV	Lockheed C-130H (L-382C-88E) Hercules	5162		130AW/WV ANG
88-1302 / WV	Lockheed C-130H (L-382C-88E) Hercules	5163		130AW/WV ANG
88-1303 / WV	Lockheed C-130H (L-382C-88E) Hercules	5164		130AW/WV ANG
88-1304 / WV	Lockheed C-130H (L-382C-88E) Hercules	5165		130AW/WV ANG
88-1305 / WV	Lockheed C-130H (L-382C-88E) Hercules	5166		130AW/WV ANG
88-1306 / WV	Lockheed C-130H (L-382C-88E) Hercules	5167		130AW/WV ANG
88-1307 / WV	Lockheed C-130H (L-382C-88E) Hercules	5168		130AW/WV ANG
88-1308 / WV	Lockheed C-130H (L-382C-88E) Hercules	5169		130AW/WV ANG
88-1803	Lockheed MC-130H (L-382C-89E) Hercules	5173		353SOG
88-2101	Lockheed HC-130H(N) (L-382C-98E) Hercules	5202		106RQW/NY ANG
88-2102	Lockheed HC-130H(N) (L-382C-98E) Hercules	5210		106RQW/NY ANG
88-4401	Lockheed C-130H (L-382C-88E) Hercules	5154		440AW
88-4402	Lockheed C-130H (L-382C-88E) Hercules	5155		440AW
88-4403	Lockheed C-130H (L-382C-88E) Hercules	5156		440AW
88-4404	Lockheed C-130H (L-382C-88E) Hercules	5157		440AW
88-4405	Lockheed C-130H (L-382C-88E) Hercules	5158		440AW
88-4406	Lockheed C-130H (L-382C-88E) Hercules	5159		440AW
88-4407	Lockheed C-130H (L-382C-88E) Hercules	5160		440AW
89-0280	Lockheed MC-130H (L-382C-01F) Hercules	5236		16SOW
89-0281	Lockheed MC-130H (L-382C-01F) Hercules	5237		16SOW
89-0282	Lockheed MC-130H (L-382C-01F) Hercules	5243		16SOW
89-0283	Lockheed MC-130H (L-382C-01F) Hercules	5244		16SOW
89-0284 / VN	Beech T-1A Jayhawk (Beechjet 400)	TT-5	N2876B	71FTW
89-0460	Fairchild C-26B Metro III (SA227AC)	BC-762B		Std Rickenbacker ANGB
89-0509	Lockheed AC-130U (L-382C-97E) Hercules	5228		16SOW
89-0510	Lockheed AC-130U (L-382C-97E) Hercules	5229		16SOW
89-0511	Lockheed AC-130U (L-382C-97E) Hercules	5230		16SOW
89-0512	Lockheed AC-130U (L-382C-97E) Hercules	5231		16SOW
89-0513	Lockheed AC-130U (L-382C-97E) Hercules	5232		16SOW
89-0514	Lockheed AC-130U (L-382C-97E) Hercules	5233		16SOW
89-1051	Lockheed C-130H (L-382C-96E) Hercules	5198		164AW/TN ANG
89-1052	Lockheed C-130H (L-382C-96E) Hercules	5199		164AW/TN ANG
89-1053	Lockheed C-130H (L-382C-96E) Hercules	5201		164AW/TN ANG
89-1054	Lockheed C-130H (L-382C-96E) Hercules	5203		164AW/TN ANG
89-1055 / HH	Lockheed C-130H (L-382C-96E) Hercules	5204		154Wg/HI ANG
89-1056	Lockheed C-130H (L-382C-96E) Hercules	5205		139AW/MO ANG
89-1181	Lockheed C-130H (L-382C-96E) Hercules	5188		164AW/TN ANG
89-1182	Lockheed C-130H (L-382C-96E) Hercules	5190		164AW/TN ANG
89-1183	Lockheed C-130H (L-382C-96E) Hercules	5192		164AW/TN ANG
89-1184	Lockheed C-130H (L-382C-96E) Hercules	5193		164AW/TN ANG
89-1185	Lockheed C-130H (L-382C-96E) Hercules	5194		164AW/TN ANG
89-1186	Lockheed C-130H (L-382C-96E) Hercules	5195		164AW/TN ANG
89-1187	Lockheed C-130H (L-382C-96E) Hercules	5196		164AW/TN ANG
89-1188	Lockheed C-130H (L-382C-96E) Hercules	5197		164AW/TN ANG
89-1189	McDonnell Douglas C-17A Globemaster III	P-3		97AMW
89-1190	McDonnell Douglas C-17A Globemaster III	P-4		437AW
89-1191	McDonnell Douglas C-17A Globemaster III	P-5		437AW
89-1192	McDonnell Douglas C-17A Globemaster III	P-6		437AW
89-9101	Lockheed C-130H (L-382C-96E) Hercules	5216		910AW
89-9102	Lockheed C-130H (L-382C-96E) Hercules	5217		910AW
89-9103	Lockheed C-130H (L-382C-96E) Hercules	5218		910AW
89-9104	Lockheed C-130H (L-382C-96E) Hercules	5220		910AW
89-9105	Lockheed C-130H (L-382C-96E) Hercules	5221		910AW
89-9106	Lockheed C-130H (L-382C-96E) Hercules	5223		910AW
90-0161	Lockheed MC-130H (L-382C-05F) Hercules	5265		16SOW
90-0162	Lockheed MC-130H (L-382C-05F) Hercules	5266		16SOW
90-0163	Lockheed AC-130U (L-382C-19F) Hercules	5256		16SOW
90-0164	Lockheed AC-130U (L-382C-19F) Hercules	5257		16SOW
90-0165	Lockheed AC-130U (L-382C-19F) Hercules	5259		16SOW
90-0166	Lockheed AC-130U (L-382C-19F) Hercules	5261		16SOW
90-0167	Lockheed AC-130U (L-382C-19F) Hercules	5262		16SOW
90-0168	CASA 212 Aviocar srs 200	CC60-6-336	N216TA	6SOS
90-0169	CASA 212 Aviocar srs 200	CC60-8-348	N218TA	427SOS
90-0175 / JS	Boeing E-8C (707-338C)	19621 / 652	N526SJ	
90-0300	GAC C-20G (Gulfstream IV)	1181	N473GA	89AW
90-0400 / XL	Beech T-1A Jayhawk (Beechjet 400)	TT-3	N2892B	47FTW
90-0401 / XL	Beech T-1A Jayhawk (Beechjet 400)	TT-7	N2896B	47FTW
90-0402 / XL	Beech T-1A Jayhawk (Beechjet 400)	TT-8	N2868B	47FTW
90-0403 / VN	Beech T-1A Jayhawk (Beechjet 400)	TT-9		71FTW
90-0404 / RA	Beech T-1A Jayhawk (Beechjet 400)	TT-6	N2872B	12FTW
90-0405 / RA	Beech T-1A Jayhawk (Beechjet 400)	TT-4		12FTW
90-0406 / XL	Beech T-1A Jayhawk (Beechjet 400)	TT-11		47FTW
90-0407 / CB	Beech T-1A Jayhawk (Beechjet 400)	TT-10		14FTW
90-0408 / CB	Beech T-1A Jayhawk (Beechjet 400)	TT-12		14FTW

Serial	Type	C/n	Reg	Unit
90-0409 / CB	Beech T-1A Jayhawk (Beechjet 400)	TT-13		14FTW
90-0410 / VN	Beech T-1A Jayhawk (Beechjet 400)	TT-14		71FTW
90-0411 / VN	Beech T-1A Jayhawk (Beechjet 400)	TT-15		71FTW
90-0412 / CB	Beech T-1A Jayhawk (Beechjet 400)	TT-2/RK-15	N2887B	14FTW
90-0413 / CB	Beech T-1A Jayhawk (Beechjet 400)	TT-16		14FTW
90-0523	Fairchild C-26B Metro III (SA227DC)	DC-784B	N3003F	VA ANG
90-0524	Fairchild C-26B Metro III (SA227DC)	DC-790M	N3003U	
90-0525	Fairchild C-26B Metro III (SA227DC)	DC-792M	N3004K	MN ANG
90-0526	Fairchild C-26B Metro III (SA227DC)	DC-793M	N3004T	AZ ANG
90-0532	McDonnell Douglas C-17A Globemaster III	P-7		437AW
90-0533	McDonnell Douglas C-17A Globemaster III	P-8		97AMW
90-0534	McDonnell Douglas C-17A Globemaster III	P-9		437AW
90-0535	McDonnell Douglas C-17A Globemaster III	P-10		97AMW
90-1057	Lockheed C-130H (L-382C-14F) Hercules	5240		154Wg/HI ANG
90-1058	Lockheed C-130H (L-382C-14F) Hercules	5241		154Wg/HI ANG
90-1791 / OH	Lockheed C-130H (L-382C-14F) Hercules	5242		179AW/OH ANG
90-1792 / OH	Lockheed C-130H (L-382C-14F) Hercules	5245		179AW/OH ANG
90-1793 / OH	Lockheed C-130H (L-382C-14F) Hercules	5246		179AW/OH ANG
90-1794 / OH	Lockheed C-130H (L-382C-14F) Hercules	5247		179AW/OH ANG
90-1795 / OH	Lockheed C-130H (L-382C-14F) Hercules	5248		179AW/OH ANG
90-1796 / OH	Lockheed C-130H (L-382C-14F) Hercules	5249		179AW/OH ANG
90-1797 / OH	Lockheed C-130H (L-382C-14F) Hercules	5250		179AW/OH ANG
90-1798 / OH	Lockheed C-130H (L-382C-14F) Hercules	5251		179AW/OH ANG
90-2103	Lockheed HC-130H(N) (L-382C-24F) Hercules	5294		176Wg/AK ANG
90-9107	Lockheed C-130H (L-382C-14F) Hercules	5238		757AS
90-9108	Lockheed C-130H (L-382C-14F) Hercules	5239		757AS
91-0075 / XL	Beech T-1A Jayhawk (Beechjet 400)	TT-18		47FTW
91-0076 / XL	Beech T-1A Jayhawk (Beechjet 400)	TT-17		47FTW
91-0077 / VN	Beech T-1A Jayhawk (Beechjet 400)	TT-1/RK-12	N2886B	71FTW
91-0078 / XL	Beech T-1A Jayhawk (Beechjet 400)	TT-19		47FTW
91-0079 / XL	Beech T-1A Jayhawk (Beechjet 400)	TT-20		47FTW
91-0080 / VN	Beech T-1A Jayhawk (Beechjet 400)	TT-21		71FTW
91-0081 / XL	Beech T-1A Jayhawk (Beechjet 400)	TT-22		47FTW
91-0082 / XL	Beech T-1A Jayhawk (Beechjet 400)	TT-23		47FTW
91-0083 / XL	Beech T-1A Jayhawk (Beechjet 400)	TT-24		47FTW
91-0084 / VN	Beech T-1A Jayhawk (Beechjet 400)	TT-25		71FTW
91-0085 / XL	Beech T-1A Jayhawk (Beechjet 400)	TT-26		47FTW
91-0086 / XL	Beech T-1A Jayhawk (Beechjet 400)	TT-27		47FTW
91-0087 / XL	Beech T-1A Jayhawk (Beechjet 400)	TT-28		47FTW
91-0088 / VN	Beech T-1A Jayhawk (Beechjet 400)	TT-29		71FTW
91-0089 / XL	Beech T-1A Jayhawk (Beechjet 400)	TT-30		47FTW
91-0090 / XL	Beech T-1A Jayhawk (Beechjet 400)	TT-31		47FTW
91-0091 / XL	Beech T-1A Jayhawk (Beechjet 400)	TT-32		47FTW
91-0092 / XL	Beech T-1A Jayhawk (Beechjet 400)	TT-33		47FTW
91-0093 / XL	Beech T-1A Jayhawk (Beechjet 400)	TT-34		47FTW
91-0094 / XL	Beech T-1A Jayhawk (Beechjet 400)	TT-35		47FTW
91-0095 / VN	Beech T-1A Jayhawk (Beechjet 400)	TT-36		71FTW
91-0096 / RA	Beech T-1A Jayhawk (Beechjet 400)	TT-37		12FTW
91-0097 / XL	Beech T-1A Jayhawk (Beechjet 400)	TT-38		47FTW
91-0098 / VN	Beech T-1A Jayhawk (Beechjet 400)	TT-39		71FTW
91-0099 / RA	Beech T-1A Jayhawk (Beechjet 400)	TT-40		12FTW
91-0100 / CB	Beech T-1A Jayhawk (Beechjet 400)	TT-41		14FTW
91-0101 / RA	Beech T-1A Jayhawk (Beechjet 400)	TT-42		12FTW
91-0102 / RA	Beech T-1A Jayhawk (Beechjet 400)	TT-43		12FTW
91-1231	Lockheed C-130H (L-382C-22F) Hercules	5278		123AW/KY ANG
91-1232	Lockheed C-130H (L-382C-22F) Hercules	5282		123AW/KY ANG
91-1233	Lockheed C-130H (L-382C-22F) Hercules	5283		123AW/KY ANG
91-1234	Lockheed C-130H (L-382C-22F) Hercules	5284		123AW/KY ANG
91-1235	Lockheed C-130H (L-382C-22F) Hercules	5285		123AW/KY ANG
91-1236	Lockheed C-130H (L-382C-22F) Hercules	5286		123AW/KY ANG
91-1237	Lockheed C-130H (L-382C-22F) Hercules	5287		123AW/KY ANG
91-1238	Lockheed C-130H (L-382C-22F) Hercules	5288		123AW/KY ANG
91-1239	Lockheed C-130H (L-382C-22F) Hercules	5289		123AW/KY ANG
91-1651	Lockheed C-130H (L-382C-22F) Hercules	5290		123AW/KY ANG
91-1652	Lockheed C-130H (L-382C-22F) Hercules	5291		123AW/KY ANG
91-1653	Lockheed C-130H (L-382C-22F) Hercules	5292		123AW/KY ANG
91-9141	Lockheed C-130H (L-382C-22F) Hercules	5293		910AW
91-9142	Lockheed C-130H (L-382C-22F) Hercules	5295		910AW
91-9143	Lockheed C-130H (L-382C-22F) Hercules	5296		910AW
91-9144	Lockheed C-130H (L-382C-22F) Hercules	5297		910AW
92-0253	Lockheed AC-130U (L-382C-40F) Hercules	5279		16SOW (2000th C-130)
92-0330 / RA	Beech T-1A Jayhawk (Beechjet 400)	TT-44		12FTW
92-0331 / RA	Beech T-1A Jayhawk (Beechjet 400)	TT-45		12FTW
92-0332 / RA	Beech T-1A Jayhawk (Beechjet 400)	TT-46		12FTW

92-0353 / RA	Beech T-1A Jayhawk (Beechjet 400)	TT-47		12FTW	
92-0354 / RA	Beech T-1A Jayhawk (Beechjet 400)	TT-48		12FTW	
92-0355 / RA	Beech T-1A Jayhawk (Beechjet 400)	TT-49		12FTW	
92-0356 / RA	Beech T-1A Jayhawk (Beechjet 400)	TT-50		12FTW	
92-0357 / RA	Beech T-1A Jayhawk (Beechjet 400)	TT-51		12FTW	
92-0358 / RA	Beech T-1A Jayhawk (Beechjet 400)	TT-52		12FTW	
92-0359 / RA	Beech T-1A Jayhawk (Beechjet 400)	TT-53		12FTW	
92-0340 / RA	Beech T-1A Jayhawk (Beechjet 400)	TT-54		12FTW	
92-0341 / VN	Beech T-1A Jayhawk (Beechjet 400)	TT-55		71FTW	
92-0342 / XL	Beech T-1A Jayhawk (Beechjet 400)	TT-56		47FTW	
92-0343 / VN	Beech T-1A Jayhawk (Beechjet 400)	TT-57		71FTW	
92-0344 / XL	Beech T-1A Jayhawk (Beechjet 400)	TT-58		47FTW	
92-0345 / XL	Beech T-1A Jayhawk (Beechjet 400)	TT-59		47FTW	
92-0346 / XL	Beech T-1A Jayhawk (Beechjet 400)	TT-60		47FTW	
92-0347 / XL	Beech T-1A Jayhawk (Beechjet 400)	TT-61		47FTW	
92-0348 / XL	Beech T-1A Jayhawk (Beechjet 400)	TT-62		47FTW	
92-0349 / XL	Beech T-1A Jayhawk (Beechjet 400)	TT-63		47FTW	
92-0350 / XL	Beech T-1A Jayhawk (Beechjet 400)	TT-64		47FTW	
92-0351 / VN	Beech T-1A Jayhawk (Beechjet 400)	TT-65		71FTW	
92-0352 / XL	Beech T-1A Jayhawk (Beechjet 400)	TT-66		47FTW	
92-0353 / RA	Beech T-1A Jayhawk (Beechjet 400)	TT-67		12FTW	
92-0354 / XL	Beech T-1A Jayhawk (Beechjet 400)	TT-68		47FTW	
92-0355 / XL	Beech T-1A Jayhawk (Beechjet 400)	TT-69		47FTW	
92-0356 / XL	Beech T-1A Jayhawk (Beechjet 400)	TT-70		47FTW	
92-0357 / XL	Beech T-1A Jayhawk (Beechjet 400)	TT-71		47FTW	
92-0358 / XL	Beech T-1A Jayhawk (Beechjet 400)	TT-72		47FTW	
92-0359 / RA	Beech T-1A Jayhawk (Beechjet 400)	TT-73		12FTW	
92-0360 / XL	Beech T-1A Jayhawk (Beechjet 400)	TT-74		47FTW	
92-0361 / XL	Beech T-1A Jayhawk (Beechjet 400)	TT-75		47FTW	
92-0362 / XL	Beech T-1A Jayhawk (Beechjet 400)	TT-76		47FTW	
92-0363 / CB	Beech T-1A Jayhawk (Beechjet 400)	TT-77		14FTW	
92-0375	GAC C-20H (Gulfstream IVSP)	1256	N438GA	89AW	
92-0547	Lockheed C-130H (L-382C-33F) Hercules	5332		463AG	
92-0548	Lockheed C-130H (L-382C-33F) Hercules	5335		463AG	
92-0549	Lockheed C-130H (L-382C-33F) Hercules	5337		463AG	
92-0550	Lockheed C-130H (L-382C-33F) Hercules	5321		463AG	
92-0551	Lockheed C-130H (L-382C-33F) Hercules	5346		463AG	
92-0552	Lockheed C-130H (L-382C-33F) Hercules	5348		463AG	
92-0553	Lockheed C-130H (L-382C-33F) Hercules	5350		463AG	
92-0554	Lockheed C-130H (L-382C-33F) Hercules	5352		463AG	
92-1094	Lockheed LC-130H (L-382C-47F) Hercules	5402		109AW/NY ANG	
92-1095	Lockheed LC-130H (L-382C-47F) Hercules	5405		109AW/NY ANG	
92-1451 / NC	Lockheed C-130H (L-382C-33F) Hercules	5343		145AW/NC ANG	
92-1452 / NC	Lockheed C-130H (L-382C-33F) Hercules	5329		145AW/NC ANG	
92-1453 / NC	Lockheed C-130H (L-382C-33F) Hercules	5330		145AW/NC ANG	
92-1454 / NC	Lockheed C-130H (L-382C-33F) Hercules	5333		145AW/NC ANG	
92-1531	Lockheed C-130H (L-382C-33F) Hercules	5310		153AW/WY ANG 'City of Cheyenne'	
92-1532	Lockheed C-130H (L-382C-33F) Hercules	5328		153AW/WY ANG 'City of Sheridan'	
92-1533 / WY	Lockheed C-130H (L-382C-33F) Hercules	5322		153AW/WY ANG 'City of Cody'	
92-1534 / WY	Lockheed C-130H (L-382C-33F) Hercules	5323		153AW/WY ANG 'City of Riverton'	
92-1535 / WY	Lockheed C-130H (L-382C-33F) Hercules	5324		153AW/WY ANG 'City of Laramie'	
92-1536 / WY	Lockheed C-130H (L-382C-33F) Hercules	5325		153AW/WY ANG 'City of Casper'	
92-1537 / WY	Lockheed C-130H (L-382C-33F) Hercules	5326		153AW/WY ANG 'City of Guernsey'	
92-1538 / WY	Lockheed C-130H (L-382C-33F) Hercules	5327		153AW/WY ANG 'City of Rock Springs'	
92-3021	Lockheed C-130H (L-382C-35F) Hercules	5312		910AW	
92-3022	Lockheed C-130H (L-382C-35F) Hercules	5313		910AW	
92-3023	Lockheed C-130H (L-382C-35F) Hercules	5314		910AW	
92-3024	Lockheed C-130H (L-382C-35F) Hercules	5315		910AW	
92-3031	Lockheed C-130H (L-382C-33F) Hercules	5331		914AW	
92-3032	Lockheed C-130H (L-382C-33F) Hercules	5334		914AW	
92-3033	Lockheed C-130H (L-382C-33F) Hercules	5336		914AW	
92-3034	Lockheed C-130H (L-382C-33F) Hercules	5338		914AW	
92-3035	Lockheed C-130H (L-382C-33F) Hercules	5347		914AW	
92-3036	Lockheed C-130H (L-382C-33F) Hercules	5349		914AW	
92-3037	Lockheed C-130H (L-382C-33F) Hercules	5351		914AW	
92-3038 / NF	Lockheed C-130H (L-382C-33F) Hercules	5353		914AW	
92-3039 / WR	Boeing E-8C (707-338C)	19622 / 660	N4131G	93ACW	

92-3290 / WR	Boeing E-8C (707-338C)	19295 / 617		93ACW	
92-3291	McDonnell Douglas C-17A Globemaster III	P-11		437AW	
92-3292	McDonnell Douglas C-17A Globemaster III	P-12		437AW	
92-3293	McDonnell Douglas C-17A Globemaster III	P-13		437AW	
92-3294	McDonnell Douglas C-17A Globemaster III	P-14		437AW	
92-9000	Boeing VC-25A (747-2G4B)	23825 / 685	N60659	89AW	Presidential Aircraft
93-0011	Boeing GE-8C (707-384C)	18949 / 497	JY-AEC		
93-0597 / WR	Boeing E-8C (707-338C)	19294 / 550	G-EOCO	93ACW	
93-0599	McDonnell Douglas C-17A Globemaster III	P-15		437AW	
93-0600	McDonnell Douglas C-17A Globemaster III	P-16		97AMW	
93-0601	McDonnell Douglas C-17A Globemaster III	P-17		437AW	
93-0602	McDonnell Douglas C-17A Globemaster III	P-18		97AMW	
93-0603	McDonnell Douglas C-17A Globemaster III	P-19		437AW	
93-0604	McDonnell Douglas C-17A Globemaster III	P-20		97AMW	
93-0621 / XL	Beech T-1A Jayhawk (Beechjet 400)	TT-78		47FTW	
93-0622 / XL	Beech T-1A Jayhawk (Beechjet 400)	TT-79		47FTW	
93-0623 / XL	Beech T-1A Jayhawk (Beechjet 400)	TT-80		47FTW	
93-0624 / XL	Beech T-1A Jayhawk (Beechjet 400)	TT-81		47FTW	
93-0626 / XL	Beech T-1A Jayhawk (Beechjet 400)	TT-83		47FTW	
93-0627 / XL	Beech T-1A Jayhawk (Beechjet 400)	TT-84		47FTW	
93-0628 / XL	Beech T-1A Jayhawk (Beechjet 400)	TT-85		47FTW	
93-0629 / XL	Beech T-1A Jayhawk (Beechjet 400)	TT-86		47FTW	
93-0630 / RA	Beech T-1A Jayhawk (Beechjet 400)	TT-87		12FTW	
93-0631 / XL	Beech T-1A Jayhawk (Beechjet 400)	TT-88		47FTW	
93-0632 / XL	Beech T-1A Jayhawk (Beechjet 400)	TT-89		47FTW	
93-0633 / XL	Beech T-1A Jayhawk (Beechjet 400)	TT-90		47FTW	
93-0634 / XL	Beech T-1A Jayhawk (Beechjet 400)	TT-91		47FTW	
93-0635 / XL	Beech T-1A Jayhawk (Beechjet 400)	TT-92		47FTW	
93-0636 / XL	Beech T-1A Jayhawk (Beechjet 400)	TT-93		47FTW	
93-0637 / XL	Beech T-1A Jayhawk (Beechjet 400)	TT-94		47FTW	
93-0638 / VN	Beech T-1A Jayhawk (Beechjet 400)	TT-95		71FTW	
93-0639 / VN	Beech T-1A Jayhawk (Beechjet 400)	TT-96		71FTW	
93-0640 / XL	Beech T-1A Jayhawk (Beechjet 400)	TT-97		47FTW	
93-0641 / VN	Beech T-1A Jayhawk (Beechjet 400)	TT-98		71FTW	
93-0642 / VN	Beech T-1A Jayhawk (Beechjet 400)	TT-99		71FTW	
93-0643 / VN	Beech T-1A Jayhawk (Beechjet 400)	TT-100		71FTW	
93-0644 / VN	Beech T-1A Jayhawk (Beechjet 400)	TT-101		71FTW	
93-0645 / VN	Beech T-1A Jayhawk (Beechjet 400)	TT-102		71FTW	
93-0646 / VN	Beech T-1A Jayhawk (Beechjet 400)	TT-103		71FTW	
93-0647 / VN	Beech T-1A Jayhawk (Beechjet 400)	TT-104		71FTW	
93-0648 / VN	Beech T-1A Jayhawk (Beechjet 400)	TT-105		71FTW	
93-0649 / VN	Beech T-1A Jayhawk (Beechjet 400)	TT-106		71FTW	
93-0650 / VN	Beech T-1A Jayhawk (Beechjet 400)	TT-107		71FTW	
93-0651 / XL	Beech T-1A Jayhawk (Beechjet 400)	TT-108		47FTW	
93-0652 / XL	Beech T-1A Jayhawk (Beechjet 400)	TT-109		47FTW	
93-0653 / VN	Beech T-1A Jayhawk (Beechjet 400)	TT-110		71FTW	
93-0654 / VN	Beech T-1A Jayhawk (Beechjet 400)	TT-111		71FTW	
93-0655 / VN	Beech T-1A Jayhawk (Beechjet 400)	TT-112		71FTW	
93-0656 / VN	Beech T-1A Jayhawk (Beechjet 400)	TT-113		71FTW	
93-1036 / LK	Lockheed C-130H (L-382C-42F) Hercules	5368		463AG	
93-1037 / LK	Lockheed C-130H (L-382C-42F) Hercules	5369		463AG	
93-1038 / LK	Lockheed C-130H (L-382C-42F) Hercules	5372		463AG	
93-1039 / LK	Lockheed C-130H (L-382C-42F) Hercules	5373		463AG	
93-1040 / LK	Lockheed C-130H (L-382C-42F) Hercules	5375		463AG	
93-1041 / LK	Lockheed C-130H (L-382C-42F) Hercules	5376		463AG	
93-1096	Lockheed LC-130H (L-382C-47F) Hercules	5410		109AW/NY ANG	
93-1097 / WR	Boeing E-8C (707-338C)	19296 / 630	N6546L	93ACW	
93-1455 / NC	Lockheed Martin C-130H (L-382C-42F) Hercules	5360		145AW/NC ANG	
93-1456 / NC	Lockheed Martin C-130H (L-382C-42F) Hercules	5361		145AW/NC ANG	
93-1457 / NC	Lockheed Martin C-130H (L-382C-42F) Hercules	5362		145AW/NC ANG	
93-1458 / NC	Lockheed Martin C-130H (L-382C-42F) Hercules	5363		145AW/NC ANG	
93-1459 / NC	Lockheed Martin C-130H (L-382C-42F) Hercules	5364		145AW/NC ANG	
93-1561 / NC	Lockheed Martin C-130H (L-382C-42F) Hercules	5365		145AW/NC ANG	
93-1562 / NC	Lockheed Martin C-130H (L-382C-42F) Hercules	5366		145AW/NC ANG	
93-1563 / NC	Lockheed Martin C-130H (L-382C-42F) Hercules	5367		145AW/NC ANG	
93-2041	Lockheed Martin C-130H (L-382C-42F) Hercules	5370		154Wg/HI ANG	
93-2042	Lockheed Martin C-130H (L-382C-42F) Hercules	5371		154Wg/HI ANG	
93-2104	Lockheed HC-130H(N) (L-382C-43F) Hercules	5381		176Wg/AK ANG	
93-2105	Lockheed HC-130H(N) (L-382C-43F) Hercules	5388		176Wg/AK ANG	
93-2106	Lockheed HC-130H(N) (L-382C-43F) Hercules	5387		176Wg/AK ANG	
93-7311 / CR	Lockheed Martin C-130H (L-382C-42F) Hercules	5374		302AW	
93-7312 / CR	Lockheed Martin C-130H (L-382C-42F) Hercules	5377		302AW	
93-7313 / CR	Lockheed Martin C-130H (L-382C-42F) Hercules	5379		302AW	
93-7314	Lockheed Martin C-130H (L-382C-42F) Hercules	5380		302AW	

94-0065	McDonnell Douglas C-17A Globemaster III	P-21		437AW	
94-0066	McDonnell Douglas C-17A Globemaster III	P-22		437AW	
94-0067	McDonnell Douglas C-17A Globemaster III	P-23		437AW	
94-0068	McDonnell Douglas C-17A Globemaster III	P-24		437AW	'Spirit of Airborne'
94-0069	McDonnell Douglas C-17A Globemaster III	P-25		97AMW	
94-0070	McDonnell Douglas C-17A Globemaster III	P-26		437AW	
94-0114 / CB	Beech T-1A Jayhawk (Beechjet 400)	TT-114		14FTW	
94-0115 / VN	Beech T-1A Jayhawk (Beechjet 400)	TT-115		71FTW	
94-0116 / VN	Beech T-1A Jayhawk (Beechjet 400)	TT-116		71FTW	
94-0117 / VN	Beech T-1A Jayhawk (Beechjet 400)	TT-117		71FTW	
94-0118 / VN	Beech T-1A Jayhawk (Beechjet 400)	TT-118		71FTW	
94-0119 / VN	Beech T-1A Jayhawk (Beechjet 400)	TT-119		71FTW	
94-0120 / VN	Beech T-1A Jayhawk (Beechjet 400)	TT-120		71FTW	
94-0121 / VN	Beech T-1A Jayhawk (Beechjet 400)	TT-121		71FTW	
94-0122 / VN	Beech T-1A Jayhawk (Beechjet 400)	TT-122		71FTW	
94-0123 / VN	Beech T-1A Jayhawk (Beechjet 400)	TT-123		71FTW	
94-0124 / VN	Beech T-1A Jayhawk (Beechjet 400)	TT-124		71FTW	
94-0125 / VN	Beech T-1A Jayhawk (Beechjet 400)	TT-125		71FTW	
94-0126 / VN	Beech T-1A Jayhawk (Beechjet 400)	TT-126		71FTW	
94-0127 / VN	Beech T-1A Jayhawk (Beechjet 400)	TT-127		71FTW	
94-0128 / VN	Beech T-1A Jayhawk (Beechjet 400)	TT-128		71FTW	
94-0129 / VN	Beech T-1A Jayhawk (Beechjet 400)	TT-129		71FTW	
94-0130 / VN	Beech T-1A Jayhawk (Beechjet 400)	TT-130		71FTW	
94-0131 / CB	Beech T-1A Jayhawk (Beechjet 400)	TT-131		14FTW	
94-0132 / VN	Beech T-1A Jayhawk (Beechjet 400)	TT-132		71FTW	
94-0133 / VN	Beech T-1A Jayhawk (Beechjet 400)	TT-133		71FTW	
94-0134 / CB	Beech T-1A Jayhawk (Beechjet 400)	TT-134		14FTW	
94-0135 / CB	Beech T-1A Jayhawk (Beechjet 400)	TT-135		14FTW	
94-0136 / CB	Beech T-1A Jayhawk (Beechjet 400)	TT-136		14FTW	
94-0137 / CB	Beech T-1A Jayhawk (Beechjet 400)	TT-137		14FTW	
94-0138 / CB	Beech T-1A Jayhawk (Beechjet 400)	TT-138		14FTW	
94-0139 / CB	Beech T-1A Jayhawk (Beechjet 400)	TT-139		14FTW	
94-0140 / CB	Beech T-1A Jayhawk (Beechjet 400)	TT-140		14FTW	
94-0141 / CB	Beech T-1A Jayhawk (Beechjet 400)	TT-141		14FTW	
94-0142 / CB	Beech T-1A Jayhawk (Beechjet 400)	TT-142		14FTW	
94-0143 / CB	Beech T-1A Jayhawk (Beechjet 400)	TT-143		14FTW	
94-0144 / CB	Beech T-1A Jayhawk (Beechjet 400)	TT-144		14FTW	
94-0145 / CB	Beech T-1A Jayhawk (Beechjet 400)	TT-145		14FTW	
94-0146 / CB	Beech T-1A Jayhawk (Beechjet 400)	TT-146		14FTW	
94-0147 / CB	Beech T-1A Jayhawk (Beechjet 400)	TT-147		14FTW	
94-0148 / CB	Beech T-1A Jayhawk (Beechjet 400)	TT-148		14FTW	
94-0284 / WR	Boeing E-8C (707-338C)	19293 / 546	N2178F	16ACCS	
94-0285	Boeing E-8C (707-373C)	19442 / 609	67-30054		
94-1569	IAI C-38A (1125 Astra SPX)	088	N398AG	113Wg/DC ANG	
94-1570	IAI C-38A (1125 Astra SPX)	090	N399AG	113Wg/DC ANG	
94-6703 / WV	Lockheed Martin C-130H (L-382C-53F) Hercules	5393		167AW/WV ANG	
94-6704 / WV	Lockheed Martin C-130H (L-382C-53F) Hercules	5394		167AW/WV ANG	
94-6705 / WV	Lockheed Martin C-130H (L-382C-53F) Hercules	5397		167AW/WV ANG	
94-6706 / WV	Lockheed Martin C-130H (L-382C-53F) Hercules	5398		167AW/WV ANG	
94-6707 / WV	Lockheed Martin C-130H (L-382C-53F) Hercules	5399		167AW/WV ANG	
94-6708 / WV	Lockheed Martin C-130H (L-382C-53F) Hercules	5400		167AW/WV ANG	
94-7320 / CR	Lockheed Martin C-130H (L-382C-53F) Hercules	5401		302AW	
94-7321 / CR	Lockheed Martin C-130H (L-382C-53F) Hercules	5403		302AW	
94-7310 / CR	Lockheed Martin C-130H (L-382C-53F) Hercules	5396		302AW	
94-7315 / CR	Lockheed Martin C-130H (L-382C-53F) Hercules	5389		302AW	
94-7316 / CR	Lockheed Martin C-130H (L-382C-53F) Hercules	5390		302AW	
94-7317 / CR	Lockheed Martin C-130H (L-382C-53F) Hercules	5391		302AW	
94-7318 / CR	Lockheed Martin C-130H (L-382C-53F) Hercules	5392		302AW	
94-7319 / CR	Lockheed Martin C-130H (L-382C-53F) Hercules	5395		302AW	
94-7320 / CR	Lockheed Martin C-130H (L-382C-53F) Hercules	5401		302AW	
94-7321 / CR	Lockheed Martin C-130H (L-382C-53F) Hercules	5403		302AW	
94-8751	Lockheed Martin C-130H (L-382C-53F) Hercules	5413	94-3026 (USAF)	403Wg	
94-8752	Lockheed Martin C-130H (L-382C-53F) Hercules	5415	94-3027 (USAF)		
95-0040 / CB	Beech T-1A Jayhawk (Beechjet 400)	TT-149		14FTW	
95-0041 / CB	Beech T-1A Jayhawk (Beechjet 400)	TT-150		14FTW	
95-0042 / CB	Beech T-1A Jayhawk (Beechjet 400)	TT-151		14FTW	
95-0043 / CB	Beech T-1A Jayhawk (Beechjet 400)	TT-152		14FTW	
95-0044 / CB	Beech T-1A Jayhawk (Beechjet 400)	TT-153		14FTW	
95-0045 / CB	Beech T-1A Jayhawk (Beechjet 400)	TT-154		14FTW	
95-0046 / CB	Beech T-1A Jayhawk (Beechjet 400)	TT-155		14FTW	
95-0047 / XL	Beech T-1A Jayhawk (Beechjet 400)	TT-156		47FTW	
95-0048 / CB	Beech T-1A Jayhawk (Beechjet 400)	TT-157		14FTW	
95-0049 / CB	Beech T-1A Jayhawk (Beechjet 400)	TT-158		14FTW	
95-0050 / CB	Beech T-1A Jayhawk (Beechjet 400)	TT-159		14FTW	

95-0051 / CB	Beech T-1A Jayhawk (Beechjet 400)	TT-160		14FTW
95-0052 / CB	Beech T-1A Jayhawk (Beechjet 400)	TT-161		14FTW
95-0053 / CB	Beech T-1A Jayhawk (Beechjet 400)	TT-162		14FTW
95-0054 / CB	Beech T-1A Jayhawk (Beechjet 400)	TT-163		14FTW
95-0055 / CB	Beech T-1A Jayhawk (Beechjet 400)	TT-164		14FTW
95-0056 / CB	Beech T-1A Jayhawk (Beechjet 400)	TT-165		14FTW
95-0057 / CB	Beech T-1A Jayhawk (Beechjet 400)	TT-166		14FTW
95-0058 / CB	Beech T-1A Jayhawk (Beechjet 400)	TT-167		14FTW
95-0059 / CB	Beech T-1A Jayhawk (Beechjet 400)	TT-168		14FTW
95-0060 / CB	Beech T-1A Jayhawk (Beechjet 400)	TT-169		14FTW
95-0061 / CB	Beech T-1A Jayhawk (Beechjet 400)	TT-170		14FTW
95-0062 / CB	Beech T-1A Jayhawk (Beechjet 400)	TT-171		14FTW
95-0063 / RA	Beech T-1A Jayhawk (Beechjet 400)	TT-172		12FTW
95-0064 / CB	Beech T-1A Jayhawk (Beechjet 400)	TT-173		14FTW
95-0065 / CB	Beech T-1A Jayhawk (Beechjet 400)	TT-174		14FTW
95-0066 / XL	Beech T-1A Jayhawk (Beechjet 400)	TT-175		47FTW
95-0067 / XL	Beech T-1A Jayhawk (Beechjet 400)	TT-176		47FTW
95-0068 / CB	Beech T-1A Jayhawk (Beechjet 400)	TT-177		14FTW
95-0069 / VN	Beech T-1A Jayhawk (Beechjet 400)	TT-178		71FTW
95-0070 / VN	Beech T-1A Jayhawk (Beechjet 400)	TT-179		71FTW
95-0071 / VN	Beech T-1A Jayhawk (Beechjet 400)	TT-180		71FTW
95-0102	McDonnell Douglas C-17A Globemaster III	P-27		437AW
95-0103	McDonnell Douglas C-17A Globemaster III	P-28		437AW
95-0104	McDonnell Douglas C-17A Globemaster III	P-29		437AW
95-0105	McDonnell Douglas C-17A Globemaster III	P-30		437AW
95-0106	McDonnell Douglas C-17A Globemaster III	P-31		437AW
95-0107	McDonnell Douglas C-17A Globemaster III	P-32		437AW
95-0121 / WR	Boeing E-8C (707-321C)	20016 / 752	68-11174	93ACW
95-0122 / WR	Boeing E-8C (707-3D3C)	20495 / 852	71-1841	93ACW
95-1001 / MN	Lockheed Martin C-130H (L-382C-57F) Hercules	5421		133AW/MN ANG
95-1002 / MN	Lockheed Martin C-130H (L-382C-57F) Hercules	5422		133AW/MN ANG
95-6709 / WV	Lockheed Martin C-130H (L-382C-57F) Hercules	5417		167AW/WV ANG
95-6710 / WV	Lockheed Martin C-130H (L-382C-57F) Hercules	5418		167AW/WV ANG
95-6711 / WV	Lockheed Martin C-130H (L-382C-57F) Hercules	5419		167AW/WV ANG
95-6712 / WV	Lockheed Martin C-130H (L-382C-57F) Hercules	5420		167AW/WV ANG
96-0001	McDonnell Douglas C-17A Globemaster III	P-33		437AW
96-0002	McDonnell Douglas C-17A Globemaster III	P-34		437AW
96-0003	McDonnell Douglas C-17A Globemaster III	P-35		437AW
96-0004	McDonnell Douglas C-17A Globemaster III	P-36		437AW
96-0005	McDonnell Douglas C-17A Globemaster III	P-37		437AW
96-0006	McDonnell Douglas C-17A Globemaster III	P-38		437AW
96-0007	McDonnell Douglas C-17A Globemaster III	P-39		437AW
96-0008	McDonnell Douglas C-17A Globemaster III	P-40		437AW
96-1003 / MN	Lockheed Martin C-130H (L-382C-57F) Hercules	5423		133AW/MN ANG
96-1004 / MN	Lockheed Martin C-130H (L-382C-57F) Hercules	5424	N4249Y	133AW/MN ANG
96-1005 / MN	Lockheed Martin C-130H (L-382C-57F) Hercules	5425	N78235	133AW/MN ANG
96-1006 / MN	Lockheed Martin C-130H (L-382C-57F) Hercules	5426		133AW/MN ANG
96-1007 / MN	Lockheed Martin C-130H (L-382C-57F) Hercules	5427		133AW/MN ANG
96-1008 / MN	Lockheed Martin C-130H (L-382C-57F) Hercules	5428		133AW/MN ANG
96-5300	Lockheed Martin WC-130J (L-382U-04J) Hercules II	5451	N4232B	403Wg
96-5301	Lockheed Martin WC-130J (L-382U-04J) Hercules II	5452	N4107F	403Wg
96-5302	Lockheed Martin WC-130J (L-382U-04J) Hercules II	5453	N4161T	403Wg
96-6049	Airtech/CASA CN235			427SOS
96-7322	Lockheed Martin C-130H (L-382C-57F) Hercules	5431		302AW
96-7323	Lockheed Martin C-130H (L-382C-57F) Hercules	5432		302AW
96-7324	Lockheed Martin C-130H (L-382C-57F) Hercules	5433		302AW
96-7325	Lockheed Martin C-130H (L-382C-57F) Hercules	5434		302AW
96-8153	Lockheed Martin C-130J (L-382U-02J) Hercules II	5454		403Wg
96-8154	Lockheed Martin C-130J (L-382U-02J) Hercules II	5455		403Wg
97-0041	Boeing C-17A Globemaster III	P-41		437AW
97-0042	Boeing C-17A Globemaster III	P-42		97AMW
97-0043	Boeing C-17A Globemaster III	P-43		437AW
97-0044	Boeing C-17A Globemaster III	P-44		437AW
97-0045	Boeing C-17A Globemaster III	P-45		437AW
97-0046	Boeing C-17A Globemaster III	P-46		437AW
97-0047	Boeing C-17A Globemaster III	P-47		437AW
97-0048	Boeing C-17A Globemaster III	P-48		437AW
97-0400	GAC C-37A (Gulfstream V)	521	N521GA	89AW
97-0401	GAC C-37A (Gulfstream V)	542	N642GA	89AW

97-0402	GAC C-37A (Gulfstream V)	571	N671GA	89AW	
97-1351	Lockheed Martin C-130J (L-382U-08J) Hercules II	5469		175Wg/MD ANG	
97-1352	Lockheed Martin C-130J (L-382U-08J) Hercules II	5470		175Wg/MD ANG	
97-1353	Lockheed Martin C-130J (L-382U-08J) Hercules II	5471		175Wg/MD ANG	
97-1354	Lockheed Martin C-130J (L-382U-08J) Hercules II	5472		175Wg/MD ANG	
97-1931	Lockheed Martin EC-130J (L-382U-09J) Hercules II	5477		193SOW	
97-5303	Lockheed Martin WC-130J (L-382U-07J) Hercules II	5473		403Wg	
97-5304	Lockheed Martin WC-130J (L-382U-07J) Hercules II	5474		403Wg	
97-5305	Lockheed Martin WC-130J (L-382U-07J) Hercules II	5475		403Wg	
97-5306	Lockheed Martin WC-130J (L-382U-07J) Hercules II	5476		403Wg	
98-0001	Boeing C-32A (757-2G4)	29025 / 783	N3519L	89AW	
98-0002	Boeing C-32A (757-2G4)	29026 / 787	N3519M	89AW	
98-0049	Boeing C-17A Globemaster III	P-49		62AW	
98-0050	Boeing C-17A Globemaster III	P-50		62AW	
98-0051	Boeing C-17A Globemaster III	P-51		62AW	
98-0052	Boeing C-17A Globemaster III	P-52		62AW	
98-0053	Boeing C-17A Globemaster III	P-53		62AW	
98-0054	Boeing C-17A Globemaster III	P-54		62AW	
98-0055	Boeing C-17A Globemaster III	P-55		62AW	
98-0056	Boeing C-17A Globemaster III	P-56		62AW	
98-0057	Boeing C-17A Globemaster III	P-57		62AW	
98-1355	Lockheed Martin C-130J (L-382U-16J) Hercules II	5491		175Wg	
98-1356	Lockheed Martin C-130J (L-382U-16J) Hercules II	5492		175Wg	
98-1357	Lockheed Martin C-130J (L-382U-16J) Hercules II	5493		175Wg	
98-1358	Lockheed Martin C-130J (L-382U-16J) Hercules II	5494		175Wg	
98-1932	Lockheed Martin EC-130J (L-382U-17J) Hercules II	5490		193SOW	
98-5307	Lockheed Martin WC-130J (L-382U-12J) Hercules II	5486		403Wg	
98-5308	Lockheed Martin WC-130J (L-382U-12J) Hercules II	5487		403Wg	
99-0003	Boeing C-32A (757-2G4)	29027 / 824		89AW	
99-0004	Boeing C-32A (757-2G4)	29028 / 829		89AW	
99-0058	Boeing C-17A Globemaster III	P-58		62AW	
99-0059	Boeing C-17A Globemaster III	P-59		62AW	
99-0060	Boeing C-17A Globemaster III	P-60		62AW	
99-0061	Boeing C-17A Globemaster III	P-61		62AW	
99-0062	Boeing C-17A Globemaster III	P-62		62AW	
99-0063	Boeing C-17A Globemaster III	P-63		62AW	
99-0064	Boeing C-17A Globemaster III	P-64		62AW	
99-0165	Boeing C-17A Globemaster III	P-65		62AW	
99-0166	Boeing C-17A Globemaster III	P-66		62AW	
99-0167	Boeing C-17A Globemaster III	P-67		62AW	
99-0168	Boeing C-17A Globemaster III	P-68		62AW	
99-0169	Boeing C-17A Globemaster III	P-69		62AW	
99-0170	Boeing C-17A Globemaster III	P-70		62AW	
99-0402	GAC C-37A (Gulfstream V)	571	N671GA	89AW	
99-0404	GAC C-37A (Gulfstream V)	590	N590GA	86AW	
99-0405	GAC C-37A (Gulfstream V)	596	N596GA		Operating as N596GA
99-1431	Lockheed Martin C-130J-30 (L-382V-30J) Hercules II	5517		143AW/RI ANG	
99-1432	Lockheed Martin C-130J-30 (L-382V-30J) Hercules II	5518		143AW/RI ANG	
99-1433	Lockheed Martin C-130J-30 (L-382V-30J) Hercules II	5519		143AW/RI ANG	
99-1933	Lockheed Martin EC-130J (L-382U-17J) Hercules II	5502		193SOW	
99-5309	Lockheed Martin WC-130J (L-382U-12J) Hercules II	5501		403Wg	
00-0001	Boeing YAL-1 (747-4G4)	30201 / 1238			On order
00-0171	Boeing C-17A Globemaster III	P-71		62AW	

00-0172	Boeing C-17A Globemaster III	P-72		62AW	
00-0173	Boeing C-17A Globemaster III	P-73		62AW	
00-0174	Boeing C-17A Globemaster III	P-74			
00-0175	Boeing C-17A Globemaster III	P-75			
00-0176	Boeing C-17A Globemaster III	P-76			
00-0177	Boeing C-17A Globemaster III	P-77			
00-0178	Boeing C-17A Globemaster III	P-78			
00-0179	Boeing C-17A Globemaster III	P-79			
00-0180	Boeing C-17A Globemaster III	P-80			
00-0181	Boeing C-17A Globemaster III	P-81			
00-0182	Boeing C-17A Globemaster III	P-82			
00-0183	Boeing C-17A Globemaster III	P-83			
00-0184	Boeing C-17A Globemaster III	P-84			
00-0185	Boeing C-17A Globemaster III	P-85			
-	Lockheed Martin EC-130J (L-382U-32J) Hercules II				
		5522		193SOW	
00-1934	Lockheed Martin EC-130J (L-382U-32J) Hercules II				
		5524		193SOW	
01-0028	GAC C-37A (Gulfstream V)	620	N535GA	310AS	
01-0029	GAC C-37A (Gulfstream V)	624	N624GA	310AS	
01-0030	GAC C-37A (Gulfstream V)				On order 2002
01-0086	Boeing C-17A Globemaster III	P-86			
01-0087	Boeing C-17A Globemaster III	P-87			
01-0088	Boeing C-17A Globemaster III	P-88			
01-0089	Boeing C-17A Globemaster III	P-89			
01-0090	Boeing C-17A Globemaster III	P-90			
01-0091	Boeing C-17A Globemaster III	P-91			
01-0092	Boeing C-17A Globemaster III	P-92			
01-0093	Boeing C-17A Globemaster III	P-93			
01-0094	Boeing C-17A Globemaster III	P-94			
01-0095	Boeing C-17A Globemaster III	P-95			
01-0096	Boeing C-17A Globemaster III	P-96			
01-0097	Boeing C-17A Globemaster III	P-97			
01-0098	Boeing C-17A Globemaster III	P-98			
01-0099	Boeing C-17A Globemaster III	P-99			
01-0100	Boeing C-17A Globemaster III	P-100			
-	Lockheed Martin C-130J-30 (L-382V-30J) Hercules II				
		5525		ANG	On order 2002
-	Lockheed Martin C-130J-30 (L-382V-30J) Hercules II				
		5526		ANG	On order 2002
02-0101	Boeing C-17A Globemaster III	P-101			
02-0102	Boeing C-17A Globemaster III	P-102			
02-0103	Boeing C-17A Globemaster III	P-103			
02-0104	Boeing C-17A Globemaster III	P-104			
02-0105	Boeing C-17A Globemaster III	P-105			
02-0106	Boeing C-17A Globemaster III	P-106			
02-0107	Boeing C-17A Globemaster III	P-107			
02-0108	Boeing C-17A Globemaster III	P-108			
02-0109	Boeing C-17A Globemaster III	P-109			
02-0110	Boeing C-17A Globemaster III	P-110			
02-0111	Boeing C-17A Globemaster III	P-111			
02-0112	Boeing C-17A Globemaster III	P-112			
02-0113	Boeing C-17A Globemaster III	P-113			
02-0114	Boeing C-17A Globemaster III	P-114			
02-0115	Boeing C-17A Globemaster III	P-115			
03-0116	Boeing C-17A Globemaster III	P-116			
03-0117	Boeing C-17A Globemaster III	P-117			
03-0118	Boeing C-17A Globemaster III	P-118			
03-0119	Boeing C-17A Globemaster III	P-119			
03-0120	Boeing C-17A Globemaster III	P-120			
86005	Boeing 707-300				
86008	Boeing 757-200				
25001	Boeing 757-23A	25494 / 611	N987AN		
N105TB	Grumman G-1159 Gulfstream II	31	N200CC		AFMCESC
N991L	Cessna OT-47B (Citation V Ultra)	560-0350	N51522	Aviation Development Corp	
N712L	Cessna OT-47B (Citation V Ultra)	560-0365	N7547P	Aviation Development Corp	
N163L	Cessna OT-47B (Citation V Ultra)	560-0374	N7728T	Aviation Development Corp	
N214L	Cessna OT-47B (Citation V Ultra)	560-0381	N2762J	Aviation Development Corp	
N615L	Cessna OT-47B (Citation V Ultra)	560-0386	N7274A	Aviation Development Corp	

EG&G Special Projects Inc

N654BA	Beech Super King Air 200C	BL-54	N6563C		
N661BA	Beech Super King Air 200C	BL-61	N6564C		
N662BA	Beech Super King Air 200C	BL-62	N6566C		
N20RC	Beech 1900C Airliner	UB-42	(N272HK)		
N27RC	Beech 1900C Airliner	UB-37	N7214K		
N5175J	Boeing CT-43A (737-200)	20689 / 334	72-0282 (USAF)	Cvtd T-43A	
N5176V	Boeing CT-43A (737-200)	20692 / 339	72-0285 (USAF)	Cvtd T-43A	
N5177C	Boeing CT-43A (737-200)	20693 / 340	72-0286 (USAF)	Cvtd T-43A	
N5294E	Boeing CT-43A (737-200)	20691 / 337	72-0284 (USAF)	Cvtd T-43A	
N5294M	Boeing CT-43A (737-200)	20694 / 343	72-0287 (USAF)	Cvtd T-43A	
N4529W	Boeing 737-275	20785 / 335	C-FPWB		

United States Navy - USN

UNITS/BASES

		tail code/notes	
VAW-77, 'Night Wolf', NAS Atlanta, GA	E-2C	AF, (Reserve CVW-20)	
VAW-78, 'Fighting Escargots', NAS Norfolk, VA	E-2C	AF, (Reserve CVW-20)	
VAW-112, 'Golden Hawks', NAS Point Mugu, CA	E-2C	Assigned to CVW-9	AEW
VAW-113, 'Black Hawks', NAS Point Mugu, CA	E-2C	Assigned to CVW-14	AEW
VAW-115, 'Sentinels', NAF Atsugi, Japan	E-2C	Assigned to CVW-5	AEW
VAW-116, 'Sun Kings', NAS Point Mugu, CA	E-2C	Assigned to CVW-2	AEW
VAW-117, 'Wallbangers', NAS Point Mugu, CA	E-2C	Assigned to CVW-11	AEW
VAW-120 (FRS), 'Greyhawks', NAS Norfolk, VA	E-2C, TE-2C, C-2A	AD	Training
VAW-121, 'Bluetails', NAS Norfolk, VA	E-2C	Assigned to CVW-7	AEW
VAW-123, 'Screwtops', NAS Norfolk, VA	E-2C	Assigned to CVW-1	AEW
VAW-124, ' Bear Aces', NAS Norfolk, VA	E-2C	Assigned to CVW-8	AEW
VAW-125, 'Tigertails', NAS Norfolk, VA	E-2C	Assigned to CVW-17	AEW
VAW-126, 'Seahawks', NAS Norfolk, VA	E-2C	Assigned to CVW-3	AEW
VP-1, 'Screaming Eagles', NAS Whidbey Island, WA	P-3C	YB	
VP-4, 'Skinny Dragons', MCAF Kaneohe Bay, HI	P-3C	YD	
VP-5, 'Mad Foxes', NAS Jacksonville, FL	P-3C	LA	
VP-8, 'Tigers', NAS Brunswick, ME	P-3C	LC	
VP-9, 'Golden Eagles', MCAF Kaneohe Bay, HI	P-3C	PD	
VP-10, 'Red Lancers', NAS Brunswick, ME	P-3C	LD	
VP-16, 'War Eagles', NAS Jacksonville, FL	P-3C	LF	
VP-26, 'Tridents', NAS Brunswick, ME	P-3C	LK	
VP-30 (FRS) 'Pro's Nest', NAS Jacksonville, FL	VP-3, P-3C, TP-3	LL	Training, VIP (CinCLANT)
VP-40, 'Fighting Marlins', NAS Whidbey Island, WA	P-3C	QE	
VP-45, 'Pelicans', NAS Jacksonville, FL	P-3C	LN	
VP-46, 'Gray Nights', NAS Whidbey Island, WA	P-3C	RC	
VP-47, 'Golden Swordsman', MCAF Kaneohe Bay, HI	P-3C	RD	
VP-62 (RPW), 'Broadarrows', NAS Jacksonville, FL	P-3C	LT	
VP-64 (RPW), 'Condors', NAS Willow Grove, PA	P-3C	LU	
VP-65 (RPW), 'Tridents', NAS Point Mugu, CA	P-3C	PG	
VP-66 (RPW), 'Liberty Bells', NAS Willow Grove, PA	P-3C	LV	
VP-69 (RPW), 'Totems', NAS Whidbey Island, WA	P-3C	PJ	
VP-92 (RPW), 'Minutemen', NAS Brunswick, ME	P-3C	LY	
VP-94 (RPW), 'Crawfish', NAS New Orleans, LA	P-3C	PZ	
VPU-1, 'Old Buzzards', NAS Brunswick, ME	P-3B, P-3C	OB	Special Projects
VPU-2, 'Wizards', MCAF Kaneohe Bay, HI	P-3C, UP-3A	SP	Special Projects
VQ-1, 'World Watchers', NAS Whidbey Island, WA	EP-3E, P-3C, UP-3	PR	SIGINT
VQ-2, 'Dons', NS Rota, Spain	EP-3E, P-3C	JQ	SIGINT
VQ-3, 'Ironmen', Tinker AFB, OK (det. Travis AFB, OK)	E-6A/B	TZ	Strategic Comms
VQ-4, 'Shadows', Tinker AFB, OK (det. NAS Pa River, MD)	E-6A/B	HL	Strategic Comms
VQ-11 (RPW), 'Bandits', NAS Brunswick, ME	P-3C, EP-3J	LP	Deactivated in 1999?
VR-1, 'Stalifters', NAF Washington, DC	C-20D	JK	VIP
VRC-30 (RW), 'Providers' NAS North Island, CA	C-2A, UC-12B	C-2A assigned to CVW as required	
VRC-40, 'Rawhides', NAS Norfolk, VA	C-2A	C-2A assigned to CVW as required	
VR-46, 'Peach Airliners', NAS Atlanta, GA	C-9B, DC-9	JS	
VR-48, 'Capital Skyliners', NAF Washington, DC	C-20G	JR	VIP
VR-51, 'Windjammers', MCAF Kanehoe Bay, HI	C-20G	RG	VIP
VR-52, 'Taskmasters', NAS Willow Grove, PA	DC-9	JT	
VR-53, 'Capital Express', NAF Washington, DC	C-130T	WV	
VR-54, 'Revelers', NAS New Orleans, LA	C-130T	CW	
VR-55, 'Bicentennial Minutemen', NAS Point Mugu, CA	C-130T	RU	
VR-56, 'Globemasters', NAS Norfolk, CA	C-9B	JU	
VR-57, 'Conquistadors', NAS North Island, CA	C-9B, DC-9	RX	
VR-58, 'Sun Seekers', NAS Jacksonville, FL	C-9B, (C-40A)	JV	
VR-59, 'Lone Star Express', NAS Ft.Worth JRB, TX	C-9B, DC-9, C-40A	RY	

VR-61, 'Islanders', NAS Whidbey Island, WA	DC-9	RS		
VR-62, 'Downeasters', NAS Brunswick, ME	C-130T	JW		
VS-21, 'Fighting Redtails', NAF Atsugi, Japan	S-3B		Assigned to CVW-5	ASW, AAR
VS-22, 'Checkmates', NAS Jacksonville, FL	S-3B		Assigned to CVW-3	ASW, AAR
VS-24, 'Scouts', NAS Jacksonville, FL	S-3B		Assigned to CVW-8	ASW, AAR
VS-29, 'Screaming Dragonfires', NAS North Island, CA	S-3B		Assigned to CVW-11	ASW, AAR
VS-30, 'Diamondcutters', NAS Jacksonville, FL	S-3B		Assigned to CVW-17	ASW, AAR
VS-31, 'Topcats', NAS Jacksonville, FL	S-3B		Assigned to CVW-7	ASW, AAR
VS-32, 'Maulers', NAS Jacksonville, FL	S-3B		Assigned to CVW-1	ASW, AAR
VS-33, 'Screwbirds', NAS North Island, CA	S-3B		Assigned to CVW-9	ASW, AAR
VS-35, 'Blue Wolves', NAS North Island, CA	S-3B		Assigned to CVW-14	ASW, AAR
VS-38, 'Red Griffins', NAS North Island, CA	S-3B		Assigned to CVW-2	ASW, AAR
VS-41 (FRS), 'Shamrocks', NAS North Island, CA	S-3B	NJ		Training
VT-31, 'Wise Owls', NAS Corpus Christi, TX	TC-12B	G		Training
VT-86, 'Sabre Hawks', NAS Pensacola, FL	T-39N	F		Training
VX-1, 'Pioneers', NAS Patuxent River, MD	P-3C	JA		Evaluation
VXE-6, 'Ice Pirates', NAS Point Mugu, CA	LC-130F/R	XD		Disestablished Mar99?
Admin Support Unit, Bahrain	UC-12B	8K		
CSCW-1, Offutt AFB, NB	E-6A/B		Drawn from VQ-3/4 as required	
FSD, NAS Patuxent River, MD	NP-3D	NRL		Evaluation
NAF Atsugi, Japan	UC-12F	8A		
NAF El Centro, CA	UC-12B	8N		
NAF Kadena, Okinawa, Japan	UC-12F	8H		
NAF Mildenhall, United Kingdom	UC-12M	8G		
NAF Misawa, Japan	UC-12F	8M		
NAF Washington, DC	UC-12B	7N		
NARC Santa Clara, CA	UC-12B	7Y		
NAS Atlanta, GA	UC-12B	7B		
NAS Barbers Point, HI (CinC Pacific)	UP-3A			
NAS Corpus Christi, TX	UC-12B	G		
NAS Fallon, NV	UC-12B	7H		
NAS Ft.Worth, TX	UC-12B	7D		
NAS Jacksonville, FL	UC-12B	7E		
NAS Keflavik, Iceland (CinC)	UP-3A			
NAS Key West, FL	UC-12B	7Q		
NAS Lemoore, CA	UC-12B	7S		
NAS New Orleans, LA	UC-12B	7X		
NAS Norfolk, VA	UC-12B/M	7C		Training, Liasion
NAS North Island, CA	UC-12B	7M		
NAS Patuxent River, MD	UC-12B	7A		
NAS Pensacola, FL	UC-12B	F		
NAS Sigonella, Sicily, Italy (CinC South)	UC-12M, VP-3A	8C		Liaision, VIP
NAS Whidbey Island, WA	UC-12B	7G		
NAS Willow Grove, PA	UC-12B	7W		
NFDS, 'Blue Angels', NAS Pensacola, FL	TC-130G		Support to F-18 team	
NFWATS, NAS Patuxent River, MD	Various			Evaluation
NS Guantanamo Bay, Cuba	UC-12B	8F		
NS Roosevelt Roads	RC-12M	8E		
NS Rota, Spain	UC-12M	8D		
NSA Mid-South/Memphis, TN	UC-12B	6M		
NSA Naples, Italy	UC-12M			
NTSU (FRS), Tinker AFB, OK	TC-18F			Training
NWTS China Lake, NAWS China Lake, CA	T-39D			Evaluation
NWTS Point Mugu, NAS Point Mugu, CA	NP-3D			Evaluation
Pacific Missile Range Facility, Barking Sands, HI	RC-12F			
USNTPS, NAS Patuxent River, MD	Various			Evaluation

Current Carrier Air Wing Disposition

US Atlantic Fleet

CVW-1, USS Theodore Roosevelt (CVN-71), Norfolk, VA	AB
CVW-3, USS Harry S Truman (CVN-75), Norfolk, VA	AC
CVW-7, USS John F Kennedy (CV-67), Mayport, FL	AG
CVW-8, USS Enterprise (CVN-65), Norfolk, VA	AJ
CVW-17, USS George Washington (CVN-73), Norfolk, VA	AA
none , USS Dwight D Eisenhower (CVN-69), Norfolk, VA	
none , USS Nimitz (CVN-68), on overhaul at Newport News, VA	

US Pacific Fleet

CVW-2, USS Constellation (CV-64), North Island, CA	NE
CVW-5, USS Kitty Hawk (CV-63), Yokosuka, Japan	NF
CVW-9, USS John C Stennis (CVN-74), North Island, CA	NG
CVW-11, USS Carl Vinson (CVN-70), Bremerton, WA	NH
CVW-14, USS Abraham Lincoln (CVN-72), Everett, WA	NK
none , USS Ronald Reagan (CVN-76), to replace CV-64 in 2002/3	

PLANS	21 new Hawkeye 2000s due between November 2001 and 2006. A retrofit programme on 54 earlier E-2s is being considered, but more new aircraft may be bought instead.		

One C-37A has been ordered for July 2001 delivery.

Further C-40A (737-700) orders are planned under the UFEAR (Unique Fleet Essential Airlift Replacement) programme.

Serial	Type	No.	Unit/Disposition
144670 / 30	DeHavilland Canada NU-1B (DHC-3)		USNTPS
148147	Grumman C-2A Greyhound	1	
148148 / RW-30	Grumman C-2A Greyhound	2	Std AMARC [1C005]
148883	Lockheed NP-3D (L-185) Orion	5001	Std Patuxent River
148887 / PR-33	Lockheed EP-3E (L-185) Orion	5005	Std AMARC [2P159]
148888	Lockheed EP-3E (L-185) Orion	5006	NADEP Alameda
148889	Lockheed UP-3A (L-185) Orion	5007	VPU-2 NFATS
149670	Lockheed RP-3A (L-185) Orion	5011	Std AMARC [2P147]
149671	Lockheed EP-3E (L-185) Orion	5012	Std China Lake NAWC, CA
149673 / LL-25	Lockheed UP-3A (L-185) Orion	5014	Std AMARC [2P078]
149674	Lockheed NP-3D (L-185) Orion	5015	NRL
149675	Lockheed VP-3A (L-185) Orion	5016	CINCPAC
149676	Lockheed VP-3A (L-185) Orion	5017	VP-30
149790 / JL-02	Lockheed C-130F (L-282B-3B) Hercules	3645	Std AMARC [2G020]
149797 / JL-00	Lockheed C-130F (L-282B-3B) Hercules	3666	Std AMARC [2G019]
149806	Lockheed KC-130F (L-282B-3B) Hercules	3703	NAWC-AD
150495	Lockheed UP-3A (L-185) Orion	5021	Keflavik *'Valkyrja'*
150496	Lockheed VP-3A (L-185) Orion	5022	VP-30 CinCAFSE/CinCUSNFE
150499 / 337	Lockheed NP-3D (L-185) Orion	5025	NWTSPM
150511	Lockheed VP-3A (L-185) Orion	5037	VP-30 CinCLANT
150515	Lockheed VP-3A (L-185) Orion	5041	VP-30 CinCAFSE
150517 / LL-66	Lockheed P-3A (L-185) Orion	5043	VP-30
			GI NADEP Jacksonville, FL
150519	Lockheed UP-3A (L-185) Orion	5045	Std AMARC [2P088]
150521 / 341	Lockheed NP-3D (L-185) Orion	5047	NWTSPM
150522 / 340	Lockheed NP-3D (L-185) Orion	5048	NWTSPM
150524 / 335	Lockheed NP-3D (L-185) Orion	5050	NWTSPM
150525 / 336	Lockheed NP-3D (L-185) Orion	5051	NWTSPM
150526 / 01	Lockheed UP-3A (L-185) Orion	5052	VQ-1
150527 / JB-04	Lockheed UP-3A (L-185) Orion	5053	Std AMARC [2P041]
150528 / JB-05	Lockheed UP-3A (L-185) Orion	5054	Std AMARC [2P043]
150538	Grumman E-2B Hawkeye		Std AMARC [2E019]
150542	North American T-39D Sabreliner	277-1	Std NAWS China Lake
150543	North American T-39D Sabreliner	277-2	Std AMARC [7T027]
150544 / F-18	North American T-39D Sabreliner	277-3	Std AMARC [7T006]
150546 / F-201	North American T-39D Sabreliner	277-5	Std AMARC [7T014]
150547 / F-211	North American T-39D Sabreliner	277-6	Std AMARC [7T021]
150548 / F-10	North American T-39D Sabreliner	277-7	Std AMARC [7T008]
150604	Lockheed P-3A (L-185) Orion	5056	Std AMARC [2P021]
150608 / PJ-1	Lockheed P-3A (L-185) Orion	5060	Std AMARC [2P006]
150969	North American T-39D Sabreliner	285-1	Std AMARC [7T026]
150972	North American T-39D Sabreliner	285-4	Std Pensacola NAS, FL
150973 / F-203	North American T-39D Sabreliner	285-5	Std AMARC [7T013]
150974 / F-204	North American T-39D Sabreliner	285-6	Std AMARC [7T015]
150976 / F-205	North American T-39D Sabreliner	285-8	Std AMARC [7T016]
150977	North American T-39D Sabreliner	285-9	Std Pensacola NAS, FL
150978 / F-13	North American T-39D Sabreliner	285-10	Std AMARC [7T009]
150979 / F-206	North American T-39D Sabreliner	285-11	Std AMARC [7T017]
150984 / F-208	North American T-39D Sabreliner	285-16	Std AMARC [7T010]
150988 / F-209	North American T-39D Sabreliner	285-20	Std AMARC [7T005]
150989	North American T-39D Sabreliner	285-21	Std NAWS China Lake
150990 / F-213	North American T-39D Sabreliner	285-22	Std AMARC [7T024]
150991 / F-17	North American T-39D Sabreliner	285-23	Std AMARC [7T003]
150992	North American T-39D Sabreliner	285-24	NWTS Weapons test-bed
151336 / F-214	North American T-39D Sabreliner	285-25	Std AMARC [7T025]
151337	North American T-39D Sabreliner	285-26	Std NAS Pensacola
151341 / F-217	North American T-39D Sabreliner	285-30	Std AMARC [7T019]
151342 / F-218	North American T-39D Sabreliner	285-31	Std AMARC [TG097]
151352 / LL-21	Lockheed TP-3A (L-185) Orion	5065	Std AMARC [2P180]
151353	Lockheed UP-3A (L-185) Orion	5066	Std AMARC [2P060]
151356	Lockheed P-3A (L-185) Orion	5069	Std AMARC [2P025]
151357 / LL-26	Lockheed TP-3A (L-185) Orion	5070	Std AMARC [2P187]
151358	Lockheed P-3A (L-185) Orion	5071	Std AMARC [2P020]
151360	Lockheed P-3A (L-185) Orion	5073	Std AMARC [2P059]
151368	Lockheed UP-3A (L-185) Orion	5081	Std AMARC [2P073]
151371 / LL-23	Lockheed TP-3A (L-185) Orion	5084	Std AMARC [2P179]
151376 / LL-22	Lockheed TP-3A (L185) Orion	5089	Std AMARC [2P163]
151378	Lockheed P-3A (L-185) Orion	5091	Std AMARC [2P028]

Serial / Code	Type	C/N	Status
151379 / LL-25	Lockheed TP-3A (L-185) Orion	5092	Std AMARC [2P183]
151383	Lockheed P-3A (L-185) Orion	5096	Std AMARC [2P023]
151386	Lockheed P-3A (L-185) Orion	5099	Std AMARC [2P010]
151388	Lockheed P-3A (L-185) Orion	5101	Std AMARC [2P018]
151393	Lockheed P-3A (L-185) Orion	5106	Std AMARC [2P026]
151396	Lockheed P-3A (L-185) Orion	5109	Std AMARC [2P007]
151702 / NJ-324	Grumman E-2B Hawkeye		Std AMARC [2E012]
151706 / AF-010	Grumman E-2B Hawkeye		Std AMARC [2E010]
151717 / NJ-326	Grumman E-2B Hawkeye		Std AMARC [2E013]
151720	Grumman E-2B Hawkeye		Std AMARC [2E017]
151722 / AF-013	Grumman E-2B Hawkeye		Std AMARC [2E007]
151891	Lockheed TC-130G (L-382-4B) Hercules	3878	Blue Angels
152140	Lockheed P-3A (L-185) Orion	5110	Std AMARC [2P051]
152146	Lockheed P-3A (L-185) Orion	5116	Std AMARC [2P046]
152147	Lockheed P-3A (L-185) Orion	5117	Std AMARC [2P089]
152148 / LV-11	Lockheed P-3A (L-185) Orion	5118	Std AMARC [2P029]
152150 / 150	Lockheed NP-3D (L-185) Orion	5120	NFATS
152154 / LU-7	Lockheed P-3A (L-185) Orion	5124	Std AMARC [2P031]
152157	Lockheed P-3A (L-185) Orion	5127	Std AMARC [2P052]
152162 / LV-7	Lockheed P-3A (L-185) Orion	5132	Std AMARC [2P053]
152167	Lockheed P-3A (L-185) Orion	5137	Std AMARC [2P039]
152168 / PJ-12	Lockheed P-3A (L-185) Orion	5138	Std AMARC [2P034]
152173	Lockheed P-3A (L-185) Orion	5143	Std AMARC [2P038]
152174	Lockheed P-3A (L-185) Orion	5144	Std AMARC [2P048]
152175	Lockheed P-3A (L-185) Orion	5145	Std AMARC [2P033]
152176	Lockheed P-3A (L-185) Orion	5146	Std AMARC [2P044]
152179	Lockheed UP-3A (L-185) Orion	5149	Std AMARC [2P009]
152180	Lockheed P-3A (L-185) Orion	5150	Std AMARC [2P037]
152185	Lockheed P-3A (L-185) Orion	5155	Std AMARC [2P057]
152186	Lockheed P-3A (L-185) Orion	5156	Std AMARC [2P032]
152187	Lockheed P-3A (L-185) Orion	5157	Std AMARC [2P035]
152719	Lockheed EP-3J (L-185) Orion	5159	Std AMARC [2P188]
152721	Lockheed P-3B LW (L-185) Orion	5161	Std AMARC [2P069]
152723	Lockheed P-3B LW (L-185) Orion	5163	Std AMARC [2P063]
152725 / 5	Lockheed P-3B LW (L-185) Orion	5165	Std AMARC [2P099]
152726	Lockheed P-3B LW (L-185) Orion	5166	Std AMARC [2P091]
152727 / PR-43	Lockheed UP-3B (L-185) Orion	5167	Std AMARC [2P173]
152728	Lockheed P-3B LW (L-185) Orion	5168	Std AMARC [2P185]
152730	Lockheed P-3B LW (L-185) Orion	5170	Std AMARC [2P083]
152734	Lockheed P-3B LW (L-185) Orion	5174	Std AMARC [2P068]
152736	Lockheed P-3B LW (L-185) Orion	5176	Std AMARC [2P066]
152737	Lockheed P-3B LW (L-185) Orion	5177	Std AMARC [2P080]
152738	Lockheed RP-3D (L-185) Orion	5178	Std AMARC [2P110]
152739	Lockheed NP-3B (L-185) Orion	5179	NAWC-23
152740	Lockheed UP-3B (L-185) Orion	5180	Std AMARC [2P133]
152742	Lockheed P-3B LW (L-185) Orion	5182	Std AMARC [2P125]
152743 / PL-2	Lockheed P-3B LW (L-185) Orion	5183	Std AMARC [2P079]
152750	Lockheed P-3B LW (L-185) Orion	5191	Std AMARC [2P086]
152751	Lockheed P-3B LW (L-185) Orion	5193	Std AMARC [2P117]
152753	Lockheed EP-3B (L-185) Orion	5195	Std AMARC [2P084]
152754	Lockheed P-3B LW (L-185) Orion	5196	Std AMARC [2P118]
152755	Lockheed UP-3B (L-185) Orion	5197	Std AMARC [2P100]
152756	Lockheed P-3B LW (L-185) Orion	5198	Std AMARC [2P064]
152758 / 3	Lockheed P-3B LW (L-185) Orion	5201	Std AMARC [2P094]
152759	Lockheed P-3B LW (L-185) Orion	5203	Std AMARC [2P134]
152762	Lockheed P-3B LW (L-185) Orion	5206	Std AMARC [2P071]
152786 / RW-31	Grumman C-2A Greyhound	3	Std AMARC [1C002]
152787	Grumman C-2A Greyhound	4	
152788	Grumman C-2A Greyhound	5	
152790	Grumman C-2A Greyhound	7	Std AMARC [1C001]
152791 / RW-32	Grumman C-2A Greyhound	8	Std AMARC [1C004]
152794 / RW-33	Grumman C-2A Greyhound	11	Std AMARC [1C003]
153416 / LZ-1	Lockheed P-3B LW (L-185) Orion	5213	Std AMARC [2P146]
153417	Lockheed P-3B LW (L-185) Orion	5214	Std AMARC [2P067]
153418	Lockheed P-3B LW (L-185) Orion	5215	Std AMARC [2P036]
153420	Lockheed P-3B LW (L-185) Orion	5217	Std AMARC [2P121]
153421	Lockheed P-3B LW (L-185) Orion	5218	Std AMARC [2P122]
153422	Lockheed P-3B LW (L-185) Orion	5219	Std AMARC [2P114]
153426 / LH-11	Lockheed P-3B LW (L-185) Orion	5223	Std AMARC [2P085]
153430	Lockheed P-3B LW (L-185) Orion	5227	Std AMARC [2P087]
153432	Lockheed P-3B LW (L-185) Orion	5229	Std AMARC [2P062]
153433	Lockheed UP-3B (L-185) Orion	5230	Std AMARC [2P189]
153435	Lockheed P-3B LW (L-185) Orion	5232	Std AMARC [2P123]
153436	Lockheed P-3B LW (L-185) Orion	5233	Std AMARC [2P142]

15343⁷	Lockheed P-3B LW (L-185) Orion	5234	Std AMARC [2P097]
15344₂ / 442	Lockheed NP-3D (L-185) Orion	5239	NRL
15344₃ / 443	Lockheed NP-3D (L-185) Orion	5500	USNTPS
15344₈ / PL-67	Lockheed P-3B HW (L-185) Orion	5244	Std AMARC [2P132]
15344₉ / LX-90	Lockheed P-3B HW (L-185) Orion	5245	Std AMARC [2P139]
15345₀	Lockheed EP-3B (L-185) Orion	5246	VPU-1
15345	Lockheed P-3B HW (L-185) Orion	5247	Std AMARC [2P115]
15345₃	Lockheed P-3B HW (L-185) Orion	5249	Std AMARC [2P131]
15345₅ / LX-2	Lockheed P-3B HW (L-185) Orion	5251	Std AMARC [2P138]
15345₆	Lockheed P-3B HW (L-185) Orion	5252	Std AMARC [2P155]
15345⁷ / LS-5	Lockheed P-3B HW (L-185) Orion	5253	Std AMARC [2P143]
15345₈	Lockheed P-3B HW (L-185) Orion	5254	Std AMARC [2P156]
15457⁷	Lockheed EP-3B (L-185) Orion	5258	VPU-1
154574 / LS-1	Lockheed P-3B HW (L-185) Orion	5259	Std AMARC [2P137]
154579	Lockheed P-3B HW (L-185) Orion	5260	Std AMARC [2P154]
15458₀	Lockheed P-3B HW (L-185) Orion	5261	Std AMARC [2P127]
15458₂	Lockheed P-3B HW (L-185) Orion	5263	Std AMARC [2P106]
15458₄	Lockheed P-3B HW (L-185) Orion	5265	Std AMARC [2P098]
15458₆	Lockheed P-3B HW (L-185) Orion	5267	Std AMARC [2P108]
15458⁷	Lockheed NP-3D (L-185) Orion	5268	NRL
15458₈	Lockheed P-3B HW (L-185) Orion	5269	Std AMARC [2P157]
15458₉	Lockheed NP-3D (L-185) Orion	5270	NRL
15459₀ / LU-00	Lockheed P-3B HW (L-185) Orion	5271	Std AMARC [2P158]
15459₂ / LV-00	Lockheed P-3B HW (L-185) Orion	5273	Std AMARC [2P105]
15459₃ / LU-03	Lockheed P-3B HW (L-185) Orion	5274	Std AMARC [2P145]
15459₄	Lockheed P-3B HW (L-185) Orion	5275	Std AMARC [2P148]
15459₅	Lockheed P-3B HW (L-185) Orion	5276	Std AMARC [2P150]
15459⁷	Lockheed P-3B HW (L-185) Orion	5278	Std AMARC [2P153]
15459₈	Lockheed P-3B HW (L-185) Orion	5279	Std AMARC [2P151]
15459₉	Lockheed P-3B HW (L-185) Orion	5280	Std AMARC [2P152]
15460₀	Lockheed RP-3D (L-185) Orion	5281	Std AMARC [2P102]
15460₁ / LZ-03	Lockheed P-3B HW (L-185) Orion	5282	Std AMARC [2P140]
15460₂	Lockheed P-3B HW (L-185) Orion	5283	Std AMARC [2P129]
15460₃	Lockheed P-3B HW (L-185) Orion	5284	Std AMARC [2P119]
15460₄ / PL-1	Lockheed P-3B HW (L-185) Orion	5285	Std AMARC [2P128]
15512 / RG-422	Grumman C-2A Greyhound	16	VRC-50
15512₄	Grumman C-2A Greyhound	19	NADEP North Island
15572₂	Grumman TC-4C Academe (G-159)	176	Std NMNA
15572₄ / AD-576	Grumman TC-4C Academe (G-159)	180	Std AMARC [4G002]
15572₅ / NJ-852	Grumman TC-4C Academe (G-159)	182	Std AMARC [4G007]
15572₆ / NJ-851	Grumman TC-4C Academe (G-159)	183	Std AMARC [4G006]
15572₇ / AD-575	Grumman TC-4C Academe (G-159)	184	Std AMARC [4G004]
15572₈ / AD-574	Grumman TC-4C Academe (G-159)	185	Std AMARC [4G003]
15572₉ / AD-577	Grumman TC-4C Academe (G-159)	186	Std AMARC [4G001]
15573₀ / NJ-853	Grumman TC-4C Academe (G-159)	187	Std AMARC [4G005]
15650₇ / PR-31	Lockheed EP-3E (L-285A) Orion	5501	VQ-1 'Aries II'
15650₉	Lockheed P-3C (L-285A) Orion	5503	VP-8
15651₀ / LL-510	Lockheed P-3C-IIIR (L-285A) Orion	5504	VP-30
15651₁ / PR-32	Lockheed EP-3E (L-285A) Orion	5505	Lockheed, Marietta 'Aries II'
15651₂	Lockheed P-3C (L-285A) Orion	5506	Std AMARC [2P169]
15651₃ / LE-513	Lockheed P-3C (L-285A) Orion	5507	Std AMARC [2P170]
15651₄ / PR-33	Lockheed EP-3E (L-285A) Orion	5508	VQ-1 'Aries II'
15651₅ / LY-515	Lockheed P-3C CDU (L-285A) Orion	5509	VP-92
15651₆ / LL-38	Lockheed P-3C-IIIR (L-285A) Orion	5510	VP-30
15651₇ / PR-34	Lockheed EP-3E (L-285A) Orion	5511	VQ-1 'Aries II'
15651₈ / LL-518	Lockheed P-3C-IIIR (L-285A) Orion	5512	VP-30
15651₉ / 21	Lockheed EP-3E (L-285A) Orion	5513	VQ-2 'Aries II'
15652₀ / 10	Lockheed P-3C (L-285A) Orion	5514	VQ-2
15652₁ / LY-521	Lockheed P-3C-IIIR (L-285A) Orion	5515	VP-65
15652₂ / LL-522	Lockheed P-3C-IIIR (L-285A) Orion	5516	VP-30
15652₂ / LL-523	Lockheed P-3C-IIIR (L-285A) Orion	5517	VP-30
15652₄	Lockheed P-3C (L-285A) Orion	5518	Std AMARC [2P177]
15652₅ / 11	Lockheed P-3C (L-285A) Orion	5519	VQ-2
15652₆ / PD-00	Lockheed P-3C (L-285A) Orion	5520	Std AMARC [2P172]
15652₇ / LT-527	Lockheed P-3C-IIIR (L-285A) Orion	5521	VP-62
15652₈ / PR-36	Lockheed EP-3E (L-285A) Orion	5522	VQ-1 'Aries II'
15652₉ / 24	Lockheed EP-3E (L-285A) Orion	5523	VQ-2 'Aries II'
15653₀ / LL-530	Lockheed P-3C-IIIR (L-285A) Orion	5524	VP-30
157310 / LL-310	Lockheed P-3C-IIIR (L-285A) Orion	5525	VP-30
157311 / 311	Lockheed P-3C CDU (L-285A) Orion	5526	VP-45
157312 / LN-312	Lockheed P-3C-IIIR (L-285A) Orion	5527	VP-45
157313 / LC-313	Lockheed P-3C-IIIR (L-285A) Orion	5528	VP-8
157314 / LD-314	Lockheed P-3C CDU (L-285A) Orion	5529	VP-10
157315 / LD-315	Lockheed P-3C-IIIR (L-285A) Orion	5530	VP-10

157316 / 23	Lockheed EP-3E (L-285A) Orion	5531		VQ-2	'Aries II'
157317 / YB-317	Lockheed P-3C-IIIR (L-285A) Orion	5532		VP-1	
157318 / PR-35	Lockheed EP-3E (L-285A) Orion	5533		VQ-1	'Aries II'
157319 / LD-319	Lockheed P-3C AIP (L-285A) Orion	5534		VP-10	
157321 / LK-321	Lockheed P-3C-IIIR (L-285A) Orion	5536		VP-26	
157322 / YB-322	Lockheed P-3C-IIIR (L-285A) Orion	5537		VP-1	
157323	Lockheed P-3C-IIIR (L-285A) Orion	5538		VP-65	
157324 / PD-324	Lockheed P-3C (L-285A) Orion	5539		VP-9	
157325 / 25	Lockheed EP-3E (L-285A) Orion	5540		VQ-2	'Aries II'
157326 / 22	Lockheed EP-3E (L-285A) Orion	5541		VQ-2	'Aries II'
157327 / LD-327	Lockheed P-3C (L-285A) Orion	5542		VP-10	
157328 / LL-328	Lockheed P-3C-IIIR (L-285A) Orion	5543		VP-30	
157329 / 329	Lockheed P-3C-IIIR (L-285A) Orion	5544		VP-47	
157330 / YB-330	Lockheed P-3C-IIIR (L-285A) Orion	5545		VP-1	
157331 / LL-47	Lockheed P-3C-IIIR (L-285A) Orion	5546		VP-30	
157353 / RW-353	North American CT-39E Sabreliner	282-84			Std AMARC [ND001]
157992	Lockheed YS-3A Viking	3001			Std NATC Lakehurst
157994	Lockheed US-3A Viking	3003			Std AMARC [2S031]
157995	Lockheed US-3A Viking	3004			Std AMARC [2S034]
157997	Lockheed US-3A Viking	3006			Std AMARC [2S033]
158204 / 204	Lockheed NP-3C (L-285A) Orion	5548		NFATS	
158205 / YB-205	Lockheed P-3C-IIIR (L-285A) Orion	5549		VP-1	
158206 / JA-03	Lockheed P-3C (L-285A) Orion	5550		VX-1	
158207 / LC-207	Lockheed P-3C-IIIR (L-285A) Orion	5552		VP-26	
158208 / RD-208	Lockheed P-3C-IIIR (L-285A) Orion	5553		VP-47	
158209 / YD-209	Lockheed P-3C-IIIR (L-285A) Orion	5554		VP-4	
158210 / LD-210	Lockheed P-3C AIP (L-285A) Orion	5555		VP-10	
158211 / 211	Lockheed P-3C-IIIR (L-285A) Orion	5556		VP-1	
158212 / RD-212	Lockheed P-3C-IIIR (L-285A) Orion	5557		VP-47	
158214 / LL-214	Lockheed P-3C-IIIR (L-285A) Orion	5559		VP-30	
158215 / YD-215	Lockheed P-3C AIP (L-285A) Orion	5560		VP-4	
158216	Lockheed P-3C (L-285A) Orion	5561			
158218 / RD-218	Lockheed P-3C-IIIR (L-285A) Orion	5563		VP-47	
158219 / LN-219	Lockheed P-3C-IIIR (L-285A) Orion	5564		VP-45	
158220 / YD-220	Lockheed P-3C-IIIR (L-285A) Orion	5565		VP-4	
158221 / RC-221	Lockheed P-3C-IIIR (L-285A) Orion	5566		VP-46	
158222 / QE-222	Lockheed P-3C AIP (L-285A) Orion	5567		VP-40	
158223 / 223	Lockheed P-3C-IIIR (L-285A) Orion	5568		VP-4	
158224 / LD-224	Lockheed P-3C AIP (L-285A) Orion	5569		VP-10	
158225 / 225	Lockheed P-3C AIP (L-285A) Orion	5570		VP-9	
158226 / 226	Lockheed P-3C-IIIR (L-285A) Orion	5571		VP-47	
158227 / 227	Lockheed NP-3D (L-285A) Orion	5551		NRL	
158228	Lockheed DC-130A (L-182-1A) Hercules	3048	55-0021 (USAF)		Std AMARC [2G003]
158383	North American CT-39E Sabreliner	282-96	N4705N	VRC-40	
158563 / LL-563	Lockheed P-3C AIP (L-285A) Orion	5572		VP-30	
158564 / LK-564	Lockheed P-3C-IIIR (L-285A) Orion	5573		VP-26	
158565 / LD-565	Lockheed P-3C-IIIR (L-285A) Orion	5574		VP-10	
158566 / LN-566	Lockheed P-3C-IIIR (L-285A) Orion	5575		VP-45	
158567 / LF-567	Lockheed P-3C-IIIR (L-285A) Orion	5576		VP-16	
158568 / LC-568	Lockheed P-3C (L-285A) Orion	5577		VP-8	
158569 / 569	Lockheed P-3C CDU (L-285A) Orion	5578		VP-10	
158570	Lockheed P-3C-IIIR (L-285A) Orion	5579		VX-1	
158571	Lockheed P-3C AIP (L-285A) Orion	5580		VP-8	
158572 / LA-572	Lockheed P-3C-IIIR (L-285A) Orion	5581		VP-5	
158573 / LD-573	Lockheed P-3C-IIIR (L-285A) Orion	5582		VP-8	
158574	Lockheed P-3C-IIIR (L-285A) Orion	5583		NASC-FS	
158640 / AG-600	Grumman E-2C Hawkeye	A52-3			Std AMARC [2E031]
158645	Grumman E-2C Hawkeye	A52-8			Std AMARC [2E024]
158647	Grumman E-2C Hawkeye	A52-10			Std AMARC [2E025]
158843	North American CT-39G Sabreliner	306-52			Std AMARC [7T031]
158844 / F-19	North American T-39G Sabreliner	306-55	N5419	TW-6	Std AMARC [7T034]
158861 / AA-706	Lockheed S-3B Viking	3009		VS-30	
158862 / NH-722	Lockheed ES-3A Viking	3010		VQ-5	
158863 / NF-707	Lockheed S-3B Viking	3011		VS-21	
158864 / AB-701	Lockheed S-3B Viking	3012		VS-32	
158865 / AC-703	Lockheed S-3B Viking	3013		VS-22	
158866 / AJ-702	Lockheed S-3B Viking	3014		VS-24	
158867 / AJ-704	Lockheed S-3B Viking	3015		VS-24	
158868	Lockheed US-3A Viking	3016			Std AMARC [2S032]
158869	Lockheed S-3A Viking	3017			Std AMARC [2S026]
158870 / NF-706	Lockheed S-3B Viking	3018		VS-21	
158871 / NH-704	Lockheed S-3B Viking	3019		VS-29	
158872 / NF-700	Lockheed S-3B Viking	3020		VS-21	
158873 / AJ-700	Lockheed S-3B Viking	3021		VS-24	

1589̄2	Lockheed P-3C-III (L-285A) Orion	5584	NFATS	
1589̄3 / QE-913	Lockheed P-3C-IIIR (L-285A) Orion	5585	VP-40	
1589̄4 / RC-914	Lockheed P-3C-IIIR (L-285A) Orion	5586	VP-46	
1589̄5 / 915	Lockheed P-3C-IIIR (L-285A) Orion	5587	VP-40	
158916 / LL-916	Lockheed P-3C-IIIR (L-285A) Orion	5588	VP-30	
158917 / LC-917	Lockheed P-3C-IIIR (L-285A) Orion	5589	VP-8	
158918 / YD-918	Lockheed P-3C-IIIR (L-285A) Orion	5590	VP-47	
158919 / LN-919	Lockheed P-3C AIP (L-285A) Orion	5591	VP-45	
158920 / LN-920	Lockheed P-3C-IIIR (L-285A) Orion	5592	VP-45	
158921 / YD-921	Lockheed P-3C-IIIR (L-285A) Orion	5593	VP-47	
158922 / RD-922	Lockheed P-3C AIP (L-285A) Orion	5594	VP-47	
158923 / 923	Lockheed P-3C-IIIR (L-285A) Orion	5595	VP-4	
158924 / LN-924	Lockheed P-3C-IIIR (L-285A) Orion	5596	VP-45	
158925 / LD-925	Lockheed P-3C-IIIR (L-285A) Orion	5597	VP-10	
158926 / LD-926	Lockheed P-3C-IIIR (L-285A) Orion	5598	VP-10	
158927 / 927	Lockheed P-3C-IIIR (L-285A) Orion	5599	VP-5	
158928 / LA-928	Lockheed P-3C-IIIR (L-285A) Orion	5600		China Lake
158929 / LD-929	Lockheed P-3C-IIIR (L-285A) Orion	5601	VP-10	
158931 / 931	Lockheed P-3C CDU (L-285A) Orion	5603	VP-16	
158932 / 932	Lockheed P-3C-IIIR (L-285A) Orion	5604	VP-16	
158933 / LN-933	Lockheed P-3C CDU (L-285A) Orion	5605	VP-16	
158934 / 934	Lockheed P-3C AIP (L-285A) Orion	5606	VP-1	
158935 / LL-43	Lockheed P-3C AIP (L-285A) Orion	5607	VP-30	
159106	Grumman E-2C Hawkeye	A52-13		Std AMARC [2E022]
159111	Grumman E-2C Hawkeye	A52-18		Std NADEP North Island
159112 / 603	Grumman E-2C Hawkeye	A52-19	3503 (USCG)	Std NAS Norfolk, bu?
159113 / RX	Douglas C-9B Skytrain II	47577 / 686	VR-57	
159114 / JS	Douglas C-9B Skytrain II	47584 / 696	VR-46	
159115 / RX	Douglas C-9B Skytrain II	47587 / 700	VR-57	
159116 / RX	Douglas C-9B Skytrain II	47580 / 704	VR-57	
159117 / JU	Douglas C-9B Skytrain II	47581 / 692	VR-56	
159118 / JU	Douglas C-9B Skytrain II	47585 / 698	VR-56	
159119 / JU	Douglas C-9B Skytrain II	47578 / 702	VR-56	
159120 / JU	Douglas C-9B Skytrain II	47586 / 707	VR-56	
159318 / LA-318	Lockheed P-3C AIP (L-285A) Orion	5608	VP-5	
159319 / LA-319	Lockheed P-3C-IIIR (L-285A) Orion	5609	VP-5	
159320 / 320	Lockheed P-3C AIP (L-285A) Orion	5610	VP-45	
159321 / 321	Lockheed P-3C-IIIR (L-285A) Orion	5611	VP-40	
159322 / LN-322	Lockheed P-3C AIP (L-285A) Orion	5612	VP-45	
159323 / RC-323	Lockheed P-3C AIP (L-285A) Orion	5613	VP-46	
159324 / YB-324	Lockheed P-3C-IIIR (L-285A) Orion	5614	VP-1	
159326 / PD-326	Lockheed P-3C AIP (L-285A) Orion	5616	VP-9	
159327 / PD-327	Lockheed P-3C-IIIR (L-285A) Orion	5617	VP-9	
159328 / RC-328	Lockheed P-3C-IIIR (L-285A) Orion	5618	VP-46	
159329 / RC-329	Lockheed P-3C AIP (L-285A) Orion	5619	VP-46	
159362 / F-21	North American CT-39G Sabreliner	306-66	VT-86	Std AMARC [7T032]
159363	North American CT-39G Sabreliner	306-67		Std Edwards AFB, CA
159364 / F-25	North American CT-39G Sabreliner	306-69	TW-6	
159387 / NH-700	Lockheed S-3B Viking	3023	VS-29	
159388 / NJ-720	Lockheed S-3B Viking	3024	VS-41	
159389 / AB-706	Lockheed S-3B Viking	3025	VS-32	
159390 / AA-703	Lockheed S-3B Viking	3026	VS-30	
159391 / AC-767	Lockheed ES-3A Viking	3027	VQ-6	
159392 / NE-706	Lockheed S-3B Viking	3028	VS-38	
159393 / SS-724	Lockheed ES-3A Viking	3029	VQ-5	
159394	Lockheed ES-3A Viking	3030		Std AMARC [2S037]
159395	Lockheed S-3A Viking	3031		Std AMARC [2S027]
159396	Lockheed S-3A Viking	3032		Std AMARC [2S030]
159397 / NF-726	Lockheed ES-3A Viking	3033	VQ-5	
159398 / NH-707	Lockheed S-3B Viking	3035	VS-29	
159400	Lockheed ES-3A Viking	3036		Std AMARC [2S040]
159401	Lockheed ES-3A Viking	3037		Std AMARC [2S036]
159402 / AC-705	Lockheed S-3B Viking	3038	VS-22	
159403 / SS-720	Lockheed ES-3A Viking	3039	VQ-5	
159404 / NK-727	Lockheed ES-3A Viking	3040	VS-35	
159405 / SS-725	Lockheed ES-3A Viking	3041	VQ-5	
159407 / NJ-742	Lockheed S-3B Viking	3043	VS-41	
159409 / NJ-720	Lockheed S-3B Viking	3045	VS-41	
159410	Lockheed S-3A Viking	3046		Std AMARC [2S019]
159413 / NF-700	Lockheed S-3B Viking	3049	VS-21	
159414 / AC-765	Lockheed ES-3A Viking	3050	VQ-6	
159415 / NH-723	Lockheed ES-3A Viking	3051	VQ-5	
159416 / NJ-724	Lockheed S-3B Viking	3052	VS-41	
159417	Lockheed S-3A Viking	3053		Std AMARC [2S028]

159419 / AB-760	Lockheed ES-3A Viking	3055		VQ-6	
159420	Lockheed ES-3A Viking	3056			Std AMARC [2S038]
159497 / 3502	Grumman E-2C Hawkeye	A52-23	3502 (USCG)		Std AMARC [2E027]
159500	Grumman E-2C Hawkeye	A52-26		NADEP NAS Norfolk	
159502	Grumman E-2C Hawkeye	A52-28	3505 (USCG)		
159503 / LN-503	Lockheed P-3C AIP (L-285A) Orion	5620		VP-45	
159504	Lockheed P-3C-I (L-285A) Orion	5621		VPU-2	
159505	Lockheed P-3C-I (L-285A) Orion	5623			Std AMARC [2P174]
159506 / 568	Lockheed P-3C-I (L-285A) Orion	5624		VPU-1	
159507 / RD-507	Lockheed P-3C AIP (L-285A) Orion	5625		VP-47	
159508 / PZ-508	Lockheed P-3C-I (L-285A) Orion	5626			Std AMARC [2P178]
159509 / PJ-509	Lockheed P-3C-I (L-285A) Orion	5627			Std AMARC [2P176]
159510 / PJ-510	Lockheed P-3C-I (L-285A) Orion	5628			Std AMARC [2P175]
159511 / LW-02	Lockheed P-3C-I (L-285A) Orion	5629			Std AMARC [2P165]
159512	Lockheed P-3C-I (L-285A) Orion	5630		VP-5	
159513 / LL-513	Lockheed P-3C-I (L-285A) Orion	5631		VP-30	
159514 / LL-514	Lockheed P-3C-I (L-285A) Orion	5632		VP-30	
159729 / NE-705	Lockheed S-3B Viking	3058		VS-38	
159730	Lockheed S-3A Viking	3059			
159731 / NH-703	Lockheed S-3B Viking	3060		VS-29	
159732 / AJ-701	Lockheed S-3B Viking	3061		VS-24	
159733 / AC-706	Lockheed S-3B Viking	3062		VS-22	
159734	Lockheed S-3B Viking	3063			
159737 / NJ-727	Lockheed S-3B Viking	3066		VS-41	
159738 / AB-762	Lockheed ES-3A Viking	3067		VQ-6	
159741 / AC-702	Lockheed S-3B Viking	3070		VS-22	
159742	Lockheed S-3B Viking	3071			
159743 / 743	Lockheed S-3B Viking	3072		NAWC-AD	
159744 / AB-705	Lockheed S-3B Viking	3073		VS-32	
159745 / NG-707	Lockheed S-3B Viking	3074		VS-33	
159746 / NJ-731	Lockheed S-3B Viking	3075		VS-41	
159747 / AJ-705	Lockheed S-3B Viking	3076		VS-24	
159749	Lockheed S-3A Viking	3078			Std AMARC [2S025]
159750 / NG-700	Lockheed S-3B Viking	3079		VS-33	
159751 / AB-705	Lockheed S-3B Viking	3080		VS-32	
159752 / 761	Lockheed ES-3A Viking	3081		VQ-6	
159753	Lockheed S-3B Viking	3082		VS-41	
159754	Lockheed S-3A Viking	3083			
159755 / AG-700	Lockheed S-3B Viking	3084		VS-31	
159756 / NG-703	Lockheed S-3B Viking	3085		VS-33	
159758 / AA-701	Lockheed S-3B Viking	3087		VS-30	
159760 / AC-706	Lockheed S-3B Viking	3089		VS-22	
159761 / NJ-721	Lockheed S-3B Viking	3090		VS-41	
159762 / AB-700	Lockheed S-3B Viking	3091		VS-32	
159763 / NK-702	Lockheed S-3B Viking	3092		VS-35	
159764 / AC-700	Lockheed S-3B Viking	3093		VS-22	
159765 / AJ-701	Lockheed S-3B Viking	3094		VS-24	
159766 / AJ-707	Lockheed S-3B Viking	3095		VS-24	
159769 / AG-710	Lockheed S-3B Viking	3098		VS-31	
159770	Lockheed S-3B Viking	3099		NAWC-AD	
159771 / NG-701	Lockheed S-3B Viking	3100		VS-33	
159883	Lockheed P-3C-I (L-285A) Orion	5634			Std AMARC [2P171]
159884 / LD-884	Lockheed P-3C-I (L-285A) Orion	5635		VP-10	
159885 / 885	Lockheed P-3C-IIIR (L-285A) Orion	5636		VP-9	
159886 / 09	Lockheed P-3C-I (L-285A) Orion	5637		VQ-6	
159887 / JA-04	Lockheed P-3C-IIIR (L-285A) Orion	5638		NASC-FS	
159888	Lockheed P-3C-I (L-285A) Orion	5639			Std AMARC [2P168]
159889 / 04	Lockheed P-3C-IIIR (L-285A) Orion	5640		VX-1	
159890 / PJ-6	Lockheed P-3C-I (L-285A) Orion	5641			Std AMARC [2P166]
159891 / LN-891	Lockheed P-3C-IIIR (L-285A) Orion	5642		VP-45	
159893	Lockheed EP-3E (L-285A) Orion	5644			
159894 / LL-894	Lockheed P-3C AIP (L-285A) Orion	5645		VP-30	
160008 / AF-601	Grumman E-2C Hawkeye	A52-30		VAW-78	
160011	Grumman E-2C Hawkeye	A52-33	3504 (USCG)		Std AMARC [2E030]
160048 / JV	Douglas C-9B Skytrain II	47681 / 784		VR-58	
160049 / JV	Douglas C-9B Skytrain II	47698 / 809		VR-58	
160050 / JT	Douglas C-9B Skytrain II	47699 / 801		VR-52	
160051 / JS	Douglas C-9B Skytrain II	47700 / 811		VR-46	
160053 / F-18	North American CT-39G Sabreliner	306-104	N65795	TW-6	
160054 / F-22	North American CT-39G Sabreliner	306-105	N65796	TW-6	
160055 / F-24	North American CT-39G Sabreliner	306-106	N65797	TW-6	
160121 / NH-701	Lockheed S-3B Viking	3103		VS-29	
160122 / AC-704	Lockheed S-3B Viking	3104		VS-22	
160123 / NF-705	Lockheed S-3B Viking	3105		VS-21	

160124 / NE-701	Lockheed S-3B Viking	3106		VS-38	
160125 / AB-704	Lockheed S-3B Viking	3107		VS-32	
160126 / NE-701	Lockheed S-3B Viking	3108		VS-38	
160127 / NJ-741	Lockheed S-3B Viking	3109		VS-41	
160128 / NJ-722	Lockheed S-3B Viking	3110		VS-41	
160129 / NK-701	Lockheed S-3B Viking	3111		VS-35	
160130	Lockheed S-3B Viking	3112		VS-33	
160131 / NJ-740	Lockheed S-3B Viking	3113		VS-41	
160132 / NJ-725	Lockheed S-3B Viking	3114		VS-41	
160133 / NF-702	Lockheed S-3B Viking	3115		VS-21	
160134 / NJ-750	Lockheed S-3B Viking	3116		VS-41	
160135 / NF-707	Lockheed S-3B Viking	3117		VS-21	
160136 / NE-702	Lockheed S-3B Viking	3118		VS-38	
160138 / AG-701	Lockheed S-3B Viking	3120		VS-31	
160139 / NF-706	Lockheed S-3B Viking	3121		VS-21	
160140 / AC-702	Lockheed S-3B Viking	3122		VS-22	
160141 / AA-702	Lockheed S-3B Viking	3123		VS-30	
160142 / AC-707	Lockheed S-3B Viking	3124		VS-22	
160143 / AJ-704	Lockheed S-3B Viking	3125		VS-24	
160144	Lockheed S-3B Viking	3126		VS-32	
160145 / AB-701	Lockheed S-3B Viking	3127		VS-32	
160147 / AB-703	Lockheed S-3B Viking	3129		VS-32	
160148 / AC-701	Lockheed S-3B Viking	3130		VS-22	
160149	Lockheed S-3B Viking	3131		VX-1	
160151 / AJ-703	Lockheed S-3B Viking	3133		VS-24	
160152 / AA-703	Lockheed S-3B Viking	3134		VS-30	
160153	Lockheed S-3B Viking	3135		VX-1	
160155 / NJ-744	Lockheed S-3B Viking	3137		VS-41	
160156 / NG-705	Lockheed S-3B Viking	3138		VS-33	
160157 / NG-704	Lockheed S-3B Viking	3139		VS-33	
160158 / NE-701	Lockheed S-3B Viking	3140		VS-38	
160159 / NH-706	Lockheed S-3B Viking	3141		VS-29	
160160 / NJ-737	Lockheed S-3B Viking	3142		VS-41	
160161 / NJ-734	Lockheed S-3B Viking	3143		VS-41	
160162 / NF-702	Lockheed S-3B Viking	3144		VS-21	
160163 / NE-703	Lockheed S-3B Viking	3145		VS-38	
160283 / 283	Lockheed P-3C-IIIR (L-285A) Orion	5646		VP-9	
160284 / LL-284	Lockheed P-3C-I (L-285A) Orion	5647		VP-30	
160285	Lockheed P-3C-I (L-285A) Orion	5648			
160286 / LK-286	Lockheed P-3C-IIIR (L-285A) Orion	5649		VP-26	
160287 / LC-287	Lockheed P-3C-I (L-285A) Orion	5650		VP-8	
160288	Lockheed P-3C-I (L-285A) Orion	5651		NASC-FS	
160289 / LL-11	Lockheed P-3C-I (L-285A) Orion	5652			Std AMARC [2P184]
160290 / 290	Lockheed P-3C-IIIR (L-285A) Orion	5653		NFATS	
160291 / JA-05	Lockheed P-3C-II (L-285A) Orion	5654		VX-1	
160292	Lockheed P-3C-II (L-285A) Orion	5655		VPU-2	
160293 / 293	Lockheed P-3C-IIIR (L-285A) Orion	5656		VP-4	
160415 / 3508	Grumman E-2C Hawkeye	A52-35	3508 (USCG)		Std AMARC [2E023]
160416	Grumman E-2C Hawkeye	A52-36			Std AMARC [2E032]
160417 / NF-602	Grumman E-2C Hawkeye	A52-37			Std AMARC [2E021]
160567 / NH-700	Lockheed S-3B Viking	3147		VS-29	
160568	Lockheed S-3A Viking	3148			Std AMARC [2S014]
160569 / NH-700	Lockheed S-3B Viking	3149		VS-29	
160570	Lockheed S-3A Viking	3150			Std AMARC [2S016]
160571	Lockheed S-3B Viking	3151		VS-38	
160572 / NF-704	Lockheed S-3B Viking	3152		VS-21	
160573 / NJ-730	Lockheed S-3B Viking	3153		VS-41	
160574	Lockheed S-3A Viking	3154			Std AMARC [2S018]
160575 / NJ-736	Lockheed S-3B Viking	3155		VS-41	
160576 / NG-710	Lockheed S-3B Viking	3156		VS-33	
160577 / NJ-723	Lockheed S-3B Viking	3157		VS-41	
160578 / NK-707	Lockheed S-3B Viking	3158		VS-35	
160580 / NG-702	Lockheed S-3B Viking	3160		VS-33	
160581 / AA-701	Lockheed S-3B Viking	3161		VS-30	
160582 / NK-703	Lockheed S-3B Viking	3162		VS-35	
160583 / NJ-747	Lockheed S-3B Viking	3163		VS-41	
160584 / NE-704	Lockheed S-3B Viking	3164		VS-38	
160585	Lockheed S-3A Viking	3165			Std AMARC [2S020]
160586	Lockheed S-3A Viking	3166			Std AMARC [2S024]
160588 / AB-707	Lockheed S-3B Viking	3168		VS-32	
160589 / NJ-745	Lockheed S-3B Viking	3169		VS-41	
160591	Lockheed S-3B Viking	3171			Std AMARC [2S029]
160592 / AJ-705	Lockheed S-3B Viking	3172		VS-24	
160593	Lockheed S-3A Viking	3173			Std AMARC [2S017]

160594	Lockheed S-3A Viking	3174		Std AMARC [2S015]
160595	Lockheed S-3A Viking	3175		Std AMARC [2S023]
160596 / NH-701	Lockheed S-3B Viking	3176	VS-29	
160597	Lockheed S-3A Viking	3177		Std AMARC [2S022]
160598	Lockheed S-3A Viking	3178		Std AMARC [2S021]
160600 / AC-704	Lockheed S-3B Viking	3180	VS-22	
160601 / NG-706	Lockheed S-3B Viking	3181	VS-33	
160602 / AG-704	Lockheed S-3B Viking	3182	VS-31	
160603 / AG-703	Lockheed S-3B Viking	3183	VS-31	
160604 / NF-710	Lockheed S-3B Viking	3184	VS-21	
160605 / NF-703	Lockheed S-3B Viking	3185	VS-21	
160606 / AJ-706	Lockheed S-3B Viking	3186	VS-24	
160607	Lockheed S-3B Viking	3187	NAWC-AD	
160610 / RC-610	Lockheed P-3C-II (L-285A) Orion	5659	VP-46	
160611 / LU-611	Lockheed P-3C CDU (L-285A) Orion	5661	VP-64	
160612 / YB-612	Lockheed P-3C-II (L-285A) Orion	5663	VP-1	
160699	Grumman E-2C Hawkeye	A52-47		
160703	Grumman E-2C Hawkeye	A52-51		
160740 / XD-02	Lockheed LC-130R (L-382C-65D) Hercules	4725	VXE-6	
160761 / LU-761	Lockheed P-3C-II (L-285A) Orion	5665	VP-9	
160762 / LV-762	Lockheed P-3C-II (L-285A) Orion	5667	VPU-2	Std due corrosion
160763 / LT-763	Lockheed P-3C-II (L-285A) Orion	5669	VP-62	
160764 / 764	Lockheed P-3C-II (L-285A) Orion	5670	NRL	
160765 / LK-765	Lockheed P-3C CDU (L-285A) Orion	5671	VP-26	
160766 / 766	Lockheed P-3C CDU (L-285A) Orion	5673	VPU-2	
160767 / 767	Lockheed P-3C CDU (L-285A) Orion	5675	VP-66	
160768 / PR-51	Lockheed P-3C-II (L-285A) Orion	5677	VQ-1	
160769	Lockheed P-3C CDU (L-285A) Orion	5678	VP-10	
160770	Lockheed P-3C CDU (L-285A) Orion	5679	VP-10	
160840 / G-462	Beech T-44A (King Air H90)	LL-2	VT-31	
160841 / G-471	Beech T-44A (King Air H90)	LL-3	VT-31	
160842 / G-882	Beech T-44A (King Air H90)	LL-4	VT-31	
160843 / G-843	Beech T-44A (King Air H90)	LL-5	VT-31	
160844 / G-544	Beech T-44A (King Air H90)	LL-6	VT-31	
160845 / G-945	Beech T-44A (King Air H90)	LL-7	VT-31	
160846 / G-046	Beech T-44A (King Air H90)	LL-8	VT-31	Std Corpus Christi NAS
160847 / G-967	Beech T-44A (King Air H90)	LL-9	VT-31	
160848 / G-448	Beech T-44A (King Air H90)	LL-10	VT-31	
160849 / G-940	Beech T-44A (King Air H90)	LL-11	VT-31	
160850 / G-800	Beech T-44A (King Air H90)	LL-12	VT-31	
160851 / G-801	Beech T-44A (King Air H90)	LL-13	VT-31	
160852 / G-032	Beech T-44A (King Air H90)	LL-14	VT-31	
160853 / G-553	Beech T-44A (King Air H90)	LL-15	VT-31	
160854 / G-854	Beech T-44A (King Air H90)	LL-16	VT-31	
160855 / G-055	Beech T-44A (King Air H90)	LL-17	VT-31	
160856 / G-956	Beech T-44A (King Air H90)	LL-18	VT-31	
160968 / G-827	Beech T-44A (King Air H90)	LL-20	VT-31	
160969 / G-459	Beech T-44A (King Air H90)	LL-21	VT-31	
160970 / G-531	Beech T-44A (King Air H90)	LL-22	VT-31	
160971 / G-911	Beech T-44A (King Air H90)	LL-23	VT-31	
160972 / G-522	Beech T-44A (King Air H90)	LL-24	VT-31	
160973 / G-013	Beech T-44A (King Air H90)	LL-25	VT-31	
160974 / G-934	Beech T-44A (King Air H90)	LL-26	VT-31	
160976 / G-437	Beech T-44A (King Air H90)	LL-28	VT-31	
160977 / G-577	Beech T-44A (King Air H90)	LL-29	VT-31	
160978 / G-978	Beech T-44A (King Air H90)	LL-30	VT-31	
160979 / G-519	Beech T-44A (King Air H90)	LL-31	VT-31	
160981 / G-020	Beech T-44A (King Air H90)	LL-33	VT-31	
160982 / G-821	Beech T-44A (King Air H90)	LL-34	VT-31	
160983 / G-403	Beech T-44A (King Air H90)	LL-35	VT-31	
160984 / G-484	Beech T-44A (King Air H90)	LL-36	VT-31	
160985 / G-595	Beech T-44A (King Air H90)	LL-37	VT-31	
160986 / G-414	Beech T-44A (King Air H90)	LL-38	VT-31	
160990	Grumman E-2C Hawkeye	A52-55		Std AMARC [2E028]
160992	Grumman E-2C Hawkeye	A52-57	NAS Point Mugu	
160999 / LL-999	Lockheed P-3C-II (L-285A) Orion	5680	VP-30	
161000 / LF-000	Lockheed P-3C-II (L-285A) Orion	5681	VP-16	
161001 / LU-001	Lockheed P-3C-II (L-285A) Orion	5683	VP-64	
161002 / LF-002	Lockheed P-3C CDU (L-285A) Orion	5684	VP-16	
161003 / 003	Lockheed P-3C-II (L-285A) Orion	5685	VP-9	
161004 / LK-004	Lockheed P-3C-II (L-285A) Orion	5686	VP-26	
161005	Lockheed P-3C-II (L-285A) Orion	5687	VX-1	
161006 / LD-006	Lockheed P-3C CDU (L-285A) Orion	5688	VP-10	
161007 / PZ-007	Lockheed P-3C-II (L-285A) Orion	5690	VP-94	

Serial / Code	Type	BuNo/Code	Unit/Status
161008 / LL-008	Lockheed P-3C-II (L-285A) Orion	5691	VP-30
161009	Lockheed P-3C CDU (L-285A) Orion	5692	VP-5
161010 / LL-010	Lockheed P-3C-II (L-285A) Orion	5694	VP-30
161011 / LK-011	Lockheed P-3C-IIIR (L-285A) Orion	5695	VP-26
161012 / YD-012	Lockheed P-3C-IIIR (L-285A) Orion	5696	VP-4
161013 / LT-013	Lockheed P-3C CDU (L-285A) Orion	5698	VP-62
161014 / LV-014	Lockheed P-3C CDU (L-285A) Orion	5699	VP-66
161057 / G-857	Beech T-44A (King Air H90)	LL-39	TW-4
161058 / G-858	Beech T-44A (King Air H90)	LL-40	TW-4
161060 / G-900	Beech T-44A (King Air H90)	LL-42	VT-31
161061 / G-901	Beech T-44A (King Air H90)	LL-43	VT-31
161062 / G-912	Beech T-44A (King Air H90)	LL-44	VT-31
161063 / G-026	Beech T-44A (King Air H90)	LL-45	VT-31
161064 / G-864	Beech T-44A (King Air H90)	LL-46	VT-31
161065 / G-865	Beech T-44A (King Air H90)	LL-47	VT-31
161066 / G-566	Beech T-44A (King Air H90)	LL-48	VT-31
161068 / G-038	Beech T-44A (King Air H90)	LL-50	VT-31
161069 / G-989	Beech T-44A (King Air H90)	LL-51	VT-31
161070 / G-400	Beech T-44A (King Air H90)	LL-52	VT-31
161071 / G-401	Beech T-44A (King Air H90)	LL-53	VT-31
161072 / G-072	Beech T-44A (King Air H90)	LL-54	VT-31
161073 / G-923	Beech T-44A (King Air H90)	LL-55	VT-31
161074 / G-804	Beech T-44A (King Air H90)	LL-56	VT-31
161075 / G-075	Beech T-44A (King Air H90)	LL-57	VT-31
161076 / G-876	Beech T-44A (King Air H90)	LL-58	VT-31
161077 / G-087	Beech T-44A (King Air H90)	LL-59	VT-31
161078 / G-808	Beech T-44A (King Air H90)	LL-60	VT-31
161079 / G-890	Beech T-44A (King Air H90)	LL-61	VT-31
161095	Grumman E-2C Hawkeye	A52-59	Std NADEP North Island
161096	Grumman E-2C Hawkeye	A52-60	Std AMARC [2E026]
161097	Grumman E-2C Hawkeye	A52-61	VAW-77
161112	Lockheed P-3C-II (L-285A) Orion	5700	VQ-65
161122 / 226	Lockheed P-3C-II.3 (L-285A) Orion	5701	VPU-1
161123 / LU-123	Lockheed P-3C-II (L-285A) Orion	5702	VP-64
161124 / 124	Lockheed P-3C-II (L-285A) Orion	5703	VP-16
161125 / LV-125	Lockheed P-3C-II (L-285A) Orion	5705	VP-66
161126 / PR-50	Lockheed P-3C-II (L-285A) Orion	5707	VQ-1
161127 / LU-127	Lockheed P-3C-II (L-285A) Orion	5710	VP-64
161128 / 128	Lockheed P-3C-II (L-285A) Orion	5713	VP-5
161129 / 129	Lockheed P-3C-II (L-285A) Orion	5716	NAWC-AD
161130 / RC-130	Lockheed P-3C CDU (L-285A) Orion	5718	VP-46
161131 / LU-131	Lockheed P-3C CDU (L-285A) Orion	5721	VP-64
161132 / 132	Lockheed P-3C CDU (L-285A) Orion	5724	VP-9
161185	Beech UC-12B Super King Air	BJ-1	TW-4
161186 / 7G	Beech UC-12B Super King Air	BJ-2	Std AMARC [5G011]
161188	Beech TC-12B Super King Air	BJ-4	TW-4 Cvtd UC-12B
161190 / 7A	Beech UC-12B Super King Air	BJ-6	NAS Patuxent River
161191 / 7E	Beech UC-12B Super King Air	BJ-7	NAS Jacksonville
161192	Beech TC-12B Super King Air	BJ-9	TW-4 Cvtd UC-12B
161194 / G-303	Beech UC-12B Super King Air	BJ-10	TW-4
161195 / 8F	Beech UC-12B Super King Air	BJ-11	NAS Guantanamo Bay
161196 / 8N	Beech UC-12B Super King Air	BJ-12	NAS El Centro
161197 / G-327	Beech TC-12B Super King Air	BJ-13	TW-4 Cvtd UC-12B
161198 / 7X	Beech UC-12B Super King Air	BJ-14	Std AMARC [5G005]
161199	Beech TC-12B Super King Air	BJ-15	VT-31 Cvtd UC-12B
161200	Beech TC-12B Super King Air	BJ-16	VT-31 Cvtd UC-12B
161201	Beech TC-12B Super King Air	BJ-17	VT-31 Cvtd UC-12B
161202 / 7L	Beech UC-12B Super King Air	BJ-18	Std AMARC [5G003]
161203 / 7C	Beech UC-12B Super King Air	BJ-19	NAS Norfolk
161205	Beech TC-12B Super King Air	BJ-21	TW-4 Cvtd UC-12B
161206 / 7G	Beech UC-12B Super King Air	BJ-22	NAS Whidbey Island
161223	Lockheed EC-130Q (L-382C-85D) Hercules	4867	Std MCAS Cherry Point
161224	Grumman E-2C Hawkeye	A52-64	NADEP North Island
161228 / NJ-321	Grumman E-2C Hawkeye	A52-68	Std AMARC [2E029]
161229 / AF-600	Grumman E-2C Hawkeye	A52-69	VAW-78
161266 / JS	Douglas C-9B Skytrain II	48137 / 982	VR-46
161306 / 8K	Beech UC-12B Super King Air	BJ-23	COMMIDEASTFOR
161310	Beech TC-12B Super King Air	BJ-27	TW-4 Cvtd UC-12B
161311 / 7M	Beech UC-12B Super King Air	BJ-28	
161312 / 7H	Beech UC-12B Super King Air	BJ-29	NAS Fallon
161313 / 7M	Beech UC-12B Super King Air	BJ-30	NAS North Island
161314	Beech TC-12B Super King Air	BJ-31	VT-31 Cvtd UC-12B
161315	Beech TC-12B Super King Air	BJ-32	VT-31 Cvtd UC-12B
161316	Beech TC-12B Super King Air	BJ-33	VT-31 Cvtd UC-12B

161319 / 7S	Beech UC-12B Super King Air	BJ-36		NAS Leemore	
161321 / 7Q	Beech UC-12B Super King Air	BJ-38			Std AMARC [5G007]
161322 / 7X	Beech UC-12B Super King Air	BJ-39		NAS New Orleans	
161323 / RW	Beech UC-12B Super King Air	BJ-40		VRC-30	NAS North Island
161326 / 7G	Beech UC-12B Super King Air	BJ-43		NAS Whidbey Island	
161329 / LU-329	Lockheed P-3C-II.5 (L-285A) Orion	5726		VP-64	
161330 / YB-330	Lockheed P-3C-II.5 (L-285A) Orion	5727		VP-46	
161331 / LY-331	Lockheed P-3C-II.5 (L-285A) Orion	5728		VP-65	
161332 / PG-332	Lockheed P-3C-II.5 (L-285A) Orion	5729		VP-65	
161333 / PG-333	Lockheed P-3C-II.5 (L-285A) Orion	5730		VP-65	
161334 / PZ-334	Lockheed P-3C-II.5 (L-285A) Orion	5731		VP-94	
161335 / PZ-335	Lockheed P-3C-II.5 (L-285A) Orion	5732		VP-94	
161336 / LY-336	Lockheed P-3C CDU (L-285A) Orion	5734		VP-92	
161337 / PZ-337	Lockheed P-3C-II.5 (L-285A) Orion	5735		VP-94	
161338	Lockheed P-3C-II.5 (L-285A) Orion	5736		VP-5	
161339 / YD-339	Lockheed P-3C CDU (L-285A) Orion	5738		VP-4	
161340 / LC-340	Lockheed P-3C CDU (L-285A) Orion	5739		VP-8	
161341 / AF-02	Grumman E-2C Hawkeye	A52-70		VAW-77	
161342 / AF-605	Grumman E-2C Hawkeye	A52-72	3506 (USCG)	VAW-78	Std Norfolk NAS
161345	Grumman E-2C Hawkeye	A52-78			Std AMARC [2E033]
161346 / AF-603	Grumman E-2C Hawkeye	A52-79		VAW-78	
161404 / LL-404	Lockheed P-3C-II.5 (L-285A) Orion	5740		VP-30	
161405 / 405	Lockheed P-3C CDU (L-285A) Orion	5742		VP-40	
161406 / 406	Lockheed P-3C-II.5 (L-285A) Orion	5743		VP-40	
161407 / PG-407	Lockheed P-3C CDU (L-285A) Orion	5744		VP-65	
161408 / PZ-408	Lockheed P-3C-II.5 (L-285A) Orion	5746		VP-94	
161409 / LV-409	Lockheed P-3C-II.5 (L-285A) Orion	5747		VP-66	
161410	Lockheed P-3C-III (L-285A) Orion	5748		NAWC-23	
161411 / LL-411	Lockheed P-3C-II.5 (L-285A) Orion	5749		VP-30	
161412 / LU-412	Lockheed P-3C-II.5 (L-285A) Orion	5751		VP-64	
161413 / LL-30	Lockheed P-3C-II.5 (L-285A) Orion	5752		VP-30	
161414	Lockheed P-3C-II.5 (L-285A) Orion	5753		VP-16	
161415 / LL-415	Lockheed P-3C-II.5 (L-285A) Orion	5755		VP-30	
161497	Beech TC-12B Super King Air	BJ-45		TW-4	Cvtd UC-12B
161498	Beech TC-12B Super King Air	BJ-46		VT-31	Cvtd UC-12B
161499 / 7Z	Beech UC-12B Super King Air	BJ-47			Std AMARC [5G004]
161500 / 7E	Beech UC-12B Super King Air	BJ-48		NAS Jacksonville	
161501 / 7A	Beech UC-12B Super King Air	BJ-49		NAS Patuxent River	
161502 / 7Q	Beech UC-12B Super King Air	BJ-50		NAS Key West	
161503 / 7D	Beech UC-12B Super King Air	BJ-51		NAS Fort Worth	
161504 / 7B	Beech UC-12B Super King Air	BJ-52		NAS Atlanta	
161505 / G-312	Beech TC-12B Super King Air	BJ-53		VT-31	
161508 / G-508	Beech TC-12B Super King Air	BJ-56		VT-31	
161509	Beech TC-12B Super King Air	BJ-57		VT-31	Cvtd UC-12B
161510 / G-315	Beech TC-12B Super King Air	BJ-58		VT-31	
161511 / 7W	Beech UC-12B Super King Air	BJ-59		NAS Willow Grove	
161512 / 7Y	Beech UC-12B Super King Air	BJ-60		NAS New Orleans	
161513	Beech UC-12B Super King Air	BJ-61		NAS Fallon	
161514 / G-316	Beech TC-12B Super King Air	BJ-62		VT-31	
161516 / 7W	Beech UC-12B Super King Air	BJ-64			Std AMARC [5G002]
161518	Beech TC-12B Super King Air	BJ-66		VT-31	Cvtd UC-12B
161529 / JS	Douglas C-9B Skytrain II	48165 / 1081		VR-46	
161530 / JS	Douglas C-9B Skytrain II	48166 / 1084		VR-46	
161548 / AJ-603	Grumman E-2C Hawkeye			VAW-124	Std NAS Norfolk
161550 / AC-604	Grumman E-2C Hawkeye			VAW-126	
161552	Grumman E-2C Hawkeye			VAW-126	Std NAS Norfolk
161572	Convair UC-880 (CV-880)	22-7-3-55	N84790		Std NAS Patuxent River
161585 / 585	Lockheed P-3C-II.5 (L-285A) Orion	5756		VPU-1	
161586 / LL-586	Lockheed P-3C-II.5 (L-285A) Orion	5757		VP-30	
161587 / YD-587	Lockheed P-3C-II.5 (L-285A) Orion	5759		VP-4	
161588 / LL-588	Lockheed P-3C-II.5 (L-285A) Orion	5760		VP-30	
161589 / 589	Lockheed P-3C-II.5 (L-285A) Orion	5761		VP-9	
161590 / LL-590	Lockheed P-3C-II.5 (L-285A) Orion	5763		VP-30	
161591 / PZ-591	Lockheed P-3C CDU (L-285A) Orion	5764		VP-94	
161592 / PZ-592	Lockheed P-3C CDU (L-285A) Orion	5766		VP-94	
161593 / LL-593	Lockheed P-3C-II.5 (L-285A) Orion	5767		VP-30	
161594 / LL-594	Lockheed P-3C-II.5 (L-285A) Orion	5768		VP-30	
161595 / LV-595	Lockheed P-3C-II.5 (L-285A) Orion	5770		VP-66	
161596 / LL-596	Lockheed P-3C-II.5 (L-285A) Orion	5771		VP-30	
161763 / RD-763	Lockheed P-3C AIP (L-285G) Orion	5775		VP-47	
161764 / YD-764	Lockheed P-3C AIP (L-285G) Orion	5777		VP-4	
161765 / PG-765	Lockheed P-3C-III (L-285G) Orion	5779		VP-65	
161766 / PJ-766	Lockheed P-3C CDU (L-285G) Orion	5781		VP-69	
161767 / 767	Lockheed P-3C-III (L-285G) Orion	5783		VP-9	

Serial / Code	Type	c/n	Reg	Unit	Status
161730	Grumman E-2C Hawkeye			NADEP North Island	
161732 / AC-602	Grumman E-2C Hawkeye			VAW-126	
161733 / AF-00	Grumman E-2C Hawkeye			VAW-77	
161735 / AD-600	Grumman E-2C Hawkeye				Std AMARC [2E034]
162140 / 42	Grumman C-2A Greyhound	20		VRC-40	
162141 / NG-23	Grumman C-2A Greyhound	21			
162143 / 52	Grumman C-2A Greyhound	23		VRC-40	
162144	Grumman C-2A Greyhound	24		NADEP North Island	
162145 / 53	Grumman C-2A Greyhound	25		VRC-40	
162146 / NK-34	Grumman C-2A Greyhound	26			
162147 / NF-430	Grumman C-2A Greyhound	27		VRC-30	
162148 / NF-430	Grumman C-2A Greyhound	28		VRC-30	
162149 / NE-33	Grumman C-2A Greyhound	29			
162150 / NH-31	Grumman C-2A Greyhound	30			
162151	Grumman C-2A Greyhound	31			Std AMARC [1C007]
162152	Grumman C-2A Greyhound	32			
162153 / 51	Grumman C-2A Greyhound	33		VRC-40	
162154 / RW-36	Grumman C-2A Greyhound	34			
162155 / AD-633	Grumman C-2A Greyhound	35		VAW-120	
162157	Grumman C-2A Greyhound	37			
162158 / AD-631	Grumman C-2A Greyhound	38		VAW-120	
162159 / 56	Grumman C-2A Greyhound	39		VRC-40	
162160	Grumman C-2A Greyhound	40		NADEP North Island	
162161 / NK-24	Grumman C-2A Greyhound	41			
162162 / RW-22	Grumman C-2A Greyhound	42			
162163 / RW-25	Grumman C-2A Greyhound	43			
162164 / NF-431	Grumman C-2A Greyhound	44		VRC-30	
162165 / RW-30	Grumman C-2A Greyhound	45			
162166 / 40	Grumman C-2A Greyhound	46		VRC-40	
162167 / NE-32	Grumman C-2A Greyhound	47		VRC-30	
162168 / AD-634	Grumman C-2A Greyhound	48		VAW-120	
162169 / AD-630	Grumman C-2A Greyhound	49		VAW-120	
162170 / 43	Grumman C-2A Greyhound	50		VRC-40	
162171 / NH-37	Grumman C-2A Greyhound	51		VRC-30	
162172 / 57	Grumman C-2A Greyhound	52		VRC-40	
162173 / NF-431	Grumman C-2A Greyhound	53		VRC-30	
162174 / 54	Grumman C-2A Greyhound	54		VRC-40	
162175 / RW-35	Grumman C-2A Greyhound	55			
162176 / AD-632	Grumman C-2A Greyhound	56		VAW-120	
162177 / AD-635	Grumman C-2A Greyhound	57		VAW-120	
162178 / 57	Grumman C-2A Greyhound	58		VRC-40	NADEP North Island
162314 / LY-314	Lockheed P-3C-III (L-285G) Orion	5786		VP-92	
162315 / YB-315	Lockheed P-3C-III (L-285G) Orion	5788		VP-1	
162316 / LY-316	Lockheed P-3C-III (L-285G) Orion	5790		VP-92	
162317 / YB-317	Lockheed P-3C AIP (L-285G) Orion	5792		VP-1	
162318 / PJ-318	Lockheed P-3C CDU (L-285G) Orion	5794		VP-69	
162614 / AA-601	Grumman E-2C Hawkeye			VAW-125	
162615 / AF-01	Grumman E-2C Hawkeye			VAW-77	
162616 / AC-600	Grumman E-2C Hawkeye				Std AMARC [2E038]
162618 / AC-603	Grumman E-2C Hawkeye			VAW-126	
162619 / AF-601	Grumman E-2C Hawkeye			VAW-78	
162753 / JT	Douglas DC-9-33RC	47410 / 480	N909DC	VR-52	
162754 / JT	Douglas DC-9-33RC	47476 / 569	N907DC	VR-52	
162770	Lockheed P-3C AIP (L-285G) Orion	5796		VP-40	
162771 / YD-771	Lockheed P-3C-III (L-285G) Orion	5797		VP-4	
162772 / 772	Lockheed P-3C AIP (L-285G) Orion	5798		VP-40	
162773 / QE-773	Lockheed P-3C-III (L-285G) Orion	5799		VP-40	
162774 / RD-04	Lockheed P-3C AIP (L-285G) Orion	5800		NFATS	
162775 / QE-775	Lockheed P-3C-III (L-285G) Orion	5801		VP-40	
162776 / LA-776	Lockheed P-3C-III (L-285G) Orion	5802		VP-5	
162777 / 777	Lockheed P-3C AIP (L-285G) Orion	5803		VP-1	
162778 / 778	Lockheed P-3C AIP (L-285G) Orion	5804		VP-16	
162782	Boeing E-6B Mercury (707-300)	23430 / 983		VQ-3	
162783	Boeing E-6B Mercury (707-300)	23889 / 986		VQ-3	
162784	Boeing E-6B Mercury (707-300)	23890 / 987		VQ-3	
162797 / AJ-603	Grumman E-2C Hawkeye				Std AMARC [2E036]
162798 / AF-03	Grumman E-2C Hawkeye			VAW-77	
162799 / AJ-602	Grumman E-2C Hawkeye				Std NAS Norfolk
162800 / AD-606	Grumman E-2C Hawkeye				Std AMARC [2E037]
162801 / AD-602	Grumman E-2C Hawkeye				Std AMARC [2E039]
162802 / AF-602	Grumman E-2C Hawkeye			VAW-78	
162998 / RD-998	Lockheed P-3C-III (L-285G) Orion	5805		VP-47	
162999 / PJ-999	Lockheed P-3C-III (L-285G) Orion	5806		VP-69	
163000 / PG-000	Lockheed P-3C-III (L-285G) Orion	5807		VP-69	

163001 / LT-001	Lockheed P-3C CDU (L-285G) Orion	5808		VP-62	
163002 / LT-002	Lockheed P-3C CDU (L-285G) Orion	5809		VP-62	
163003 / PJ-003	Lockheed P-3C-III (L-285G) Orion	5810		VP-69	
163004 / PG-004	Lockheed P-3C-III (L-285G) Orion	5811		VP-65	
163005 / LT-005	Lockheed P-3C CDU (L-285G) Orion	5812		VP-62	
163006 / JA-06	Lockheed P-3C-III (L-285G) Orion	5813		VX-1	
163024 / AC-601	Grumman E-2C Hawkeye	A52-117		VAW-126	
163025 / AJ-601	Grumman E-2C Hawkeye				Std AMARC [2E035]
163026 / AD-601	Grumman E-2C Hawkeye			VAW-120	
163027 / AC-600	Grumman E-2C Hawkeye			VAW-126	
163028 / AC-602	Grumman E-2C Hawkeye			VAW-126	
163029 / AD-625	Grumman TE-2C Hawkeye			VAW-120	
163036 / JT	Douglas DC-9-32CF	47041 / 200	N59T	VR-52	
163037 / JT	Douglas DC-9-32F	47221 / 305	N938F	VR-52	
163050	Douglas EC-24A (DC-8-54F)	45881 / 276	N8048U		Std AMARC [2C001]
163208 / JU	Douglas DC-9-32F	47639 / 735	N4549V	VR-56	
163289 / LT-289	Lockheed P-3C-III (L-285G) Orion	5814		VP-62	
163290 / PJ-290	Lockheed P-3C-III (L-285G) Orion	5815		VP-69	
163291 / PG-291	Lockheed P-3C-III (L-285G) Orion	5816		VP-65	
163292 / LF-292	Lockheed P-3C-III (L-285G) Orion	5821		VP-16	
163293 / LF-293	Lockheed P-3C-III (L-285G) Orion	5822		VP-16	
163294 / LY-294	Lockheed P-3C-III (L-285G) Orion	5823		VP-92	
163295 / LY-295	Lockheed P-3C-III (L-285G) Orion	5824		VP-92	
163511 / JS	Douglas DC-9-32	47431 / 520	N506MD	VR-46	
163512 / RX	Douglas DC-9-32	47474 / 600	N507MD	VR-57	
163513 / JV	Douglas DC-9-32	47477 / 613	N508MD	VR-58	
163535	Grumman E-2C Hawkeye			NAWC-AD	
163536	Grumman E-2C Hawkeye				
163537	Grumman E-2C Hawkeye			NAWC-AD	
163538 / AB-601	Grumman E-2C Hawkeye			VAW-123	
163539 / AB-622	Grumman E-2C Hawkeye			VAW-123	
163540 / AJ-600	Grumman E-2C Hawkeye	A57-128		VAW-124	
163553 / 8M	Beech UC-12F Super King Air	BU-1		NAF Misawa	
163554 / 8A	Beech UC-12F Super King Air	BU-2		NAF Atsugi	
163555	Beech UC-12F Super King Air	BU-3		NAF Atsugi	
163556	Beech UC-12F Super King Air	BU-4		NAF Kadena	
163557	Beech UC-12F Super King Air	BU-5		NAF Kadena	
163562	Beech UC-12F Super King Air	BU-10		NAF Kadena	
163563	Beech RC-12F Super King Air	BU-11		PMRF Barking Sands	
163564	Beech RC-12F Super King Air	BU-12		PMRF Barking Sands	
163691	GAC C-20D (Gulfstream III)	480	N302GA	VR-1	
163693 / AB-600	Grumman E-2C Hawkeye	A52-129		VAW-123	
163694 / AG-601	Grumman E-2C Hawkeye	A52-130		VAW-121	
163695	Grumman E-2C Hawkeye	A52-131			
163696 / AJ-603	Grumman E-2C Hawkeye	A52-132		VAW-124	
163697	Grumman E-2C Hawkeye	A52-133		NADEP	
163698 / NF-602	Grumman E-2C Hawkeye	A52-134		VAW-115	
163836 / 7C	Beech UC-12M Super King Air	BV-1		NAF Mildenhall	
163837	Beech UC-12M Super King Air	BV-2		COMMIDEASTFOR	
163838	Beech UC-12M Super King Air	BV-3		COMMIDEASTFOR	
163839	Beech UC-12M Super King Air	BV-4		NAS Rota	
163840	Beech UC-12M Super King Air	BV-5			
163841	Beech UC-12M Super King Air	BV-6		COMMIDEASTFOR	
163842	Beech UC-12M Super King Air	BV-7		NAS Rota	
163843 / 8G	Beech UC-12M Super King Air	BV-8		NAF Mildenhall	
163844 / 8E	Beech UC-12M Super King Air	BV-9		NAS Roosevelt Roads	
163845 / 8E	Beech UC-12M Super King Air	BV-10		NAS Roosevelt Roads	
163846 / 8E	Beech RC-12M Super King Air	BV-11		NAS Roosevelt Roads	
163847 / 8E	Beech RC-12M Super King Air	BV-12		NAS Roosevelt Roads	
163848 / AD-611	Grumman TE-2C Hawkeye	A52-135		VAW-120	
163849	Grumman E-2C Hawkeye	A52-136			
163850 / AJ-602	Grumman E-2C Hawkeye	A52-137		VAW-124	
163851	Grumman E-2C Hawkeye	A52-138			
163918	Boeing E-6B Mercury (707-300)	23891 / 988		VQ-3	
163919	Boeing E-6B Mercury (707-300)	23892 / 989		VQ-3	
163920	Boeing E-6B Mercury (707-300)	23893 / 990		VQ-3	
164107 / NF-602	Grumman E-2C Hawkeye	A52-139		VAW-115	
164108 / AJ-601	Grumman E-2C Hawkeye	A52-140		VAW-124	
164109	Grumman E-2C Hawkeye	A52-141		NAWC-AD	
164110 / AD-623	Grumman E-2C Hawkeye	A52-142		VAW-120	
164111 / NH-601	Grumman E-2C Hawkeye	A52-143		VAW-117	
164112 / NH-603	Grumman E-2C Hawkeye	A52-144		VAW-117	
164352	Grumman E-2C Hawkeye	A52-145			
164353	Grumman E-2C Hawkeye	A52-146			

164354 / NE-600	Grumman E-2C Hawkeye	A52-147		VAW-116	
164355	Grumman E-2C Hawkeye	A52-148			
164386	Boeing E-6B Mercury (707-300)	23894 / 991		VQ-4	
164387	Boeing E-6B Mercury (707-300)	24500 / 992		VQ-3	
164388	Boeing E-6B Mercury (707-300)	24501 / 994		VQ-4	
164404	Boeing E-6B Mercury (707-300)	24502 / 995		VQ-4	
164405	Boeing E-6B Mercury (707-300)	24504 / 997		VQ-4	
164406	Boeing E-6B Mercury (707-300)	24505 / 998		VQ-3	
164407	Boeing E-6B Mercury (707-300)	24506 / 999		VQ-4	
164408	Boeing E-6B Mercury (707-300)	24507 / 1002		VQ-4	
164409	Boeing E-6B Mercury (707-300)	24508 / 1005		VQ-4	
164410	Boeing E-6B Mercury (707-300)	24509 / 1008		VQ-4	
164433 / NH-600	Grumman E-2C Hawkeye	A52-149		VAW-117	
164434 / NE-601	Grumman E-2C Hawkeye	A52-150		VAW-116	
164435 / NE-602	Grumman E-2C Hawkeye	A52-151		VAW-116	
164436	Grumman E-2C Hawkeye	A52-152		VAW-116	
164437 / NK-600	Grumman E-2C Hawkeye	A52-153		VAW-113	
164438 / AD-620	Grumman E-2C Hawkeye	A52-154		VAW-120	
164432 / NK-603	Grumman E-2C Hawkeye	A52-155		VAW-113	
164433 / NK-601	Grumman E-2C Hawkeye	A52-156		VAW-113	
164434 / NH-602	Grumman E-2C Hawkeye	A52-157		VAW-117	
164435 / NG-604	Grumman E-2C Hawkeye	A52-158		VAW-112	
164436 / AD-622	Grumman E-2C Hawkeye	A52-159		VAW-120	
164437 / NE-603	Grumman E-2C Hawkeye			VAW-116	
164525 / 35	DeHavilland Canada U-6A (DHC-2)			USNTPS	
164605 / RS	Douglas DC-9-33RC	47545 / 671	N538MD	VR-61	
164606 / RS	Douglas DC-9-33RC	47496 / 673	N536MD	VR-61	
164607 / RS	Douglas DC-9-33RC	47428 / 669	N521MD	VR-61	
164608 / RS	Douglas DC-9-33RC	47565 / 675	N539MD	VR-61	
164762	Lockheed C-130T (L-382C-21F) Hercules	5255		NAWC-AD	
164763	Lockheed C-130T (L-382C-21F) Hercules	5258		NAWC-AD	
164993 / CW	Lockheed C-130T (L-382C-21F) Hercules	5298		VR-54	
164994 / WV	Lockheed C-130T (L-382C-21F) Hercules	5299		VR-53	
164995 / CW	Lockheed C-130T (L-382C-21F) Hercules	5300		VR-54	
164996 / WV	Lockheed C-130T (L-382C-21F) Hercules	5301		VR-53	
164997 / WV	Lockheed C-130T (L-382C-21F) Hercules	5304		VR-53	
164998 / WV	Lockheed C-130T (L-382C-21F) Hercules	5305		VR-53	
165033 / JR	GAC C-20G (Gulfstream IV)	1187	N481GA	VR-48	
165034 / JR	GAC C-20G (Gulfstream IV)	1189	N402GA	VR-48	
165151 / RG	GAC C-20G (Gulfstream IV)	1199	N428GA	VR-51	
165152 / RG	GAC C-20G (Gulfstream IVSP)	1201	N431GA	VR-51	
165158 / CW	Lockheed C-130T (L-382C-36F) Hercules	5341		VR-54	
165159 / CW	Lockheed C-130T (L-382C-36F) Hercules	5342		VR-54	
165160 / CW	Lockheed C-130T (L-382C-36F) Hercules	5344		VR-54	
165161 / RU	Lockheed C-130T (L-382C-36F) Hercules	5345		VR-55	
165293 / AB-601	Grumman E-2C Hawkeye	A52-164		VAW-123	
165294 / NF-601	Grumman E-2C Hawkeye	A52-165		VAW-115	
165295 / NF-600	Grumman E-2C Hawkeye	A52-166		VAW-115	
165296 / NF-603	Grumman E-2C Hawkeye	A52-167		VAW-115	
165297 / AD-642	Grumman E-2C Hawkeye	A52-168		VAW-120	
165298 / AB-603	Grumman E-2C Hawkeye	A52-169		VAW-123	
165299 / AA-600	Grumman E-2C Hawkeye	A52-170		VAW-120	
165300 / AD-641	Grumman E-2C Hawkeye	A52-171		VAW-120	
165301 / AA-601	Grumman E-2C Hawkeye	A52-172		VAW-125	
165302 / AD-640	Grumman E-2C Hawkeye	A52-173		VAW-120	
165303	Grumman E-2C Hawkeye	A52-174			
165304	Grumman E-2C Hawkeye	A52-175			
165313 / JW	Lockheed C-130T (L-382C-52F) Hercules	5383		VR-62	
165314 / JW	Lockheed C-130T (L-382C-52F) Hercules	5384		VR-62	
165342	Boeing TC-18F (707-382B)	18961 / 456	N45RT	SCW-1	Std AMARC [3C001]
165348 / JW	Lockheed C-130H (L-382C-55F) Hercules	5404		VR-62	
165349 / JW	Lockheed C-130H (L-382C-55F) Hercules	5406		VR-62	
165350 / RU	Lockheed C-130H (L-382C-55F) Hercules	5407		VR-55	
165351 / RU	Lockheed C-130H (L-382C-55F) Hercules	5409		VR-55	
165378 / RU	Lockheed C-130T (L-382C-59F) Hercules	5429		VR-55	
165379 / RU	Lockheed C-130T (L-382C-59F) Hercules	5430		VR-55	
165507 / AA-602	Grumman E-2C Hawkeye			VAW-125	
165508 / AA-603	Grumman E-2C Hawkeye			VAW-125	
165509 / F-01	North American T-39N Sabreliner	282-9	N301NT	TW-6	
165510 / F-02	North American T-39N Sabreliner	282-81	N302NT	TW-6	
165511 / F-03	North American T-39N Sabreliner	282-29	N303NT	TW-6	
165512 / F-04	North American T-39N Sabreliner	282-2	N304NT	TW-6	
165513 / F-05	North American T-39N Sabreliner	282-66	N305NT	TW-6	
165514 / F-06	North American T-39N Sabreliner	282-30	N306NT	TW-6	

165515 / F-07	North American T-39N Sabreliner	282-72	N307NT	TW-6	
165516 / F-08	North American T-39N Sabreliner	282-90	N308NT	TW-6	
165517 / F-09	North American T-39N Sabreliner	282-61	N309NT	TW-6	
165518 / F-10	North American T-39N Sabreliner	282-77	N310NT	TW-6	
165519 / F-11	North American T-39N Sabreliner	282-19	N311NT	TW-6	
165520 / F-12	North American T-39N Sabreliner	282-32	N312NT	TW-6	
165521 / F-13	North American T-39N Sabreliner	282-94	N313NT	TW-6	
165522 / F-14	North American T-39N Sabreliner	282-28	N314NT	TW-6	
165523 / F-15	North American T-39N Sabreliner	282-20	N40YA	TW-6	Also wears N315NT
165524 / F-16	North American T-39N Sabreliner	282-60	N316NT	TW-6	
165525 / F-17	North American T-39N Sabreliner	282-100	N317NT	TW-6	
165647 / AD-645	Grumman E-2C Hawkeye			VAW-120	
165648	Grumman E-2C Hawkeye				
165649	Grumman E-2C Hawkeye				
165650	Grumman E-2C Hawkeye				
165829 / RY	Boeing C-40A (737-7AF) Clipper	29979 / 496	N1003N	VR-59	
165830 / RY	Boeing C-40A (737-7AF) Clipper	29980 / 568	N1003M	VR-59	
165831 / RY	Boeing C-40A (737-7AF) Clipper	30200 / 651	N1786B	VR-59	'City of Fort Worth'
165832	Boeing C-40A (737-7AF) Clipper	30781 / 742			
	Boeing C-40A (737-7AF) Clipper				
	Boeing C-40A (737-7AF) Clipper				
103208	Cessna 421			NWEF	
553134	Boeing NKC-135A Stratotanker	17250 /T0017	55-3134 (USAF)		Std AMARC [6G002]
563596	Boeing NKC-135A Stratotanker	17345 /T0035	56-3596 (USAF)		Std AMARC [6G001]
570461	Lockheed DC-130A (L-182-1A) Hercules	3168	57-0461 (USAF)	NWTSPM	
570496	Lockheed DC-130A (L-182-1A) Hercules	3203	57-0496 (USAF)	NWTSPM	
570497	Lockheed DC-130A (L-182-1A) Hercules	3204	57-0497 (USAF)	NWTSPM	
68-10865	Cessna O-2A Super Skymaster	M337-0230			Std AMARC [2L041]
68-10971	Cessna O-2A Super Skymaster	M337-0247			Std AMARC [2L046]
68-11155	Cessna O-2A Super Skymaster	M337-0380			Std AMARC [2L042]
68-11167	Cessna O-2A Super Skymaster	M337-0392			Std AMARC [2L050]
68-6889	Cessna O-2A Super Skymaster	M337-0178			Std AMARC [2L054]
68-6900	Cessna O-2A Super Skymaster	M337-0189			Std AMARC [2L052]
69-7608	Cessna O-2A Super Skymaster	M337-0406			Std AMARC [2L048]
69-7612	Cessna O-2A Super Skymaster	M337-0410			Std AMARC [2L043]
70-15909 / 36	Beech U-21F	B-96		USNTPS	
70-15910 / 37	Beech U-21F	B-97		USNTPS	
70-15911 / 38	Beech U-21F	B-98		USNTPS	
70-15912 / 39	Beech U-21F	B-99		USNTPS	
76-0172	Beech C-12C Huron (Super King Air 200)	BD-29			
76-22563	Beech C-12C Huron (Super King Air 200)	BC-40	N7066D (USCS)		
87-0157	Lockheed NC-130H (L-382C-84E) Hercules	5121	1721 (USCG)	NAS Pax River/Rotordome	
900528	Fairchild C-26D Metro III (SA227AC)	DC-795M	90-0528 (USAF)	NAS Sigonella	
900530	Fairchild C-26D Metro III (SA227AC)	DC-796M	90-0530 (USAF)	NAS Sigonella	
900531	Fairchild C-26D Metro III (SA227AC)	DC-798M	90-0531 (USAF)	NAS Sigonella	
907038	Fairchild C-26D Metro III (SA227DC)	DC-836M		PMRF	
910502	Fairchild C-26B Metro III (SA227AC)	DC-801M	91-0502 (USAF)	NAS Naples	
910512	Fairchild C-26D Metro III (SA227DC)	DC-814M			
910514	Fairchild C-26B Metro III (SA227AC)	DC-816M	91-0514 (USAF)	PMRF	
920370	Fairchild C-26B Metro III (SA227DC)	DC-832M			Std San Antonio, TX
920371	Fairchild C-26D Metro III (SA227DC)	DC-833M	N3018P	PMRF	
920373	Fairchild C-26B Metro III (SA227DC)	DC-835M			Std San Antonio, TX

United States Marine Corps   - USMC

UNITS/BASES			tail code
	FMFPAC, VIP Flt, Camp Smith, CA	UC-12B	BZ
	HQMC, VIP flt, Andrews AFB-Washington, DC	UC-12B, C-20G	5A
	MWHS-1, MCAS Futenma, Okinawa	CT-39G	SZ
	MWHS-4, NAS New Orleans, LA	UC-12B, UC-35C	EZ
	SOES, MCAS Cherry Point, NC	C-9B, CT-39G	5C
	VMGR-152, MCAS Futenma, Okinawa	KC-130F/R	QD
	VMGR-234 'Thundering Herd', NAS Ft. Worth JRB, TX	KC-130T/T-30	QH
	VMGR-252 'Heavy Haulers' , MCAS Cherry Point, NC	KC-130F/R/J	BH
	VMGR-352, MCAS Miramar, CA	KC-130F/R	QB
	VMGR-452, Stewart IAP, NY	KC-130T/T-30	NY
	VMGRT-253, MCAS Cherry Point, NC	KC-130F	GR
	Base Flight, MCAS Beaufort, SC	UC-12B	5B
	Base Flight, MCAS Cherry Point, NC	UC-12B	5C
	Base Flight, MCAS Futenma, Okinawa	UC-12B	5F
	Base Flight, MCAS Iwakuni, Japan	UC-12B	5G
	Base Flight, MCAS New River, NC	UC-12B	5D
	Base Flight, MCAS Yuma, AZ	UC-12B	5Y

PLANS   Up to 51 tankers (probably KC-130Js) needed to replace the current fleet, some orders placed.

Serial / Code	Type	C/N	Reg	Unit
147572 / QB	Lockheed KC-130F (L-282B-3B) Hercules	3554		VMGR-352
147573 / QD	Lockheed KC-130F (L-282B-3B) Hercules	3555		VMGR-352
148246 / GR	Lockheed KC-130F (L-282B-3B) Hercules	3566		VMGRT-253
148247 / QD	Lockheed KC-130F (L-282B-3B) Hercules	3573		VMGR-152
148248 / QD	Lockheed KC-130F (L-282B-3B) Hercules	3574		VMGR-152
148249 / GR	Lockheed KC-130F (L-282B-3B) Hercules	3577		VMGRT-253
148891 / BH	Lockheed KC-130F (L-282B-3B) Hercules	3605		VMGR-252
148893 / QD	Lockheed KC-130F (L-282B-3B) Hercules	3607		VMGR-152
148894 / BH	Lockheed KC-130F (L-282B-3B) Hercules	3608		VMGR-252
148895 / BH	Lockheed KC-130F (L-282B-3B) Hercules	3619		VMGR-252
148896 / BH	Lockheed KC-130F (L-282B-3B) Hercules	3623		VMGR-252
148897 / BH	Lockheed KC-130F (L-282B-3B) Hercules	3627		VMGR-252
148898 / BH	Lockheed KC-130F (L-282B-3B) Hercules	3631		VMGR-252
148899 / BH	Lockheed KC-130F (L-282B-3B) Hercules	3632		VMGR-252
149788 / BH	Lockheed KC-130F (L-282B-3B) Hercules	3640		VMGR-252
149789 / BH	Lockheed KC-130F (L-282B-3B) Hercules	3644		VMGR-252
149791 / QB	Lockheed KC-130F (L-282B-3B) Hercules	3657		VMGR-352
149792 / QB	Lockheed KC-130F (L-282B-3M) Hercules	3658		VMGR-352
149795 / QB	Lockheed KC-130F (L-282B-3B) Hercules	3664		VMGR-352
149796 / QB	Lockheed KC-130F (L-282B-3B) Hercules	3665		VMGR-352
149798 / QB	Lockheed KC-130F (L-282B-3B) Hercules	3680		VMGR-352
149799 / QD	Lockheed KC-130F (L-282B-3B) Hercules	3684		VMGR-152
149800 / QB	Lockheed KC-130F (L-282B-3B) Hercules	3685		VMGR-352
149804 / GR	Lockheed KC-130F (L-282B-3B) Hercules	3695		VMGRT-253
149808 / BH	Lockheed KC-130F (L-282B-3B) Hercules	3705		VMGR-252
149811 / GR	Lockheed KC-130F (L-282B-3B) Hercules	3711		VMGRT-253
149812 / QD	Lockheed KC-130F (L-282B-3B) Hercules	3718		VMGR-152
149815 / QB	Lockheed KC-130F (L-282B-3B) Hercules	3725		VMGR-352
149816 / QD	Lockheed KC-130F (L-282B-3B) Hercules	3726		VMGR-152
150686 / BH	Lockheed KC-130F (L-282B-3B) Hercules	3733		VMGR-252
150687 / GR	Lockheed KC-130F (L-282B-3B) Hercules	3734		VMGRT-253
150688 / GR	Lockheed KC-130F (L-282B-3B) Hercules	3740		VMGRT-253
150689 / QB	Lockheed KC-130F (L-282B-3B) Hercules	3741		VMGR-352
150690 / QD	Lockheed KC-130F (L-282B-3B) Hercules	3742		VMGR-152
159365	North American CT-39G Sabreliner	306-70		VMR-2
160013 / QD	Lockheed KC-130R (L-382C-43D) Hercules	4615		VMGR-152
160014 / QD	Lockheed KC-130R (L-382C-43D) Hercules	4626		VMGR-152
160015 / QB	Lockheed KC-130R (L-382C-43D) Hercules	4629		VMGR-352
160016 / QB	Lockheed KC-130R (L-382C-43D) Hercules	4635		VMGR-352
160017 / QB	Lockheed KC-130R (L-382C-43D) Hercules	4677		VMGR-352
160018 / QD	Lockheed KC-130R (L-382C-43D) Hercules	4683		VMGR-152
160019 / QD	Lockheed KC-130R (L-382C-43D) Hercules	4689		VMGR-152
160020 / QD	Lockheed KC-130R (L-382C-43D) Hercules	4696		VMGR-152
160021 / QB	Lockheed KC-130R (L-382C-58D) Hercules	4702		VMGR-352
160046	Douglas C-9B Skytrain II (DC-9)	47684 / 786		VMR-1
160047	Douglas C-9B Skytrain II (DC-9)	47687 / 795		VMR-1
160056	North American CT-39G Sabreliner	306-107	N65798	MCAS Futenma
160240 / QB	Lockheed KC-130R (L-382C-58D) Hercules	4712		VMGR-352
160625 / BH	Lockheed KC-130R (L-382C-68D) Hercules	4768		VMGR-252
160626 / BH	Lockheed KC-130R (L-382C-68D) Hercules	4770		VMGR-252
160627 / BH	Lockheed KC-130R (L-382C-68D) Hercules	4773		VMGR-252
160628 / BH	Lockheed KC-130R (L-382C-68D) Hercules	4776		VMGR-252
161187	Beech UC-12B Super King Air	BJ-3		HQUSMC
161192 / 5Y	Beech UC-12B Super King Air	BJ-8		MCAS Yuma
161204 / 5T	Beech UC-12B Super King Air	BJ-20		MCAS Miramar
161307 / EZ	Beech UC-12B Super King Air	BJ-24		MWHS-4
161308	Beech UC-12B Super King Air	BJ-25		MCAS Yuma
161309 / 7N	Beech UC-12B Super King Air	BJ-26		Washington
161317 / 5A	Beech UC-12B Super King Air	BJ-34		HQUSMC
161318 / EZ	Beech UC-12B Super King Air	BJ-35		MWHS-4
161320 / 5T	Beech UC-12B Super King Air	BJ-37		MCAS Miramar
161324 / 5T	Beech UC-12B Super King Air	BJ-41		MCAS Miramar
161325 / 5D	Beech UC-12B Super King Air	BJ-42		New River
161506 / 7N	Beech UC-12B Super King Air	BJ-54		Washington
161507 / 5D	Beech UC-12B Super King Air	BJ-55		New River
161515 / 5B	Beech UC-12B Super King Air	BJ-63		Beaufort
161517 / 7U	Beech UC-12B Super King Air	BJ-65		MCAS Cherry Point
162308 / QH	Lockheed KC-130T (L-382C-34E) Hercules	4972		VMGR-234
162309 / QH	Lockheed KC-130T (L-382C-34E) Hercules	4974		VMGR-234
162310 / QH	Lockheed KC-130T (L-382C-34E) Hercules	4978		VMGR-234
162311 / QH	Lockheed KC-130T (L-382C-34E) Hercules	4981		VMGR-234
162785 / QH	Lockheed KC-130T (L-382C-48E) Hercules	5009		VMGR-234

162786 / QH	Lockheed KC-130T (L-382C-48E) Hercules	5011		VMGR-234	
163022 / QH	Lockheed KC-130T (L-382C-58E) Hercules	5040		VMGR-234	
163023 / QH	Lockheed KC-130T (L-382C-58E) Hercules	5045		VMGR-234	
163310 / QH	Lockheed KC-130T (L-382C-70E) Hercules	5085		VMGR-234	
163311 / NY	Lockheed KC-130T (L-382C-70E) Hercules	5087		VMGR-452	
163558	Beech UC-12F Super King Air	BU-6		MCAS Iwakuni	
163559	Beech UC-12F Super King Air	BU-7		MCAS Iwakuni	
163560	Beech UC-12F Super King Air	BU-8		MCAS Futenma	
163561	Beech UC-12F Super King Air	BU-9		MCAS Futenma	
163591 / NY	Lockheed KC-130T (L-382C-83E) Hercules	5143		VMGR-452	
163592 / NY	Lockheed KC-130T (L-382C-83E) Hercules	5145		VMGR-452	
163692	GAC C-20D (Gulfstream III)	481	N304GA	VR-1	
164105 / NY	Lockheed KC-130T (L-382C-83E) Hercules	5147		VMGR-452	
164106 / NY	Lockheed KC-130T (L-382C-83E) Hercules	5149		VMGR-452	
164180 / NY	Lockheed KC-130T (L-382C-95E) Hercules	5174		VMGR-452	
164181 / NY	Lockheed KC-130T (L-382C-95E) Hercules	5176		VMGR-452	
164441 / NY	Lockheed KC-130T (L-382C-11F) Hercules	5219		VMGR-452	
164442 / NY	Lockheed KC-130T (L-382C-11F) Hercules	5222		VMGR-452	
164597 / NY	Lockheed KC-130T-30 (L-382C-18F) Hercules	5260		VMGR-452	
164598 / QH	Lockheed KC-130T-30 (L-382C-18F) Hercules	5263		VMGR-234	
164999 / QH	Lockheed KC-130T (L-382C-32F) Hercules	5302		VMGR-234	
165000 / QH	Lockheed KC-130T (L-382C-32F) Hercules	5303		VMGR-234	
165153	GAC C-20G (Gulfstream IVSP)	1200	N430GA	HQMC	
165162 / QH	Lockheed KC-130T (L-382C-39F) Hercules	5339		VMGR-234	
165163 / QH	Lockheed KC-130T (L-382C-39F) Hercules	5340		VMGR-234	
165315 / NY	Lockheed KC-130T (L-382C-51F) Hercules	5385		VMGR-452	
165316 / NY	Lockheed KC-130T (L-382C-51F) Hercules	5386		VMGR-452	
165352 / NY	Lockheed KC-130T (L-382C-56F) Hercules	5411		VMGR-452	
165353 / NY	Lockheed KC-130T (L-382C-56F) Hercules	5412		VMGR-452	
165735 / BH	Lockheed Martin KC-130J (L-382U-11J) Hercules II				
		5488		VMGR-252	
165736 / BH	Lockheed Martin KC-130J (L-382U-11J) Hercules II				
		5489		VMGR-252	
165737 / BH	Lockheed Martin KC-130J (L-382U-11J) Hercules II				
		5499		VMGR-252	
165738 / BH	Lockheed Martin KC-130J (L-382U-11J) Hercules II				
		5506		VMGR-252	
165739 / BH	Lockheed Martin KC-130J (L-382U-11J) Hercules II				
		5507		VMGR-252	
165740	Cessna UC-35A (Citation V Ultra)	560-0524	N5091J	MWHS-4	
165741	Cessna UC-35A (Citation V Ultra)	560-0529	N5097H	VMR-2	
165809 / BH	Lockheed Martin KC-130J (L-382U-11J) Hercules II				
		5508		VMGR-252	
165810 / BH	Lockheed Martin KC-130J (L-382U-11J) Hercules II				
		5509		VMGR-252	
165957	Lockheed Martin KC-130J (L-382U-33J) Hercules II				
		5515		VMGR-252	On order
166380	Lockheed Martin KC-130J (L-382U-33J) Hercules II				
		5516		VMGR-252	On order
166381	Lockheed Martin KC-130J (L-382U-33J) Hercules II				
		5527		VMGR-252	On order 2002
166382	Lockheed Martin KC-130J (L-382U-33J) Hercules II				
		5528		VMGR-252	On order 2002

United States Coast Guard

UNITS/BASES	1st CGD, CGAS Cape Cod-Otis ANGB, MA	HU-25A/B
	5th CGD, CGAS Elizabeth City, NC	HC-130H, EC-130E, HU-25A/C, VC-4A
	(aircraft deployed to St.Johns NFD for ice survey)	
	5th CGD, CGAS Washington, DC	VC-11
	7th CGD, Borinquen, PR	HC-130H, HU-25A
	7th CGD, Clearwater-St.Petersberg IAP, FL	HC-130H
	7th CGD, Miami-Opa Locka IAP, FL	HU-25C
	8th CGD, CGAS Corpus Christi, TX	HU-25B, HC-130H
	11th CGD, CGAS Sacramento-McClellan AFB, CA	HU-25B, HC-130H
	11th CGD, CGAS San Diego-Lindbergh Field, CA	HU-25
	13th CGD, CGAS Astoria, OR	HU-25
	14th CGD, CGAS Barbers Point-NAS Barbers Point, HI	HC-130H
	17th CGD, CGAS Kodiak, AK	HC-130H
	Coast Guard Aviation Training Center,	
	Bates Field-Mobile, AL	HU-25A/B
PLANS	Approval received to purchase a Gulfstream V, A sixth HC-130J-30 is also on order.	

01	GAC VC-20B (Gulfstream III)	477	86-0205 (USAF)	VIP	Washington
02	Grumman VC-4A (Gulfstream I)	91	1380 (USCG)		
1500	Lockheed HC-130H (L-382C-27D) Hercules	4501		5 CGD	Elizabeth City
1501	Lockheed HC-130H (L-382C-27D) Hercules	4507		5 CGD	Elizabeth City
1502	Lockheed HC-130H (L-382C-27D) Hercules	4513		5 CGD	Elizabeth City
1503	Lockheed HC-130H (L-382C-27D) Hercules	4528		5 CGD	Elizabeth City
1504	Lockheed HC-130H (L-382C-27D) Hercules	4529		5 CGD	Elizabeth City
1602	Lockheed HC-130H (L-382C-70D) Hercules	4762			AR&SC
1603	Lockheed HC-130H (L-382C-70D) Hercules	4764		11 CGD	Sacramento
1700	Lockheed HC-130H (L-382C-37E) Hercules	4947		11 CGD	Sacramento
1701	Lockheed HC-130H (L-382C-37E) Hercules	4958		7 CGD	Clearwater
1702	Lockheed HC-130H (L-382C-37E) Hercules	4966		14 CGD	Barbers Point
1703	Lockheed HC-130H (L-382C-37E) Hercules	4967		7 CGD	Clearwater
1704	Lockheed HC-130H (L-382C-37E) Hercules	4969		14 CGD	Barbers Point
1705	Lockheed HC-130H-7 (L-382C-50E) Hercules	4993			
1706	Lockheed HC-130H-7 (L-382C-50E) Hercules	4996		17 CGD	Kodiak
1707	Lockheed HC-130H-7 (L-382C-50E) Hercules	4999		17 CGD	Kodiak
1708	Lockheed HC-130H-7 (L-382C-50E) Hercules	5002		17 CGD	Kodiak
1709	Lockheed HC-130H-7 (L-382C-50E) Hercules	5005			
1710	Lockheed HC-130H (L-382C-57E) Hercules	5028		17 CGD	Kodiak
1711	Lockheed HC-130H (L-382C-61E) Hercules	5031		14 CGD	Barbers Point
1712	Lockheed HC-130H (L-382C-61E) Hercules	5033		7 CGD	Clearwater
1713	Lockheed HC-130H (L-382C-61E) Hercules	5034		7 CGD	Clearwater
1714	Lockheed HC-130H (L-382C-57E) Hercules	5035		14 CGD	Barbers Point
1715	Lockheed HC-130H (L-382C-64E) Hercules	5037		7 CGD	Clearwater
1716	Lockheed HC-130H (L-382C-76E) Hercules	5023		7 CGD	Clearwater
1717	Lockheed HC-130H (L-382C-79E) Hercules	5104		7 CGD	Clearwater
1718	Lockheed HC-130H (L-382C-79E) Hercules	5106		7 CGD	Clearwater
1719	Lockheed HC-130H (L-382C-79E) Hercules	5107		7 CGD	Clearwater
1720	Lockheed HC-130H (L-382C-84E) Hercules	5120		7 CGD	Clearwater
2101	Dassault HU-25B Guardian (Falcon 20)	374	N1045F		Corpus Christi
2102	Dassault HU-25B Guardian (Falcon 20)	386	N149F		Miami
2103	Dassault HU-25B Guardian (Falcon 20)	394	N178F		Corpus Christi
2104	Dassault HU-25C Guardian (Falcon 20)	390	N173F		Miami
2105	Dassault HU-25A Guardian (Falcon 20)	398	N183F		Std AMARC [41011]
2106	Dassault HU-25A Guardian (Falcon 20)	402	N187F		Std AMARC [41007]
2107	Dassault HU-25A Guardian (Falcon 20)	409	N407F		Cape Cod
2108	Dassault HU-25A Guardian (Falcon 20)	405	N405F		Std AMARC [41015]
2109	Dassault HU-25A Guardian (Falcon 20)	407	N406F		ARSC Elizabeth City
2110	Dassault HU-25C Guardian (Falcon 20)	411	N408F		
2111	Dassault HU-25B Guardian (Falcon 20)	413	N410F		Corpus Christi
2112	Dassault HU-25C Guardian (Falcon 20)	415	N413F		Miami
2113	Dassault HU-25A Guardian (Falcon 20)	417	N416FJ		Borinquen
2114	Dassault HU-25A Guardian (Falcon 20)	418	N417F		Std AMARC [41014]
2115	Dassault HU-25A Guardian (Falcon 20)	419	N419F		Cape Cod
2116	Dassault HU-25A Guardian (Falcon 20)	420	N420F		Std AMARC [41005]
2117	Dassault HU-25A Guardian (Falcon 20)	421	N422F		ARSC
2118	Dassault HU-25B Guardian (Falcon 20)	423	N423F		Miami
2119	Dassault HU-25A Guardian (Falcon 20)	424	N424F		Std AMARC [41002]
2120	Dassault HU-25A Guardian (Falcon 20)	425	N425F		Borinquen
2121	Dassault HU-25A Guardian (Falcon 20)	431	N429F		Cape Cod
2122	Dassault HU-25B Guardian (Falcon 20)	433	N432F		Mobile
2123	Dassault HU-25A Guardian (Falcon 20)	435	N433F		Std AMARC [41003]
2124	Dassault HU-25A Guardian (Falcon 20)	437	N435F		Mobile
2125	Dassault HU-25B Guardian (Falcon 20)	439	N443F		Corpus Christi
2126	Dassault HU-25B Guardian (Falcon 20)	441	N445F		Cape Cod
2127	Dassault HU-25A Guardian (Falcon 20)	443	N447F		Std AMARC [41001]
2128	Dassault HU-25A Guardian (Falcon 20)	445	N449F		Miami
2129	Dassault HU-25C Guardian (Falcon 20)	447	N455F		Miami
2130	Dassault HU-25A Guardian (Falcon 20)	450	N458F		Std AMARC [41004]
2131	Dassault HU-25C Guardian (Falcon 20)	452	N459F		Miami
2132	Dassault HU-25A Guardian (Falcon 20)	454	N461F		Mobile
2133	Dassault HU-25C Guardian (Falcon 20)	456	N462F		Miami
2134	Dassault HU-25A Guardian (Falcon 20)	458	N465F		Borinquen
2135	Dassault HU-25C Guardian (Falcon 20)	459	N466F		Miami
2136	Dassault HU-25B Guardian (Falcon 20)	460	N467F		Mobile
2137	Dassault HU-25A Guardian (Falcon 20)	462	N470F		Std AMARC [41008]
2138	Dassault HU-25A Guardian (Falcon 20)	464	N472F		Std AMARC [41009]
2139	Dassault HU-25C Guardian (Falcon 20)	466	N473F		Miami
2140	Dassault HU-25C Guardian (Falcon 20)	467	N474F		Miami
2141	Dassault HU-25C Guardian (Falcon 20)	371	N1039F		Miami
3501	Grumman E-2C Hawkeye	A52-45	Bu160698 (USN)		
	Lockheed Martin HC-130J (L-382U-35J) Hercules II				
		5532			On order 2002

Lockheed Martin HC-130J (L-382U-35J) Hercules II		
	5533	On order
Lockheed Martin HC-130J (L-382U-35J) Hercules II		
	5534	On order
Lockheed Martin HC-130J (L-382U-35J) Hercules II		
	5535	On order
Lockheed Martin HC-130J (L-382U-35J) Hercules II		
	5541	On order 2003

United States Army

US Army Forces, Central Command, Third US Army - THREEUSA

224th AVN BDE, 2-228th AVN, A Co, NAS Willow Grove, PA (USARC)	C-12R
224th AVN BDE, Det 1, ASF Johnstown-Cambria AP, PA (USARC)	C-12R
224th AVN BDE, 192 AVN, F Co, Isla Grande AP, PR (ARNG)	C-23A
224th AVN BDE, Det 1, Muir AAF-Ft.Indiantown Gap, PA	C-23B/B+
224th AVN BDE, Det 2, Quonset State Airport, RI	C-23B/B+
224th AVN BDE, Det 3, Indianapolis IAP, IN	C-23B+
224th AVN BDE, Det 4, Hamilton AP, St.Croix, Virgin Islands	C-23B+
224th AVN BDE, 2-228th AVN, C Co, Simmons AAF-Ft.Bragg, NC	C-12D, UC-35A
224th AVN BDE, Det A, MacDill AFB, FL	C-12D/F
224th AVN BDE, Det B, Sherman AAF-Ft.Leavenworth, KS	C-12D

US Army South - USARSO

513th MIBDE, 204th MIB, Biggs AAF, Ft.Bliss, TX	O-5A, EO-5B, C-12F

US Army Europe/Seventh Army - USAREUR/7A

7th ATC, AVN Det, Grafenwoehr AAF, Germany	C-12F
USLSE, Flt Det, Cigli AB-Izmir, Turkey	C-12F
HQ EUCOM, Flt Det, Echterdingen AAF-Stuttgart, Germany	C-12F/J
1-168th AVN, 207th AVN Co, Heidelberg AAF, Germany (ARNG)	C-12F, UC-35A, c/s Duke****
1-168th AVN, 249th AVN, A Co, Eastern Oregon RAP-Pendleton, OR (ARNG)	C-23B
1-168th AVN, Det 1, Will Rogers WAP-Oklahoma City, OK	C-23B
1-168th AVN, Det 2, Gray AAF-Ft.Lewis, WA	C-23B
1-168th AVN, Det 3, Rapid City RAP, SD	C-23B
1-168th AVN, 185th AVN, I Co, Gulfport-Biloxi Regional APMS, MS (ARNG)	C-23B
1-168th AVN, Det 1, Groton-New London AP, CT	C-23B
1-168th AVN, Det 2, Fresno-Yosemite AP, CA	C-23B
1-168th AVN, Det 3, Springfield Regional AP, MO	C-23B
V Corps, 12th AVN BDE, 5-158th AVN, A Co, Wiesbaden AAF, Germany	C-12F
Southern Europe Task Force (SETAF), 6th AVN Det, Vicenza AB, Italy	C-12F

US Army Alaska

207th IG, 1-207th AVN, D Co, Bryant AHP-Ft.Richardson, AK (ARNG)	C-23B+

US Army Pacific - USARPAC

US Army Japan (USAJ), 78th AVN Battalion, Kastner AAF- Camp Zena, Tokyo, Japan	C-12J, UC-35A

Eighth US Army - EUSA/8th Army

17th Theater AVN BDE, 6-52nd AVN, A Co, K-16 Seoul AB, Korea	C-12F
17th Theater AVN BDE, 6-52nd AVN, B Co, ASF Dobbins ARB- Marietta, GA (USARC)	C-12F, UC-35A
17th Theater AVN BDE, 6-52nd AVN, B Co, Det, Cairns AAF- Ft.Rucker, AL (USARC)	C-12R
17th Theater AVN BDE, 6-52nd AVN, C Co, ASF Los Alamitos AAF, CA (USARC)	C-12R
17th Theater AVN BDE, 6-52nd AVN, C Co, Det, Gray AAF-Ft.Hood, TX	C-12F, UC-35A
17th Theater AVN BDE, 2-228th AVN, B Co, ASF McCoy AAF- Ft.McCoy, WI (USARC)	C-12R
17th Theater AVN BDE, 2-228th AVN, B Co, Det 1, Godman AAF- Ft.Knox, KY (USARC)	C-12R
17th Theater AVN BDE, 171st AVN, H Co, Dobbins ARB, GA (ARNG)	C-23B+
17th Theater AVN BDE, 171st AVN, H Co, Det 1, Lakeland-Linder RAP, FL	C-23B+
17th Theater AVN BDE, 171st AVN, H Co, Det 2, Robert Mueller MAP, TX	C-23B+
17th Theater AVN BDE, 171st AVN, H Co, Det 3, Capital City AP- Frankfurt, KY	C-23B/B+

US Army Intelligence and Security Command - INSCOM

205th MIBDE, 1st MIB, B Co, Wiesbaden AAF, Germany	
(assigned to VCORPS/USAREUR)	RC-12D/K, c/s Argus/Sparky**"
501st MIBDE, 3rd MIB, A Co, Desiderio AAF-Camp Humphries,	
Korea (assigned to EUSA)	RC-7B
501st MIBDE, 3rd MIB, B Co, Desiderio AAF-Camp Humphries, Korea	RC-12D/H
504th MIBDE, 15th MIB, B Co, Robert Gray AAF-Ft.Hood, TX	
(assigned to IIICORPS)	RC-12P/Q
525th MIBDE, 224th MIB, B Co, Hunter AAF-Savannah, GA	
(assigned to XVIIIABNCORPS)	RC-12N

US Army Medical Command - MEDCOM

USAARL, Cairns AAF-Ft.Rucker, AL	C-12D

US Army Training and Doctrine Command - TRADOC

1-223rd AVN, Det 1, Dothan MAP, AL (ARNG)	C-12C
FWATS, Det 1, Bennedum AP-Bridgeport-WV	C-12C, C-23B+, C-26B
111th MIBDE, 304th MIB, B Co, Libby AAF-Ft.Huachuca, AZ	RC-12D/N

Operational Test & Evaluation Command - OPTEC

OTSA, Biggs AAF-Ft.Bliss, TX	Antonov An-2
Test and Experimentation Command (TEXCOM),	
IEWTD, Libby AAF-Ft.Huachuca, AZ	O-2A

US Army Material Command - USAMC

USAAMCOM, RTTC, Flight Ops Divn, Redstone AAF-Huntsville, AL	C-23A
USAAMCOM, USNTPS, NAS Patuxent River, MD	U-21F
USAAMCOM, AATD, Felker AAF-Ft.Eustis, VA	C-23B
USACBDCOM, CBDCOM, Flt Det, Phillips AAF-	
Aberdeen Proving Ground, MD	Beech 1900D
USACECOM, AEESB, NAWC-AD Lakehurst, NJ	C-12C, C-23A
USACECOM, NVDAAB, Davison AAF-Ft.Belvoir, VA	Islander, UV-18B
USAIOC, 185th AVN, 1106th AVCRAD, Fresno-Yosemite IAP, CA	C-23B
USAIOC, 185th AVN, 1107th AVCRAD, Springfield MAP, MO	C-23B
USAIOC, 185th AVN, 1108th AVCRAD, Gulfport-Biloxi RAP, MS	C-23B
USAIOC, 185th AVN, 1109th AVCRAD, Groton-New London AP, CT	C-23B
USATECOM, ATTC, Cairns AAF-Ft.Rucker, AL	C-12C, JC-23A, JU-21H
USATECOM, EPG, Flt Det, Libby AAF-Ft.Huachuca, AZ	C-12C
USATECOM, WSMR, Air Ops Divn, Holloman AFB, NM	C-12D
USAKAMR, Flt Det, Dyess AAF-Kwajalein Atoll, Marshall Islands	DHC-7

XVIII Airborne Corps

18th AVN BDE, US Army Parachute Team, Simmons AAF-Ft.Bragg, NC	C-12C, C-31A, UV-18B, UV-20A
(XVIII Airborne Corps, operate as the 'Golden Knights').	

US Army National Guard - ARNG

OSACOM, USA PATD, Andrews AFB, MD	C-20E/F, C-21A, UC-35A
OSACOM, Atlanta RFC, Fulton County AP-Brown Field, GA	C-12F
OSACOM, Ft.Belvoir RFC, Davison AAF-Ft.Belvoir, VA	C-12F
OSACOM, Ft.Hood RFC, Robert Gray AAF-Ft.Hood, TX	C-12F
OSACOM, Ft.Lewis RFC, Gray AAF-Ft.Lewis, WA	C-12F
OSACOM, Alaska RFC, Elmendorf AFB, AK	C-12F
OSACOM, Hawaii RFC, Hickam AFB, HI	C-12D, C-20E

National Guard State Area Command (ARNG STARC), State Flight Detachments (SFD):	
Det 4, Davison AAF-Ft.Belvoir, VA	C-26B
Det 5, Montgomery RAP, AL	C-12F
Det 6, Bradley IAP-Windsor Locks, CT	C-12D
Det 7, Newcastle CAP, DE	C-12D
Det 8, St Augustine AP, FL	C-12F
Det 9, Dobbins ARB, Marietta, GA	C-26B
Det 10, Shelbyville MAP, IN	C-12F
Det 11, Capital City AP-Frankfurt, KY	C-12F
Det 12, Otis ANGB-Falmouth, MA	C-26B
Det 13, Phillips AAF, Aberdeen Proving Ground, MD	C-12F
Det 14, Bangor IAP, ME	C-12D
Det 15, Capital City AP-Lansing, MI	C-12F

Det 16, Hawkins Field, Jackson, MS			C-12R
Det 17, Raleigh-Durham AP, NC			C-26B
Det 18, Concord MAP, NH			C-12F
Det 19, Mercer CAP- W Trenton, NJ			C-12D
Det 20, Albany County AP, NY			C-12F
Det 21, Rickenbacker IAP, OH			C-26B
Det 22, Muir AAF, Ft.Indiantown Gap, PA			C-12F
Det 23, Quonset State AP, Kingston, RI			C-12D
Det 24, McEntire ANGS, SC			C-26B
Det 25, Smyrna AP, TN			C-12F
Det 26, Richmond IAP, VA			C-12F
Det 27, Burlington IAP, VT			C-12D
Det 28, Wood CAP-Parkersburg,			C-12D
Det 30, Robinson AAF-Little Rock, AR			C-26B
Det 31, Papago AAF-Phoenix, AZ			C-12R
Det 32, Mather AP-Sacramento, CA			C-12F
Det 33, Buckley ANGB, Aurora, CO			C-26B
Det 34, Boone MAP-Des Moines, IA			C-12D
Det 35, Boise Air Terminal, ID			C-12F
Det 36, Decatur AP, IL			C-12F
Det 37, Forbes Field ANGB, Topeka, KS			C-12F
Det 38, Lakefront AP, New Orleans, LA			C-12D
Det 39, St.Paul Downtown AP, MN			C-12F
Det 40, Jefferson City MAP, MO			C-12D
Det 41, Helena Regional AP, MT			C-12R
Det 42, Bismark Municipal AP, ND			C-12F
Det 43, Lincoln Municipal AP, NE			C-12F
Det 44, Santa Fe County MAP, NM			C-12R
Det 45, Reno-Stead AP, NV			C-12F
Det 46, Westheimer AP-Norman, OK			C-12F
Det 47, McNary Field-Salem, OR			C-12F
Det 48, Rapid City Regional AP, SD			C-12F
Det 49, Robert Mueller MAP-Austin, TX			C-12F
Det 50, West Jordan AP, UT			C-12F
Det 51, Gray AAF-Ft.Lewis, WA			C-12R
Det 52, Dane County RAP-Madison, WI			C-26B
Det 53, Cheyenne AP, WY			C-12F
Det 54, Elmendorf AFB, AK			C-12F
Det 55, Wheeler AAF-Schofield Barracks, HI			C-26B
Det 56, Isla Grande AP-San Juan, PR			C-12F

Civilian Contractors

SEAIR, Yuma Proving Ground, Laguna Army Airfield, AZ			O-2A

66-15361	Beech VC-6A (King Air A90)	LJ-153	N901R		Missile Center
66-18003	Beech U-21A Ute (King Air A90-1)	LM-4			Std
66-18035	Beech U-21A Ute (King Air A90-1)	LM-36			Std
67-18064	Beech U-21A Ute (King Air A90-1)	LM-65			
67-18070	Beech U-21A Ute (King Air A90-1)	LM-71			
67-18077	Beech RU-21B Ute (King Air A90-2)	LS-1			
67-18082	Beech U-21A Ute (King Air A90-1)	LM-82			
67-18087	Beech RU-21B Ute (King Air A90-2)	LS-2			
67-18093	Beech RU-21B Ute (King Air A90-2)	LS-3			
67-18113	Beech RU-21A Ute (King Air A90-1)	LM-109			
67-18114	Beech RU-21A Ute (King Air A90-1)	LM-110			
67-18115	Beech RU-21A Ute (King Air A90-1)	LM-111			
67-18118	Beech U-21A Ute (King Air A90-1)	LM-114			Std Selma, AL
67-21349	Cessna O-2A Super Skymaster	M337-0055			Yuma Proving Ground
67-21414	Cessna O-2A Super Skymaster	M337-0140			Yuma Proving Ground
68-6903	Cessna O-2A Super Skymaster	M337-0192			Std AMARC [YB001]
68-11158	Cessna O-2A Super Skymaster	M337-0383			Std AMARC [YB002]
70-15888	Beech RU-21E Ute (King Air A90-4)	LU-14		TECOM/ATTC	
70-15908	Beech U-21J Ute (King Air 100)	B-95/LM-142			Std Wichita, KS
73-22250	Beech C-12C Huron (Super King Air 200)	BC-01			Std Guthrie, AL
76-22551	Beech C-12C Huron (Super King Air 200)	BC-27			Std Dothan, AL
76-22555	Beech C-12C Huron (Super King Air 200)	BC-31			
76-22559	Beech C-12C Huron (Super King Air 200)	BC-36			Std Dothan, AL
76-22561	Beech C-12C Huron (Super King Air 200)	BC-38			Std Dothan, AL
76-22565	DeHavilland Canada UV-18A Twin Otter (DHC-6)	495		NVDAAB	
76-22566	DeHavilland Canada UV-18A Twin Otter (DHC-6)	496			
77-22932	Beech C-12C Huron (Super King Air 200)	BC-43			Std Dothan, AL
77-22941	Beech C-12C Huron (Super King Air 200)	BC-52			Std Dothan, AL

Serial	Type	Code	Reg.	Unit	ARNG
77-22942	Beech C-12C Huron (Super King Air 200)	BC-53		Std	
77-22944	Beech C-12C Huron (Super King Air 200)	BC-55		Std Dothan, AL	
77-22949	Beech C-12C Huron (Super King Air 200)	BC-60		Std Dothan, AL	
78-23128	Beech C-12C Huron (Super King Air 200)	BC-64		Det.1 EAATS	WV ARNG
78-23130	Beech C-12C Huron (Super King Air 200)	BC-66		OSACOM	VT ARNG
78-23132	Beech C-12C Huron (Super King Air 200)	BC-68		Det.1 EAATS	WV ARNG
78-23133	Beech C-12C Huron (Super King Air 200)	BC-69		USAAVNC	
78-23135	Beech C-12C Huron (Super King Air 200)	BC-71		USAAVNC	
78-23140	Beech JC-12D Huron (Super King Air 200)	BP-01		USAATCA	
78-23141	Beech RC-12D Huron (Super King Air 200)	GR-06		B/304th MI BN (AE)	
78-23142	Beech RC-12D Huron (Super King Air 200)	GR-07		B/15th MI BN (AE)	
78-23143	Beech RC-12D Huron (Super King Air 200)	GR-08		B/15th MI BN (AE)	
78-23144	Beech RC-12D Huron (Super King Air 200)	GR-09		B/3rd MI BN (AE)	
79-23253	Pilatus UV-20A Chiricahua (PC-6)	802		Golden Knights	
79-23254	Pilatus UV-20A Chiricahua (PC-6)	803		Golden Knights	
79-23255	DeHavilland Canada UV-18A Twin Otter (DHC-6)	680		Golden Knights	
79-23256	DeHavilland Canada UV-18A Twin Otter (DHC-6)	681		Golden Knights	
80-23371	Beech RC-12D Huron (Super King Air 200)	GR-02		B/3rd MI BN (AE)	
80-23372	Beech RC-12G Huron (Super King Air 200)	FC-03		138th MI CO	
80-23373	Beech RC-12D Huron (Super King Air 200)	GR-04		B/3rd MI BN (AE)	
				'CECOM Flight Activity'	
80-23374	Beech RC-12D Huron (Super King Air 200)	GR-12		B/1st MI BN (AE)	
80-23376	Beech RC-12D Huron (Super King Air 200)	GR-11		B/15th MI BN (AE)	
80-23377	Beech RC-12D Huron (Super King Air 200)	GR-03		B/15th MI BN (AE)	
80-23378	Beech C-12D Huron (Super King Air 200)	GR-13		WSMR Air Operations Div	
80-23380	Beech RC-12G Huron (Super King Air 200)	FC-02		138th MI CO	
81-23541	Beech C-12D Huron (Super King Air 200)	BP-22		USAARL	
81-23542	Beech RC-12D Huron (Super King Air 200)	GR-01		B/15th MI BN (AE)	
81-23543	Beech C-12D Huron (Super King Air 200)	BP-24		OSACOM Det.18	NH ARNG
81-23544	Beech C-12D Huron (Super King Air 200)	BP-25		EAATS Det.1	
81-23545	Beech C-12D Huron (Super King Air 200)	BP-26		Atlanta RFC	GA ARNG
81-23546	Beech C-12D Huron (Super King Air 200)	BP-27		OSACOM Det.6	CT ARNG
82-23559	Beech 65 Queen Air	LC-72			
82-23780	Beech C-12D Huron (Super King Air 200)	BP-28		OSACOM Det.14	ME ARNG
82-23781	Beech C-12D Huron (Super King Air 200)	BP-29		Hawaii RFC	HI ARNG
82-23782	Beech C-12D Huron (Super King Air 200)	BP-30		Fort Hood RFC	
82-23783	Beech C-12D Huron (Super King Air 200)	BP-31		OSACOM Det.23	RI ARNG
82-23784	Beech C-12D Huron (Super King Air 200)	BP-32		OSACOM Det.38	LA ARNG
82-23785	Beech C-12D Huron (Super King Air 200)	BP-33		OSACOM Det.40	MO ARNG
82-23786	Cessna 310				
82-23835	DeHavilland Canada UV-18A Twin Otter (DHC-6)	800		340G/98FTS	
82-23836	DeHavilland Canada UV-18A Twin Otter (DHC-6)	801		NVDAAB	CECOM
82-24054	Beech 65 Queen Air	LC-62			
82-24101	Cessna 402B				
83-24128	Beech 65 Queen Air				
83-24145	Beech C-12D Huron (Super King Air 200)	BP-34		OSACOM Det.19	NJ ARNG
83-24146	Beech C-12D Huron (Super King Air 200)	BP-35		OSACOM Det.15	MI ARNG
83-24147	Beech C-12D Huron (Super King Air 200)	BP-36		OSACOM Det.39	MN ARNG
83-24148	Beech C-12D Huron (Super King Air 200)	BP-37		Fort Lewis RFC	WA ARNG
83-24149	Beech C-12D Huron (Super King Air 200)	BP-38		Atlanta RFC	GA ARNG
83-24150	Beech C-12D Huron (Super King Air 200)	BP-39		Fort Hood RFC	TX ARNG
83-24151	Cessna 310				
83-24188	Beech 65 Queen Air	LC-70			
83-24313	Beech RC-12H Huron (Super King Air 200)	GR-14		B/3rd MI BN (AE)	
83-24314	Beech RC-12H Huron (Super King Air 200)	GR-15		B/3rd MI BN (AE)	
83-24315	Beech RC-12H Huron (Super King Air 200)	GR-16		B/3rd MI BN (AE)	
83-24316	Beech RC-12H Huron (Super King Air 200)	GR-17		B/3rd MI BN (AE)	
83-24317	Beech RC-12H Huron (Super King Air 200)	GR-18		B/3rd MI BN (AE)	
83-24318	Beech RC-12H Huron (Super King Air 200)	GR-19		B/3rd MI BN (AE)	
84-0063	Gates C-21A Learjet	35A-509	N7263C	OSACOM/USAPAT	
84-0067	Gates C-21A Learjet	35A-513	N7263H	OSACOM/USAPAT	
84-0143	Beech C-12F Huron (Super King Air 200)	BL-73		B/6-52nd AVN	
84-0144	Beech C-12F Huron (Super King Air 200)	BL-74		7th ATC CMD FLT DET	
84-0145	Beech C-12F Huron (Super King Air 200)	BL-75		Alaska RFC	AK ARNG
84-0146	Beech C-12F Huron (Super King Air 200)	BL-76		204th MI BN (AE)	
84-0149	Beech C-12F Huron (Super King Air 200)	BL-79		Alaska RFC	AK ARNG
84-0150	Beech C-12F Huron (Super King Air 200)	BL-80		OSACOM Det.42	ND ARNG
84-0151	Beech C-12F Huron (Super King Air 200)	BL-81		ATTC	
84-0152	Beech C-12F Huron (Super King Air 200)	BL-82		207th AVN CO (TA)	
84-0153	Beech C-12F Huron (Super King Air 200)	BL-83		207th AVN CO (TA) / 1st MIBtn	
84-0154	Beech C-12F Huron (Super King Air 200)	BL-84		OSACOM Det 38	LA ARNG
84-0155	Beech C-12F Huron (Super King Air 200)	BL-85		207th AVN CO (TA)	
84-0156	Beech C-12F Huron (Super King Air 200)	BL-86		207th AVN CO (TA)	
84-0157	Beech C-12F Huron (Super King Air 200)	BL-87		A/5-158th AVN	

84-0158	Beech C-12F Huron (Super King Air 200)	BL-88		HQ EUCOM FLT DET	
84-0159	Beech C-12F Huron (Super King Air 200)	BL-89		OSACOM Det.43	NE ARNG
84-0160	Beech C-12F Huron (Super King Air 200)	BL-90		HQ EUCOM FLT DET	
84-0161	Beech C-12F Huron (Super King Air 200)	BL-91		6th AVN CO	
84-0162	Beech C-12F Huron (Super King Air 200)	BL-92		6th AVN CO	
84-0163	Beech C-12F Huron (Super King Air 200)	BL-93		204th MI BN (AE)	
84-0164	Beech C-12F Huron (Super King Air 200)	BL-94		LSE AVN BDE	
84-0165	Beech C-12F Huron (Super King Air 200)	BL-95		LSE AVN BDE	
84-0166	Beech C-12F Huron (Super King Air 200)	BL-96		A/6-52nd AVN (TA)	
84-0167	Beech C-12F Huron (Super King Air 200)	BL-97		A/6-52nd AVN (TA)	
84-0168	Beech C-12F Huron (Super King Air 200)	BL-98		A/6-52nd AVN (TA)	
84-0169	Beech C-12F Huron (Super King Air 200)	BL-99		A/6-52nd AVN (TA)	
84-0170	Beech C-12F Huron (Super King Air 200)	BL-100		A/6-52nd AVN (TA)	
84-0171	Beech C-12F Huron (Super King Air 200)	BL-101		OSACOM Det 37	KS ARNG
84-0172	Beech C-12F Huron (Super King Air 200)	BL-102		Det. C/6-52nd AVN	
84-0173	Beech C-12F Huron (Super King Air 200)	BL-103		OSACOM Det. 46	OK ARNG
84-0174	Beech C-12F Huron (Super King Air 200)	BL-104		Fort Lewis RFC	WA ARNG
84-0175	Beech C-12F Huron (Super King Air 200)	BL-105		Fort Lewis RFC	WA ARNG
84-0176	Beech C-12F Huron (Super King Air 200)	BL-106		OSACOM Det.13	MD ARNG
84-0177	Beech C-12F Huron (Super King Air 200)	BL-107		Det.A C/2-228th AVN	USAR
84-0178	Beech C-12F Huron (Super King Air 200)	BL-108		Atlanta RFC	GA ARNG
84-0179	Beech C-12F Huron (Super King Air 200)	BL-109		Det. C/6-52nd AVN	
84-0180	Beech C-12F Huron (Super King Air 200)	BL-110		204th MI BN (AE)	
84-0181	Beech C-12F Huron (Super King Air 200)	BL-111		204th MI BN (AE)	
84-0182	Beech C-12F Huron (Super King Air 200)	BL-112		OSACOM Det.10	IN ARNG
84-0463	Shorts C-23A Sherpa (SD-330UTT)	SH.3110		AMCOM Tech Test Center	
84-0464	Shorts C-23A Sherpa (SD-330UTT)	SH.3111		AEESB	
84-0467	Shorts C-23A Sherpa (SD-330UTT)	SH.3114		AMCOM Tech Test Center	
84-0471	Shorts C-23A Sherpa (SD-330UTT)	SH.3118		ATTC	
84-0484	Beech C-12F Huron (Super King Air 200)	BL-118		OSACOM Det.48	SD ARNG
84-0485	Beech C-12F Huron (Super King Air 200)	BL-119		OSACOM Det.11	KY ARNG
84-0486	Beech C-12F Huron (Super King Air 200)	BL-120		OSACOM Det.47	OR ARNG
84-0487	Beech C-12F Huron (Super King Air 200)	BL-121		OSACOM Det.53	WY ARNG
84-0488	Beech C-12F Huron (Super King Air 200)	BL-122		OSACOM Det.54	AK ARNG
84-0489	Beech C-12F Huron (Super King Air 200)	BL-123		OSACOM Det.45	NV ARNG
84-24320	Beech 80 Queen Air	LD-338			
84-24375	Beech C-12D Huron (Super King Air 200)	BP-46		Det.A C/2-228th AVN	
84-24376	Beech C-12D Huron (Super King Air 200)	BP-47		C/2-228th AVN	
84-24377	Beech C-12D Huron (Super King Air 200)	BP-48		C/2-228th AVN	
84-24378	Beech C-12D Huron (Super King Air 200)	BP-49		C/2-228th AVN	
84-24379	Beech C-12D Huron (Super King Air 200)	BP-50		ARCENT (SA)	
84-24380	Beech C-12D Huron (Super King Air 200)	BP-51		Det. B C/2-228th AVN	
85-0147	Beech RC-12K Huron (Super King Air 200)	FE-1		B/1st MI BN (AE)	
85-0148	Beech RC-12K Huron (Super King Air 200)	FE-2		B/1st MI BN (AE)	
85-0149	Beech RC-12K Huron (Super King Air 200)	FE-3		B/1st MI BN (AE)	
85-0150	Beech RC-12K Huron (Super King Air 200)	FE-4		B/1st MI BN (AE)	
85-0151	Beech RC-12K Huron (Super King Air 200)	FE-5		B/1st MI BN (AE)	
85-0152	Beech RC-12K Huron (Super King Air 200)	FE-6		B/1st MI BN (AE)	
85-0153	Beech RC-12K Huron (Super King Air 200)	FE-7		B/1st MI BN (AE)	
85-0154	Beech RC-12K Huron (Super King Air 200)	FE-8		B/1st MI BN (AE)	
85-0155	Beech RC-12K Huron (Super King Air 200)	FE-9		B/1st MI BN (AE)	
85-1262	Beech C-12F Huron (Super King Air 200)	BP-53		OSACOM Det.26	TN ARNG
85-1263	Beech C-12F Huron (Super King Air 200)	BP-54		OSACOM Det.56	PR ARNG
85-1264	Beech C-12T Huron (Super King Air 200)	BP-55		Fort Belvoir RFC	
					VA ARNG, Cvtd C-12F
85-1265	Beech C-12F Huron (Super King Air 200)	BP-56		OSACOM Panama RFC	
85-1266	Beech C-12F Huron (Super King Air 200)	BP-57		Fort Belvoir RFC	VA ARNG
85-1267	Beech C-12F Huron (Super King Air 200)	BP-58		Fort Belvoir RFC	VA ARNG
85-1268	Beech C-12F Huron (Super King Air 200)	BP-59		Fort Belvoir RFC	VA ARNG
85-1270	Beech C-12F Huron (Super King Air 200)	BP-61		OSACOM Panama RFC	
85-1271	Beech C-12F Huron (Super King Air 200)	BP-62		OSACOM Det.50	UT ARNG
85-1272	Beech C-12F Huron (Super King Air 200)	BP-63		OSACOM Det.35	ID ARNG
85-1607	Fokker C-31A Troopship (F.27-400M)	10652	PH-FUA	Golden Knights	
85-1608	Fokker C-31A Troopship (F.27-400M)	10668	PH-FUB	Golden Knights	
85-1609	Piper PA-31T Cheyenne II	31T-7720051	N27KM	HHC 1-58th AVN	
85-24370	Beech 65 Queen Air	LC-165			
85-25343	Shorts C-23C Sherpa (SD3.30 conversion)	SH.3011	N331GW		
85-25344	Shorts C-23C Sherpa (SD3.30 conversion)	SH.3019	N332GW		
85-25345	Shorts C-23C Sherpa (SD3.30 conversion)	SH.3027	N334GW		
85-25349	Beech 65 Queen Air	LC-84			
85-25350	Cessna 310				
86-0079	Beech C-12J Huron (B1900)	UC-2		HQ EUCOM FLT DET	
86-0082	Beech C-12J Huron (B1900)	UC-5		78th AVN BN	
86-0084	Beech C-12F Huron (Super King Air 200)	BP-64		OSACOM Det.26	VA ARNG

86-0085	Beech C-12F Huron (Super King Air 200)	BP-65		OSACOM Det.20	NY ARNG
86-0086	Beech C-12F Huron (Super King Air 200)	BP-66		OSACOM Det.32	CA ARNG
86-0087	Beech C-12F Huron (Super King Air 200)	BP-67		OSACOM Det.22	PA ARNG
86-0088	Beech C-12F Huron (Super King Air 200)	BP-68		OSACOM Det.8	FL ARNG
86-0089	Beech C-12F Huron (Super King Air 200)	BP-69		OSACOM Det.36	IL ARNG
86-0450	Fairchild C-26A Metro III (SA227AC)	AC-734B			
87-0026	Gates C-21A Learjet	35A-280		OSACOM / USAPAT	
87-0139	GAC C-20E (G-1159A Gulfstream III)	497	N7096G	OSACOM / Hawaii RFC	
87-0140	GAC C-20E (G-1159A Gulfstream III)	498	N7096E	OSACOM/USAPAT	
87-0160	Beech C-12F Huron (Super King Air 200)	BP-70		OSACOM Det.49	TX ARNG
87-0161	Beech C-12F Huron (Super King Air 200)	BP-71		OSACOM Det.5	AL ARNG
87-1000	Fairchild C-26A Metro III (SA227BC)	BC-764B			
87-1001	Fairchild C-26A Metro III (SA227BC)	BC-766B			
88-0325	Beech RC-12K Huron (Super King Air 200)	FE-10		B/224th MI BN (AE)	
88-0326	Beech RC-12K Huron (Super King Air 200)	FE-11		B/224th MI BN (AE)	
88-0327	Beech RC-12K Huron (Super King Air 200)	FE-12		B/224th MI BN (AE)	
88-1361	Shorts C-23B Sherpa (SD-330)	SH.3201	G-BSJI	1107th AVCRAD	MO ARNG
88-1362	Shorts C-23B Sherpa (SD-330)	SH.3202	G-BSJJ	F/192nd AVN (TA)	PR ARNG
88-1363	Shorts C-23B Sherpa (SD-330)	SH.3203	G-BSJK	1109th AVCRAD	CT ARNG
88-1364	Shorts C-23B Sherpa (SD-330)	SH.3204	G-BSJL	1106th AVCRAD	CA ARNG
88-1365	Shorts C-23B Sherpa (SD-330)	SH.3205	G-BSJM	1108th AVCRAD	MS ARNG
88-1366	Shorts C-23B Sherpa (SD-330)	SH.3206	G-BSJN	EAATS Det 1	WV ARNG
88-1367	Shorts C-23B Sherpa (SD-330)	SH.3207	G-BSJO	A/249th AVN (TA)	OR ARNG
88-1368	Shorts C-23B Sherpa (SD-330)	SH.3208	G-BSJP	H/171st AVN Det 3	KY ARNG
88-1369	Shorts C-23B Sherpa (SD-330)	SH.3209	G-BSJR	EAATS Det 1	WV ARNG
88-1370	Shorts C-23B Sherpa (SD-330)	SH.3210	G-BSJS	AMCOM	
89-0268	Beech RC-12K Huron (Super King Air 200)	FE-14		B/224th MI BN (AE)	
89-0269	Beech RC-12K Huron (Super King Air 200)	FE-15		B/224th MI BN (AE)	
89-0270	Beech RC-12N Huron (Super King Air 200)	FE-16		B/224th MI BN (AE)	
89-0271	Beech RC-12N Huron (Super King Air 200)	FE-17		B/224th MI BN (AE)	
89-0273	Beech RC-12N Huron (Super King Air 200)	FE-19		B/304th MI BN (AE)	
89-0274	Beech RC-12N Huron (Super King Air 200)	FE-20		B/304th MI BN (AE)	
89-0275	Beech RC-12N Huron (Super King Air 200)	FE-21		B/224th MI BN (AE)	
89-0276	Beech RC-12N Huron (Super King Air 200)	FE-22		B/304th MI BN (AE)	
89-0515	Fairchild C-26B Metro III (SA227AC)	DC-799M		OSACOM Det 55	HI ARNG
90-0527	Fairchild C-26B Metro III (SA227DC)	DC-794M	N3004V	EAATS Det 1	WV ARNG
90-7011	Shorts C-23B Sherpa (SD-330)	SH.3211	G-BUCU	1109th AVCRAD	CT ARNG
90-7012	Shorts C-23B Sherpa (SD-330)	SH.3212	G-BUCV	1107th AVCRAD	MO ARNG
90-7013	Shorts C-23B Sherpa (SD-330)	SH.3213	G-14-3213	1106th AVCRAD	CA ARNG
90-7014	Shorts C-23B Sherpa (SD-330)	SH.3214	G-BUCX	H/171st AVN Det 3	KY ARNG
90-7015	Shorts C-23B Sherpa (SD-330)	SH.3215	G-BUCY	1108th AVCRAD	MS ARNG
90-7016	Shorts C-23B Sherpa (SD-330)	SH.3216	G-BUCZ	F/192nd AVN Det 4	VI ARNG
91-0074	Antonov An-2			OPTEC/TSA	
91-0108	GAC C-20F Gulfstream IV	1162	N7096B	OSACOM / USAPAT	
91-0503	Fairchild C-26B Metro III (SA227DC)	DC-802M		OSACOM Det52	WI ARNG
91-0505	Fairchild C-26B Metro III (SA227DC)	DC-804M		OSACOM Det17	NC ARNG
91-0506	Fairchild C-26B Metro III (SA227DC)	DC-806M		OSACOM Det33	CO ARNG
91-0507	Fairchild C-26B Metro III (SA227DC)	DC-807M		OSACOM Det9	GA ARNG
91-0509	Fairchild C-26B Metro III (SA227DC)	DC-810M		OSACOM Det21	OH ARNG
91-0511	Fairchild C-26B Metro III (SA227DC)	DC-813M		OSACOM Det12	MA ARNG
91-0513	Fairchild C-26B Metro III (SA227DC)	DC-815M		OSACOM Det24	SC ARNG
91-0516	Beech RC-12N Huron (Super King Air 200)	FE-23		B/224th MI BN (AE)	
91-0517	Beech RC-12N Huron (Super King Air 200)	FE-24		B/304th MI BN (AE)	
91-0518	Beech RC-12N Huron (Super King Air 200)	FE-25		TRW (SID)	
91-0519	Beech RC-12N Huron (Super King Air 200)	FE-26			
91-0572	Fairchild C-26B Metro III (SA227DC)	DC-828M		OSACOM Det30	AR ARNG
92-13120	Beech RC-12P Huron (Super King Air 200)	FE-26		TRW (SID)	
92-13121	Beech RC-12P Huron (Super King Air 200)	FE-27		TRW (SID)	
92-13122	Beech RC-12P Huron (Super King Air 200)	FE-28		TRW (SID)	
92-13123	Beech RC-12P Huron (Super King Air 200)	FE-29		TRW (SID)	
92-13124	Beech RC-12P Huron (Super King Air 200)	FE-30		TRW (SID)	
92-13125	Beech RC-12P Huron (Super King Air 200)	FE-31		TRW (SID)	
92-3327	Beech C-12R Huron (Super King Air 200)	BW-1	N2843B	A/2-228th AVN	USAR
92-3328	Beech C-12R Huron (Super King Air 200)	BW-2	N2844B	A/2-228th AVN	USAR
92-3329	Beech C-12R Huron (Super King Air 200)	BW-3	N2845B	A/2-228th AVN	USAR
93-0697	Beech RC-12P Huron (Super King Air 200)	FE-32		TRW (SID)	
93-0698	Beech RC-12P Huron (Super King Air 200)	FE-33		TRW (SID)	
93-0699	Beech RC-12Q Huron (Super King Air 200)	FE-34		TRW (SID)	
93-0700	Beech RC-12Q Huron (Super King Air 200)	FE-35		TRW (SID)	
93-0701	Beech RC-12Q Huron (Super King Air 200)	FE-36		TRW (SID)	
93-1317	Shorts C-23B+ Sherpa (Cvtd SD-360)	SH.3401/SH.3624	N418SA	F/192nd AVN Det 1	PA ARNG
93-1318	Shorts C-23B+ Sherpa (Cvtd SD-360)	SH.3402/SH.3695	N419SA	A/249th AVN (TA)	OR ARNG
93-1319	Shorts C-23B+ Sherpa (Cvtd SD-360)	SH.3403/SH.3629	N403SA	F/192nd AVN Det 2	RI ARNG
93-1320	Shorts C-23B+ Sherpa (Cvtd SD-360)	SH.3404/SH.3628	N424SA	D/1-207th AVN	AK ARNG

93-1321	Shorts C-23B+ Sherpa (Cvtd SD-360)	SH.3405/SH.3634	N404SA	D/1-207th AVN	AK ARNG
93-1322	Shorts C-23B+ Sherpa (Cvtd SD-360)	SH.3406/SH.3645	N406SA	F/192nd AVN Det 1	PA ARNG
93-1323	Shorts C-23B+ Sherpa (Cvtd SD-360)	SH.3407/SH.3643	N407SA	H/171st AVN Det 2	TX ARNG
93-1324	Shorts C-23B+ Sherpa (Cvtd SD-360)	SH.3408/SH.3636	N408SA	F/192nd AVN Det 3	IN ARNG
93-1325	Shorts C-23B+ Sherpa (Cvtd SD-360)	SH.3409/SH.3646	N409SA	D/1-207th AVN	AK ARNG
93-1326	Shorts C-23B+ Sherpa (Cvtd SD-360)	SH.3410/SH.3649	N410SA	EAATS Det 1	WV ARNG
93-1327	Shorts C-23B+ Sherpa (Cvtd SD-360)	SH.3411/SH.3650	N432SA	D/1-207th AVN	AK ARNG
93-1328	Shorts C-23B+ Sherpa (Cvtd SD-360)	SH.3412/SH.3657	N412SA	A/249th AVN Det 1	OK ARNG
93-1329	Shorts C-23B+ Sherpa (Cvtd SD-360)	SH.3413/SH.3660	N413SA	D/1-207th AVN	AK ARNG
93-1330	Shorts C-23B+ Sherpa (Cvtd SD-360)	SH.3414/SH.3687	N426SA	A/249th AVN Det 3	SD ARNG
93-1331	Shorts C-23B+ Sherpa (Cvtd SD-360)	SH.3415/SH.3708	N435SA	D/1-207th AVN	AK ARNG
93-1332	Shorts C-23B+ Sherpa (Cvtd SD-360)	SH.3416/SH.3664	N428SA	A/249th AVN Det 2	WA ARNG
93-1333	Shorts C-23B+ Sherpa (Cvtd SD-360)	SH.3417/SH.3647	N427SA	D/1-207th AVN	AK ARNG
93-1334	Shorts C-23B+ Sherpa (Cvtd SD-360)	SH.3418/SH.3654	N369MQ	H/171st AVN	GA ARNG
93-1335	Shorts C-23B+ Sherpa (Cvtd SD-360)	SH.3419/SH.3658	N371MQ	D/1-207th AVN	AK ARNG
94-0307	Shorts C-23B+ Sherpa (Cvtd SD-360)	SH.3421/SH.3682	N373MQ	F/192nd AVN Det 3	IN ARNG
94-0308	Shorts C-23B+ Sherpa (Cvtd SD-360)	SH.3422/SH.3683	N374MQ	F/192nd AVN Det 2	RI ARNG
94-0309	Shorts C-23B+ Sherpa (Cvtd SD-360)	SH.3423/SH.3685	N376MQ	A/249th AVN Det 1	OK ARNG
94-0310	Shorts C-23B+ Sherpa (Cvtd SD-360)	SH.3424/SH.3666	N403SA	A/249th AVN Det 2	WA ARNG
94-0311	Shorts C-23B+ Sherpa (Cvtd SD-360)	SH.3425/SH.3644	N418SA	A/249th AVN Det 3	SD ARNG
94-0312	Shorts C-23B+ Sherpa (Cvtd SD-360)	SH.3426/SH.3662	N362SA	H/171st AVN	GA ARNG
94-0313	Shorts C-23B+ Sherpa (Cvtd SD-360)	SH.3427/SH.3663	N360SE	H/171st AVN Det 1	FL ARNG
94-0314	Shorts C-23B+ Sherpa (Cvtd SD-360)	SH.3428/SH.3689	N6368X	F/192nd AVN Det 3	IN ARNG
94-0315	Beech C-12R Huron (Super King Air 200)	BW-4		A/2-228th AVN	USAR
94-0316	Beech C-12R Huron (Super King Air 200)	BW-5		A/2-228th AVN	USAR
94-0317	Beech C-12R Huron (Super King Air 200)	BW-6		A/2-228th AVN	USAR
94-0318	Beech C-12R Huron (Super King Air 200)	BW-7		A/2-228th AVN	USAR
94-0319	Beech C-12R Huron (Super King Air 200)	BW-8		A/2-228th AVN	USAR
94-0320	Beech C-12R Huron (Super King Air 200)	BW-9		B/2-228th AVN	USAR
94-0321	Beech C-12R Huron (Super King Air 200)	BW-10		B/2-228th AVN	USAR
94-0322	Beech C-12R Huron (Super King Air 200)	BW-11		OSACOM Det 16	MS ARNG
94-0323	Beech C-12R Huron (Super King Air 200)	BW-12		OSACOM Det 44	NM ARNG
94-0324	Beech C-12R Huron (Super King Air 200)	BW-13		OSACOM Det 31	AZ ARNG
94-0325	Beech C-12R Huron (Super King Air 200)	BW-14		OSACOM Det 51	WA ARNG
94-0326	Beech C-12R Huron (Super King Air 200)	BW-15		OSACOM Det 41	MT ARNG
95-0088	Beech C-12R Huron (Super King Air 200)	BW-16		B/2-228th AVN	USAR
95-0089	Beech C-12R Huron (Super King Air 200)	BW-17		A/2-228th AVN Det A	USAR
95-0090	Beech C-12R Huron (Super King Air 200)	BW-18		A/2-228th AVN	USAR
95-0091	Beech C-12R Huron (Super King Air 200)	BW-19		6-52nd AVN Det B	
95-0092	Beech C-12R Huron (Super King Air 200)	BW-20		6-52nd AVN Det B	
95-0093	Beech C-12R Huron (Super King Air 200)	BW-21		6-52nd AVN Det B	
95-0094	Beech C-12R Huron (Super King Air 200)	BW-22		C/6-52nd AVN Det B	
95-0095	Beech C-12R Huron (Super King Air 200)	BW-23		C/6-52nd AVN Det B	
95-0096	Beech C-12R Huron (Super King Air 200)	BW-24		C/6-52nd AVN Det B	
95-0097	Beech C-12R Huron (Super King Air 200)	BW-25		B/2-228th AVN	USAR
95-0098	Beech C-12R Huron (Super King Air 200)	BW-26		6-52nd AVN Det B	
95-0099	Beech C-12R Huron (Super King Air 200)	BW-27		B/2-228th AVN	USAR
95-0100	Beech C-12R Huron (Super King Air 200)	BW-28		B/2-228th AVN	USAR
95-0101	Beech C-12R Huron (Super King Air 200)	BW-29		A/2-228th AVN	USAR
95-0123	Cessna UC-35A (Citation V Ultra)	560-0387	N5108G	207th AVN CO	
95-0124	Cessna UC-35A (Citation V Ultra)	560-0392	N5124F	207th AVN CO	
96-0107	Cessna UC-35A (Citation V Ultra)	560-0404	N5201M	C/2-228th AVN (TA)	
96-0108	Cessna UC-35A (Citation V Ultra)	560-0410	N5211A	C/6-52 AVN	
96-0109	Cessna UC-35A (Citation V Ultra)	560-0415	N52457	78th AVN BN	US Army Japan
96-0110	Cessna UC-35A (Citation V Ultra)	560-0420	N51942	78th AVN BN	US Army Japan
96-0111	Cessna UC-35A (Citation V Ultra)	560-0426	N5101J	C/6-52nd AVN (TA)	
96-0112	Beech C-12J Huron (Be1900D)	UE-256	N10931	CBDCOM AVN DET	
97-0049	GAC C-37A (Gulfstream V)	566	N466GA		
97-0101	Cessna UC-35A (Citation V Ultra)	560-0452	N5130J	207th AVN Co	
97-0102	Cessna UC-35A (Citation V Ultra)	560-0456	N51444	B/6-52nd AVN	
97-0103	Cessna UC-35A (Citation V Ultra)	560-0462	N5183U	B/6-52nd AVN	
97-0104	Cessna UC-35A (Citation V Ultra)	560-0468	N51042	B/6-52nd AVN	
97-0105	Cessna UC-35A (Citation V Ultra)	560-0472	N5097H	B/6-52nd AVN	
98-0006	Cessna UC-35A (Citation V Ultra)	560-0495		OSACOM/PATD	
98-0007	Cessna UC-35A (Citation V Ultra)	560-0501	N51896		
98-0008	Cessna UC-35A (Citation V Ultra)	560-0505	N52229		
98-0009	Cessna UC-35A (Citation V Ultra)	560-0508	N5085E		
98-0010	Cessna UC-35A (Citation V Ultra)	560-0513	N5061W	B/6-52nd AVN	
99-0100	Cessna UC-35A (Citation V Ultra)	560-0532	N5268V	B/6-52nd AVN	
99-0101	Cessna UC-35A (Citation V Ultra)	560-0534	N5112K	B/6-52nd AVN	
99-0102	Cessna UC-35A (Citation V Ultra)	560-0538	N51143	B/6-52nd AVN	
99-0103	Cessna UC-35B (Citation V Ultra)	560-0545	N5091J	OSACOM	
99-0104	Cessna UC-35B (Citation V Ultra)	560-0548	N5097H		

16555	Antonov An-2				OPTEC/TSA
22253	Antonov An-2				OPTEC/TSA
N441EL	Beech King Air B100	BE-67	N522CF		US Army Avtn&Missile Cmd
N75AH	Beech Super King Air 200	BB-741			
N59A6	DeHavilland Canada RC-7B (DHC-7)	59	C-GYMC		A/3rd MIBtn (AE)
N158CL	DeHavilland Canada RC-7B (DHC-7)	58	N42RA		A/3rd MIBtn (AE)
N176RA	DeHavilland Canada RC-7B (DHC-7)	76	C-GFOD		
N177RA	DeHavilland Canada RC-7B (DHC-7)	85	C-GFOD		INSCOM California Microwave
N273EP	DeHavilland Canada DHC-7-103 Dash 7	11			Raytheon Corp Range Sys Engr Div
N341DS	DeHavilland Canada DHC-7-102 Dash 7	57	C-GTAZ		Raytheon Corp Range Sys Engr Div
N7C2GG	DeHavilland Canada DHC-7-102 Dash 7	44			Raytheon Corp Range Sys Engr Div
N7C5GG	DeHavilland Canada EO-5B (DHC-7)	48			204th MI BN (AE)
N765MG	DeHavilland Canada RC-7B (DHC-7)	65	N2655P		INSCOM California Microwave
N53953	DeHavilland Canada EO-5B (DHC-7)	104	C-GFUM		204th MI BN (AE)
N89CE8	DeHavilland Canada RC-7B (DHC-7)	88	HK-3112G		A/3rd MIBtn (AE)
N797CD	GAC Gulfstream IV	1145			
N10759	Raytheon Beech 1900D	UE-264			Kwajalein
N11015	Raytheon Beech 1900D	UE-274			Kwajalein
N11254	Raytheon Beech 1900D	UE-280			Kwajalein

United States Customs Service - USCS

P-3AEW

82-0637	Cessna U-26A				
N783MC	Beech C-12C Huron (Super King Air 200)	BC-02	73-22251 (US Army)		
N1546	Beech C-12C Huron (Super King Air 200)	BC-58	77-22947 (US Army)		
N154T	Beech C-12C Huron (Super King Air 200)	BC-50	77-22939 (US Army)		
N1549	Beech C-12C Huron (Super King Air 200)	BC-45	77-22934 (US Army)		
N155E	Beech C-12C Huron (Super King Air 200)	BC-39	76-22562 (US Army)		
N155C	Beech C-12C Huron (Super King Air 200)	BC-30	76-22554 (US Army)		
N155A	Beech JC-12C Huron (Super King Air 200)	BC-21	76-22545 (US Army)		
N1558	Beech C-12C Huron (Super King Air 200)	BC-20	73-22269 (US Army)		
N1559	Beech C-12C Huron (Super King Air 200)	BC-13	73-22262 (US Army)		
N156C	Beech C-12C Huron (Super King Air 200)	BC-14	73-22263 (US Army)		
N65CB	Beech Super King Air 200	BB-498	N23707		
N70EB	Beech C-12C Huron (Super King Air 200)	BC-35	76-22558 (US Army)		
N70E9A	Beech C-12C Huron (Super King Air 200)	BC-54	77-22943 (US Army)		
N707G	Beech C-12C Huron (Super King Air 200)	BC-17	73-22266 (US Army)		
N724C0	Beech C-12C Huron (Super King Air 200)	BC-04	73-22253 (US Army)		
N724C2	Beech C-12C Huron (Super King Air 200)	BC-11	73-22260 (US Army)		
N724C6	Beech C-12C Huron (Super King Air 200)	BC-26	76-22550 (US Army)		
N724CY	Beech C-12C Huron (Super King Air 200)	BC-03	73-22252 (US Army)		
N120CN	Cessna 550 Citation II	550-0681/681	(N6776Y)		
N1259	Cessna 550 Citation II	550-0501/501			
N125X	Cessna 550 Citation II	550-0494/494			
N1255K	Cessna 550 Citation II	550-0505/505			
N125B	Cessna 550 Citation II	550-0497/497	(N12549)		
N253K	Cessna 550 Citation II	550-0594/594	N1302X		
N263Y	Cessna 550 Citation II	550-0602/602			
N273K	Cessna 550 Citation II	550-0595/595			
N322M	Cessna 550 Citation II	550-0652/652	(N1311P)		
N372C1	Cessna 550 Citation II	550-0655/655			
N461N	Cessna 550 Citation II	550-0659/659			
N531J	Cessna 550 Citation II	550-0663/663			
N54CBG	Cessna 550 Citation II	550-0666/666			
N60CL	Cessna 550 Citation II	550-0169/185	XC-HHA		
N663G	Cessna 550 Citation II	550-0670/670			
N6775C	Cessna 550 Citation II	550-0677/677			
N6776T	Cessna 550 Citation II	550-0680/680			
N26494	Cessna 550 Citation II	550-0605/605			
N26496	Cessna 550 Citation II	550-0607/607			
N26521	Cessna 550 Citation II	550-0593/593	N1302V		
N1551	Grumman E-2C Hawkeye	A52-4	Bu158641 (USN)		
N9735	Gulfstream 1000B (Commander)	96206	N9915S		
N142CS	Lockheed P-3B (L-185) AEW Orion	5248	Bu153452 (USN)		Cvtd P-3B
N143CS	Lockheed P-3B (L-185) AEW Orion	5243	Bu153447 (USN)		Cvtd P-3B
N144CS	Lockheed P-3B (L-185) AEW Orion	5242	Bu153446 (USN)		Cvtd P-3B
N145CS	Lockheed P-3B (L-185B) AEW Orion	5409	A9-299 (RAAF)		Cvtd P-3B
N146CS	Lockheed P-3B (L-185) AEW Orion	5286	A9-605 (RAAF)		Cvtd P-3B
N147CS	Lockheed P-3B (L-185) AEW Orion	5162	Bu152722 (USN)		Cvtd P-3B

N148CS	Lockheed P-3B (L-185) AEW Orion	5256	Bu154575 (USN)	Cvtd P-3B
N149CS	Lockheed P-3B (L-185) AEW Orion	5262	Bu154581 (USN)	Cvtd P-3B
N423SK	Lockheed P-3B LW (L-185) Orion	5220	Bu153423 (USN)	Cvtd P-3B
N431SK	Lockheed P-3B LW (L-185) Orion	5228	Bu153431 (USN)	Cvtd P-3B
N741SK	Lockheed P-3B LW (L-185) Orion	5181	Bu152741 (USN)	Cvtd P-3B
N769SK	Lockheed P-3B LW (L-185) Orion	5169	Bu152729 (USN)	Cvtd P-3B
N15390	Lockheed UP-3A (L-185) Orion	5103	Bu151390 (USN)	Cvtd P-3A
N16295	Lockheed UP-3A (L-185) Orion	5108	Bu151395 (USN)	Cvtd P-3A
N16370	Lockheed UP-3A (L-185) Orion	5140	Bu152170 (USN)	Cvtd P-3A
N18314	Lockheed UP-3A (L-185) Orion	5040	Bu150514 (USN)	Cvtd P-3A
N9085U	Piper PA-42 Cheyenne IIIA	42-5501034	N9532N	
N9091J	Piper PA-42 Cheyenne IIIA	42-5501035	N9520N	
N9116Q	Piper PA-42 Cheyenne IIIA	42-5501037	N9528N	
N9142B	Piper PA-42 Cheyenne IIIA	42-5501038	N9536N	
N9150T	Piper PA-42 Cheyenne IIIA	42-5501024	N41182	
N9279A	Piper PA-42 Cheyenne IIIA	42-5501036	N9522N	
N3225F	GAF N22SL Nomad	162	VH-HVY	
N5056D	GAF N22SL Nomad	164	VH-HMZ	
N6302W	GAF N22SL Nomad	159	VH-HWB	
N6313P	GAF N22SL Nomad	161	VH-HQC	
N6338C	GAF N22SL Nomad	165	VH-JQM	

National Aeronautics & Space Administration - NASA

UNITS/BASES

Office of Aeronautics
Ames Research Center, Moffett Field, CA
Dryden Flight Research Center, Edwards AFB, CA
Langley Research Center, Langley Field-Hampton, VA
Lewis Research Center, Cleveland, OH

Office of Space Flight
George C Marshall Space Center, Huntsville, AL
John C Stennis Space Center, Bay St.Louis, MS
John F Kennedy Space Center, Cape Canaveral, FL
Lyndon B Johnson Space Center, Ellington ANGB-Houston, TX

Office of Space Sciences
Jet Propulsion Laboratory, Pasadena, CA

Mission to Planet Earth
Goddard Center, Wallops Flight Facility, Wallops Island, VA

153429	Lockheed P-3B (L-185) Orion	5226		Wallops Island
N1NA	GAC G-1159A Gulfstream III	309	N18LB	Johnson
N2NA	Grumman G-159 Gulfstream I	96	N1NA	Johnson
N3NA	Grumman G-159 Gulfstream I	92	NASA3	Johnson
N4NA	Grumman G-159 Gulfstream I	151	NASA4	Kennedy
N7NA	Beech Super King Air B200	BB-997		Dryden
N8NA	Beech Super King Air B200	BB-950		Wallops Island
N145UA	Boeing 747SP-21	21441 / 306	N536PA	Ames
N425NA	North American T-39E Sabreliner	282-95	Bu158380 (USN)	Wallops Island
N426NA	Lockheed P-3B (L-185) Orion	5175	Bu152735 (USN)	Wallops Island
N427NA	Lockheed EC-130Q (L-382C) Hercules	4901	Bu161495 (USN)	Wallops Island
N429NA	Lockheed L-188C Electra	1103	N97	
N430NA	Shorts SC.7 Skyvan srs 200	SH.1844	N30DA	Wallops Island
N432NA	Fairchild F-27F	35	N768RL	Wallops Island
N503NA	Cessna 402B	402B-0313	N719NA	Langley
N529NA	Beech Super King Air B200	BB-1091	N9NA	Langley
N557NA	Boeing 757-225	22191 / 2	N501EA	Langley
N607NA	DeHavilland DHC-6 Twin Otter 100	4	N508NA	Lewis
N616NA	Learjet 25	035	N33TR	Lewis
N635NA	Cessna O-2A Super Skymaster	M337-0236	68-10871 (USAF)	Lewis
N707NA	Lockheed NC-130B (L-282) Hercules	3507	N929NA	Dryden
N714NA	Lockheed L-300-50A (Starlifter)	300-6110	N4141A	Ames
N715NA	DeHavilland UC-8A (DHC-5)	2	63-13687 (USArmy)	Ames
N801NA	Beech Super King Air B200	BB-1164	N701NA	
N805NA	Learjet 24A	102	N705NA	Dryden
N810NA	Convair 990A	29	N710NA	Std Mojave
N814NA	Lockheed L-1329 Jetstar 6	5003	NASA414	Std Dryden
N817NA	Douglas DC-8-72	46082 / 458	N717NA	Dryden
N905NA	Boeing 747-123	20107 / 86	N9668	Johnson
N911NA	Boeing 747SR-46	20781 / 221	N747BL	Johnson

N931~A	Boeing KC-135A Stratotanker	18615 /T0654	63-7998 (USAF)	Johnson
N933~A	Learjet 23	049	N701NA	Stennis
N941~A	Airbus Industrie Super Guppy 377SGT-201F	004	F-GEAI	Johnson
N944~A	Grumman G-1159 Gulfstream II	144	HB-ITR	Johnson
N945~A	Grumman G-1159 Gulfstream II	118	N650PF	Johnson
N946~A	Grumman G-1159 Gulfstream II	146	N897GA	Johnson
N947~A	Grumman G-1159 Gulfstream II	147	N898GA	Johnson
N948~A	Grumman G-1159 Gulfstream II	222	N5253A	Johnson

URUGUAY
República Oriental del Uruguay   S America

Uruguay has operated military aircraft since 1916 but today operates primarily in a transport role including the obligatory South American Air Force airline, in this case TAMU. Funding for desperately needed new equipment is not forthcoming following a period of military rule in the 1970s and 80s and with no external aggressors this is unlikely to change.

SERIAL SYSTEM The Air Force uses three digit serials allocated with transports beginning 5** and liasion types 7**, the Navy uses a similar system with patrol aircraft commencing 8** and communictions 2**. TAMU aircraft also wear civil regis trations in the normal sequence.

Fuerza Aérea Uruguaya
Uruguayan Air Force

UNITS/BASES
Brigada Aérea 1, Grupo de Aviación 3, Montevideo-Carrasco; Aviocar, C-130B, Bandeirante,
includes operation of Transporte Aéro Militar Uruguayo (TAMU) F-27
Brigada Aérea II, Escuadrón de Enlace, Durazno-Santa Bernadina C206 (support to attack sqn)
Brigada Aérea III, Escuadrón de Aviación 7, Montevideo-Melilla C206
EMA, Escuela Basico, Aeropuerto Militar General Artigas, Pando Queen Air
Brigada de Mantenimiento y Abastecimiento, Montevideo-Carrasco AC680, C210, C182
Instituto de Adiestramiento Aeronáutico, Melilla Queen Air, C310, C182

501	Aero Commander 680	499-169	LV-FYE	BMA	
531 / CX-BOG	CASA 212-200 Aviocar	CC28-2-187		TAMU	
532 / CX-BPI	CASA 212-200 Aviocar	A28-1-189		TAMU	
533 / CX-BPJ	CASA 212-200 Aviocar	A28-1-198		TAMU	
540 / CX-BPB	Beech Queen Air A65	LC-325		IAA	
541 / CX-BKP	Beech Queen Air A65	LC-326		EMA	
550 / CX-BTZ	Embraer EMB-120R Brasilia (C-120)	120089	N12705	TAMU	
561 / CX-BHW	Fokker F.27 Friendship 100	10202	PH-FDR	TAMU	
580 / CX-BJJ	Embraer EMB-110C Bandeirante	110076	PT-GJI	TAMU	
582 / CX-BJB	Embraer EMB-110C Bandeirante	110081	PT-GJK		Std
583 / CX-BJC	Embraer EMB-110C Bandeirante	110082	PT-GJL	TAMU	
585 / CX-BKF	Embraer EMB-110B1 Bandeirante	110187		TAMU	Survey
591 / CX-BQW	Lockheed C-130B (L-282-1B) Hercules	3668	61-0971 (USAF)	TAMU	
592 / CX-BQX	Lockheed C-130B (L-282-1B) Hercules	3596	60-0295 (USAF)	TAMU	
710	Cessna 206H Stationair	2068003	N4149B	BA II, E d E	
711	Cessna 206H Stationair	2068004		BA II, E d E	
712	Cessna 206H Stationair	2068005		BA II, E d E	
713	Cessna 206H Stationair	2068006		BA II, E d E	
714	Cessna 206H Stationair	2068007		BA III, EA 7	
715	Cessna 206H Stationair	2068008		BA III, EA 7	
716	Cessna 206H Stationair	2068009	N4076J	BA III, EA 7	
717	Cessna 206H Stationair	2068010		BA III, EA 7	
718	Cessna 206H Stationair	2068011		BA III, EA 7	
719	Cessna 206H Stationair	2068012		BA III, EA 7	
744	Cessna 206 Super Skywagon	206-0262	CX-BDP	BA II	
746	Cessna 210 Centurion			BMA	
790	Raytheon Beech Baron 58	TH-1860	N2314P		
791	Raytheon Beech Baron 58	TH-1863	N2316N		

Aviación Naval Uruguaya - ARMADA
Uruguayan Naval Aviation

UNITS/BASES All units are based at BA 2 Capitan Curbelo, Laguna del Sauce.
Escuadrón Antisubmarino y Exploración Super King Air
Escuadrón de Entrenamiento Avanzado PA-34

PLANS With the S-2s effectively non-operational surplus USN P-3s are being sought.

210	Piper/Chincul PA-34-200T Seneca	AR34-7570074	LV-LRY
211	Piper/Chincul PA-34-200T Seneca	AR34-7870142	LV-MGO

853	Grumman S-2A Tracker	233	Bu133262	Std Laguna del Sauce
854	Grumman S-2G Tracker		Bu152372	Std Laguna del Sauce
855	Grumman S-2G Tracker		Bu152374	Std Laguna del Sauce
856	Grumman S-2G Tracker		Bu152376	Std Laguna del Sauce
871	Beech Super King Air 200T	BT-4/BB-408	N2067D	
875	Scottish Aviation Jetstream T.2	268	XX485 (RN)	
876	Scottish Aviation Jetstream T.2	271	XX490 (RN)	

UZBEKISTAN
Ozbekiston Respublikasy   C Asia

Uzbekistan has retained ties with Russia since the formation of the CIS with a bilateral military agreement. Serviceability is reported as good compared with some of its neighbours. The majority of transports are operated jointly with the national airline although the acquisition of more pure freighters is planned.

SERIAL SYSTEM   Most aircraft appear to have retained their Soviet identities just changing the registration prefix, note the lack of a dash between the prefix and serial, this is intentional reflecting the presentation on the aircraft.

Uzbekistan Air Force

UNITS/BASES   Most transports are based at Tashkent IAP, ICAO code UZB denotes Uzbekistan Airways.

UK85050	Tupolev Tu-154B	73A-050	CCCP-85050	UZB cs
UK11372	Antonov An-12BP	5343204		Lst UZB
11513	Antonov An-12BP			Aeroflot cs
RA-11666	Antonov An-12BP			Aeroflot cs
05 red	Ilyushin Il-76			

Government of the Republic of Uzbekistan

UK75700	Boeing 757-23P	28338 / 731		
UK80001	Avro RJ85	E2312	G-6-312	UZB cs
UK85600	Tupolev Tu-154B-2	84A-600	YA-TAT	UZB cs
UK86569	Ilyushin Il-62M	1356234		
UK86579	Ilyushin Il-62M	2951636	CCCP-86579	Opf UZB
UK87923	Yakovlev Yak-40	9741455	CCCP-87923	

VENEZUELA
República de Venezuela   S America

With its oil reserves Venezuela should be one the richest South American countries but a late 1980s economic crisis led to two attempted but unsuccessful military coups in 1992, both featuring FAV participation. The Air Force has not acquired much in the way of new equipment since.

SERIAL SYSTEM   The Air Force serial system appears random although the VIP aircraft are currently sequential from 0001. The Navy, Army and National Guard use their own sequences commencing with their initials, the last two air arms including the year of acquisition as the first two digits.

Fuerza Aérea Venezolana - FAV
Venezuelan Air Force

UNITS/BASES   Grupo Aéreo de Transporte 4, 'BA Generalisimo Francisco de Miranda' Caracas-La Carlota
              Escuadrón 41   A319, 737, G-1159, G-1159A   Presidential transport

              Grupo Aéreo de Transporte 5, 'BA Generalisimo Francisco de Miranda' Caracas-La Carlota
              Escuadrón 51   B200   VIP, medevac
              Escuadrón 52   Citation, Falcon 20, Metro, Learjet
                                                                                VIP, medevac, survey, ECM

              Grupo Aéreo de Transporte 6, 'Pegasos', Palo Negro/BA El Libertador
              Escuadrón T1   C-130H, 707   Transport. AAR
              Escuadrón T2   G222   Transport

PLANS   Another A319 is believed to be required as a VIP transport, continued operation of the 737 is therefore uncertain.

0001	Airbus A319-133(CJ)	1468	D-AVYQ	Gr 4/Esc41
0002	Cessna 550 Citation II	550-0011/012	N98876	Gr 5/Esc52
0004	Grumman G-1159 Gulfstream II	124	N203GA	Gr 4/Esc41
0005	GAC G-1159A Gulfstream III	400	N17585	Gr 4/Esc41

0006	Learjet 24D	24D-250	N85CD	Gr 5/Esc52	
0009	Fairchild C-26A Metro (SA.227AC)	AC-745B	86-0455 (USAF)	Gr 5/Esc52	
0207	Boeing 737-2N1 Advanced	21167 / 442	0001 (FAV)	Gr 4/Esc41	
0222	Cessna 500 Citation 1	500-0092/092	N592CC	Gr 5/Esc52	
0442	Dassault Falcon 20DC	235	N20FE		Std El Libertador
0675	Aeritalia G-222	4042	EV-8227 (Ejerctio)		Std El Libertador
1258	Aeritalia G-222	4055			Std El Libertador
1650	Dassault Falcon 20F	476	F-ZJTD	Gr 5/Esc52	
1952	Shorts 360-300	SH.3727	YV-O-GURI-2		
1964	Fairchild C-26A Metro (SA.227AC)	AC-740B	86-0452 (USAF)	Gr 5/Esc52	
1967	Cessna 550 Citation II	550-0449/449	YV-2338P	Gr 5/Esc52	
2222	Cessna 550 Citation II	550-0224/251	YV-O-MTC20	Gr 5/Esc52	
2414	Aeritalia G-222	4073			Std El Libertador
2716	Lockheed C-130H (L-382C-03F) Hercules	5137		Gr 6 /Esc T1	
2840	Beech Super King Air 200	BB-520			Std La Carlota
3134	Lockheed C-130H (L-382C-84D) Hercules	4801		Gr 6 /Esc T1	
3150	Beech Super King Air 200	BB-522	(YV-261CP)	Gr 5/Esc51	
3280	Beech Super King Air 200C	BL-18		Gr 5/Esc51	
3526	Aeritalia G-222	4080			Std El Libertador
4224	Lockheed C-130H (L-382C-42D) Hercules	4556		Gr 6 /Esc T1	
4402	Aeritalia G-222	4081		Gr 6 /Esc T2	
4951	Lockheed C-130H (L-382C-20D) Hercules	4407			Std El Libertador
5320	Lockheed C-130H (L-382C-42D) Hercules	4577		Gr 6 /Esc T1	
5761	Dassault Falcon 20C	23	N582G		Std El Libertador
5802	Aeritalia G-222	4082			Std El Libertador
5840	Dassault Falcon 20D	216	N9FE		Std El Libertador
6620	Aeritalia G-222	4083			Std El Libertador
6944	Boeing 707-384C	19760 / 715	SX-DBD		Std El Libertador
8747	Boeing 707-384C	18950 / 504	SX-DBC	Gr 6 /Esc T1	AAR
9508	Lockheed C-130H (L-382C-20D) Hercules	4409			Std El Libertador
YV-403CP	Beech Super King Air 200C	BL-23		Min. of Defensa Nacional	

Armada República Venezolana - ARV
Comando de la Aviación Naval (Naval Aviation Command)

UNITS/BASES	Escuadrón Aeronavale de Patrulla, Puerto Cabello/				
	Aeropuerto General Bartelome Salom		Aviocar		MR/ASW
	Escuadrón Aeronavale de Transporte				
	Grupo de Apoya, Caracas/La Carlota/				
	BA Generalisimo Francisco de Miranda		King Air, Super King Air, Commander		
	Grupo de Transporte Tactico, Caracas/				
	Maiquetia/Simon Bolivar IAP		Aviocar, Dash 7		
	Escuadrón Aeronavale de Adiestramiento, Puerto				
	Cabello/Aeropuerto General Bartelome Salom		C210, C310, C402		Liaision, Training

ARV-0201	Beech King Air E90	LW-264	TR-0201	EAdT/GrA	
ARV-0202	Cessna 402C	402C0352	TR-0202		Std Puerto Cabello
ARV-0203	DeHavilland Canada DHC-7-102 Dash Seven	68	C-GFBW	EAdT/GrTT	
ARV-0204	CASA 212 Aviocar srs 200	A27-1-177	TR-0204		Std Puerto Cabello
ARV-0205	Cessna 310R	310R-0062		EAdA	
ARV-0206	CASA 212 Aviocar srs 200	AV27-1-183	TR-0206	EAdT/GrTT	
ARV-0208	Cessna T310R	310R2124	TR-0208	EAdA	
ARV-0211	Gulfstream 695 (Jetprop 980)	95007	YV-581CP	EAdT/GrA	
ARV-0212	Beech Super King Air 200	BB-906	TR-0212	EAdT/GrA	
ARV-0215	Cessna 402B	402B0311	YV-125CP		Std Puerto Cabello
ARV-0216	CASA 212 Aviocar srs 400	462		EAdT/GrTT	
ARV-0217	CASA 212 Aviocar srs 400	463		EAdT/GrTT	
ARV-0218	CASA 212 Aviocar srs 400	464		EAdT/GrTT	
ARV-0401	CASA 212 Aviocar srs 200ASW	S43-1-351		EAdP	ASW
ARV-0403	CASA 212 Aviocar srs 200ASW	S43-1-353		EAdP	ASW
ARV-0404	CASA 212 Aviocar srs 200ASW	S43-1-354		EAdP	ASW
ARV-0501	Cessna 210E Centurion	21058664			

Ejercito de Venezuela - EV
Comando Aéreo del Ejercito (Army Air Command)

UNITS/BASES	811 Grupo a Aereo de Logistica, 'BA Generalisimo	
	Francisco de Miranda' Caracas-La Carlota	King Air, Super King Air
	812 Grupo de Transporte ' Gen Tomas Montilla',	
	Caracas/Dr Oscar Machado Zuloaga	Various

EV-7702	Beech King Air E90	LW-229			Std La Carlota
EV-7910	Beech Super King Air 200	BB-495		811 Gr	
EV-8014	IAI Arava srs 201	0063	4X-ICJ	812 Gr	
EV-8118	IAI Arava srs 202	0102	4X-CVC	812 Gr	
EV-8119	IAI Arava srs 202	0103	4X-CVD	812 Gr	
EV-8223	Cessna TU206G Turbo Stationair 6 II	U20606655	N9778Z	812 Gr	
EV-8224	Cessna TU206G Turbo Stationair 6 II	U20606642	N9748Z	812 Gr	
EV-8225	Cessna TU206G Turbo Stationair 6 II			812 Gr	
EV-8226	Cessna T207A Turbo Stationair 8	20700755	N9941M	812 Gr	
EV-9047	IAI Arava srs 201	0087	4X-CUG	812 Gr	
EV-9960	PZL-Mielec M-28 Skytruck	AJE001-19	SP-DFR	812 Gr	
EV-9961	PZL-Mielec M-28 Skytruck	AJE001-20	SP-DFS	812 Gr	
EV-0062	PZL-Mielec M-28 Skytruck	AJE002-01	SP-DFT	812 Gr	
EV-0063	PZL-Mielec M-28 Skytruck	AJE002-02	SP-DFU	812 Gr	
EV-0064	PZL-Mielec M-28 Skytruck	AJE002-03	SP-DFW	812 Gr	
EV-0065	PZL-Mielec M-28 Skytruck	AJE002-04	SP-DFZ		
EV-0068	PZL-Mielec M-28 Skytruck	AJE002-07	SP-DFV		
EV-0069	PZL-Mielec M-28 Skytruck	AJE002-08	SP-DGA		
EV-0070	PZL-Mielec M-28 Skytruck	AJE002-09	SP-DGB		
EV-0071	PZL-Mielec M-28 Skytruck	AJE002-10	SP-DGC		

Guardia Nacional
National Guard

UNITS/BASES	DAA-1, Santa Barbara de Barinas	C206, Seneca
	DAA-2, Santa Barbara de Zulia	C206
	DAA-3, Maracaibo	Baron, Skytruck
	DAA-4, Barquisimeto	King Air, C402
	DAA-5, Caracas/La Carlota	King Air, Arava, Super King Air, Skytruck
	DAA-6, San Fernando de Apure	Arava
	DAA-7, Porlamar, Isla Margarita	C206
	DAA-8, Tucupita	C206, Queenair, Arava
	DAA-9, Puerto Ayacucho	Skytruck
	CAAGN, Porlamar, Isla Margarita	C182
PLANS	Options on a futher six Skytrucks are held.	

GN-7224	Cessna U206F Stationair	U20601819	(YV-1767P)	DAA-8	
GN-7325	Beech 65 Queenair B80	LD-466	(YV-TACC)	DAA-8	
GN-7428	Beech 58 Baron	TH-418		DAA-3	
GN-7593	Beech King Air E90	LW-154	N211DG		Std Barquisimeto
GN-7839	Beech King Air E90	LW-260	(YV-171CP)		Std Barquisimeto
GN-7948	Cessna 402C	402C0104		DAA-4	
GN-7954	Cessna U206G Stationair 6 II	U20605019		DAA-1	
GN-8063	Cessna U206G Stationair 6 II	U20605402		DAA-2	
GN-8168	IAI Arava srs 201	0071	4X-ICS	DAA-5	
GN-8197	Cessna U206G Stationair 6 II	U20606156		DAA-7	
GN-8199	Cessna 206			DAA-8	
GN-8270	Beech Super King Air B200C	BL-51	(YV-487CP)	DAA-5	
GN-8274	Beech Super King Air B200	BB-980	YV-466CP		Std La Carlota
GN-8575	IAI Arava srs 201	0088	4X-CUG	DAA-6	
GN-8576	IAI Arava srs 201	0089	4X-CUH	DAA-5	
GN-8595	IAI Arava srs 201	0099	4X-CST	DAA-8	
GN-96105	PZL M-28 Skytruck	AJE001-03	SP-DFD	DAA-9	
GN-96106	PZL M-28 Skytruck	AJE001-04	SP-DFE	DAA-3	
GN-96107	PZL M-28 Skytruck	AJE001-05	SP-DFF	DAA-5	
GN-96108	PZL M-28 Skytruck	AJE001-06	SP-DFG	DAA-5	
GN-96109	PZL M-28 Skytruck	AJE001-07	SP-DFH	DAA-5	
GN-96110	PZL M-28 Skytruck	AJE001-08	SP-DFI	DAA-5	
GN-97119	PZL M-28 Skytruck	AJE001-13	SP-DFK		
GN-97120	PZL M-28 Skytruck	AJE001-14	SP-DFL		
GN-97121	PZL M-28 Skytruck	AJE001-15	SP-DFM		
GN-97122	PZL M-28 Skytruck	AJE001-16	SP-DFN		
GN-97123	PZL M-28 Skytruck	AJE001-17	SP-DFO		
GN-97124	PZL M-28 Skytruck	AJE001-18	SP-DFP		VIP
GN-	Piper PA-34-200T Seneca	34-7970393	YV-2090P	DAA-1	

VIETNAM
Cong Hoa Xa Hoi Chu Nghia Viet Nam / Socialist Republic of Viet Nam   SE Asia

1995 saw Vietnam's relations with the USA normalised twenty years after the fight to keep the Communist North and Southern Republic apart were given up. In the same year Vietnam achieved ASEAN membership. Despite initial alliance with China most post war acquisitions came from the Soviet Union (as well as the use of abandoned US equipment).

SERIAL SYSTEM No system is evident although the An-26s appear to be wearing the last three of their former Soviet identity.

Khong Quan Nhan Dan Viet Nam
Vietnamese People's Air Force

UNITS/BASES   Transport Brigade, 918 'Hong Ha' Regiment, Hanoi-Gialam.

02101	Antonov/PZL-Mielec An-2TD	1G187-32		
02102	Antonov/PZL-Mielec An-2TD	1G187-33		Std
02104	Antonov/PZL-Mielec An-2TD	1G187-30		Std
02105	Antonov/PZL-Mielec An-2TD	1G187-31		
02106	Antonov/PZL-Mielec An-2TD	1G187-32		
214	Antonov An-26			Std Saigon
215	Antonov An-26			Std Saigon
216	Antonov An-26		CCCP-26216?	Std Saigon
217	Antonov An-26			Std Saigon
218	Antonov An-26		CCCP-26218?	Std Saigon
219	Antonov An-26			Std Saigon
239	Antonov An-26			
240	Antonov An-26		CCCP-26092	
241	Antonov An-26			
242	Antonov An-26			
243	Antonov An-26			
245	Antonov An-26			
246	Antonov An-26			Std Saigon
248	Antonov An-26			Std Saigon
249	Antonov An-26			
250	Antonov An-26			Std Nha-Trang
251	Antonov An-26			
254	Antonov An-26			Std Saigon
256	Antonov An-26			Std Saigon
257	Antonov An-26			Std Saigon
258	Antonov An-26			Std Saigon
259	Antonov An-26			Std Saigon
260	Antonov An-26			
261	Antonov An-26			
262	Antonov An-26			
267	Antonov An-26	11201		
268	Antonov An-26			
269	Antonov An-26			
270	Antonov An-26		CCCP-26270?	
271	Antonov An-26			
272	Antonov An-26			
274	Antonov An-26			Std Saigon
276	Antonov An-26		CCCP-26276?	
279	Antonov An-26			
281	Antonov An-26			
282	Antonov An-26	12105		
283	Antonov An-26			
284	Antonov An-26			Std Saigon
285	Antonov An-26			
286	Antonov An-26			
287	Antonov An-26			
291	Antonov An-26			
590	Antonov An-26B		CCCP-26590	
902	Antonov An-26			
906	Antonov An-26			

YEMEN

al-Jumhouriya al-Yamania / Republic of Yemen   SW Asia

The Aden protectorate was once a very important staging post in the supply chain to Britain's Far East Empire. After it was relinquished in 1967 Yemen existed as two states, the Yemen Arab Republic (North) and the People's Democratic Republic of Yemen (South). The two halves were united in 1990 after two decades of border fighting and a further uprising in 1994 saw the Northern forces win over-all control. With little oil Yemen has little wealth, what is left of the mainly Soviet supplied equipment carries on with little immediate prospect of renewal.

SERIAL SYSTEM Three or four digit serials are displayed in arabic on the aircraft. Civil registrations are also applied but it is thought that they may change and appear on different aircraft at different times.

Al Quwwat al Jawwiya al Yemeniya
Yemen Air and Air Defence Force

UNITS/BASES   Sana'a   Il-76, C-130H, An-24, An-26

601	Antonov An-24			
602	Antonov An-24			
603	Antonov An-24			
604	Antonov An-24			
611 / 7O-ABH	Antonov An-26	9503		Yemenia titles
612	Antonov An-26			Yemenia titles
613 / 7O-ABJ	Antonov An-26	9507		Yemenia titles
615	Antonov An-26			Yemenia titles
616 / 7O-ABM	Antonov An-26	9505		Yemenia titles
617 / 7O-ABN	Antonov An-26	12302		Yemenia titles
618 / 7O-ABO	Antonov An-26			Yemenia titles
621	Antonov An-12			Yemenia titles
622	Antonov An-12			Yemenia titles
625 / 7O-ACJ	Antonov An-12			Yemenia titles
626 / 7O-ACI	Antonov An-12			Yemenia titles
1150 / 7O-ADE	Lockheed C-130H (L-382C-86D) Hercules	4825		Yemenia cs
1153	Shorts SC.7 Skyvan srs 3M-400	SH.1921	G-BBRR	Std?
1154	Shorts SC.7 Skyvan srs 3M-400	SH.1922	G-BBRU	Std?
1160 / 7O-ADD	Lockheed C-130H (L-382C-86D) Hercules	4827		Yemenia cs
1177	Antonov An-26	6507		Yemen Repubic Aviation cs
1178	Antonov An-26	6504		Yemen Repubic Aviation cs
1190	Antonov An-24RV	77310809		Yemen Repubic Aviation titles
2016	Antonov An-24TV	1022016?	966 (Sud AF)	
9503	Antonov An-26			
7O-ADF	Ilyushin Il-76TD	1033418578	RA-76380	Yemenia cs
7O-ADG	Ilyushin Il-76TD	1023412402	RA-76405	Yemenia cs
7O-ADH	Ilyushin Il-76TD	1033415497	RA-76361	Yemenia cs

Government of the Yemen Republic

7O-ADA	Boeing 727-2N8 Advanced	21842 / 1512	4W-ACJ	Yemenia cs
7O-YMN	Boeing 747SP-27	21786 / 413	A7-AHM	

YUGOSLAVIA

Savezna Republica Jugoslavija / Federal Republic of Yugoslavia   SE Europe

Yugoslavia now consists of the Republics of Serbia and Montenegro together with the autonomous regions of Kosovo and Vojvodina. The change of leadership in 2000 eventually came about though an almost peaceful revolution and the trade sanctions imposed against Milosovic's regime are being lifted. Damage inflicted during the NATO air operations on the fleet listed below has not been taken into account due to lack of substantive reports.

SERIAL SYSTEM Five digit serials are allocated to all aircraft with the first digit determining role (ie 7****, for transports). The serials are then issued in batches by type.

Ratno Vazduhoplovstvo i Prtiv Vazdushna Odbrana - RViPVO
Military Air Force and Air Defence

UNITS/BASES   677th TRAE, Nis   An-26, An-2
                 SUKL, Belgrade IAP   Yak-40

71351	Antonov An-26
71352	Antonov An-26

71356	Antonov An-26			
71359	Antonov An-26	3606		
71363	Antonov An-26			
71364	Antonov An-26			
71365	Antonov An-26			
71366	Antonov An-26			
71367	Antonov An-26			
71369	Antonov An-26	3702		
71371	Antonov An-26			
71374	Antonov An-26			
71376	Antonov An-26			
71377	Antonov An-26			
71379	Antonov An-26			
71382	Antonov An-26			
71383	Antonov An-26			
71385	Antonov An-26	3807		
71386	Antonov An-26			
71501	Yakovlev Yak-40	9120717		
71502	Yakovlev Yak-40	9120817		
71504	Yakovlev Yak-40	9231523		
71506	Yakovlev Yak-40	9731255		

Government of the Federal Republic of Yugoslavia

UNITS/BASES   Formerly with the Air Force 675 Transport Sqn, the VIP aircraft remain based at Belgrade-Batajnica.

YU-BJG	Learjet 25B	25B-187		
YU-BKR	Learjet 25D	25D-221	N3819G	
YU-BNA	Dassault Falcon 50	43	72102 (JRV)	
YU-BPZ	Dassault Falcon 50	25	72101 (JRV)	

ZAMBIA
Republic of Zambia   C Africa

Known as Northern Rhodesia until independence within the Commonwealth in 1964. The Air Force was initially established with British assistance but later support came from the Soviet Union, Yugoslavia and most recently China.

SERIAL SYSTEM   Serials are allocated in blocks by type and are prefixed with the initals AF (for Air Force).

Zambia Air Force and Air Defence Command

UNITS/BASES   Transports are reported as flying from Lusaka IAP and Livingstone.

PLANS   Up to 6 Airtech CN235Ms are required to replace the stored DHC Buffalos.

AF111	Douglas C-47	25339/13894	43-48078		
AF203	Dornier 28D Skyservant	4042	D-IBBE		
AF204	Dornier 28D Skyservant	4040	D-IBBC		
AF205	Dornier 28D Skyservant	4044	D-IBBG		
AF206	Dornier 28D Skyservant	4043	D-IBBF		
AF207	Dornier 28D Skyservant	4041	D-IBBD		
AF208	Dornier 28D Skyservant	4045	D-IBBH		
AF209	Dornier 28D Skyservant	4046	D-IBIG		
AF210	Dornier 28D Skyservant	4047	D-IBIH		
AF211	Dornier 28D Skyservant	4048	D-IBIK		
AF212	Dornier 28D Skyservant	4049	D-IBIL		
AF213	Yunshuji/Harbin Y-12 II				
AF214	Yunshuji/Harbin Y-12 II			22 Sqn	
AF215	Yunshuji/Harbin Y-12 II			22 Sqn	
AF216	Yunshuji/Harbin Y-12 II			22 Sqn	
AF217	Yunshuji/Harbin Y-12 II		B-501L	22 Sqn	
AF314	DeHavilland Canada DHC-5D Buffalo	61	C-GGQA		Std Lusaka
AF315	DeHavilland Canada DHC-5D Buffalo	65	C-GGQB		Std Lusaka
AF316	DeHavilland Canada DHC-5D Buffalo	66	C-GGQC		Std Lusaka
AF317	DeHavilland Canada DHC-5D Buffalo	67	C-GGQD		Std Lusaka
AF318	DeHavilland Canada DHC-5D Buffalo	68	C-GGQE		Std Lusaka
AF320	DeHavilland Canada DHC-5D Buffalo	70	C-GGQF		Std Lusaka
AF602	Hawker Siddeley HS.748-265 srs 2A	1688/set160			
AF605	Yakovlev Yak-40	9532042			Std Lusaka
	Antonov An-26				

Antonov An-26
Antonov An-26
Antonov An-26

Government of the Republic of Zambia

9J-DCF	Beech King Air C90		LJ-575	N12RF	Comms Flight

ZIMBABWE
Republic of Zimbabwe   S Africa

Possessing no coast line, Zimbabwe was the British colony of Southern Rhodesia until unilaterally declaring independence as Rhodesia in 1965, followed by full indepencence under its new name in 1980. The inherited air arm consisted of primarily British equipment but acquisitions have come from anywhere but the UK since then, including China. Recently internal problems derived from the land ownership issue could mean a resumption of a trade embargo, much depending on the outcome of the 2002 elections and the way in which they are handled.

SERIAL SYSTEM   Thankfully a system introduced by Rhodesia involving three digit serials having an extra type-defining digit inserted at random within them appears to have been abandoned. New acquisitions receive three digit serials in blocks by type.

Air Force of Zimbabwe

UNITS/BASES   3 'Falcon' Sqn, Manyame AFB   Aviocar, Islander
4 'Hornet' Sqn, Thornhill AFB   F337, O-2

PLANS   Former USAF C-130Bs have been offered but not yet taken up or at least delivered.
DC-3s were reported back in service in early 2001 in addition to an An-12 (probably a Chinese Y-8).

321	Cessna O-2A Super Skymaster	M337-0459	69-7661 (USAF)	4 Sqn	
322	Cessna O-2A Super Skymaster	M337-0416	69-7618 (USAF)	4 Sqn	
800	CASA 212 Aviocar srs 200	A45-1-288		3 Sqn	
803	CASA 212 Aviocar srs 200	A45-4-300		3 Sqn	
804	CASA 212 Aviocar srs 200	AV45-5-312		3 Sqn	VIP, White cs
805	CASA 212 Aviocar srs 200	A45-6-329		3 Sqn	
806	CASA 212 Aviocar srs 200	A45-7-358	ECT-134	3 Sqn	
807	CASA 212 Aviocar srs 200	A45-8-364	EC-411	3 Sqn	
808	CASA 212 Aviocar srs 200	A45-9-365		3 Sqn	
810	CASA 212 Aviocar srs 200	A45-11-367		3 Sqn	
811	CASA 212 Aviocar srs 200	A45-12-368		3 Sqn	
812	CASA 212 Aviocar srs 200	A45-13-321		3 Sqn	
813	CASA 212 Aviocar srs 200	A45-14-186	T530 (FAU)	3 Sqn	
3034	Reims/Cessna FTB337G Lynx	FTB3370039	F-BXXD	4 Sqn	
3094	Reims/Cessna FTB337G Lynx	FTB3370045	F-BXXJ	4 Sqn	
3140	Reims/Cessna FTB337G Lynx	FTB3370046	F-BXXK	4 Sqn	
3144	Reims/Cessna FTB337G Lynx	FTB3370050	F-BXXO	4 Sqn	
3146	Reims/Cessna FTB337G Lynx	FTB3370052	F-BXXQ	4 Sqn	
3154	Reims/Cessna FTB337G Lynx	FTB3370051	F-BXXP	4 Sqn	
3240	Reims/Cessna FTB337G Lynx	FTB3370059		4 Sqn	
3401	Reims/Cessna FTB337G Lynx	FTB3370037	F-BXXB		Std Manyame
3405	Reims/Cessna FTB337G Lynx	FTB3370041	F-BXXF	4 Sqn	
3407	Reims/Cessna FTB337G Lynx	FTB3370043	F-BXXH	4 Sqn	
3411	Reims/Cessna FTB337G Lynx	FTB3370047	F-BXXL		Std Manyame
3419	Reims/Cessna FTB337G Lynx	FTB3370058		4 Sqn	
4300	Reims/Cessna FTB337G Lynx	FTB3370036	F-BXXA		Std Manyame
4318	Reims/Cessna FTB337G Lynx	FTB3370057	(5T-MAR)	4 Sqn	
7136	Britten-Norman BN-2A-6 Islander	707	CR-AQF	3 Sqn	
7213	Britten-Norman BN-2A-21 Islander	412	ZS-ORD	3 Sqn	
7317	Britten-Norman BN-2A-6 Islander	658	CR-ANH	3 Sqn	
7319	Britten-Norman BN-2A-8 Islander	656	CR-ANJ	3 Sqn	
7323	Britten-Norman BN-2A-21 Islander	678	ZS-JZO	3 Sqn	

Summary by type and operating country

Each type is listed by its most recent or best known manufacturer with a summary of the countries currently maintaining at least one in Military, Government or Civil Contractor service. Aircraft on order are shown in brackets.

Aircraft Type	*Operator*
Aeritalia G-222 / LMATTS C-27J	Argentina, Italy, Libya, Nigeria, Thailand, Tunisia, Venezuela.
Aero/Rockwell/GAC Commander	Argentina, Australia, Benin, Burkina Faso, Colombia, Honduras, Indonesia, Iran, S.Korea, Mexico, Pakistan, Peru, Philippines, Thailand, USA, Uruguay, Venezuela.
Aerospatiale Corvette	Congo PR, France."
Aerospatiale TBM-700	France.
Airbus Industrie A300/310	Belgium, Brunei, Canada, France, Germany, Kuwait, (Portugal), (Spain), Thailand, UAE.
Airbus Industrie A319/A320	France, Italy, Qatar, UAE, Venezuela.
Airbus Industrie A340	Brunei, Egypt, Jordan, Qatar, Saudi Arabia.
Airbus Industrie A400M	(Belgium, France, Germany, Luxembourg, Portugal, Spain, Turkey, UK).
Airbus Industrie 377SGT Super Guppy	USA.
Airtech CASA/IPTN CN235	Austria, Botswana, Brunei, Chile, Colombia, Ecuador, France, Gabon, Indonesia, Ireland, Jordan, S.Korea, Malaysia, Mexico, Morocco, Oman, Panama, Papua New Guinea, Saudi Arabia, South Africa, Spain, Switzerland, Thailand, Turkey, UAE, USA.
AMD-BA Atlantic/Atlantique 2	France, Germany, Italy, Pakistan.
Antonov An-2/Yunshuji Y-5	Albania, Angola, Armenia, Belarus, Bulgaria, China, Croatia, Cuba, Estonia, Indonesia, Kazakstan, N.Korea, Latvia, Lithuania, Moldova, Nicaragua, Poland, Romania, Russia, Turkmenistan, Ukraine, USA, Vietnam.
Antonov An-12/Shaanxi Y-8	Afghanistan, Angola, Azerbaijan, Belarus, China, Ethiopia, Guinea, Kazakstan, N.Korea, Myanmar, Russia, Sri Lanka, Sudan, Turkmenistan, Ukraine, Uzbekistan, Yemen.
Antonov An-22	Russia.
Antonov An-24	Armenia, Azerbaijan, Belarus, Bulgaria, Cambodia, Congo PR, Cuba, Czech Rep, Equatorial Guinea, Kazakstan, Mali, Mongolia, Romania, Russia, Slovakia, Syria, Turkmenistan, Ukraine, Yemen.
Antonov An-26	Afghanistan, Angola, Belarus, Bulgaria, Cape Verde Isl., Chad, China, Cuba, Czech Rep, Hungary, Iraq, Kazakstan, Laos, Libya, Lithuania, Madagascar, Mali, Mongolia, Mozambique, Nicaragua, Niger, Poland, Romania, Russia, Slovakia, Sri Lanka, Syria, Ukraine, Vietnam, Yemen, Yugoslavia, Zambia.
Antonov An-28/PZL M-28 Skytruck	Djibouti, Peru, Poland, Venezuela
Antonov An-30	Bulgaria, China, Cuba, Czech Rep, Kazakstan, Romania, Russia, Ukraine.
Antonov An-32	Afghanistan, Angola, Armenia, Bangladesh, Croatia, Equatorial Guinea, Ethiopia, India, Mexico, Peru, Sri Lanka.
Antonov An-72/74/76	Angola, Chad, Iran, Kazakstan, Laos, Moldova, Peru, Russia, Ukraine.
Antonov An-70	(Russia, Ukraine)
Antonov An-124	(Libya), Russia.
ATR42	Gabon, Italy.
BAC One-Eleven	Oman, Romania, UK.
Beagle Bassett	UK.
Beech 18	Indonesia, Tonga.
Beech Queen Air 65	Argentina, Colombia, Israel, Peru, Philippines, USA, Uruguay, Venezuela.
Beech Duke 60	Dominican Rep.
Beech 99	Chile.
Beech/Raytheon Baron 55/58	Bolivia, Chile, Colombia, Haiti, Mexico, Namibia, Pakistan, Paraguay, UK, Uruguay, Venezuela.
Beech/Raytheon King Air 90/100/T-44/U-21/C-6	Argentina, Algeria, Bolivia, Canada, Chile, Colombia, Ecuador, Guatemala, Haiti, India, Jamaica, Japan, Morocco, Mexico, Peru, Tanzania, Thailand, USA, Venezuela, Zambia.
Beech/Raytheon Super King Air 200/300/C-12	Algeria, Argentina, Australia, Bolivia, Botswana, Burkina Faso, Canada, Chile, Colombia, Dominican Rep., Ecuador, Egypt, France, Greece, Guatemala, India, Ireland, Israel, Japan, Macedonia, Malaysia, Mexico, Morocco, Netherlands, New Zealand, Pakistan, Papua New Guinea, Peru, South Africa, Sri Lanka, Sweden, Switzerland, Taiwan, Thailand, Togo, Turkey, UAE, USA, Uruguay, Venezuela.
Beech/Raytheon 400 Beechjet/T-1	Japan, Pakistan, South Africa, USA.
Beech/Raytheon 1900/C-12J	Algeria, Egypt, Seychelles, Taiwan, Thailand, USA.
Boeing 707/C-137/E-3/E-6/E-8/C-18	Angola, Argentina, Australia, Brazil, Chile, Colombia, Congo DR, Egypt, France, India, Indonesia, Iran, Israel, Italy, Libya, NATO, Pakistan, Paraguay, Peru, Saudi Arabia, South Africa, Spain, Togo, UK, USA, Venezuela.
Boeing 727/C-22	Bahrain, Burkina Faso, Cameroon, Colombia, Congo DR, Djibouti, Ecuador, Iran, Mexico, New Zealand, Nigeria, Tatarstan, Saudi Arabia, Senegal, Taiwan, USA, Yemen.

Boeing 737/BBJ/T-43/C-40	(Australia), Brazil, Chile, China, India, Indonesia, Iran, S.Korea, Mexico, Niger, Peru, Philippines, Saudi Arabia, South Africa, Taiwan, Thailand, Tunisia, (Turkey), Turkmenistan, UAE, USA, Venezuela.
Boeing 747/747SP/E-4/C-25/AL-1	Bahrain, Brunei, Iran, Japan, Kuwait, Oman, Saudi Arabia, UAE, USA, Yemen.
Boeing 757/C-32	Argentina, Kazakstan, Mexico, Saudi Arabia, Turkmenistan, USA, Uzbekistan.
Boeing 767	Brunei, China, Japan, UAE.
Boeing C-135 series	France, Singapore, Turkey, USA..
Boeing/McDonnell Douglas C-17 Globemaster III	UK, USA.
Bombardier/Canadair CL-215/415	Canada, Croatia, France, Greece, Spain, Thailand.
Bombardier/Canadair CL-600/601/604 Challenger	Canada, Croatia, Czech Rep., Denmark, Germany, Jordan, S.Korea, Palestine, Saudi Arabia.
Bombardier/Canadair Regional Jet	China.
Bombardier Global Express	Malaysia, (UK).
Bombardier/DeHavilland DHC-8 DASH Eight/E-9	Australia, Canada, Kenya, Mexico, USA.
Bombardier/Gates Learjet/C-21	Argentina, Australia, Bolivia, Brazil, Chile, China, Finland, Germany, India, Japan, Macedonia, Mexico, Namibia, Pakistan, Peru, Saudi Arabia, Singapore, Slovenia, Switzerland, Thailand, UAE, USA, Venezuela, Yugoslavia.
British Aerospace 146/Avro RJ	Bahrain, Uzbekistan, UK.
British Aerospace Jetstream 31/41	China-Hong Kong, Saudi Arabia, Thailand, UK, Uruguay.
Britten-Norman BN-2 Islander/Defender	Angola, Australia, Belgium, Belize, Botswana, Cambodia, Central African Republic, Cyprus, Falkland Isl., Ghana, Guyana, India, Indonesia, Ireland, Jamaica, Jordan, Malawi, Mali, Malta, Mauritania, Mauritius, Morocco, Pakistan, Peru, Philippines, Seychelles, Surinam, Thailand, UK, Zimbabwe.
CASA 212 Aviocar	Angola, Argentina, Botswana, Chile, Colombia, Congo DR, Dominican Rep, France, Indonesia, Jordan, Lesotho, Mexico, Panama, Paraguay, Portugal, South Africa, Spain, Surinam, Sweden, Thailand, UAE, USA, Uruguay, Venezuela, Zimbabwe.
CASA C295	(Poland), Spain.
Cessna 206	Argentina, Bolivia, Cameroon, Chile, Colombia, Costa Rica, Djibouti, Ecuador, Guatemala, Guyana, Indonesia, Liberia, Malaysia, Paraguay, Peru, Philippines, Tanzania, Thailand, Turkey, Uruguay, Venezuela.
Cessna 207 Skywagon	Argentina, Austria, Dominican Rep., Venezuela.
Cessna 208 Caravan	Brazil, Canada, Chile, Colombia, Djibouti, Liberia, Malaysia, South Africa, Thailand.
Cessna 210 Centurion	Bolivia, Colombia, Guatemala, Jamaica, Paraguay, Peru, Philippines, Uruguay, Venezuela.
Cessna 310/U-3	Canada, Colombia, Congo PR, Congo DR, France, Honduras, Kenya, Madagascar, Paraguay, Surinam, Trinidad & Tobago, Uruguay, USA, Venezuela.
Cessna 320 Skyknight	Ecuador.
Cessna 337 Super Skymaster/Skymaster/O-2/ F337/FTB337G/Summit T-337	Botswana, Burkina Faso, Canada, Chad, Chile, Costa Rica, El Salvador, Ethiopia, France, Gabon, Guinea Bissau, Haiti, Ivory Coast, S.Korea, Madagascar, Mauritania, Namibia, Niger, Portugal, Solomon Isl., Thailand, Togo, USA, Zimbabwe.
Cessna 340	Colombia.
Cessna 401	Colombia, Ethiopia, Honduras, Indonesia, Paraguay, Trinidad & Tobago.
Cessna 402	Barbados, Bolivia, Colombia, Djibouti, Haiti, Malaysia, Paraguay, South Africa, Tanzania, USA, Venezuela.
Cessna 404 Titan	Colombia, France, Kenya, Mexico, Nicaragua, Tanzania.
Cessna/Reims F406 Caravan II	Australia, (Brazil), France, Greece, S.Korea, Namibia, Seychelles.
Cessna 411	France.
Cessna 421 Golden Eagle	Bahamas, Bolivia, Cambodia, Ivory Coast, Pakistan, Peru, Philippines, Sri Lanka, Turkey, USA.
Cessna 441 Conquest II	Colombia, Mexico, UK.
Cessna Citation 500/525/550/560 /T-47/C-35	Argentina, Bosnia-Herzegovina, Canada, Chile, China, Colombia, Ecuador, Mexico, Morocco, Myanmar, Nigeria, Pakistan, Saudi Arabia, South Africa, Spain, Sweden, Turkey, USA, Venezuela.
Cessna Citation 650/670	Chile, China, Turkey.
Consolidated PBY Catalina/Canso	Canada.
Convair 440/580	Bolivia, Colombia.
Convair 880/990	USA.
Dassault Falcon 10	France.
Dassault Falcon 20/HU-25	Belgium, Cambodia, Egypt, France, Iran, Iraq, Mexico, Morocco, Norway, Pakistan, Peru, Portugal, Spain, Sudan, Syria, UK, USA, Venezuela.
Dassault Falcon 50	Burundi, France, Iran, Italy, Libya, Morocco, Portugal, South Africa, Spain, Sudan, Switzerland, Yugoslavia.
Dassault Falcon 900	Australia, Belgium, Equatorial Guinea, France, Gabon, Greece, Italy, Japan, Namibia, Nigeria, Saudi Arabia, South Africa, Spain, Sudan, Syria, UAE.
Dassault Falcon 2000	Bulgaria.
DeHavilland DHC-2 Beaver/Turbo Beaver/U-6	Canada, USA.
DeHavilland DHC-3 Otter/U-1	Canada, USA.
DeHavilland DHC-4 Caribou/C-7	Australia, Costa Rica, Liberia, Malaysia.

DeHavilland DHC-5 Buffalo/C-8	Brazil, Cameroon, Canada, Congo DR, Ecuador, Egypt, Indonesia, Kenya, Mexico, Sudan, Tanzania, Togo, USA, Zambia.
DeHavilland DHC-6 Twin Otter/V-18	Argentina, Australia, Benin, Canada, Chile, Colombia, Ecuador, Ethiopia, France, Mexico, Norway, Paraguay, Peru, Saudi Arabia, Senegal, Switzerland, USA.
DeHavilland DHC-7 DASH Seven/O-5	USA, Venezuela.
Dinfia IA.50	Argentina.
Dornier 27/CASA 127	Spain, Switzerland, Togo, Turkey.
Dornier 28/128 Skyservant	Benin, Cameroon, Croatia, Ethiopia, Greece, Israel, Kenya, Morocco, Niger, Nigeria, Turkey, Zambia.
Dornier 228/HAL228	Bhutan, Cape Verde Isl., Eritrea, Finland, Germany, India, Iran, Italy, Mauritius, Niger, Nigeria, Oman, Thailand, UK.
Dornier 328	Colombia.
Douglas C-47/DC-3/C-53/BT-67/DC-3TP	Bolivia, Colombia, El Salvador, Guatemala, Haiti, Honduras, Indonesia, Israel, Madagascar, Malawi, Mali, Mauritania, Paraguay, South Africa, Thailand, Zambia.
Douglas DC-8/C-24	France, Gabon, Peru, Saudi Arabia, USA.
Embraer EMB-110/EMB-111 Bandeirante	Angola, Brazil, Cape Verde Isl., Chile, Colombia, Gabon, Uruguay.
Embraer EMB-120 Brasilia	Brazil, Uruguay.
Embraer EMB-121 Xingu	Brazil, France.
Embraer ERJ-135/145	Belgium, Brazil, Greece, (Mexico).
Fairchild F-27/FH-227	Angola, Mexico, Myanmar, USA.
Fairchild Merlin	Argentina, Belgium, Colombia, El Salvador, Thailand.
Fairchild Metro/C-26	Argentina, Barbados, Colombia, Mexico, Peru, Trinidad & Tobago, USA, Venezuela.
Fokker 50/60	Netherlands, Singapore, Taiwan, Thailand.
Fokker 70/100	Ivory Coast, Kenya, Netherlands.
Fokker F27 Friendship/Troopship/C-31	Algeria, Argentina, Bolivia, Canada, Chad, Finland, France, Ghana, Guatemala, Iceland, Indonesia, Iran, Myanmar, Pakistan, Peru, Philippines, Senegal, Spain, Thailand, Uruguay, USA.
Fokker F28 Fellowship	Argentina, Colombia, Ecuador, Ghana, Indonesia, Iran, Malaysia, Peru, Philippines, Tanzania, Togo.
GAF Nomad	Indonesia, Papua New Guinea, Philippines, Thailand, USA.
Gavilan 358	Colombia.
Grumman S-2 Tracker/Firecat	Argentina, Canada, France, Taiwan, Thailand, Uruguay.
Grumman C-2 Greyhound	USA.
Grumman E-2 Hawkeye	Egypt, France, Israel, Japan, Singapore, Taiwan, USA.
Grumman V-1 Mohawk	Argentina.
Grumman Gulfstream 1/C-4	Mexico, USA.
Grumman/GAC Gulfstream II / III/C-20A-E	Angola, Bahrain, Cameroon, Chad, Denmark, Egypt, Ghana, India, Nigeria, Italy, Ivory Coast, Mexico, Morocco, Panama, Saudi Arabia, USA, Venezuela.
GAC Gulfstream IV/V/C-20F-H/C-37	Algeria, Bahrain, Botswana, Brunei, Chile, Egypt, Gabon, Ireland, Ivory Coast, Japan, Kuwait, Malaysia, Netherlands, Nigeria, Oman, Saudi Arabia, Sweden, Turkey, Uganda, UAE, USA.
Hawker Siddeley HS.748/HAL 748/Andover	Australia, Belgium, Brazil, Burkina Faso, Ecuador, India, S.Korea, Madagascar, Nepal, Sri Lanka, Thailand, UK, Zambia.
Hawker Siddeley/British Aerospace Nimrod	UK.
IAI Arava	Bolivia, Cameroon, Colombia, Ecuador, Guatemala, Haiti, Israel, Liberia, Mexico, Papua New Guinea, Surinam, Thailand, Venezuela.
IAI Astra/C-38	USA.
IAI Westwind	Germany, Honduras, Israel.
Ilyushin Il-14	Albania.
Ilyushin Il-18/20/22	Kazakstan, Russia, Ukraine.
Ilyushin Il-38	India, Russia.
Ilyushin Il-62	N.Korea, Russia, Ukraine, Uzbekistan.
Ilyushin Il-76/78/82/A-50	Algeria, Azerbaijan, Belarus, China, Cuba, Russia, India, Iran, Iraq, N.Korea, Libya, Syria, Ukraine, Uzbekistan, Yemen.
Ilyushin Il-86/80	Russia.
Ilyushin Il-96	Russia.
Kawasaki C-1	Japan.
Let 410	Bulgaria, Czech Rep., Estonia, Latvia, Libya, Lithuania, Peru, Russia, Slovakia, Slovenia, Tunisia.
Let 610	Czech Rep.
Lockheed C-130/L-100 Hercules	Algeria, Argentina, Australia, Bangladesh, Belgium, Bolivia, Botswana, Brazil, Cameroon, Canada, Chad, Chile, Colombia, Congo DR, Denmark, Ecuador, Egypt, Ethiopia, France, Gabon, Greece, Honduras, Indonesia, Iran, Israel, Italy, Japan, Jordan, S.Korea, Kuwait, Libya, Malaysia, Mexico, Morocco, Netherlands, New Zealand, Niger, Nigeria, Norway, Oman, Pakistan, Peru, Philippines, Portugal, Romania, Saudi Arabia, Singapore, South Africa, Spain, Sri Lanka, Sudan, Sweden, Taiwan, Thailand, Tunisia, Turkey, UAE, UK, USA, Uruguay, Venezuela, Yemen.
Lockheed C-141 Starlifter	USA.
Lockheed C-5 Galaxy	USA.

Lockheed L-1011 TriStar	Jordan, Saudi Arabia, UK.
Lockheed L-1329 JetStar/C-140	Iran, Iraq, Mexico, Palestine, USA.
Lockheed L-188 Electra	Argentina, Bolivia, Honduras, Mexico, USA.
Lockheed P-3 Orion/CP-140 Aurora	Argentina, Australia, (Brazil), Canada, Chile, Greece, Iran, Norway, Netherlands, Japan, S.Korea, New Zealand, Pakistan, Portugal, Spain, Thailand, USA.
Lockheed S-3 Viking	USA.
Max Holste Broussard	Madagascar.
McDonnell Douglas DC-9/C-9/MD-80	Italy, Kuwait, USA.
McDonnell Douglas DC-10/KC-10	Netherlands, USA.
McDonnell Douglas MD-11	Saudi Arabia.
Mitsubishi Mu-2	Japan, Mexico.
Morane-Saulnier MS.760 Paris	Argentina, France.
NAMC YS-11	Greece, Japan.
Nord 262	Burkina Faso, France, Gabon.
Partenavia P-68	Italy.
Piaggio P-166	Italy.
Piaggio P-180	Italy.
Piaggio PD-808	Italy.
Pilatus PC-6 Turbo Porter/V-21/Fairchild U-23	Algeria, Argentina, Austria, Chad, Ecuador, France, Indonesia, Iran, Malaysia, Mexico, Myanmar, Peru, Slovenia, Thailand, South Africa, Switzerland, Thailand, UAE, USA.
Pilatus PC-XII	Argentina, Canada, South Africa.
Piper PA-23 Apache/Aztec	Argentina, Cameroon, Colombia, Liberia, Madagascar, Mexico, Paraguay.
Piper PA-31 Navajo/Colemill Panther	Argentina, Bahamas, Canada, Chile, Colombia, Costa Rica, Dominican Rep, Finland, France, Gabon, Guatemala, Mexico, Nigeria, Peru, Syria, Trinidad & Tobago, UK.
Piper PA-31T/PA-42 Cheyenne	Bangladesh, Canada, Chile, Colombia, Honduras, Mauritania, Panama, USA.
Piper PA-34 Seneca/EMB-810/PZL M-20	Argentina, Brazil, Colombia, Costa Rica, Ecuador, Haiti, Pakistan, Panama, Paraguay, Peru, Poland, Uruguay, Venezuela.
Piper PA-44 Seminole	Colombia.
Piper PA-60 Aerostar	Canada.
Raytheon Hawker/BAe/HS125	Brazil, Japan, S.Korea, Malawi, Malaysia, Nigeria, Saudi Arabia, Turkmenistan, UK.
Rockwell Sabreliner/North American T-39	Argentina, Bolivia, Ecuador, Mexico, Sweden, USA.
Saab 340	Greece, Japan, Sweden.
Shin Mewa US-1	Japan.
Shorts SC.7 Skyvan	Austria, Ghana, Guyana, Indonesia, Mexico, Nepal, Oman, Thailand, UAE, UK, USA, Yemen.
Shorts 330/360/C-23	Thailand, UAE, USA, Venezuela.
SIAI-Marchetti SF.600 Canguro	Philippines.
Transall C-160	France, Germany, South Africa, Turkey.
Tupolev Tu-134/Tu-135	Angola, Armenia, Azerbaijan, Belarus, Bulgaria, Georgia, Kazakhstan, Moldova, Russia, Syria, Ukraine.
Tupolev Tu-142	India.
Tupolev Tu-154	Azerbaijan, Belarus, Bulgaria, China, Czech Rep, Kazakhstan, Poland, Russia, Slovakia, Ukraine, Uzbekistan.
Tupolev Tu-204	Russia.
Vickers VC-10/Super VC-10	UK.
Yakovlev Yak-40	Angola, Belarus, Cuba, Czech Rep, Equatorial Guinea, Ethiopia, Kazakhstan, Laos, Madagascar, Poland, Russia, Slovakia, Syria, Ukraine, Uzbekistan, Yugoslavia, Zambia.
Yakovlev Yak-42	China, Russia.
Yunshuji/Harbin Y-12 II	Cambodia, China, Eritrea, Iran, Kenya, Laos, Mauritania, Namibia, Pakistan, Peru, Sri Lanka, Tanzania, Zambia.
Yunshuji/Xian Y-7	China, Laos.

Abbreviations and translations

AAB	Army Air Base	USA
AACS	Airborne Air Control Squadron	USA
AAF	Army Air Force	USA
AAR	Air-Air Refuelling (Tanker aircraft)	universal abbreviation
AB	Air Base	USA
ABG	Air Base Group	USA
ABS	Air Base Squadron	USA
ABW	Air Base Wing	USA
ACG	Air Control Group	USA
ACW	Air Control Wing	USA
AEW	Airborne Early Warning	universal abbreviation
AFAF	Air Force Auxillary Field	USA
AFB	Air Force Base	USA
AG	Airlift Group	USA
ALF	Airlift Flight	USA
AMARC	Aerospace Maintenance & Regeneration Centre (Davis-Monthan AFB, Arizona)	USA
AMW	Air Mobility Wing	USA
ANG	Air National Guard	USA
ANGB	Air National Guard Base	USA
AP	Airport	USA
APSZ	Air Refuelling Aviation Regiment	Russia
ARB	Air Reserve Base	USA
ARG	Air Refuelling Group	USA
ARNG	(US) Army National Guard	USA
ARS	Air Refuelling Squadron	USA
ARS	Air Reserve Station	USA
ARW	Air Refuelling Wing	USA
AS	Airlift Squadron	USA
ASEAN	Association of South East Asian Nations	
ASW	Anti-Submarine Warfare	universal abbreviation
AW	Airlift Wing	USA
CEV (Centre d'Essais en Vol)	Flight Test Centre	France
CGAS	Coast Guard Air Station	USA
CGD	Coast Guard District	USA
COIN	COunter INsurgency	universal abbreviation
COMINT	Communications Intelligence	universal abbreviation
Corpus Takticheska Aviatzia	Tactical Aviation Corps	Bulgaria
Cvtd	Converted (modified)	
Dam	Damaged	
Densi-sen Sien-tai	ECM Support Squadron	Japan
Det / det	Detachment	universal abbreviation
Diikissi Aeroporikis Ipostirixis	Support Command	Greece
DoD	Department of Defense	USA
Dopravne Letecke Kridlo	Transport Wing	Slovakia
ECM	Electronic Counter Measures	universal abbreviation
École du Personnel Navigants d'Essais et de Réception	Navigators' Test and Reception School	France
ECS	Electronic Combat Squadron	USA
Enlace	Liaison	Spain and Latin America
Eskadrila Transportinih Zrakoplova	Combat Transport Squadron	Croatia
EU	European Union	Europe
EW	Electronic Warfare	universal abbreviation
EWG	Electronic Warfare Group	USA
FAC	Forward Air Control	universal abbreviation
Flachenstaffel	Fixed-wing Squadron	Austria
Fliegerregiment	Aviation Regiment	Austria
Flotila Militara de Transport	Military Transport Regiment	Romania
FLTS	Flight Test Squadron	USA
FMFPAC	Fleet Marine Force Pacific	USA
FS	Fighter Squadron	USA
FTS	Flying Training Squadron	USA
FTW	Flying Training Wing	USA
FW	Fighter Wing	USA
FWATS	Fixed Wing ARNG Training Site	USA
GAF	German Air Force (post 1990)	Germany
Hiko Kaihatsu Jikken-dan	Air Development and Test Wing	Japan
Hiko Tenken-tai	Flight Check Squadron	Japan
Hiko-tai	Squadron	Japan
IAP	International Airport	universal abbreviation

JRB	Joint Reserve Base	USA
Keikai Koku-tai	Airborne Early Warning Wing	Japan
Koku Kyunan-dan	Air Rescue Wing	Japan
Koku-dan	Air Wing	Japan
Koku-gun	Fleet Air Wing	Japan
Koku-tai	Fleet Air Squadron	Japan
Kyunan-tai	Air Rescue Squadron	Japan
Letka	Squadron	Slovakia
Lsf / Lst	Leased from / to	
MAP	Memorial Airport	USA
MATS	Materials Squadron	USA
MCAS	Marine Corps Air Station	USA
MIB	Military Intelligence Brigade	USA
Mira Nafikis Aeroporikis Sinergasias	Naval Co-operation Sqn	Greece
Mira Taktikon Metaforon	Tactical Transport Squadron	Greece
NAF	Naval Air Facility	USA
NAS	Naval Air Station	USA
OG	Operations Group	USA
Opb / Opf	Operated by / for	
OSACOM	Operational Support Airlift Command	USA
OSAE	Independent Composite Aviation Sqn	Russia
OSAP (Otdel'nyi Smeshan'nyi Aviatsion'nyi Polk)	Independent Composite Aviation Regiment	Russia
OVTAE	Independent Military Transport Aviation Sqn	Russia
OVTAP	Independent Military Transport Aviation Regiment	Russia
PATD	Priority Air Transport Detachment	USA
Pievalve Lennu Eskadril	Air Operations Squadron	Estonia
Pteriga Machis	Combat Wing	Greece
Pulk Lotnictwa Transportowego	Air Transport Regiment	Poland
RFC	Regional Flight Center	USA
RQG	Rescue Group	USA
RQS	Rescue Squadron	USA
RQW	Rescue Wing	USA
RRAF	Royal Rhodesian Air Force	Zimbabwe
SIGINT	Signals Intelligence	universal abbreviation
Smaldeel	Squadron	Belgium
SOES	Station Engineering and Operations Squadron	USA
SOG	Special Operations Group	USA
SOLL	Special Operations Low Level	USA
SOS	Special Operations Squadron	USA
SOW	Special Operations Wing	USA
Specjalny Pulk Lotnictwa Transportowego	Special Air Transport Regiment	Poland
Sqn	Squadron	various
Staffel	Squadron	various
Std	Stored	
Stihaci Letecke Kridlo	Fighter Wing	Slovakia
SUKL	Federal Air Traffic Control	Yugoslavia
Szallito Repulo Szazad	Transport Aircraft Squadron	Hungary
Taktiki Aeroporikis Dynamis	Tactical Air Force	Greece
Tokubetu Koku Yuso-tai	Special Air Transport Group	Japan
TRAE	Transport Aviation Squadron	Yugoslavia
TRS	Training Squadron	USA
TRW	Training Wing	USA
TS	Test Squadron	USA
TSS	Test Support Squadron	USA
TT	Target Towing	universal abbreviation
Tukilentclavue	Operational Support Squadron	Finland
TW	Test Wing	USA
USAAMCOM	US Army Aviation and Missile Command	USA
USACBDCOM	US Army Chemical and Biological Defense Command	USA
USACECOM	US Army Communications-Electronics Command	USA
USAIOC	US Army Industrial Operations Command	USA
USAKAMR	US Army Kwajalein Atoll Missile Range	USA
USATECOM	US Army Test and Evaluation Command	USA
VAW	Carrier Airborne Early Warning Squadron	USA
Vegyes Szallito Repulo Dandar	Mixed Transport Aircraft Brigade	Hungary
VIP	Very Important Person	universal abbreviation
VMGR	Marine Aerial Refueler Transport Squadron	USA
VMGRT	Marine Aerial Refueler Transport Training Squadron	USA
VP	Patrol Squadron	USA
VPU	Patrol Squadron, Special Operations	USA
VQ	Fleet Air Reconnaissance Squadron	USA
VR	Fleet Logistic Support Squadron	USA
VRC	Fleet Tactical Support Squadron	USA
VS	Air Anti-Submarine Squadron	USA

VT	Training Squadron	USA
VTAD	Military Transport Aviation Division	Russia
VTAE	Military Transport Aviation Sqn	Russia
VTAP	Military Transport Aviation Regiment	Russia
VX	Air Test and Evaluation Squadron	USA
VXE	Antarctic Development Squadron	USA
VXN	Oceanographic Development Squadron	USA
Vycvikove Stredisko Letectva	Flying Training Centre	Slovakia
W	Wing	universal abbreviation
WGAF	West German Air Force (pre 1990)	Germany
WRS	Weather Reconnaissance Squadron	USA
Yuso-Koku-tai	Tactical Airlift Group	Japan
Zmiesany Doprany Kridlo	Mixed Transport Wing	Slovakia

Reading Arabic and Thai numerals

A large number of Middle East air arms display the serial information reported in the main body of the text in arabic character numerals. Similar presentation occurs in Thailand. In some cases either the serial or a code is shown in westernised form but the guide is included below for completeness and as an aid to identification.

Arabic numerals

٠	١	٢	٣	٤	٥	٦	٧	٨	٩
0	1	2	3	4	5	6	7	8	9

Thai numerals

๑	๒	๓	๔	๕	๖	๗	๘	๙	๐
0	1	2	3	4	5	6	7	8	9

Aircraft Type and Role designations

Introduced in 1962, all three main services within the US Armed Forces share a common designation system. A single letter is used to indicate the aircraft's prime role. This is followed by an aircraft model number and then by a suffix indicating series or modification status. In some cases an aircraft may be modified from its original primary role and will receive an additional prefix letter.

eg.,	Boeing C-135	'C' indicates Transport and '135' the model number
	Boeing C-135A	'A' indicates the series
	Boeing KC-135A	'K' indicates a modified mission (Tanker)
	Boeing NKC-135A	'N' shows a further modification to special Test (Permanent)

Most other Western countries employ either the same system or a variation of it if they have developed a designation system of their own. Individual variations include those shown below:

Country	Prefix	Description	Example
UK	CC	Communications	British Aerospace 125 CC.3
UK	AL	Army Liaison	PBN BN-2T Islander AL.1
Brazil	C-98	Transport type 98	Cessna C-98 Caravan 1
Canada	CC-142	Canadian Transport type 142	DHC-8 CC-142 Dash 8
Sweden	Tp100	Transport type 100	Tp100A, (Saab 340B)

Primary Mission Symbols

Prefix	Role	Example
A	Attack	A-10 Thunderbolt II
B	Bomber	B-1 Lancer
C	Transport (Cargo)	C-141 Starlifter
E	Electronics Installation	E-3 Sentry
F	Fighter	F-18 Hornet
H	Helicopter	H-3 Seaking
O	Observation	O-2 Super Skymaster
P	Patrol	P-3 Orion
S	Anti Submarine	S-3 Viking
T	Trainer	T-43
U	Utility	U-2
V	VTOL/VSTOL	V-22 Osprey
X	Experimental/Research	X-31

Model Number

A sequential model number follows the primary mission prefix. The series numbers were restarted in the 1960s when separate USAF and USN systems were combined. This is apparent on aircraft such as the C-17 and C-23, which though significantly lower numerically than a C-141, appeared some 20 years after the Starlifter entered service.

Modified Mission Symbols

Prefix	Role	Example
C	Transport	CT-39 Sabreliner
D	Drone Director	DC-130 Hercules
E	Electronics Installation	EP-3 Orion
H	Search/Rescue	HC-130 Hercules
K	Tanker (Kerosene)	KC-135 Stratotanker
L	Cold weather ops	LC-130 Hercules
M	Special Mission	MC-130 Hercules
O	Observation	OC-135 Stratotanker
Q	Drone	QF-4 Phantom
R	Reconnaissance	RC-135 Stratotanker
T	Trainer	TP-3 Orion
U	Utility	US-3 Viking
V	Admin/Staff Transport/VIP	VC-137
W	Weather	WC-130 Hercules

Status Prefix

The primary and secondary mission symbols may further be prefixed by one of the following letters. Many new types under evaluation or which have undergone a major modification may receive the prefix 'Y'. As the aircraft enters into production the 'Y' prefix is dropped, for example, the new laser equipped Boeing 747-400F is currently designated YAL-1. When it enters service it will do so as a Boeing AL-1. Any airframe/electronic systems updates will result in a suffix alteration.

In addition to the above mission roles and prefixes, another prefix is given to an aircraft that becomes a Ground Instructional Airframe. These are generally used for the training of maintenance personnel or in the case of transports as loading trainers. These aircraft are usually at the end of their flying days when they receive this prefix.

Prefix	Role	Example
J	Special Test (Temporary)	JC-130 Hercules
N	Special Test (Permanent)	NC-135 Stratotanker
Y	Prototype/Pre-production	YAL-1 (Boeing 747-400F)
G	Ground Instructional Airframe	GC-141 Starlifter

Commonality between the same type operated by different parts of the US Armed Forces does not exist as they may perform a completely different role. For example, the Beechcraft 90 King Air is operated by the US Navy as a trainer (as the T-44), while the same basic type is also operated by the US Army and designated U-21, reflecting its utility transport role.

Some pure civilian types operated by the different services appear to retain their basic manufacturers' model numbers, through clever allocation. For example the Douglas DC-9s built specifically for the USAF and US Navy are designated C-9, but the USN also operate ex civilian DC-9s that have not been re-identified. The original C-10 was to be the Handley Page Jetstream for the USAF but come the arrival of the McDonnell Douglas DC-10 aerial tanker the designation C-10 was revived with a 'K' modified mission symbol.

No doubt there is scope here for a book in its own right.

AIR-BRITAIN MEMBERSHIP

If you are not currently a member of Air-Britain, the publishers of this book, you may be interested in what we have on offer to provide for your interest in aviation.

About Air-Britain

Formed over 50 years ago, we are the world's most progressive aviation society, and exist to bring together aviation enthusiasts with every type of interest. Our members include aircraft historians, aviation writers, spotters and pilots – and those who just have a fascination with aircraft and aviation. Air-Britain is a non-profit organisation, which is independently audited, and any financial surpluses are used to provide services to the ever-growing membership. In each of the last 7 or more years, our membership has increased annually, and our current membership now stands at over 4,000.

Membership of Air-Britain

Membership is open to all. A basic membership fee is charged and every member receives a copy of the quarterly house magazine, Air-Britain Digest, and is entitled to use all the Air-Britain specialist services and buy **Air-Britain publications at discounted prices**. A membership subscription includes the choice to add any or all of our other 3 magazines, News &/or Archive &/or Aeromilitaria. Air-Britain publishes 15-20 books per annum (around 70 titles in stock at any one time).

Air-Britain Digest is the quarterly 40-page house magazine containing not only news of Air-Britain activities, but also a wealth of features, often illustrated in colour, on many different aviation subjects, contemporary and historical, contributed by our 4,000 members.

Air-Britain News is the world aviation news monthly, containing data on aircraft registrations worldwide, and news of Airlines, Business Jets, Air Shows and Military Intelligence. 160 pages of lavishly–illustrated information for the dedicated enthusiast

Air-Britain Archive is the quarterly 36-page specialist journal of civil aviation history. Packed with the results of historical research by Air-Britain specialists into aircraft types, overseas registers and previously unpublished photographs and facts about the rich past of civil aircraft.

Air-Britain Aeromilitaria is the unique source for meticulously researched details of military aviation history edited by the acclaimed authors of Air-Britain's military monographs. Quarterly, illustrated in colour and black & white.

Other Benefits

Additional to the above, members have access to the Air-Britain e-mail Information Exchange Service (ab-ix) where members can exchange information, or ask others for information they may have at their fingertips; access to Branches and the Specialists' Information Service; Air-Britain trips; slide and photograph sales libraries. During the summer we also host our own popular FLY-IN. Each autumn, we host an aircraft recognition contest.

Membership Subscription Rates – from £10 per annum.

Membership subscription rates start from as little as £10 per annum, and this amount provides a copy of 'Digest' quarterly as well as all the other benefits covered above. Subscriptions to include any or all of our other three magazines vary between £18 and £48 per annum (slightly higher to overseas).

**Join on-line at www.air-britain.co.uk.
or, write to 'Air-Britain' at 1 Rose Cottages, 179 Penn Road, Hazlemere, High Wycombe, Bucks HP15 7NE, UK, or telephone/fax on 01394 450767 (+44 1394 450767) and ask for a membership pack containing the full details of subscription rates, samples of our magazines and a book list.**

AIR-BRITAIN SALES

Companion publications to World Military Transport Fleets 2002 are also available by post-free mail order from

Air-Britain Sales Department (Dept WMTF02)
41 Penshurst Road, Leigh,
Tonbridge, Kent TN11 8HL

For a full list of current titles and details of how to order, visit our e-commerce site at www.air-britain.com
Visa / Mastercard / Delta / Switch accepted - please give full details of card number and expiry date.

ANNUAL PUBLICATIONS - AVAILABLE EARLY 2002: (Prices to be announced)

UNITED KINGDOM & IRELAND CIVIL AIRCRAFT REGISTERS 2002

Acknowledged to be the leading publication of its type, now over 600 pages, with all current UK and Irish regist-ered civil aircraft, gliders, microlights, non-British aircraft based in the UK, type index and many other features.

UK & IRELAND QUICK REFERENCE 2002

New, basic easy-to-carry registration and type listing, UK-based foreign aircraft, base index. A5 size.
Buy **BOTH** the above titles together for considerable discount.

AIRLINE FLEETS 2002

Almost 3000 fleets listed by country plus numerous appendices including airliners in non-airline service, IATA and ICAO airline and base codes, operator index, short-lived airlines, etc. Over 750 pages A5 size hardback.

AIRLINE FLEETS QUICK REFERENCE 2002

New pocket guide to airliners over 40 seats likely to visit UK, Europe & North America; regn, type, c/n, fleet nos.
Buy **BOTH** the above titles together for considerable saving.

EUROPEAN REGISTERS HANDBOOK 2002

Current civil registers of 36 European countries, all powered aircraft, balloons, gliders, microlights. Full previous identities and many extra permit and reservation details. Over 700 pages, hardback.

BUSINESS JETS INTERNATIONAL 2002

Complete production lists of all purpose-built business jets with 48,000+ entry registration and c/n cross-refer ence. Approx 400 pages. Available in hardback or softback:

PUBLICATIONS AVAILABLE NOW:

JET AIRLINERS OF THE WORLD 1949-2001 £16.00 (Members) £20.00 (Non-members)

Detailed production lists of over 70 jet airliner types with expanded coverage of Russian-built types and purely military jet transports. Full cross-reference index containing over 56,000 registrations and serials.

BUSINESS TURBOPROPS INTERNATIONAL 2000 £15.00 (Members) £19.00 (Non-members)

Complete production lists of over 75 types including all B-N Islanders, with 42,000+ cross-reference index. 360 pages, hardback.

TURBOPROP AIRLINERS AND MILITARY TRANSPORTS OF THE WORLD 1948-2000

£16.00 (Members) £20.00 (Non-members)   528 pages
Detailed production lists of 112 turboprop airliner types including Eastern European and military transports with full cross-reference master index containing over 47,000 entries.

OTHER MILITARY TITLES

Air-Britain also publishes a comprehensive range of military titles, please check for latest details of -
RAF Serial Registers
Detailed RAF aircraft type "Files"
Squadron Histories
Royal Navy Aircraft Histories

IMPORTANT NOTE - Members receive substantial discounts on prices of all the above Air-Britain publications.
For details of membership - see page 277 or visit our website at http://www.air-britain.com